The Dai

HON
MOTORING
YEARBOOK
2002–2003

The Daily Telegraph

Honest John's

MOTORING
YEARBOOK
2002–2003

ROBINSON
London

Constable & Robinson Ltd
3 The Lanchesters
162 Fulham Palace Road
London W6 9ER

www.constablerobinson.com

First published by Robinson Publishing Ltd 1997
This edition published by Robinson,
an imprint of Constable & Robinson Ltd 2002

A copy of the British Library Cataloguing in Publication Data is
available from the British Library

ISBN 1–84119–621–5

Designed and typeset by WordSpace, Lewes, East Sussex
Printed and bound in the EU

10 9 8 7 6 5 4 3 2 1

Contents

Introduction

These days, car buyers have never had it so good.

We have never had so much choice. There have never been so many different makes and models to suit every conceivable need and desire. Everything from microcars to vast seven-seater 4x4s. We can have 67mpg with 105mph performance (Yaris D-4D), or we can have 200mph with 12mpg (Ferrari 575M). We can buy a practical utility car (Berlingo) for less than a hatchback (Xsara). We can have a four-seater sports car (MINI) for less than a two-seater (MX5). And every six months the goalposts shift. The pace of change is now so fast it's almost impossible to keep up with.

In real terms, value for money has never been so good. Long gone are the days when cheap and nasty tin boxes could be foisted upon us at ridiculously inflated prices. We're not stupid anymore. If a car's nothing special, we don't buy it until the price has dropped so far it becomes a bargain. And if a car is the one to have but the price is lower in another country, we'll go to the other country to buy it.

We'll do this for new cars. And we'll do it for second-hand cars. In 2002, reps' specials such as Mondeos, Vectras, Lagunas and 406s fell to rock bottom. Yet status-enhancing sportscars actually rose a bit. So the wise money went to Germany and picked up an LHD there.

But if you're not clued up about what car does what, how reliable they are and what to watch out for, you can stitch yourself up with a money pit of a lemon more easily than ever before.

That's why you need this book.

Honest John

Frequently Asked Questions

After seven and a half years, I have to confess I get a bit tired of answering the same old questions over and over again.

Equally, most readers would rather get a quick answer to their question by looking it up than by having to type me a letter or email.

So here are my answers to the 32 questions I am asked the most.

The first answer is by far the most useful to anyone with a computer because it lists all the best motor related websites I have found over the past year. We haven't categorised them. They're in plain, simple alphabetical order according to what they offer.

Next we get into importing and sources of cheap cars.

We cover running-in, maintenance regimes, hiring something unusual, which cars have five proper three-point seatbelts, even finding somewhere to store a car you wish to cherish.

If what you want isn't here in the printed list, it might have arrived in the FAQ answers online at www.honestjohn.co.uk, which are updated weekly, daily and sometimes even hourly.

And don't forget, this is interactive. If I haven't included something you think I should have, please email me direct at letters@honestjohn.co.uk

1 Website directory

"Do you have a list of links to useful motor related websites?"

You bet. Here they are, in simple alphabetical order (some are duplicated). See also the other FAQs, many of which contain separate directories.

Accessories: www.saxonind.co.uk; www.speeding.co.uk/acatalog

Acoustic improvements: bjacoustics.com; www.noisekiller.com

Advanced Driving: www.iam.org.uk; www.rospa.org.uk/CMS

Advertise your car for sale: www.exchangeandmart.co.uk; www.autotrader.co.uk

Air conditioning installation and repairs: www.readerair.co.uk; tel: 01483 726300.

Airflow battery conditioner: www.airflow.uk.com

> **Honest's Opinion:** I bought one of these myself years ago. Paid the man my own £40 and have used it ever since. The Airflow Battery Conditioner is a small trickle charger that gently recharges a battery and automatically keeps it at the maximum 13.5 volts without spiking any of the car's electronics. Can be left like that all winter. Product now comes with a socket kit which removes the need to connect crocodile clips each time.

Alloy wheels: www.mswuk.com; www.bbsdirect.co.uk

American models: 'Autotrader' type site, with lots of info about current US models: www.cars.com

Association of British Drivers: www.abd.org.uk

Auction buying service: www.carauctionbuyer.co.uk

Automatic transmission repairs: www.sussexautos.co.uk

Automobile Association (AA): www.theaa.com

Back Room photos: Independent picture gallery (set up by contributors to The Back Room, Honest John's online forum) at http://communities.msn.com/honestjohn

Bangers: http://bangernomics.tripod.com

BIK (Benefit in Kind) cash for car alternatives: www.e-drive.uk.com; www.honda.co.uk; www.cashforcarclub.com; www.cash4carclub.com;

> **Honest's Opinion:** www.cashforcarclub.com; www.cash4carclub.com (same site, different spelling) is run by a chap called Nick Moger, for whom I have great respect. It gives you the information you need and shows you exactly how to work out your company car benefit in kind tax liability. Also offers club membership at £60 a year, which entitles you to be sourced with a personal lease car at minimum cost with all the figures up-front.

BIK (Benefit in Kind) company car tax: www.inlandrevenue. gov.uk/pdfs/ir172.htm; www.lvl.co.uk (rates).

BIK (Benefit in Kind) tax and London Congestion Charge calculator: www.comcar.co.uk

BIK (Benefit in Kind) tax calculator: www.citroen.co.uk/fleet

Biodiesel: www.ukbiodiesel.biz

BMW body and engine codes: www.unixnerd.demon.co.uk/ bmw.html

BMW engine bore liner degradation issue: www.lestac.co.uk/bmw/ nikasil.htm

Breakdown cover: www.theaa.com; www.directline.co.uk; www.europe-assistance.co.uk; www.greenflag.co.uk; www.rac.co.uk

Camera car: www.cameracar.se

Honest's Opinion: Bertil Gustafsson's incredible six-wheeler air-suspended SAAB 9-5-based camera car provides a stable platform for car-to-car filming and photography. 5ft x 4ft platforms can be fitted front or rear approximately 12ins from the ground. Sweden-based; website is in Swedish, but Bertil speaks excellent English.

Campaign for motorists rights: www.abd.org.uk

Car status checks: www.hpicheck.com; www.theaa.com; www.carwatchuk.com

Honest's Opinion: Visit www.carwatchuk.com to check that the car you are thinking of buying is all it seems to be. Simple web-based check for £9.99 tells you if the car is stolen or wanted by the police; has been an insurance write-off; has had a registration plate change. Also tells you the date of first UK registration, any colour change, recorded chassis/VIN and engine numbers, number of previous keepers, late or last keeper change and if the car is recorded as an independent import.

Caravans: Matching caravan weight to safe towing weight of cars; also checking Caravan Identification Register for stolen caravans: www.crischeck.com

Carburettors and fuel injection: www.webcon.co.uk

Cash for Car Alternative to BIK (Benefit in Kind tax): See under BIK, above.

Cheap cars: http://bangernomics.tripod.com

Cherished registration transfers: www.dvla.gov.uk/vehicles/cherish.htm.

Citroën 2CV: buying advice: www.geocities.com/MotorCity/8243/index.html

Citroën 2CV: electric conversion: www.stephenbarnes.com

Citroën 2CV specialist: http://subscriber.scoot.co.uk/2cv/

Citroën and Peugeot parts: www.andyspares.co.uk

Classic lawnmowers: www.lawnmowerworld.co.uk

Cleaning products and polishes: www.autoglym.co.uk

Climate change: www.john-daly.com

CO_2 ratings: www.smmt.co.uk

CO_2: the Con: www.techcentralstation.com/1051/envirowrapper. jsp?PID=1051-450&CID=1051-042202A (See also under Climate change and Global warming.)

CO_2: the Truth: www.co2science.org/carbon/2002/v5n9com.htm (See also under Climate change and Global warming.)

Company car information: www.fleetworld.net

Company car tax comparisons for companies and individuals: www.comcar.co.uk

Company car tax: (includes classics) www.inlandrevenue.gov.uk/ pdfs/ir172.htm

Congestion charging: www.transportaction.org.uk; www.comcar.co.uk

Convertible hood maintenance products: www.renovointernational. com

Convertible hood replacement: www.autohoods.co.uk

Crash test results: www.euroncap.com; www.crashtest.com

Diesel damage: damage to seals from low sulphur diesel: www. americansweeper.com/v3n1/v3n1lowsulph.html#do

Direction/location finder (UK): www.streetmap.co.uk

Disability: advice and mobility roadshow: www.justmobility.co.uk

Disability: converted vehicle exchange: www.en-abled.com

Frequently Asked Questions

Disability: mobility conversions for the disabled: www.brotherwood.com

Discounted UK-supplied cars: www.broker4cars.co.uk

Driving test theory papers: www.driving-tests.co.uk; www.carnetlive.co.uk/trivia

DVLA: www.dvla.gov.uk

Electric Citroën 2CV: www.stephenbarnes.com

Electrical/electronic components: testing and reconditioning: www.fsvo.com/esalternators.

Electrical problems on classic vehicles solved: www.alexclassics.com.

Electronic bits and pieces: www.maplin.co.uk

Emissions ratings: To find out how much CO_2 a new car emits, and therefore how much you will pay in VED or BIK tax: www.vcacarfueldata.org.uk

Engine rebuilds: www.fer.co.uk; www.ivor-searle.co.uk

Ergonomics: www.drivingergonomics.com

European breakdown cover: www.theaa.com; www.directline.co.uk; www.europe-assistance.co.uk; www.greenflag.co.uk; www.rac.co.uk

European travel advice: www.theaa.com/allaboutcars/overseas/europe_advice.html

Expert Witnesses Register: www.jspubs.com

Ferrari maintenance and race preparation: www.racecar.co.uk/dk-eng

Fuel consumption: Official EC figures: www.vcacarfueldata.org.uk

Fuel injection and carburettors: www.webcon.co.uk

Geodesy: GPS speed camera locator: www.morpheous.com

Glass's Guide: www.glass.co.uk

Global warming: web.archive.org/web/20001019081322/indigo.

col-ed.org/mine/trojan.htm/ also www.globalwarming.org/sciup/ sci6-27-01.htm and www.stats.org/spotlight/ceid4.htm and www.stats.org/ newsletters/9903/warming.htm (See also 'CO$_2$' and 'Climate change', above.)

Headlamp beam deflectors: www.saxonind.co.uk

History checks: www.hpicheck.com

Hood maintenance products: www.renovointernational.com

Hood replacements: www.autohoods.co.uk

How things work: The lowdown on how everything works: www.howstuffworks.com

HPI checks: www.hpicheck.com

Imports: European imports and discounted UK supplied cars: www.showroom4cars.com

Imports: help with Japanese imports: www.importedvehicles.co.uk

Imports: help with SVA compliance: www.protech-uk.co.uk

Imports: used LHD sportscars: www.premiercarsearch.com

Imports: warranted history checks: www.bimta.com

Inspection pit moulded liners: www.mech-mate.com

Institute of Advances Motorists: www.iam.org.uk

Insurance: direct insurers: www.churchill.com; www.privilege.com; www.admiral.com; www.axamotor.co.uk; www.directline.com; www.esure.com

Insurance: compensation for injury by uninsured drivers: www.mib.org.uk

Insurance: private multi-car policies: www.bluesure.com

ISOFIX seat fittings: www.britax.co.uk/isofix/isofix_vcg_2.htm

Italian car information and forums: www.carsfromitaly.com

Japanese imports: help over SVA compliance, rustproofing, parts: www.protech-uk.co.uk; www.importedvehicles.co.uk

Japanese import tuning: www.blitz-uk.co.uk

Kit cars: American kit car site: www.kitcar.com

Kit Cars: Kit-car website at www.totalkitcar.com run by Steve Hole. Gives details of everything currently on offer and is updated daily.

Lawnmowers (including Atco car): www.lawnmowerworld.co.uk

Left-hand-drive anything: www.lhdplace.co.uk

Left-hand-drive sportscars: www.premiercarsearch.com

Locksmiths (specialist auto locksmiths): www.home-own.co.uk/ala/index.htm

Low-sulphur diesel damage to seals: www.americansweeper.com/v3n1/v3n1lowsulph.html#do

Machine tools: Second-hand: http://site.voila.fr/danielmachinery

Manual gearbox reconditioning: www.ivor-searle.co.uk

Mats: Autostyle carmats: www.autostyle.co.uk

Mazda MX5 parts, accessories and £190 cats: www.mx5parts.co.uk

Mercedes Benz model numbers and parts in Australia: www.mbspares.com.au/whatmodel.html

MG-Rover unofficial website: www.mg-rover.org

Miller's Oils: For Miller's DieselPower Plus stockists and information on other Millers products, tel: 0800 281 053. Or go to: www.millersoils.co.uk

Mobility conversions for the disabled: www.brotherwood.com

Motor Show (UK): www.motorshow.co.uk

Motorists' protest page: www.itsyourduty.org.uk

Motorway stats and pix: www.abd.org.uk/green_and_pleasant_land.htm

Movie cars: Make your car a Hollywood movie star: www.movievehicles.com

Mystery Motors: For nostalgic family pictures of old cars and to get an old car identified go to www.mysterymotors.com

New Zealand classics: Nice amateur site with pix of some rare and unusual veteran and vintage cars: kiwibear.netfirms.com

Nostalgia: For nostalgic family pictures of old cars and to get an old car identified go to www.mysterymotors.com

Number plates: Made up with national symbols at £22.50 a pair: www.euronumberplates.co.uk

Oil: Everything you need to know about engine oil: www.fernblatt.com/longhurst/engineoil_bible.html

Old cars: For nostalgic family pictures of old cars and to get an old car identified go to www.mysterymotors.com

Older drivers: For a website specifically designed for the needs of older drivers go to www.olderdriver.com

Ombrello windscreen treatment: www.weathertec.co.uk/ telegraph.htm

Parking ticket trouble: www.hackneynet.com/parking.htm; www.croydon.gov.uk/tpsec/news/parking_plan2001.htm; www.snowdonia2002.fsnet.co.uk/English/observation15.htm; www.tcfl.gov.uk/parking_appeals/what1.html; www.hants.gov.uk/scrmxn/c30652.html; www.parkingticket.co.uk

Parts (European makes): For sensibly priced German, Swedish and French car parts: www.gsfcarparts.com; www.eurocarparts.com; www.parts4peugeot.com

Parts (general): www.findapart.co.uk

 Honest's Opinion: The best car parts finding service, whether for an engine, a boot-lid or some obscure piece of trim.

Personalised registration numbers: www.dvla-som.co.uk (for transfers: www.dvla.gov.uk/vehicles/cherish.htm)

Polish: www.autoglym.com

> **Honest's Opinion:** My favourite range of car cleaning products and polishes. I recommend Autoglym Super Resin Polish topped off with two or three coats of Autoglym Extra Gloss Protection for a lasting shine that also repels many of the nasty things that eat into paintwork. Use it myself. It works. So I don't bother with anything else.

Polish: www.merproducts.com

Price comparisons: Car price comparisons: www.carpricecheck.com; car price and options comparisons across Europe: www.eurocote.net/eurocote/index.asp

Price guide: www.glass.co.uk

RAC used-car website: www.yourautochoice.com

Registration plate origins: For marks issued before 1963: www.pre63.co.uk

Registration year and area information: www.new-reg.co.uk/index.plate

Replacement hoods: www.autohoods.co.uk

Road tax: VED rate for your vehicle: www.dvla.gov.uk/newved.htm

Roof racks, bars and top boxes: www.thule.co.uk

SAAB tuning and suspension upgrades: www.abbottracing.com

Scratch removal products: www.meguiars.co.uk

Seat comfort: www.drivingergonomics.com

Seatbelts: Third rear lap/diagonal seatbelt when not originally fitted: www.securon.co.uk

Security glass: Laminate treatments: www.pentagon-supaglass.com

Security: New car security ratings: www.ncsr.co.uk

Security: Steering wheel bars: www.saxonind.co.uk

Honest's Opinion: Not only protects the car, it also prevents increasing theft of airbags. Special versions available for 4x4s and cars with airbags.

Seven-seater estate car conversions: www.option7.co.uk

Shoestring cars: http://bangernomics.tripod.com

S.M.M.T. (Society of Motor Manufacturers and Traders): www.smmt.co.uk

Smashed-up supercars: www.wreckedexotics.com

S.O.R.N. forms: www.dvla.gov.uk/forms/pdf/v890online.pdf

Soundproofing: bjacoustics.com; www.noisekiller.com

Spain: Buying a car there; special offers, etc.: www.km77.com

Spare parts (European makes): See under Parts, above.

Spare parts (general): See under Parts, above.

Spare parts (second-hand): www.universal-salvage.com

Spares, tools, old bits or manuals: Bid for them or auction them off at www.ebay.com

Speed camera anarchists in Holland: www.tuftufclub.com

Speed camera locator (Geodesy GPS): www.morpheous.com

Speed trap bible: www.speed-trap.co.uk

Status checks: See under Car status checks, above.

Stolen car recovery: www.thankstotracker.com

Storage for cars: www.carbank.co.uk; www.classicarstorage.co.uk; www.classic-reserve.co.uk; www.northerncarstorage.co.uk

Stunt driving site: www.russswift.co.uk

SVA information, CO_2 ratings: www.vca.gov.uk

Swedish car site: www.autosite.se/engelskann/carsell.htm

Tickets to motor sports events: www.sportscotickets.com

Frequently Asked Questions

Tools: www.international-tool.com; www.saxonind.co.uk

Towing advice: www.rydertowing.co.uk

Towsafe: Matching caravan weight to safe towing weight of cars and also checking Caravan Identification register for stolen caravans: www.crischeck.com

Tracking stolen cars: www.thankstotracker.com

Transmission reconditioning (manuals): www.ivor-searle.co.uk

Transmission repair (automatics): www.sussexautos.co.uk

Twingo: Renault Twingo parts, service and cars: www.twingo.co.uk

Tyre information: www.tyresafety.co.uk; www.tyres-online.co.uk; www.mytyres.net

Tyre pressure gauges: www.international-tool.com

Tyre pressure valve indicators: www.auto-unique.co.uk

Tyres and laser alignment: Great discounts: www.micheldever.co.uk

Ugly cars: www.uglycars.co.uk

Unmarked police cars: www.drive.to/unmarked.com

USA: For driving in the USA: usa.dedas.com/driving.html/

Vauxhall Omega specialists: www.dkcarsales.co.uk; www.niddvale.co.uk

VED rate for your vehicle: www.dvla.gov.uk/newved.htm

Vehicle Identification Number decoding: www.autobaza.pl

Vehicle Inspectorate: www.via.gov.uk

VW independent specialist: www.wheelbase.uk.com

Wind deflectors (sunroof and side window): www.climair.co.uk

Windscreen treatment: www.weathertec.co.uk/telegraph.htm

Witnesses: the Expert Witnesses Register: www.jspubs.com

Workshop manuals: www.haynes.co.uk

14

2 Buying from mainland Europe

"Where can I buy cars in the UK at close to mainland European prices? Also tell me about import warranties and import finance."

Online import specialists with supersites

Trade Sales of Slough, 353-357 Bath Road, Slough, Berks SL1 6JA; tel: 0870 127 3763; website: www.trade-sales.co.uk

Motorpoint, Chartwell Drive, West Meadows, Derby; tel: 0870 1209611; website: www.motorpoint.co.uk

Motorhouse 2000, Wryly Brook Retail Park, Walkmill lane, Cannock WS11 3XE; tel: 0845 345 6777; website: www.motorhouse2000ltd.co.uk

The Car People; tel: 01924 887654; website: www.thecarpeople.co.uk

CP Motor Company; tel: 01443 218400; website: www.cpmotors.co.uk

Online import and discount UK-supplied specialists
(Note that NONE of these are checked out. This is merely information. You use it entirely at your own risk)

www.showroom4cars.com
www.broker4cars.co.uk (cars UK supplied and warranted)
www.drivethedeal.co.uk (cars UK supplied and warranted)
www.autoaalbersonline.com or **www.autoaalbers.co.uk**
www.broadspeed.com
www.cars4importing.net
www.intermotive-car.nl
www.virgincars.com
www.alliancecarimports.co.uk
www.cancelledorders.com
www.oneswoop.com (£10 search fee)
www.autobytel.co.uk (UK supplied. Run by Inchcape Group)
www.autohit.com
www.carpricecheck.com (compares a basket of prices, not all)

Frequently Asked Questions

www.paragon-euro.com
www.jamjar.com
www.eurekar.com
www.tins.co.uk
www.carimportsuk.com
www.wundercars.co.uk
www.carfaxinternational.com
www.marketvehicles.com
www.brownsnw.com
www.bobgerard.co.uk
www.pentagoncars.com
www.carpartnership.com
www.ford-calais.com
www.sportimport.co.uk
www.europsave.co.uk

Independent import warranties
www.carimportwarranty.com

Independent import finance
www.currencies4less.com
a-plan; tel: 0845 071 1234

Independent import step-by-step guide with dealer contacts
www.4circle.com

3 Personal imports from Europe

"I want to personally import a car from Europe. What do I need to know?"

a Get the relevant Government booklets and forms. First phone the DVLA on 01792 772134 and ask for the pack on personal imports. This includes: the booklet 'How to Import a Vehicle Permanently into Great Britain'; Form V100, which explains registering and licensing procedures and gives a list of Vehicle Registration Offices; and Form V55/5, which is an application form to license a vehicle in the UK for the first time. (Alternatively, phone the DETR on 0207 676 2094, write to DETR VSE1, Zone 2/01, Great Minster House, 76 Marsham Street, London SW1 4DR, or visit the DETR website at: www.roads.detr.gov.uk) Then phone your local VAT enquiry line, listed under 'Customs & Excise' in the telephone directory, and ask for the 'VAT Notice 728 Pack' which includes form VAT 415, 'New Means of Transport – Notification of Acquisition'. (Please don't phone Customs & Excise on either 020 7864 3000 or 01304 224372, as these lines have become overwhelmed with enquiries.)

b Decide which makes and models you are interested in and obtain the UK brochures for these cars. Then phone the manufacturers' UK customer helpline, asking for a current list of continental service dealers.

c Choose the car and specification you want, then start phoning. When you find a receptive dealer, fax the exact specification of car you want and ask for a quote, to include temporary registration and export plates. The best countries to buy in are likely to be Holland, Belgium, Germany and France. Remember, if you buy in Europe, you will be buying a Europe-spec. car with RHD as an extra. Other things, such as a radio, tinted glass, alarm/immobiliser (and seven seats in an MPV), may be extras too.

d Order your car from the dealer offering the best combination of price and delivery date. Delivery could easily be 6 to 8 months for a car such as a VW, Mercedes Benz or Alfa Romeo. You will be asked to pay a deposit of between 10 and 30 per cent on receipt of order, either by credit card, Switch or by international bank credit transfer. Make sure the dealer faxes, emails or posts you a receipt for this and a confirmation of your order.

e Decide on whether you are going to gamble on Sterling rising or falling against the currency in which you will be buying the car. If you gamble on Sterling rising, leave your funds in a high-interest Sterling account. If you gamble on Sterling falling, open a Foreign Currency Call Account at your bank. This is a deposit account in a foreign currency offering interest based on the much lower base rates for the foreign currency.

f Keep in touch with the dealer by phone, fax or email to make sure your order is being processed. Within two months of the delivery date, start asking for a scheduled build date for your car.

g Once the dealer gives you a delivery date, ask him to arrange temporary insurance for you to drive the car back (this insurance will be Third Party only). A new EU rule now requires you to insure the car in the country of purchase. But if you want to arrange additional comprehensive insurance on the Vehicle Identification Number (VIN) from the point of purchase back to the UK, speak to Footman James on 0121 561 4196. Then organise your flight out and ferry back, and arrange for a bank draft to pay for the car.

h When you go to collect the car, inspect it carefully to make sure it complies with the specification you have ordered. Make sure the dealer gives you: a Certificate of Conformity to European Type Approval (a 'C of C'); a Registration Certificate naming you as the keeper; an insurance document to prove the car was insured in the country of origin (often combined with the temporary registration); and, of course, the dealer's invoice. Make sure you buy some petrol in the country of origin and keep the receipt. Keep any hotel and restaurant receipts. And keep the ferry ticket.

i As soon as possible (this must be within seven days of arriving back in the UK with your new car), fill in the form 'New Means of Transport – Notification of Acquisition' (Appendix 'D') which came with VAT 728, and take it, together with completed form C55/5, the dealer's invoice, foreign registration document, the Certificate of Type Approval Conformity, your petrol receipts and any other foreign receipts to prove you have driven the car abroad, your ferry ticket and your UK insurance certificate based on the VIN number, to your nearest Vehicle Registration Office. On payment of a £25 first registration fee, and either six months' or twelve months' VED, the VRO will issue you with a registration

number and a VED disc. The date of first registration will now be the date the car was first registered in the UK, provided this is within 14 days of the purchase date, or within 30 days of the purchase date if this immediately precedes a registration letter change. Your V5 registration document will then be sent to you from Swansea.

j The VRO will send form NMT – Notification of Acquisition – on to Customs & Excise, who will then send you invoice VAT 413 for UK VAT at 17.5% of the cost of the car, which you have 30 days to settle. Once settled, you will receive a receipted VAT 413.

k Order a set of plates. Phone the manufacturer's customer helpline to put the car on the manufacturer's UK data bank for warranty purposes and in case of any recalls. Though C&E only insist you keep the purchase invoice and the receipted VAT for 6 years as proof that VAT has been paid, it's advisable to keep all the documentation, including petrol receipts and ferry tickets, in a safe place with them to pass on to the new owner when you sell the car.

Imports from outside the EU

On 1 August 2000 the Government announced that it was to relax SVA quotas, which had previously restricted trade imports of non-EU Type Approved vehicles to a total of 50 a year for any one make and model. These quota restrictions were lifted as from 18 August 2000. By January 2001, personal import rules were tightened up so that only people who have lived overseas for more than a year and owned the car overseas for more than six months can bring it to the UK as a personal import which, if it is more than 3 years old, is not subject to a Single Vehicle Approval test. All other imports up to ten years old will be subject to the SVA test.

4 Cheapest places to buy 'nearly new' in the UK

"Where are the cheapest places to buy nearly-new cars in the UK, which are the best used car supersites and where is the best online used car advertising?"

Trade Sales of Slough, 353-357 Bath Road, Slough, Berks SL1 6JA. Tel: 01753 773763, website: www.trade-sales.co.uk

The Great Trade Centre, Hythe Road (off Scrubbs Lane: continuation of Wood Lane); White City, London NW10 6JR, tel: 020 8969 5511; website: www.greattradecentre.co.uk

Motorpoint, Chartwell Drive, West Meadows, Derby, tel: 01332 347357, website: www.motorpoint.co.uk

Motorhouse 2000, Wryly Brook Retail Park, Walkmill Lane, Cannock WS11 3XE, tel: 01543 462300; website: www. motorhouse2000ltd.co.uk

The Car People, tel: 01924 887654; website: www.thecarpeople.co.uk

CP Motor Company, tel: 01443 218400; website: www.cpmotors.co.uk

Fords of Winsford, Wharton Retail Park, Weaver Valley Road, Winsford, Cheshire, tel: 0845 345 1016; website: www.fow.co.uk

The Members Motoring Club gives free quotations on new and nearly new cars, so members can see what sort of a deal they're getting from their local showroom. The club can also source vehicles on request. Contact Steve West, Members Motoring Club, 1 Cardiff Rd, Cardiff CF5 2DN; tel: 02920 555543; website: www.members-motoring-club.com

Nearly new and used car buying supersites

Motorpoint, Chartwell Drive, West Meadows, Derby; tel: 0870 1209611; website: www.motorpoint.co.uk

Trade Sales of Slough, 353-357 Bath Road, Slough, Berks SL1 6JA; tel: 0870 127 3763; website: www.trade-sales.co.uk

Motorhouse 2000, Wryly Brook Retail Park, Walkmill Lane, Cannock WS11 3XE, tel: 01543 462300; website: www. motorhouse2000ltd.co.uk

The Great Trade Centre, Hythe Road (off Scrubbs Lane: continuation of Wood Lane), White City, London NW10 6JR; tel: 020 8969 5511; website: www.greattradecentre.co.uk

Fords of Winsford, Wharton Retail Park, Weaver Valley Road, Winsford, Cheshire; tel: 0845 345 1016; website: www.fow.co.uk

Stephen Rayns Ltd, Leicester; tel: 0116 261 2200.

Fleetlease Direct, Union House, Kennetside Industrial Estate (off Bone Lane), Newbury, Berks RG14 5PX; tel: 0800 294 1948; website: www.fleetleasedirect.co.uk

Used car buying websites
www.autotrader.co.uk
www.exchangeandmart.co.uk
www.CarChase.co.uk
www.fish4cars.co.uk
www.autohit.com
www.autolocate.co.uk
www.used-car-buyer.co.uk

5 VED changes from March 2001

"Please summarise the Vehicle Excise Duty (Road Tax) changes as from March 2001."

The CO_2-based VED tax bands for new cars first registered on or after 1 March 2001 are as follows: up to 150g/km CO_2 the owner pays £90 for a gas-fuelled car, £100 for a petrol-fuelled car or £110 for a diesel. Up to 165g/km the rates are £110 for gas, £120 for petrol and £130 for diesel. Up to 185g/km the rates are £130 for gas, £140 for petrol and £150 for diesel; and over 185g/km (anything from a Nissan Primera III 1.6 at 186g/km to an Aston Martin V8 Vantage at 511g/km) the rates are £150 for gas, £155 for petrol and £160 for diesel. From July 2001 all cars under 1,549cc first registered before 1/1/2001 qualify for the reduced £105 VED rate and this was backdated with rebates to November 2000. From the April 2002 Budget, VED for cars emitting less than 120g/km CO_2 was reduced by a further £30 to £60pa for alternative fuel cars, £70pa for petrol cars and £80 for diesel cars. There is a website where you can find out how much tax will be due for your particular car at www.dvla.gov.uk/newved.htm, or you can obtain a leaflet by telephoning 0845 605 2222.

6 Changes to BIK tax from April 2002

"Please summarise the changes to company car benefit in kind (BIK) tax from April 2002."

This is the tax drivers of company cars pay for the benefit of their private use of the car. The system for calculating this tax will change from 6 April 2002 and there will no longer be any discount for high business mileage. Instead, drivers will be taxed on 15 per cent of the car's 'list price', with the tax base increasing by 1 per cent for each 5g/km CO_2 the car emits over and above 165g/km. For tax year 2003–2004, the base CO_2 will be 155g/km, and for tax year 2004–2005 the base CO_2 will be 145g/km. So, effectively, the tax base for a £15,000 car emitting 185g/km CO_2 will rise from 19 per cent (or £2,850) in 2002–2003 to 23 per cent (or £3,450) in 2004–2005. Because they emit less CO_2, diesels will be hit with a 3 per cent surcharge (though a diesel whose engine meets Euro-4 standards will be exempt from the surcharge), and no driver will be taxed on a base of more than 35 per cent of the car's list price. So, as with VED, there is no benefit to be had from driving a company car with an ultra-low CO_2 rating, even though the tax is supposed to be CO_2-based. Instead it has become a complicated banding exercise – though it does have the environmental benefit of abolishing discounts for high business miles. List prices and CO_2 tables can be found in *What Car?* and *Diesel Car* magazines, but drivers will need to subtract registration tax and VED to arrive at the taxable 'list price'.

From April 2002, cars first registered before 1 January 1998 for which no CO_2 figure is available will be charged on the basis of 15% of the car's new price up to 1,400cc; 22% up to 2,000cc and 32% for bigger engines and rotaries. For cars first registered after 1 January 1998 these rates rise slightly to 25% for cars up to 2,000cc and 35% for bigger engines and rotaries.

Classic cars are taxed on the basis of the above percentages of their original list price, or if they are 15 years old or older and their current market value is £15,000 or more, on the above percentages of their current market value.

For example: 1989 VW Golf GTi 16v, original price £13,885, taxed on basis of 22% of £13,885, i.e. £3,055. Tax at 40% = £1,222 a year.

But: 1971 Alfa Romeo 1,750 GT, original price £2,450, taxed on basis of 22% of £2,450, i.e. £539. Tax at 40% = £216 a year.

Vans and pick ups used as company vehicles are currently taxed on the basis of a straight £500, but abuse of this is likely to lead to a change.

From April 2002, tax-free allowances for business use of a car owned by an employee have been a universal 40p a mile up to 10,000 miles and 25p a mile thereafter. This encourages a shift to economical low-CO_2 privately owned cars and discourages business use of thirsty high-CO_2 cars.

Further information is available online at www.vca.gov.uk; www.ukcashforcar.com; www.businesscarsolutions.co.uk; www.lvl.co.uk; and www.honda.co.uk (which runs an excellent and very 'friendly' BIK tax calculator: click on the 'Cars' icon, wait for the page to load, then click on 'cash for cars' at the bottom of the page).

7 The new licensing system by area

"Please summarise the new car licensing system by area."

From 1 September 2001, new vehicle registrations have begun with one letter denoting the region, followed by one letter denoting the vehicle registration office (each VRO has 5 to 25 letters available, depending on how many of them there are in each region). This is followed by two numbers giving the period of registration. In turn this is followed by three random letters.

So 'AA 51 ABC' means that the car was registered in the Anglia region at the Norwich VRO between 1 September 2001 and 28 February 2002, and is the only 'AA 51'-registered car with the random letters 'ABC'.

Because of the twice-yearly registration change, the year figures get a bit complicated:

02 denotes 1 March 2002 to 31 August 2002;

52 denotes 1 September 2002 to 28 February 2003;

03 denotes 1 March 2003 to 31 August 2003;

53 denotes 1 September 2003 to 29 February 2004; and so on.

The regional letters are:

A: Anglia

B: Birmingham

C: Cymru

D: Deeside to Shrewsbury

E: Essex

F: Forest and Fens

G: Garden of England

H: Hampshire and Dorset

K: Luton

L: London

M: Manchester

N: North

O: Oxford

P: Preston

R: Reading

S: Scotland

V: Severn Valley

W: West Country

Y: Yorkshire.

8 Rear seat belts

"Which cars have three lap/diagonal three-point belts in the back seats?"

Alfa 156 (£97.53 option); BMW E46 3-Series; BMW E46 Compact; BMW 5-Series; Audi A3 5-door; Audi A4 from 2001 MY; Audi A6;

25

Audi A8; Chrysler Neon II from Oct 1999; Chrysler PT Cruiser; Citroën C3; Citroën Berlingo Multispace Forte 5-door; Citroën Xsara from 2001 MY; Citroën Picasso; Citroën Xantia Estate; Citroën C5; Citroën Picasso; Citroën C8; Fiat Punto from 2000 MY (standard in HLX and above; £75 option in base models); Fiat Doblo Combi ELX model; Fiat Stilo; Fiat Multipla; Ford Fiesta Fusion; Ford Focus; Ford Mondeo (from 1997 MY), Ford Galaxy (from 2001 MY); Honda Jazz; Honda Civic 5-dr from 2001 MY; Honda Accord from 1999 MY; Honda Accord Coupe from 1998 MY; Honda CRV from 2002 MY; Hyundai Getz (from autumn 2002); Hyundai Santa Fe; Kia Magentis; Land Rover Freelander 5-door; Land Rover Discovery from 1999 MY; Lexus IS200; Lexus RX300; Lexus LS430; Mazda 626 from July 1997; MB C Class estate; MB C Class from 2000 MY; MB E Class estate from May 1996; MB E Class from June 1998; MB M Class ('family' model all 7); Mitsubishi Galant from 1998 MY; Mitsubishi Space Star; Nissan Almera 4-door; Nissan Almera Tino; Nissan Almera from 2000 MY; Nissan Primera III SLX; Nissan Primera IV; Nissan X-Trail; Peugeot Partner Combi; Peugeot 206 hatchbacks (from June 2002); Peugeot 206 SW; Peugeot 306 Sedan; Peugeot 307; Peugeot 307 SW (all 7 seats); Peugeot 406; Peugeot 607; Peugeot 807; Proton Impian; Renault new Clio from May 1998 (not base models); Renault Kangoo Combi RXE model; Renault Megane and Scenic; Renault Laguna from 95M; Renault Espace from 2003; new Rover 200; Rover 25; Rover 45; Rover 600 from 1997 MY; Rover 75; Rover 800 4-door from 94M; SAAB 900 from 94L; SAAB 9-3; SAAB 9-5 (saloon and estate); SEAT Alhambr (from 2001MY); SEAT Toledo (from 1999 MY); SEAT Leon; Subaru Legacy (from 2001 MY); Toyota Corolla from July 1997; Toyota Avensis; Toyota Avensis Verso; Toyota Camry from 1997 MY; Vauxhall Corsa C from 2001 MY; Vauxhall Meriva from 2003; Vauxhall Astra from April 1998 (not Zafira); Vauxhall Vectra from 1997 MY; Vauxhall Omega; 2002 VW Polo (£75 optional extra); 1998 VW Golf IV and Bora (£100 optional extra; but standard on Golf V5 Estate); new VW Passat (£100 optional extra to 2002: standard from 2002MY); VW Sharan (from 2001MY). Volvo S40; Volvo V40; Volvo S60; Volvo S70; Volvo V70; Volvo 850; Volvo S80; Volvo

940; Volvo 960; Volvo S90; Volvo V90.

If the car deos not have three three-point belts across the back seats, in many cases an aftermarket centre three-point belt by Securon can be fitter for around £70. Details online at www.securon.co.uk, or tel: 01494 434455.

9 Manufacturers' websites

"Can you give a list of car manufacturers' websites and brochure lines?"

It follows, in alphabetical order.

AC CAR GROUP LTD www.accars.co.uk Brochure-line: 01932 336033.

AIXAM LTD Brochure-line 01926 886100.

ALFA ROMEO (GB) LTD www.alfaromeo.co.uk Brochure-line: 0800 718000.

ASTON MARTIN LAGONDA LTD www.astonmartin.co.uk Brochure-line: 01908 610620.

AUDI UK www.audi.co.uk (Used cars: www.audi.co.uk/usedcars) Brochure-line: 0345 699777.

BENTLEY www.rolls-royceandbentley.co.uk Tel: 01270 255155.

BMW (GB) LTD www.bmw.co.uk Brochure-line: 0800 325600.

BRISTOL CARS www.bristolcars.co.uk HQ tel: 020 7603 5554.

CADILLAC www.cadillaceurope.com UK HQ tel: 01582 721122.

CATERHAM www.caterham.co.uk Brochure-line: 07000 00 0077.

CHEVROLET www.chevroleteurope.com UK HQ tel: 01582 721122.

CHRYSLER JEEP IMPORTS UK www.chryslerjeep.co.uk (Used cars: www.genuinejeep.co.uk) Brochure-line: 0800 616159.

CITROEN (UK) LTD www.citroen.co.uk Brochure-line: 0800 262262.

DAEWOO CARS LTD www.daewoo-cars.co.uk Brochure-line: 0800 666222.

DAIHATSU (UK) LTD www.daihatsu.co.uk Brochure-line 0800 521700.

FERRARI www.ferrari.co.uk Tel: 01784 436222.

FIAT AUTO (UK) LTD www.fiat.co.uk Brochure-line: 0800 717000.

FORD MOTOR CO. LTD www.ford.co.uk (Used cars: www.forddirect.co.uk) Brochure-line: 0345 111888.

HONDA (UK) LTD www.honda.co.uk Brochure-line: 0345 159159.

HYUNDAI CAR (UK) LTD www.hyundai-car.co.uk Brochure-line: 0800 981981.

ISUZU (UK) LTD www.isuzu.co.uk Brochure-line: 0990 100586.

JAGUAR CARS LTD www.jaguar.co.uk Brochure-line: 0800 708060.

KIA (UK) LTD www.kia.co.uk Brochure-line: 0800 775777.

LAMBORGHINI www.lamborghini.co.uk Tel: 0118 925 2870.

LAND ROVER LTD www.landrover.co.uk Brochure-line: 0800 110110.

LEXUS c/o Toyota GB www.lexus.co.uk Brochure-line: 0800 343434.

LIGIER c/o Reliant Cars Ltd www.reliant-motors.co.uk Brochure-line: 01543 459222.

LOTUS CARS LTD www.lotuscars.co.uk HQ tel: 01953 608000.

MASERATI www.maserati.co.uk Brochure-line: 01784 436222.

MAZDA CARS (UK) LTD www.mazda.co.uk Brochure-line: 0345 484848.

MCC SMART www.thesmart.co.uk Brochure-line: 0800 037 9966.

MERCEDES-BENZ www.mercedes-benz.co.uk and www.mercedesretail.co.uk (Used cars: www.directmercedes.co.uk) Brochure-line: 020 7536 3540.

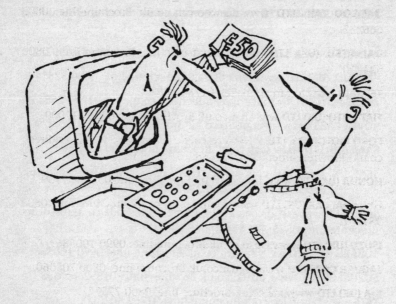

MG CARS www.mg-cars.com Brochure-line: 0800 620820.

MICROCAR UK HQ tel: 01789 730095.

MINI www.mini.co.uk

MITSUBISHI www.mitsubishi-cars.co.uk Brochure-line; 0845 0702000.

MORGAN MOTOR CAR CO www.morgan-motor.co.uk Brochure-line: 01684 573104.

NISSAN MOTOR (GB) LTD www.nissan.co.uk Brochure-line: 0345 669966.

PERODUA UK LTD Tel: 020 8961 1255.

PEUGEOT MOTOR CO PLC www.peugeot.co.uk Brochure-line: 0345 565556.

PORSCHE CARS (GB) LTD www.porsche.co.uk Brochure-line: 08457 911911.

Frequently Asked Questions

PROTON CARS (UK) LTD www.proton.co.uk Brochure-line: 0800 0521 521.

RELIANT www.reliant-motors.co.uk Brochure-line: 01543 459222.

RENAULT (UK) LTD www.renault.co.uk Brochure-line: 0800 525150.

ROLLS-ROYCE www.rolls-royceandbentley.co.uk Tel: 01270 255155.

ROVER CARS www.rovergroup.co.uk Brochure-line: 0800 620820.

SAAB (GB) LTD www.saab.co.uk Brochure-line: 0800 626556.

SEAT UK www.seat-cars.co.uk (Used cars: www.seat-cars.co.uk/usedcars) Brochure-line: 0500 222222.

SKODA UK www.skoda.co.uk (Used cars: www.skoda.co.uk/usedcars) Brochure-line: 0845 774 5745.

SUBARU (UK) LTD www.subaru.co.uk Brochure-line: 0990 100568.

SUZUKI GB PLC www.suzuki.co.uk Brochure-line: 01892 100568.

TATA www.tata-telco.com Brochure-line: 01262 402200.

TOYOTA GB LTD www.toyota.co.uk Brochure-line: 0800 777555.

TVR ENGINEERING LTD www.tvr-eng.co.uk Brochure-line: 01253 509055.

VAUXHALL MOTORS LTD www.vauxhall.co.uk (Used cars: www.networkq.co.uk) Brochure-line: 0345 400800.

VOLKSWAGEN www.volkswagen.co.uk (Used cars: www.volkswagen.co.uk/usedcars) Brochure-line: 0800 333666.

VOLVO CAR UK LTD www.volvocars.co.uk Brochure-line: 0800 400430.

WESTFIELD www.westfield-sportscars.co.uk Brochure-line 01384 400077.

10 Conversion to LPG

"Where can I get my car converted to run on LPG?"

UK LPG (Liquified Petroleum Gas) is wellhead gas, rather than refined from crude oil, and current estimates are that there is enough under the North Sea to last 40 to 60 years. Usually a petrol-engined car running on LPG suffers a 10% to 20% increase in fuel consumption. If it uses more LPG in comparison to petrol the reason might be the siting of a crucial part of the conversion, or it may be that the fuel stations are short-changing the amount of LPG they supply.

There is now a standard conversion of the Perkins 180 diesel engine for buses and trucks, enabling them to run on LPG at the increased consumption rate of 25 to 50 per cent, but using a fuel which is less than half the price of diesel. Typical conversion costs for cars and vans can be found online at www.est-powershift.org.uk New Citroën Xantias, Ford Mondeos, Vauxhall Vectras and Volvos with LPG conversions all qualify. The LP Gas Association (tel: 01425 461612; website: www.lpga.co.uk) can recommend LPGA-accredited converters whose conversions on new cars qualify for the Powershift grant. Without the benefit of the grant, conversions for older vehicles cost between £850 and £2,000. Tanks are available to fit the car's spare wheel well.

LPG conversion specialists include: Autogas 2000 of Thirsk, tel: 01845 523213; Autogas Conversion Co. of Hythe, Kent, tel: 01303 840901/07970 919092, email: gasman@autogas.fsnet.co.uk; Hendy Lennox Ltd of Chandlers Ford, tel: 02380 363301; Key Autogas of Leicester, tel: 0116 2608813; Marine Ecopower Ltd of Lymington, tel: 01590 688444; Autogas Northwest Ltd of Frodsham, Warrington, tel: 01928 787110; Millennium Autogas of Basingstoke, tel: 07771 993459; LPG Auto Power UK of Bradford, tel: 01274 729425, and finally GasCar, online at www.gascar.ltd.uk.

The Natural Gas Vehicle Association, tel: 020 7388 7598, can supply a list of CNG (Compressed Natural Gas) 'Gas Stations'. The phone number for British Gas for vehicles is: 01784 646030. The Autogas Installers and Retailers Association (01663 732030) claims to supply 'the only completely accurate and up-to-date list of outlets'.

11 Running-in

"What is your advice about running-in a new car and changing the oil for the first time?"

To run a car engine in, it is vital to vary engine speeds during the first 1,000 to 4,000 miles. If you are cruising on a motorway, vary your cruising speed by 10 to 20 mph every 15 minutes or so. Don't over-rev the engine, but don't under-rev it either. Never labour the engine by driving in too high a gear. Unless it is a super-high-performance car, current thinking is to leave the factory filled oil in the engine for the first 12 months or 10,000 miles in order to promote some wear and enable the piston rings and bores to bed themselves in. After that, change the engine oil and filter and consider switching from the semi-synthetic oil the car came with to fully synthetic. Also, have the manual gearbox oil changed to get rid of any swarf thrown off while the box was bedding itself in before the swarf grinds itself into minute particles which get into the bearings and shorten their lives.

12 Running-in a diesel

"What's the best way to run-in a diesel?"

For the first 1,000 miles do not exceed 3,000rpm, but make sure you reach 3,000rpm regularly. For the next 1,000 miles (to 2,000 miles) do not exceed 3,500rpm, but make sure you reach 3,500rpm regularly. For the next 1,000 miles (to 3,000 miles) do not exceed 4,000rpm, but make sure you reach 4,000rpm regularly. For the next 1,000 miles (to 4,000 miles) do not exceed 4,500rpm, but make sure you reach 4,500rpm at least a couple of times a week. After that, no limit, but make sure you continue to hit 4,500rpm

through the gears several times a week. The benefit of this is it helps to self-clean the injectors, it blows any accumulated soot out of the exhaust system, and it helps to free off the piston rings making the engine more efficient and less likely to use engine oil.

13 Lubricant and cambelt change intervals

"Some car manufacturers are specifying oil changes at 20,000-mile or two-year intervals, and give no indication of when things like timing belts should be changed. What is your advice?"

After the first year or 10,000 miles, whichever comes first, I recommend using either a good semi-synthetic oil such as Texaco Havoline 5w/30 (Ford dealer 'bulk' oil), or a fully-synthetic such as Mobil 1, and changing it every 5,000 miles or every six months, whichever comes first. If you are a higher-mileage driver doing 15,000 miles a year or more, consider stretching your oil changes to 6,000 miles. If you do 25,000 miles or more and use fully-synthetic oil, consider stretching to 7,500 miles but no further. Always change the filter as well. Change the manual gearbox oil once after the first 12 to 18 months, or 10,000 to 15,000 miles. Change the coolant every 3 years if it is an MEG coolant, or every 4 years if it is an MPG coolant. Change the brake fluid every 2 years unless it is Dot 5 silicon brake fluid (unlikely on a mass-produced car). If the engine has a timing belt, change that every 3 to 4 years or every 40,000 miles, whichever comes first, unless the engine has no history of pre-mature timing belt failures (Ford Zetec E and Zetec S engine timing belts generally exceed their design life of 80,000 miles, so can be changed at 5 years or 80,000 miles, whichever comes first.) Change the timing belt tensioner and any weeping camshaft or jackshaft oil seals at 80,000 miles (every second timing belt change for non-Ford Zetecs).

14 Crashworthiness

"Where can I obtain information about the crashworthiness of vehicles?"

Online, at www.crashtest.com

15 Advertising a car online

"Which are the best websites to advertise a car I want to sell?"

www.autotrader.co.uk (£7.50 for a fortnight)
www.ixM.co.uk
www.loot.com
www.classic-car-mart.co.uk (for classic and collectors' cars)
www.fish4cars.co.uk
www.CarChase.co.uk
www.autohit.com

www.autolocate.co.uk
www.used-car-buyer.co.uk

16 Buying online from the USA

"Are there any websites for buying cars and getting information about cars in the USA?"

Like its UK counterpart, www.autotrader.com is a listing of both new and used cars. You'll need a zip code, the equivalent of the UK post code, to price vehicles locally, but if you are seriously considering working or studying in the US you'll probably already have one. Alternatively, clone one to get the search working.

For make and model information, www.edmunds.com is a very interesting site devoted to new and used car reports. There is a massive amount of data here and certainly no bias towards local offerings. One thing to remember when looking at the prices is that they typically exclude tax, licence and registration fees, which can add another 10 per cent

A final piece of advice is that the DMV, Department of Motor Vehicles (www.dmv.ca.gov for California), is even more of a bureaucracy than our DVLA, so if you intend to do anything other than what's super straightforward, then be prepared for a very long wait and possible additional expense. It took Andy Kearl 6 months to be issued a driving licence despite passing the test first time.

Massive thanks to Andy Kearl for these useful links.

17 Electronic reversing aids

"Who makes the best electronic car reversing aids? And where can I get them?"

Auto Express magazine tested a range of these devices in issue 646. The one they rated best value was the Quanan 2030 at £89.50 including post and packing, from Cleargate Ltd, tel: 0870 729 3949. Next, scoring four stars, came last year's winner: Autosonics' Backminder at a price of £160 for the DIY kit, including p&p, VAT and a drill bit, tel: 01259 217004 (website: www.autosonics.co.uk). Next, also scoring four stars, was Safety Eye at £83.98 including p&p, from APS Marketing on 01341 450690. Next, scoring three stars, the C-Back at around £150 from Dutch Company CPL on 0031 621 532 726 (website: www.c-back.com). Next, with three stars, Ultrapark at an expensive £339.57 from Laver Technology, tel: 01279 436080. Next, with three stars, the Cobra ParkMaster 0166 at £170, including installation, from Ital Audio, tel: 01923 240525. Next, also with three stars, the Meta SR2C at £249 including installation, from Metasystem UK, tel: 01905 791700. Next, the VTD MB4 at £293.75 installed from Toad VTD, tel: 01928 570500 (website: www.toadplc.com). Finally, the Meta SR2C Targa at £249 installed, from Metasystem UK, tel: 01905 791700.

Another product which uses coloured lights as well as 'beeps' was originally designed for reversing caravans. It is made by

Brigade Electronics, is called the 'Backscan RI-OS', costs around £200 installed and worked well when fitted as an optional extra to a Ford Scorpio I tried. Brigade Electronics can be contacted on 020 8852 3261.

18 Aircon maintenance

"What do I need to know about servicing my car's air-conditioning?"

You should leave the a/c on all the time, even if not using it to cool the car. You should also turn the system to full cold for ten minutes once a week – even through the winter if you can – in order to circulate refrigerant which contains lubricants for the system and its seals. Then switch to full heat through the same pipes to thoroughly dry them out. This also blows out any moisture in the ventilation passages where mould and bacteria might be accumulating.

Opinions are divided on servicing. Aircon specialists looking for business will tell you it needs servicing, preferably by a visit to an air-conditioning system specialist, every year. That way they can keep a record of how much gas is being lost from the system. But the only way to test the gas is to draw some off and lab-test it.

Re-gassing a typical air-conditioning system costs around £80 + VAT. A service and a new accumulator/dryer costs around £150 + VAT. Some a/c specialists argue that this needs to be done otherwise the silica gel dessicant in the dryer could break up and circulate through the system, severely damaging it. Refrigeration engineer Keith Wood believes that replacing the accumulator is not necessary and could be responsible for introducing harmful dirt or dust to the system. It should only be replaced if the system has lost gas and needs to be re-gassed. In his opinion the only regular checks should be for leaks. A pool of water under the car is, of course, not the result of a leak but of condensation dripping off the condenser and is entirely normal.

The two main causes of failure are lack of gas and component breakdown. Low refrigerant means low lubricant, which is contained in the refrigerant, and this can lead to seals drying out, thus

losing even more refrigerant and leading to failure of the compressor. Properly repairing a failed system is a four-figure job.

For more information online: www.autoair.co.uk

Air conditioning specialists include:

Coolair UK Ltd (guarantees its work), head office: Kingsley Road, Lincolnfields, Lincoln LN6 3TA, tel: 01522 682288, and ask for Emma Hayward or Nikki Miller to put you onto your local branch.

David Norton, Kingsfold Garage, Dorking Road, Kingsfold, West Sussex RH12 3SB, tel: 01403 750202.

Readerair www.readerair.co.uk, tel: 01483 726300.

Motor Climate, tel: 0121 766 5006.

Alpinair, 174 Honey Pot Lane, Stanmore, Middlesex, tel: 020 8204 9633.

Vehicle Air Conditioning Services, Service Centre: Unit 8, Wintersells

Road, Byfleet, Weybridge, Surrey KT14 7LF; Parts: Unit A, 120 Oyster Lane, Byfleet, Surrey, tel: 01932 355825.

Vehvac Ltd, Fircroft Way, Edenbridge, Kent TN8 6AJ, tel: 01732 868080.

Halfords Garages (see local Yellow Pages for numbers).

Autoclimate, Battlefield Enterprise Park, March Way, Harlescott, Shrewsbury, SY1 3TE, tel: 01743 445566, website: www.autoclimate.com

ColdStart, Little Tennis Street in Nottingham (a recommendation from The Back Room, the online forum at www.honestjohn.co.uk).

19 ECU testing and chipping

"Where can I have the Engine Control Unit of my car re-mapped or 'chipped' to give better performance? And where can I have my car's ECU tested for faults, and repaired rather than simply replaced?"

'Chipping' is the generic term for re-programming an engine's electronic management system for increased performance, different performance characteristics, better fuel economy, or to run on a lower grade of fuel. This can be done internally, by dismantling the engine's ECU and either replacing or re-programming the chips inside, or externally, by altering the signals from the ECU to the fuel injection system and ignition igniter.

Both petrol and turbo-diesel engines can be 'chipped'. Prices start at around £100, but are more usually in the £300 to £400 bracket.

Practitioners include:

BBR of Brackley (petrol and diesel Starchips), tel: 01280 700800 (website: www.bbr.gti.demon.co.uk)

Superchips of Buckingham (petrol and diesel), tel: 01280 816781 (website: www.superchips.co.uk)

Milford Microsystems of Kidlington (system developments), tel: 01865 331552; AMD, Oxon, tel: 01865 331226

Tim Styles Racing, Somerset, tel: 01278 453036;

Siegerland (UK), tel: 0191 4286226 (website: www.tuningbox.com)

Power-Box, tel: 01603 722698 (website: www.dieselchiptuning.com)

Prima Racing, tel 0115 949 1903;

Van Aaken Developments of Crowthorne, tel: 01344 777553 (website: www.vanaaken.com)

Jetex of Stratford-upon-Avon, tel: 01789 298989 (website: www.jetexlimited.freeserve.co.uk)

Webcon of Sunbury (Diesel Torqmaster), tel: 01932 788630 (Website: www.webcon.co.uk)

Darley Specialist Services (Diesel Powerchip), tel 01332 553143.

ATP's Network 500 offers a nationwide ECU testing service, tel: 01543 467466. But remember, apparent ECU faults are often simply due to a poor contact in the multipin plug.

Carelect (website: www.carelect.demon.co.uk) offer a repair service for injection ECUs.

(**Please note** If you alter the specification of your car in any way you must inform your insurer or your insurance could be void.)

20 Minor bodywork repairs

"Who repairs minor damage to my car, its trim and its wheels at less cost than a garage or bodyshop?"

For minor dents of the supermarket carpark variety, call 'Dentmaster' (0800 433687), or 'Dent Devils' (0870 241 5679; website www.dentdevils.co.uk), both of whom will put you onto their nearest operator. You might also check out S.M.A.R.T. Repair's website, www.smartrepair.com. DENTS 2 GO!!! is a mobile dent and light scratch removal service in South Wales and the South West.

The repair needs no filling or painting. Call 07977 069149 or 01495 756985, or email leeburston@dents-2-go.co.uk (website: www.dents-2-go.co.uk). Dent-Magician comes highly recommended. For your local guy, check the Yellow Pages.

For stone chips and upholstery repairs, try 'Chips Away' on 01562 755678. For plastic trim and upholstery repairs call 'Magic Mend' on 0800 901 902 or Trimline Systems on 01202 480 881. And for chipped or scratched windscreens, call Glas Weld Systems on 0800 243 274 or 01372 362362 in Surrey; or Laminex Windscreen Repair (tel: 01895 675174; mobile: 07850 400826) in the Heathrow area. On modern cars with bonded windscreens this is better than having the entire screen replaced because removing the old one can damage the car body leading to leaks and rust. (Autoglass and Auto Windscreens and many others offer a similar service.)

For repairs to damaged alloy wheels, try A1 Wheel Renovations of 345 Bilston Road, Wolverhampton (01902 871422); 'Spit & Polish' of Tonbridge, Kent (01732 367771); or 'Wheelbrite' of London (0171 431 9015). The cost is likely to be £30–£50 per wheel.

For an in-house service combining bumper repairs, glass repairs, paintless dent removal, interior and exterior plastic and vinyl repairs, leather upholstery and trim repairs and Connolising, velour upholstery and trim repairs, alloy wheel refurbishment, wheel trim refurbishment, and general valeting, visit the Smart Car Centres at Bircholt Road, Maidstone, Kent ME15 9YP, tel: 01622 609 360 and at 1 Lea Valley Road, Chingford, Essex. Smart Car Centres, freephone: 0800 298 54 55; website: www.smart-car-centres.com

21 Speciality hire

"Where can I hire something special? A Ferrari, or a car which is completely out of the ordinary?"

The Classic Car Club is a sort of 'classic car timeshare', which costs £500 to join and then £1,750 a year. This gives access to around 40 days' hire of a range of 50 classic cars, from Fiats to Ferraris, according

to the number of points per day required for each car; tel: 020 7713 7313; fax: 020 7713 7316. A good classic car rental company is Bespokes on 020 8421 8686, fax: 020 8421 8588. Its fleet includes E-Types, older 911s, Aston Martins and Ferraris, at prices from £350 a day. It also does long-term contract hire. Modena offers Lotus, Ferrari and Porsche; tel: 01676 535596. Northern Sportscar Hire has a TVR Tuscan Speed Six, among others; tel: 01977 668068. Express Vehicle Rentals has Mercedes, BMW, Porsche, Lexus, Land Rover, Jeep, Jaguar and Audi; tel: 020 7383 3440; website: www.expressrentacar.co.uk Eurostyle has Ferraris, TVRs, Porsche 996s, Porsche Boxters, Mercs and BMWs, tel: 020 7624 1313; website: www.eurostyle.uk.com Miles & Miles Prestige Car Rental offers new BMWs, Jaguars and Mercedes; tel: 020 7591 0555. Carriages Vehicle Agency offers a wide variety of 'classic' vehicles, from a 1920s Dennis bus, through 1930s Rolls Royces, to a 1970s VW Beetle cabriolet; tel: 01737 353926. Ray Tomkinson offers a range of 'classic taxis' from 1930s Austin Landaulettes to late `70s Checker Cabs; tel: 01204 533447. Hanwells of London W7 have a late-model RR and Bentley rental fleet; tel: 020 8567 9729; website: www.hanwells.com Budget Rent-a-Car (now owned by Team Rental) aims to offer anything from a Harley Davidson motorcycle to a Jaguar XK8 convertible (see Yellow Pages). Euro Style in London offers TVRs, Boxters, SLKs, Range Rover 4.6HSEs and even a Bentley Azure; tel: 020 7624 1313. Tangerine (0800 975 7299) offers every kind of track day and off-road driving experience you can think of; tel: 0800 975 7299; website: www.tangerineuk.com

In the south-west, AutoInvest classic car hire has a Mercedes SL500, a Daimler 420 auto, a Porsche 911SC and an MGB roadster, tel: 01363 83909.

(**Warning** If hiring a car for road use and paying a substantial deposit, inspect the car with a fine-tooth comb before taking delivery, so you cannot be charged for damage you did not do.)

22 Autobox specialists

"Could you recommend any automatic gearbox specialists prepared to service and rebuild automatic boxes rather than simply replace them?"

King Automatics, The Chalk Pit, College Road, Epsom, Surrey, tel: 01372 728769.

Automatic Transmissions (Tattersall), Tattersall Bridge, near Coningsby, Lincoln, tel: 01526 342956.

Ivor Searle, www.ivor-searle.co.uk

23 Secondhand spares

"Which are the best sources for second-hand parts for cars?"

Find a Part One Call, tel: 0891 662706 www.findapart.co.uk
Universal Salvage, website: www.universal-salvage.com

National Parts Locator, tel: 0800 525 030
Premier Spares, tel: 0800 092 6700
1st Choice Spares, tel: 0906 910 8400

24 Electric cars

"Does anyone make an electric car which I can actually buy in the UK?"

Ford's contribution to the urban environment, first seen at the 1999 Frankfurt Motor Show, is the Think City. A small, two-seater plastic-bodied car less than 3 metres long, the Think reaches 30mph in 7 seconds and has a top speed of 56mph. Power is from 19 NiCd batteries and the car's range is 53 miles. More information is available at these websites: www.thinkmobility.com and www.thinkaboutlondon.co.uk (Incidentally, the Metropolitan Police Force now has two of these in its fleet.)

Alternative Vehicles Technology (AVT) has written to say that it offers 'affordable electric cars'. Unfortunately, 'affordable' is only relative, because its 'lowest-cost complete conversion' works out at £5,500 including batteries and charger but excluding the cost of the car to be converted – either a Mini or the old-model, sump-gearbox Metro, now at least nine years old. However, kits are available for home conversions from £2,995, excluding charger and batteries. The company also offers a conversion of the later and better Rover Metro or Rover 100, and of micro-vans, including the Bedford Rascal, Daihatsu Hijet and Suzuki Supercarry. AVT is in the process of developing its own AVT 100E electric car, but quotes prices from £16,995 to £19,995, plus batteries which cost from £1,481 to £2,070, including VAT. AVT claims top speeds from 56mph for its £16,995 plus battery PM2 model, to 'over 120mph' for its £17,996 plus battery S192 model.

For those keen on the retro look, Feel Good Cars, based in Toronto, Canada (www.feelgoodcars.com), build electric conversions of early-1960s Renault Dauphines.

The theory of electric cars is spot-on for people who use their cars for short journeys only, a job for which internal combustion engines are particularly unsuited. Unfortunately, as yet, AVT's complete vehicle prices are still too high to attract the levels of interest that the vehicles themselves should justify. AVT can be contacted at Blue Lias House, Station Road, Hatch Beauchamp, Somerset TA3 6SQ, tel: 01823 480196; website: www.avt.uk.com The Electric Car Association also operates from the same offices. There have been unfavourable reports on Varta semi-traction batteries, and you would be advised to source batteries from a British supplier instead. For more advice on electric vehicles, contact The Electric Vehicle Society on 01933 276618, website: www.evn.co.uk, and the Battery Vehicle Society on 01258 455470.

25 Microcars: where can I buy one?

"Where can I buy a 500cc automatic microcar in the UK?"

Reliant is now importing Ligier microcars from France. They are right-hand-drive, UK and Euro Type-Approved, have 505cc 2-cylinder Lombardini petrol or diesel engines and open-belt Variomatic transmission. In de-restricted UK specification, they should have a top speed of 55 to 65mph and give 65 to 85mpg. They also qualify for an extremely low CO_2-based rate of VED. And, after changes in licence regulations in 1996, they can also be driven on the same motorcycle licence as a Reliant three-wheeler. Price from £6,495. More details from Reliant Cars Ltd, Cannock Road, Chase Terrace, Burntwood, Staffs WS7 8GB, tel: 01543 459222; fax: 01543 459444. Reliant is also importing Piaggio Ape micro pick-up trucks and vans and will probably take on the cheaper Ligier Due Microcar in the near future. A second microcar contender is Aixam Ltd, Units 2 & 3, Tachbrook Link, Tachbrook Park Drive, Royal Leamington Spa, Warwicks, tel: 01926 886100. Aixam has been building microcars since 1975 and offers a range of convertibles and two- and four-seater hatchbacks with diesel engines from 276cc to 479cc. The UK range is all RHD and is powered by the 479cc Kubota diesel engine which gives up to 55mph and up to 90mpg. Prices start at £6,530 on the road with a year's VED for the 2-seater Utility, or £6,630 OTR for the

4-seater Economy, rising to £8,050 for the 4-seater Super. Ex-Reliant Boss Jonathan Heynes is importing a range of right-hand-drive fibreglass monocoque models called Microcar Virgo. These are available with two seats, 505cc petrol or diesel Lombardini engines giving up to 68mph and up to 80mpg, and cost from £5,995 on the road, including a 3-year warranty: Microcar UK, Park House, The Grange, Wolverton, Stratford-on-Avon CV37 0HD, tel: 01789 730094. Other microcar makers include JRD and Erad, who will be watching the UK market to see how sales go. We shouldn't forget the LHD 599cc 6-speed 87mph MCC SMART car, now also available as a 799cc common rail direct-injected diesel or a convertible, from MB UK, at prices from £5,995, tel: 0800 037 9966; or from KSB MotorGroup, website: www.ksb.co.uk New on the scene is the American 'Sparrow', a single-seater three-wheeler electric microcar capable of up to 70mph, but costing £8,750. Finally, the incredible two-seater 50cc three-wheeler and 350cc four-wheeler Fun Tech buggies seen at the Barcelona Motor Show can now be obtained in the UK from SMC Scooters of Torquay, tel 01803 200670, or Fun Tech UK on 01803 666610, website: www.fun-tech.co.uk; prices £2,995 and £3,995.

26 Making the change to automatic

"What is your advice to the elderly who are contemplating buying an automatic for the first time?"

Often it's too late to make the change safely. The problem with automatic transmission is that, unless the driver drives 'two-footed', he or she has far less control over the car than over a manual – which is why we read of around 20 deaths a year caused by 'out of control' automatics. What usually happens is that during the engine's warm-up phase, or if the engine has been over-fuelling, the electronic control unit raises engine revs to above the point at which drive is taken up in the transmission, and the car starts to move. The driver may then panic, attempt to brake heavily, but hit the accelerator instead of the brake, and the car either crashes or runs someone over. (The phenomenon even has a name: 'Sudden

Acceleration Syndrome'.) You cannot predict precisely when the car's ECU will increase revs independently, so my advice is only buy an automatic if you can teach yourself to brake with your left foot at least while manoeuvring, which keeps the car fully under control. Skilled drivers left-foot-brake automatics – and even manuals – all the time, but not everyone can get their heads around the technique for everyday driving, especially if they switch between the two types of transmission.

27 Soft top maintenance

"What are the best products for reconditioning the canvas hood of a convertible and for restoring transparency to a plastic rear screen?"

I reckon Renovo, which offers a range of products for reconditioning and re-proofing soft-tops. These include a new-formula Ultra

47

Proofer at £11.95 for 500ml or £19.95 for a litre, a Soft Top Dry Cleaner at £11.95 for 300ml (canvas or mohair hoods only), and a Plastic Window Polish at £4.99 for 30ml (tel: 01444 443277 or visit: www.renovointernational.com).

Autocar magazine's favourite is Autoglym's Cabriolet Hood Cleaner and Protector Kit, which comes as two 500ml spray bottles for £19.95 and an abrasive sponge (tel: 01462 677766 if not stocked by your local accessory shop).

Halfords also sells its own brand Soft Top Renovation Kit, which consists of 500ml of cleaner, 400ml of Fabric Guard, a small brush and a sponge for £15.99 (neither is suitable for mohair cloth hoods). Halfords also sells an own-brand plastic window cleaning cream. Available at all branches of Halfords.

28 Honest John's gadgets

"Where can I buy the tyre pressure gauge and battery charger that Honest John keeps mentioning?"

The Accu-Gauge S60X circular-dial tyre pressure gauge, 0-60psi, costs £13.25, plus £2.95 for a protective rubber cover, and plus carriage. Buy online from www.international-tool.com, or telephone 01604 646433.

The Airflow Battery Conditioner costs £40 from Airflow Products, tel: 01635 569569. The advantage is it trickle charges so gently up to 13.5 volts (then recharges as and when necessary) that it can be left attached more or less permanently without the need to disconnect the battery or remove the vent plugs, even if the car has an alarm/immobiliser unit.

29 VCAR?

"What is a VCAR?"

VCAR was the old name for an Insurance Damage Write-off.

A 'write off' is a colloquial term for a vehicle which has been

declared a total loss by an insurer, either following accident damage or theft. There are some 450,000 accident-related write-offs
every year and another 150,000 insurance thefts, many of which
are subsequently recovered damaged and re-classified. Many
write-offs are legitimately allowed back on the roads following a
repair; the safest ones to buy are those which have passed an
independent vehicle inspection, such as those on HPI's
Condition Inspected register. However, almost half of all write-
offs are so badly damaged that qualified insurance inspectors
determine that they should never go back on the road. To assist
the industry and the used car buyer, the Association of British
Insurers (ABI) has since 1997 provided the following classifica-
tion of damage to vehicles that have been deemed an insurance
write-off:

Category A Scrap only – this vehicle should have been crushed. It
should never reappear on the road and there are no economically
salvageable parts. It is of value only for scrap metal – e.g. a totally
burnt-out vehicle.

Category B The bodyshell should have been crushed. The vehicle
should never reappear on the road, but it can be broken for spare
parts plus any residual scrap metal.

Category C Vehicle extensively damaged and insurer has decided
not to repair.

Category D Vehicle damaged and insurer has decided not to repair.

Category F Vehicle damaged by fire and insurer has decided not to
repair.

Check if the car you are looking at is on one of these registers by
visiting www.hpicheck.com

30 Four-star availability

"Where can I still find four-star leaded petrol?"

You will find a full list online at www.bayfordthrust.co.uk

31 Four-star alternatives

"I have an older car designed to run on four-star leaded petrol. What should I be using now?"

If your car is post-1990 it should be capable of running on unleaded petrol of the correct octane without any additives. Nearly all 1980s Japanese cars or 1980s cars with Japanese engines are designed to run on unleaded. Many cars with aluminium cylinder heads have been fitted with hard exhaust valve seat inserts made of chrome steel rather than cast iron.

The oil companies have agreed that all UK Lead Replacement Petrol (LRP) will contain potassium instead of lead, now dosed at 10 to 12 mg per litre (which may still not be enough to properly protect the exhaust valve seats). If your car has a compression ratio of 9:1 or higher, you may find it both cheaper and safer to run your car on premium unleaded (always the same brand), octane-boosted with exactly the correct quantity of either Castrol Valvemaster Plus (phosphorus-based, from Halfords) or Millers VSP Plus or Carplan Nitrox 4-Lead (both manganese-based – the favoured additive in Canada).

If your car has a compression ratio of less than 9:1, you can use 95Ron unleaded petrol (preferably Shell or Texaco) dosed with a wider choice of additives which include: standard Valvemaster (phosphorus-based), Millers VSP Plus (manganese-based), Superblend Zero Lead 2000 (potassium-based), Nitrox 4-Star (potassium-based), Redline (sodium-based) or Wynns (sodium-based).

If your engine has hard exhaust valve seats but is unhappy on 95Ron or even 97Ron petrol, you can boost the octane from 95 to 97+ and from 97 to 98+ by using Millers Octane +. This costs around £3.00 for enough to boost 40 to 50 litres of petrol.

All the additives mentioned have been extensively lab-tested and approved by the FBHVC at the Motor Industry Research Association.

Contact numbers Castrol (Valvemaster): 01793 452222; Superblend: 0116 291 1700; Redline: 01732 866885; Millers: 0800 281 053; Carplan Nitrox: 0161 764 5981.

(**Please note** Sodium can damage turbochargers. Never mix petrol containing one LRP additive with petrol containing another, and never overdose it. Never mix manganese-based Nitrox 4-Lead with potassium-based Nitrox 4-Star.)

32 Pedal extenders

"My legs are not long enough to allow me to sit a safe minimum of 10" from the steering wheel of my car and reach the foot pedals. Where can I buy pedal extenders to enable me to sit further back?"

Eze Drive Limited of 169 London Road, Leicester LE2 1EG, tel: 07970 571407; email: EzeDrive@aol.com. Alternatively, a range of adjustable, removable and permanent pedal extenders is available from Roland Kerr Ltd, P.O. Box 8896, London SW15 3ZA, tel: 020 8546 8125; fax: 020 8546 7145.

De-mystified Motors

All too often, car people sound like they're talking out of their exhaust pipes. Have you ever wondered what their technical terms, car jargon and dealer slang really mean? De-mystified Motors gives you the plain English anwers so you need never feel baffled again.

Fuel consumption

We buy our fuel in litres. So why do we persist in using 'miles per gallon' as a basis for comparing economy? The answer is that most of us simply would not understand or relate to the metric method of measuring fuel consumption. When excited engineers refer to 'the three-litre car' they're not talking about the cubic capacity of its engine. Instead, they mean that the car will require just three litres of fuel to travel 100 kilometres. 'Litres per 100 km' is how fuel consumption is measured throughout Europe. But it's not too hard for us to start measuring this way as well.

For a start, your till receipt shows how many litres you have bought, not how many gallons. Mark your mileage on the receipt after you have filled your tank to the brim. Then brim it again next time you fill up and mark the mileage on that receipt. Subtract the first mileage from the second mileage and multiply the answer by 0.0161. Then divide the litres you have used by the answer and you get your fuel consumption in terms of litres per 100 kilometres. For example, I recently travelled 391 miles on 32.94 litres of diesel fuel in a SEAT Toledo TDI 110. Multiply 391 by 0.0161 and you get 6.295. Divide 32.94 by 6.295 and you get 5.23 litres per 100km.

For simplicity's sake, 8 litres per 100km = 35.31mpg; 5 litres per 100km = 56.5mpg; and 3 litres per 100km = 94.16mpg. To convert mpg to litres per 100km, a booklet from Citroën tells us to divide 282.5 by the mpg achieved, and to convert litres per 100km to mpg divide 282.5 by the number of litres used.

What are 'understeer' and 'oversteer'?

Readers have offered at least a dozen different definitions of these two characteristics. Leaving wit at the roadside, the simplest is what the car does in relation to what you ask it to do with the steering wheel. If the car turns less than you ask it to, it 'understeers'. If it turns more, it 'oversteers'. Depending on how fast it is asked to take a corner, every car will do one or the other at some point and might even switch from one to the other. The faster it can take corners without either, the more 'neutral' the handling is deemed to be. Skilled drivers usually hate understeer and prefer a car to handle neutrally, then gradually oversteer at the limits of adhesion. One of the best in this respect was the Porsche 968 Club Sport. But because oversteer can be dangerous in the hands of unskilled drivers, manufacturers have collectively taken the decision to design it out of the handling of most cars. Legendary Swedish rally driver Eric

Carlsson told me that the Vauxhall Vectra-based SAAB 9–5 is designed to understeer consistently (like the Vectra) and demonstrated how hard it is to provoke any sort of oversteer from this car. A 'Legends' racing car, on the other hand, with its locked and off-set solid back axle, oversteers luridly at the earliest opportunity and takes a lot of getting used to.

What's 'lean burn'?

Lean burn is a generic term for engines which are capable of running on a considerably higher proportion of air to fuel than the stoichiometric level 14.7:1 (known as Lambda 1). Honda V-Tech E engines, Toyota Carina E and Avensis 1.6 litre and 1.8 litre engines, and Mitsubishi's 1.8 litre and 2.4 litre GDIs, are all capable of running with air-to-fuel ratios of up to 40:1. The obvious benefits are reduced fuel consumption and reduced emissions through more complete burning of the fuel. Unfortunately, in Europe, lean burn engines have been legislated against in favour of catalytic converters, the testing of which requires all engines to be capable of running at very close to Lambda 1 in a specified rev band between 2,000 and 3,200 rpm, and this has compromised the effectiveness of lean burn. Driving a lean burn engine requires a different technique from normal economy driving: comparatively high revs with small throttle openings rather than low revs with early upchanges. The reason why so many Carina Es and Avensises tend to need very expensive Lambda sensor replacements early in their lives could be the failure of their owners to drive them as instructed by Toyota, instead adopting time-honoured economy driving techniques which are harmful to the extra-sensitive lambda sensor.

What's a 'chip shop'?

'Chipping' is the generic term for re-programming a car engine's electronic management system for increased performance, different performance characteristics, better fuel economy, or to run on a lower grade of fuel. This can be done internally, by dismantling the engine ECU and either replacing or re-programming the chips inside; or externally, by altering the signals from the ECU to the fuel injection system and ignition igniter. Both petrol and turbo-diesel engines can be 'chipped'. Prices start at £100, but are more usually in the £300–£400 bracket. Practitioners of the art include BBR of Brackley (petrol and diesel Starchips), tel: 01280 700800 (website: www.bbr.gti.demon.co.uk); Superchips of Buckingham (petrol and diesel), tel: 01280 816781 (website: www.superchips. co.uk); Milford Microsystems of Kidlington (system developments), tel: 01865 331552; AMD, Oxon, tel: 01865 331226; Tim Styles Racing, Somerset, tel: 01278 453036; Siegerland (UK), tel: 0191 4286226 (website: www.tuningbox.com); Prima Racing, tel 0115 949 1903; Van Aaken Developments of Crowthorne, tel: 01344 777553 (website: www.vanaaken.com); Jetex of Stratford upon Avon, tel: 01789 298989 (website: www.jetexlimited.freeserve.co.uk); Webcon of Sunbury (Diesel Torqmaster), tel: 01932 788630 (website: www.webcon.co.uk); and Darley Specialist Services (Diesel Powerchip), tel: 01332 553143.

(**Please note** If you alter the specification of your car in any way you must inform your insurer or your insurance could be void.)

How do I read my tyres?

Modern tyres are covered in hieroglyphics. Where the main ones read something like '195/60 R 15 87V', '195' is the tyre width in millimetres; '/60' is the ratio of tyre height to width expressed as a percentage (the lower the figure, the less cushion in the tyre and the harder the car's ride will be); 'R 15' signifies that the tyre has a radial ply and is meant for a 15-inch wheel rim; '87' is the carrying load index; and 'V' is the speed rating. A speed rating of 'R' is up to a maximum of 105 mph; 'S' up to 113 mph; 'T' up to 118 mph; 'U' up to 124 mph; 'H' up to 130 mph; 'V' up to 150 mph; 'W' up to 169 mph; 'Y' up to 175 mph; and 'ZR' 150 mph plus with no upper limit. (Some of these ratings are now obsolete and no longer apply to new tyres.) Obviously we don't all drive at these speeds, but if a

car comes with 'V'-rated tyres, any replacement tyres should be also be 'V'-rated. Though these are the main symbols, a tyre may be sold anywhere in the world, from Swindon to San Francisco, and markings applicable to other markets also appear. In the USA, for example, tyres are tested for tread wear, so a wear rating may be included. (Many thanks to Brian at Micheldever Tyres for his help with this.)

How do I rate an engine oil?

Readers keep asking me, and, thanks to Adrian at Castrol's Technical Department, this should provide all the answers. Eighty per cent of an oil is the base oil, which may be mineral, synthetic or a mixture called 'semi-synthetic' (the other 20 per cent is comprised of additives). Undesirable compounds cannot be completely refined out of mineral oil, so the purest base oil is fully synthetic. The Society of Automobile Engineers (SAE) ratings (0W/40, 20W/50, etc.) refer to the oil's viscosity (or resistance to flow) at minus 20 degrees centigrade compared with its viscosity at 100 degrees centigrade. A low cold viscosity oil (e.g. 0W) has its viscosity at high temperature increased by viscosity improving additives, which is how 0W/40 or 5W/40 is achieved. Matters have been complicated by new ratings systems devised by the American Petroleum Institute (API) and the Association de Constructeurs Europeans d'Automobiles (ACEA). These are arrived at by testing the oils in engines. For oils for petrol engines, the API rating of SG corresponds with the ACEA A1, SH with A2 and SJ with A3. For oils for diesel engines the API CD rating corresponds with ACEA B1, CE with B2 and CF with B3. The telephone numbers of Castrol's Technical Help Desk are 01793 452222 (for modern cars) or 01954 231668 (for older cars).

When is a 'write-off' not written off?

The answer is, when it's a Category C or Category D insurance 'write-off'. An insurance assessor will 'write a car off' when it is stolen and not recovered, or when the cost of repairing any damage to it exceeds 60 per cent of the car's trade value. The insured owner is then paid the car's private sale value, while the car is registered on the national 'Vehicle Condition Alert Register' and becomes the property of the insurer. If the assessor has deemed it a Category A write-off, that's the end of it and the remains of the car must be crushed. If it's deemed a Category B, it cannot be put back on the road, but it can be used as a donor car to yield spare parts for other vehicles. Category C means 'damaged, but repairable', so the car can be sold with a V5 for repair. Depending on the car's value, a professional repairer may then have his repair checked by an alignment specialist such as Autolign (01604 859424) or Popplewells (01992 561571), and a 'pass' will be entered on the VCAR register. Category D is where damage is confined to windows, locks and, possibly, a few bent panels, but the car remains roadworthy. This is often the state in which stolen cars are recovered after the insurer has paid out. These cars are the easiest to fix. HPI Equifax (01722 422422) and AA Experian (0800 234999) each offer history checks on vehicles which include their VCAR status (have a credit card handy when you phone).

What's the difference between diesels?

These days you can buy a diesel car with one of at least nine different types of injection system. The first is indirect injection (IDI), where diesel fuel is pumped to the injectors by a distribution pump, then fed through to the combustion chamber via a pre-combustion antichamber. IDI engines can be made more efficient by compressing the air fed into the combustion chamber with a turbocharger. And a turbocharged diesel engine can be made still more efficient by cooling the turbocharged air with an intercooler. This explains badges such as D, TD and TDi on the backs of cars. But badging has been complicated by the advent of direct injected diesel engines, first built for cars by Perkins, where the fuel is fed directly into the combustion chamber. Direct injected diesels may also be turbocharged and charge-cooled, and may be badged SD, DI, DT, DTI or TDI. VAG has taken direct injection a big step further by introducing 'pumpe duse' injector pumps where each individual injector contains a pump to increase the pressure at which fuel is pumped into the combustion chamber, enabling the dosage to be more finely controlled.

The other method of achieving this at slightly lower pressure is 'Common Rail Direct Injection', the route favoured by BMW, Mercedes Benz, Fiat and PSA. Instead of distributing the fuel charge to each injector, the pump feeds a 'common rail' of fuel from which each injector is fed at high pressure and the dosage fed into each combustion chamber is finely controlled. The air supply to common rail direct injected engines is invariably turbocharged, and for more efficient, more powerful versions it is turbocharged and intercooled. CD tends to mean common rail direct injected. CDI usually means intercooled as well.

What's the difference between an automatic gearbox and a CVT?

A lot of readers are still confused about the difference between conventional automatic transmissions and continuously variable transmissions (CVT). I'll try to explain. Instead of a clutch, a conventional automatic box uses a 'torque converter'. In very simplified terms, oil is thrown by one turbine wheel onto another, creating a flexible drive which becomes more positive as engine speed increases. This allows sequential gearchanges up or down two, three, four or five ratios according to road speed, the extent to which the accelerator is pressed, an electronic programme, or a manual override. The advantage is reliability. The disadvantages are a fixed set of ratios, a sometimes sluggish response, and overheating when the car is heavily laden or towing. Instead of a torque converter, most current-generation transaxle CVT boxes use a pair of multi-plate clutches or an electromagnetic clutch to take up drive from standstill much more positively than a conventional autobox. Instead of having fixed gear ratios, a steel belt runs between two pulleys which expand and contract in diameter, theoretically giving continuously variable ratios between the lowest and highest. However, the latest CVTs have six or seven lockable ratios, so upshifts and downshifts can be manually controlled if the driver desires. Confusing matters further, for the latest 'Hypertronic CVT M6' transmission fitted to some Primeras, Nissan has adopted a torque converter instead of an electromagnetic clutch. The new 'Torotrak' CVT does away with belts, feeding drive directly from an input cone to an output cone.

What's a 'small child' in the eyes of the law?

A reader from Stratford-upon-Avon asked if I could clarify the law concerning small children riding in the front seats of cars. Sections 15(2) and 15(4) of The Road Traffic Act 1988 state that it is an offence for any person without reasonable excuse to drive a motor vehicle on a road unless any children under 14 in the front or rear

seats of the vehicle are wearing seat belts which conform to the regulations. A child under 1 year old can travel in the front in a carrycot restrained by straps. Children under 3 years old can travel in the front seats if they are wearing approved child restraints. A 'small child', defined as aged 3–12 and less than 1.5 metres tall (4' 11"), can travel in the front or rear using an adult belt if no approved child restraint is available. If there are no belts in the back and the front passenger seat is unoccupied, the 'small child' must travel belted in the front. There are further exceptions for disabled children and children holding medical certificates. There are more exceptions for motor vehicles first registered before 1 January 1965, if the vehicle has no rear seats, or if no seats apart from the driver's are fitted with seat belts appropriate for a child. And, of course, there are yet more exceptions for buses, vans, trucks, etc. Rear belts must be fitted to all cars first registered on or after 1 April 1987. Many thanks to the 'Hughes Guide to Road Traffic Law for the Enforcement Officer', copies of which can be obtained from Motorvation Consultants on 01908 639233 in file form or on CD Rom.

What's 'fuel tax'?

'Fuel tax' is the fixed amount of tax you pay per litre of fuel before the cost of the fuel itself is added and VAT is imposed on both the fuel tax and the petrol. The current rates are: ultra-low-sulphur unleaded ('city' petrol): 47.82p per litre; premium unleaded 48.82p per litre; superunleaded and LRP 50.89p per litre; and unleaded low-sulphur diesel 48.82p per litre. If you pay a pump price of 79.9p a litre for premium unleaded, 19.18p pays for the petrol, 48.82p is the fuel tax and 11.9p is the VAT, so 76 per cent of the cost of the petrol is tax and the actual tax rate on the petrol works out at 316.58 per cent. The SMMT has provided CO_2-based VED tax bands for new cars as from 1 March 2001. Up to 150g/km CO_2, the owner will pay £90 for a gas-fuelled car, £100 for a petrol-fuelled car or £110 for a diesel. Up to 165g/km CO_2 the rates will be £110 for gas, £120 for petrol and £130 for diesel. Up to 185g/km CO_2 the rates will be £130 for gas, £140 for petrol and £150 for diesel; and over 185g/km (anything from a Nissan Primera 1.6 at 186g/km to an Aston Martin V8 Vantage at 511g/km) the rates will be £150 for gas, £155 for petrol and £160 for diesel. So the owner of a low-CO_2 'Y' prefix car, such as a VW Polo 1.4 TDI which puts out 119g/km, will only benefit financially by 29 per cent compared to the owner of a 'Y' prefix Aston Martin V8 Vantage, despite the fact that the Aston puts out 329 per cent more CO_2 than the Polo. The chancellor has, however, brought all older cars under 1,549cc into the same £105-a-year tax band.

What are 'regional registrations'?

From 1 September 2001, new vehicle registrations have started with one letter denoting the region, followed by one letter denoting the vehicle registration office (each VRO will have 5 to 25 letters, depending on how many of them there are in each region). This will be followed by two numbers giving the period of registration. And this will be followed by three random letters. So 'AA 51 ABC' will mean that the car was registered in the Anglia region at the Norwich VRO between 1 September 2001 and 28 February 2002 and is the only 'AA 51' registered car with the random letters 'ABC'. Because of the twice-yearly registration change, the year figures get a bit complicated. 02 will mean 1 March 2002 to 31 August 2002; 52 will mean 1 September 2002 to February 28 2003; 03 will mean 1 March 2003 to 31 August 2003; 53 will mean 1 September 2003 to 29 February 2004 – and so on. The regional letters will are A: Anglia; B: Birmingham; C: Cymru; D: Deeside to Shrewsbury; E: Essex; F: Forest and Fens; G; Garden of England; H: Hampshire and Dorset; K: Luton; L: London; M: Manchester; N: North; O: Oxford; P: Preston; R: Reading; S: Scotland; V: Severn Valley; W: West Country; Y: Yorkshire.

What is a 'three litre car'?

In mainland Europe the standard for vehicle fuel consumption is obviously not 'miles per gallon'. But it's not 'kilometres per litre' either. Instead, fuel consumption is measured in terms of 'litres per 100 kilometres'. Taking a reader from Oakhampton's formula, it is relatively easy to translate 'mpg' into 'l/100km' by dividing the figure 282.5 by the mpg achieved. Thus 30 miles per gallon translates to 9.4 litres per 100 kilometres; 40 mpg translates to 7.05 l/100km and 94mpg translates to 3.0 l/100km. This is the target figure set by VAG engineers for a new generation of super-economical diesel cars such as the VW Lupo 1.2TDI. It's actually quite easy for us to start thinking in terms of litres per 100kms rather than mpg, and obviously a lot more relevant than some halfway-house figure such as 'miles per litre'. All we have to do is make sure we brim our tanks on every fill-up and note the odometer mileage on our till receipts. Subtract the previous mileage from the mileage on the latest receipt; either divide by 5 and multiply by 8 (to convert miles to kilometres) or, more accurately, multiply by 1.60934; divide the result by 100; then divide that into the litres shown on the till receipt. Thus, on a recent series of 'brim-to-brim' fills while travelling through France, Belgium and Holland, my 836 miles translated to 1,345 kilometres, which, on 97.39 litres of Shell Premium Unleaded, worked out at 7.24 litres per 100 kilometres, or 38.95

miles per gallon. To convert mpg to litres/100 kms, divide 282.481 by the mpg; to convert litres/100 kms to mpg divide 282.481 by the litres/100kms.

What is 'Benefit In Kind' tax?

This is the tax drivers of company cars pay for the benefit of their private use of the car. The system for calculating this tax has changed from 6 April 2002 and there will no longer be any discount for a high business mileage. Instead, drivers will be taxed on 15 per cent of the car's 'list price', with the tax base increasing by 1 per cent for each 5g/km CO_2 the car emits over and above 165g/km. For tax year 2003–2004, the base CO_2 will be 155g/km, and for tax year 2004–2005 the base CO_2 will be 145g/km. So, effectively, the tax base for a £15,000 car emitting 185g/km will rise from 19 per cent (or £2,850) in 2002–2003 to 23 per cent (or

£3,450) in 2004–2005. Because they emit less CO_2, diesels will be hit with a 3 per cent surcharge, and no driver will be taxed on a base of more than 35 per cent of the car's list price. So, as with VED, there is no benefit to be had from driving a company car with an ultra-low CO_2 rating, which is extraordinarily hypocritical for a tax which is supposed to be CO_2-based. Instead it has merely become an over-complicated banding exercise but with the environmental benefit of abolishing discounts for high business miles. List prices and CO_2 tables can be found in *What Car?* and *Diesel Car* magazines, but drivers will need to subtract registration tax and VED to arrive at the taxable 'list price'.

What's 'GEODESY'?

Everyone has heard of radar and laser speed trap detectors, which may soon be outlawed. But GEODESY is an entirely different dash-top system which relies on Global Positioning System (GPS) technology to alert a driver that he or she is approaching the location of a known electronically mapped speed trap. If a user spots a speed trap which the GEODESY has not alerted them to, a press of a button will store its location in the unit's memory. The user then plugs the GEODESY into a self-dialling land-line interface to both upload the latest speed trap location data into the GEODESY and download the locations of any new ones into the data bank (every confirmed new location earns the user £50). Of course, GEODESY cannot identify which speed traps are active but, assuming the traps have been set up in known accident black spots, it will encourage users to take extra care when approaching them and thus makes a valuable contribution to road safety. Obviously, if the speed trap is simply there to earn revenue, then the GEODESY helps prevent it from doing so. GEODESY costs £380 including VAT, next-day delivery and a 12-month warranty. For more information, contact Morpheous Ltd, tel: 0870 2401701, website: www. morpheous.co.uk; e-mail: info@morpheous.co.uk; product test on www.speed-trap.co.uk; product description on www.speed-trap.co.uk/geodesy.doc.

What's 'Transport 2000'?

'Transport 2000' is a small but well linked pressure group that favours punitive anti-motoring measures such as high petrol taxes, high vehicle taxes, inefficient vehicle speed restrictions and draconian speed limit enforcement. Yet time and time again, its spokespeople are fronted on radio and television news programmes as the voices of reason. Fortunately, with the price of a litre of unleaded approaching 89.9p and Tony Blair telling us he needs 70 per cent of that to pay for our hospitals and schools, the public has finally woken up and turned against anti-car campaigners. So what organisations can honestly be said to truly represent the average road user, each of whom is forced to contribute 10p towards our hospitals and schools for every mile he or she drives? The Association of British Drivers is one, even though a name change to The Association of Road Users might give it greater stature. The ABD has a very helpful website at www.abd.org.uk, or (for those who don't have internet connection) membership enquires can be phoned through to 0700 781 544. Fellow columnist Mike Rutherford founded The Motorists Association, PO Box 325, Longfield DA3 7JU. The AA joined the fight against petrol tax while it was still 80 per cent of the pump price, while the RAC has the very able Edmund King speaking up for the motorist at every chance he gets.

What is 'cost per mile'?

Various organisations, including the AA and *Glass's Guide*, publish figures estimating vehicle cost per mile. While these are extremely useful to fleet managers and to drivers who cover average mileages, they aren't so much help to readers who are interested in the cost per mile of running a small 1,200cc car for a small annual mileage so as to compare it with taxi fares. Assuming the car is two years old and under 1,200cc, the biggest annual cost from March 2001–February 2002 was depreciation of around £1,250. Loss of interest on capital of £5,000 was about £400. With petrol at £4.50

a gallon and assuming 35 mpg, each mile cost 12.86p, so 2,000 miles of petrol came to £257. Insurance came to about £250. The car needed at least an annual service which, with running repairs, probably worked out at around £200 a year. At the new rate for cars under 1,200cc, VED is £105 a year. And a low-cost breakdown insurance such as that offered by the Guild of Experienced Motorists (GEM) will be around £50. So, as a basis of comparison with taxi fares, the car cost roughly £2,500 a year, or £1.25 a mile.

What is 'Multitronic'?

This is Audi's interpretation of the CVT (Continuously Variable Transmission). Despite the good sense of dispensing with the need for a conventional set of separate gear ratios, CVTs have acquired an unenviable reputation for unreliability. Part of it comes from sensor failure in those which employ an electro-magnetic clutch between the engine and the gearbox itself. Part of it arises from band failure, though the old composite bands are now mostly replaced by steel bands. And part of it is due to transmission fluid leaks, to which CVTs are particularly sensitive. To overcome all this, and to develop a CVT suitable for relatively large, high-torque engines, Audi's transmission engineering team under Reinhard Gesenhaus developed a new type of CVT. Instead of an electromagnetic clutch, Audi's Multitronic has a multi-plate wet clutch which engages automatically as engine revs rise and does not suffer the power sapping of, for example, Nissan's torque converter CVT. And instead of composite or steel bands, Audi has come up with a 'link-plate' chain, similar to the timing chain of Ford's Duratec V6, but much wider. This rides on two very special pulleys which fit over each other and the hydraulically controlled relative movement between them gives a spread of gearing ratios of over 6.1, compared to under 5.0 for a conventional five-speed automatic. The result is an extremely flexible and responsive drive which is completely jerk and jolt free, and is actually faster than the same car fitted with a five-speed Tiptronic or manual transmission. Multitronic transmissions, with steering wheel pushbutton-selectable ratios, are now available on the new Audi A4 and A6 models.

What's an 'ESVA'?

Single Vehicle Approval (SVA) is a means of testing and certificating imported vehicles up to ten years old which are not already European Type Approved. It was imposed by Gavin Strang from July 1998 to provide a means of quality control over imports, mainly from Japan and the USA, but it was also used to impose quantity restrictions by restricting trade imports to no more than fifty a year of any one make and model of vehicle. Traders instantly got round this by 'personally importing' cars 3–10 years old, thus absolving them from the trade restrictions and tests, and the entire system became an unsatisfactory mess. However, on 1 August 2000 the DETR issued a press release announcing that, as from 18 August 2000, the 50-car-a-year trade quota would be lifted. From 1 February 2001 the rules about what constitutes a 'personal import' were tightened and, to qualify, the importer must have resided in the country he is exporting from for more than a year and owned the vehicle there for more than six months. As from 1 September 2001, the SVA test itself has been 'enhanced' (Enhanced SVA: ESVA) to cover safety, anti-theft security and tougher emissions standards, and to extend the full test to commercial vehicles previously subject to an abbreviated SVA. All vehicles purchased in other EU countries will normally be EU Type Approved and exempt from ESVA. ESVA public enquiries, tel: 020 7944 3000; website: www.via.gov.uk.

What's a 'jump-start'?

Almost everyone knows the answer to this. But not everyone knows the correct way to use a set of jump leads to start a car with a flat battery. What most garages and yard men at the auctions do is as follows. First connect the positive terminal (+) of the good battery to the positive terminal (+) of the flat battery. Then connect the

negative terminal (–) of the good battery to a metal (negative earth) engine part of the car with the flat battery. If instead they are connected negative to negative directly, or worse still positive to negative, they could feed too much current into the Engine Control Unit and burn it out. To try and make the whole process of jumpstarting a lot safer than it otherwise might be, Airflow products has developed a fool-proof jump lead kit called the Kangoo, with LED lights that tell you if you have done the job correctly at each stage. They come in a circular plastic container from Airflow, the people who market my recommended Battery Trickle Charger/Conditioner; tel: 01635 569569.

Why should I worry about Freon?

Freon is the CFC refrigerant also known as R12, which the DETR has banned from sale since 1 October 2000. While this would seem to be all very well and good for the environment, it poses two rather serious problems. The first is that most owners of air-conditioned cars built before the end of 1993 will have R12 systems. And, while it was originally thought that the R12 in their systems could simply be replaced by CFC-free R134a refrigerant, this cannot be done easily due to the incompatibility of the lubricating oils contained in R12 and R134a. Blends of R134a with the older type of lubricating oil have been tried on a trial-and-error basis, with mixed success, often leading to leaking seals and loss of refrigerant. Worse still, R12 systems refilled with R134a or with one of the blends have not necessarily been marked with what they contain. On top of all of this, R12 refrigerant removed from a system needs to be properly disposed of or its disposal creates, rather than solves, an environmental problem. Many thanks to Dave Norton of Auto Air for this. More online at www.honestjohn.co.uk (Honest John's FAQs) and at www.autoair.com.

What is a 'timing belt tensioner'?

Even some dealers remain ignorant of the danger to engines posed by plastic timing belt tensioner pulleys. These pulleys run on sealed bearings at up to 15,000 revs per minute. If the pulley is made of steel or cast iron, the heat generated by the bearing is dissipated throughout the pulley itself, so the bearing runs much cooler than does the bearing in the centre of a plastic pulley. Normally it should therefore have a much longer life. When the bearing of a steel or cast iron pulley starts to reach the end of its life it shrieks, giving the owner plenty of warning that something is amiss and that he should stop before the thing seizes up, throwing off the belt. But when the bearing of a plastic timing belt tensioner pulley nears the end of its life, the additional heat this creates before it starts shrieking cannot be dissipated into the plastic so, without warning, the plastic cracks and shatters, throwing off the timing belt with disastrous consequences. That is why plastic timing belt tensioner pulleys should be replaced when the belt is replaced, at 40,000-mile or four-year intervals, whichever comes first.

What is 'Torotrak'?

This is a tough new type of Infinitely Variable Transmission which dispenses with the need for a clutch or torque converter and the drive belts used in CVTs. Instead, it relies on a system of cones and wheels to deliver a continuous range of drive ratios from full reverse through to high overdrive. As a result, the vehicle is always in the right gear ratio for the circumstances rather than a compromise ratio, as is the case even with a six-speed manual gearbox. The huge benefit of this is a fuel saving of more than 17 per cent compared to a manual transmission. Torotrak was first developed for transverse-engined cars and has been extensively road-tested, first in 2.0 litre Rovers and later in the 2.0 litre Ford Mondeo. Now a third-generation Torotrak has been developed specifically for rear-drive and four-wheel-drive Sports Utility Vehicles such as the Ford Explorer, Ford Expedition, Ford F-Series, Chevrolet Suburban, Chevrolet CK Series and Dodge Ram. Transmission manufacturers throughout the world have Torotrak systems on test. For more information contact Torotrak (Development) Ltd, tel: 01772 900900, website: www.torotrak.com.

What's an 'A Class' car?

Different car makers used different jargon to describe the sizes of cars they make. Though they have become a bit blurred at the edges, they start with 'Sub A', or mini, which includes the old Mini, Matiz, Amica, Ford Ka, SEAT Arosa, VW Lupo, etc. Next is the 'A' or 'supermini' class which includes the new MINI, Fiesta, 106, 206, Mercedes A Class, Micra, Yaris, Ibiza, Corsa, Polo, etc., and which, confusingly, is dubbed 'basse' or 'B Class' in France. Next, the 'B', 'small family' or 'lower medium' class of Xsara, Focus, 323, Almera, 306, Corolla, Astra, Golf, etc., known in France as 'M1'. Next, our 'C', 'large family' or 'upper medium' class of Audi A4, Xantia, Mondeo, 626, Mercedes C Class, Primera, Laguna, Avensis, Vectra, Passat, etc., known in France as 'M2'. Then comes our 'D' or 'Executive' class of Audi A6, BMW 5-Series, Mercedes E Class, Volvo S80, etc. And finally our 'E' or 'Luxury' class of Audi A8, BMW 7 Series, Mercedes S Class, etc., known collectively with the D Class in France as 'Classe H' for 'haut de game'. It's all so confusing, with cars like the Rover 25, Rover 75, BMW 3 Series and Mitsubishi Galant difficult to pigeon-hole. This is one piece of industry jargon best forgotten.

What's the difference between 'MEG' and 'MPG'?

It's always a wise precaution to get the strength of your engine coolant anti-freeze checked before winter. (Vauxhall dealers offer cut-price 'Winter Check Ups'.) However, because engines are inevitably made of different metals in close proximity to each other they are what is known as 'corrosion batteries'. To prevent internal engine corrosion and the sludge this causes blocking water galleries, coolant also contains corrosion inhibitors. In normal Mono Ethylene Glycol (MEG) coolant, the inhibitors last two to three years before they are too degraded to work and internal engine corrosion beings to set in. However, around six years ago a different type of coolant, Mono Propylene Glycol (MPG) became widely available. The brand name for the additive package is 'Trigard', the corrosion inhibitors last at least four years, the coolant is best bought pre-mixed with purified water and, because it is environmentally friendly, old coolant can be safely flushed down a storm drain. Some brand names for pre-mixed MPG Trigard coolants are Comma Coldstream, Esso Ready Mixed, Quantum (VW/Audi) Ready Mixed Coolant, Bluecol Protex Anti Freeze, Unipart Super Plus Anti Freeze, Batoyle Masterfrost and Silkolene Iceguard. 'Forlife' pre-mix from Toyota dealers (£13.61 + VAT) for 5 litres is also recommended by readers.

What's 'Powershift'?

Powershift is a government-backed initiative run by the Energy Saving Trust to provide grants to buyers on new 'clean fuel' vehicles

such as the Honda Insight and Toyota Prius hybrids and the LPG-
or CNG-converted cars being offered by Citroën, Ford, Vauxhall
and Volvo, among others. Powershift has written to tell us that it
now has a website, www.est-powershift.org.uk, which contains a
map showing all UK LPG refuelling stations, a buyer's guide to new
clean fuel vehicles, a directory of approved gas conversion specialists, links to other relevant sites and answers to Frequently Asked
Questions about LPG and CNG conversions. For those not yet with
access to the Internet, there is also a telephone hotline: 0845 602
1425. I should add that anyone considering an LPG or CNG conversion should first check with the car manufacturer that the
engine is suitable for conversion. From the experience of one reader we know that Honda VTEC engines, and high performance
engines generally, definitely are not.

What's a 'hot rod'?

We're not talking here of the Spanish 'polla caliente', which means
something very rude indeed. We're talking about a generic term for
boring old cars which have been made a bit more exciting.
According to a wonderful 1994 book, *Authentic Hot Rods*, by Don
Montgomory (ISBN 0-9626454-4-3), the foundations of hot rodding lay in speed trials on Muroc Dry Lake in 1932. Most of the cars
were fenderless Ford V8s and hopped-up earlier 4-cylinder Model
'A's. By 1938 the Southern California Timing Association (SCTA)
had been set up, but by 1941 its activities were curtailed by the war.
But in the years 1946–49 the sport of time trials on the dry lakes
blossomed. In 1949 the sport took an alternative direction in the
form of drag racing. What's particularly interesting is a craze which
grew in the UK about ten years ago to recreate late 1940s and early
1950s hot rods as authentically as possible, then set up a meet and
race them on an old airfield. 'Hot Rod' racing, on the other hand,
is the quick category of UK stock car racing and bears little relation
to the origins of hot rodding.

What's a 'fender'?

A tired old cliché asserts that Britain and the USA are separated by a common language. But in the automotive (motor) industry, there are more linguistic differences than most people realise. In alphabetical order (with the British version in brackets), here are some of the more common ones: top (hood); hood (bonnet); trunk (boot); engine displacement (engine capacity); motor (engine); rumble seat (dickey seat); fender (mudguard or wing); nerf bar (bumper); station wagon (estate car or shooting brake); transmission (gearbox); gasoline (petrol); sedan (saloon); trailer (caravan); windshield (windscreen); tire (tyre); muffler (silencer); kerosene (paraffin); hard top (pillarless coupe); phaeton (tourer); stocker (touring car racer); rig (articulated truck); clunker (banger); top fuel (runs on nitro methane).

What is 'horsepower'?

Horsepower was a very strange measurement adopted by the British for the purpose of motor vehicle taxation. Many believe it was deliberately developed to penalise cheap, large-engined cars such as the Model T Ford in favour of smaller engined vehicles of British manufacture. The RAC formula for calculating horsepower is the square of the cylinder bore in millimetres multiplied by the number of cylinders in the engine, divided by 1613. This meant that a Model T Ford with a swept engine capacity of 2,890cc, a bore of 95mm and a stroke of 101.5mm was classed as a 22.4HP car and taxed accordingly. On the other hand, a Morris Cowley with a swept engine capacity of 1,548cc, a bore of 69.5mm and a stroke of 120mm was classed as an 11.9HP car, with the obvious tax benefit this brought. In Britain's strangely protected market, small-capacity, narrow-bore, long-stroke engines became the order of the day and Herbert Austin was able to get away with selling us the miniature 747cc 7.7HP Austin Seven for much the same price as Henry Ford had been charging for twice as much motor car. It was hardly surprising that, on the developing world markets of the 1920s and 1930s, the tough, large-engined, short-stroke American cars were much preferred to the fragile, small-engined, long-stroke British cars.

What's 'Pass Plus'?

With insurance rates for young drivers as much as ten times the price of their old bangers, any kid with a brain wants to know how he or she can get a better deal. The answer is 'Pass Plus', a post-driving-test instruction course backed by the Driving Standards Agency and designed to prepare young drivers for the reality of driving in all weathers, in and out of town, on motorways and at night. There's no test to get cold sweats about. Simply, once the instructor is satisfied, he or she issues a pass certificate which is not just a lifesaver in itself, it can entitle youngsters to reductions of up to 25 per cent on their insurance premiums. Over four years this could easily add up to a £1,000 saving. Insurers which offer discounts to Pass Plus certificate holders include Churchill, CGNU, Direct Line, Norwich Union and Ecclesiastical Direct (young women only). The Pass Plus hotline is 0115 901 2633; website: www.passplus.org.uk.

What is 'electronic ignition'?

These days, most cars are fitted with some form of electronic ignition or 'ignition igniter' in place of the old-fashioned distributor and points system. The disadvantage of a distributor is that the rotor arm contact and the points in the distributor are inevitably subject to wear. So what an electronic ignition system kit does is replace them with an optical switch which feeds firing information through to a power module without any physical contact. Basically, an infra red light beam is detected by a silicon photo-transistor and this beam is interrupted by a revolving chopper with wings for each cylinder replacing the rotor arm on the distributor shaft. The optical switch is fitted to the same base plate as the points were, so that speed and vacuum advance are unchanged. The earthed power module (or amplifier) receives the electronic pulses from the optical switch and charges the coil. These systems rarely go wrong, but when they do the fault tends to be either in the distributor shaft or its bearing or, more commonly, in the ignition amplifier which can malfunction intermittently.

What's a 'Hamburger' junction?

The Transport Research Laboratory has been experimenting with various alternatives to roundabouts, some of which it has now introduced to real road situations. A 'Hamburger' junction is where a major road crosses a minor road and a roundabout formerly dealt with traffic flow. Instead of having to drive round the roundabout, cars on the main road drive straight across it. Then, when traffic starts to build up on the minor roads into the roundabout or on the major road from traffic wishing to turn right, lights stop the through traffic to allow the other vehicles on their way. A 'Hot Cross Bun' junction takes this a stage further, allowing traffic at a crossroads between two major roads to treat the junction either as a roundabout or as a crossroads with slip roads for traffic wishing to turn left or right. A 'Signabout' does away with the roundabout altogether, dividing traffic entering the junction which wishes to turn right from traffic intending to go straight ahead or turn left. Instead of driving round the backs of each other, vehicles making turns pass left-side to left-side. Unfortunately, the new schemes seem to be causing enormous confusion, nowhere more so than at the former dosser's palace Waterloo roundabout, where, to the great surprise of many drivers, roundabout traffic suddenly became two-way with one side blocked off so there was no longer any possibility of correcting a directional error – the great boon of every roundabout.

What's a 'Christmas tree'?

To launch the company's 8.2 litre, 1,183bhp, supercharged drag racing PT 'Bruiser', Chrysler has kindly supplied a list of drag racing jargon. A 'drag race' is a race between two cars, usually down a quarter-mile drag-strip. The first car to pass the finish line wins. A 'Christmas tree' is the stack of lights used to tell the drivers when to start their race. A 'dragster' or 'rail' is a long, low drag-racing car with an engine usually developing well over 1,000bhp; a 'blower' is a supercharger; a 'burnout' is spinning the tyres on the line prior to the race to get them as hot and sticky as possible for maximum traction off the line; an 'ET' is the elapsed time the car takes to cover the quarter mile strip; a 'bump spot' is the lowest qualifying elapsed time; a 'funny car' is a short wheelbase dragster with a plastic body resembling that of a current car; a 'holeshot' is when one racer leaves the startline before his opponent; a 'red light' is a disqualification for leaving the line before the green light on the Christmas tree; a 'pro stock' is a category for steel-bodied race cars like the PT Bruiser.

What's a 'pre-heater'

Diesel fuel has a high 'wax' content which can crystallise at low temperatures and clog the fuel filter. Although winter-grade diesel now has additives to help prevent 'waxing' down to around minus 20 degrees Celsius, most diesel cars are fitted with a fuel pre-heater in the fuel line before the fuel filter. It is thermostatically controlled to switch on whenever the temperature drops to just above zero. Other types of pre-heater, such as VAG's, are incorporated into the fuel pump. In cold weather, indirect injected diesel engines also require pre-heating of the combustion chambers because the heat created by the initial ignition of the fuel is soaked away through the cold engine cylinder walls. This is achieved by means of 'glow plugs' which introduce a heated element into the combustion chamber. The high compression of an IDI diesel engine and the need to heat glow plugs helps explain why they need a high-capacity battery and why the life of that battery can be short if the vehicle does lots of short runs from cold. Though direct injected diesels don't usually need pre-heaters, some do have glow plugs, but these are smaller, heat up more quickly and take less out of the battery.

What's an 'alternator'

This is the piece of engine-driven kit which generates a car's electricity supply. The 'stator' is a circular laminated iron core on which three separate lengths of wire are wound, and which remains static in the casing. The 'rotor' is a coil of wire wound on an iron core pressed onto a shaft. When current from the battery is passed through the rotor a magnetic field is created and, as it rotates inside the stator, an AC current is produced. This is converted to the DC current required by the car using six diodes which allow current to flow in only one rather than two directions. The advantage of an alternator over a dynamo is that it can be geared up to be driven at higher speeds than the engine, enabling the car battery to be re-charged more quickly at low engine speeds. Typical alternators produce useful current at around 1,500rpm up to a maximum of about 7,000rpm, and most are driven at about twice the engine speed.

What is 'smoke opacity'

This is the density of the exhaust emissions of a diesel-fuelled engine. For all diesel-fuelled cars and light commercial vehicles first used on or after 1 August 1979, it is tested annually as part of the MOT test by a probe which measures absorption coefficient per metre and is placed in the vehicle's exhaust tailpipe. Controversy still surrounds the actual method of testing. First the engine must be brought up to its running temperature, measured by a probe placed down the oil dipstick tube. Engine revs are then very gradually increased until they reach a governed maximum. If the fuel pump governor is not working then the test will be abandoned. The engine is then revved to its maximum governed revs three times and three measurements of its exhaust smoke opacity are taken. The maximum permitted is an absorption coefficient of 3.0 per metre for a turbocharged diesel and 2.5 per metre for a non-turbo diesel. If the average of the three tests is below the permitted figures, the engine passes the test. If not, further tests take place up

to a maximum of six accelerations until the average of the last three tests is below the permitted figures. If it isn't, the engine fails its MOT 'smoke opacity' test.

What's an 'MOT Refusal to Test'?

This is where an MOT examiner can refuse to examine a vehicle submitted for testing on one or more of the following grounds: the V5 registration document is not provided to prove the date of first registration if this is necessary for testing purposes (usually when the vehicle has a non-dating cherished registration); the vehicle is presented in such a dirty condition that examination would be unreasonably difficult; the vehicle cannot be driven, or has insufficient fuel or oil to enable the test to be completed; an authorised examiner considers that an insecure load or other items would prevent a proper test being carried out; the vehicle is of a size or weight that cannot properly be tested at the testing station; the vehicle emits substantial quantities of avoidable smoke; a proper examination cannot be carried out because a door, tailgate, boot lid, engine cover, fuel cap or other device designed to be readily opened cannot be; the condition of the vehicle is such that, in the opinion of the examiner, a proper examination would involve danger of injury to any person or damage to the vehicle or other property.

What's an MOT 'screen test'?

This is the procedure an MOT inspector uses to check a windscreen as part of a car's annual test. He will first look at the area swept by the wipers in a 290mm vertical band centred on the centre of the steering wheel. Reasons for MOT failure are: damage not contained within a 10mm diameter circle; a windscreen sticker or other obstruction encroaching more than 10mm; or a combination of minor damage areas which seriously restricts the driver's view. He will then look at the entire area of the screen swept by the wipers and will fail the car if there is any damage not contained within a 40mm circle, or a windscreen sticker or other obstruction encroaching more than 40mm. Remember, it is far better to repair a windscreen if at all possible, or simply leave the damage if the car will still pass the MOT. Removing and replacing bonded screens often damages paintwork and enables rust to take hold with a vengeance.

What's an MOT 'brake test'?

Readers may be wondering exactly what sort of MOT examination the hydraulic 'foot brake' system on their car is put to. First the examiner looks for leaks in the system and checks that rigid brake and flexible pipes are securely held and are not corroded, fouled, kinked, chafed, twisted or damaged in any way. He then checks the individual brake discs and drums for corrosion and fluid leaks, and makes sure the callipers and back plates are securely fitted. He makes sure that the master cylinder is securely mounted, is free of corrosion, has an adequate fluid level, is capped and is not leaking.

He then checks the servo and associated pipework. After that, on most cars, he performs a Roller Brake Test, but cars with more than one driven axle permanently engaged, with a limited slip differential or with a belt-driven transmission cannot be tested on a roller. The test includes both retardation performance and any imbalance in the braking system. Cars which cannot be tested in this way must be tested with a decelerometer on a road. For most cars, the foot brake (service brake) must have a minimum brake efficiency of 50 per cent and the hand brake (parking brake) 25 per cent.

What's a 'MacPherson Strut'

With a few exceptions, car suspension is composed of coil or leaf springs, damper units to absorb bounce, and various arms, links and bushes to hold the system together. The idea of the MacPherson Strut was to eliminate as many separate components as possible, particularly in the front suspension of a car – though MacPherson Struts can also be used at the rear. Very simply, strut suspension combines a coil spring, a telescopic damper and a vertical suspension arm in one. When used at the front of a car the spring and damper fit into a bearing set into a strengthened section of the top inner wing of the car. This allows it and the hub it is attached to at the bottom to rotate, so the car can be steered. A single arm containing a lower bearing for the strut provides up and down movement and is held in place by a leading or trailing arm running at right angles to it. One of the first British cars to have MacPherson Strut front suspension was the 1950 Ford Consul.

What's a 'Trade Licence'?

These are what the public usually refer to as 'trade plates' and are subject to some surprisingly draconian restrictions. Essentially they allow unregistered or untaxed vehicles to be driven on public roads for the purposes of delivery, demonstration or testing. They do not allow the holder to make any personal journeys in a vehicle on trade plates, and traders dropping their kids off at school on their way to an auction have been fined for this. Currently the design of trade plates is under consultation. It is proposed to change them from pressed metal plates with a pointy bit on top to carry the tax triangle to simple oblong shapes with the tax disc incorporated. Consultees are being asked if they would prefer the plates to be plastic, to be designed to be clipped or fastened over existing registration plates, or to be fitted inside the windows of the vehicles using suckers.

What's 'CO_2 Benefit Tax'?

This is the tax drivers of company cars pay for the benefit of their private use of the car, as from 6 April 2002. Many company drivers remain unaware of the new regime and will be in for a shock. There will no longer be any discount for a high business mileage. Instead, drivers will be taxed on 15 per cent of the car's 'list price', with the tax base increasing by 1 per cent for each 5g/km CO_2 the car emits over and above 165g/km. For tax year 2003–2004, the base CO_2 will be 155g/km and for tax year 2004–2005 the base CO_2 will be 145g/km. So, effectively, the tax base for a £15,000 car emitting 185g/km will rise from 19 per cent (or £2,850) in 2002–2003 to 23 per cent (or £3,450) in 2004–2005. Because they emit less CO_2, diesels will be hit with a three per cent surcharge, and no driver will be taxed on a base of more than 35 per cent of the car's list price. So, as with CO_2-based VED, there is no benefit to be had from driving a company car with an ultra-low CO_2 rating. Automatics emit around 10 per cent more CO_2 than manuals. List prices, VED bands and CO_2 tables can be found in *What Car?* magazine.

What's a three-point belt?

This is a quicker way of describing a lap and diagonal safety belt. Over the years more and more cars have been fitted with three three-point belts across the back seat. These include: Alfa 156 (£97.53

option) Alfa 147, BMW 5-Series, Chrysler PT Cruiser, Citroën Berlingo Multispace Forte 5-door; Citroën Xantia Estate, Citroën C5, Citroën Picasso, Fiat Punto from 2000 MY (standard in HLX and above; £75 option in base models), Fiat Multipla, Ford Mondeo from 1997 MY, Honda Accord from 1999 MY; Hyundai Santa Fe, Jaguar S Type, Jaguar X Type, KIA Magentis, Land Rover Freelander 5-door; Land Rover Discovery from 1999 MY, Mazda 626 from July 1997, MB C Class estate; all new MB C Class; MB E Class estate from May 1996; MB E Class from June 1998; MB S Class; Mitsubishi Galant from 1998 MY, Mitsubishi Space Star, Nissan Almera 4-door; Nissan Almera Tino; new Nissan Primera SLX, Peugeot 306 Sedan, Peugeot 307; Peugeot 406, Proton Impian, Renault new Clio from May 1998 (not base models), Renault Kangoo Combi RXE model, Renault Megane and Scenic, Renault Laguna from 95M, Renault Espace from 1997 MY, new Rover 200, Rover 25, Rover 45, Rover 600 from 1997 MY, Rover 75, Rover 800 4-door from 94M, SAAB 900 from 94L, SAAB 9-3, SAAB 9-5 (saloon and estate), SEAT Leon, new SEAT Toledo (from 1999 MY), new SEAT Alhambra (from August 2000), Toyota Corolla from July 1997, Toyota Avensis, Toyota Camry from 1997 MY, Vauxhall Corsa from 2001 MY, Vauxhall Astra from April 1998 (not Zafira), Vauxhall Vectra from 1997 MY, Vauxhall Omega, 1998 VW Golf IV and Bora (£100 optional extra, but standard on Golf V5 Estate), VW Passat (£100 optional extra), VW Sharan from 2001 MY, Volvo S40, Volvo V40, Volvo S60, Volvo S70, Volvo V70, Volvo 850, Volvo S80, Volvo 940, Volvo 960, Volvo S90, Volvo V90.

What's 'motormilk'?

This is what the Society of Motor Manufacturers and Traders has calculated is being extracted from car owners by the government. In a calculation tracing all costs from the purchase of a new £8,000 car in 1992 to its scrappage after 110,000 miles in 2000, the SMMT calculates that the car will have generated no less than £11,712 in tax revenue. This sum includes VAT on the original sale and re-sale of the car, Vehicle Excise Duty, Fuel Tax and VAT on fuel and Fuel Tax, Insurance Premium Tax and VAT on service, parts and repair costs. This means that out of a total of £50,984 generated within the economy by the car over its eight-year life, 22.97 per cent was tax. Apart from booze and fags, which are allegedly heavily taxed because of the health risk, nothing else is taxed as heavily and nothing else generates a tax income for the government of 146 per cent of its original purchase price.

What is 'satisfactory quality'?

This is the definition used in The Sale and Supply of Goods Act 1994 as the legitimate reason for a purchaser to reject goods sold to him by a supplier. The 1994 Act modified the Sale of Goods Act 1979 which defined the reason for rejection as not being of 'merchantable quality'. The later Act should have made life a lot easier for all of us but, of course, Britain being Britain and lawyers being lawyers, it didn't. We are forced to rely on case law precedents as to what constitutes 'satisfactory quality' and what doesn't. Even where a precedent is set, it can be overruled by a higher court, so every court case involving The Sale and Supply of Goods Act 1994 involves legal argument on the technicalities as to whether a previous judgment sets a precedent for the case being heard. Very broadly, you probably won't be able to reject a car you have owned for more than six months, you won't be able to reject it for a trivial reason and, most importantly, the only way to start the proceedings is to return the car to the supplier. You cannot reject a car while still remaining in possession of it.

What is 'congestion charging'?

This is a means by which city councils hope to limit the number of vehicles entering their cities and thus reduce vehicle congestion on city streets. The intention is to create a central zone with limited numbers of streets leading into it, and controlled by cameras. Vehicle drivers have to obtain electronic permits costing, for example, £5 per day to enter this central zone, otherwise the registered

keeper of the vehicle will be subject to, for example, an £80 fine. Objectors to congestion charging point out that the areas immediately outside the central zone will become even more congested with parked vehicles and confused drivers; that city centre public transport will be unable to transport the extra passengers created by the schemes; that the movement of goods and packages within the central zone will become more expensive; that business people who need flexible transport at all hours will either be hard hit or will simply pass the charges on to their customers; and that, instead of travelling into the central zone by public transport, many potential visitors will simply avoid it and take their money elsewhere.

What is 'EBD'?

There are quite a lot of new abbreviations being applied to vehicle braking systems these days. We've got used to 'ABS' meaning Antilock Braking System, whereby electronic sensors detect losses of traction by individual wheels and release the brakes on that wheel in a series of pulses until traction is regained. Then we got 'TCS' which stands for Traction Control System and electronically releases the power fed to a wheel which has lost traction. An 'EDL' or Electronic Differential Lock performs a slightly different function by preventing the slippage of one wheel at the same end of the car depriving the other wheel of drive through the differential effect. Comparative newcomers are 'HBA', or Hydraulic Brake Assist, which provides additional braking effort on top of that of the driver and the servo assistance; 'EBD' or Electronic Brakeforce Distribution, which evens out the front-to-back braking forces and is particularly helpful in MPV-type vehicles; and finally we have 'ESP' which has nothing to do with extra sensory perception and everything to do with Electronic Stability Programme which harnesses the ABS, TCS, EDL, HBA, EBD and suspension componentry to prevent the car getting out of shape on a corner, whatever shape the driver happens to be in.

What is 'automotive ageism'?

We're starting to shun older cars. In its 2001 Used Car Market Report, British Car Auctions revealed that sales of cars nine years old or more have dropped by over half a million a year. Total used car sales dropped by 550,000, so the vast bulk was accounted for by falling sales of older cars. Against this, sales of used cars under two years old actually grew by 3% to 1,030,000. Internet sales have grown enormously with 49% saying they would use the Internet to research or buy their next car compared to just 9% three years ago. Surprisingly, the survey showed that 64% of used car buyers were 'very satisfied' with their purchases and a further 28% were 'quite satisfied', and that 78% of car buyers would buy another used rather than a new car. Only 4% were either 'quite dissatisfied' or 'very dissatisfied', but all of them seem to write to Honest John giving a distorted picture of satisfaction levels in general.

What are the new rules on number plates?

Script and altered-space number plates have irritated *Telegraph* readers for years. Now new rules contained in the Road Vehicles (Display of Registration Marks) Regulations 2001 have outlawed this for all new registration plates made on or after 1 September 2001. Regulation 15 specifies the Charles Wright typeface. Serifs may be added but the typeface must not be: italic; non-vertical; substantially different in curvature or alignment from the Charles Wright font; formed in such a way as to make characters appear to be different (no S for 5; no T for 7, etc.); and must not involve multiple or broken strokes. The prescribed height is now slightly smaller than before at 79mm for 'all vehicles' and 69mm for motorcycles, etc. 'Classics' (vehicles first registered before 1 January 1973) are exempted and may continue to display 'white, silver or light grey letters and numbers on a black surface', even if the plates are freshly made up.

What is a company 'cash for car' scheme?

The MD of a small advertising agency with ten company cars asked for a simple way to offer his employees a cash alternative when the new BIK taxes started in April 2002. From that date the benefit of a company car is calculated on the basis of a percentage of its list price, progressively increased by percentage points according to its CO_2 output up to a maximum of 35% of the list price. Higher-rate tax-paying employees are required to pay tax at 40% of that amount. CO_2 figures are listed online at www.vca.gov.uk/fcb.htm. Alternatively, employees can check their BIK liability for any car online by visiting www.honda.co.uk, which runs an excellent and very 'friendly' BIK tax calculator (click on the 'Cars' icon, wait for the page to load, then click on 'cash for cars' at the bottom of the page). What the MD needs to think about is the cost to his company of each car, including lease costs, insurance, maintenance, repairs, fuel and employer's NIC on all of this. Once he has that figure and the BIK liability figure of the employee, he can work out a

cash alternative plus a tax-free Business Approved Mileage Rate of 40p a mile to 10,000 miles and 25p thereafter. Or he can have it all packaged for him by a company such as Delta Leasing on 01487 773322, website: www.ukcashforcar.com

What's 'flashcan'?

This is a kid's game involving a tin can, a length of string or rope and a Gatso speed camera. First, the kids peel the label from the can so it's nice and shiny. Then they punch a hole in the bottom, push a knotted string through and tie another knot on the outside of the can. They then find that, after a bit of practice, they can swing the can on the string at such speed in front of the camera's radar that it triggers the flash. Obviously, if any *Daily Telegraph* reader witnesses children wasting valuable police electricity and film in such a manner they should immediately report the young ruffians to the police.

What are 'telematics'?

This is a term you may have heard Murray Walker mention at the top of his voice during a Grand Prix commentary. It's the method by which the on-board computers of a racing car convey information to the computers and the engineers in the pits. So the driver does not need a fuel gauge because the engineers in the pits know exactly how much fuel he has got left and how much fuel he is using. If the engine is suffering a misfire the engineers know exactly which cylinder. They can even see if an individual tyre is losing pressure. Formula One is the test bed for technology that eventually filters through to the cars you and I drive. So it won't be long before the ECU in your new car sends telematic messages directly to your servicing garage, the staff of which will then call you up to tell you your oil is getting a bit dirty, your front offside tyre is losing pressure, your engine is using too much fuel, or whatever. Let's just hope the same gizmos aren't also transmitting to your local police station.

What's 'telediagnosis'?

We've already seen (above) how the term 'telematics' is used to describe the means by which every aspect of the way a Formula 1 car is performing is transmitted back to the engineers in the pits. It was only a matter of time before this technology was applied to cars. Most modern engines have diagnostic plugs. Many modern cars also have mobile phones. By connecting the car's diagnostics to its mobile phone system, anything wrong with the car can be picked up in real time by a service centre. In the case of the new Mercedes E Class, 'Teleaid' is a system which automatically sends an SOS signal to the MB Customer Assistance Centre in the event of an accident. 'Telediagnosis' takes this a stage further by relaying any faults in the car's systems to the service centre at the touch of a button.

What's the law on licence display?

Regulation 16 of the Road Vehicle (Registration & Licensing) Regs 1971 states that on vehicles with windscreens extending across the front of the driver to the nearside, the VED disc must be displayed on or adjacent to the nearside and clearly visible in daylight from the nearside of the road. Section 33 of the Vehicle Excise and Registration Act 1994 imposes a level one fixed penalty fine for failing to exhibit the VED disc in the prescribed manner.

What's 'Distronic'?

This is Mercedes' name for what Bosch calls 'Adaptive Cruise Control'. Its purpose is to prevent your car getting too close to the car in front when using cruise control, by automatically either reducing engine revs or applying the brakes. In theory this should be a life-saver, but there is one situation in which it can be a killer. You are on a wide slip road from one motorway to another. A second car is up close to your back bumper. A second slip road then feeds into your slip road and a third car peels onto it in front of you. What could then happen is that the sensors pick up this third car as too close, send a panic signal to your brakes, apply your brakes hard, and you get a bootfull of car number two. The answer is never switch on this type of cruise control on a slip road while you are joining a motorway and always switch it off at any sort of motorway interchange.

What exempts you from wearing a seatbelt?

I obviously don't want to encourage the non-wearing of seatbelts, but Regulation 6 of the Motor Vehicle (Wearing Seat Belts) Regulations 1993 allows the following exemptions for adults:
- The driver if no adult seatbelt is provided.
- A person in the front if no adult belt is available in the front.
- A person in the rear if no adult belt is available in the rear.
- A person holding a medical exemption certificate.
- A person using a goods or mail delivery vehicle while engaged in making local rounds of deliveries or collections.
- A person driving a vehicle while performing a manoeuvre which includes reversing.
- A qualified driver supervising a provisional driver while performing a manoeuvre which includes reversing.
- A person conducting a test of competence to drive and the wearing of the belt would endanger himself or any other person.
- A person driving or riding in a vehicle while it is being used for fire brigade or police purposes, or for carrying a person in lawful custody including the detained person himself.
- The driver of a licensed taxi while being used for seeking hire, or answering a call for hire, or carrying a passenger for hire, or a private hire vehicle while it is being used to carry a passenger for hire.
- A person riding in a vehicle being used under a trade licence for

the purposes of investigating or remedying a mechanical fault in the vehicle.
- A disabled person wearing a disabled person's belt.
- A person riding in a vehicle while taking part in a procession organised by or on behalf of the Crown, or which is commonly or customarily held, or a procession for which a notice under Section 11 of the Public Order Act 1986 has been issued.

What's the law on speedometers?

Regulation 35 of the Road Vehicles (Construction and Use) Regs 1986 stipulates that every motor vehicle shall be fitted with a speedometer except: those that can't do more than 25mph; motorbikes under 100cc; invalid carriages and works trucks first used before 1 April 1984; any vehicle first used before 1937. On vehicles first used on or after 1 April 1984, the speedometer must indicate speed in mph and kph, or must comply with EC Directive 97/39 or ECE reg 39. The most important bit is that all speedometers must never indicate less than the true speed of the vehicle, and between 40kph and 120kph the error must not exceed 10% + 2.5mph (or 4kph) over the true speed. This means that at a true speed of 25mph or 40kph the Speedo may read up to 5mph (8kph) high. That's why you can and do get stuck behind drivers holding a steady 25mph in a 30 zone.

What's the 120g/km cutoff

This is the VED concession granted by Chancellor Gordon Brown in his April 2002 budget to cars first registered on or after 1 March 2001 which emit less than 120g/km CO_2. It brings the VED of some petrol engined cars previously taxed at £100 down to £70, of some diesels previously taxed at £110 down to £80 and of some alternative fuel cars previously taxed at £90 down to £60. Cars which qualify for the cut include the Honda Insight hybrid, Toyota Prius hybrid, MCC Smart petrol models and Vauxhall Corsa 1.0 Eco.

Diesels cut to £80 are: Audi A2 1.4 TDi, Citroën C3 1.4HDI, Ford Fiesta 1.4 TDCi, Peugeot 206 1.4 HDI, Renault Clio 1.5dCi 65 and dCi 80, SEAT Arosa 1.4 TDi, Toyota Yaris 1.4 D-4D, VW Lupo 1.7SDi and VW Lupo 1.4TDi. The new Polo 1.4TDi misses out by a whisker.

What's a 'Power-Box'?

This is a neat little German TUV-approved gizmo that can increase the power of a VAG TDI engine by as much as 37bhp. What it does is intercept the signals from the engine's Electronic Control Unit to the fuel pump and modulate the fuel pump timing much more accurately than the standard very conservative set-up. The result is an average increase of 20bhp for a TDI 90, 25bhp for a TDI 110, 24bhp for a TDI PD 115, 30bhp for a TDI PD 130 and up to 37bhp for a TDI V6 155. Telephone Power-Box on 01603 722698; website: www.dieselchiptuning.com Telephone Van Aaken, which offers a similar Smart Box, on 01344 777557; website: www.vanaaken.com

What's 'Ackerman' steering?

Rudolf Ackerman is the 1818 patentee of a steering design, still used on all vehicles, based on the geometric principle that all wheels must describe different circles around a common centre; hence the wheel on the inside of a curve must turn through a greater angle than the wheel on the outside of the curve.

What's a 'bootlegger turn'?

This is the technique of inducing a controlled 180 degree spin at speed as an emergency escape manoeuvre. It can be done by braking hard from speed to encourage a rear wheel skid then, at about 30mph, turning the steering wheel rapidly to induce a U turn while continuing to brake hard and, as the vehicle turns, countersteering and accelerating hard in 2nd gear. The manoeuvre is ideally suited to a rear wheel drive car that will naturally oversteer. Some vehicles may require application of the parking brake, thereby converting the manoeuvre into a 'handbrake turn'.

(**Caution** Do not try this in a vehicle with a high centre of gravity such as a pickup, SUV, 4x4 or MPV.)

What's a De Dion axle?

This is an axle and suspension system comprising a driven axle where the differential or transaxle is mounted on the chassis so that it is sprung weight and does not comprise part of the unsprung weight of the vehicle. The driveshafts from diff to hubs have universal joints at each end in order that the wheels can remain vertical when the vehicle is cornering. It was designed by Count Albert de Dion in 1894 and was a distinguishing advanced feature of the cars which bore his name.

Good Garage Guide

In the summer of 1996 the 'Motoring' section of the *Daily Telegraph* ran a reader's story about the differences between big garages in Britain and small garages in France. I felt that the contrast was more likely to be between bad garages and good garages generally, so I asked for readers' recommendations. The list continues to grow, and the most recent version is published here.

Remember, the list is based purely on readers' recommendations,* and inclusion is no guarantee of quality, competence or good value.

---

* Do you have a recommendation for the Good Garage Guide? Send it to Honest John care of the publishers, Constable-Robinson, at the address shown on page iv opposite the Contents list.

Nevertheless, many of the testimonials were fulsome in their praise, so if you are looking for good service from your garage, this list may be the right place to start.

The London Area

Bromley
Ted and Neil Craker, The Vehicle Test Centre, 107 Southlands Road, Bromley, Kent BR2 9QT, tel: 020 8460 6666. (Very well equipped and sensibly priced servicing workshop/MOT test centre, with two 'rolling road' brake testers and full diagnostic equipment.)

Catford
Gilbert's Motors, 304–312 Sangley Road, London SE6 2JX, tel: 020 8698 7067. (Honda agent prepared to repair expensive components rather than replace them.)

Enfield
Stephen James, Clock Parade, London Road, Enfield EN2 6JG, tel: 020 8367 2626. (Friendly BMW agent with sensibly priced servicing.)

London N4
Nick Sandamas, G & N Garages Ltd, 54–58 Wightman Road, Harringay, London N4 1RU, tel: 020 8340 3311. (Independent Saab specialist.)

London SE6

Gonella Brothers, 9–13 Catford Hill, Catford, London SE6 4NU, tel: 0208 690 0060. (Alfa, Fiat and Lancia specialists.)

London SW2

Hearn Bros Ltd, The Hill Garage, 94 Brixton Hill, London SW2, tel: 0208 674 2888.

London SW17

Carpenters Garage, 69–71 Bickersteth Road, Tooting, London SW17 9SH, tel: 0208 672 4891. (Small, family run independent garage and MOT testing station.)

London W8

ACE Cars of Kensington, 18–23 Radley Mews, London W8 6JP, tel: 0207 938 4333. (Subaru dealer specialising in the SVX. Also specialises in older Saabs: 900, 99, 96. Very well thought of.)

London W12

AC Automotive, 247–251 Goldhawk Road, London W12, tel: 0208 741 9993. (American car parts and servicing.)

Perivale

AC Delco, Unit 14, 19 Wadsworth Road, Perivale, Middx., tel: 020 8810 4595. (American car parts and servicing.)

South of the Thames

Alton

Neil Carpenter, Farringdon Industrial Centre, Alton, Hants, tel: 01420 587 403.

Andover

Chris Monaghan and Martin Dix, Intech GB Ltd, Unit 12B, Thruxton Industrial Estate, Thruxton Circuit, near Andover, Hants, tel: 01264 773888. (Service and repair specialists for Japanese 'grey' imports, from Honda Beat to Lexus 'Soarer' Coupe.)

97

Bexhill-On-Sea

Peter Johnson Motor Engineer, Unit 3, de la Warr Mews, Station Road, Bexhill-on-Sea, East Sussex TN40 1RD, tel: 01424 224169.

Bexleyheath

Paul at PDQ Car Services, Bexleyheath, Kent (best to phone first for directions), tel: 020 8303 1618, mobile: 07831 138463.

Billinghurst

Geoffrey Sizzy (Automobiles), Wisborough Green, Nr Billingshurst, West Sussex, tel: 01403 700661. (Independent Peugeot specialist – sales, service, very good after-sales service.)

Bognor Regis

Middleton Garage, 169 Middleton Road, Middleton on Sea, Bognor Regis, tel: 01243 58276. (Very helpful Fiat franchise.)

Bournemouth

Horizon Motors, tel: 01202 294341. (Honda agents.)

Canterbury

Ashford Road Service Station, Chilham, Canterbury, Kent CT4 8EE, tel: 01227 730223.

Hewitt Motors Ltd, Rhodans Town, Canterbury, Kent, tel: 01227 464386.

Chandlers Ford

Hendy Lennox, Chandlers Ford, Hants, tel: 023 8048 3100. (Good, helpful Ford agent.)

Chertsey

Speedtest, Unit A, Gogmore Lane, Chertsey, Surrey, tel: 01932 568921. (Non-rip-off servicing and MOT centre. Good with Citroëns and Renaults.)

Chessington

Mole Valley TVR, Chessington, Surrey, tel: 020 8394 1114. (Good TVR dealer.)

Chislehurst

Paul and Tony at PDQ, 1a Albany Road, Chislehurst, Kent, tel: 020 8295 0121. (BMW and Jaguar specialists.)

Croydon

The Silver Wing Garage, 25 Horatius Way, Silverwing Industrial Estate, Stafford Road, Croydon, Surrey CR0 4RU, tel: 020 8680 6959. (Much-praised independent garage operating a National Auto Service franchise.)

Parker Bros (Croydon) Ltd, tel: 0208 654 1923. (General repairs and servicing, in business for over 70 years. Will do jobs in the most economic way possible.)

Crowborough

John Cottenham, Care's Garage, School Lane, St Johns, Crowborough, Sussex TN6 1SE, tel: 01892 653519.

Dorking
Steve Bradstock, The Coach House, Beare Green, Dorking, Surrey, tel: 01306 713424.

Dover
Elms Vale Garage, Elms Vale Road, Dover, tel: 01304 201077. (Good small independent local garage.)

Eastbourne
Visick Cars Ltd, Birch Close, Lottbridge Drove, Eastbourne BN23 6PE, tel: 01323 722244.

Emsworth
Lillywhite Bros Ltd, 40 Queen Street, Emsworth, Hants PO10 7BL, tel: 01243 372336.

Epsom
King Automatics, 'The Chalk Pit', College Road, Epsom, Surrey KT17 4JA, tel: 01372 728769. (Automatic transmissions of all types, including CVTs).

Kwik-Fit, 166 East Street, Epsom, Surrey, tel: 01372 739955.

Drift Bridge Garage Ltd, Reigate Road, Epsom, Surrey, tel: 01737 360111.

Erith
Erith Garage Services, Maypole Crescent, Darent Industrial Park, Erith, Kent, tel: 01322 331150. (Good independent garage which also carries out restorations.)

Fareham
Peter Cooper, Fareham, Hants, tel: 01329 288233. (Good, helpful VW franchise.)

Ferring
John Cooper Garages, Ferring, West Sussex, tel: 01903 504455. (Very helpful Honda franchise.)

Finchampstead
Cresswells, California Crossroads, Finchampstead, Berks, tel: 01734 732201.

Guildford
A.H. Autos, Unit 11, Foundation Units, Westfield Road, Slyfield Green, Guildford, tel: 01483 303942. (VW/Audi specialists.)

Hersham
Colin Marshall or Keith Rhoods, Wheelbase Garage, 43 Queen's Road, Hersham, Surrey, tel: 01932 252515/252881. (VW/Audi specialists.)

Sunbury Coachworks, Unit R3, Lyon Road, Hersham Industrial Estate, Hersham, Surrey, tel: 01932 254057. (Good bodyshop offering excellent Autocolor paint finish at reasonable prices.)

East Horsley
Philip Stonely, The Body Workshop, Forest Road Garage, Forest Road, Effingham Junction, Surrey KT24 5HE, tel: 01483 284805.

Hythe
Auto Pat, 3 Hardley Industrial Estate, Hardley, Nr Hythe, Hants, tel: 023 8080 4163.

Isle of Wight
Harwoods, Lushington Hill, IOW, tel: 01983 885500. (Very helpful Renault agent, not averse to imports.)

Kingston
Top One International, Unit 11, Park Works, Borough Road, Kingston, Surrey KT2 6BD, tel: 020 8549 8188. (Very good for independent spares, supply and servicing of MCC Smart cars.)

Leatherhead
Kingscraft Volvo, Leatherhead, Surrey KT22 7DL, tel: 01372 371900. (Helpful Volvo dealer which has picked up the pieces left by other Volvo franchises.)

Lewes
Morris Road Garage, Western Road, Lewes, East Sussex, tel: 01273 472434. (Independent Bosch fuel injection specialists.)

Lymington
Dory's Garage Ltd, Sway Park, Station Road, Sway, Hants, tel: 01590 683432. (Citroën specialists.)

Maidenhead

Delta Motors, tel: 01628 675064. Contacts: Jerry Houdret – sales; Roger Towers – parts. (Efficient Renault agents.)

Merstham

John Witty, Witmun Engineering, 67 Nutfield Road, Merstham, Surrey RH1 3ER, tel: 01737 644828. (Citroën specialists.)

New Romney

Dave Allchin, Marsh Citroën Repairs, Unit 11, Mountfield Road, New Romney, Kent TN28 8LH, tel: 01797 361234. (Dave is a fount of knowledge who gives excellent service at sensible prices.)

Orpington

Chelsfield Motor Works, Court Lodge Farm, Warren Road, Orpington, Kent BR6 6ER, tel: 01689 823200.

Petersfield

Collins and White, 52c College Street, Petersfield, Hants, tel: 01730 262654. (Highly recommended longstanding family business.)

Poole

Connellys, Ashley Road, Upper Parkstone, Poole, Dorset, tel: 01202 738700.

Grand Parade Motors, Poole Road, Poole, Dorset, tel: 01202 763361. (Good Vauxhall agent).

Reading

Clever Cars Ltd, Prospect Mews, Prospect Street, Reading, tel: 01734 576405. (Citroën specialist.)

Ripley

Colbourne Garages Ltd, Portsmouth Road (old A3), Ripley, Surrey, tel: 01483 224361. (Oldest-established UK VW agent, still good.)

Sanderstead

Steven Pengelly, Vorne Motorsport, 145 Limpsfield Road, Sanderstead, Surrey, tel: 020 8651 5344.

Sidcup
Steve King, King's Auto Services, 313–315 Blackfen Road, Blackfen, Sidcup, Kent SA15 9NG, tel: 020 8298 9225.

Southampton
E. & J. Jarvis, Motor Engineers, Onslow Road, Southampton, tel: 023 8022 9297.

Hilton Motors, Bond Road Garage, Bitterne Park, Southampton SO18 1LH, tel: 023 8055 5600. (General service, repair, sales garage and automatic transmission specialist.)

Southsea
John Skerratt, Owl Motor Services, Richmond Road, Southsea, Hants, tel: 023 9273 6393.

Tankerton
Tankerton Garage, Tankerton Road, Whitstable, Kent CT5 2AJ, tel: 01227 771108. (Owner Simon does an excellent job at exceptional prices, often well into the evenings and at weekends.)

West Malling
B. Butler, The Saab Sanctuary, 'Almandene', Woodgate Road, Ryarsh, West Malling, Kent ME19 5LH, tel: 01732 872722.

Weybridge
S.S. Motors. 16c Hanwell Lane, Weybridge Business Park, Weybridge, Surrey KT15 2SD, tel: 01932 821555. (Mercedes specialist run by Mercedes-trained ex-franchise service manager.)

Dagenham Motors (Weybridge), Wintersalls Road, Byfleet, Surrey, tel: 01932 332933. (Good official Ford service agent.)

Q Motors Workshop, Hare Hill, Addlestone, Weybridge KT15 1D, tel: 01932 873 726; website: www.qmotors.co.uk (An outstanding reference for this garage. Prices well below those of franchised dealers but customers have every confidence in Douglas Millard's ability.)

Weymouth
Tyre & Exhaust World, Weymouth, tel: 0345 419937. (Friendly, values its customers.)

Windsor

New and Son, West End Service Station, Dadworth Road, Windsor, Berks, tel: 01753 862078/851685.

Woking

Colbourne Garages Ltd, 76 Maybury Road, Woking, Surrey, tel: 01483 722415. (Oldest-established UK VW agent, still good.)

Worcester Park

Glen Brown, GB Autos, 16a Cheam Common, Worcester Park, Surrey KT4 8RW, tel: 020 8330 6090. (Independent Volvo and air-conditioning servicing specialists.)

Worthing

Rod Denton, Denton Motors, 1–3 Park Road, Worthing, W. Sussex, tel: 01903 233790.

Throughout the region

Association of TUNE-UP Technicians. PO Box 3028, East Preston, West Sussex, BN16 1TD. Mobile engine servicing, Tuning, and Diagnostics. Operators call to your home or place of work. For areas covered and contact telephone numbers see 'Car Engine Tuning' in the Yellow Pages, or for the outh East area online visit www.uktuneup.co.uk (click your location on the map to find your nearest operator).

North of the Thames

Amersham

T and F Motors, White Lion Road, Amersham, Bucks HP7 9JB, tel: 01494 765286.

Aylesbury

Ivor Miles, Churchway Garage, Churchway, Haddenham, Aylesbury, Bucks HP17 8HA, tel: 01844 291263.

Lodge Garage (Aylesbury Mazda) Ltd, Bicester Road, Kingswood, Aylesbury, Bucks HP18 0QJ, tel: 01296 770245.

C.D. Bramall (Aylesbury Toyota – formerly BMG Aylesbury), 156 Wendover Road, Stoke Mandeville, Aylesbury, Bucks HP22 5TE, tel: 01296 615656.

Bishops Stortford
Maltings Garage, Station Road, Sawbridgeworth, Herts CM21 9JX, tel: 01279 723671; fax: 01279 725555. (General servicing, repairs and MOTs. Long-standing customers.)

Franklins Garage Ltd, Stansted Road, Bishop's Stortford CM23 2BT, tel: 01279 757220. (Renault main dealer who, though extremely busy, fixed an overheated Renault miles from its home and charged a tiny £3.15.)

Gravenhurst
Chris Case, Town Farm Garage, Campton Road, Gravenhurst, Beds MK45 4JB, tel: 01462 711017.

Harlington

Exchange Gearboxes, 228 Manor Parade, High St, Harlington, Hayes, Middlesex UB3 5DS, tel: 020 8897 0601.

Harrow

Goodwood Autos, 53b Springfield Road, Harrow, Middlesex HA1 1QF, tel: 020 8427 1343. (Always, helpful, efficient and thorough, and never do unnecessary work just to inflate the bill.)

Hemel Hempstead

V.P. Autos, 559 London Road, Hemel Hempstead, Herts , tel: 01442 268163.

Henlow

Henlow Car Centre, Bedford Road, Lower Standen, Henlow, Beds SG16 6DZ, tel: 01462 814668.

Hounslow

Franco Motors, 29 Vine Place, Hounslow, Middlesex TW3 3UE, tel: 020 8570 3798.

Letchworth

Autolube, 12–13 Woodside Industrial Park, Works Road, Letchworth, Herts SG6 1LA, tel: 01462-481342. (State-of-the-art diagnostic kit, helpful and knowledgeable staff.)

Lower Basildon

Les Allum, Allum Auto Services, Reading Road, Lower Basildon, Berks RG8 9NL, tel: 01491 671726.

Ruislip

Autobahn Services, Victoria Road, South Ruislip, Middlesex HA4 0JE; tel: 0208 845 2337. (Gary Woollatt is a top-quality independent BMW specialist.)

St Albans

Godfrey Davis (St Albans), 105 Ashley Road, St Albans, Herts AL1 5GD, tel: 01727 791300. (Good Ford servicing facility capable of correctly diagnosing problems.)

Wraysbury

George Williams, Lakeside Garage, 48 Welley Road, Wraysbury, Middx TW19 5DJ, tel: 01784 482158.

Eastern England

Aldeburgh

Chris Copeman, Copeman & Son Eng., Hazelwood Farm, Aldringham, Nr Aldeburgh, Suffolk, tel: 01728 830640 (mobile: 0860 614518).

Barton

Wallis and Son, Barton, Cambs., website: www.wallisandson.co.uk (Independent garage, excellent service at reasonable prices.)

Boston

Mick Barsley, Barsley Motor Engineers, 78 High Street, Boston, Lincs, tel: 01205 355396.

Bourne

Eurorescue, The Drift, Bourne, Cambs CP3 7TE, tel: 01954 719844. (Honest M11 rescue service with capability to make good-quality permanent repairs at reasonable prices.)

Chelmsford

Mr & Mrs John Plumb and their son Steve, Central Garage, Latchingdon, nr Chelmsford, Essex, tel: 01621 740284.

Grantham

TMS Garages, Spittlegate Level, Grantham, Lincs, tel: 01476 564114. (Volvo specialist.)

Hull

Jordans of Hull, 45–52 Witham, Hull, tel: 01482 222500. (Various dealerships including Mazda. Sensible service policy.)

Ilford

Whichford Rover, 404 Eastern Avenue, Gants Hill, Ilford, Essex IG2 6NW, tel: 020 8554 8888. (Rover dealer; fixes faults on recently purchased used cars at no charge and without question.)

Langworth

Paul Schmitt, Langworth Service Station, Station Road, Langworth, Lincs. tel: 01522 754291. (Paul is an excellent and helpful mechanic with longstanding customers.)

Lincoln

Riccardo Emiliani, Lincoln, tel: 01522 531735. (Helpful Honda agent.)

Loddon

Autotechnic, Unit 9, Langley Road Trading Estate, Loddon, Norfolk (off A146 between Norwich and Beccles), tel: 01508 522995. (Independent Mercedes servicing and repairs by fully trained ex-Mercedes franchise mechanics.)

Needham Market

Richard Robinson, Robinson's Motor Engineers, Debtrac Centre, Needham Market, Suffolk, tel: 01449 722240.

Norwich

Peter Whitley Motor Services, 7 Low Road, Drayton, Norwich NR8 6AA, tel: 01603 860154.

Duff Morgan, Earlham Road, Norwich, tel: 01603 621393. (Citroën dealer offering sensibly priced servicing and tyres.)

Oulton Broad

John Pope, Pope Brothers, Station Garage, Bridge End, Oulton Broad, Lowestoft, tel: 01502 573797.

Peterborough

Brian Pitts, 'The Complete Automobilist', 35–37 Main Street, Baston, Peterborough PE6 9NX, tel: 01778 560444.

Soham

Crown Garage Ltd, 1–5 High Street, Soham, Cambridgeshire, CB7 5HB, tel: 01353 720779, fax: 01353 723392, website: www. crowngarage.co.uk (Rover dealership giving outstanding, efficient and very polite and courteous service.)

Stebbing

Bob Rains, Drakeswell Garage, Bran End, Stebbing, Essex, 01371 856391.

Westcliff-on-Sea

J. Harold Penny of Westcliff on Sea, Essex. (Ford agent with longstanding loyal customers.)

Wroxham

Stewart Tubby, SMT Motors, Station Road, Wroxham, Norfolk NR12 8UR, tel: 01603 783966. (Always helpful and always honest, many a holidaymaker has reason to be grateful to Stewart.)

Central England

Abberley

Alan Hole, P. Owen & Sons Ltd, Motor & Agricultural Eng., The Abberley Garage, Abberley, Worcs WR6 6AY, tel: 01299 896209.

Ashbourne
Hulland Ward Garage, Main Street, Hulland Ward, Nr Ashbourne, Derbyshire DE6 3EF, tel: 01335 370209.

Ashton-under-Lyne
H & J Quicks Ltd, Manchester Road, Ashton-under-Lyne OL7 0DG, tel: 0161 330 0121. (Ford Agent with loyal customers of long standing.)

Birmingham
R. Newman Motor Engineers, Alcester Road (rear of J.H. Hancox Ltd), Portway, Birmingham B48 7JA, tel: 01564 824996.

G. & B. Clements, Baldwins Lane Service Station, Baldwins Lane, Hall Green, Birmingham B28 0XB, tel: 0121 744 5453.

Ken Hunt Auto Services, 536 Hobmoor Road, Yardley, Birmingham B25 8TN, tel: 0121 789 7273.

Avonway Services, Pershore Road Service Station, 582–588 Pershore Road, Birmingham B29 7QH, tel: 0121 472 0244. (Fair, reliable and inexpensive. Ray Johnson heads a team of really nice guys.)

Broadway
Alan Aston Motor Engineers, Eastwick Garage, Eastwick Drive, Evesham, Worcs WR11 6LG, tel: 01386 760700; fax: 01386 760701.

Burton-on-Trent
Peter Sharp, European Car Specialists, Unit 3, APS Industrial Park, Wetmore Road, Burton-on-Trent, Staffs DE14 1QL, tel: 01283 540414.

Chesterfield
Bridgegate Ltd, Pottery Lane, West Chesterfield, Derbys S41 9BN, tel: 01246 208681. (Very helpful BMW agent, notwithstanding age of car.)

Coalville
Mick Rolfe and Ian Whattom, Scotlands Garage, Scotlands Industrial Estate, London Road, Coalville, Leicestershire, tel: 01530 817277. (Ian is the bodywork/paint specialist, Mick the repairs/servicing specialist. Excellent work at reasonable rates.)

Daventry

Dave Carvell Cars, Badby Lane, Staverton, Nr Daventry, Northants NN11 6DE, tel: 01327 300739.

Derby

Citronome Derby Ltd, Great Northern Road, Derby DE1 1LT, tel: 01332 345869. (Citroën specialists.)

Evesham

Evesham Volkswagen/Audi, Unit 15, St Richard's Road, Evesham, Worcestershire WR11 6XJ, tel: 01386 48195. (Contact: Kevin.)

Leamington Spa

Midland Autocar Co., 8–16 Russell Street, Leamington Spa, Warks CV32 5QB, tel 01926 421171. (General repairs and service.)

Bull Ring Garage, Church Terrace, Harbury, Leamington Spa, Warks CN33 9HL, tel: 01926 612275. (Excellent local garage.)

Lichfield

Central Garage (Lichfield) Ltd, Queen Street, Lichfield, Staffs WS13 6QD, tel: 01543 262826.

Mansfield Woodhouse

Leeming Car Centre, Edge Hill Service Station, Warsop Road, Mansfield Woodhouse, Notts NG19 9LF, tel: 01623 635735. (Independent garage, but specialises in Toyota Corolla GTi models and can offer reduced-cost repairs to these cars.)

Nottingham

John Harrison (Lowdham) Ltd, Southwell Road, Lowdham, Nottingham NG14 7DS, tel: 0115 966 4112. (Helpful, straight Peugeot franchise.)

Oxford

North Oxford Garage Ltd, 280 Banbury Road, Oxford, OX2 7EB, tel: 01865 319000. (Helpful BMW franchise.)

Motor World Mitsubishi, New Barclay House, 234 Botley Road, Oxford OX2 0HP, tel: 01865 722444. (Mitsubishi agent offering excellent after-sales service).

Sutton Coldfield

G. Chamberlain & Sons, Four Oaks Garage, Lichfield Road, Four Oaks, Sutton Coldfield, W. Midlands B74 2UH, tel: 0121 308 0309.

Dave Buckland, D.J. Buckland (Motor Engineer), rear of 162 Birmingham Road, Wylde Green, Sutton Coldfield, W. Midlands B72 4JP, tel: 0121 355 7634 (out of hours tel: 0121 350 6881).

Wantage

Paul Rivers, Hillcrest Garage, Reading Road, West Hendred (nr Wantage), Oxon OX12 8RH, tel: 01235 833363.

T.A. Collins Motor Engineers, Grove Technology Park, Grove, Wantage, Oxon OX12 9TA, tel: 01235 768321. (Volvo specialist.)

West Bromwich

The Sun Garage Company, Sandwell Road, West Bromwich, West Midlands B70 8TG, tel: 0121 553 0296.

Wolverhampton

Roger Williams, Oxley Service Station, Fordhouse Road, Bushbury, Wolverhampton, W. Midlands WV10 9EY, tel: 01902 787386.

The South West

Bath

Ron Cray Automatics (Prop. Ian Chant), High Littleton Garage, High Street, High Littleton, Bath BS39 6HW, tel: 01761 472295. (Recommended automatic gearbox specialist.)

Grants of Bath, London Road West, Bath, tel: 01225 858 147. (Small and outwardly rather chaotic private garage, but always knowledgeable, helpful and very reasonably priced. Ask for Nigel.)

Bridgwater

Tim Stiles Racing, Units 5 & 6, Transform Estate, Wylds Road, Bridgwater, Somerset TA6 4DH, tel: 01278 453036. (VW/Audi performance modifications at reasonable prices and labour rates.)

Stogursey Motors, High Street, Stogursey (8 miles from Bridgwater near Hinkley Point power station), tel: 01278 732237. (Car, van and motorcycle repairs and MOTs.)

Bristol
All Audi Used Part Stores, Unit 26, Hanham Business Park, Memorial Road, Hanham, Bristol BS15 3JE, tel: 0117 949 4136; mobile: 0860 259567. (Good source of parts for obsolete Audis.)

R.J. Auto Engineers, Whitehouse Lane, Bedminster, Bristol, tel: 01179 632029. (SAAB and Alfa specialists.)

Cotswold Sports Cars, A38 at Thornbury, Nr Bristol, tel: 01454 412413. (General maintenance and repairs.)

Castle Carey
Moff Motors, Castle Carey, Somerset (nr Castle Carey Station on Shepton Mallet road), tel: 01963 350310. (Independent dealers with good after-sales service.)

Corfe Mullen
Westover Nissan, 149–153 Wareham Road, Corfe Mullen, Dorset, tel: 01202 693681. (Former Rover dealer, now Nissan. Very highly recommended.)

Crewkerne
Misterton Garage, Misterton, Crewkerne, Somerset, tel: 01460 72997. (Ford retail dealer, good for servicing and repairs, reasonable prices.)

Dorchester
Loders, Dorchester, Dorset, tel: 01305 267881. (Good franchised Audi dealer service.)

Old's Jeep, Dorchester. (Good franchised Chrysler dealer service.)

Exeter
Volkswagen Services, 11 Coombe Street, Exeter, Devon EX1 1DB, tel: 01392 493737.

Carrs of Exeter, tel: 01392 823988. (Good Mercedes and Porsche service.)

113

Reg and Paul Stephens, Snow and Stephens, King Edward Street, Exeter, tel: 01392 256552.

Rockbeare Motor Services, Rockbeare, Exeter EX5 2DZ, tel: 01404 822410.

Best Tyres, Verney Street, Exeter, tel: 01392 411100. (Low prices, good service and excellent for suspension alignment.)

Exmouth

Karl Brigham, KB Auto Services and Repairs, Victoria Way, Exmouth, Devon, tel: 01395 223330.

Bentleys Garage, Chapel Hill (High Street), Exmouth, Devon, tel: 01395 272048.

Frenchay

Frenchay Garage, Frenchay Common, Frenchay, Bristol BS16 1NB, tel: 0117 956 7303.

Frome

Marston MOT Centre, Whitworth Road, Marston Trading Estate, Frome, Somerset BA11 4BY, tel: 01373 452352. (Proprietor Stewart Herridge. Very reasonably-priced local independent garage.)

Langport

J.A. Scott, Langport Motor Co., Westover Trading Estate, Langport, Somerset, tel: 01458 251100. (Citroën specialist.)

Liskeard

Ken Rowe, Rowe's Garage Ltd, Dobwalls, Liskeard, Cornwall PL14 6JA, tel: 01579 320218. (Citroën franchise, but will gladly help owners of other makes in trouble.)

Newton Abbot

K. Tapper, Decoy Motors, Unit 10, Silverhills Road, Decoy Trading Estate, Newton Abbot TQ12 5LZ, tel: 01626 68701.

Paignton

Geoff Norman, G M Motors, Unit 1, Miglo Industrial Estate, Yalberton Road, Paignton, Devon TQ4 7QW, tel: 01803 664466. (Excellent, small, non-franchised repairs and servicing plus MOTs and tyres.)

Penzance

Autostop Service Centre, Longrock, Nr Penzance, Cornwall, tel: 01736 330300. (Excellent, non-franchised service and repair garage.)

Plymouth

Simon Rouse, Peverell Garage, Weston Park Road, Peverell, Plymouth, Devon PL3 4NS, tel: 01752 266099.

South Molton

Andrew Geen, Geen's Garage, South Molton, North Devon, tel: 01769 572395.

Taunton

Paul Lyall, Fairwater Garage, Staplegrove Road, Taunton, Somerset TA1 1DF, tel: 01823 277268.

Wadebridge

John Smith, Old Forge Garage, St Miniver, Wadebridge, Cornwall, tel: 01208 863323.

Wellington

Grants Repairs, Mantle Street, Wellington, Somerset, tel: 01823 662067. (Independent BMW specialist; chief mechanic Trevor Klimpke.)

Weston-Super-Mare

Howards Citroën (tel: 01934 644644) and Howards Rover (tel: 01934 643434), both of Hildersheim Bridge, Weston-Super-Mare BS23 3PT.

Howards Peugeot, Searle Crescent, Weston-Super-Mare BS23 3YX, tel: 01934 636049.

Howards Nissan, Herluin Way, Weston-Super-Mare BS23 3YN, tel: 01934 416454. (Howards are franchised agents for Citroën, Rover, Peugeot and Nissan – all, very unusually, in the same town.)

Yeovil

Eastside Garage, Lufton Trading Estate, Yeovil, Somerset, tel: 01935 31412. (Citroën specialist.)

Auto Wizard, Penhill Trading Estate, Yeovil, Somerset, tel: 01935 410532.

Douglas Seaton Ltd, White Post Garage, West Coker Road, Yeovil, Somerset BA22 9AA, tel: 01935 863008; fax: 01935 863047. (Longstanding and loyal customer base.)

Philip Sargent Vehicle Services, Goldcroft, Yeovil, Somerset, tel: 01935 427554. ('Ever ready to go the "extra mile" when you are in a fix.')

Wales and The West

Abergavenny
Abergavenny Autos, Monmouth Road, Abergavenny, Mon. NP7 5HF, tel: 01873 852712. (Reliable Renault franchise.)

Aberystwyth
Anthony Motors Ltd, Llanbadarn Road, Aberystwyth SY23 3QP, tel: 01970 624444. (Good Mazda agents.)

Bridgnorth
Faintree Garage, Ludlow Road, Faintree, Bridgnorth WV16 6RQ, tel: 01746 789275. (Friendly Skoda agents, for whom nothing is ever too much trouble.)

Caerleon
Autotech, Panthir Road, Caerleon, Gwent NP18 3NY, tel: 01633 423717. (One of semi-official Autotech chain of independent BMW specialists.)

Cardiff
Continental Cars (Cardiff) Ltd, Pentwyn Road, Pentwyn, Cardiff CF23 7XH, tel: 029 2054 2400. (Mercedes franchise, treats elderly drivers with extra consideration.)

Chester
Crane Bank Garage, New Crane Street, Chester CH1 4JE, tel: 01244 317191. (One of three general garages: together, winners of *Daily Telegraph* Customer Service Award 2001.)

Manor Garage, Lightfoot Street, Hoole, Chester CH2 3AL, tel: 01244 346886. (One of three general garages: together, winners of *Daily Telegraph* Customer Service Award 2001.)

Newgate Motors, Countess Way, Chester CH1 4DU, tel: 01244 374473. (Expensive but fair Mercedes agent. Labour charges £58.75 an hour (at time of recommendation).)

Colwyn Bay

Meredith and Kirkham, 394 Abergely Road, Colwyn Bay, tel: 01492 515292. (Rover agent with longstanding loyal customers.)

Cwmcarn

Bijou Motor Services, rear of 99–101 Newport Road, Cwmcarn, Gwent NP1 7LZ, tel: 01495 271033. (Citroën specialists, offering enhanced servicing for this manufacturer.)

Eastham
Mitchell Mitsubishi, New Chester Road, Eastham, Wirral, Cheshire CH62 8HJ, tel: 0151 328 5555/0151 625 4555.

Gloucester
Bathwick Tyres, Great Western Road, Gloucester GL1 3PZ; tel: 01452 304499; website: www.bathwicktyres.co.uk

Holt
Castle Street Garage, Castle Street, Holt, Clwyd LL13 9YL, tel: 01829 271400. (Down-to-earth, non-patronising approach coupled with brilliant service.)

Ledbury
R. & J. Mathews, Blacklands Garage, Canon Frome (near Ledbury), Hereford & Worcester HR8 2TB, tel: 01531 670440.

Llangollen
Kenrick's Garage, Market Street, Llangollen, North Wales LL20 8RA, tel: 01978 861382. (Friendly local garage with excellent and reasonably priced 'rescue' service.)

Minsterley
Minsterley Garage, Station Road, Minsterley, Shropshire SY5 0BE, tel: 01743 790000. (Refit specialists. Reasonably priced, extremely good and efficient service.)

Monmouth
County Garages, Wye Valley Road, Monmouth, Monmouthshire; tel: 01600 712366. (A small Ford main agent, always giving very good service.)

Moreton-in-Marsh
N.E. Repairs, Hospital Road, Moreton-in-Marsh, Gloucs GL56 0BN, tel: 01608 650405.

Oswestry
Arthurs of Oswestry Ltd, Lower Brook Street, Oswestry, Shropshire SY11 2HJ, tel: 01691 652235. (Vauxhall franchise prepared to do small jobs for regular customers for the parts cost alone.)

Penarth
Bernard Cody Motor Engineers, Station Approach, Penarth, Mid-Glamorgan CF64 3EE, tel: 029 20704293.

Penrhyndeudraeth
Dafydd Williams, Garreg Lwyd, Penrhyndeudraeth, Gwynedd, LL48 6AW, tel: 01766 770203. (Second-hand Twingos, servicing, advice and 'hard to get' parts.)

Pewsey
Stevens Cars, Nicol's Yard (rear of Post Office), Pewsey SN9 5EF, tel: 01672 563330.

Pontyberem
Raymond Garage Ltd, 4A Station Road, Pontyberem, Carmarthenshire SA15 5LF, tel: 01269 870955. (Good independent garage.)

Porthcawl
John Rogers, Station Hill Garage, Porthcawl, Mid-Glamorgan CF36 5DL, tel: 01656 786705.

Portmadoc
The Glanaber Garage, Borth-y-Gest, Portmadoc, Gwynedd LL49 9TP, tel: 01766 512364.

Swindon
Fish Bros, Addington Drive, Swindon, Wilts SN5 7SB, tel: 01793 512685. (Several recommendations: Fiat, Alfas Romeo and Mitsubishi franchise – good at diagnosing faults on Alfa Romeos. Also Skoda, Nissan and Renault.)

Dick Lovett Specialist Cars, Rushey Park, Swindon SN5 8WO, tel: 01793 615999. (Honest and decent BMW franchise.)

Greenmeadow Service Station, Thames Avenue, Greenmeadow, Swindon, tel: 01793 534501. (Long-standing and well recommended.)

Weobley
John Simpson, Whitehill Garage, Weobley, Hereford HR4 8QZ, tel: 01544 318268.

Wirral
Crane Bank Garage, Poulton Road, Wallasey, Wirral CH44 4BZ, tel: 0151 638 1469. (One of three general garages: together, winners of *Daily Telegraph* Customer Service Award 2001.)

Durley Garage, Units 12–14, Badger Way, North Cheshire Trading Estate, Prenton, Wirral CH43 3HQ, tel: 0151 608 0788.

Wrexham
Brian Jones Garage Services Ltd, Queensway, Wrexham LL13 8UN, tel: 01978 352077. (General garage. Happy to save a customer money wherever possible.)

The North

Bedale
John Gill Ltd, Aiskew Garage, Aiskew, Bedale, N. Yorks DL8 1DD, tel: 01677 423124. (Daihatsu dealer and general repairs.)

Bishop Auckland
S.G. Petch, Milford Garage, South Church, Bishop Auckland, tel: 01388 774545. (Rover specialist for service over and above the normal.)

Blackburn
Slater Motors, Brunswick Street Garage, Appleby Street, Blackburn, Lancs, tel: 01254 57934. (Mercedes-trained independent MB specialist.)

Carnforth
The Mountain family, Lune View Garage, Melling, Carnforth, Lancs LA6 2RB, tel: 015242 21457.

Castleford
Castleford VW Spares, Methley Road, Castleford, W. Yorks, tel: 01977 518254. (VW/Audi servicing and parts.)

Durham
Volksparts, Langley Moor, Nr Durham DH7 8LZ, tel: 0191 378 0284. (German car specialists: Audi, BMW, Mercedes, VW.)

Garstang

H. & J. Kitching, Hornby's Garage, Lydiate Lane, Claughton on Brock, Garstang, Preston, Lancs PR3 0QL, tel: 01995 640229.

Harrogate

Mr Greenwood, Western Garage, 54 Valley Mount, Harrogate, N. Yorks H62 0JG, tel: 01423 502902.

Nidd Vale Motors, Westmoreland Street, Harrogate, N. Yorks HG1 5AS, tel: 01423 500005. (Vauxhall agents.)

David Fox Ltd, 118–122 Wetherby Road, Harrogate HG2 7AB, tel: 01423 545454. (Authorised Citroën dealer. Service is always good and prompt. Very helpful, fair service costs, doesn't seem to overcharge or "find" things to repair.)

Hexham

Fred Almond, Haugh Lane Garage, Haugh Lane, Hexham, Northumberland NE46 3PT, tel: 01434 604163.

Holmfirth

M & M Engineering Services, Clarence Mills, Holmbridge, Holmfirth HD9 2NE, tel: 01484 687706.

Jarrow

David Ellis, Jarrow Coachworks, Curlew Road, Jarrow, Tyne and Wear NE32 2DX, tel: 0191 4892715; mobile: 0776 417 8390.

Leeds

IVC (Independent VW/Audi Centre), Globe Road, off Water Lane, Leeds LS11 5QS, tel: 0113 242 0875.

Leek

Andy Jackson, of A&C Vehicle Services, The Yard, Ball Haye Road, Leek, Staffs ST13 6AF, tel: 01538 398227.

Littleborough

J. Stanton, Stanton's Motor Garage, Brookfield Mill, Canal Street, Littleborough, Nr Rochdale, Lancs OL15 0HA, tel: 01706 370166.

Liverpool

Philip Walker, Dudlow Motor Company, Menlove Gardens West,

Liverpool L18 2ET, tel: 0151 722 2396.

Manchester
Derek Boardman, Units 12–15, Morton Street Industrial Estate, Failsworth, Manchester M35 0BN, tel: 0161 681 0456.

Middlesbrough
Dave Stott Motors, Charlotte Street, Middlesbrough TS2 1DT, tel: 01642 224805. (Independent Citroën specialists.)

Preston
J.C. and M. Davis, Garstang Road Garage, Garstang Road, Pilling, Preston PR3 6AQ, tel: 01253 790322 (General repairs, but good with diesels and Citroëns.)

I.J. Woodburn, Unit 4 Garage, Langley Lane, Goosnargh (nr Preston), Lancs PR3 2JP, tel: 01772 861126. (Reliable independent BMW specialist.)

Rotherham
Dearnside Motor Co. Ltd, 106 Barnsley Rd, Goldthorpe, Rotherham, South Yorkshire S63 9AE; tel: 01709 893864. (Citroën specialists, always found to be honest and very obliging...and they do know their Citroëns.)

Saddleworth
Greenfield Service Station, Chew Valley Road, Greenfield, Saddleworth, Nr Oldham, Lancs OL3 7DB, tel: 01457 873700.

Salford
Leyden Bros Ltd, Chapel Street, Salford, Lancs. M3 7AA, tel: 0161 832 3838. (Reasonable and fair prices.)

Sheffield
Bridgco Garage, 160 Broad Oaks, Sheffield 9, tel: 0114 2441775.

Cemetery Road Motors, Cemetery Road, Sheffield S11 8FT, tel: 0114 266 6500. (Specialists in high-mileage Mercedes sales and service.)

S P Motors, Cross Smithfields, off Allen St, Sheffield S3 7AU, tel: 0114 272 1128. (Independent for servicing and bodywork.)

Stockport

Chris or Ben, Tenby Garage, Lavenders Brow, Churchgate, Stockport, Cheshire SK1 1YW, tel: 0161 480 5075.

The Dave Arnitt Citroën Repair Centre, Arthur Street, Reddish, Stockport SK6 1PE, tel: 0161 432 0636. (Citroën specialist.)

The General Motor Co. Ltd, Cooke Street, Hazel Grove, Stockport SK7 4EG, tel: 0161 483 3883. (Independent Audi/VW specialists.)

Ryland Honda, 35 Buxton Road, Stockport SK2 6LZ, tel: 0161 480 4244. (Very helpful and efficient, even in sourcing parts for grey-imported Hondas.)

Stockton

Shearborne Eng., 1a Norton Avenue, Norton, Stockton-on-Tees, Cleveland TS20 2JH, tel: 01642 860080. (Independent Jaguar specialists.)

Wallsend

Priory Cars, The Silverlink, Wallsend, Tyne and Wear NE28 9ND, tel: 0191 295 1295; fax: 0191 295 1123; e-mail: priory.bmw@dial.pipex.com (BMW franchise.)

Warrington

Stan Woods, Horseshoe Garage, Hollow Lane, Kingsley, Frodsham, Cheshire WA6 8ET, tel: 01928 787323. (Well-equipped independent, capable of servicing anything from a Mini to a BMW 7-Series, labour rate just £25 an hour (at time of recommendation).)

David Roundell Services, Milner Street, Warrington, Cheshire WA5 1AD, tel: 01925 635958.

Whitley Bay

John Gallagher, Collingwood Garage, Rockcliffe Street, Whitley Bay, Tyne and Wear NE26 2NW, tel: 0191 252 2244.

Widnes

Widnes Car Centre, Moor Lane, Widnes, Cheshire WA8 7AL, tel: 0151 420 2000. (Independently owned Nissan agent.)

D & M Motors, Waterloo Road, Widnes, Cheshire WA8 0PY, tel: 0151 420 2646.

Wigan

K. Brown & Partner Motor Engineers, 131 Upholland Road, Billinge, Nr Wigan WN5 7EG, tel: 01942 519522. (Independent garage, experienced in VWs.)

Windermere

Keith Donnelly, Oldfield Road Garage, Oldfield Road, Windermere, Cumbria LA23 2BY, tel: 015 394 46710.

York

John Galley Motors, Pocklington Industrial Estate, Pocklington, York, tel: 01759 303716. (VW/Audi.)

Dixon MG and Rover, Jockey Lane, Monk's Cross, York YO32 9XX, tel: 01904 667300, fax: 01904 667316 (parts, tel: 01904 636666). (Credited with 'absolutely first-class service, every time'.)

Scotland

Ballater

J. Pringle, Victoria Garage, Ballater, Grampian AB35 5QQ, tel: 013397 55525.

Drumndrochit

J.E. Menzies & Son Ltd, Lewiston Garage, Drumndrochit, Inverness, tel: 01456 450212.

Elvanfoot

Car and Truck Services, Elvanfoot, Lanarkshire MH2 6KF (adjacent to A74M), tel: 01864 502236. (General repairs and service, bodywork, breakdown and recovery.)

Forres

Pedigreed Cars, Bogton Place, Forres, Morayshire IV6 1EP, tel: 01309 672555.

Kirkwall

A.T.S., Junction Road, Kirkwall, Orkney KW15 1AX, tel 01856 872361. (Tyre specialists and general servicing.)

Largs
Waterside Motors, 24 Waterside Street, Largs, Ayrshire, KA30 9LN, tel: 01475 675020. (Excellent service and superb customer relations.)

Loanhead
McLennan Garage, 16 Park Avenue, Loanhead, Midlothian EH20 9AZ, tel: 0131 440 0597.

Skye
Ewan MacRae, Dunvegan Road, Portree, Isle of Skye IV51 9HD, tel: 01478 612554.

Stirling
Arnold Clark, Kerse Road, Stirling FK7 7RU, tel: 01786 472212; fax: 01786 464733. (Good Renault franchise: 'a pleasure to recommend them.')

Northern Ireland

Bushmills, Co. Antrim
James Wylie Auto Repairs, 48A Ballyclogh Road, Bushmills, Co. Antrim BT57 8UZ, tel: 028207 32096. (Citroën specialist, as well as other makes.)

On the Continent

Calais, France
Midas, 112 Blvd La Fayette, 62100 Calais, tel: (0033) 321 82 38 80.

Speedy Europe, 1 Place Nations, 62100 Calais, tel: (0033) 321 34 38 16. (Recommended tyre and exhaust specialists.)

Cherbourg, France
Garage Pichard, 124 Rue du Val de Saire, 51000 Cherbourg. (Rover agent.)

Valencia, Spain
Imperauto, Valencia, tel: (0034) 96 342 06 22. (Land Rovers.)

Car Clubs Directory

We're crazy about our cars in the UK. What's more, we love to share our mania with others. There are hundreds of Car Clubs across the country, celebrating both current and long-lost (but never forgotten) marques, and some even dedicated to a single model.*

This list is classified in alphabetical order of manufacturer, from AC to Zil (OK, to Wolseley). A final section lists specialist clubs not allied to a specific manufacturer.

---

* Do you run a car club that is not listed in the Directory? Send your details to Honest John care of the publishers, Constable-Robinson, at the address shown on page iv opposite the Contents list.

AC

AC Owners Club Ltd, Eric Gates, 8 Netherway, Upper Poppleton, York YO2 6JQ, tel: 01904 793563.

AEC

AEC Society, c/o L. Harris, 32 Kingscroft Road, Hucclecote, Glos GL3 3RG.

Aixam

Aixam Owners Club, c/o Brian J.Hampton, 21 Bounds Croft, Greenleys, Milton Keynes MK12 6AW, tel: 01908 316991, e-mail: battery@zetnet.co.uk.

AJS

AJS 9 Car Club, c/o Peter Hubbard, The Chestnuts, Chequers Road, Tharston, Norwich NR15 2YA, tel: 01508 530072; website: www.ajscar.freeserve.co.uk.

Alfa Romeo

Alfa Romeo Owners Club, 9 Green Lane, Wootton, Northants NN4 6LH, tel: 01604 761813; website: www.aroc-uk.com.

Allard

Allard Owners Club, c/o Michelle Wilson, 10 Brooklyn Court, Woking, Surrey GU22 7TQ, tel: 01483 773428.

Alvis

Alvis Owners Club, c/o Charles Mackonochie, 2 Sunny Bank Cottage, Colts Hill, Capel, Tonbridge, Kent TN12 6SW, tel: 01892 832118; website: www.alvisoc.org.

The Alvis Register, c/o John Willis, The Vinery, Wanborough Hill, Guildford, Surrey GU3 2JB, tel: 01483 810308.

Armstrong Siddeley

Armstrong Siddeley Owners Club Ltd, c/o Peter Sheppard, 57 Berberry Close, Birmingham B30 1TB, tel: 0121 459 0742 (eve); website: www.siddeley.com.

Aston Martin

Aston Martin Owners Club Ltd, c/o Secretary, John Burslem, Drayton, St Leonard, Wallingford, Oxon OX10 7BJ, tel: 01865 400400; website: www.amoc.org.

Audi

Audi-Sport Club, John Robins, 17 Masefield Road, Stratford-upon-Avon CV37 7JT, tel: +44 (0) 1789 298529; mobile: +44 (0) 7976 729884; website: www.audi-sport.net; email: John@Audi-Sport.net.

Austin

The Vintage Austin Register Ltd, c/o Frank Smith, The Briars, Four Lane Ends, Oakerthorpe, Nr Alfreton, Derbyshire DE55 7LH, tel: 01773 831646.

Austin 7 Owners Club (London), c/o Yvonne King (Membership Secretary), PO Box 77, Esher, Surrey KT10 8WZ, tel: 01372 466134; email: king_yvonne@hotmail.com; website: www.austinsevenownersclub.co.uk.

The Pre-War Austin Seven Club Ltd, c/o Steve Jones, 1 The Fold, Doncaster Road, Whiteley, nr Goole, East Yorks DN14 0JF, tel: 01977 662828.

Midlands Austin 7 Club, c/o John Roberts, 18 Oaktree Lane, Cookhill, Alcester, Warks B49 5LH, tel: 01789 765349 (before 9pm).

South Wales Austin Seven Club, c/o H. and G. Morgan, 90 Ammanford Road, Llandybie, Ammanford, Carmarthenshire SA18 2JY, tel: 01269 850528.

Austin Swallow Register, School House, Rectory Road, Gt. Haseley, Oxford OX44 7JP.

Austin Big 7 Register, c/o R. Taylor, 101 Derby Road, Chellaston, Derby DE73 1SB, tel: 01332 700629.

The Austin Eight Register, c/o Ian Pinniger, 3 La Grange Martin, St. Martin, Jersey, Channel Islands JE3 6JB, e-mail: mail@pinniger. fsnet.co.uk.

Austin Ten Drivers Club Ltd (Pre-War 10s, 12s, 14s, 16s, 18s, 20s), c/o Ian Dean, PO Box 12, Chichester, West Sussex PO20 7PH, tel: 01243 641284.

British Austin Society, c/o Barry Martin, Park Gate Oast, Cranbrook Road, Tenterden, Kent TN30 6UP. Membership £14 a year. Caters mainly for pre-war 7s, 10s and 12s but all Austin owners welcome.

North East Club for Pre-War Austins (NECPWA), contact George Halliday, 67 Balliol Avenue, Westmoor, Newcastle-upon-Tyne NE12 0PN, or the membership secretary, Tom Gatenby, e-mail: PG9882@aol.com; website: www.necpwa.demon.co.uk.

Austin J40 Car Club, Marcia Blake, 9 Spades Bourne Road, Lickey End, Bromsgrove, West Midlands B60 1JW, tel: 01527 876152.

Austin Counties Car Club, c/o Ian Coombes, 44 Vermeer Crescent, Shoeburyness, Essex SS3 9JT, tel: 01702 295385; website: www. austincounties.org.uk. Includes the Austin Atlantic Owners Club.

Austin Sheerline and Princess Owners Register, c/o Ian Coombes, 44 Vermeer Crescent, Shoeburyness, Essex SS3 9JT, tel: 01702 295385.

Austin Healey Club, c/o Colleen Holmes, 4 Saxby Street, Leicester LE2 0ND.

Austin Gipsy Register, c/o Miles Gilbert, 24 Green Close, Rixon, Sturminster Newton, Dorset DT10 1BJ, tel: 01258 472680.

Cambridge/Oxford Farina Owners Club (1959-1971), c/o Malcolm Padbury, 32 Reservoir Road, Southgate, London N14 4BG; e-mail: coocmem@padburym.freeserve.co.uk.

Austin Cambridge/Westminster Car Club, c/o J. Curtis, 4 Russell Close, East Budleigh, Budleigh Salterton, Devon EX9 7EX, tel: 01395 446210.

Austin A40 Farina Club, 75 Tennal Toad, Harborne, Birmingham B32 2JB.

1100 Club (all 1100 and 1300 variants), c/o Andrew Morton, 18 Ullswater Close, North Anston, Sheffield S25 4GH.

Austin Maxi Club, Send SAE to Ms C. Jackson, 27 Queen Street, Bardney, Lincs LN3 5XF.

Landcrab Owners Club International, c/o Bill Fraser, 10 Eastcott Road, Welling, Kent DA16 2SX, website: www.landcrab.net.

Allegro Club International, 20 Stoneleigh Crescent, Stoneleigh, Epsom, Surrey KT19 0RP, website: www.uk-classic-cars.com/allegro.htm.

Princess and Ambassador Owners Club, c/o Peter Maycroft, 26 Castlehall, Glascote, Tamworth, Staffs B77 2EJ, website: www.princessandambassador.btinternet.co.uk.

Austin Maestro Owners Club (includes Montego), Jonathan Sellars, 6 Grailands Close, Fernhurst, Haslemere, Surrey GU27 3HU, tel: 07932 997770; websites: www.maestro.org.uk; e-mail: jpsellars@maestro.org.uk.

Autocycle and Cyclemotor
National Autocycle and Cyclemotor Club: membership secretary: David Freeman, 81 High Road, Trimley, Felixstowe, Suffolk IP11 0TA.

Autovia
Autovia Car Club, club secretary: Gordon Thomas, 43 Tilbury Road, Tilbury Juxta Clare, Halstead, Essex CO9 4JJ, tel: 01787 237676.

Bedford
Bedford Owners Club, c/o Ron Ruggins, 27 Northville Drive, Westcliff-on-Sea, Essex SS0 0QA.

Bedford CA UK, c/o P. Oakham, 2 Banmore Avenue, Higher Openshaw, Manchester M11 1BS.

Belsize

Useful contact for Belsize information: Rodney Fowler, Tithe House, Chelford Road, Knutsford, Cheshire WA16 8LY, tel: 01565 651051; fax: 01565 754204.

Bentley

Bentley Drivers Club Ltd, c/o Patricia Gee, Secretary, 16 Chearsley Road, Long Crendon, Aylesbury, Bucks HP18 9AW, tel: 01844 208233; website: www.bdcl.co.uk.

Bitter

Bitter Owners Club, c/o P. Griffith, Medina Garden Centre, Staplers Road, Wootton, Isle of Wight PO33 4RW, tel: 01983 883430; website: www.uk-classic-cars.com/bitter.htm.

BMC

British Made Car Club (BMCC), c/o 6 Caulfield Court, East Street, Newton Abbot, Devon, tel: 01626 351007; e-mail: britishmadecarclub @hotmail.com; website: www.britishmadecarclub.co.uk. (All British-made classic cars, though with an emphasis on the Austin Cambridge and Westminster.)

Scottish BMC Car Club, c/o Euan Smith, 111 Stewart Avenue, Bo'ness, EH51 9NN, website: www.geocities.com/motorcity/ speedway5705/.

BMC J2/150 Register, c/o Matt and Joanne Traxton, 10 Sunnyside Cottages, Woodford, Kettering, Northants NN14 4HX, tel: 01832 734441; website: www.brmmbrmm.com/bmcj2152; e-mail: matt. traxton@tesco.net.

BMC JU 250 Register, c/o Stuart Cook, 34 Thorncliffe Drive, Darwen, Lancs BB3 3QA, tel: 01254 772372.

BMC LD Register, 86 Manica Crescent, Fazakerley, Liverpool L10 9NA, tel: 0151 525 3907.

BMW

BMW Car Club (GB) Ltd, Andrew Dale, Club Secretary, PO Box 328, Melksham, Wilts, tel: 01225 709009, fax: 01225703885, email: enquiries@bmwccgb.org , website: www.bmwcarclub.co.uk.

BMW Car Club Historic Section, c/o Mark Garfitt, 126 Llantarnam Road, Cwmbran, Gwent NO44 3BD, tel: 01633 871704.

BMW Drivers Club International, c/o Samantha Easton, 41 Norwich Street, Dereham, Norfolk NR19 1AD, tel: 01362 691144.

Bond

Bond Owners Club, c/o Stan Cormack, 42 Beaufort Avenue, Hodge Hill, Birmingham B34 6AE, tel: 0121 784 4626; website: www. bondownersclub.co.uk.

Borgward

Borgward Drivers Club, c/o The Secretary, Derek Farr, 19 Highfield Road, Kettering, Northants NN15 6HR, tel: 01536 510771; website: www.borgward.org.uk ; e-mail: borgward@bigfoot.com.

Bristol

Bristol Owners Club, c/o John Emery, Vesutor Ltd, Marringdean Road, Billingshurst, West Sussex RH14 9EH, tel: 01403 784028, website: www.boc.net/bristol.

BSA

BSA Front Wheel Drive Club, c/o Barry Baker, 164 Cottimore Lane, Walton-on-Thames, Surrey KT12 2BL, tel: 01932 225270; website: members.aol.com/bsafwdc/home.htm.

Buckler

Buckler Car Register, c/o Stanley Hibberd, 42 Stepping Road, Long Lawford, Rugby CV23 9SG, tel: 01788 573319.

Bugatti

Bugatti Owners Club Ltd, c/o Sue Ward, Prescott Hill, Gotherington, Cheltenham, Glos GL52 4RD.

Cadillac

Cadillac Owners Club of Great Britain, c/o Bill Greenwood, "Dunvegan", Lynn Road, King's Lynn, Norfolk PE33 0HG; website: www.cocgb.dircon.co.uk/

Calcott

Calcott Register, c/o Anthony Wilson, "Willerby", 61 Ridgewood Drive, RD1 New Plymouth, New Zealand, fax: 00 64 67537461.

Chevrolet

Classic Chevrolet Club, c/o Chris Richards, Secretary, PO Box 2222, Braintree, Essex CM7 9TW, tel: 0208 244 4893.

Classic Corvette Club (UK) Ltd, c/o Andy Greenfield, 8 New England Crescent, Great Wakering, Essex SS3 0DU, tel: 01702 217075, website: www.corvetteclub.org.uk.

Citroën

Citroën Traction Owners Club, c/o Peter Riggs, 2 Appleby Gardens, Dunstable, Beds LU6 3DB.

Citroën Traction Enthusiasts Club, c/o Robin Rother, Preston House Studio, Preston, Canterbury, Kent CT3 1DZ.

Citroën Car Club, c/o Derek Pearson, PO Box 348, Bromley, Kent BR2 8QT, tel: 0700 0248258, website: www.citroencarclub.org.uk.

2CV GB, PO Box 602, Crick, Northampton NN6 7UW, tel: 07770 228602, email: enquiries@2cvgb.co.uk, website: www.2cvgb.co.uk.

Citroën XM 2.1TD Group, c/o John Cownley, fax: 01635 202643.

For all things Citroën: www.citroenet.org.uk (an amenity website for Citroën enthusiasts).

Clan

Clan Owners Club, c/o Fred Brooks, 19 Greenacres, South Cornelly, Mid-Glam CF33 4SE, tel: 01656 744741, email: clanclubmembership @tesco.net

Clyno

Clyno Register, c/o R. Surman, Swallow Cottage, Langton Farm, Burbage Common Road, Elmesthorpe, Leicester LE9 7SE, tel: 01455 842178; fax: 01455 850584.

Commer

CommerCAR (Commer Archive and Register) c/o Peter Daniels (archivist), Fairway View, Netherhampton, Salisbury, Wilts SP2 8PX, tel: 01722 744766; fax: 01722 744767; e-mail: commercar @active.uk.com.

Cougar

Cougar Club of America, c/o Barrie Dixon, 11 Dean Close, Partington, Manchester M31 4BI, tel: 0161 775 0820.

Crossley

Crossley Register, c/o Malcolm Jenner, Willow Cottage, Lexham Road, Great Dunham, Kings Lynn, Norfolk PE32 2LS, tel: 01328 701240.

Crossley Climax Register, c/o M. Sims, 10 Longbridge Road, Bramley, Hampshire RG26 5AN.

DAF

DAF Owners Club, c/o Steve Bidwell, 56 Ridgedale Road, Bolsover, Chesterfield, Derbyshire S44 6TX, email: dafownersclub @bolsover.co.uk, website: www.dafownersclub.co.uk.

Daimler/Lanchester (*see also* Jaguar)

Daimler Enthusiasts Club, c/o Greville Taverner, Beech House, Northwell Pool Road, Swaffham, Norfolk PE37 7HW, tel/fax: 01760 721685, email: GTaverner@onetel.net.uk.

Daimler and Lanchester Owners Club, PO Box 276, Sittingbourne, Kent ME9 7GA, tel/fax 07000 356285; e-mail: DaimlerUK@aol.com.

Daimler SP250 Owners Club 1998, c/o G. Frost, 15 Broom Mead, Bexleyheath, Kent DA6 7NZ, tel: 01322 522958, email: grahamfrost@gmfltd.freeserve.co.uk.

Datsun

Datsun Owners Club, c/o Jon Rodwell, Secretary, 26 Langton Road, Wraughton, Wilts SN4 0QN, tel: 01793 845271, website: www.datsunworld.com.

Datsun Z Club, c/o Steve Kemp, Membership Secretary, 12 Palmerston Way, Biddulph, Stoke-on-Trent ST8 7SX, tel: 01782 518992; website: www.jwa.co.uk/zclub.

Classic Z Register, c/o J. Newlyn, 11 Lawday Link, Upper Hale, Farnham, Surrey GU9 0BS, tel: 01252 711297.

DB/David Brown

David Brown Owners Club, Secretary: Martin George, Champney Hill Farm, Silkstone Common, Barnsley S75 4PH. Chairman: Daryl Clegg, Hays Barn, The Hays, Helm, Huddersfield HD7 3RN.

Davrian

Davrian Register, c/o J. Rawlins, 4 Browns Lane, Uckfield, East Sussex TN22 1RS, tel: 01825 763638.

Delage

Delage Section of the VSCC, c/o Peter Jacobs, "Clouds Reach", The Scop, Almondsbury, Bristol BS32 4DU, tel: 01454 612434, website: www.delage-world.co.uk.

Delahaye

Delahaye Club (GB) The club has ceased to exist, but Peter Jacobs is acting as a helpful contact, e-mail: peter@cloudsreach.freeserve.co.uk.

Dellow

Dellow Register, c/o John Temple, 4 Roumelia Lane, Bournemouth, Dorset BH5 1ET; tel 01202 304641; fax 01202 392170; email dellow@douglastemple.co.uk.

DeLorean

DeLorean Owners Club (GB), c/o Chris Parnham, 14 Quarndon heights, Allestree, Derby DE22 2XN, tel: 01332 230823, website: www.delorean.co.uk.

De Tomaso

De Tomaso Drivers Club, c/o Roger Brotton, Stoney Croft, Moor Lane, Birdwell, Barnsley, South Yorkshire S70 5TZ, tel 01226 292601, email: detomaso.dcuk@virgin.net.

DKW

DKW Owners Club, c/o David Simon, "Aurelia", Garlogie, Skene, Westhill, Aberdeenshire AB32 6RX, tel: 01224 743429.

Dormobile

Dormobile Owners Club, c/o Allan Horne, 23 Fairmile, Aylesbury, Bucks HP21 7JS, tel: 01296 428580.

Dutton

Dutton Owners Club. c/o Mark Young, 6 Binyon Close, Badsey, Evesham, Worcs WR11 5EY.

Elva

Elva Owners Club, c/o Roger Dunbar, 8 Liverpool Terrace, Worthing, W. Sussex BN11 1TA, tel: 01903 823710; website: www.elva.com.

Facel Vega

Facel Vega Owners Club, c/o Roy Scandrett, "Windrush", 16 Paddock Gardens, East Grinstead, Sussex RH19 4AE, tel: 01342 326655, email: www.linscan@aol.com.

Fairthorpe

Fairthorpe Sports Car Club, c/o Tony Hill, 9 Lyndhurst Crescent, Hillingdon, Middlesex UB10 9EH, tel: 01895 256799.

Ferrari

Ferrari Owners Club, c/o Peter Everingham, 35 Market Place, Snettisham, Kings Lynn PE31 7LR, tel: 01485 544500, website: www.ferrariownersclub.co.uk.

Ferrari Dino Register, c/o B. Boxall, 43 Mayswood Road, Solihull, West Midlands.

Fiat

Fiat 500 Club, c/o Janet Westcott, 33 Lionel Avenue, Wendover, Bucks HP22 6LP, tel: 01296 622880 website: www.fiat500club.org.

500 Owners Association, c/o David Docherty, 68 Upton Park, Upton-by-Chester, Cheshire CH2 1DQ, tel: 01244 382789.

Fiat Barchetta Club. Contact Geoff Bowles on geoff@bowles. force9.co.uk for further details (website: www.fiatbarchetta. com/club/uk). Or write to 39 New Road, Great Kingshill, High Wycombe. Bucks, HP15 6DR.

Fiat Motor Club (GB), c/o Sally Robins (membership secretary), 118 Brookland Road, Langport, Somerset TA10 9TH, tel: 01458 250116; Peter Jones (chairman), tel: 020 8372 4028.

Fiat X1/9 Owners Club, c/o Lyn Robertson, Membership Secretary, Bwthyn Penygroes, Penisarwaun, Caernarfon, Gwynedd LL56 3PP, tel: 016640822395; website: www.x1-9ownersclub.org.uk.

Fiat Dino Register, 59 Sandown Park, Tunbridge Wells, Kent TN2 4RY.

Fiat Osca Register, c/o Mr Elliott, 36 Maypole Drive, Chigwell, Essex.

Foden
The Foden Society, c/o Graham Donaldson, 13 Dudfleet Lane, Horbury, Wakefield, West Yorks WF4 5EX, tel: 01924 275544, website: www.thefodensociety.co.uk.

Ford
Model T Ford Register of Great Britain, c/o Julia Armer, 3 Riverside, Strong Close, Keighley, West Yorks BD21 4JP, tel: 01535 607978, website: www.t-ford.co.uk.

Model A Ford Club of Great Britian, c/o Mike Cobell, 10-14 Newland Street, Coleford, Forest of Dean, Glos GL16 8AN, tel: 01594 834321; fax: 01594 835456.

Ford Y and C Model Register, c/o Bob Wilkinson, 9 Brambleside, Thrapston, Northants NN14 4PY, tel: 01832 734463, email: bob@bwilkinson49.fsnet.co.uk, website: members.pipemedia.net/ ford-model-register/index.htm.

Early Ford V8 Club of America, c/o S. Wade, "Forge Stones", Heath Road, Boughton, Monchelsea, Maidstone, Kent ME17 4HS.

Ford 400E Owners Club, c/o Sandy Glen, 1 Maltings Cottage, Witham Road, White Notley, Witham, Essex CM8 1SE, email: sandy@thames400e.freeserve.co.uk.

Ford Sidevalve Owners Club, c/o Mike Crouch, 30 Earls Close, Bishopstoke, Eastleigh, Hants SO50 8HY, e-mail: menear @easynet.co.uk.

Pre-67 Ford Owners Club, c/o Alastair Cuninghame, Membership Secretary, 13 Drum Brae Gardens, Edinburgh EH12 8SY, tel: 0131 339 1179.

Ford Anglia 105E Owners Club, c/o M. Lewis, 81 Compton Road, North End, Portsmouth, Hants PO2 0SR.

The Sporting Escort Owners Club (all RWD cars), c/o Peter Ridgewell, Chairman, 30 Rowan Way, Thursdon, Bury St. Edmunds, Suffolk IP31 3PU, tel: 01359 231384.

Ford Classic and Capri Owners Club, c/o Ray Brandon, 1 Verney Close, Covingham, Swindon, Wilts SN3 5EF.

Capri Club International, 18 Arden Business Centre, Arden Road, Alcester B49 6HW, tel: 01789 400455; website: www.cci.planet-capri.net.

Capri II Register, c/o Kevin Hickling. 14 Beechfield Road, Welwyn Garden City, Herts AL7 3RF, tel: 07949 949297, email: capri2reg@hotmail.com.

Capri Drivers Association, c/o Moira Farelly, 9 Lyndhurst Road, Coulsdon, Surrey CR5 3HU.

Ford Capri Enthusiasts Register, c/o Glyn Watson, 7 Louis Avenue, Bury, Lancs BL9 5EQ, tel: 0161 762 9952.

Capri Club Scotland, c/o P. Lewis, 7 Logan Lea Crescent, Addlewell, West Lothian EH55 8HP.

Capri 280 Register: for details send SAE to Mark Smith, Capri 280 Register, Manchester Capri Club, Box No 5, Manchester M28 7HB, tel: 0161 790 4726 (day) 0860 568188 (eve) email: bob@bwilkinson.49fsnet.uk, website: www.geocities.com/fastfordcar/capri280register.htm.

Ford Corsair Owners Club, c/o Liz Checkley, 7 Barnfield, New Malden, Surrey KT3 5RH, tel: 020 8395 4089, website: members.aol.com/fcoc/index.htm.

Ford Cortina Owners Club, c/o Ken Wylson, 56 Barrowfield Road, Woodhouse Park, Manchester M22 1RT, tel: 0161 028 600647 (after 6pm).

Mk I Cortina Owners Club, c/o Karen Clarke, 6 Hobson's Acre, Gunthorpe, Nottingham NG14 7FF, tel: 0115 966 3995; e-mail: 106553.456@compuserve.com.

Ford Cortina Mk II Owners Club, c/o L. Willis, 7 Underdown Road, Herne Bay, Kent.

Ford Cortina 1600E Owners Club, c/o D. Johnson, 16 Woodlands Close, Sarisbury Green, Southampton SO31 7AQ, tel: 01489 602576; website: www.uk-classic-cars.com/fordcortina1600E.htm.

Ford Cortina Mk III Owners Club, c/o Steve Brookes, 146 Tudor Road, Hinckley, Leics LE10 0EH, tel: 01455 619905.

Ford Cortina Mk III Owners Register, c/o Keith Macey, 4 Fron Dirion, Brion Eeyn, Nebo, Caernarfon, Gwynned LL54 6EN, tel: 01286 881424.

Mk I Consul, Zephyr and Zodiac Owners Club, c/o V. Pell, 180 Gipsy Road, Welling, Kent DA16 1JQ.

Mk II Consul/Zephyr/Zodiac Owners Club, c/o Del Rawlins, tel: 01286 831291.

Ford Mk II Independent Owners Club International, c/o J. Enticknap, 173 Sparrow Farm Drive, Feltham, Middlesex TW14 0DG, tel: 020 8890 3741.

Ford Mk III Zephyr and Zodiac Owners Club, c/o Dave Barnes, 27 Shurley Grove, Edmonton, London N9 8ES, tel: 020 8443 2648.

Zephyr and Zodiac Mk IV Owners Club, c/o John Glaysher, 94 Claremont Road, Rugby CV21 3LU, tel: 01788 574884.

Ford Executive Owners Register, c/o George Young, 31 Brian Road, Chadwell Heath, Romford, Essex EM6 5DA.

Ford Granada Mk I Owners Club, c/o Paul Stones, 10 Wayland Road, Grove, Wantage, Oxon OX12 0BQ, tel: 01235 768399.

Ford Granada Mk I and Mk II Drivers Guild, General Secretary: Maureen Kennedy, 26 Brent Road, Bourne End, Bucks SL8 5LU; tel: 01628 530784; website: www.ford-granadaguild.co.uk; e-mail: martin@ford-granadaguild.co.uk.

Ford Granada Mk II Owners Club, c/o P. Farrer, 58 Jevington Way, Lee, London SE12 9NQ, tel: 020 8857 4356.

Granada Mk II Collection, c/o Rod Bamford, 11 Tolton Road, Stocking Farm, Leicester LE4 2HG, tel: 0116 299 7409.

Ford Granada Mk I, Mk II and Mk III Club, c/o Cliff Robinson, 29 Rowlands Close, Cheshunt, Herts EN8 9NW.

Ford Granada Enthusiasts Club, c/o Philip Snow, 116 Whitmore Road, Hanchurch Crossroads, Newcastle, Staffs ST5 4DG, tel: 01782 657697; website: www.granada-enthusiasts.co.uk.

Mustang Owners Club of Great Britain, c/o A. Keighley, 21 Raleigh Close, Eaton Socon, Cambs PE19 3NN, tel: 01480 477254; website: www.geocities.com/MotorCity/3380/index.html.

Ford RS Owners Club, PO Box 4044, Pangbourne, Reading, Berks RG8 7XL, tel: 01189 841583 website: www.rsownersclub.co.uk.

Ford XR Owners Club, PO Box 47, Loughborough, Leics LE11 1XS; tel: Les Gent 01509 881015.

Ford Fiesta Club of GB, c/o Mrs S. Church, 145 Chapel Lane, Farnborough, Hants GU14 9BN, tel: 01276 35422; website: www.fiestaclubgb.co.uk.

Ford Drivers Register, c/o Neil Jones, 86 Muncaster Gardens, East Hunsbury, Northampton NN4 0XR, tel: 01604 768909.

Frisky

Frisky Register, c/o J. Meadows, Graces Cottage, Tregagle, Monmouth, Gwent NP5 4RZ, tel: 01600 860420.

FSO/Polski Fiat

FSO Owners Club (including Polski Fiat register), c/o Simon McDonald-Elliott, Cottage Workshops, The Graig, Water-Trough Lane, Llanwenarth Citra, Abergavenny NP7 7EN, tel: 01873 810517, email fsofriends@smartgroup.com.

Gentry

Gentry Register, c/o Barbera Reynolds, Barn Close Cottage, Cromford Road, Woodlinkin, Notts NG16 4HD, tel:01773 719874, website: www.gentry-owners.co.uk.

Gilbern

Gilbern Owners Club, c/o Peter Daye, Membership Secretary, Castlebrook, Compton Dundon, Somerton, Somerset TA11 6PR, tel: 01458 442025; e-mail: pvdaye@netscapeonline.co.uk.

Gordon Keeble

Gordon Keeble Owners Club, 26 Burford Park Road, Birmingham B38 8PB, tel: 0121 459 9587, website: www.gordonkeeble.com.

Gwynne and Albert

Gwynne and Albert Register, c/o Ian Walker, 8 Baines Lane, Knebworth, Herts SG3 6RA, tel: 01438 812041.

Healey

Association of Healey Owners, c/o John Humphreys, 2 Kingsbury's Lane, Ringwood, Hants BH24 1EL, tel: 01425 480243.

Heinkel/Trojan

Heinkel Trojan Club Ltd., c/o Peter Jones, 37 Brinklow Close, Matchborough West, Redditch, Worcs B98 0HB, tel: 01527 501318, website: homepages.tesco.net/~heinkeljb/HTCltd/main.htm.

Hillman

Hillman Register 1907-1932, c/o Clive Baker, Waterloo Mill, School Road, Wotton-under-Edge, Glos GL12 7JN, tel: 01453 843438.

Hillman Owners Club, c/o Christine Gore, 6 Askham Grove, Upton, Pontefract WF9 1LT.

Avenger and Sunbeam Owners Club, c/o Malcolm Wood, 40 Stanbeck Meadows, Workington, Cumbria. e-mail: Marcus@avenger72. freeserve.co.uk.

Imp Cruising Club, 28 Marrion Crescent, Orpington, Kent BR5 5DD.

The Imp Club. Keith and Mary Robbins, The Imp Club Ltd, 21 Elmwood Close, Retford, Notts DN22 6SL, tel: 01777 703146; website: www.theimpclub.co.uk.

Hillman Minx and Hunters Galore, c/o Mrs Janet Thorpe, 3 The Pinfold, Newton Burgoland, Goalville, Leicester LE67 2SQ, tel: 01530 273511; e-mail: althorpe@aol.com (Chairman and Magazine: c/o Gerald Bostock, 17 Fennel Drive, The Fallows, Stafford ST17 7HA, tel: 01785 255586.)

Holden
Holden UK Register, c/o Guy Hardy, Membership Secretary, Cawdron House, 111 Charles Street, Milfrod Haven, Pembrokeshire SA73 2HW, tel: 01646 692254, e-mail: holdenuk@ndirect.co.uk; website: www.geocities.com/ikiloh.

Honda
Honda Beat Club, c/o Stephen Finegan, 4 Leeson Walk, Harborne, Birmingham B17 0LU.

Hotchkiss
British Hotchkiss Society, c/o Michael Edwards, Yew Cottage, Old Boars Hill, Oxford OX1 5JJ, tel: 01865 735180; fax: 01865 730698. President: Paul Hickson, 20 Eldon Road, Reading, Berks RG1 4DL, tel: 0118 957 6193.

Humber
Humber Register (1896–1932), c/o Richard Arman, Northbrook Cottage, 175 York Road, Broadstone, Dorset BH18 8ES, tel: 01202 695937.

Post-Vintage Humber Car Club, c/o Harvey Cooke, 1 Hilbery Rise, Northampton NN3 5ER, tel: 01604 404363, website: www.pvhcc. fsnet.co.uk.

Invicta
Invicta Car Club, Stanley Hall, Selsey, Stroud, Gloucs GL5 5LJ, fax: 01453 791363; e-mail: renall@selseyswinternet.co.uk.

Isetta
Isetta Owners Club of Great Britain, c/o Mick and Kay West, 137 Prebendal Avenue, Aylesbury, Bucks HP21 8LD.

Jaguar/Daimler (*see also* Daimler/Lanchester)
Jaguar Car Club, c/o Jeff Holman, Membership Secretary, Barbary, Chobham Road, Woking, Surrey GU21 4AS, tel: 01483 763811, website: www.geocities.com/ikiloh.

Jaguar Drivers Club Ltd., Mrs Kathy Beech, Company Secretary, Jaguar House, 18 Stuart Street, Luton, Beds LU1 2SL, tel: 01582 419332; website: www.jaguardriver.co.uk.

Jaguar Enthusiasts Club, The Old Library, 113A Gloucester Road North, Filton, Bristol BS34 7PU. tel: 0117 969 8186; website: www.jec.org.uk.

Jensen
Jensen Owners Club, c/o Keith Andrews, 2 Westgate, Fulshaw Park, Wilmslow, Cheshire SK9 1QQ, tel: 01625 525699.

Jensen Club, PO Box 334, Aylesbury, Bucks HP22 5GL, tel: 01296 614072 e-mail: jensenclub@btinternet.com, website: www. jensenclub.com.

Jowett
Jowett Car Club, Membership Secretary: Pauline Winteringham, 33 Woodlands Road, Gomersal, West Yorks BD19 4SF, tel: 01274 873959.

Jupiter

Jupiter Owners Automobile Club, c/o Geoff Butterwick, Cowlishaw Cottage, Yarmouth Road, Melton,Woodbridge, Suffolk IP12 1QF, tel: 01394 385709; website: www.jowettjupiter.co.uk; e-mail: ed@jowettjupiter.co.uk.

Lada

Lada Owners Club of Great Britain, c/o Heather Rogers, Secretary, 10 Carnaby Close, Godmanchester, Huntingdon, Cambs PE29 2EE, tel: 01480 391343, email: p.rogers@lada-owners-club.co.uk.

Lagonda

Lagonda Club, c/o Colin Bugler, Wintney House, London Road, Hartley Wintney, Hants RG27 8RN, tel: 01252 845451, website: www.lagonda-club.com.

Lagonda Rapier Register, c/o Mrs J. Williams, The Smithy, Tregynon, Newtown, Powys SY16 3EH, tel: 01686 650396.

The Lanchester Register 1895–1931, c/o Chris Clark, The Lanches, Ledbury Road, Dymock, Gloucestershire GL18 2AG, tel: 01531 890204.

Lancia

Lancia Motor Club, PO Box 51, Wrexham LL11 5ZE, website: www.lanciamotorclub.co.uk.

Land Rover

Land Rover 1947–1951 Register, c/o Frank Mall, 10 Rowan Mount, Wheatley Hills, Doncaster, South Yorkshire DN2 5PJ, tel: 01302 367349.

Land Rover Series One Club, c/o Tim Webb, Secretary, Overmeade, Arches Farm, Malmesbury, Wiltshire SN16 0EJ, tel: 01666 823449.

Land Rover Series Two Club, PO Box 251, Barnsley S70 5YN, tel: 01226 241483, e-mail: series2club@freenetname.co.uk.

148

Discovery Owners Club. Membership Secretary: Steve Clive, 77 Northfield Road, Thatcham, Berkeshire RG18 3ER; e-mail: sclive@bciplc.com; website: www.discoveryownersclub.com.

Lea Francis

Lea Francis Owners Club, c/o Robin Sawers, "French's", Long Wittenham, Abingdon, Oxon OX14 4QQ, tel: 01865 407515.

Lincoln

Lincoln Zephyr Owners Club, c/o Colin Spong, 22 New North Road, Hainault, Ilford, Essex IG6 2XG.

Lotus

The Official Lotus Club, c/o Deborah Marsh, Club Coordinator, Lotus Cars Ltd, Potash Lane, hethel, Norwich NR14 8EZ, tel: 01953 608149, website: www.lotuscars.co.uk.

Lotus Drivers Club, PO Box 387, St. Albans, Herts AL4 9BJ.

Club Lotus, PO Box 8, Dereham, Norfolk NR19 1AD, tel: 01362 694459.

Historic Lotus Register, c/o Graham Capel, Nyes Place, Newdigate, Surrey RH5 5BX, tel: 01293 871541.

Lotus Cortina Register, c/o Andy Morrell, 64 The Queen's Drive, Chorleywood, Rickmansworth, Herts WD3 2LT, tel: 01923 836520 (day); 01923 776219 (eve).

Sunbeam Lotus Owners Club, c/o The Secretary, 7 Church Road, Maulden, Bedford MK45 2AU, tel: 01525 840331; website: www.sunbeamlotus.com.

Marcos

Marcos Owners Club, 51 London Road, Bromley, Kent BR1 4HB, tel: 020 8460 3511, e-mail: ABS.Labs@dial.pipex.com.

Mini Marcos Owners Club, c/o Roger Garland, 28 Meadow Road, Claines, Worcester WR3 7PP, tel: 01905 458533, website: www.argonet.co.uk/minimarcos.

Club Marcos International, c/o Isobel Chivers, The Spinney, Littleworth Lane, Whitley, Melksham, Wilts SN12 8RE, tel: 01225 707815.

Marendaz

Marendaz Special Car Register, c/o Mrs J. Shaw, 107 Old Bath Road, Cheltenham GL54 7DA, tel: 01242 526310.

Marlin

Marlin Owners Club, c/o J. Neeld, Sewdish Bungalow, School Lane, Wheaton Ashton, Staffs ST19 9NH, tel: 01785 841439.

Maserati

Maserati Club, c/o Michael Miles, The Paddock, Abbotts Ann, Andover, Hants SP11 7NT.

Matra

Matra Enthusiasts Club, c/o Greg Dalgleish, The Hollies, Crowborough Hill, Crowborough, East Sussex TN6 2HH, tel: 01892 652964, website: www.matra-club.co.uk.

Mazda

MX5 Owners Club UK. Mike Hayward, Membership Secretary, 17 Knights Close, Bishop's Stortford, Hertfordshire, CM23 4BZ, tel (before 10pm): 01279 656914, Fax: 07715 700747, E-Mail: Mx5.mike@virgin.net, website: www.mx5oc.co.uk.

Mazda RX7 Owners Club, c/o M. Hocknull, 65 Coyne Road, West Bromwich, W. Mids B70 7HJ, tel: 07071 797797, website: www.rx7club.co.uk.

Mazda Rotary Club. Includes all Mazda cars powered by the revolutionary rotary engine. Quarterly newsletter by email or post; discounts from various providers of specialist rotary spares, performance parts and insurance. Mazda Rotary Club, 41 Elizabeth Court, St James Road, Gravesend, Kent DA11 0HH, tel: 01474 333099; email: info@mazdarotaryclub.com; website: www.mazdarotaryclub.com.

Mercedes-Benz

Mercedes-Benz Club Ltd., c/o Paddy Long, Whitefriars, Ashton Keynes SN6 6QR, website: www.mercedes-benzownersclub.co.uk.

Mercedes-Benz Owners Association, Merceded House, Langton Road, Langton Green, Tunbridge Wells, Kent TN3 0EG, tel: 01892 860922; fax: 01892 861363; e-mail: Join@mercedesclub.org.uk.

Messerschmitt

Messerschmitt Owners Club, c/o Eileen Hallam, Membership Secretary, Birches, Ashmores Lane, Rusper, W. Sussex RH12 4PS, tel: 01293 871417; website: www.messerschmitt.co.uk.

Metropolitan

Metropolitan Owners Club, c/o Nick Savage, The Old Pump House, Nutbourne Common, Pulborough, West Sussex RH20 2HB, tel: 01798 813713, email: metclubuk@aol.com, website: www.stevvia. demon.co.uk/metro.htm.

MG

MG Car Club, PO Box 251, Kimber House, Cemetery Road, Abingdon, Oxon OX14 1FF, tel: 01235 555552; website: www. mgcars.org.uk.

MGA Register of the MG Car Club, c/o David De Saxe, Ivy Cottage, Axford, Marlborough, Wilts SN8 2HA.

MG Owners Club, Freepost, Swavesey, Cambridge CB4 5QZ, tel: 01954 231125; fax: 01954 232106; e-mail: mginfo@mgownersclub.co.uk.

MG Octagon Car Club, Unit 1–2 Parchfields Enterprise Park, Parch-fields Farm, Colton Road, Trent Valley, Rugeley, Staffs WS15 3HB, tel: +44 (0)1889 574666; fax: +44 (0)1889 574555; website: www. mgoctagoncarclub.com; e-mail: info@mgoctagoncarclub.com.

MG 'Y' Type Register, c/o J. Lawson, 12 Nithsdale Road, Liverpool L15 5AX.

Midget and Sprite Club, c/o Nigel Williams, 15 Foxcote, Kingswood, Bristol BS15 2TX, tel: 0117 961 2759.

Mini

British Mini Club, c/o David Hollis, The Mini House, 18 Aldgate Drive, Brierley Hill, West Midlands DY5 3NT, tel: 01384 897779; email: british.miniclub@lineone.net; website: www.britishminiclub. co.uk.

National Mini Owners Club, c/o C. Cheal, 15 Birchwood Road, Lichfield, Staffs WS14 9UN, tel: 01543 257956; website: www.miniownersclub.co.uk.

Club Mini Classics, c/o Phil Kershaw, 15 Macclesfield Road, Wilmslow, Cheshire SK9 1BZ, tel: 01625 532969. Club magazine: 'Sliding Window'. (NB: the club promotes originality.)

Mini Cooper Club, c/o Mary Fowler, 59 Giraud Street, Poplar, London E14 6EE, tel: 020 7515 7173.

Mini Cooper Register, c/o Clive Ludden, The Spirals, Barton Road, Farndon, Chester CH3 6NL, website: www.minicooper.org.

Mini Moke Club, c/o Philip Mitchell, 53 Yarmouth Road, Ellingham, Bungay, Suffolk NR35 2PN, tel: 01508 518265, website: www.mokeclub.org.uk.

Mini Seven Racing Club, c/o Mike Jackson, Membership Secretary, 345 Clay Lane, S. Yardley, Birmingham B26 1ES, tel: 0121 707 5881, website: www.mini7.co.uk.

Mini Special Register, c/o Adrian Boyns, 30 Dalton Lane, Barrow in Furness, Cumbria LA14 4LE.

Mitsubishi

Mitsubishi Motors Owners Club, c/o Lesley Jensen, The Colt Car Company Ltd., Watermoor, Cirencester, Gloucestershire GL7 1LF, tel: 01481 850348.

Mitsubishi Sapporo Register (1974–84), c/o Graham Haswell, The Old Winchester Street, Botley, Southampton SO30 2AA, tel: 01489 785293.

Morgan

Morgan Sports Car Club, c/o Mrs Carol Kennett, Secretary, Old Ford Lodge, Ogston, Highham, Alfreton, Derbyshire DE55 6EL, tel: 01773 830281, fax: 01773 521816, website: www.itmc.net/mscc.

Morgan Three Wheeler Club Ltd., c/o E. Eyes, 280 Commonwealth Way, Abbey Wood, London SE2 0LD, tel: 020 8311 7282.

Morris

Bullnose Morris Club, c/o Richard Harris, PO Box 383, Hove, East Sussex BN3 4FX.

Morris Register, Secretary Michael Thomas, 5 Woodland Rise, Oxted, Surrey RH8 9HW; Historian Harry Edwards, Wellwood Farm, Lower Stocks Road, West Hanningfield, Chelmsford, Essex CM2 8UY, tel: 01277 840697; website: www.morrisregister.co.uk/

Morris Commercial Club, c/o Gordon Payley, 32 Daniell Way, Great Boughton, Cheshire CH3 5XH. (All types of Morris Commercial and BMC-built commercial vehicles 1924-1973, from 10cwt J type to 7 tons, but excluding Minors and car-derived vans. Membership £10).Morris Cowley and Oxford Club, c/o Derek Andrews, 202 Chantry Gardens, Southwick, Trowbridge, Wilts BA14 9QX, tel: 07971 071 0292.

Morris J-Type Register, c/o Harvey Pircher, 31 Queenswood Road, Moseley, Birmingham B13 3AU.

Morris Minor Owners Club, PO Box 1098, Derby DE23 8ZX, tel: 01332 291675, fax: 01332 290661, website: www.MorrisMinorOC.co.uk.

Morris Minor LCV Register, c/o D. Thomas, 61 Zeals Rise, Warminster, Wilts BA12 6PL, tel: 01747 840990; e-mail: LCVReg@aol.com.

Morris Marina Owners Club and Ital Register, 39 Portley Road, Dawley, Telford, Shropshire TF4 3JW, tel: 01952 504900; e-mail: ajmmarina@aol.com.

Marina and Ital Drivers Club, c/o John Lawson, 12 Nithsdale Road, Liverpool LS15 5AX (35 members).

Morris Marina Enthusiasts Club, 45 Oak Drive, Acton Vale, Acton, London W3 7LD; e-mail: alan@mmec.freeserve.co.uk; website: www.mmec.freeserve.co.uk/mmec.htm.

Morris Oxford MO and Wolseley 6/80 Club, c/o D. Gould, 2 Barleyfield Close, Heighington, Lincs LN4 1TX: fax only: 01522 793994; e-mail: sixeightymo@tesco.net.

Napier

Napier Power Heritage Trust (NPHT), Hon. Secretary Alan Vessey, 188 London Road, Aston Clinton, Aylesbury, Bucks HP22 5LE.

Naylor

Naylor Car Club, c/o Freda Taylor, Naylor and Hutson Register, 21 Anglesey Place, Great Barton, Bury St. Edmunds, Suffolk IP31 2TW, tel: 01284 787539; email: freda.naylorcarclub@btinternet.com, website: www.naylorcarclub.org.uk. (Naylor Parts: Airedale Garage, Hollins Hill, Shipley, W. Yorkshire BD17 7QN.)

Nobel

Nobel Register, c/o K. Wagstaff, Keepers Cottage, The Green, Kelling, Holt, Norfolk NR25 7EN.

NSU

Ro80 Club GB, Membership Secretary Mr E. Strong, Round Barn, Blackburn Road, Entwistle, Turton, Lancashire BL7 0QB, tel: 01204 852425, website: www.ro80club.freeserve.co.uk.

Oakland (*see also* Pontiac)

International Oakland Register, 105 Summers Road, Farncombe, Godalming, Surrey GU7 3BE, tel: 01483 861177; e-mail: oakland@dial.pipes.com.

Ogle

Ogle Register, c/o Chris Gow, The Stack Yard, Malt House Lane, Burgess Hill, West Sussex RH15 9HA, tel: 01444 248439.

Opel

Opel Monza: Autobahnstormers: David Waddington, 19 Olivers Drive, Witham, Essex CM8 1QJ, tel: 01376 516034, e-mail: dwgsi24v@aol.com.

Opel Group, c/o Andrew Lee, 93 Bradgate Road, Barwell, Leics LE9 8FB.

Opel Manta Owners Club, c/o Richard Miller, 186 Norman Place Road, Coundon, Coventry CV6 2BU.

Packard

Packard Automobile Club of Great Britain, c/o John Bath, 16 Ruskin Drive, Worcester Park, Surrey KT4 8LG, tel: 020 7398 9000/020 8330 0013, e-mail: andrewb@clara.net; and Stuart Broatch, Guy Cottage, Chicklade, Hindon Salisbury SP3 5SU, tel: 01747 820545.

Panhard et Levassor

Les Amis de Panhard et Levassor GB, 'La Dyna', 11 Arterial Avenue, Rainham, Essex RM13 9PD, tel: 01708 524425.

Panther

Panther Car Club, Secretary Fraser Robertson, Plas Yn Coed, Llandegla, Wrexham LL11 3AL, website: www.panthercarclub.com.

Panther Car Club UK, c/o George Newell, 91 Fleet Road, Farnborough, Hants GU14 9RE, tel: 01252 540217.

Paramount

Paramount Equipe Etrange, 4 Wool Road, Wimbledon, London SW20 0HW.

Peugeot

Club Peugeot UK, c/o Peter Beale, 49 Upper Green, Tewin, Welwyn, Herts AL6 0LX, tel: 01778 422274.

Piper

Piper Sports and Racing Car Club, PO Box 55, Bourne, Lincolnshire, PE10 9FX; email: thepiperclub@u.genie.co.uk.

Pontiac (*see also* Oakland)

Pontiac and Oakland Club International, 105 Summers Road, Farncombe, Godalming, Surrey GU7 3BE, tel: 01483 861177; e-mail: davidjones@dial.pipes.com.

Porsche

Porsche Club of Great Britain, Cornbury House, Cotswold Business Village, Moreton-in-Marsh, Glos GL56 0JQ, tel: 01608 652911.

The Independent Porsche Enthusiasts Club, Manora, 31 The Grove, Hartlepool TS26 9LZ, tel: 07000 924 968 911.

Radford

Radford Register, c/o Chris Gow, 108 Potters Lane, Burgess Hill, West Sussex, tel: 01444 248439.

Railton

Railton Owners Club, c/o Barrie Mckenzie, Fairmiles, Barnes Hall Road, Buncross, Sheffield S35 1RF, tel: 0114 246 8357. Club Mag Editor: Mike Stenhouse, 17 Pease Hill Close, Rowdon, Leeds LS19 6EF.

Reliant/Raleigh

Raleigh Safety Seven and early Reliant Owners Club, c/o Mick Sleap, 17 Courtland Avenue, Chingford, London E4 6DU.

Reliant Owners Club, c/o Graham Chappell, 19 Smithey Close, High Green, Sheffield S30 4FQ, tel: 0114 284 8138.

Reliant Kitten Register, c/o Brian Marshall, 16 Glendee Gardens, Renfrew PA4 0AL, tel (after 6pm): 0141 886 6117; website: www.uk-classic-cars.com/kitten.htm.

Reliant Scimitar Drivers Club International, c/o Steven Lloyd, 74 Bradley Avenue, Winterbourne, Bristol BS17 1HR, tel: 01454 775282, website: www.scimitardriver.co.uk.

Reliant Sabre and Scimitar Owners Club, PO Box 67, Teddington, Middx TW11 8QR, tel: 020 8977 6625; website: www.scimweb.com.

Renault

Renault Freres Club for pre-1940 Renaults, c/o Mrs Pam Mills, 54 High Street, Durrington, Salisbury, Wilts PS4 8AQ.

Renault Owners Club, c/o J. Cowgill, 89 Queen Elizabeth Drive, Beccles, Suffolk NR34 9LA.

Club Alpine Renault, c/o Peter Whitehouse, I Bloomfield Close, Wombourne, Wolverhampton WV5 8HQ, tel (after 7pm): 01902 895590.

Rear Engine Renault Club. Advice from Kevin Gould, 2 Barleyfield Close, Heighington, Lincoln LN4 1TX, tel/fax 01522 874990, website: www.rerc.co.uk.

Renault Twingo Club, Dafydd Williams, tel: 01766 770203; website: www.twingo.co.uk/

Riley Motor Club Ltd., c/o J.S. Hall, 'Treelands', 127 Penn Road, Wolverhampton WV3 0DU, tel: 01902 773197.

Riley Register, c/o Jim Clarke, 56 Cheltenham Road, Bishop's Cleve, Cheltenham, Glos GL52 4LY, tel: 01242 673598, website: www.rileyregister.com.

Scottish Riley Register, c/o Eric Stewart, 27 Rockfield Street, Dundee, Tayside DD2 3LD.

Riley RM Club 1946–1955, c/o Jacque Morris, Y Fachell, Ruthin Road, Gwernymynydd, Flintshire CH7 5LQ, tel: 01352 700427, website: www.rileyrmclub.org.uk.

Rochdale
Rochdale Owners Club, c/o Alaric Spendlove, 7 Whiteleigh Avenue, Crownhill, Plymouth PL5 3BQ, tel: 01752 791409, website: www.rochdale-owners-club.com.

Rolls Royce
Rolls Royce Enthusiasts Club, c/o Captain Peter Baines, The Hunt House, Paulerspury, Towcester, Northants NN12 7NA, tel: 01327 811788, email: admin@rrec.co.uk, website: www.rrec.co.uk.

Rover
Rover Sports Register, c/o C. Evans, 8 Hilary Close, Great Broughton, Chester CH3 5QP.

Rover Owners Club, c/o Ian Derby, 20 Heathbank Drive, Huntington, Staffs WS12 4NY, tel: 01543 468103.

Rover P4 Drivers Guild, c/o Colin Blowers, 32 Arundel Road, Luton, Beds LU4 8DY, tel: 01582 572499, website: www.roverp4.com.

Rover P5 Owners Club, c/o G. Moorshead, 13 Glen Avenue, Ashford, Middx TW15 2JE, tel: 01784 258166.

Rover P5 Alive Owners Club, c/o Rikki Woolf, 1 Bank Street, Faversham, Kent ME12 8PR.

Rover P6 Owners Club, c/o Brenda Griffin, Secretary, PO Box 120, Feltham, Middlesex TW13 4JN, tel (evenings only): 020 8890 9094.

Rover P6 Drivers Club, PO Box 1477, Walsall WS5 3XY, fax: 01922 648133, emails: membership@p6club.com or secretary@p6club.com, website: www.p6club.com. (Membership of 900-plus.)

Rover SD1 Club, PO Box 255, Woking, Surrey GU21 1GJ, tel: 01483 888432.

Rover SD1 Mania, c/o Tom Willis, 59 Third Avenue, Enfield, Middx EN1 1BU, tel: 020 8482 7387, website: www.roversd1mania.co.uk.

Saab

Saab Enthusiasts Club, c/o William Glander, 4 Rochdale Avenue, Calne, Wilts SN11 9AX, tel: 01249 815792; e-mail: enthusiasts @saabenthusiasts.co.uk; website: www.saabenthusiasts.co.uk.

Saab Owners Club of Great Britain Ltd., c/o John Wood, PO Box 900, Durham DH1 2GF, tel: 070 7 171 9000; e-mail: membership@saabclub.co.uk; website: www.saabclub.co.uk.

Salmson

British Salmson Owners Club, c/o D. Cannings, 61 Holyrood Gardens, Edgware, Middlesex HA8 5LS.

Tickford Owners Club, c/o Neville Clark, 5 The Elms Paddock, Clifton upon Dunsmore, Rugby CV23 0TD, tel: 01788 537695, email: mark.richardson@btclick.com. (Includes Salmson Tickford from 1820s.)

Scott

Scott Owners Club, c/o Brian Marshall, PR Officer, Walnut Cottage, Abbey Lane, Aslockton, Nottingham NG13 9AE, website: home.clara.net/g.harland/soc.htm.

SEAT

SEAT, all models. Lee Shand, 52 Ten Acre Close, Rainham, Kent; tel: 07703 593710; email: lee@seatcupra.net; websites: www.seatcupra.net and www.forums-seatcupra.net.

Simca

Simca Club UK, c/o David Chapman, 18 Cavendish Gardens, Redhill, Surrey RH1 4AQ, tel: 01737 765331.

Singer

Singer Owners Club. c/o Martin Wray, 11 Ermine Riase, great Casterton, Stamford, Lincs PE9 4EJ, tel (evenings): 01780 762740, email: martin@singeroc.free-online.co.uk, website: www.singeroc.free-online.co.uk.

Association of Singer Car Owners, c/o Anne Page, 39 Oakfield, Rickmansworth, Herts WD3 2LR, tel: 01923 778575. website: www.uk-classic-cars.com/singer.htm.

Skoda

Skoda Owners Club of Great Britain, c/o B. Challis, 12 Millfields, Stansted, Essex CM24 8AS, tel: 01279 815183; email: skodaclubgb@dial.pipex.com; website: www.skoda-owners-club.co.uk. Technical and Publishing Officer Simon McDonal-Elliott, email: techoffice@llanwenarth.com.

Smart

MCC Smart Club: c/o Al Young: www.thesmartclub.co.uk (Also Rob Eatwell, 9 Honeysuckle Court, 43 Grove Road, Sutton, Surrey SM1 2AW; e-mail rob@thesmartclub.co.uk)

Smart Owners Club UK, c/o Andrew Moss, 265-267 Burnley Road, Colne, Lancs BB8 8JD, tel: 01282 868806; website: smartownersclubuk.com (offers a driver's manual in English at £19.95).

Spartan

Spartan Owners Club, c/o Steve Andrews, 28 Ashford Drive, Ravenhead, Notts NG15 9DE, tel: 01623 409351, website: www.spartan-oc.demon.co.uk.

Standard

Standard Register (1903–1930), c/o Leonard Barr, 30 The Walled Garden, West Way, Cirencester, Gloucs GL7 1JA, e-mail: Standardregist@aol.com.

Standard Motor Club, c/o Tony Pingriff, 57 Main Road, Meriden, Coventry CV7 7LP, tel: 01676 522181, e-mail: pingriff@cwcom.net, website: www.standardmotorclub.org.uk.

Standard Vanguard Owners Club, c/o Ken Holstead, 7 Priory Close, Wilton, Salisbury, Wilts SP2 0LD.

Vanguard 3 Owners Club, c/o Martin Holstead, PO Box 1581, Marlborough, Wiltshire SN8 2UA, tel: 01672 520154; website: www.the-vanguard-ph3-owners-club.co.uk.

Star, Starling, Stuart and Briton

Star, Starling, Stuart and Briton Register, c/o D. Evans, 2A Hyperion Road, Stourton, Stourbridge DY7 6SB, tel: 01384 374329.

Studebaker Owners Club UK, c/o Doug Priston, 5 Kingsway Manor Lodge Road, Rowlands Castle, PO9 6AZ.

Stutz

The Stutz Club, c/o Norman C. Barrs, 54 Canonbury Road, London NW, tel: 020 7226 8483, fax: 020 7359 6812.

Sunbeam/Darracq

Sunbeam Talbot Darracq Register, c/o J. Donovan, Membership Secretary, Blackwell House, 21 Stubbs Wood, Chesham Bois, Amersham HP6 6EY, tel: 01494 721972; or Mrs Gill Brett, Secretary,, 9 Hallet's Close, Stubbington, Fareham, Hants PO14 2JS, tel: 01329 663809.

Sunbeam Register, c/o Bruce Dowell, The Maples. Badger's Cross, Somerton TA11 7JD, tel: 01458 274700; fax: 01458 274600.

Sunbeam Rapier Owners Club, Mike Kingston, Chairman, tel (evenings): 01928 788583.

Sunbeam Alpine Owners Club, c/o Sarah Jarrett, 25 Willow Drive, Hutton, Weston-super-Mare, Avon BS24 9TJ.

Sunbeam Talbot Alpine Register, c/o Derek Cook, 47 Crescent Wood Road, Sydenham, London SE26 6SA, tel: 020 8693 1045.

Sunbeam Tiger Owners Club, c/o Brian Postle, Beechwood, 8 Villa Real Estate, Consett, County Durham DH8 6BJ, tel: 01207 508296.

Suzuki

Suzuki SC100 Enthusiasts Club, c/o Tim Smith, 57 Wordsworth Mead, Redhill, Surrey RH1 1AH. Tel: 01737 766263.

Suzuki Cappucino Owners Register, c/o Alex Clouter, 6 Blenheim Fields, Riverside, Forest Row, East Sussex RH18 5EW, tel (7pm–9pm): 01342 823951, website: www.score.org.uk.

The Swift Club (1901-31), c/o John Harrison, 70 Eastwick Drive, Great Bookham, Leatherhead, Surrey KT23 3NX, tel: 01372 452120, email: john-harrison@bookham36.freeserve.co.uk.

Talbot

79-86 Talbot Owners Register, c/o David Chapman, 18 Cavendish Gardens, Redhill, Surrey RH1 4AQ, tel: 01737 765331.

Tatra

Tatra Register UK, c/o Derrick Moores, The Manse, Stratford Road, Watford, Herts WD17 4QG, tel 01923 225863, website: www.tatra-register.co.uk.

Tornado

Tornado Register, c/o Dave Malins, 48 St Monica's Avenue, Luton, Beds LU3 1PN, tel: 01582 737641, email: tornado_register@aol.com, website: www.astruc.s.easynet.co.uk/tornado_register.

Torcars

Torcars Sun-Tor Register c/o Jim Matthews, 28 Woodfield Road, Gainsborough, Lincs DN21 1RF, tel: 01427 614128.

Toyota

Toyota Enthusiasts Club, c/o Billy Wells, 28 Park Road, Feltham, Middx TW13 6PW, tel: 020 8898 0740.

Toyota MR2 Mk 1 Club, 35 Alma Street, Luton, Beds LU1 2PL, tel: 01582 454971, website: www.mr2mk1club.com.

Toyota MR2 Drivers Club, c/o Kew Kinnersley MBE, PO Box 999, Huntingdon PE17 2PX, tel: 01487 710010.

Toyota Sera UK Register, c/o Andrew Cliffe, 31, Dalbier Close, Norwich, Norfolk NR7 0RP; tel: 07798 651441; website: www.toyotasera.co.uk; e-mail: andrew@omicron.co.uk.

Toyota Landcruiser 4x4 Club, c/o J. Boatwright, 61 Graham Street, Swindon, Wilts SN1 2HA, tel: 07831 201596.

Trident

Trident Car Club, c/o Dave Rowlinson, 23 Matlock Crescent, Cheam, Sutton, Surrey SM3 9SS, tel: 020 8644 9029.

Triumph

Pre-1940 Triumph Owners Club, Mem Sec: Jon Quiney, 2 Duncroft Close, Reigate, Surrey RH2 9DE, tel: 01737 247218.

Triumph Razoredge Owners Club, c/o David Wickens, 12 Cornwall Close, Camberley, Surrey GU15 3UA, tel: 01276 65958.

Triumph Roadster Club, c/o John Cattaway, Membership Secretary, 59 Cowdray Park Road, Little Common, Bexhill-on-Sea, East Sussex TN39 4EZ, tel: 01424 844608.

Triumph Mayflower Club, c/o John Oaker, 19 Broadway North, Walsall, West Midlands WS1 2QG, tel: 01922 633042, website: www.mayflower99.freeserve.co.uk.

Triumph Dolomite Club (all derivatives from 1300/1500 FWD through Toledo to Dolomite and Sprint), PO Box 2886, Cannock, WS12 5WW, tel/fax: 08700 111737; e-mail: info@triumphdolomiteclub.com; website: www.triumphdolomiteclub.com.

Triumph Sporting Owners Club, c/o P. Utratny, 57 Rothiemey Road, Flixton, Urmston, Manchester M41 6JY, tel: 0161 747 3618.

Club Triumph, Membership Secretary, FREEPOST (SWB20389), Christchurch BH23 4ZZ, tel/fax: 01425 274193, e-mail: club.triumph@btinternet.com; website: club.triumph.org.uk/.

Triumph Spitfire Club, c/o Corwin van Heteren, Waltersingel 34a, 7314 NT Apeldoorn, The Netherlands.

Triumph Sports Six Club Ltd.(all Herald-based Triumphs from Herald to GT6), Main Street, Lubbenham, Market Harborough, Leics LE16 9TF, tel: 01858 434424, e-mail: tssc@tssc.uk.com, website: www.tssc.uk.com.

Stag Owners Club, The Old Rectory, Aslacton, Norfolk NR15 2JN, tel: 01379 677362, fax: 01379 677735; e-mail: stagmemsec @compuserve.com.

Triumph Stag Owners Club; website: www.stag.org.uk; e-mail: martin@ford-granadaguild.co.uk.

Triumph Stag Register, c/o Mike Wattam, 18 Hazel Close, Highcliffe, Dorset BH23 4PS, tel: 01425 274638, website: www.tristagreg.org.

TR Drivers Club, c/o Jeff Black, 3 Blackberry Close, Abbeymead, Gloucester GL4 7BS, tel: 01452 614234.

TR Register, 1B Hawksworth, Southmead Industrial Park, Didcot, Oxon OX11 7HR, tel: 01235 818866; e-mail: TR.Register @onlyxnet.co.uk.

Triumph 2000, 2500, 2.5 Register, c/o A. Crussell, 10 Gables Close, Chalfont St. Peter, Bucks SL9 0PR, tel: 01494 582673/873264; website: www.kvaleberg.com/t2000.html.

Triumph 2000 and 2500 Owners Club, c/o Jim Barry, 164 Polwell Lane, Barton Seagrave, Kettering, Northants NN15 6UB, tel: 01536 724512.

Turner
Turner Register. c/o Tony Hill, 9 Lyndhurst Crescent, Hillingdon, Middx UB10 9EF, tel: 01895 256799.

TVR
TVR Car Club, c/o Carol Folkard, PO Box 36, Telford TF6 6WF, tel: 01952 770635; website: www.tvrcc.com/.

Vanden Plas
Vanden Plas Owners Club, c/o Brian Peebles, Vice Chairman/Membership Secretary, Cherrytrees, Llandyfaelog, Kidwelly, Carmarthenshire SA17 5PS, email: bryanpeebles @aol.com, website: www.vpoc.org.

Vauxhall
Vauxhall Owners Club, c/o Roy Childers, 31 Greenbanks, Melbourne, nr Royston, Cambridge SG8 6AS, tel: 01763 220179.

Vauxhall Convertible Car Club, c/o Phil Homer, 42 The Ridgeway, St. Albans, Herts AL4 9NR, tel: 01727 868405; e-mail: homerp @btsales.bt.com.

Vauxhall Cavette Club (Mk 1 Cavaliers and Chevettes), c/o Peter Norrish, Membership Secretary, 67 Riley Lane, Bradshaw, Halifax HX2 9QE, tel: 01422 245124, email: norrish@cavetteclub.org.uk, website: www.cavetteclub.org.uk.

Vauxhall Opel Drivers Club, c/o Peter and Sue Hicks, PO Box 65, Dereham, Norfolk NR19 1UD, tel/fax: 01362 692020, email: vodriversclub@bigfoot.com.

Vauxhall Cresta PA, PB, PC, E Owners Club, c/o Steve Chapman, 333 Eastcote Lane, South Harrow, Middx HA2 8RY, tel: 020 8423 2440.

Droop Snoot Group, c/o John Smerdon, 17 Priors Road, Tadley, Herts RG26 4QJ, tel: 01189 815238.

Vauxhall Royale Opel Monza Owners Club International, c/o Martin Yardley, 71 Polmear Parc, Par, Cornwall PL24 2AU, tel: 01726 815749; e-mail: cgodfrey4@aol.com.

Vauxhall Senator: Autobahnstormers, (new address): David Waddington, 19 Olivers Drive, Witham, Essex CM8 1QJ, tel: 01376 516034, e-mail: dwgsi24v@aol.com.

Vauxhall Viva Owners Club, c/o Adrian Miller, 'The Thatches', Snetterton North End, Snetterton, Norwich NR16 2LD, tel: 01953 498818.

Viva Outlaw Club, c/o Keith Laxton, 92 Churchill Crescent, Thame, Oxon)X9 3JP, tel: 01844 217928, e-mail: eddv6@klaxton. freeserve.co.uk.

Vauxhall VX 4/90 Drivers Club, c/o Jason Callear, 1 Milverton Drive, Uttoxeter ST14 7RE.

Vauxhall Victor 101 Club. c/o Joan Caldwell, 43 Princess Street, Widnes, Cheshire WA8 6NT, tel: 0151 510 0251.

Vincent-HRD

Vincent-HRD Owners Club. Membership secretary: Mary Bagley, 9 Whitworth Close, Gosport, Hants PO12 3PF, tel: 023 9242 2320; Registrar: Gordon Powell, 7 Church Street, Upwey, Weymouth DT3 5QB, tel: 01305 812303, e-mail: gopow@globalnet.co.uk.

VW

Volkswagen Owners Club of Great Britain, PO Box 7, Burntwood, Walsall, Staffs WS7 8SB.

Volkswagen Type 2 Owners Club, a club for 'Vans with Fans' and 'Fans with Vans'. Club Secretary, Phil Shaw, 57 Humphrey Avenue, Charford, Bromsgrove, Worcestershire; tel 01527 872194; email: PhilShawVW@cs.com; website: www.vwt2oc.org.uk).

Historic Volkswagen Club, c/o Rod Sleigh, 28 Lognor Road, Brooklands, Telford, Shropshire TF1 3NY, tel: 01952 242167.

Association of British Volkswagen Clubs, c/o J. Daniel, 66 Pinewood Green, Iver Heath, Bucks, tel: 01753 651538; website: www.uk-classic-cars.com/abvwc.htm.

Split Screen Van Club, c/o Robert Neekings, Membership Secretary, 21 Nabwood Road, Shipley, Yorkshire BD18 4AG, tel: 01274 596564, website: www.ssvc.org.uk. (VW vans, 1950–1967.)

VW Type 3 and 4 Club, c/o Jim Bourne, 'Brookside', Hamsey Road, Barcombe, Lewes, East Sussex BN8 5TG, tel: 01273 400463.

Club GTi: Alan Bell, Membership Secretary, PO Box 6506, Sutton-in-Ashfield, Nottinghamshire NG17 1NG, tel: 01454 626118, website: www.clubgti.com.

VW Corrado Club of Great Britain, Membership Secretary, VW Corrado Club of GB. PO Box 10346, Halesowen B63 3XU; website: www.vw-corrado-club.co.uk

Essex Vee Dubbers Volkswagen Club. Open to owners of all models of VW. Brian Walker, 53 Louise Gardens, Rainham, Essex RM13 8LH, tel: 01708 520669.

Volvo

Volvo Enthusiasts Club, c/o Kevin Price, 4 Goonbell, St. Agnes, Cornwall TR5 0PH, tel: 01872 553740.

Volvo Owners Club, c/o John Smith, 18 McCaulay Avenue, Portsmouth, Hants PO6 4NY, tel: 023 9238 1494, email: voc@dircon.co.uk, website: www.volvoclub.org.uk.

Wolseley

Wolseley Register, c/o Mike Schilling, 46 Mansewood Road, Glasgow G43 1TN; website: www.wolseley.dircon.co.uk; e-mail: mschilling @46mansewood.freeserve.co.uk or SisEightyMO@btinternet.com.

Wolseley Hornet Special Club 1930-35, c/o Chris Hyde, 'Kyelmor', Crown Gardens, Fleet, Hants GU51 3LT, tel: 01252 622411, e-mail: whsc.sec@btinternet.com, website: www.whsc.co.uk.

Wolseley 680/Morris Oxford Club, c/o Dave Robinson, 6 Kings Drive, Wigston, leicester LE8 1AG, tel: 0116 212 9972.

Specialist Clubs

American Automobile Club (UK), Freepost (MID00017), Tamworth, Staffs SY13 3DL. Contact: David Sword, tel: 01827 284538, website: www.uk-classic-cars.com/americanauto.htm.

Anglo American Classic Car Club, c/o Steve Seeby, 12 Davy's Close, Wheathampstead, Herts, tel: 01582629667. (This is a very small club.)

The Association of American Car Clubs UK, Trevor Lynn, PO Box 2222, Braintree, Essex CM7 6TW, tel: 01376 552478, website: www.motorvatinusa.org.uk.

Association of Old Vehicle Clubs of Northern Ireland, c/o T. Mitchell, 38 Ballymacconnell Road, Bangor, County Down BT20 5PS, tel: 02891 467886, website: www.aovc.co.uk.

Battery Vehicle Society, c/o Mr McPhee, Secretary, 29 Armour Road, Tilehurst, Reading, Surrey RG31 6HA, tel: 0118 941 4873.

British Ambulance Society, c/o Roger Leonard, 21 Victoria Road, Horley, Surrey RH6 9BN, tel: 01293 776636.

Checker Cars. Advice from A. Pritchard, 1 Curbar Road, Great Bar, Birmingham B42 2AT, tel: 0121 608 2737.

Cirencester Car Club, c/o John Knott, Safflower House, London Road, Stroud GL5 2AT; tel 01453 763737; website www.cirencestercarclub.co.uk.

Classic & Historic Motor Club Ltd, Celia Sheppard, 01749 676330.

Classic Camper Club, Secretary: M. Smith, PO Box 3, Amlwch, Anglesey LL68 9ZE, e-mail: ClassicCamperClub@btinternet.com; website: www.ClassicCamperClub.co.uk

Classic Crossbred Club, 7 Wills Hill, Stanford-le-Hope, Essex, tel: 01375 679943.

Classic Hearse Register, c/o Mark Josey, 58 Winchester Street, Overton, Basingstoke, Hants RG25 3HY, tel: 01256 771158.

Classic Motor Sports Club, c/o Stephanie Taylor, 37D Heathfield Road, Wandsworth Common, London SW18 2PH.

Classic Saloon Car Club, 15 Biddenham Turn, Garston, Herts WD2 6PU.

Club of Ancient Automobiles and Rallies, c/o Nigel Woodyer, 152 Ware Road, Hoddesdon, Herts EN11 9EX, tel : 01992 444502, e-mail: caargb@btinternet.com, website: www.caeargb.com.

Commercial Vehicle and Road Transport Club, c/o Steve Wimbush, 8 Tachbrook Road, Uxbridge, Middx UB8 2QS.

Enfield & District Veteran Vehicle Society, c/o S. Clinton, Whitewebbs Museum, White Webbs Road, Enfield, Middlesex EN2 9HW, tel: 020 8367 1898.

Federation of British Historic Vehicle Clubs, c/o Mike Holt-Chasteauneuf, PO Box 2506, Henfield, W. Sussex BN5 9QW, tel: 01273 495051.

Fire Service Preservation Group, c/o Andrew Scott, 50 Old Slade Lane, Iver, Bucks SL0 9DR, tel: 01753 652207.

Friends of the British Commercial Vehicle Museum, King Street, Leyland, Preston PR5 1LE.

Friends of the National Motor Museum, Beaulieu, Brokenhurst, Hants SO42 7ZN, tel: 01590 614650, email: nmmt@beaulieu.co.uk, website: www.beaulieu.co.uk.

Historic Rally Car Register Ltd., c/o Tony Bardon, 113 Locke Road, Spondon, Derby DE21 7AP, tel: 01332 372533.

Historic Sports Car Club, c/o Philip Parfitt, HSCC, Silverstone Circuit, Silverstone, Towcester, Northants NN12 8TN, tel: 01327 858400 website: www.hscc.org.uk.

Italian Car Club (UK), The Brackens, Vicarage Court, Vicarage Drive, Kinver, West Midlands DY7 6HJ.

London Bus Preservation Trust, c/o Mike Nash, 43 Stroudwater Park, Weybridge, Surrey KT13 0DT, tel: 01932 856810.

London Vintage Taxi Association, c/o Steve Dimmock, 51 Ferndale Crescent, Cowley, Uxbridge UB8 2AY.

Mechanical Horse Club, c/o Dan Madeley, 2 The Poplars, Horsham, West Sussex RH13 5RH, tel: 01483 269051.

Micro Maniacs, c/o Roger Bentley, 3 Pine Tree Lane, Hillam, Leeds LS25 5HY.

Midlands Classic Car Club, c/o John Langham, Abbey Business Centre, Keats Lane, Earl Shilton, Leicestershire LE9 7JL, tel: 01455 444450, fax: 01455 444451, email: midclass@btinternet.com, website: www.midlandsclassic.com.

Military Vehicle Trust, c/o Nigel Godfrey, PO Box 6, Fleet, Hants GU13 9PE, tel: 01264 392951, fax: 01257 515211; website: www.mvt.org.uk

Motorvatin' USA American Car Club, c/o Trevor Lynn, PO Box 2222, Braintree, Essex CM7 6TW, tel: 01376 552478, website: www.motorvatinusa.org.uk.

National 39/45 Military Vehicle Group, c/o Adrian Hardgrave, 9 Cordelia Way, Rugby, Warks CV22 6JU, tel: 01788 812250.

Pedal Car Collector's Club, 4/4a Chapel Terrace Mews, Kemp Town, Brighton, East Sussex BN2 1HJ, tel: 01273 601960, website: www.brmmbrmm.com/pedalcars.

Period and Classic Caravan Club, 128 Fulbourn, Old Drift, Cherry Hinton, Cambs CB1 9LR, tel: 01223 248187.

Period Motorcaravan Guild, c/o Mrs J. Lund, House 3, Connaught Court, St Oswalds Road, Fulford, York YO1 4QA, tel: 01904 651526, e-mail: mjjl@btinternet.com; website: www.brmmbrmm.com/periodmcg

Police Vehicle Enthusiasts Club, c/o John Oliver, 42 Walkers Way, South Bretton, Peterborough, Cambs PE3 9AX.

Post Office Vehicle Club, c/o John Targett, 7 Bignal Rand Drive, Wells, Somerset BA5 2EU, tel: 01749 675168.

Post-War Thoroughbred Car Club, 87 London Street, Chertsey, Surrey KT16 8AN, tel: 01932 562933.

Pre-1950 American Automobile Club and Ford V8 Register, c/o C. Nolson, 23 High Street, Twyford, Berks RG10 9AB.

Preston and District Vintage Car Club, c/o Mark Hindle, 4 Glendene Park, Wilpshire, Blackburn BB1 9JQ, tel: 01254 245245.

Register of Unusual Microcars, c/o Jean Hammond, School House Farm, Hawkenbury, Staplehurst, Kent, tel: 01580 891377.

Road Roller Association, D A Rayner, Vice Chairman and Archivist, Invicta, 9 Beagle Ridge Drive, Acomb, York YO24 3JH, tel: 01904 781519.

Scootacar Register, c/o Stephen Boyd, 18 Holman Close, Aylesham, Norfolk NR11 6DD, tel: 01263 733861.

Scottish Rally Car Register, c/o A Johnstone, The Clachan, Main Street, St Boswells, Melrose TD6 0BG, tel: 01835 822266.

Sprite Motorhome Owners Club, c/o Bert Raspin, 156 Farebrother Street, Grimsby, Lincs DN32 0JR.

Surrey Vintage Vehicle Society, website: www.restored-classics. com/surrey.

750 Motor Club Ltd, c/o Neil Carr-Jones, Lewes Enterprise Centre, 112 Malling Street, Lews, East Sussex BN7 2RJ, tel 01273 488750, website: www.750mc.co.uk.

Teesside Yesteryear Motor Club, c/o Graham Armstrong, 3 Tewesbury Avenue, Marton, Middlesbrough, Teesside TS7 8NB, tel: 01642 320999.

The Steam Car Club of Great Britiain, c/o Diana Goddard, 29 Nins Heath, Montford Bridge, Shrewsbury SY4 1HL, tel: 01939 260595.

United States Army Vehicle Club, c/o Simon Johnson, 7 Carter Fold, Mellor, Lancs BB2 7ER, tel: 01254 812894.

Unloved Soviet and Socialist Register, c/o Julian Nowill, Earlsland House, Bradninch, Exeter, Devon EX5 4QP, tel: 01392 881748.

Veteran Car Club of Great Britain, c/o Margaret Golding, Jassamine Court, 15 High Street, Ashwell. Herts SG7 5NL, tel: 01462 742818; fax: 01462 742997.

Vintage Motor Cycle Club, c/o Dr Derek Foxton, 4 Helensdale Close, Hereford HR1 1DP, tel: 01432 357315.

Vintage Sports Car Club of Calgary, c/o Colin Martindale, 90 Canova Road SW, Calgary, Alberta, Canada T2W 2A7; website: www.cadvision.com/vintage.

Vintage Sports Car Club, c/o Neil Murray, The Old Post Office, West Street, Chipping Norton, Oxon OX7 5EL, tel: 01608 644777; fax: 01608 644888.

How to Buy and Sell Cars

In this chapter Honest John tells you everything you need to know about the new and used car market. Topics covered include: finance; buying a new car abroad and importing it yourself; buying second-hand from a dealer, at auction or through a private ad; how to check out a prospective purchase; how to advertise a car for sale; and how to prepare your car for an auction.

Buying new

Beating the system

Though the real gap between continental car prices and UK car prices is closing, it's still possible to save thousands of pounds on a new car purchase.

One way is by buying a car imported from mainland Europe, either by yourself or by a specialist. The best deals from around twenty different sources are regularly compared at www.carpricecheck.com. Sometimes UK dealers can actually offer a better price than an import, with the added benefit of a three-year UK dealer warranty.

Always look for deals: www.honestjohn.co.uk features news of new car deals on a day-to-day basis.

You can buy 'pre-registered' cars from franchised dealers. These are cars registered by the dealer to earn a monthly or quarterly volume bonus. Depending on how old the cars are at the time of sale, savings can be as much as 20%. However, your choice will be strictly limited to oversupplied cars. There would be no chance of obtaining a much-desired new model such as a MINI, an Audi cabrio or a W211 Mercedes E Class in this way.

Alternatively, forget new and buy 'nearly new', either at auction or from a car supermarket such as The Great Trade Centre or Fords of Winsford. This way you can obtain a 6–12-month-old car with 5,000–15,000 miles on the clock at a saving of between 20% and 50% of the new car list price.

Other methods save you less money, but involve less risk, less hassle and usually give a greater degree of choice.

Buying from a franchised dealer

If you are a good negotiator, during comparatively slack months such as December you might get 10% to 12% off 'list price'. The best way to achieve this is to know precisely what the 'on-the-road' price of the car should be, take off the cost of Vehicle Excise Duty and the £25 First Registration tax, then subtract 15% from the remainder. On the premise that 3%–5% profit is better than no profit at all, many dealers will play ball, particularly towards the end of the month.

On the other hand, where they have more customers than cars, they won't play this game. You are unlikely to get more than 4% or 5% off a car you have to order and then wait several months for.

The part-exchange trick

If you have a car you want to part-exchange for a new one, it's no good getting a decent discount then giving it all back by accepting too little for your trade-in.

Be very well aware of what your existing car is worth. Compare it with similar models of similar age and mileage which the dealer has for sale, and don't accept less than £1,000 or 10% (whichever is the greater) less than the sticker price on these cars. This £1,000 or 10% may sound a lot, but remember the dealer will usually have to negotiate downwards from sticker prices when selling his used stock.

Also remember, what you get for your part-exchange is not the most important factor. The 'cost to switch' is. Always compare the total financial outlay involved in one deal compared to another.

For example, dealer 'A' has a new Mondeo which lists at £15,000. He offers you £4,000 for your part-exchange, but no discount on the Mondeo, so the cost to switch is £11,000.

Dealer 'B' has a Laguna which lists at £15,000. He offers you £3,500 for your part-exchange, plus £1,000 off the price of the Laguna. The cost to switch is therefore £10,500, so the Laguna is £500 cheaper than the Mondeo even though you get less for your part exchange.

Is the Mondeo worth £500 more than the Laguna? Or can you use the Laguna deal to chip £500 or more off the price of the Mondeo?

This is the way you should be thinking. It's not hard, is it?

Importing

Importing a car yourself

It is against European Community Law for any manufacturer to place any impediment upon any EU citizen buying any car at the pre-tax price in any other European country.

EC Regulation No. 1475/95 states: 'The consumer's freedom to buy anywhere in the Common Market is one of the fundamental achievements of the European Community and the Regulation reinforces this right.'

But it goes on to state: 'The consumer's right is not accompanied by an obligation imposed on dealers to sell since it is normally in a dealer's interest to maximise its profits.'

Where a model of car is in short supply, a continental dealer may take the view that he will generate more profit from selling the car to a local who will probably insure, finance and service the car through the dealer and even part-exchange it in a few years time.

But where the model is freely available and the dealer simply wants to maximise turnover, he will usually be happy to play ball.

You will find a lists of the cheapest sources of cars in the UK in the FAQ answers online at www.honestjohn.co.uk

You will also find a step-by-step guide to importing a car from Europe in the FAQ answers online at www.honestjohn.co.uk

Where to shop for an import

Order the relevant car magazines from an international newsagent, or pick them up at the airport when you land – *DAZ*, *Motor Markt*, *Auto Motorrad Freizeit* and *Auto Motor und Sport* for Germany; *Auto Week* for Holland; *Coche Actual*, *Autopista* or *Top Auto* for Spain; *Irish Auto Trader* for Eire – and start phoning dealers with the intention of buying a car already in stock, either pre-tax or with the forms to reclaim the local taxes. (One very good reason for choosing Dutch or Irish dealers, of course, is that they all speak English.) Once you have located a car, send your deposit by telegraphic transfer (which takes three days). Send the rest of the money by telegraphic transfer (once again, allow three working days), take a flight to the relevant country, get the dealer to fix you up with 'export plates' and third party insurance, and make sure that the car comes with an EU Type Approval 'Certificate of Conformity' (C-of-C) or you won't be able to register it in the UK. Then simply drive to the nearest ferry and follow the rest of this 'step-by-step' guide. You can now arrange import insurance in the UK using A-Plan, tel: 0800 731 7666.

If you have bought an LHD it's a relatively simple matter to change over the lights and foglamp, have the speedo altered to mph by Reap Automotive Design (020 8863 2305), arrange for the car to be inspected and get it registered via your local VRO. With Europe-wide Type Approval for European cars dating from January 1998 there is no need for an SVA for a new European car, but you must make sure you get a 'Certificate of Conformity' with it, otherwise it will be subject to SVA.

If you order a car from a mainland Europe dealer, the biggest worry you are likely to face is that he may demand a substantial deposit – up to 30%. If his franchise is pulled or he goes bust before you take delivery of your car, the situation is the same as in the UK. Your deposit becomes one of the assets of the company and you will be way down the list of creditors and therefore unlikely to get it back.

If a continental dealer tells you he would like to sell you an RHD car but is being pressurised by the manufacturer not to, report the matter to: Mario Monti, Competition Commissioner, DG IV, European Commission, 200 Rue de la Loi, 1049 Brussels, Belgium. He doesn't have a full set of teeth because he caved in to lobbying by German and French manufacturers to maintain the system which helps to keep UK prices relatively high. But he may still take up a case where overt discrimination is applied.

Warranty claims with euro-imports

As long as you have registered your car with the UK manufacturer or official UK importer, the car will be subject to the same pan-European warranty that applies in the country of origin and which must give at least 12 months' cover.

It will not be subject to a UK three-year warranty unless a three-year warranty applies in the country of origin. (In the case of VAG and BMW, this warranty is 24 months, while Mazda, Mitsubishi, Nissan and Toyota apply a 36-month pan-European warranty – all as long as the UK company can be supplied with a copy of the original invoice.)

The catch is, if you buy the car in the UK, the warranty will only date from when the car was first purchased in the country from which it was exported to the UK. So you could buy a 'new' car with no more than a 7-month pan-Euro warranty.

If a car bought in Europe proves to be seriously faulty, it is not covered by the UK's 'Sale and Supply of Goods Act 1994' which, subject to case law, allows you to reject it. The car will only be covered by consumer protection law in the country of origin. If this allows for rejection, then the car must be returned to the supplying dealer in that country.

However, if you buy your car directly from an independent import supplier in the UK, and the car is first registered in the UK rather than collected by you from mainland Europe, then you can invoke the UK's 'Sale and Supply of Goods Act 1994' and reject the car by returning it to the UK importer.

The EC might eventually introduce new pan-European consumer protection laws, but there is no Directive to this effect at the moment.

Independent import warranties

Wherever you purchase an import, you can buy an aftermarket warranty for it online from www.carimportwarranty.com

Japanese and American imports

In 1997 and 1998 the strong pound made new RHD imports from Japan very attractive – especially super-quick Mitsubishi and Subaru four-wheel-drive saloons. But the rising Yen has been making Japanese imports progressively more expensive. And the Enhanced Single Vehicle Approval Test from November 2001 has made compliance more complex and expensive, so it is vital that, before laying out any money on a vehicle, you contact experts such as Protech (www.protech-uk.co.uk) and find out what will be involved to get the vehicle through its Enhanced SVA Test.

A useful website on importing from Japan is www.importedvehicles. co.uk

Import agents' deposits

Agents usually ask for a deposit of at least 10% and sometimes as much as 30%. You can protect this deposit against the agent going bust or doing a runner by paying it by credit card (credit card, not charge card) or by insisting it is paid into a UK 'escrow' account where the agent cannot touch it until the deal is done and it does

not form part of his assets if he goes bust. Do not pay by credit card cheque, which carries no protection.

Financing an import
If you find it difficult to get finance for an import, try online www.carfinance4less.com, or ring a-plan on 0845 071 1234.

To forward-buy your foreign currency online and protect yourself against currency fluctuations try www.currencies4less.com

Buying on finance
Personal contract purchase
This is a form of lease purchase which sprang up during the 1990s and now seems to be offered by many dealers over periods of two or three years.

You pay a deposit (either cash or your trade-in). You then make monthly repayments which pay off roughly half the amount of money borrowed and the interest on all of it. At the end of the two or three years, you have three options: pay off the remaining lump sum and keep the car; use any equity you have in the car (the difference between the lump sum to clear the debt and the trade value of the car) as the deposit on another PCP on another car; or simply walk away with no debts but no car.

PCPs are best for people who are in steady, secure jobs, who are happy leasing rather than owning, and who don't mind both the dealers and the finance companies profiting from this. If you're worried about your job, you can take out redundancy insurance on the debt, but this is expensive and makes the car even dearer to buy.

Always remember, if the market slumps against the price you paid for your car on a PCP, as happened in thousands of cases over the last three years, you may be left with no equity in it to finance the deposit of your next PCP. (See 'Straight hire purchase', below, on this point.)

50/50 finance

This is another form of lease purchase. You cough up 50% of the car's price straight away, and the remaining 50% in two years time.

It looks like a free loan for two years but, of course, it isn't. In this world, nothing is for nothing. The car that is on the 50/50 deal is usually the sort of car which will be worth 40% of the price you paid for it in two years time. So it isn't really worth 100% of the price being asked for it.

I'm well aware that many people feel that a 50/50 deal suits them. All I want to be sure of here is that you know what you're getting into.

Straight hire purchase

APRs vary and dealers earn commission on finance. Even with base rate at 5%, the true APR could be 25% or more, especially if you are buying from a finance house which specialises in financing purchases by people with poor credit records where the rate is often more than 50% APR.

All you have to do is follow the golden rule of comparing your total outlay on the deal with your total outlay on any other deal.

Also, whatever you do, don't get caught out by the financed debt insurance trick. If you insure your ability to pay off the debt, you may be charged a one-off four-figure premium which is itself financed at a near-criminal rate of interest.

If you buy a car on hire purchase, the law says that the supplier (i.e. the dealer) and the finance house are jointly liable for any defects. If the car proves to be faulty and you reject it under the Sale and Supply of Goods Act 1994, and the supplier accepts the rejection, don't take any heavy-handed treatment from the finance house.

However, until the rejection is accepted by the supplier, you must keep up the payments or you could find yourself in serious financial trouble.

One final point: if you buy on hire purchase, pay off half the total finance cost (including any deposit you have made or been allowed on a part exchange), then discover that you owe more than the car is worth, you are legally entitled to return it to the finance house and walk away debt-free. This can make straight finance at a sensible APR a much better deal than personal contract purchase which ties you into a fixed contract you can't get out of.

Buying used

Buying used privately
Buying from someone you know

How well do you know this person? How well do you know the car?

You wouldn't be the first to buy a disaster zone just because someone in the family was selling it. Nor would you be the first to overlook faults because you didn't want to upset Uncle Albert and Auntie Gwen and your entire mother's side of the family.

So think about this very carefully. Obviously, if the car is literally being given away, take it. If it's being offered to you at a knockdown price, make sure the price really is knockdown by looking it up in 'Parker's Guide' or the '*What Car?* Price Guide'. If the price is merely a fair price, weigh up what you know about the car against what you're being asked to pay. How long has the owner owned it? Is the mileage genuine? How often was the car serviced? Is there anything wrong with it? How much will the faults cost to put right?

I accept you may have private reasons for giving too much for a car to an impecunious, elderly or sick member of the family. It's a diplomatic way of helping them out. But otherwise you should not let your relationship with the seller colour your judgement. The car is a purchase you are going to have to live with and if it proves to be a money pit you'll have to live with that too.

Buying used from an advertisement or website

Websites are an excellent means of finding out how sellers are pricing the car you want. So in addition to buying 'Parker's Guide' and the 'What Car? Used Car Price Guide', check the asking prices for the make and model you're after on www.autotrader.co.uk This incorporates its own search engine and lists the model by asking prices at progressively greater distances from your postcode.

Once you find the car, first you need to establish the status of who you are buying from. If he is a trader, he is required by law to put a 'T' or the word 'trade' in his small ad. Don't be put off if he has. It gives you rights you do not have against a private seller; in fact the very same rights you have when buying from a swanky, carpeted car showroom.

To try and get out of this, some low-life 'home traders' try to hide the fact that that is what they are. So when you call a number in the advertisement which does not contain a 'T' or the word 'trade', say you are calling about 'the car'. A private seller is unlikely to have half a dozen parked up and down the street, so will immediately know which car you mean. A trader who has more than one car will have to ask you, 'Which car?' But even if there is only one car for sale, the seller could still be a small-time trader.

So your next question should be, 'How long have you owned it?' (You may well sense the vendor squirming at the other end of the line.) Anything less than six months should then prompt your next question, 'Are you a private seller or a trader?'

If the answer to this is something evasive or a final admission of trader status, ask yourself a question. Do you really want to deal with someone who has already lied in his advertisement?

Assuming from now on we are dealing with a genuine private seller rather than a trader, you need to establish some more facts about the car. First, concentrate on the content of the advertisement.

By 'P reg', does he mean 1996P or 1997P? Which 'model year' is the car? For example, a 1996 model 'P' reg Mondeo was the dull original shape, but a 1997 model had received a glamorous facelift, even if it had been registered in 1996.

Ask how many previous keepers are listed on the V5 registration document, and add that number to the vendor for the true figure. Ask if the advertised mileage is genuine, and if the answer is 'Yes', ask how the vendor knows it is genuine.

By now, you'll be starting to feel the measure of the person you are dealing with and your instincts will be starting to work. Trust these instincts. They are what you were born with and have developed through your life to protect yourself against danger.

If you're happy about the car and the person selling it, make an appointment to view. Unless the car is something rare and really special, don't be rushed into a hasty twilight or nocturnal encounter. You want broad daylight and you don't want rain. Rain is the most effective disguise for a chameleon colour scheme, paint chips and a host of other defects.

Used car buying websites
- www.autotrader.co.uk
- www.exchangeandmart.co.uk
- www.CarChase.co.uk
- www.fish4cars.co.uk
- www.autohit.com
- www.autolocate.co.uk
- www.used-car-buyer.co.uk

Buying from a company
Buying your 'company car'
Your company car may be owned by your company, or it may be leased.

If it's the company's own car, the company may have a policy of offering it to an employee at a favourable price as a perk. But if whoever runs the fleet gets performance-related pay for saving the company money, forget about getting an excellent deal.

And if the car is leased, you can expect the first price the leasing company quotes you to be close to retail. They want to make money and you're a captive market, so you can't blame them.

Be very sure of your ground. You know your car better than they do. Is it so good that you want to lay out your own money on it?

It may have been reliable during your tenure over three years and maybe sixty thousand miles. But fleets love low maintenance schedules which keep running costs down at the expense of storing up problems for future owners. Over the next forty thousand miles your cheap-to-run company car could need tyres, exhaust, clutch, water pump, timing belt and all the other things that fail just after fleets get rid of their cars.

And if it's a high performance car on an intensive maintenance schedule take a look at the service bills. Can you afford to pay them yourself?

'Cold buying' from a company

Traders constantly phone the fleet and 'human resources' managers of companies to try to buy company-owned cars as they come off the company fleets. The bad news is there are a lot of closed 'sweetheart' deals involving bungs which keep outsiders out. Or the company's accounts may be so strictly audited that it is compelled either to sell its cars by tender or to put them up for auction.

But you never know unless you try. So check the businesses in your locality and spend a morning phoning them.

Inevitably, you will get a lot of brush-offs, but if you 'score' just one car in a morning at £1,000 below trade book, you've done rather well. That £1,000 below book will probably finance running the car for the next six months. No wonder traders are thicker-skinned than the average rhinoceros.

Buying used from a dealer
'Franchised' dealers

Most franchised dealers now offer used car schemes supported by manufacturers, such as Ford's 'Ford Direct', Vauxhall's 'Network Q'

and VW's Retailer Approved Used Cars. Where the warranty is backed by the manufacturer (Ford Direct) rather than being simply an insured warranty, these give peace of mind but can come at a fairly high price.

Nevertheless, once you've shopped around a bit and got the feel of prices in the car supersites, it's worth paying the franchised dealers a visit. They have been known to beat supersite prices, and if their prices, inclusive of a cast-iron warranty, are only a few hundred more than the supersites, you may be better off with the franchised dealer.

Many also have their own websites, enabling you to browse their stocks from your living room.

Where you want to part-exchange your old car, franchised dealers almost always give better part-exchange allowances than the supersites. But here you need to compare the total 'cost to switch', not merely the part-exchange allowance offered.

Manufacturers' websites

- **ALFA ROMEO (GB) LTD** www.alfaromeo.co.uk
- **ASTON MARTIN LAGONDA LTD** www.astonmartin.co.uk
- **AUDI UK** www.audi.co.uk/usedcars
- **BENTLEY** www.rolls-royceandbentley.co.uk
- **BMW (GB) LTD** www.bmw.co.uk
- **BRISTOL CARS** www.bristolcars.co.uk
- **CADILLAC** www.cadillaceurope.com
- **CATERHAM** www.caterham.co.uk
- **CHEVROLET** www.chevroleteurope.com
- **CHRYSLER JEEP IMPORTS UK** www.chryslerjeep.co.uk
- **CITROEN (UK) LTD** www.citroen.co.uk
- **DAEWOO CARS LTD** www.daewoo-cars.co.uk
- **DAIHATSU (UK) LTD** www.daihatsu.co.uk
- **FERRARI** www.ferrari.co.uk
- **FIAT AUTO (UK) LTD** www.fiat.co.uk
- **FORD MOTOR CO. LTD** www.ford.co.uk
- **HONDA (UK)** LTD www.honda.co.uk
- **HYUNDAI CAR (UK) LTD** www.hyundai-car.co.uk
- **ISUZU (UK) LTD** www.isuzu.co.uk
- **JAGUAR CARS LTD** www.jaguar.co.uk
- **KIA (UK) LTD** www.kia.co.uk
- **LAMBORGHINI** www.lamborghini.co.uk
- **LAND ROVER LTD** www.landrover.co.uk
- **LEXUS** www.lexus.co.uk
- **LIGIER** c/o Reliant Cars Ltd www.reliant-motors.co.uk
- **LOTUS CARS LTD** www.lotuscars.co.uk
- **MASERATI** www.maserati.co.uk
- **MAZDA CARS (UK) LTD** www.mazda.co.uk
- **MCC SMART** www.thesmart.co.uk
- **MERCEDES-BENZ** www.mercedes-benz.co.uk
- **MG CARS** www.mg-cars.com
- **MINI** www.mini.co.uk
- **MITSUBISHI** www.mitsubishi-cars.co.uk
- **MORGAN MOTOR CAR CO.** www.morgan-motor.co.uk
- **NISSAN MOTOR (GB) LTD** www.nissan.co.uk
- **PERODUA UK LTD** www.perodua-uk.com

- **PEUGEOT MOTOR CO. PLC** www.peugeot.co.uk
- **PORSCHE CARS (GB) LTD** www.porsche.co.uk
- **PROTON CARS (UK) LTD** www.proton.co.uk
- **RELIANT CARS LTD** www.reliant-motors.co.uk
- **RENAULT (UK) LTD** www.renault.co.uk
- **ROLLS-ROYCE** www.rolls-royceandbentley.co.uk
- **ROVER CARS** www.rovergroup.co.uk
- **SAAB (GB) LTD** www.saab.co.uk
- **SEAT UK** www.seat.co.uk/usedcars
- **SKODA UK** www.skoda.co.uk/usedcars
- **SUBARU (UK) LTD** www.subaru.co.uk
- **SUZUKI GB PLC** www.suzuki.co.uk
- **TATA** www.tata-telco.com
- **TOYOTA GB LTD** www.toyota.co.uk
- **TVR ENGINEERING LTD** www.tvr.co.uk
- **VAUXHALL MOTORS LTD** www.vauxhall.co.uk
- **VOLKSWAGEN** www.volkswagen.co.uk/usedcars
- **VOLVO CAR UK LTD** www.volvocars.co.uk
- **WESTFIELD** www.westfield-sportscars.co.uk

Supersites

By far the biggest is the one that started it all: The Great Trade Centre in White City, London, which has now taken over most of Hythe Road Industrial Estate and offers between 3,500 and 5,000 cars. The GTC sells both 'nearly new' ex-rental and pre-registered cars, and ex-fleet cars up to 5 years old. The choice is so huge and the prices are so low that, for many private buyers, it's not worth the time and effort of trying to beat them by buying at auction.

Nearly new and used car supersites

- The Great Trade Centre, Hythe Road (off Scrubbs Lane: continuation of Wood Lane), White City, London NW10 6JR, tel: 020 8969 5511; website: www.greattradecentre.co.uk
- Trade Sales of Slough, 353-357 Bath Road, Slough, Berks SL1 6JA, tel: 0870 127 3763, website: www.trade-sales.co.uk
- Motorpoint, Chartwell Drive, West Meadows, Derby, tel: 0870 1209611, website: www.motorpoint.co.uk

- Motorhouse 2000, Wryly Brook Retail Park, Walkmill Lane, Cannock WS11 3XE, tel: 0845 345 6777; website: www. motorhouse2000Ltdco.uk
- Fords of Winsford, Wharton Retail Park, Weaver Valley Road, Winsford, Cheshire, tel: 0845 345 1016; website: www.fow.co.uk
- Stephen Rayns Ltd, Leicester (now specialising in Peugeot), tel: 0116 261 2200.
- Fleetlease Direct, Union House, Kennetside Industrial Estate (off Bone Lane), Newbury, Berks RG14 5PX, tel: 0800 294 1948; website: www.fleetleasedirect.co.uk

Specialist dealers

These are dealers who specialise in a particular type of car, usually sports cars, prestige cars or 4x4s, but you also find '7-seater Centres', 'Mini Centres', 'Cavalier Centres' and so on.

To maintain attractive stock levels, they usually have to pay more for their cars, especially at auction, and this is likely to be reflected in the prices they ask.

You have to weigh up the convenience and time-saving they offer you against these slightly higher prices. And if they have any sports or prestige cars on offer which are less than three years old, you should question the wisdom of buying from them rather than from a franchised dealer.

The best specialists are keen enthusiasts of a marque, such as Porsche, BMW or Volkswagen, with workshops on the premises.

Independent dealers

These are your old-school car dealers, seen by the hundred on London's Romford Road and stretches of the A24 through Tooting, Balham and Clapham.

Some of them are really nice people. Some of them are right old rogues.

'Home' traders

These people are much maligned, usually by magazines with a vested interest in maligning them. (Obviously if a magazine's main source of income is from advertising by dealers, it isn't going to recommend the little guys who undercut those dealers.)

A proper trader who openly trades from a home of his own is bound by all the same consumer protection laws as a dealer with large, expensive premises. He'll be watched fairly carefully by the local Trading Standards Office. The only way he can make an honest living is by offering deals that beat those on offer from the big boys.

That 'home of his own' bit is important. If he's operating from rented accommodation you may have no more comeback against him than from a 'traveller' working from a big shiny caravan.

Make sure he invites you into the house (it may not be his house). And if he's the least bit aggressive, shifty, bad tempered or has a vicious looking dog on a chain, make a polite excuse and get the hell out of there.

Never buy a car in a car park or a lay-by, or from a dealer working from a mobile phone number who brings the car round to your house. Always make a check (CarwatchUK, HPI or AA/Experian) on cars offered by home traders, and look for verification that the mileage is genuine.

For this purpose, a fleet car's computerised service history printout is a far better bet than a lot of stamps in a service book. For example, unless the car is a notorious tyre eater such as a manual Volvo T5, if the tyres seem to have been changed every 5,000 miles you'll know something isn't quite right.

Checking the car out
Getting the car's history checked

Several organisations will check the car's history for you to make sure it is not on any registers as having been an insurance damage write off, a finance bad debt, or stolen. All you need is the car's make, model and registration, so this is something you can do before you even make a trip to view the car.

The checks are provided over the phone for a fee, payable by credit card, of around £32.50. The organisations are: HPI on 01722 422422 (website: www.hpicheck.com); AA/Experian Car Check on 0800 234999; ABS on 0800 3895169; and *What Car?* History Check on 0845 601 0804. The AA/Experian insured check (insured that the information given is correct) for cars up to £10,000 costs AA members £34.99 and non-members £36.99 (website: www.theaa.com) and an insured check for cars £10,000 to £30,000 costs from £44.99, tel: 0800 056 9090. Another website check is at www. carwatchuk.com and costs just £9.99.

AA/Experian and *What Car?* have extended their services to a limited mileage check (where past mileages have been recorded). But gathering mileage information has been a nightmare, largely due to the reluctance of some fleets (the prime source of relatively young but high-mileage cars) to divulge mileages on disposal. These fleets know that if they have a reputation in the trade for not divulging mileages, they stand a better chance of getting high 'clockers' money' for their cars at auction. The worry is whether the data registers are getting the correct information in the first place. If a vendor and a trader conspire to register a lower mileage than a vehicle has actually covered, then that's what goes on the DVLA records and gets entered onto the data registers. Still, some record of mileage has to be better than none at all.

The best advice is to treat all odometer readings as suspicious and to get in touch with previous owners listed on the car's V5. If you are buying from the first owner of the car and he is a man of the cloth, then the mileage is probably correct. If you are buying from a freelance commercial traveller, then, if the mileage is low, it is probably not correct.

For what to look for in individual models see the Car by Car Breakdown starting on page 219 (and updated daily online at www. honestjohn.co.uk).

First impressions

When you first see the car, what do your instincts tell you? Do you get a funny feeling in the pit of your stomach, or do you feel happy and excited?

Trust these feelings, because they are your natural defence mechanisms at work. All too often we ignore our instincts and talk ourselves into making a bad decision.

That's what salesmanship is all about: getting you to think nice thoughts about what you're going to do with the car or how easy it will be to pay for it, and to put out of your head the obvious fact that the car is a heap of junk.

Beware the car dealer who pre-qualifies your financial status over the phone so that, when you arrive at the car lot, the finance is set up and all you have to do is choose a car. By that time, you are pre-sold on buying a car from that dealer come what may and, when you leave home, you leave your brain and your instincts behind.

Assuming, and only assuming, you have a good feeling about the car, you can check it out yourself or have it independently inspected. The downside of an independent inspection, of course, is that it may take some time to get an appointment, the vendor may sell the car in the meantime, and you'll still have to fork out the inspection fee.

So, even if you're not mechanically minded, it makes sense to carry out some preliminary checks before you go to the expense of an independent inspection.

Inspecting a car yourself

First and foremost, does the paint match? If every panel is a different shade of red, for example, the car has been in several accidents. If the paint is fresh and new and all the same colour, the car has been in a big accident and has been rebuilt. If just part of the car has fresh paint, for example the bonnet, it may merely have had a minor scrape or been repainted because it was badly stone-chipped. Other tips for looking for signs of repaired accident damage are to peel back bits of rubber trim and look for 'tide marks' underneath, to open and close all the doors and check for even shut lines, to look under the boot carpet for fresh paint and a lack of the usual manufacturer's stickers, to look under the bonnet at the inner wings and on the engine, gearbox and suspension, for flecks of spray dust, to crouch down in front of the car and look for ripples in its sides. It's not that hard, is it? One final tip: when a front wing is replaced it is resprayed in situ and they don't usually make much of a job of the section hidden behind the closed door. Feel the paint there, and if it's rough the car's had a new front wing. Rust is less of a problem than it used to be and paint is now so expensive it's simply not worth filling a car with pudding and giving it a 'blow over'. But if the car is getting on, check all the usual places – round the wheel arches, under the valences (if they're steel), round the edges of the boot floor, under the carpets if they will lift, in the bottoms of the doors, round the headlights and along the outer tops of the doors.

Next job, check the tyres. Uneven wear may be due to incorrect alignment settings, or it may be due to bent suspension components from kerbs, pot holes or road humps. So be particularly wary of uneven front tyre wear. Check the nearside front wheel for rim damage. Has it got a new wheeltrim? Does the wheeltrim match the others? Are all the wheeltrims wrong? (A cheap set of four costs less than one correct wheeltrim from the manufacturer's dealer.)

You've done paint and tyres. Now on to the interior. Dirt cleans off but tears in the seats and broken bits of trim are notoriously difficult and expensive to put right. One fag burn can be invisibly repaired using new techniques, but a lot of fag burns will cost you £50 each and the repairs won't be invisible. If the entire interior stinks of tobacco smoke you'll be up against it to get rid of the lingering odour. Has there been a dog in the car? Has it scratched the paint? Has it left a smell? Don't feel you have to be polite about this to the car's owners, however nice they may be. It's your money they're after, not your friendship.

Open the bonnet and check all the fluids. Makers like Ford very helpfully put yellow paint on all the things to check. But what you want to look at is the oil on the end of the dipstick. Is it up to the mark? What colour is it? Castor-oil yellow is excellent; light brown is good; dark brown is okay; a tar-like black in a petrol engine spells disaster, though lubricating oil in all but the latest HDI diesel engines will always be black.

Unscrew the oil filler cap. If there is a deposit of whitish or creamy-grey 'mayonnaise' underneath, it means one of two things. The car has led a life of very short runs from cold starts, has never warmed up properly and the condensation this has created has mixed with the oil. Engines run like this have less than a quarter of the life of engines run properly, so a little old lady's car with 10,000 miles on the clock has really worn to the equivalent of at least 50,000 miles and should be valued accordingly.

The second problem 'mayonnaise' can symptomise is a blown

cylinder head gasket. It may be straightforward to replace this, or the head may need to be skimmed because it has warped. This gives the car a higher compression ratio and may mean that it simply won't run on 95Ron unleaded petrol. Have a look under the radiator cap or in the radiator expansion tank for similar emulsion to confirm this, and also look for white smoke (steam) from the exhaust.

Have a look at the condition of the power steering fluid. It should be red, not black. Same goes for the automatic transmission fluid (most autoboxes have a dipstick). It is vital that the ATF level is kept up to the mark. It is also a good idea for automatic transmission fluid to be changed every year (essential with CVT automatics).

Look under the car for leaks. Is there oil on the vendor's driveway? A leak from a cam-cover gasket is common and no big deal, but a bad oil leak from a cylinder head gasket means the head has to come off and, if it does, manifold studs may break and stretch bolts will have to be replaced. A leak from the timing belt cover is bad news because it means that the camshaft end seal or a jackshaft seal has gone, contaminating the timing belt – so you won't just need a new seal, you'll need a new belt. If the gearbox/final drive is leaking from an output shaft seal, the lack of oil in the transmission may have led to premature wear.

Now ask to see the service history. Not a book full of stamps; the actual bills for all the work on the car which the owner has paid for, or, if a fleet car, a computer print-out of its service history. If, from this, you find that the car has been 'overserviced' (had its oil and filter changed every 4–6 months), then be willing to pay more for it than the guides suggest. If, on the other hand, it has been 'underserviced' (with gaps of more than a year), then pay substantially less than guide price. If the car has a timing belt rather than a chain, in general this needs to be replaced every 35,000–40,000 miles or every 3-4 years. On some cars, such as Fords with Zetec engines, the replacement cycle can be pushed to up to 5 years or 80,000 miles whichever comes first, but no longer. If the service bills don't show a timing belt change, then budget £60–£200 to have it done. (The job is more expensive on Peugeots and Citroëns because there is an engine mounting in the way.) Automatic transmission fluid should have been changed at least every 2 years; brake and power steering fluid every 2 years, or 3 years at a push, but every year if the car is fitted with ABS. If the car has a manual gearbox and the oil in that has been changed within its first 18 months on the road, this is a valuable plus point worth paying more for.

You have now made a number of checks which will have provided you with a lot of information without having to pay anyone. Now we'll get onto the road test of the car.

The road test

First, are you insured? If you own and insure a car yourself, your policy will usually cover you to drive another insured car third party only. But this means you will be personally liable for any damage you do to the car.

Switch on the ignition and look at the lighting display. If there is an ABS light, make sure it goes off within seconds of starting the engine. The engine should start instantly and, when it does, are there any rattles? With hydraulic tappets you may hear a brief rattle before the tappets pump up, but this is nothing to worry about unless it persists.

If the car is manual, where does the clutch take up? If near the top of the pedal travel, there is likely to be less than 10,000 miles of life left in the clutch. If you can get it to slip, reckon on less than 2,000 miles.

If the car is front-wheel-drive, do a full lock reverse turn in both directions. This will tell you more about the condition of the clutch, but if you also hear clonking, there is wear in the driveshaft universal joints and these are expensive to replace.

Does the car accelerate smoothly? If it's an automatic, do the gears change smoothly? But don't expect all automatics to change into 4th or even 3rd at town speeds. If it's a manual, do the gears change easily with no graunching and can you change down smoothly, particularly from 3rd to 2nd, without having to double de-clutch? Is there any gearbox whine or whirring noises? A lot of gearboxes do whine slightly and, though it's an irritant, it may be nothing to worry about. Similarly, a bit of diff lash may be terminal, or the diff may soldier on for years. But the likelihood of a transmission repair should be budgeted for and the price you pay for the car chipped down unless it already accounts for this.

Do the brakes stop the car straight and true? If you feel juddering, the discs may be warped. If retardation is slow, the discs, pads, drums, linings may be worn or grooved. Do the brakes lock up front or back during an emergency stop? If so, the rear brake compensator may be u/s.

Finally, check all the electrics: wipers, sunroof, windows, everything. If the car has a trip computer, get the owner to run through its functions. (But, obviously, if the car is cheap, you don't worry about a non-functioning trip computer.)

Having the car inspected

The four main used car inspection organisations are AA: 0345 500610; ABS: 0345 419926; Green Flag/National Breakdown: 01254 355606; RAC: 0800 333660. Others are AAA Motor Vehicle Inspections (London area only): 0705 0158123; Autocheck GB Ltd: 020 8678 7060; D.S. Crawford (Central Scotland only) 0131 453 4393. ABS also offers a Helpline on 01625 576441. (ABS is by far the best for 'grey-imported' Japanese cars because they know what to look for.)

Inspections tend to cost £50–£150 for the average car, the inspectors 'come to the car', and you are provided with a written report afterwards. Some, such as D.S. Crawford in Scotland, include an HPI status check in their price of £89 plus VAT. The RAC has charged up to £250 for inspecting personally imported cars. Alternatively, phone the Institute of Automotive Assessors on 01543 251346 to get the number of your local Assessor. They use a standard 171-point check list, supply a next-day telephone appraisal and a 5-page report within 48 hours for around half the cost of the motoring organisations.

A new service operating in Edinburgh but hoping to roll out nationwide is Carscan at 81 Dundee Street, tel: 0131 228 2882. This offers a sophisticated performance and condition check at its premises, which includes a wheels-off visual inspection on a hoist, a proper rolling road performance analysis and even a wheel geometry check for a very reasonable £33 + VAT. A full HPI check can also be incorporated for an additional charge.

Sports and high-performance cars need specialist inspections by experts in the particular make and model. An AA or RAC inspection of a Porsche, for example, simply isn't enough. Best to get a written report from a Porsche dealer or Porsche specialist and to pay the extra for a compression test on all six cylinders.

The problem is, no vendor with any sense will give you right of first refusal on a car subject to inspection at a later date unless you pay them a non-refundable deposit. If you can't cut a deal like this with the vendor, they will simply sell the car to the first buyer who comes up with the right money and you could end up forking out an inspection fee for a non-existent 'sold' car.

Condition of older cars

Where cars are more than ten years old, whatever the make, there is likely to be some rust somewhere.

In general, German cars with metallic paint finishes seem to rust the least. But this is an oversimplification because German build-quality slipped quite a bit between 1988 and 1992. Since 1986, all Audis have incorporated hot-dip or electro-galvanised panels, but, since 1988, so have most FIATs, starting with the Tipo and carrying on even with Unos and Pandas from around 1990.

Where the car has spent its life also affects its propensity to rust. Nothing rusts a car worse than a saline solution which allows corrosion batteries to form on a car's body and suspension. In northern counties such as Northumberland, roads are heavily salted from November to March, and if you go into any Northumbrian market town you can see the effect this has on the cars. Cars in coastal areas are affected by airborne salt and sea spray.

In general, cars that have spent their lives in the South East and at least 20 miles from the coast are least likely to have been affected by premature rusting.

Keeping a car in a garage does not necessarily prevent rusting. If a car is put away wet and salty in a poorly ventilated garage, the atmosphere in there will accelerate the rusting process. On the other hand, a warm, dry car driven into a dry, well-ventilated and possibly even heated garage is least likely to rust while stored. Remember, though, the floors of most garages, even integral garages, are usually below the damp course of the house and condensation is likely inside such garages during the winter.

Agreeing a price

How good are you at negotiating? Most used car sellers will have checked the value of their car as a 'private sale' in one of the consumer car price guides available from newsagents. ('Parkers', the '*What Car?* Price Guide', etc.) They are likely to have followed the guide advice to build an amount into the price for negotiation.

The simplest way to check out their bottom line is to ask, 'OK, I know the advertised price, but what's the lowest you're prepared to take for the car?' They may smile sheepishly and tell you straight away, or getting to their bottom line might be like pulling teeth.

Remember, though, that even when you get to what they have told themselves is their 'bottom line', it might not be as low as they are prepared to go. Much will depend on circumstances, such as the urgency of the sale, how long the car has been on the market, and/or how few people have come to see it. So think like a detective. If the bloke's bags are already packed, his furniture gone and his curtains down, he's probably leaving for Australia that afternoon. If he's already bought a replacement car, he may need to sell the older one urgently. Just chatting to the fellow may elicit little hints that tell you the true circumstances.

It's hardly a moral approach, but it's up to you to take advantage of whatever you can.

Obtaining a warranty

Even if you buy a used car privately or at auction, you can still purchase an aftermarket warranty for it from Warranty Direct, tel: 0800 731 7001, website: www.usedcarwarranty.co.uk

Buying at auction
Advantages and disadvantages

Auctions can be the best places to source a car (see the full list of auction sites online in the Directories section at www.honestjohn. co.uk). After all, unless its a 'classic car auction' aimed at the public, the cars there should sell for the trade prices the market puts on them on the day.

Auctions, especially 'classic car auctions', are also a lion's den for the naive and unwary. Remember, from a seller's point of view, auctions provide quick sales with no comebacks.

In the old days it was common for traders to buy a car either in the trade or at auction, strip all the good bits off (tyres, battery, upgraded stereo, etc.), replace them with duff bits, then put the car back through the auction. This still happens and the more luxurious the car the worse it can be. Often it's the little things, like good electric mirrors swapped for u/s bits. Occasionally, big things like a good engine and transmission or a good diff are swapped for a bad one. And, of course, if a car is coming up for a £2,000 service, it will be put through the auction before rather than after.

Different types of car auction

There are a lot of different types of car auction and some are much safer for the private buyer than others.

Manufacturer Sales of nearly new, ex-rental and ex-demonstration fleet cars can be a good bet. The cars are clean, usually have some warranty left and you know where they're coming from. However, such sales are increasingly aimed at the private buyer as well as the trade and it can be difficult for obvious private buyers to actually buy at true trade money. Either rival trade bidders or the auctioneer may 'run up' your bids, and if the auctioneer runs you past your limit, the car will simply be re-entered in a subsequent auction.

True trade money for a car changes through the course of the sale and self-tracks to a variation of no more than £100 for a given make, model and mileage in a similarly desirable colour. If you write down all the prices paid, you will be able to see this for yourself.

With manufacturer sales, listen carefully to the auctioneer (what he says is taped) because some of the cars may be faulty and returned to the manufacturer for a refund, either under a special scheme or simply under the Sale and Supply of Goods Act 1994.

Dedicated Fleet Sales can be good too. These are where a section of the sale is given over to cars from a single named fleet source. MFL

(Motability Finance Ltd) has the largest fleet in Europe and, for obvious reasons, its cars tend to be low-mileage, less than three years old, with a good sprinkling of power-steered automatics.

You need to be a bit more wary where the named fleet also has its own retail outlets (I'd better not name any names here) because you have to ask yourself why it has not retailed the cars itself rather than consigned them to auction. Some fleets retail their ex-fleet cars from their own sites, then enter the cars they take in part-exchange in their dedicated sections, so not all the cars in their dedicated sections are genuinely ex-fleet.

West Oxfordshire Motor Auctions (01993 774413) holds ex-police vehicle evening sales twice a month. Blue lights, sirens, radios, 'jam sandwich' fillings, will all have been removed, so there's no chance of impersonating a police officer on the drive home. And the specification of all but 'undercover' cars tends to be a bit basic (no sunroofs, for example). But it's a great way to pick up a high-mileage, well-maintained ex-Panda Escort or Astra, or even a full-blown 3-litre Omega, BMW 325TDS or Volvo T5. Well worth a visit. (They also do Britain's best auction house bacon rolls, with optional chilli sauce.)

Fleet/Finance Sales may offer a mix of cars from named and un-named fleets and repossessed cars from finance houses. A dedicated Finance House Sale can be an excellent source, particularly where it includes pre-registered zero-mileage dealer stock which had not been sold before the dealer's creditors pulled the plug and did a midnight swoop on his premises.

Theme sales such as 'Diesel Cars', 'MPV & 4x4', 'Japanese', 'Late-year low-mileage' are designed to help the trade shift metal and can catch private buyers out. Most of these vehicles will be traders' cars, spiffed up for the occasion, on which the trader hopes to make his living. He may even be there on the floor bidding against you. It need not be a catastrophe for a private bidder to buy such a car from a trader, especially at one of the bigger auction houses which don't tolerate 'low-lifes'. But be extra attentive to the auctioneer's description, make sure the mileage is 'warranted' and that the car comes with its V5 listing previous owners so you can check the mileage yourself within the auction house warranty time limits.

For *General Sales*, the same applies. But these sales often also include 'wrong make' dealer part-exchanges such as Mazdas from Renault dealers and vice-versa. If you happen to make the top provisional bid for a car that's already been through the halls 'over reserved' several times, the chances are the dealer will instruct the auction house to 'get it gone' and you'll lay your hands on a bargain.

Dedicated *Part-Exchange Sales* to shift generally older excess stock taken in by larger groups such as Inchcape and Hartwell can be good sources. Inchcape rarely warrants any mileages, but 'gut-feel' and some broad hints from the auctioneer should tell you which cars are right and which are wrong. If, for instance, the auctioneer reads out the car's entire service history you don't usually have to worry that the mileage is not warranted.

Classic & Historic is another form of general sale aimed principally at the public. About half the cars will be entered by traders or restorers. But the others will be genuine private and executors' entries. Pick of the bunch are often late entries on the supplementary list rather than in the catalogue. Classics are rarely sold with warranted mileages, due to the impossibility of checking them, and it really is up to the buyer to satisfy him or herself of the car's true condition prior to bidding. Remember also that the public is easily hoodwinked by shiny paintwork and glittering chrome. It can be well worth a trader's while to fill a rusty old classic with 'pudding', give it a respray and try to get bids of £3,000–£5,000 more then he paid. So classic auctions are one type of sale to which it's still worth taking a magnet.

Time of year

While we still had the August plate change there was always a price crash at some point between September and November.

After the frenzied activity of August, with around 500,000 used cars hitting the forecourts in just one month, the trade was faced with a residue of cars and a market which declined from September until Christmas.

It usually picked up in January, so the wise buys were made at the bottom of the market – at the point where retail sales had slowed down but just before the big players started buying for the new year.

But the March and September registration plate changes starting in 1999 have changed everything.

The March plate change ensures that the market is reasonably well supplied with part-exchanges for the peak Spring selling season. But it is not over-supplied, so Spring remains the most expensive time of year to buy a used car.

But the September plate change feeds a large number of used cars to the market at the wrong time of year. Any leftovers tend to be at rock bottom during November, which is when the smart, well financed big dealers stock up for the new year. Lesser dealers see this happening and start buying too in December, so prices usually rise by Christmas.

In January we no longer see a large influx of part-exchanges, so prices shoot up, often by 10% or more, until the market slows a bit in mid-February in anticipation of the March part-exchanges.

Auction buying hints and tips

When visiting an auction and particularly when bidding, it is vital for private buyers to keep a low profile. Noisy family groups carrying 'Parkers Guide' or the '*What Car?* Price Guide' are a dead giveaway. So don't wave your newsagent price guide around. Look up prices on the sly, and keep the guide hidden when bidding.

Give the cars you're interested in a good once-over in the auction marshalling yard. Look for obvious signs of a repaint (spray dust, over-bright paint, rubbing compound, tide marks under rubber trim strips). Check for matching shut-lines, especially between the bonnet and wings and front wings and doors. Crouch down in front of the car and look along the sides for ripples. Check the condition of the tyres for uneven wear. (And if it's a Renault, Citroën or Peugeot, feel under the back to make sure it still has a spare wheel.)

When they come to start it up, look for excessive smoke from the exhaust, and ask the yard boy how much clutch it has left. As it moves into a different light, you may spot faults you missed before. But don't be 'all over' the car as it drives into the auction hall.

Find a spot where the auctioneer can see you very clearly, but where most rival bidders can't. Let the bidding start, and wait until it slows down or shifts from £100s to £50s or £25s before making your bid. Do this by waving your catalogue to catch the auctioneer's eye. Then, once he knows you are in the bidding, a simple nod will suffice for each increment. If you want to get out, shake your head as soon as he looks at you for a next bid. The more you appear like a trader from out of the area, the less chance you have of being 'run up' next time you get into the bidding.

Bidding at auction for the first time can be both nerve-wracking and addictively exciting. Remember, though, you're there to buy a car as cheaply as possible, not to get high on the adrenaline rush.

Auction warranties

Auction houses usually charge a 'buyer's premium', which is higher for the public than the trade. If the car is described as 'with warranty', this will include limited cover warranting title to the car, described condition, and mileage if the vendor has warranted this. The condition warranty usually only lasts to close of business on the day of the sale, so if you can't pay straight away and drive the car you can't return it under this warranty. If the car is described as 'without warranty' or 'as seen', the only guarantee is your title to the car.

'Buyer's premiums' have risen over the past few years, and for a £20,000 car could be as much as £500, so check this carefully before starting to bid.

Employing an auction buyer

If you're nervous of buying at auction, several organisations offer to source the car for you.

J. Dowd & Son is run by the most trustworthy buyer I see regularly on the auction floor, a really good guy; tel: 01903 245171, mobile: 07768 338585; website: www.auctioncarbuyer.co.uk

Douglas Coker's Cars For Customers will source the car either directly from a fleet or from auction, with full service histories if requested; tel: 020 8351 7976, mobile: 0973 506288.

Julian Trim & Co. charges the auction hammer price plus 6%; tel: 01747 838888.

Yet another car sourcing specialist is Sam Davies of Autobarn Direct; tel: 020 8367 1647.

Used vehicle imports
Introduction
Different pre-tax pricing to compensate for heavier taxation in other countries does not help the second-hand buyer in the same way as it helps the new car buyer. Used cars are generally little cheaper in countries such as Holland than they are in the UK. So for the used buyer there are no tax killings to be made.

What will help is any comparative strength of Sterling and a differently structured market.

Used German imports
With Sterling at around Dm3.0/£1, Germany has been a good source of extremely well-cared-for high-performance cars. But a quick glance through a magazine such as *Motor Markt* soon shows you that, without the heavy supply of ex-fleet cars on its used car market, most bread-and-butter used cars aren't particularly cheap. However, sports and high performance cars can be, and LHD is no hardship if your main reason for buying a used Porsche is to enjoy yourself at race circuit trackdays.

One problem can be certification. Every car sold in most European countries since January 1998 comes with a 'Certificate of Conformity' to pan-European Type Approval. Before that date most European countries recognised most other European other countries' National Type Approval, so make sure you get that certificate.

Alternatively, use an online specialist such as www.premiercarsearch.com, or www.lhdplace.co.uk

Used Japanese imports
New cars in Japan sell for between half and two-thirds of the UK list price. But Japan also has a tough government testing regime designed to encourage Japanese owners to buy new every three, five or seven years. As a result, the already low prices of Japanese cars drop sharply once they are three years old, and once they are seven years old they are of little more than scrap value on the home market.

Until the Yen recovered, this made second-hand imports from Japan spectacularly cheap.

Unfortunately the potential fortunes to be made were spotted many years ago. So, as well as the rising Yen, the export factor has increased values of used Japanese cars and they are not the bargains they once were. The second factor is the condition of these cars. Most Japanese cars spend most of their driving lives stuck in traffic jams. After 20,000 miles of this sort of treatment, the diesel engine in a Shogun, for example, can be ruined. The third factor is that, because they don't keep their cars for long, a significant proportion of Japanese owners simply don't bother to service them. The fourth factor is that Japanese cars are set up to run on different petrol at different speeds than in the UK. The maximum speed in Japan is 55 mph, so tyres may not be suitable for the UK, suspension may be too soft, steering too light and so on.

There is an auction of used Japanese imports every month in Dublin (Windsor Car Auctions, Bewlgard Road, Dublin; tel: 00 351 1 4599 300).

You can also try using specialists who buy cars for you at Japanese auctions. These include Spectrum on 0081-48-833-0665, website: www.trade.co.jp; email: spectrum@trade.co.jp And Japan Car Direct on 0081-339 280-935; website: www.isibike.com/isicar; email: isik@crisscross.com

Specialists know how to get most Japanese cars through the SVA test for imports. The more complex the car, the more complex the modifications. The most experienced people are Protech; tel: 0117 986 1611, website: www.protech-uk.co.uk Another useful website on all aspects of importing from Japan is www.importedvehicles.co.uk But, and it's a big BUT, the rules about SVA changed on 1 November 2001 (see 'Single Vehicle Approval' on page 208).

UsedAmerican imports

Think of the USA as a happy hunting ground for 1960s–1980s muscle cars and leviathans, and for rust-free British sports cars in the dry states such as California, Arizona and New Mexico. But please note, Florida is not a 'dry state', due to the extremely high humidity and proximity to the sea.

Currency fluctuations

From 1997 to 2001 the relative strength of Sterling and the comparative weakness of domestic used car markets in other European countries made Europe a ready source of supply.

But the reasons for this were threefold. First, Britain had the highest interest rates in Europe, so currencies transferred to Sterling deposits would bring in a better return for Europeans than depositing the money in their own currencies in their own banks.

Second, the rest of Europe had its brakes on in order to qualify for the single currency. How well Sterling will fare against the Euro longterm could be a completely different matter.

Third, because Britain did not join the Euro in the first wave, Sterling remained a European hedge against it. But since the Labour election victory in June 2001, it seemed increasingly likely that Sterling would have to 'converge' with other European currencies. This led to a heavy fall against the Dollar and the Yen, making imports from Japan and the USA considerably more expensive.

Finding the car

Check websites. Buy magazines. Preferably learn the language. Make use of friends in the country. *Hemmings* is the equivalent of a national classic car *Auto Trader* for the USA.

Shipping

No problem from Europe, of course. But some tips may help if you wish to import from Japan or the USA. Be warned that, when importing from Japan, car space on the huge Wallenius Lines RORO ships may be limited and may be booked up months in advance.

A good shipper is Mann Motor Ships (tel: 023 8023 7711) which ships from Jacksonville, Charleston, Baltimore, New York and Halifax to Southampton and Liverpool, using Wallenius Lines. Mann only uses RORO ships, but you can have a car shipped as deck cargo or fully containerised. Expect to pay between $495 and $625 to ship a 'one-off' average car sized between 351 and 500 cubic feet. You'll also have to pay US wharfage of $75–$85 and UK wharfage of about £30. Insurance has to be negotiated with a Stateside broker.

Four other shippers are: Prestige Shipping Services Ltd, tel: 020 8462 0292; N.S.E.W., tel: 01394 674455; and, from the West Coast,

Farber Inc. of Long Beach, tel: 001 562 432 8748 and Binoray Ltd, tel: 020 8946 5157.

Import duties from the USA and Japan
There is 10% European import duty to pay on the invoice price of the vehicle plus the shipping costs, then a further 17.5% UK VAT. The appropriate two leaflets are: 'How to Permanently Import your Vehicle into Great Britain' (Department of Transport leaflet P12 printed December 1996) and 'The Single Vehicle Approval Scheme'. Both are available from Department of Transport VSE1, Zone 2/01, Great Minster House, 76 Marsham Street, London SW1 4DR. Public Enquiries can be directed to tel: 020 7271 4800.

Single vehicle approval
The rules about Single Vehicle Approval changed on 1 February 2001, and changed again on 1 November 2001.

Essentially, any car which was not first registered in Europe and which does not carry a European Certificate of Type Approval ('C-of-C') is required to pass a Single Vehicle Approval test at a government HGV testing centre.

The only exceptions are cars more than 10 years old and cars 3–10 years old which have been owned abroad by the importer for at least six months in a country where the importer has lived for at least 12 months.

Further changes from 1 November 2001, introducing an 'Enhanced' SVA Test, have made compliance more complex and expensive, so it is vital that, before laying out any money on a vehicle, you contact experts such as Protech (website: www.protech-uk.co.uk) and find out what will be involved to get the vehicle through its Enhanced SVA Test.

The relevant SVA and ESVA booklets can be obtained from the Vehicle Certification Agency, tel: 0117 951 5151, or check the website: www.via.gov.uk You also can buy a copy of the 'Single Vehicle Approval' Inspection Manual, priced £25, from the Vehicle Inspectorate, PO Box 12, Swansea SA1 1BP.

Importing a used car from Europe

1 Get the relevant Government booklets and forms. First phone the DVLA on 01792 772134 and ask for the pack on personal imports. This includes a booklet, 'How to Import a Vehicle Permanently into Great Britain'; Form V100, which explains registering and licensing procedures and gives a list of Vehicle Registration Offices; and Form V55/5, which is an application form to license a vehicle in the UK for the first time. (Alternatively, phone the DETR on 0207 676 2094, write to DETR VSE1, Zone 2/01, Great Minster House, 76 Marsham Street, London SW1 4DR, or visit the DETR website at www.roads. detr.gov.uk/vehicle/vse1/index.htm). Then phone your local VAT enquiry line, listed under 'Customs & Excise' in the telephone directory, and ask for the 'VAT Notice 728 Pack', which includes a form 'Appendix D: New Means of Transport – Notification of Acquisition'. (Please don't phone C&E at either 020 7864 3000 or 01304 224372, as these lines have become overwhelmed with enquiries.)

2 Make sure the car comes with a Certificate of Conformity to European Type Approval ('C-of-C') or a National Type Approval Certificate, an invoice showing that VAT has been paid in the country of purchase, and, of course, the dealer's invoice.

3 Insure the car on the VIN or on its foreign plates through A-Plan, tel: 0800 731 7666.

4 As soon as possible, fill in the form 'New Means of Transport – Notification of Acquisition' (Appendix D) which came with VAT 728 and take it, together with completed form C55/5, the dealer's invoice, foreign registration document and the Certificate of Type Approval Conformity, and an MOT if the car is more than three years old (photos of a lit offside rear foglight and mph speedo face if less than three years old), to your nearest Vehicle Registration Office. On payment of a £25 first registration fee, they will issue you with a registration number. You then have to obtain an insurance certificate containing that registration number before you can tax the car at a Post Office using form V62. Your V5 registration document will then be sent to you from Swansea.

5 Order a set of plates.

Selling

Selling privately
How to prepare the car for sale

The public are suckers for clean-looking cars. So, whatever old rubbish the car may be, if it can be made to look good, someone will inevitably buy it.

Making a car look good is a matter of thoroughly cleaning it inside and out, thoroughly polishing it – paying particular attention to the windows, treating the plastic with a restorative, touching up or 'blocking in' as many paint chips as you reasonably can and blacking the tyres to make the whole show look new. An upholstery spray such as 'Apple Fresh' also goes down well. Whatever you do, don't spray the plastic around the dashboard with shiny glop. This looks and feels hideous and will make the public suspicious.

If you are selling the car privately from your doorstep, consider servicing it and putting it through a fresh MOT. It doesn't need to be a big service, but it will give buyers confidence and make then feel much better-disposed towards you.

A couple of years ago I came across a lady with a Rover 800 Vitesse full of kids stuck by the roadside. The car was dead, I couldn't help, and Wayne from the garage round the corner was called in. A few days later I asked Wayne what had been wrong with the car. 'Plugs and throttle valve completely choked up with muck. Hell of a state', he replied. 'I asked her when she last had it serviced and she told me 16,000 miles ago. I offered to service it for her but she said, no, we're selling it next week.'

This is the worst way to sell a car because all any buyer will look at is the profit they can gain from cleaning it up and re-offering it. She'll have got about £2,000 less for it than she would have done had it been clean, freshly serviced and newly tested.

How to prepare your advertisement

If you're using a photo ad in one of the many 'Trader' publications, don't let their bloke come round and take the photograph. Especially don't let him take his snap of the car parked next to the dustbins round the back of a block of flats.

These days you get 24 prints and a free replacement film for a fiver. Obviously it's well worth a bit of time and a fiver if a good snap is going to sell your car faster and for a lot more money. So shoot the whole roll. And if you've got a digital camera the snaps cost you nothing.

Photograph the car against a variety of backgrounds. Side-on, three-quarters, against a contrasting skyline. Then pick the photo that both shows it off best and is most likely to reproduce well on fairly grotty newsprint.

Describe the car accurately and simply, using no superlatives. 'Nissan Primera 2.0SLX 5-door hatchback, 97R, 55,632 miles, full service history, met blue, electric sunroof and windows, power steering, good condition, £3,000' will go down a lot better with the public than 'Beautiful Nissan Primera, two litre, top spec SLX model, R reg, 55k, FSH, stunning metallic blue, electric roof and windows, PAS, drives superb, first to see will buy, £2,999'.

How to Buy and Sell Cars

Where to advertise

This depends on the car and the price range.

For cars under £3,000, it's always worth putting a postcard in the local newsagent's window. Local newspapers or freesheets usually have sections for this type of car. People who buy *Loot*, the London classified newspaper, expect cars advertised in it to be cheap. *Auto Trader* magazines also offer sections for cheap cars. And if the car is a bit specialist, *Exchange & Mart* is worth a stab.

The photo ad section in *Classic Car Weekly* has become the best for 'classics' at the cheaper end and charges £20 a week. For more expensive 'classics' it may be worth going for a series ad in *Classic Car Weekly*, *Practical Classics* and *Classic & Sportscar*.

Cheap cars sell well in *Loot* or *Loot Hot Car & Motorbike*, tel: 020 7644 9290; email: hotcar@loot.com

Mid-range family cars seem to go best either from the bigger local newspapers (or groups of newspapers) or from a photo ad in an *Auto Trader* (website: www.autotrader.co.uk). See tips about taking the photo on page 210.

For sports or specialist cars it might be worth trying *Top Marques*, which is an upmarket national version of *Auto Trader*. If you have something you think a dealer or an enthusiast might be interested in, *Autocar* is worth a try. If attempting to get a high price or an 'over' for a car the demand for which exceeds supply, then you'll do best with an ad in *Exchange & Mart*, *The Sunday Times* or *The Daily Telegraph* 'Motoring' which appears on Saturdays. 'Telegraph Motoring' also has a photo 'Forecourt' section which can be particularly good for reaching a high circulation with a classic car.

But I reckon that the best place of the lot is the *Auto Trader* website, www.autotrader.co.uk, which costs £7.50 a fortnight and gets cars gone for me when all else has failed. *Exchange & Mart* also has a website: www.exchangeandmart.co.uk

How to answer the phone

Though you are a private individual, it's better to sound fairly professional. Blaring television, loud pop music or kids fighting in the background are a definite turn-off to the buyer.

Answer with a polite, upbeat, 'Hello', followed by your telephone number. This immediately confirms that the caller has phoned the right number.

There is then a 95% chance that the caller will say, 'I'm calling about the car.' This is your cue to say words to the effect of, 'Yes, the Nissan Micra' (or whatever) and confirm to the caller that you are not a 'home trader' who has a lot of different cars for sale. Quickly add, 'What can I tell you about it?'

You're honest, you've put the buyer at ease, and you are welcoming his or her questions. What more could the buyer want? You must then try to answer every question as quickly and straightforwardly as you can, which is not always easy when they make ill-thought demands on you such as, 'Does it have any marks?' (Every car has marks, so your answer to this is 'Nothing significant'.) Similarly, if they ask, 'What sort of condition is it in?', you say, 'Good condition, at least I think so.'

What they should be asking are questions such as, 'Are you the owner of the car?', 'How long have you owned it?', 'Why are you selling it?', 'When did you last have it serviced?', 'Can you be sure that the mileage is genuine?', 'Do you owe anything on finance for the car?', 'Is the colour Baliol Blue, Rimini Blue, Ontario Blue, Cayman Blue, Java Blue, State Blue or Petrol Blue?' (that would indicate that the caller knew his or her Mondeos).

Remember, depending on the scarcity of the car and how competitively you have priced it, the buyer may either be working through a list or you may be the only vendor he is phoning that night. If it's obvious he is working through a list, you have to hook him and you'll do that by charm and honesty, not by a load of old flannel.

Even if the buyer does not yet want to make an appointment to view the car, be sure to get his name and phone number before you give him your address. When subsequent callers query how much interest there has been in the car you can then read out a list of names and that might make them want to come and view the car immediately. The British are a bit peculiar like that. They always seem to want something if they think everyone else wants it.

Getting the name and number of all callers also helps protects you against theft from your driveway or from the street. If you are selling a highly desirable, much-stolen sportscar, take all callers' phone numbers, then phone them back on that number before divulging any address details. Smart thieves can get your address from your phone number anyway but they're not all that smart.

How to demonstrate the car

It is illegal for anyone to drive your car if he or she is not insured to do so. In effect, most purchasers' private car policies will cover them to drive a car they wish to purchase privately on third party terms. But 'third party' means just that. If the potential purchaser wrecks your car, his insurer will pay for any damage to third parties, but not to your car. Similarly, if he steals the car from you, you will get nothing back either. And if he turns out not to be insured at all, then crashes your car, both you and he could find yourselves facing criminal charges.

So be very careful indeed about allowing other people to drive your car, and don't even contemplate it unless you see their insurance certificate or have an 'any driver' policy for your car, or a trade policy.

Assuming the insurance question is satisfactorily answered, there is not much point in you driving the car with the purchaser as passenger unless that is specifically what they want.

Why not let them drive? The procedure is for the buyer to get into the driver's seat and you to get into the passenger's seat. Both of you then make yourselves comfortable, the buyer gets familiarised with the controls and you both put your safety belts on.

Then, and only then, hand him the key.

If you drive first, there are two safe ways to carry out the swapover. You climb from the driver's seat to the passenger seat and let the buyer walk round to the driver's seat. Or you both walk round but you take the key so he doesn't get hold of it until you're both belted in.

Never, ever, take more than one male person on a test-drive unless you also take a big bloke as your own back-up and he remains in the car all the time.

How to do the deal

The buyer will try to chip you down on price. If you have accidentally underpriced the car (it can happen, I've done it) and the phone has hardly stopped ringing, you can be firm on your price. Simply and politely say you're sorry, but you know you have priced the car fairly and you know you will get the asking price, if not from the buyer in front of you then from someone else.

But, of course, if the car has stuck (this has also happened to me) you will be prepared to take a bath just to get rid of the damn thing. Whatever you do, don't make this too glaringly obvious. Still try and do a deal. Consult 'er indoors. Fight for the last £25. Do whatever you have to. But don't let the car go cheap easily, both for your own sake and the fact that it might make the buyer have second thoughts.

How to take payment

There are only three ways to take payment for a car.

The first is a Building Society Cheque issued by the Building Society itself, in which case you need to see the buyer's passbook to check the amount has in fact been withdrawn so you can satisfy yourself that the cheque is genuine.

The second is a Bank Draft, which you must only take during banking hours so you can phone the bank that issued it and check it is genuine.

The third is 'Nelsons' (Nelson Eddies = Readies). The best advice when taking cash is to swap the V5 and keys for the cash in a bank so you can bank it safely straight away. Take cash on your doorstep and you won't be the first to receive a 'cash-back' visit soon after by big, nasty men you wouldn't want to argue with or to threaten your children.

Part-exchanging

Part-exchanging for a new car

If you have a used car you want to part-exchange for a new one, it's no good getting a decent discount then giving it all back by accepting too little for your trade-in.

Be very well aware of what your existing car is worth. Compare it with similar models of similar age and mileage which the dealer has up for sale, and don't accept less than £1,000 or 10% (whichever is the greater) less than the sticker price on these cars. This £1,000 or 10% may sound a lot, but remember the dealer will usually negotiate downwards from these sticker prices when selling his used stock.

Also remember, what you get for your part-exchange is not the most important factor. The 'cost to switch' is. Always compare the total financial outlay involved in one deal compared to another.

For example, dealer 'A' has a Mondeo which lists at £15,000. He offers you £4,000 for your part exchange, but no discount on the Mondeo, so the cost to switch is £11,000.

Dealer 'B' has a Laguna which lists at £15,000. He offers you £3,500 for your part exchange, plus £750 off the price of the Laguna. The cost to switch is therefore £10,750, so the Laguna is £250 cheaper than the Mondeo even though you get less for your part exchange.

Is the Mondeo worth £250 more than the Laguna? Or can you use the Laguna deal to chip £250 or more off the price of the Mondeo?

This is the way you should be thinking. It's not hard, is it?

Part-exchanging for a used car

The same rules apply as when part-exchanging a used car for a new car. But be doubly vigilant when part-exchanging for a 'nearly new' or used car on finance. One well-known dealer used to offer two deals on his used cars. 'Deal 1' was a straight price, itself very competitive and negotiable if you found a cheaper deal for precisely the same make, model, colour, age and mileage. 'Deal 2' involved a price usually well below what you would pay at auction for the car. But the deal was subject to a minimum £500 part exchange allowance, payment of £99 and finance on the dealer's terms. The 'Deal 2' package was designed to be irresistibly tempting and the truth is it wasn't bad if you didn't mind tucking yourself up with fairly expensive finance. Even when you compare the true total cost of the deal you would probably come out better off than with a deal from a franchised dealer. Just know exactly what you're getting into.

Selling to a dealer

Unless the car is highly sought-after and selling for an 'over', this is a desperation tactic.

If the car is relatively ordinary and the dealer wants stock, he has to build in a margin on top of whatever he offers you and has to include in that margin his own insurance that the car doesn't have some secret history you and HPI don't tell him about.

If your car is over the age of the dealer's stock, then the dealership may not make you an offer, but one of its salesmen might. These sort of offers are often derisory. A few years ago, a reader was offered just £1,000 for an immaculate 50,000-mile BMW 320i Bauer cabrio. I told the reader to do what the salesman was planning to do with it. Advertise it in *Top Marques* for £4,000 and be prepared to accept up to £500 less. He did, and got £3,750.

Okay, you can't do this if you're about to leave the country. But if you are all set to emigrate, don't be too greedy. Advertise the car for a tempting price, and take an offer. Don't hold out for more money until the day before your plane flies out or you could end up forced to virtually give the car away.

Selling at auction

See Honest John's list of Auction Sites online at www.honestjohn.co.uk

Advantages and disadvantages

It's clear-cut, simple and ideal for executors, finance houses and bailiffs who may be audited and must not show any favours.

Ordinary cars sold this way usually fetch no more than trade price, less the auction house entry fee and less commission.

'Top Cars' may or may not sell to a member of the public, but they usually need a bit of 'encouraging' to fetch top money – either from Joe Public or from a franchised dealer attending the auction who has an order for precisely that car.

Specialist cars in high demand and short supply will achieve what the people in the auction house that day are prepared to pay. 'Top Car' sales are often used by specialists who deal in such cars to test market price levels so they know what to pay and what to sell for.

The classified ads in the weekend newspapers are no true indication because they are often placed by speculators who have bought in too late for too much money and missed the 'overs' market. On the other hand, a car for which demand suddenly exceeds supply may sell for considerably more than the speculators are asking.

Executors who have classic cars to dispose of as part of the deceased's estate will usually get a better price selling at auction than they will from any dealer.

Car by Car Breakdown

Thinking of buying a car? Then the chances are that as well as learning what's good about it, you'll want to know what's bad. What typically goes wrong.

Well you don't have to take my word for it. My 725-model car by car breakdown is compiled from the combined experience of everyone I know in the trade, plus the experiences of around 3,000,000 *Telegraph* readers and www.honestjohn.co.uk website visitors. So if there's any sort of problem with a car there's a strong chance you'll find it here.

Not only that, I've also listed all the official and unofficial recalls I've come to hear about so you'll know about them too. And, if you're thinking of buying new, you might also discover just how long your dream car is likely to remain a current model.

Anyone can tell you the good points of cars. Read any road test and you'll get plenty of facts and opinions about how a car goes, corners and stops. You'll get that from me too.

What you'll also get here is what the road testers don't tell you. How cars stand up to the rigours of life on the road long after they've left a magazine's 'long term fleet'. I don't borrow any 'long term cars'. I don't have any advertisers I need to keep happy to keep their advertising revenue. What you get here is the truth about cars.

But remember, things are changing all the time. This is just a snapshot of the on-line Car by Car Breakdown at www.honestjohn. co.uk at the time we went to press. Specs and prices will change. The on-line breakdown is updated daily, sometimes even hourly, with the very latest information on new cars, used cars and problems that develop with them. Before you make any decision on a car, check the Car by Car Breakdown at www.honestjohn.co.uk for the latest updates.

AC

212 S/C, Superblower, Mk IV and CRS

What's good: With 355 bhp supercharged Ford V8 putting out 385 lb ft torque, they might as well have called the Superblower the 'Mindblower'. But there's nothing to be afraid of. Take it easy, 'point and squirt' at first, and the informative chassis soon tells you that much more is possible. Original AC Cobra looks. Beautiful; hand-beaten aluminium body shared by 220 bhp Mk IV now selling at around the £25,000 mark at 18–24 months old. But new £38,000 CRS polycarbonate version with non-supercharged 240 bhp Mustang engine from Summer 1999 is a great alternative to a TVR. 212 S/C at £69,000 is fitted with the 350bhp lightweight twin-turbo 3.5 litre V8 from the Lotus Esprit V8. 0–60 is 4.0 seconds, gearbox is 6-speed. 212 S/C, CRS and Superblower have nice, central dashboard. Mamba coupe from July 2002 with 4.0 litre 192bhp LPG straight six, 230bhp petrol straight six or 350bhp V8. New 350bhp Ace also from 2002. CXRS now apparently to be built in Malta.

Website: www.accars.co.uk

What's bad: Driver and passenger get blown about a bit at over 100 mph. Nice gearchange of Superblower has a narrow gate, and first time out you may get 5th instead of 3rd. Buy new, and Mk IV and Superblower will lose money in spades. Mk IV has terrible parts-bin dashboard.

What to watch out for: Superblower and 212 S/C could blow a big hole in your finances when you come to sell.

AIXAM

MAC 500

What's good: Beach buggy version of the Aixam 500 car with 479cc two cylinder Kubota diesel engine giving 70mpg and open-belt CVT transmission. Base price just £4,550, but add £105 for VED and Registration Tax.

User group: www.aixam.org.uk

What's bad: Alloy wheels, a spare wheel, a hood and even doors are all extras. Not suitable for year round use (see catalogue of problems in the user group.)

What to watch out for: Check online at www.aixam.org.uk

Micro-Cars

What's good: Tiny French two- and four-seater micro hatchbacks. Have two-cylinder 400cc and 469cc Kubota diesel engines giving 55 mph and 75–90 mpg. Simple, exposed-belt Variomatic transmission. Under the weight limit, so can be driven on a B1 motorcycle licence. Euro Type Approved. First UK RHD sale May 1999. Can also be towed unbraked behind a large motorhome. Polycarbonate body on aluminium space frame won't rust. £80 pa VED. Online user group: www.aixam.org.uk

What's bad: Slow acceleration will take a bit of getting used to. Quite expensive for what it is. Body leaks.

What to watch out for: Wet carpets and internal condensation damage to electrics.

ALFA ROMEO

145/146 (1994 to 2000)

What's good: Fabulous two-litre Twin-Spark motor, superquick power steering on 2.0 litre versions, brilliant oddball styling of the 3–door 145, good but not great handling. (146 was more conventional 5–door). 1.8 and 1.6 Twin-Sparks also reasonable enthusiasts cars. 3-year warranty on all Twin-Sparks. Same length as 33 at 13ft 5in but slightly wider at 5ft 7in. Much heavier at from 1,100kg to 1,200kg. 1.6 flat four from 1994 to 1997 had 103bhp; 1.7 flat four from 1994 to 1997 had 129bhp; 1.6 twin-spark 1997 to 2001 had 120bhp; 1.8 twin-spark from 1997 to 2001 had 140bhp; 2.0 twin-spark had 150bhp and sounded lovely.

What's bad: The injected and catalysed flat-fours in early models are nothing like as good as the straight-four Twin-Sparks. Dashboard a bit iffy. Not much room in the back when sitting behind a long-legged driver. S and T plate 145 20th from bottom in 2001 *Top Gear*/J.D. Power Customer Satisfaction Survey. S and T plate 146 12th from bottom in 2001 *Top Gear*/J.D. Power Customer Satisfaction Survey. In June 2001 Alfa Romeo was rated by Motor Warranty Direct as Britain's worst out of 22 marques for warranty claims (check online at www.warrantydirect.co.uk)

What to watch out for: Accident damage, lack of service history. Check electrics carefully. Oil leaks from gearboxes of flat-fours. Starting problems with flat-fours. Make sure it has its 'Red Key'.

Recalls: (April 1997 build): Tyres may lose pressure.

147 (from 2001)

What's good: Stunning-looking replacement for 145/146 with front-end retro styling reminiscent of late 1940s Alfas. Based on 156/Tipo floorpan. 120 bhp 1.6 Twin-Spark, 150 bhp 2.0 TS and 110 bhp JTD. Voted European 'Car of the Year' 2001 narrowly pipping the Ford Mondeo for the title. February 2001 launch models are the 121mph 120bhp 1.6TS in Turismo or Lusso trim and the 129mph

150bhp 2.0TS with Alfa Romeo's Selaspeed semi automatic gearbox. All models are well equipped with air-conditioning and ABS as standard. Prices start at £12,985 for the 1.6TS Turismo, rising to £17,340 for the 2.0TS Selaspeed. Standard 3 year warranty included in price. 5 door version with 2.0TS manual gearbox offered from May 2001. V6 GTA version due October 2002. Online user group: www.alfaowner.com

What's bad: Poor score in 2001 NCAP crash tests. Problems with Selaspeed gearbox actuator on 156 models and long wait for replacement parts reported by two readers. Could be repeated with 147. Paddle shift arrangement for Selaspeed on 147 doesn't work very well. Not a great drive. Paint problems with solid lacquered black. FIAT/Alfa joint worst for breakdowns attended by German ADAC during 2001.

What to watch out for: Witches brew of problems. What follows is just one owner's experience:

1 Selespeed failure to engage gear. Leaving car in dangerous position. Normally happens when on roundabout or turn when engine cold. Alfa dealer has had car in 4 times and not solved problem.
2 Alarm goes off when boot is unlocked with remote control.
3 Boot plastic gutter trim not secure at rear edge, hatch not aligned.
4 Oil leak.
5 Positive terminal battery cover broken.
6 CD Player skips on normal CDs even when car stationary.
7 Front Windscreen washers very poor.
8 Power Steering fluid level below minimum.
9 Handbrake cable on left not fitted properly to floor bracket.
10 Timing belt cover not fitted correctly, gap at top and loose.
11 Carpet hanging out of passenger front lower trim.
12 Carpet loose on side of centre console.
13 Alternator fails to charge battery.
14 Only 25 to 26mpg.
15 Engine uses oil.
16 Rattles from door trims.

223

17 Rattles from rear seats.

18 Rear seats not locking in position.

19 Sunroof blind completely missing.

20 Sunroof fails to open.

21 Finish keeps coming off Selespeed Paddles on steering wheel.

22 The Climate Control keeps going to HIGH and MAX.

147 Sprint (from December 2003)

What's good: New coupe based on 147.

What's bad: Too soon to say.

What to watch out for: Too soon to say.

155 (1992 to 1998)

What's good: Brilliant later engines – both Twin-Spark and 2.6 V6. Late 'Sport' models had 'Quick-Rack' power steering. 3-year warranty on later cars. 1,773cc 1.8TS had 129bhp; 1,995cc 2.0TS had 145bhp; 2,492cc 2.5 V6 had 166bhp; Cloverleaf (92–94 only) had 190bhp turbocharged 2.0 engine.

What's bad: Front wheel drive. Terrible fall-apart dashboards. 'Italian Ape' driving position. Looks like yesterday's car compared to 156. Avoid early pre-Twin-Spark models. In June 2001 Alfa Romeo was rated by Motor Warranty Direct as Britain's worst out of 22 marques for warranty claims (check online at www. warrantydirect.co.uk) FIAT/Alfa joint worst for breakdowns attended by German ADAC during 2001. Alfa Romeo had joint highest average cost in warranty claims for cars up to 10 years old in 2002 Warranty Direct index, check online at www. performanceindex.co.uk

What to watch out for: Tattiness. Kerbed alloys. Accident damage. Duff cats. Front tyre wear. Check all electrics. Sport spec well worth having. Make sure the car does have 'Quick-Rack' (2.1 turns lock to lock) steering. If a later model, make sure it has 'Red Key'.

156 (1998 to 2004)

What's good: Fabulous styling. Brilliant engines. 1.8 and 2.0 litre Twin-Sparks are great. 190 bhp 24v 2.5 V6 is a real hooligan. All have 'Quick-Rack' steering. Pure, unadulterated handling well up to the job with Sports packs; less good without. 3-year warranty. 2.0 litre Selaspeed with thumb operated gearchange buttons on steering wheel works very well on country roads, but less satisfactory in town. 'Q' system V6 is a full automatic. Gruff but grunty 136 bhp 2.4JTD arrived in Summer 1999, offering 224 lb. ft. torque. Sport 1 spec adds carbon fibre console, bodykit, 16in alloys with 205/55 tyres, sports suspension and 'Blitz' cloth trim. Sport 2 spec adds Recaro front seats. Sport 3 spec adds Momo leather. £13,495 120 bhp 1.6TS in UK from Spring 2000. All prices cut from same date with 1.8TS down to £15,405. No missing 'Red Key' problems as it has a different immobiliser system. In June 2002 Alfa Romeo announced 156s with its new 165bhp 2.0 litre JTS direct injection petrol engine. The 2.4 litre 156 JTD direct injection diesel got a power hike to 150bhp. And first imports of the blisteringly fast 250bhp 3.2 litre GTA started to arrive. JTS stands for Jet Thrust Stoichiometric. Alfa has abandoned twin spark plugs in favour of directly injecting the fuel air mixture to the combustion chamber, running at lean burn to 1,500rpm and a stoichiometric 14.7:1 air:fuel mixture thereafter. Compression ration is raised to 11.3:1, power is up 15bhp and torque up 18 lb ft. 156 JTSs start at £17,720 for the saloon and £18,820 for the Sportwagon. Revised mapping pulled the 5-cylinder JTD up from 140bhp to 150bhp at 4,000rpm and torque to 225lb ft at 1,800rpm. Fuel economy is slightly improved at 42.8 mpg on the combined cycle v/s 42.1 mpg from the 140bhp JTD. 156 JTDs start at £17,835 for the saloon and £18,930 for the Sportwagon. The awe inspiring 3,179cc GTA V6 pumps out a class leading 250bhp at 6,200rpm and 221 lb ft torque at 4,800rpm. GTA prices start at £26,900 for the saloon and £27,900 for the Sportwagon. VDC (Vehicle Dynamic Control) is fitted to all post June 2002 156s except the GTA. The new range is distinguished from the older cars by new central console switches for the climate control incorporating LED pictograms. Range prices start with the 1.6 Turismo at £14,610. Thankfully they haven't messed around with the stunning exterior styling of the car.

More online at www.alfaromeo.co.uk

Usergroup: www.alfaowner.com

What's bad: Police Alert' spoilers optional on Sport 2 and Sport 3 spec will attract plod. Sub-20 mpg fuel consumption of V6 if you boot it. Trim quality not up to BMW standards. 5-speed gearchange on 1.8 and 2.0 can feel a bit floppy. Turn-in not as sharp as Peugeot 306 GTi-6 or even 406 2.0 litre Coupe. Usual Alfa build-quality problems with electrics. Fuel enrichment device may stick, leading to poor starting. Dealers are a very mixed bag. Resale values fell heavily in early 2000 even before price cuts. V6 and JDT can eat front tyres on the inside edge (need realigning with less toe-out). Paint problems with solid lacquered black. FIAT/Alfa joint worst for breakdowns attended by German ADAC during 2001. 9th from Bottom of 100 models for reliability in *Auto Express* 2002 survey. 18th from Bottom in 144 car 2002 JD Power/*What Car?* Customer Satisfaction Survey of V and W reg. cars. Alfa Romeo had joint highest average cost in warranty claims for cars up to 10 years old in 2002 Warranty Direct index, check online at www. performanceindex.co.uk

What to watch out for: Worn front tyres on V6. Front suspension alignment, in particular toe-out is critical. Accident damage. Kerbed alloys. Make sure aircon works properly. Feel the discs through the wheels for scoring or shouldering. Problems with 156 Selaspeed gearbox actuator and long wait for replacement parts. 'Tappety' sounding engine sign that car has been run with low or dirty oil and variable valve timing has been damaged. Clonks from rear suspension mean that bolts through he aluminium suspension components have not been tightened periodically causing wear. Make sure a/c blows cold as can leak refrigerant. Stoned glass headlight lenses cost £175 each to replace.

Recalls: June 1999: Safety recall No 4054: Modify rear hinge mounting on all four side doors to prevent hinges splitting from doors. 2000: 156, built Nov '97–Oct '98: Brake pipe connector may crack and leak.

157 (from 2004)

What's good: Will be based on GM Epsilon platform, same as Vectra and SAAB 9–3. Due in Europe May 2004. Will have four wheel drive option.

What's bad: An Alfa on a Vectra platform? Sacrilege. But remember, the 156 was based on the Tipo platform and SAAB has made quite a good job of the new 9–3.

What to watch out for: Too soon to say.

164 (1988 to 1998)

What's good: Big, fine handling front wheel drive car on shared FIAT Chroma, Lancia Thema, SAAB 9000 floorpan. 14ft 11in long by 5ft 9in wide and weighing in at from 1,200kg to 1,430kg. Brilliant engines, none more so than full-house 3.0 litre 24 valve mega-powerful 230 bhp Cloverleaf V6, good for 150 mph. Engine range started with 192bhp 3.0 V6, complemented in 1990 by 148bhp 2.0 Twin Spark four. 3.0V6 got 200bhp in 1990, 210bhp in 1993 and 230bhp in 1993.

What's bad: Old fall-apart Alfa trim, Alfa build quality and uneven quality of Alfa dealers (some brilliant and enthusiastic, others completely the opposite). In June 2001 Alfa Romeo was rated by Motor Warranty Direct as Britain's worst out of 22 marques for warranty claims (check online at www.warrantydirect.co.uk) FIAT/Alfa joint worst for breakdowns attended by German ADAC during 2001. Alfa Romeo had joint highest average cost in warranty claims for cars up to 10 years old in 2002 Warranty Direct index, check online at www.performanceindex.co.uk

What to watch out for: Electrics. Accident damage. Driveshaft wear. Gear selector problems. Worn front suspension springs, shocks and joints. Scored or lipped discs (try to feel them through the wheels). Rear suspension bush wear. Tattiness. Make sure aircon works. Go for post-May 1993 makeover improvements. Make sure cambelt has been changed within last 35,000–40,000 miles. Make sure it has its 'Red Key' (later models only).

Recalls: 1995 (to VIN 6272929): Corrosion of front suspension spring support. (Earlier TSB check of timing belt.)

166 (1999 to 2005)

What's good: Svelte front wheel drive replacement for 164. 15ft 6in long by 5ft 11in wide and weighing in from 1,420kg to 1,510kg. 2.0 litre 155 bhp Twin-Spark, 2.5 24v 190 bhp V6 or 3.0 24v 220 bhp V6. Autoboxes optional with V6s.

Usergroup: www.alfaowner.com

What's bad: Not as charismatic as 156. V6 eats front tyres. FIAT/Alfa joint worst for breakdowns attended by German ADAC during 2001.

What to watch out for: Check all tyres for wear regularly. Some 166s have gone through REAR tyres in as little as 5,000 miles indicating that they have been supplied with the tracking badly out of alignment. If you notice severe premature tyre wear, take the cat to a laser tracking specialist such as Micheldever Tyres and have them track it properly.

Recalls: 30–4–2001: Problem of loss of hydraulic power assistance to steering. All RHD 1,900 166s imported to UK by April 2001 recalled to have oil cooler and refill system replaced.

33 (1983 to 1994)

What's good: Zingy flat-four pre-cat engines. Replaced the Alfasud and not quite as rust prone. 79bhp 1,351cc flat four to quad cam 16 valve 137bhp 1,712cc 16v Cloverleaf from 1990 to 1993. Also came as a Sportshatch semi-estate and, from 1991 to 1992 as a 137bhp Permanent 4 four wheel driver. 13ft 5in long by 5ft 5in wide. Weighed 970kg to 1,070kg.

What's bad: Poor substitute for Alfasud with outboard front discs that were easier to service than Sud's inboard discs but did nothing for the handling. Similar rust problems. Gearboxes break. Condensation on flat-four causes poor starting. Seat trim falls apart. Gearboxes stiffen up and break. Electrics fail.

What to watch out for: Most have recycled themselves by now. Only the 137bhp quad cam late Sportwagons worth preserving. As for others, unless they're virtually being given away, best avoided.

75 (1986 to 1993)

What's good: Rear wheel drive with rear transaxle 5-speed gearbox for good weight distribution and balance. Replaced both Giulietta and Alfetta. 14ft 2in long by 5ft 5in wide and weighed from 1,060kg to 1,160kg. Engines were 1,779cc 1.8 with 120bhp; 1,962cc 2.0 TS with 148bhp; 2,492cc 2.5 V6 Cloverleaf (1986–1987) with 158bhp; 2,959cc 3.0 V6 with 188bhp.

What's bad: Usual Alfa rot-box bodies and fall-apart trim. Cannibalised for donor parts for specials.

What to watch out for: Not many left.

Alfasud (1974 to 1989)

What's good: Fantastic wheel in each corner design. Brilliant handling. Flat four engines grew in size from 1,186cc to 1,712cc and 118bhp. Most had 5-speed boxes. 12ft 9in long by 5.3in wide. Sprint was 13ft 2in by 5ft 4in. Last Alfasuds from 1980 came as three or five door hatchbacks. 1,351cc engine developed 79bhp with one carb or 86bhp with two. 1,490cc engine had 85bhp with one carb or 105bhp with two. Hatchback production ended in 1984, but much prettier Sprint coupe continued to December 1989 and last cars had 1,712cc 118bhp engine.

What's bad: Rusted as soon as they came off the line as built from impure steel imported as deals between Italy and both Russia and India. Prone to damp starting problems. Gearboxes weak. Structure not still (especially with hatchback and sunroof) and very easy to put front suspension out of alignment. Not a simple job to get it right again.

What to watch out for: 99.9% Have already recycled themselves, so finding one won't be easy. Rust is the main problem. Out of balance carbs is another (on twin carb engines). Don't buy if the gearchange is stiff. Haynes did a manual, no. 0290, ISBN 1 85010 445 X.

GTV (1995 to 2004/5)

What's good: We're talking about the latest model here, not the mid-60s Duetto that lasted into the 1990s. The good bits are fabulous looks, brilliant engines, 'Quick-Rack' steering, better rear suspension than the saloons. 3-year warranty. 1999 MY on 218bhp 3.0 24v V6 6-speed is as close as you'll get to a new Ferrari for under £30k. Same engine and gearbox in Spider from Spring 2001, making it an unruly hooligan of a car and capable of over 150mph with the top down. Surprisingly little buffeting at this speed, even without a cockpit air-dam.

Usergroup: www.alfaowner.com

What's bad: Virtually no boot room at all in the coupe. 'Saw their legs off' back seats. No auto options. Cylinder head gasket failed before one owner got his new car home. Rear suspension bushes apt to wear and when they do they can damage the rear subframe. S and T platers 3rd from bottom in 2001 *Top Gear*/J.D. Power Customer Satisfaction Survey. In June 2001 Alfa Romeo was rated by Motor Warranty Direct as Britain's worst out of 22 marques for warranty claims (check online at www.warrantydirect.co.uk) FIAT/Alfa joint worst for breakdowns attended by German ADAC during 2001. Alfa Romeo had joint highest average cost in warranty claims for cars up to 10 years old in 2002 Warranty Direct index, check online at www.performanceindex.co.uk

What to watch out for: Kerbed alloys. Electrics. Porous wheel rims (symptom: soft tyres). Undeclared personal imports lacking 3-year warranty. Disguised envy damage. Hood mechanism and tears in hood (don't forget to check hood if hood is down). Make sure it has 'Red Key' if supposed to. Clonks from rear suspension mean that bolts through he aluminium suspension components have not been tightened periodically causing wear both to bushes and mounting points (as per 156).

Recalls: 24/1/2000: Brake master -cylinder supply pipes may crack. 1,209 cars built May '98–July '99 recalled for replacement pipes. 10/3/2000: 122 GTV6 models built June '96–March '98: radiator fan cables could overheat, short-circuit and cause a fire. Cables to be checked and modified.

GTV (from 1978 to 1987)

What's good: Replaced beautiful Bertone 105 Series coupes. Teardrop shape, with back end sitting low on its haunches. Front engine with 5-speed rear transaxle gearbox. Began with 1,779cc 1,750 engine, then joined by a 1.6 Junior. Later cars had 1,962cc 2.0 twin cam with 130bhp, but the one to find is the V6 with either a 2,492cc 158bhp V6, or the rare 2,959cc 3.0V6 which had 192bhp. **What's bad:** Weren't as perfectly balanced as front gearbox 105 series coupes and spiders. Could snap into oversteer. Suffers from Alfa bodyrot, fall-apart trim. Things like the trim and the huge front windscreen hard to replace. **What to watch out for:** Rust.

Spider (1966 to 1993)

What's good: Lovely 'up and down' classic Alfa gearchange. Evergreen Alfa twin-cam motors. Early 1,570cc and 1,779cc boat tail cars had the looks. 1990 facelift brought with it a decent hardtop. 14ft long by 5ft 4in wide and weighing 1,110kg in 1990. **What's bad:** Scuttle shake. Progressively ruined over the years by ugly facelifts, but 1990 facelift was an improvement. Early cars rusted from new. Later cars can still rust. 'B' pillar can dig you in the back when you try to get in. Ruined by fuel injection and catalytic converter. RHD only with 'approved' Seaking conversion in later cars. Alfa Romeo had joint highest average cost in warranty claims for cars up to 10 years old in 2002 Warranty Direct index, check online at www.performanceindex.co.uk **What to watch out for:** Tears in hood and trim. Soggy carpets. Rusty 'cornflakes under the carpet'. Rust around the fuel tank in the boot which can rot through the sandwich construction and leave you with a boot full of petrol slopping around the boot mounted battery. Duff catalytic converters on later cars. Broken window-winder cables. Dripping heater matrix. Electrics. Noisy timing chain. 3,000–mile oil changes essential (I used to change mine every three months).

Spider (April 1996 to 2004)

What's good: Beautiful new front-drive Spider, initially with 150bhp 2.0TS engine and 5-speed gearbox only. decent enough handling. Enough room to perch a couple of girls in the back for seaside showing off. Finally got serious with addition of 218bhp 3.0V6 and six-speed gearbox in April 2001. Somehow the shape of the car means minimum buffeting with the top down at 150mph. 14ft long by 5ft 10in wide and 2.0TS weighed in at a hefty 1,370kg.

What's bad: Usual Alfa quality problems. Suffers from scuttle shake and doesn't handle as well as Toyota MR2, Porsche Boxter, Audi TT Roadster, etc. Virtually no boot room at all in the coupe. No auto options. Notorious for problems with the hood mechanisms and motors. Cylinder head gasket failed before one owner got his new car home. Rear suspension bushes apt to wear and when they do they can damage the rear subframe. S and T platers 3rd from bottom in 2001 *Top Gear*/J.D. Power Customer Satisfaction Survey. In June 2001 Alfa Romeo was rated by Motor Warranty Direct as Britain's worst out of 22 marques for warranty claims (check online at www.warrantydirect.co.uk) FIAT/Alfa joint worst for breakdowns attended by German ADAC during 2001. Alfa Romeo had joint highest average cost in warranty claims for cars up to 10 years old in 2002 Warranty Direct index, check online at www.performanceindex.co.uk Apparently to be replaced by new car with folding hardtop in 2004.

What to watch out for: Watch out for rejected problem cars if buying at auction at 6–18 months old. Look out for Kerbed alloys. Duff electrics. Porous wheel rims (symptom: soft tyres). Undeclared personal imports lacking 3-year warranty. Disguised envy damage. Hood mechanism and tears in hood (don't forget to check hood if hood is down). Make sure it has 'Red Key' if supposed to. Clonks from rear suspension mean that bolts through he aluminium suspension components have not been tightened periodically causing wear both to bushes and mounting points (as per 156).

Recalls: 24/1/2000: Brake master -cylinder supply pipes may crack. 1,209 cars built May '98–July '99 recalled for replacement pipes.

SZ and RZ (1990 to 1992)

What's good: Very strange looking ground-hugging wedge-shaped cope and roadster with strong performance from 207bhp 2,959cc catalysed V6 and brilliant rear drive, rear transaxle handling. Moving the engine and geabox much closer together made them almost 'front mid-engined'. Only 1000 SZs made and only 100 officially imported into the UK. SZ weighed 1,261kg. You can dump the cats because all were made before August 1992.

What's bad: So rare parts have to be specially made and body parts hand-crafted.

What to watch out for: This is a classic, so originality is very important.

ASCARI

KZ1

What's good: Stunning new 200mph carbon fibre British supercar build in Blandford Forum, Dorset. Has a BMW M5 V8 bored out to 4,928cc developing 520bhp. Six speed 'H' pattern or sequential gearbox. Top speed estimated at over 200mph. 0–60 in 3.7 seconds. 5.0 litre 400bhp £96,000 Ascari Ecosse continues.

Company website: www.ascari.co.uk

What's bad: £130,000 price. Gatso speed cameras. Otherwise too soon to say.

What to watch out for: Too soon to say.

ASTON MARTIN

DB7 (1994 on)

What's good: Nice compromise between handling and ride quality. Excellent 335 bhp supercharged 3,239cc six-cylinder engine with healthy 361 lb ft torque. Supplemented from Spring 1996 by convertible Volante and from Spring 1999 by 6.0 litre V-12 Vantage version offering 420 bhp, much praised by English motoring writers.

What's bad: Expensive compared to XK8 (but Vantage comparatively 'reasonable' at £92,500). Cabin spoiled by cheap and nasty 'parts bin' switchgear. Hood of convertible does not fold away. Most six-cylinder cars fitted with old-fashioned four-speed automatic gearbox which is difficult to override manually and changes gear half way round corners.

What to watch out for: For rich English people, chosen over XK8 for exclusivity of Aston Martin name. Must have top notch service history. Don't expect this car to be 100% niggle-free.

Recalls: 10/1/2000: 140 DB7 Vantage Coupes and Volantes recalled because of insufficient welds to front damper lower mounting brackets. Brackets to be replaced if not welded on all three sides. 9/10/2000: 478 DB7 Vantage models recalled for replacement of Power Train Control Module because original ignition software could result in misfires. 4/6/2001: DB7 coupes and Volantes recalled because steering column lighting switchgear cabling can become trapped. Switchgear to be replaced.

Vanquish (2000 on)

What's good: 6.0 litre V-12 DB7 Vantage developed to 504 bhp, launched late 2000 at £170,000 and selling for overs.

What's bad: Too soon to say.

What to watch out for: Too soon to say.

Virage and new V8

What's good: 1990 Replacement for old Aston Martin V8 which dated back to the 1960s. 5.3 litre 330bhp V8. 5-speed manual. 4 speed auto from Jan 1993. Re-named V8 in April 1996. Got 350bhp and option of 6-speed manual box. Awesome supercharged V8 Vantage had 550bhp and six-speed box. Demand picked up again and a 35,000 mile 91J auto sold for £28,000 at a BCA Top Car auction in July 2001.

What's bad: Unsuccessful. Launched during the supercar boom and went into a tailspin once the boom went bust. Auto only a 3-speeder to Jan 1993. The engine alone is an enormous piece of engineering. Potentially huge bills.

What to watch out for: Don't buy without full inspection by an Aston Martin expert.

AUDI

100 (1983 to 1991)

What's good: Big aerodynamic saloons and Avant semi-estate. 15ft 9in long, 5ft 11in wide, but not too heavy at 1,,090kg. Engines from familiar 90bhp VAG 1,781cc OHC four with 5 speed manual or 3-speed auto. Also 115bhp 1,994cc 'five', 136bhp 2,144cc 'five', 138bhp 2,226cc 'five' which grew to 2,309cc in 1989 but gained a cat so lost power back to 136bhp. 100 Turbo had 165bhp 2,225cc 'five' and came as front-drive or Quattro. Also an 87bhp 1,998cc five cylinder turbodiesel. Galvanized bodies last well. Can still get spares from specialists such as German & Swedish and Euro Car Parts.

What's bad: Five cylinders overhanging the front wheels makes them not very inspiring to drive.

What to watch out for: Things like light lenses can be expensive.

100 and 'Old' A6 (1991 to 1997)

What's good: Essentially the same car with a mid life name change and a new grille. 15ft 9in long by 5ft 10in wide and weighing from 1,325kg to 1,500kg. Galvanised against rust. Launched with catalysed 115bhp 1,984cc VAG four, 133bhp 2,309cc five, 150bhp 2,508cc V6, 164bhp 2,772cc V6 (front drive or quattro), and 230bhp 2,226cc five cylinder turbo for 100S4 quattro. 5-speed manual, but auto now has 4 speeds. Became A6 in June 1994 and acquired addition of 115bhp 2,460 five cylinder TDI diesel. S4 became S6. 2.0 litre models handle better than heavier V6 and 5-cylinder TDI. Also 90bhp 1.9 TDI from January 1995 when 2.5 TDI grew to 140bhp and gained option of six-speed manual gearbox. TDI 2.5 5-cylinder powerful and economical, especially with 6-speed manual gearbox.

What's bad: Expensive dealer servicing and parts. TDI fuelling needs re-setting regularly. TDI timing belt drives water pump and if water pump fails, so does belt. Replacing timing belt is expensive because it's hard to get engine and pump timing exactly right. TDI is front heavy.

What to watch out for: Worn autoboxes. PAS leaks and wear. Serious front tyre wear. Suspension joints. Wheel bearing rumble. Rattling cats, especially on 2.6 V6. Ex-fleet examples may be clocked. Accident damage repaired with non-galvanised panels or with bad welds which can rust. Flexible braided fuel hose of S6 passes over turbo and can eventually start to leak, depositing fuel onto red hot turbo. Needs checking regularly and replacing at the slightest sign of a leak. Check online at www.s-cars.org/Features/BurntS4/burnts4.html for details. Mixed metal corrosion at unions of flexible brake pipes to rear wheels.

Recalls: 1997 (2.8 V6): rumoured recall issued in April concerning driveline. 1997 (built Feb-March 1997): Check front seatbelt top mounting height adjusters. (Built '95–'96): Airbag may inflate while stationary.

80 Cabrio (1992 to 2002)

What's good: Launched 1992 and based on the post 1988 coupe has been very successful. 15ft 9in long by 5ft 9in wide and weighing in from 1,370kg. 5–sped manual or 4-speed automatic gearboxes. Huge engine range began with 133bhp 2,309cc five or 115bhp 2.0 8 valve. 150bhp 2.6 V6 from May 1994, 125bhp 1,8 20v from October 1997, 174bhp 2.8 V6 from May 1996. Optional hard-top. Galvanized rot proof bodies. Nice looking and strong.

What's bad: Suffers some scuttle shake. Back seat not wide enough for three. Lacks rear headroom with the top up and very claustrophobic for kids.

What to watch out for: See 80 and Coupe.

80 Coupe (1988 to 1996)

What's good: Coupe version of galvanized 80 replaced old coupe and famous Quattro coupe. 14ft 5in long by 5ft 8in wide, weighing in from 1,130kg. Complex engine range started with 138bhp 2.2 five. Could also be had as a quattro four wheel drive. 1989 saw

115bhp 2.0 four and 170bhp 2.3 litre 20v five; 1990 saw 220bhp 2.2 turbo S2; 1991 saw 174bhp 2.8 V6 manual or 4-speed auto; 1992 saw 250bhp 2.6 V6 manual or 4-speed auto; S2 got a hike to 230bhp and a six speed gearbox in September 1992.

What's bad: Handling disappointed fans of the original Quattro turbo.

What to watch out for: See 80.

80 Mk II (1991 to 1995)

What's good: Electro-galvanised body shell, hot-dip galvanised underside, so very little chance of rust unless accident damaged. Now 14ft 9in long by 5ft 7in wide and weighing from 1,220kg. Avant estate from September 1992. Has switchable ABS (A4ft s doesn't switch off). Powerful 2.0–litre 16-valve engine. Smooth and punchy 2.6 V6. Economical TDI. All had PAS, folding rear seat and better-shaped boot than previous model. Engine range started with 90bhp or 115bhp 2.0, or 137bhp 2.0 16v, or 174bhp 2.8 V6 which could be had as a quattro; then 150bhp 2.6 V6 and 90bhp TDI from September 1992; then 100bhp 1.6 from September 1993; and 230bhp turbocharged 5-cylinder S2 Avant quattro from January 1993.

What's bad: Franchised dealer service costs. Hard to sell without a sunroof. Tornado red paint oxidises in sunlight.

What to watch out for: Duff catalytic converters. Accident damage repaired with non-galvanised panels. Coolant must be changed every two years, especially on TDI, or head gasket problems can result. Valve stem seals need replacing at 100,000–130,000 miles – earlier if mileage clocked up slowly. Make sure ABS and ABS switch work properly. Rear discs rust first, leading to failed MOT. TDI may be worn out and oil-burning at 150,000 miles.

Recalls: 1997: 50,523 cars recalled due to possibility of 'inadvertent deployment of airbags'.

80/90 Mk 1 (1986 to 1991)

What's good: Electro-galvanised body shell, hot-dip galvanised underside, so very little chance of tin-worm unless accident damaged. Switchable ABS. 14ft 5in long by 5ft 7in wide and weighing from 1,020kg to 1,320kg. Engine range began with 75bhp 1.6 with 5-speed box and 3-speed auto option, up through 75bhp 1.8, 90bhp injected 1.8, 112bhp injected 1.8, 137bhp 16 valve 2.0, 80bhp 1.6TD, 115bhp 2.0 five, 136bhp 2.2 five and 170bhp 20 valve five. Quattro versions also available Powerful 2.0 litre 16-valve engine. Euro Car Parts supplies cheap parts.

What's bad: Getting old now. Strangely-shaped, short, deep boot. Hard to sell without a sunroof. Tornado red paint oxidises in sunlight. Audi replacement autoboxes cost the wrong side of £3,000. BBS Replica alloy wheels on Sport models chip easily, then oxidise.

What to watch out for: Duff catalytic converters, but can be 'de-catted' for £350. Accident damage repaired with non-galvanised panels. Rattly hydraulic tappets due to insufficient oil changes (sump only holds 3 litres). Worn CV joints. Rumbling wheel bearings. Don't buy early cars without PAS. Look for PAS leaks. Rear discs rust first, leading to failed MOT. Valve stem seals may need replacing at 100,000–130,000 miles – earlier if mileage clocked up slowly.

A1 (from late 2002?)

What's good: City car on Lupo/Arosa floorpan to be available with concertina-type electrically folding hard top. Steel and plastic panel construction with overall weight around 800kg. '3 litre' (94 mph) version with 3-cylinder 1.2 litre 61 bhp TDi, or four cylinder 1.0 litre and 1.4 litre petrol engines. Originally due 2002.

What's bad: Will be comparatively expensive in UK, probably from £10,000. May not now happen.

What to watch out for: Too soon to say.

A2 (from 2000)

What's good: High-tech aluminium space-frame constructed 12ft 4in hatchback, with low drag coefficient of 0.28, built to take on the MB A-Class. 12ft 7in long by 6ft 1in wide. 75 bhp 1.4 petrol engine offering a Euromix of 46.31 mpg or a 3-cylinder 1.4 litre 75 bhp, 144 lb ft TDI pump-injector diesel offering a Euromix of 67 mpg and up to 81 mpg touring. Both do 108 mph and 0–60 in 12 seconds, but diesel is more fun to drive. Two-deck rear luggage compartment. Rear seats completely removable. Decent ride quality and steering. High level of grip from tyres. Very comfortable multi-adjustable seats. 1.4 priced from £13,095. TDI arrived January 2001, priced from £14,000. 1.2 litre '3 litre car' which averages 94 mpg, semi-automatic gearbox and 105 bhp 1.4 16v petrol not for UK, but new ultra-economical 100bhp 1.6 FSI petrol engine arrived Spring 2002. Deep sills provide impressive side impact protection. Gained four stars in NCAP crash safety tests. Very trendy among the well heeled. Three year warranty. TDI emits 116g/km CO_2 so qualifies for £80pa VED from April 2002. Achieved an excellent four star rating for crash safety in 2002 NCAP tests.

What's bad: Looks like a chopped-up A6. High rear door sills and sunken footwells do not help access to the back seats for the elderly. Gearchange quality varies a lot. Pre-production gearboxes were noisy, but production RHD examples seem to be fine. 1.4 petrol engine is rorty, needs to be revved for performance and can feel sluggish on the motorway when the car is laden. Emergency spare wheel is an optional extra. Terrible MW and LW radio reception. Non opening bonnet foxes some people (front flap opens for checking fluids and revealing clips which allow bonnet to be lifted off). Quite a few faults emerging. To find out more, check the unofficial Audi A2 bulletin board online at pluto.beseen.com/boardroom/h/51992

What to watch out for: Accident damage and parking dings to alloy body and structure will be expensive to repair, but Audi is setting up six special repair centres for A8s and A2s. Seems to be a problem of turbo failures on the 1.4TDI.

Recalls: 26/2/2001: Air-conditioned A2s built 1/1/2000–31/12/2000 recalled because a/c components may come into contact with starter motor in a collision which could lead to a short circuit and fire.

A3 (1996 to 2001)

What's good: Image, quality, galvanised body. 3-year warranty. 100 bhp 1.6, 125 bhp 1.8, 150 bhp 1.8 Turbo, 200 bhp S3 quattro turbo. First application of Golf Mk IV platform. 13ft 7in long by 6ft wide and from 1,090kg. Front-drive alternative to the BMW Compact. Joint top-of-the-class for secondary safety in NCAP crash testing. 3–door version handles better than Golf Mk IV. 5–door has complemented 3–door from autumn 1999. Three year warranty. Engine range from 100bhp 1.6, through 125bhp 1.8 20v and 150bhp 1.8T to 180bhp 1.8 Quattro Sport. Also 90bhp and 110bhp diesels.

What's bad: Not much room in back whether 3– or 5–door. First tests seemed to indicate that 5–door A3 had lost the handling edge of the 3–door over the Golf Mk IV. Expensive compared to SEAT Leon on same floorpan. Bigger splashguards to overcome wet weather braking problems mean that later S3 brakes don't cool sufficiently under hard use and are not up to the car's performance under repeated heavy braking, for example on a track day (see online at www.sport-3.net).

What to watch out for: Demand a proper Audi dealer service history and evidence that recall work has been carried out. Sometimes bought as 'shopping cars', so be vigilant when checking the flanks for dings. Check for accident damage repaired with non-galvanised panels or with bad welds which can rust. Plastic water pump impellers on early 1.8 20v engines fail. Newer water pumps have metal impellers. Hydraulic connection to rear brake callipers can corrode due to types of metals used.

Recalls: 1997 (built Feb-March 1997): Check front seatbelt top mounting height adjusters. 1998: 2,822 cars recalled due to possible cracks in rear seatbelt brackets. 2000: A3s built Jan-May 1999: front seatbelt buckles may open in a collision. Replacement buckles to be fitted (2,855 cars). A3s built Jan-Dec 1998: seatbelt pretensioner could ignite fabric trim; A3 1.8T built Dec '97–June '98: Accelerator could jam. Official recall A3 Quattro and S3 25/9/2001: On cars built up to March 2000 the bottom rear hub carrier ball joint can corrode and seize, leading to the lower suspension arms snapping at the hub ends. Owners to call Audi Customer Services on 0800

699 888. April 2002: German recall of all A3s with standard ABS (no problem with those with ABS + EDS, ASR, ESP.)

A3 (2001 to late 2003)

What's good: Extensively revised, smoother and better looking A3 3–door and 5–door model for 2001. Engine range, from 103bhp 1.6 petrol up to 225bhp S3 quattro. Prices from £14,605 for base 1.6 3–door to £24,770 for S3 Quattro. 180bhp 1.8T Quattro Sport 5–door comes in at £21,515 and the cheapest diesel is the 3–door TDI 90 at £15,485. All models have Electronic Stability Programme, transponder immobilisers, ultrasonic interior protection and front and front-side airbags. From December 2001, six speed manual TDI PD 130 available with Haldex clutched four-wheel-drive quattro drivetrain at £20,040 for the 3–door and £20,660 for the 5–door. Torque is 229lb ft (310Nm) at 1,900rpm; 0–60 is 8.9 seconds and top speed 126mph, while CO_2 is 162g/km keeping it in the lowest 18% list price bracket for company car BIK tax. Also from December 2001, S3 Quattro benefits from full 225bhp of the TT 225 instead of its previous 210bhp, giving it a 0–60 of 6.5 seconds and a top speed of 151mph, yet the price remains £24,770, while the A3 1.8T Sport is now available with an optional 5-speed Tiptronic automatic gearbox for an extra £1,400.

What's bad: More expensive than Golf and Leon, but carries much more status.

What to watch out for: As previous A3.

Recalls: April 2002: German recall of all A3s with standard ABS (no problem with those with ABS + EDS, ASR, ESP.)

A3 (from 2003)

What's good: New car with family look based on PQ35 floorpan shared with Golf V and Leon II. Family of VAG engines to include 116bhp FSI 1.6, 150bhp FSI 2.0; 185bhp 2.0T, 150bhp TDI and 240bhp 3.2 V6 S3 plus transverse Multitronic transmission optional. Multi-link rear suspension. To be launched at Frankfurt Show in autumn 2003. Estate version in 2004.

What's bad: No 5–door hatchback this time.
What to watch out for: Too soon to say.

A4 (1995 to 2000)

What's good: Handles quite nicely. Good looking, galvanised body. 14ft 8in long by 6ft 1in wide and weighing from 1,195kg. Avant estate from March 1996. Old 150 bhp 2.6 V6 is a nice engine and easily delivers 30 mpg. TDI 90 and TDI 110 deservedly popular, delivering up to 50 mpg driven fairly carefully. 150bhp TDI V6 well liked. Other engines: 100 bhp 1.6, 125 bhp 1.8 20v, 150 bhp 20v Turbo, new 165 bhp 30v 2.4 V6; 193 bhp 2.8 30v V6; 265 bhp S4 Quattro. Comprehensively re-thought in Spring 1999. Got 115 bhp 'Pumpe Duse' TDI option from late 1999. Seventh most reliable car in 2001 Fleet News Survey of 620,000 fleet cars mostly under 3 years old. Limited production 350bhp RS4 marked end of the line.
What's bad: Takes a few days to get used to the steering, seats and over-servoed brakes. Weight of TDI V6 takes edge off handling. Limited market for 1.6s without sunroofs or aircon. Similar expensive front wishbone bush problems as A6 and Passat – eliminated late 1999. Average performance in NCAP crash tests. Heavy salted road spray may make brakes feel spongey. In Germany, deflectors are available FOC to cure this (*Auto Bild* magazine 24/11/2000) and these are coming to the UK. Poor AM radio reception. Last of the line, ultra quick RS4s suffered from 'soft' alloy wheels easily damaged by potholes.
What to watch out for: Rear discs rust first. Rattling catalytic converters (especially on 2.6, which has two costing £650 apiece). Cats also fail on 1.9 TDIs built before August 1998. Quite a few coming off the fleets, so look out for signs of clocking and inadequate maintenance. Look for accident damage repaired with non-galvanised panels or with bad welds. Plastic water pump impellers on early 1.8 20v engines fail. Newer water pumps have metal impellers. Possible oil consumption problem with 30v V6s, so have emissions checked for excessive HCs before buying. Some A4s develop a fault with the immobiliser ignition switch transmission reader coil. Some develop faults with both the reader coil and the

key transponder. If the car comes with two different keys, this is why. Creaks from front suspension indicate wishbone problem: budget for £500–£700 to replace unless carried out under recall programme. Mixed metal corrosion at unions of flexible brake pipes to rear wheels.

Recalls: 1997 (built Feb-March 1997): check front seatbelt top mounting height adjusters. (Built '95–'96): airbag may inflate while stationary. 1998: 4,574 2.4 litre V6 cars built Aug '97–Feb '98: possibility of throttle jamming. 1999: 'S' reg. 2.5 V6 TDIs recalled for brake modification; 2.5 V6 TDIs recalled for major engine modifications. 2000: A4 manuals built July '94–August '95: brake pedal may become loose; A4s built March '98 to August '98: steering ball joints could fail. Also Recall 13A9 vibration damper, Recall 17B4 oil pump and Recall 46C7 brake pads. March 2001: Worldwide recall of 560,000 1999 model year A4s, A6s, A8s and VW Passats to replace steering ball joints (track rod ends). Announced *Auto Bild* 11/3/2001: Wordwide recall of all VW Passats from 1996 to July 2001, Audi A4s from 1994, Audi A6s from 1997 to replace faulty front lower wishbones (this recall is not acknowledged or applied by Audi UK). Recall announced in *Auto Bild* 26/8/2001: The ball joint can fail and the two other flex connections can fail. (These are the long arms that go from the bottom of the front hubs to the body.)

A4 B6 (from 2001)

What's good: Code name B6. Second generation A4 on new platform with classy look about it. More leg and head room. Better ride quality. Better driving environment. Yet similar dimensions to the old A4 at 14ft 8in long by 6ft 1in. Avants arrived autumn 2001 weighing 1,485kg. Engines include a new 130bhp balancer shaft 30 valve 2.0 litre; the old 150bhp 1.8T; a 170bhpe 2.4 V6; a new 220bhp 3.0 V6; a 130bhp 1.9 litre TDI PD; a 155bhp 2.5 litre V6 TDI and a 180bhp V6 TDI for Quattro versions. Five and six speed manual gearboxes. Multitronic automatic option. Promise of a long-lived car which will still have some value left after 5–6 years. Cabrio from Spring 2002 (separate car by car entry). Three year warranty. High equipment levels throughout the range. All new A4s come complete with electronic climate control, abs, ebd, esp and alloy wheels. Excellent Four Star 30 point rating in NCAP occupant protection crash tests. On sale in UK from March 2001. A4 TDI 130PD emits 149g/km CO_2 putting it into the lowest diesel VED bracket of £110pa and also benefiting company car drivers. TDI 130PD to be combined with steering wheel pushbutton change Multitronic CVT transmission which will make this car very quick in traffic. 102bhp 1.6 litre model from September 2001 priced at £17,640. Seventh most reliable car in 2001 Fleet News Survey of 620,000 fleet cars mostly under 3 years old. Range road test at www.honestjohn.co.uk. June 2002 brought small power boost for 1.8T from 150bhp to 163bhp, while standard 155bhp 2.5 TDI V6 also went up to 163bhp.

What's bad: Prices higher than originally anticipated at from £18,640 on the road. Expensive franchised dealer servicing. On Multitronics, the steering wheel pushbutton change system is an extra, so make sure you order it when ordering the car. One report of problems with Multitronic electronics causing bangs when drive or reverse were selected and a low rpm vibration in 5th/6th.

What to watch out for: Steering wheel buttonchangers for Multitronic are an optional extra, so don't automatically assume a Multitronic will have them.

A4 Cabriolet (from July 2002)

What's good: New Audi A4 B6 based Cabriolet in UK from Spring 2002. Looks gorgeous, based on classy new A4 with a choice of 2.4 litre 170bhp or 3.0 litre 220 bhp 30 valve V6 engines. Prices of £24,620 for the 2.4 and £28,170 for the 3.0 Sport. Standard kit includes 16–inch 5–arm Aero alloy wheels with 205/55 R16 tyres, remote central locking activating an alarm with interior microwave protection, electronic climate control, a leather 4–spoke multifunction steering wheel and a Concert stereo with single CD player. An automatic roll-over protection system adds to the extensive list of safety features already fitted to A4 saloon and Avant models. Sport versions gain 17–inch 5–spoke star alloy wheels with 235/45 R17 tyres, sports suspension, a sports leather steering wheel and sports seats with electric lumbar support. The car's four-link front and trapezoidal-link rear suspension has been both lowered and tuned specifically to give a more sporting bias. An increase in body rigidity of 112 per cent compared with the old 80 based Cabriolet also brings benefits both dynamically and in terms of safety. New Cabriolet is more practical than predecessor, offering genuine four seat capability and class leading luggage capacity thanks to a wheelbase which has been extended by 100mm. Electro-hydraulically operated hood with a heated glass rear window is standard.

More online at www.audi.co.uk

What's bad: UK RHD allocation apparently sold out for 2002 (but check with your Audi dealer).

What to watch out for: Paying too much of an 'over' just to get one.

A6 (1997 to 2004)

What's good: Good looking Passat-based Audi, with Audi styled body. 15ft 9in long by 6ft 4in wide, weighing 1,390 to 1,680kg. 2.4 30-valve V6 is a nice, powerful (165–170 bhp) engine. Handling 'soft' but not floaty and grip is quite good. 150 bhp 2.5 V6 TDI available as Quattro. Estate versions. 230 bhp twin-turbo 2.7T and 340 bhp 4.2 V8 S6 launched autumn 1999. V6 TDI upped to 180 bhp in July 2000. Impressive new Multitronic CVT transmission available in UK on 2.4 litre V6s from late summer 2000. Three year warranty. Re-engineered Summer 2001. Multitronic more widely available. TDI PD 130 the most tax-efficient executive company car. Road test of new range at www.honestjohn.co.uk. Awesome 450bhp RS6 versions of its A6 saloon and Avant launched at Geneva Show March 2002 with RHD deliveries set for autumn 2002. 4.2 litre twin-turbo V8 puts out 331kW (450bhp) between 5,700 and 6,400rpm and a massive 560Nm (413 lb ft) torque from 1,950 to 5,600rpm. This is fed through a beefed up 5-speed Tiptronic autobox to the Quattro four-wheel-drive system. Performance figures are quoted at 0–100km (62mph) in 4.7 seconds, so take a couple of points off for the 0–60 time. Top speed electronically limited to 250kph (156mph), but derestricted can do 190 and the sprint to 200kph (125mph) takes just 17.6 seconds. RS6 is first Audi to be equipped with Dynamic Ride Control, which counteracts movements of the vehicle along its longitudinal and transverse axis. When a corner is taken, a flow of oil damping force is generated via the central valve between the diagonally opposed shock absorbers, almost entirely eliminating rolling and pitching. Massive 255/40 R18 tyres are standard with the option of gargantuan 255/35 R 19s. UK prices: RS6 saloon £57,000; RS6 Avant £58,000.

More online at www.audi.co.uk

What's bad: Tiptronic gearbox lever works wrong way round (forward for upshifts, backwards for downshifts). Three-Star NCAP crash test rating. Reports of heavy oil consumption of 2.4 litre V6. ADAC in Germany reported a lot of other problems with A6 generally, including fuel pump, fuel tank, air-mass meter, wheel bearings, front wishbones, air filter, instruments, heated door mirrors and timing belts. Have had reports of repeated electric window failure, driver's side. Franchised dealer servicing can be expensive.

What to watch out for: Audi dealer service history. Accident damage repaired with non-galvanised panels or with bad welds which can rust.

Recalls: A6s built March '98 to August '98: Steering ball joints (track rod ends) could fail. March 2001: Worldwide recall of 560,000 1999 model year A4s, A6s, A8s and VW Passats to replace steering ball joints (track rod ends). Announced *Auto Bild* 11/3/2001.

A8 (1994 to 2004)

What's good: Advanced all-alloy 'ASF' space frame body construction. 16ft 6in long by 6ft 6in wide but weighing just 1,500–1,815kg. Lots of room inside. 300 bhp 4.2 V8 is a high quality, quick, safe, luxurious car. S8 has 360 bhp and gets up to 140 mph very quickly, even when leaving the Tiptronic box to shift itself. Lesser versions are front-drive 174bhp 2.8 V6 and 230 bhp 3.7 V8. 2.8 went 30-valve and got power hike from 174 bhp to 193 bhp in

1996. 3-year warranty. 420 bhp 6.0 litre W12–engined version launched at September 2000 Paris Motor Show. Three year warranty.
What's bad: Body dents easily and is very expensive to repair – requiring a special jig (makes insurance expensive). Ride quality not as luxurious as expected. Hasn't sold very well against competition from Mercedes and BMW. UK did not get V8 TDI.
What to watch out for: Don't confuse a £36,000 2.8 with a £55,000 4.2 Quattro Sport or a £61,000 S8. Mark price down heavily for even the smallest dent or scratch. Quattros must have full Audi dealer servicing history, 2.8s not quite so important.
Recalls: A8s built March '98 to August '98: Steering ball joints could fail. March 2001: Worldwide recall of 560,000 1999 model year A4s, A6s, A8s and VW Passats to replace steering ball joints (track rod ends). Announced *Auto Bild* 11/3/2001.

A8 (from 2003)

What's good: Unveiled July 2002, Audi's new top car with Audi Space frame aluminium body. Launch engines are a 4.2 V8 developing 246 kW (335bhp) at 6,500rpm and 430 Nm torque at 3,500rpm (top speed limited to 155 mph; 0–60 6 seconds); and a 3.7 V8 offering 206 kW (280bhp) at 6,500rpm and 360 Nm torque at 3,750rpm (Top speed 155 mph; 0– 60 in 7 seconds. S8 which follows will have a 6.0 litre 550bhp W12 engine. Also to be a 180bhp 2.5 V6 diesel, a 280bhp 4.0 V8 diesel, a 5.0 V10 diesel and VAG's 220bhp 3.2 petrol V6. Petrol engines to feature Fuel Stratified Injection (petrol direct injection). Gearbox is six-speed Tiptronic with power to all four wheels via the Audi Quattro system. Rides on air suspension. Prices from around £40,000.
   Latest news online at www.audi.co.uk
What's bad: Too soon to say.
What to watch out for: Too soon to say.

Allroad (from 2000)

What's good: A6 Avant based 4x4 with either 180 bhp 2.5 litre TDI V6 or 250 bhp twin-turbo 2.7 litre petrol V6. Choice of 6-speed manual or 5-speed Tiptronic, with low-ratio box available as a factory fit extra on the 6-speed. Height-adjustable suspension lowers for the motorway or raises for the rough, giving as much ground clearance as a Range Rover for serious off-roading. Exhaust system well tucked away. Clever bush fenders on bottoms of doors. Amazingly capable both on the road and off with better visibility than a high bonnet traditional 4x4. Not hugely more expensive than an A6 Avant. Makes a Range Rover look like a horse and cart. Definitely one for the ski set.

What's bad: Tiptronic gearbox lever works wrong way round. Still expensive at £32,550 for the TDI and £36,630 for the 2.7T.

What to watch out for: Check for off-roading damage.

Recalls: Recall 3/9/2001 (879 cars): wipers may become entangled at high speed. Driver's side wiper arm to be replaced with modified arm.

Coupe and Quattro (1982 to 1991)

What's good: Sensational four wheel drive 200bhp turbocharged coupe, launched in Europe in LHD in 1980 and in UK with RHS from 1982. 14ft 5in long by 5ft 8in wide. Wheels and wheel-arches widened from 1984. Engine up from 2,144 to 2,260 in 1987. Power hiked to 220bhp in 1989. Continued alongside new 80 Coupe to April 1991. Meanwhile, normal Audi Coupe ran to October 1987 with front or quattro four wheel drive. Engine range ran from 90bhp 1.8 through 112bhp 1.8, 114bhp 1.9 'five', 130nhp 2.1 'five' and 136bhp 2.2 'five'.

What's bad: Early Quattros got a lot of drivers who expected miracles into trouble. Handling or roadholding was not foolproof, especially on snow and ice. Feels very old-fashioned to drive in comparison with a modern Audi TT Quattro.

What to watch out for: Accident damage. Blown turbos. Howling four wheel drive systems. Be very careful not to waste time going to see a 136bhp Quattro thinking its a Quattro Turbo. Be especially careful not to make this mistake when buying.

TT Coupe and Roadster (1999 on)

What's good: Totally individual shape. No other car looks remotely like it and you either love them or hate them. 13ft 3in long by 6ft 1in wide and 1,475kg. All UK spec cars have Haldex clutched four wheel drive with either 180 bhp or 225 bhp, which is a lot from 1.8 litres. RHD Roadsters arrived early 2000, but lots of grey imports before then. Three year warranty. 225s are very sure footed and great fun to drive on a severely twisting road. You can buy a used LHD two wheel drive German import TT 180 coupe for £14,000 from an import specialist. Revisions from Summer 2002 include 2.0 litre 245bhp engine.

What's bad: A spate of high-speed autobahn accidents led to a German recall for suspension modifications to be made, ESP system and a rear spoiler to be fitted. Some doubt as to whether these accidents were caused by the car, by lack of skill or by a rear suspension joint seizing up. A new hood for the Roadster costs £5,000.

What to watch out for: The car's history. Many are grey imports and it's important to know what you are paying for and pay accordingly. Some doubts as to longevity of the 225 bhp engine. Anything left on the rear parcel shelf could shatter the glass rear window of the Roadster when the hood is electrically lowered. It can't be replaced and means a new hood at £5k.

Recalls: All 2,430 official UK imports recalled to Germany for extensive modifications to be made, including the fitting of ESP stability and traction control and a rear spoiler. Work took several weeks. Owners were supplied with an A4 courtesy car. Source *Auto Express* 16/2/2000. Official recall notice issued 17/4/2000. Official recall 25/9/2001: On cars built up to March 2000 the bottom rear hub carrier ball joint can corrode and seize, leading to the lower suspension arms snapping at the hub ends. Owners to call Audi Customer Services on 0800 699 888.

AUSTIN (ROVER)

Maestro (1983 to 1995)

What's good: Practical size, practical shape, very economical Perkins Prima DI and TDI engines. 2.0 litre MG version by far the best. MG Maestro Turbo a bit of a hooligan. Amazingly, you can still buy 'new' 1.3s, built from CKD kits originally sent to Bulgaria and assembled with RHD and catalytic converters by Ian Yarsley of Parkway Service Station, Ledbury, tel: 01531 632320. (Also in LHD from Lifestyle Garages, Fuengirola, Malaga, Spain, tel: 00 345 952 580 077.)

What's bad: Tin shed construction. 'Red Robbo' build quality. Antediluvian 'A' Series 1.3 litre engine. 1.3s are surprisingly horrible to drive – worse than you would ever have imagined.

What to watch out for: Rust in body seams. Water leaks. Dodgy engine management systems. Oil leaks from all engines. Core plug problems with 1.3. Avoid the MG 1600 Maestro due to hopeless twin-carb set-up. 1600s and 2000s need regular cambelt replacement.

Metro (1980 to 1990)

What's good: Quite tough. Will still drag themselves along when little more than a crumbling shell. MG Metro quite well done and fun to drive. Clever separate double-folding rear seats give good luggage space. Driving position can be adapted to suit six footers. (For Rover K Series Metro, see 'Rover'.)

What's bad: Ugly (apart from MG). Parts-bin stop-gap model – more a tribute to expediency than proper all-new design. Rust badly at the front. Many began their lives with driving schools or as panda cars. Fuel splashes out of low-set filler onto rear n/s tyre. Old now, so pay no more than banger money.

What to watch out for: Rust in front bib, down front wings, in sills, in floorpan, in doors and in all body seams. Look for engine oil leaks from -cylinder head gasket, water leaking from core plugs.

Jumping out of second gear due to selector collar moving down rod. Clonking drive-shafts. Rattling timing chains. Leaking radiators and water pumps. Don't believe that they can do 10,000 miles between oil changes. Some were 'exported' to Jersey then re-registered in UK as a year younger than they really are. The last 1.0 and 1.3 'A' Series 3–door Metros had fuel tank filler directly over the rear wheel instead of in front. For automatics, see Mini.

Mini (1959 to 2000)

What's good: Classic 40-year-old design. Driving position can be adapted to suit six-footers. Outlived the Metro. Lots of specials about, some with Jack Knight 5-speed manual boxes which are good but very noisy. AP autobox works well if the combined engine/gearbox oil is changed every six months without fail. If oil not changed, it can be a disaster. Retro 'Mini Seven' with 1959 style seats and painted cream dashboard launched Spring 2000. Prices cut to from £8,495 on 6/10/2000. JKD 5-speed box was fitted to some John Cooper modified cars and is no noisier than standard (only STRAIGHT CUT 4 or 5 speed boxes are noisier). 'K' reg. Carb plus Cat cars apparently exempt from MOT advanced emissions test. Insurance friendly so can be quite a good first car. Lee temptation to go the Max Power route. (For New Mini, see 'MINI'.)
What's bad: Hard, bouncy ride (Smootharide kit from Alex Moulton helps enormously). Standard cars have just four gears. sited in the engine sump. Noisy drivetrain. Feels gutless. Prone to slipping clutch. Heavy steering on wide 12in wheels, even heavier on 13in sportspack wheels. Driving position feels strange (but is actually quite comfortable). They're so low, winter road salt gets everywhere and they rust badly underneath. Bumpers far too low to be of any use.

Fell foul of EU emissions and safety laws from 2001, so production finally ended in September 2000. S and T platers 7th from bottom in 2001 *Top Gear*/J.D. Power Customer Satisfaction Survey. 3rd Bottom of 100 models for reliability in *Auto Express* 2002 survey. Bottom in 144 car 2002 JD Power/*What Car?* Customer Satisfaction Survey of V and W reg. cars.

What to watch out for: Rust in seams was always a Mini problem. Rust also found in sills, in area in front of the doors, in rear battery box and in rear subframes which can collapse. Doors have been known to develop rust holes in as little as 5 years, but should be covered by warranty. Early 'K reg' carb plus cat didn't work (insist on a new MOT if buying one). Water leaking from core plugs of ancient 'A' Series engine. Oil leaks. Head gasket problems ('mayonnaise' under oil cap may be gone gasket, may be from short runs). Noisy timing chain. Gears jump out of second due to internal selector collar moving down rod. Clonking drive-shafts. Wear on rear trailing arm bushes. Front tie bars can bend. Never buy a Mini without a good look underneath, preferably on a garage hoist. Be careful not to get conned into paying too much. 1990 on cars suffer front suspension sagging – worse as time went on. 1996 on twin point injection cars suffer with failed coolant sensors, like other Rovers.

Recalls: 14/5/99: 5,000 Minis built from August 1999 recalled for rectification of a fault in the braking system causing it to lose fluid. 3/10/2001: Recall of 5,809 Minis from VIN XN134031 to XN169800 built from August 1996 to January 1999. Possibility of rear wheel bearings failing due to water ingress which, if left unchecked, could cause the wheel to detach from the stub axle. Vibration and noise caused will alert most owners long before the wheel falls off, but the cars are being recalled as a precaution.

Montego (1984 to 1995)

What's good: Very sensible, practical estates (7–seat 'Countryman' once quite sought-after). Not bad to drive. Economical Perkins Prima TDI engines. LX models had decent spec, but most lacked power steering. Engines can be long-lived. Diesel or catalysed 2.0 litre only from 1992K. Lots of owners loved the estates and mourn their passing.

What's bad: Rust in body seams. Hit-and-miss build quality of all but the last few years' production. Saloons difficult to re-sell for more than buttons. All are getting old and tired now.

What to watch out for: Cracked plastic bumpers. Fall-apart trim.

Oil/water leaks from -cylinder head gaskets. Cambelts need regular replacement. Valve gear wears on 'O' Series engines (if it's particularly quiet, it's about to give way). Same engine management foibles as Maestro. Petrol Turbo may spell trouble, but may have enjoyed doting enthusiast care. The last saloons went as special orders to taxi fleets and to the MOD, long since auctioned off.

BENTLEY

Arnage (from 1998)

What's good: BMW's relatively small but powerful 350 bhp/420 lb. ft. twin-turbo 4,398cc V8 engine and 5-speed auto in a very British body 17ft 8in long by 7ft 1in wide. Optional 'Red Label' 6,750cc Cosworth V8 from Turbo RT offers 400 bhp and walloping 619 lb ft torque with tougher GM 4-speed autobox.

What's bad: Doomed wedding between Rolls Royce and BMW before VW turned up like Dustin Hoffman in 'The Graduate' and whipped the bride away. Values drop like a spanner down a lift-shaft. Power characteristics of twin turbo BMW V8 disliked by traditionalist customers.

What to watch out for: Thinking you want one, when it probably isn't a very good idea at all.

Recalls: 1999: possible wiring fault in heated seat circuit. 22/3/2000: fuel return pipe may be routed too close to exhaust manifold which could lead to fuel igniting. Routing of pipe on 64 cars to be checked and modified if necessary. 8/2/2001: Recall of Arnage Red Label because engine compartment flexible fuel hoses between engine and pipes back to fuel tank may leak and fuel may ignite. To be replaced with pipes of higher specification.

Arnage T 450bhp

What's good: The 450bhp, 168mph Arnage T was, at the time, Bentley's most powerful car in history. Was the result of a three year project to re-engineer the Arnage saloon from bumper to bumper. Beneath its updated, but still familiar 17ft 8in long body lies what is in many respects a new car. The engine produces 450bhp (336kW) and 645lb ft (875Nm) of torque. Top speed 168mph (270kph), 0–60mph in 5.5 sec (0–100kph in 5.8 sec). This has meant a total redesign of 6.75–litre V8 engine with minimal component carry over, twin turbochargers and Bosch engine management. Over 50% is all new and of the remainder, over 80%

has been re-engineered. New engine fully compliant with global emissions legislation to 2004. Body monocoque has been extensively re-engineered to give dramatic improvements in torsional rigidity and therefore ride and handling. New computer controlled sports suspension transforms handling while further enhancing ride quality.

What's bad: Likely to be thirsty.

What to watch out for: Too soon to say.

Continental R and T (from 1991)

What's good: Massive Bentley coupes 17ft 6in long by 6ft 9in wide. 400bhp turbocharged V8s, and 420bhp from March 1999. Four speed autoboxes. Not as intimidating to drive as you'd think.

What's bad: Handling not up to standards of a Jaguar XJR or Mercedes S Class.

What to watch out for: Not for me to say.

Mulsanne, Eight and Turbo

What's good: Image. Huge performance from Turbo versions. Stiffer suspension than Rolls Royce. Best colours: metallic bottle green or ink black. 17ft 3in long by 6ft 2in wide and weighing from 2,245kg. Gradually improved over the years with injection and ABS in October 1986, automatic ride control in 1987, four- rather then three-speed autobox in September 1991. Cats came in during June 1990, but were initially a no-cost option. Standard Brooklands has 226 bhp and 340 ft lb torque. Continental R had 385 bhp and 553 ft. lbs torque. Turbo RT from 1997 has all of 400 bhp and 580 ft. lb torque. Continental T has a truly awesome 420 bhp, no less than 619 ft lb torque, and handles its power and bulk very well.

What's bad: Thirst. Stink of cigar smoke clings to the headlining. The Labour Government might ban them. Resentful drivers don't let you out of side roads, particularly during recessions. Apt to get vandalised with rusty nails or keys while parked. Trim choice may be in bad taste. White or cream paint is hideous and suitable only for wedding hire.

What to watch out for: Anything over £15,000 must have a proper Rolls Royce dealer or Rolls Royce specialist history. The engine is an old fashioned pushrod V8, so you don't want to hear ticking tappets or see any blue smoke from the exhaust pipe. Make sure the suspension is not unduly wallowy. Check expensive tyres for tread depth and uneven wear. With so much weight to stop, turbos can be heavy on their brakes, so check for signs of warp on your test drive. Best to have the car inspected by a different Rolls Royce specialist from the one who's selling it.

Recalls: 1997 (Rolls/Bentley general): 29 LHD cars found to have potentially defective braking system.

W12 GT coupe (from late 2003)

What's good: To be Crewe built with twin-turbo VAG 6.0 litre W12 engines developed in the Phaeton and stillborn W12 sports car. Up to 550bhp and 750lb ft torque. Quattro four wheel drive system and six-speed autobox from new Audi A8. To be capable of around 195 mph and 0–60 in under 5 seconds. To be priced around £100,000, launched Frankfurt Motor Show September 2003. Don't be surprised to see our cultural ambassador Jeremy Clarkson taking delivery of one.

What's bad: Too soon to say.

What to watch out for: Too soon to say.

BMW

1 Series (from 2004)

What's good: New small BMW with rear wheel drive, due for launch at Frankfurt Show in autumn 2003 to rival new Audi A3. 13ft 8in long by 5ft 7in wide. Will be 3 and 5 door hatchbacks. Already seen as CS1 convertible concept. Apparently to have 1.6 to 2.4 litre 4 cylinder engines with up to 250bhp.

What's bad: Too soon to say.

What to watch out for: Too soon to say.

3-Series E30 (1983 to 1991)

What's good: Nice looking. Replaced shark nose E21 3 Series. 14ft 2in long by 5ft 5in wide and weighing 990kg to 1,235kg. 316i has 90bhp 1.8, 318i had 105bhp to 115bhp 1.8, 318iS has 136bhp twin cam 16 valve 1.8; 320i had 125bhp to 129bhp six, 325i had 270bhp six, M3 had 200bhp 2.3 lite twin cam 16 valve four. No compulsory cats in the UK. 318iS, 320i, 325i and M3 still good to drive. Some galvanised panels from 1988. American spec 325i auto only car I've ever driven with more than 1,000,000 miles on the clock and it still ran to 6,000 rpm with no trouble. 136 bhp chain-cam 16v M42 powered 318iS is already achieving minor classic status. But M3 is the true classic. Convertibles carried on for a few more years alongside new E36.

What's bad: Getting old now. 316 and 318 relatively slow and over-rated. Many drivers not ready for oversteer, especially in the wet. No room in the back of two-door versions with big front seats. All models apart from 318iS and M3 had timing belts which need to be replaced every 3 years or 36,000 miles without fail. Official replacement parts for BMWs over 10 years old are being phased out from April 2002.

What to watch out for: Clocking. Rust in early cars. Make sure cambelts and tensioners were recently changed. Cylinder head studs of 6-cylinder engines can shear. Heads of 6-cylinder cars can also crack. Prime candidate for fully synthetic oil, but if the engine is old don't suddenly switch to synthetic. Check for repaired accident damage. Most convertibles have been 'customised' in questionable taste. Some nice, obviously well cared for M3s are coming over from Germany – and M3s are all LHD anyway. (It's very hard to find a genuine old 3–Series these days.)

Recalls: 1998: 170,000 E30s recalled because radiator cap pressure valve may seize up and over-pressurise cooling system, leading to coolant leak and steaming up inside car

3-Series E36 (1991 to 1998)

What's good: The 3–Series that really made big money for BMW. 14ft 7in long by 5ft 7in wide and weighing 1,190kg to 1,385kg. Engine line up: 316i 102bhp 1.6; 318i 115bhp 1.8; 318iS 140bhp twin cam 16v 1.8; 320i 150bhp 2.0 litre six; 323i 170bhp 2.5 litre six; 325i 192 bhp 2.5 litre six; 328i 193bhp 2.8 litre six; S50 B29 M3 286bhp 3.0 litre six; S50 B32 321bhp 3.2 litre six; 318TDS 90bhp 1.7 litre diesel; 325TD 115bhp 2.5 litre diesel; 325TDS 143bhp 2.5 litre diesel. Coupes from April 1992, convertibles from May 1994, Touring estates from Jan 1997. 323i is a strong performer also capable of delivering excellent mid-30s mpg. 6-cylinder cars have brilliant brakes. 140 bhp 318iS coupe and run-out special 318iS saloon (offered for just one month in 1998) by far the best 4-cylinder cars. Impressive build quality. Older iron block chain cam 325 twin-cam longest-lived of all. Generally reliable. All engines had timing chains from 1994. E36 Convertible carried on alongside E46 until May 2000. BMW, Toyota and Ford jointly suffered the fewest breakdowns attended by German ADAC during 2001. BMW had sixth lowest average cost in warranty claims for cars up to 10 years old in 2002 Warranty Direct index, check online at www.performanceindex.co.uk

What's bad: Average performance in NCAP crash tests. 4-cylinder disc/drum set ups nothing like as good as 6-cylinder's discs (318iS 1.9s had discs all round). 316i and 318i saloons over-rated, under powered and pretty ordinary to drive. M40 8-valve four-cylinder engines had timing belts up to September 1993. M43 four cylinder engines from 1994 model year had chains. Some M52 6-cylinder 320is, 323is and 328is have suffered premature bore wear. Early E36s suffered poor quality trim. Later 3 year warranty requires expensive top-up to be comprehensive. Thriving trade in M Tech body parts is leading to many front spoilers being stolen. Just six fastenings hold it on. Quentin Willson talked prices up on Channel 5 'Driven' programme, so early E36s are no longer the bargains they once were.

What to watch out for: Clocked mega mile ex-fleet cars (not all fleets registered their mileages on disposal). Lots of early E36 3–Series suffered premature dashboard failure, so mileage on the clock may not be the mileage on the car. Service light indicator can easily be re-set with a £30 tool, so a paid invoice is the only guarantee of a recent service. Earlier 4-cylinder cars still had cambelts which need changing every 3 years or 36,000 miles. Kerbed alloys may indicate front suspension damage from uncaring company driver. Lift carpets to check for result of rainwater leaks through screen seals (condensation inside windows a sure sign of this). M52–engined 320i from December 1994, 323i from May 1995 and 328i from April 1995 may suffer premature bore wear due to high amounts of sulphur in some UK petrol. Solved by replacement block with steel-lined bores. Front suspension lower ball joints and inner bushes wear, but are comparatively cheap to replace. A full BMW-dealer service history should tell you all recall work has been carried out. Check took kit is all there.

Recalls: 1997 (E36 from January 1996): tighten stub axle bolts. 1997 (E36 built Feb '91–Dec '94: 77,000 cars): possibility of corroded steering shafts. 1997 (M3): faulty bearings in Variable Valve Timing mechanism can deposit shards of metal in engine. Official recall. 400 cars affected. 1998: E36s built before Nov '94 recalled to fit new radiator cap. 26/2/2001: All E36 3 Series Jan 1991 to Dec 1998 recalled because corrosion may weaken the lower steering shaft over time. To be inspected, replacements only made if corrosion has set in.

3-Series E36 Compact (1994 to 2001)

What's good: As E36, but lighter and therefore quicker. 13ft 10in long by 5ft 7in wide and weighing 1,215 to 1,400kg. 102bhp 1.6 (replaced by 105bhp 1.9 from January 1999), 90bhp 1.7 diesel, and 140bhp 1.9 litre twin-cam 318Ti quickest of all. No RHD sixes or 'M' versions in the UK so drivers less likely to be branded as status seekers. 17th from top in 'R' reg. J.D. Power Customer Satisfaction Survey. BMW, Toyota and Ford jointly suffered the fewest breakdowns attended by German ADAC during 2001. BMW had sixth lowest average cost in warranty claims for cars up to 10 years old in 2002 Warranty Direct index

What's bad: As E36. Has simpler rear suspension based on E30 3–Series. Six-cylinder 323i engine available in LHD only. Later 2nd and 3rd year dealer warranty requires expensive top up to be effective.

What to watch out for: As E36.

Recalls: 1997 (E36 from January 1996): tighten stub axle bolts. 1997 (E36–77,000 cars): possibility of corroded steering shafts. 1998: compacts built before Nov '94 recalled to fit new radiator cap (very few cars involved, as Compact not launched until Sept '94).

3-Series E46 (from 1998)

What's good: Fairly close to perfection. More comfortable and refined than E36.14ft 8in long by 5ft 8in wide and weighing 1,360kg to 1,500kg. Good body control. 'Cornering Brake Control' makes it very safe. Up to 193 bhp in standard range at 1998 launch, but progressive update programme meant that 328i was replaced by 231 bhp 330i in UK in July 2000. All have steel bore liners eliminating problems of previous Nickasil-lined all-alloy blocks. Same 2.0 litre direct injected diesel as Rover 75, initially with 136 bhp instead of Rover's 116 bhp, later raised to 150bhp (see below). Excellent secondary safety features. 2–door CI version arrived in spring 1999; Touring in autumn 1999; 325i cabrio in spring 2000. Cabrio has very little 'scuttle shake'. 184 bhp 330D was rated by Stephen Sutcliffe of *Autocar* in 2000 as "the best 3–Series, period": offered the best combination of performance, handling and fuel economy in the business (top speed 143 mph, as timed by French police near Montpellier with Jenson Button driving). 2–door M3 boasts 340 bhp and is great fun to drive with the traction control turned off. Almost as quick on a twisting road as a Mitsubishi Lancer EVO V1. Suspension and steering improvements from April 2001 build (steering lock to lock reduced from 3.2 to 2.9 turns). 320 gained new 170bhp 2,171cc six in September 2000. Facelift September 2001 with upswept rather than downswept front indicator lenses. Underpowered 1.9 litre engine of 318i saloon replaced by new British built 143bhp 2.0 litre NG4 unit as from September 2001 facelift. This engine is also more economical with lower CO_2 emissions of 175g/km making it a better proposition for company car drivers. Air-conditioning standard across range from September 2001 facelift, plus sharper steering and uprated suspension for coupes. Facelift 320D got a power boost from 136bhp to 150bhp, with a more serious torque hike from 207 lb ft (280Nm) to 243lb ft (330Nm) at 2,000rpm. combined fuel consumption improved to an excellent 51.4mpg and CO_2 emissions are just 148g/km qualifying the car for £110pa VED and low BIK tax for company drivers. UK prices start at £21,415 including standard air-conditioning and insurance is Group 13E. Improved unlimited mileage two year full manufacturer warranty followed by one year full dealer warranty from November 2001, making total three year unlimited mileage warranty. BMW 3–Series was fifth most reliable car in 2001 Fleet News Survey of 620,000 fleet cars mostly under 3 years old. Good three star score in 2001 NCAP crash tests, but criticised for lack of a third rear lap/diagonal seatbelt. E46 316i saloon and Touring models re-launched April 2002 with same UK built N42 1,796cc 115bhp Valvetronic engine as the new Compact. New engine offers 175Nm torque, 0–60 in 10.6 seconds, a top speed of 128 mph, combined consumption of 39.8mpg and CO_2 emissions of 172g/km with the manual box. Touring is a bit slower and thirstier with 0–60 in 10.9 seconds, top speed 125mph, combined consumption 38.7 and CO_2 emissions 177g/km. List prices are: £18,450 and £19,470 for the SE. Automatics are £19,685 and £20,705 for the SE. The Touring only comes as an SE and prices are £20,440 for the manual; £21,675 for the automatic. ABI Insurance group is 12E for all. BMW, Toyota and Ford jointly suffered the fewest breakdowns attended by German ADAC during 2001. E46 voted 7th equal from Top in 144 car 2002 JD Power/*What Car?* Customer Satisfaction Survey of V and W reg. cars. BMW had sixth lowest average cost in warranty claims for cars up to 10 years old in 2002 Warranty Direct index

More online at www.bmw.co.uk

What's bad: Lacks character and visual impact of Alfa 156. Performance and driving pleasure slightly blunted compared to the best E36s. Cornering brake control on early E46s could take over, but does make car safer in unskilled hands when a corner tightens up unexpectedly. Heavier, so uses more fuel than E36. Much criticism of poor-quality conversion to RHD of early E46s. Now reports of harmonic vibrations through steering and floor of 330i. Side repeater indicators pop out and damage the front wings. Pre-November 2001 3 year warranty required expensive top up to be comprehensive in 2nd and 3rd years. Reports of a thermostat problem with 318i models; replacement parts on back order as much as 7 weeks so cars were being run without thermostat cores which meant no climate control. Heater fan resistors can fail leaving fan only running at full speed but BMW aware of this and will meet cost even though not covered by 2nd and 3rd year standard dealer warranty. Steptronic auto increases fuel consumption of 330D by around 25%. Supply problem in Autumn 2001 due to strike in South Africa from which a proportion of RHD UK market 3–Series are sourced. In Summer 2002 new M3 convertibles were selling at a £5,000 premium.

What to watch out for: Build date now shown on engine compartment label on top of front nearside wheelarch. First year's RHD production was sold out and some people paid premiums to get cars. This was not reflected in used values. Original 316 and 118bhp 318 not powerful enough. (318 cured with 143bhp from September 2001 facelift; 316i got new 115bhp engine from April 2002.) Make sure the electric engine radiator fan works. Even it does, a previous failure could have resulted in head gasket failure so check for the usual signs of this such as emulsified oil under the oil filler cap. Note that production of 316i was stopped between

Summer 2001 and Spring 2002. Any cars bought between those dates would have the OLD engine. Reports of blown turbos on 530Ds may also apply to 330Ds.

Recalls: 1999 (E46 from April 1998): safety recall over failure of brake pedal clip which can allow the pedal to become disconnected, and over-sensitive side airbag trigger switches. 15/12/1999: (E46 built Sept/Oct 1999): brake light switch may fail leading to brake lights flickering or failing and switch overheating. New switches to be fitted. 1/8/2001: 1659 E46s built 1/2/2001–18/5/2001 recalled because fault with radiator fan motor could lead electrics to overload and fan motor to fail. 3/11/2000: 887 E46 models with alloy wheels built 4/9/2000–7/10/2000 recalled because inside rims of wheel could have been damaged when tyres were fitted. 9/11/2001: Cars built 28/9/2001 to 24/10/2001 with Continental tyres may have cuts in the tyres which can lead to blowouts. w/e 23/2/2002: recall in German for all models fitted with Conti Eco Contact and Sport Contact 205/55 R16 and 225/55 R16 tyres due to a pressure problem.

3-Series E46 Compact (from 2001)

What's good: As E46, but slightly lighter and therefore a bit quicker with really good handling. 14ft long by 5ft 9in wide; weighing 1,300 to 1,430kg. Launch engines ranged from 116bhp 1.8 NG (badged 316ti) with 133lb ft torque giving EU combined economy of 40.9 mpg and 2.5 litre 192bhp '325ti' giving combined economy of 31.7mpg. 143bhp 2.0 litre NG engine (badged 318ti), 105bhp 1.6 litre and 150bhp 2.0 litre diesel arrived late 2001. Diesel is fantastic with 330Nm torque (248 lb ft), 9 second 0–60, 133mph top speed, 51.8mpg combined and just 148g/km CO_2. Will eventually be a 220bhp version of the new 2.0 litre four cylinder NG engine. Improved unlimited mileage two year full manufacturer warranty followed by one year full dealer warranty from November 2001, making total three year unlimited mileage warranty.

What's bad: Expensive for a small 3–door hatchback.

What to watch out for: Build date shown on engine compartment label on top of front nearside wheelarch. Otherwise too soon to say.

Recalls: 9/11/2001: Cars built 28/9/2001 to 24/10/2001 with Continental tyres may have cuts in the tyres which can lead to blowouts. w/e 23/2/2002: recall in Germany for all models fitted with Conti Eco Contact and Sport Contact 205/55 R16 and 225/55 R16 tyres due to a pressure problem.

5 Series E28 (1982 to 1987)

What's good: Square rigged four door saloons 15ft 2in long by 5ft 6in wide weighing 1,240kg to 1,430kg. 5-speed manual or 3-speed auto to September 1983. 4-speed auto available from then. Engines: 90bhp 1.8 four (hiked to 105bhp in Jan 1985); 125bhp 2.0 six; 129bhp 2.7 six '525E'; 150bhp 2.5 six; 184bhp 2.8 six; 218bhp 3.4 six '535i' and 'M535ft ; 286bhp 3.5 twin chain cam six 'M5ft .

What's bad: All apart from M5 had timing belt engines and the belts only safely last 3–4 years or 30,000–40,000 miles. Old cars now, not many left. Lots were modded up towards the ends of their lives, not always in the best possible taste.

What to watch out for: Rust, old car problems, when was timing belt last replaced?

5-Series E34 (1987 to 1996)

What's good: A very good looking car when launched. Replaced square rigged E28 model. Decent quality. Good looks. Good ride and handling. 15ft 6in long by 5ft 9in wide; weighs 1,330kg to 1,530kg. Originally offered with 115bhp 1.8 four, 129bhp single cam 2.0 M20 six, 170bhp single cam 2.5 M30 six, 188bhp single cam 3.0 M30 six or 211bhp 3.4 single cam E28 six. Important engine changes in 1990 when M50 twin chain cam iron block sixes replaced old belt cammers: 520i got 150bhp, 525i got 192bhp and 5-speed autoboxes. 3.0 and 3.5 gradually dropped. 315bhp 3,535cc twin chain cam S38 M5 six from 1989. E34 5–Series did not get the sometimes troublesome M52 alloy block six. Touring model is a practical estate car. IX denoted four wheel drive. 218bhp M60 530iV8 and 286bhp M60 540iV8 from Jan 1993 with optional six speed manual box from May 1994. 340bhp 3.8 litre S38 B39 M5 from Jan 1993 the top performer. 115bhp TD and 143bhp TDS iron block M51 2.5 litre diesels introduced July 1993. BMW, Toyota and Ford jointly suffered the fewest breakdowns attended by German ADAC during 2001. No M52 six cylinder bore wear problems as all E34s were fitted with M50 iron block sixes. BMW had sixth lowest average cost in warranty claims for cars up to 10 years old in 2002 Warranty Direct index

What's bad: Premature bore wear in 'M60ft 530i and 540i V8s from 1993 on. Low inertia 4-cylinder 518i ok in town, but not strong enough for heavy motorway use and can wear rapidly. Old single cam 525i, 530i and 535i engines all need cambelt replacement every 3 years or 36,000 miles. 5-speed auto not liked by autobox specialists. Dashboard printed circuit apt to break down and send the display haywire. Costs £400 to replace. From April 2002 BMW started to phase out production of official replacement parts for cars over 10 years old.

What to watch out for: Electronically 'corrected' odometer/on-board computer (clockers sometimes steal one of the chips). Make sure dash display all functioning, as new printed circuit costs £400. Accident damage. Electric window problems. Faked service indicator. Whining manual gearbox can last for years but expensive to fix. Slurry autoboxes with neglected ATF and filter changes. Accident damage to M5s. Earlier model, less powerful, imported LHD M5s. Smoke from worn valve stem seals. Overheating from cracked cylinder heads on older 6-cylinder 12 valve engines. Cylinder head studs of 12 valve engines can shear. 'Problem' M60 V8s. Duff catalytic converters. Smoking 1.8s (valve stem seals). Noisy 12-valve sixes. Misfires from faulty integrated coil units on later 24v. Rear subframe rubbers (MOT failure point – £200 to put right). Damage to front suspension and steering (look for uneven tyre wear). Duff ABS. Service light indicator can easily be re-set, so a paid invoice is the only guarantee of a recent service. Check tool kit is all there.

Recalls: 1998: 5s built 1988–Nov '94 recalled to fit new radiator cap.

5-Series E39 (1996 to 2003)

What's good: Great looks. 528i provides huge feelgood factor. Decent economy from 528i and 523i. 15ft 8in long by 5ft 11in wide; weighs 1,485 to 1,690kg. Petrol V8s overkill, but 4,398cc M62 540i can be had with six-speed manual. Top model is 5.0 litre 32-valve 400 bhp M5. Engine line-up began with M52 150bhp 2.0 six, M52 170bhp 2.5 '523i' six and M52 193bhp 2.8 six. Also old M51 149bhp iron block diesel six, M62 235bhp 3.5 V8 and M62 286bhp 4.0 V8. Steel bore liner M52 EU3 engines introduced for 520i, 523i and 528i in September 1998. M57 direct injected 184bhp 3.0D six diesel also introduced September 1998. Facelift September 2000 with clear lens headlights saw more engine changes: 170bhp 2,171 cc replace 2.0 six in 520i; 523i became 525i, now with 192bhp; 528i replaces by M52 EU3 530 six with 231bhp; smaller 163bhp direct injected 525d introduced. Four Star NCAP crash test rating, but worst in group for pedestrian safety. Quiet, refined, powerful 184 bhp 3.0 litre diesel automatic from Spring 1999 the best car in the range. New 163 bhp 525D arrived September/November 2000 along with new 170bhp 2.2 litre to replace 150bhp 2.0 litre and 192bhp 2.5 litre petrol engines, made in the UK. 18th from top in 'R' reg. J.D. Power Customer Satisfaction Survey. S and T reg. cars came 9th in 2001 *Top Gear*/JD Power Customer Satisfaction Survey. Not due to be replaced by new E60 5–Series until 2003. Improved unlimited mileage two year full manufacturer warranty followed by one year full dealer warranty from November 2001, making total three year unlimited mileage warranty. BMW, Toyota and Ford jointly suffered the fewest breakdowns attended by German ADAC during 2001. 5th Top in 144 car 2002 JD Power/*What Car?* Customer Satisfaction Survey of V and W reg. cars so seems to be improving. BMW had sixth lowest average cost in warranty claims for cars up to 10 years old in 2002 Warranty Direct index

What's bad: Have been some quibbles about build quality and paint. Dodgy door seals. Lots of electrical niggles reported, including faults with ventilation and air-conditioning system, airbags, park distance control. Engine gasket leaks. Wipers set for LHD. Old 2.5 litre diesel not significantly more economical than petrol, so best avoided. V8s not worth the extra. 2.8iSE and newer

3.0iSE is as far as you need to go. Franchised dealers know how to charge. Pre-November 2001 3 year warranty required expensive top up to be comprehensive in 2nd and 3rd years. Problem with combined navigation and telephone system of facelift 5–Series. The phones don't work and owners are being issued with hand mobiles until the fault can be corrected.

What to watch out for: Build date from 2001 shown on engine compartment label on top of front nearside wheelarch. Repaired accident damage. Excessively high franchised dealer prices for over-specified cars. M52 520i six 523i six, 528i six to September 1998 may suffer premature bore wear due to high amounts of sulphur in some UK petrol. Solved by replacement block with steel-lined bores on sixes. Production from September 1998 fitted with 'EU3ft steel-lined bores. (No such problems with newer 525i and 530i six cylinder engines, and no problems with M62 V8s in the E39) Check took kit is all there. Service light indicator can easily be re-set, so a paid invoice is the only guarantee of a recent service. Reports of blown turbos on 530Ds.

Recalls: 15/12/1999: (E39 built Sept/Oct 1999): brake light switch may fail leading to brake lights flickering or failing and switch overheating. New switches to be fitted. 9/11/2001: Cars built 28/9/2001 to 24/10/2001 with Continental tyres may have cuts in the tyres which can lead to blowouts. 16/11/2001: 5–Series diesels and V8s built 11/11/2000–30/9/2001 recalled because fault with radiator fan motor could lead electrics to overload, fan motor to fail and a small electrical fire to result. w/e 23/2/2002: recall in German for all models fitted with Conti Eco Contact and Sport Contact 205/55 R16 and 225/55 R16 tyres due to a pressure problem.

5-Series E60 (late 2003 on)

What's good: First spy pictures starting to appear of the new Five. Looks like a smaller new 7 Series. To be launched at Frankfurt Show in autumn 2003. Improved unlimited mileage two year full manufacturer warranty followed by one year full dealer warranty from November 2001, making total three year unlimited mileage warranty. Expect upgraded 218bhp 3.0 diesel engine from launch (see 7 Series). Blue car is E60 M5 with different front end from lesser E60s.

What's bad: Far too soon to say.

What to watch out for: Far too soon to say.

6-Series (from Spring 2003)

What's good: New coupe and convertible to compete with Mercedes SL. Styling cues as new 7–Series and forthcoming 5–Series. Prices to kick off at around £40,000 for 231bhp 630CI six, but rise steeply via 635CI V8 and 645CI V8 to a 200mph M6.

What's bad: Too soon to say.

What to watch out for: Too soon to say.

6-Series E24 (1982 to 1989)

What's good: Handsome four seater coupe launched June 1982 with 184bhp 2,788cc six or 220bhp 3,430cc six. 5-speed manual or 3-speed automatic boxes. 15ft 7in long, 5ft 8in wide and quite heavy at 1,460–1,490kg. 4-speed auto from September 1982 on 628 and January 1984 on 635. 286bhp M635 CSi from January 1985 with five speed manual box only. That's obviously the one to have and good ones are now appreciating strongly.

What's bad: They rust, tyres are hard to get and autoboxes can give up the struggle.

What to watch out for: Mainly rust. Take a magnet. If you're spending big money on an M635 CSi, then get an expert on them to check it out carefully. £250 to him could save you £10,000 of grief.

7-Series (From February 2002)

What's good: All new 7 Series with new 'iDrive' dashboard ergonomics which separate the cabin into a 'comfort area' and a 'driving area'. Most secondary functions are operated by a single central controller and the result is a big reduction in the number of buttons and switches. A central monitor displays the various functions and chosen settings. All the controls in the 'comfort area' of the car can be operated by either driver or front seat passenger. Gear selection of new six-speed automatic is controlled via a steering column stalk plus Steptronic buttons on the steering wheel rim. The ignition switch is controlled by a new electronic key and the engine is started and stopped by a button, like that of the Renault Laguna II. Launch choice of two V8s: a 272bhp 3.6 with 256 lb ft (360Nm) torque, or a 333bhp 4.4 with 332 lb ft (450Nm) torque. Combining VANOS variable valve timing with new Valvetronic technology and variable intake manifolding improves both power output and economy. Combined fuel consumption for the new 735i is 26.4mpg and for the 745i is 25.9mpg. Both cars are speed limited to 155mph with the 735i getting to sixty in 7.3 seconds and the 745i managing it in 6.1 seconds. Other engines to include new 3.0 straight six and diesel in 2003 and a top of the range 6.0 litre 400bhp V12 in late 2002. Prices are £52,750 for 735i and £56,950 for 745i. A one-off fee of £500 covers servicing and maintenance for the first 5 years or 75,000 miles. Price includes engine oil and filters, wiper blades, brake pads and discs, spark plugs, air filters, cabin filter, brake fluid and coolant. Improved unlimited mileage two year full manufacturer warranty followed by one year full dealer warranty, making total three year unlimited mileage warranty. Drives and handles well. 218bhp six-speed automatic 730D due in UK March 2003. Offers useful 500Nm (369lb ft) torque between relatively high 2,000–2,750rpm, 146mph top speed and 7.7 second 0–60mph, so is quicker than Mercedes S320 CDI.

More online at www.bmw.co.uk

What's bad: Its looks won't be to everyone's taste at first, but will probably grow on people. A lot of work is required to learn and adapt to the car's systems.

What to watch out for: Build date shown on engine compartment label on top of front nearside wheelarch. Otherwise too soon to say.

7-Series E32 (1987 to 1994)

What's good: Big BMW 16ft 1in long by 6ft 1in wide, weighing 1,570kg to 1,610kg. Engines: 197bhp M30 belt-cam 2,986cc six;

220bhp M3 belt-cam 3,430cc six; 300bhp M70 4,988cc V12. Then, from September 1992, 218bhp M60 2,997cc V8 and 286bhp M60 3,982cc V8. High-mileage six-cylinder 730i and 735iSE can be real bargains. Parts prices quite reasonable. Very luxurious. BMW, Toyota and Ford jointly suffered the fewest breakdowns attended by German ADAC during 2001. BMW had sixth lowest average cost in warranty claims for cars up to 10 years old in 2002 Warranty Direct index

What's bad: V12 750 guzzles fuel. V8s may suffer bore liner degradation and use oil. From April 2002 BMW started to phase out production of official replacement parts for cars over 10 years old.

What to watch out for: Avoid lower spec trim unless you like cloth interiors. Aircon system problems. Bore liner degradation in aluminium V8s. Electrical glitches. Check the on-board computer carefully (see 5–Series). Make sure the heater fan works on all speeds because replacing the resistors involved removing the dash which is a TWO DAY job. Suspension sags eventually. Make sure the ABS light goes on, then off, at the right time. Try to find one with BMW service history; if not consistent specialist history.

Recalls: 1998: 7s built 1988–Nov '94 recalled to fit new radiator cap.

7-Series E38 (1994 to 2001)

What's good: More 'modern' looking than predecessor. A bit bigger (16ft 4in long by 6ft 1in wide, but a lot heavier at 1,915kg for 740i. 193bhp 728i capable of 28–30 mpg. Better ride. Luxurious and capable. V8s re-engined in early 1996. 238bhp M62 3,498cc 735i replaced 218bhp 2,997cc M60 730i and 286bhp M62 4,398cc 740i replaced 286bhp 3,592cc M60 740i (same power output, more torque). 326bhp M73 5,379cc 750 V12. 7–Series was 15th from top in 'R' reg. J.D. Power Customer Satisfaction Survey (but well below Jaguar XJ8). S and T reg. cars came fourth in 2001 *Top Gear*/JD Power Customer Satisfaction Survey. BMW, Toyota and Ford jointly suffered the fewest breakdowns attended by German ADAC during 2001. BMW had sixth lowest average cost in warranty claims for cars up to 10 years old in 2002 Warranty Direct index

What's bad: Not a big improvement on 6 cylinder predecessors. Premature bore wear can be a problem on the earlier M60 V8 engines and the M52 2.8 six. Heavy tyre wear. Pre-November 2001 3 year warranty required expensive top up to be comprehensive in 2nd and 3rd years.

What to watch out for: Build date from 2001 shown on engine compartment label on top of front nearside wheelarch. Be very wary of M60 730i and 3,982cc 740i V8s (the engines that were dropped in 1996). Some unsold 'P' platers still had the old engines. 728i may also suffer bore liner degradation. Check all electrics, computer (see 5–Series) and aircon system carefully. Check for duff cats, condensation corroded rear silencers from chauffeured cars. Chauffeured cars also most likely to suffer premature bore wear due to long periods spent idling. Automatic transmission specialists don't like the 5-speed autobox. Solved by replacement block with steel-lined bores. UK imports from March 1998 fitted with steel- or Alusil-lined bores, but grey imports from other markets may not be. 1998: new 7s built before Nov '94 recalled to fit new radiator cap (very few cars involved, because new 7 not launched until August 1994). Electrical fault in rear tail lights causes the contact between bulb holder and bulb to erode and contact to be lost. BMW replacements from a dealer are £280 a side, fitted.

Recalls: 15/12/1999: (E38 built Sept/Oct 1999): brake light switch may fail leading to brake lights flickering or failing and switch overheating. New switches to be fitted. 16/11/2001: cars built 11/11/2000–30/9/2001 recalled because fault with radiator fan motor could lead electrics to overload, fan motor to fail and a small electrical fire to result.

850 and 840 E31 (1990 to 1999)

What's good: BMW's super coupe launched in UK October 1990 as 850Ci with 4,988cc

300bhp M70 V12. 15ft 7in long by 6ft 1in wide and weighing in at 1,830 to 1,900kg. Soon followed in June 1993 by 850CSi with 5,576cc 380bhp V12. 300bhp 850Ci dropped in September 1994; essentially replaced by 3,982cc 286bhp 840Ci from July 1993.

840Ci engine grew to 4,398cc with same 286bhp in January 1997 and this is the model to go for. Sport option also from January 1997. Size is 4,780mm long (15ft 8in) x 1,855mm wide (6ft 1in). BMW had sixth lowest average cost in warranty claims for cars up to 10 years old in 2002 Warranty Direct index

What's bad: V12 thirsty. Bore liner erosion problems with original M60 4.0 litre V8.

What to watch out for: Avoid the 4.0 V8 due to possible bore liner erosion problems.

Alpina B3 3.3 (from 1999)

What's good: Cheaper alternative to M3. 330 engine increased to 3.3 litres puts out 280bhp at 6,200rpm and 249lb ft torque at 4,500rpm. Gives it top speed of 160mph, zero to 60 of 6.6 seconds, combined mpg of 24.1 and CO_2 output of 278g/km. Price from UK BMW dealer: £39,754. BMW, Toyota and Ford jointly suffered the fewest breakdowns attended by German ADAC during 2001. BMW had sixth lowest average cost in warranty claims for cars up to 10 years old in 2002 Warranty Direct index

What's bad: Won't hold its value as well as an M3 or 330CI. Pre-November 2001 3 year warranty required expensive top up to be comprehensive in 2nd and 3rd years.

What to watch out for: Build date from 2001 shown on engine compartment label on top of front nearside wheelarch. Otherwise too soon to say.

X5 4x4 E53 (from 2000)

What's good: BMW's own Range Rover with 231bhp 3.0 litre petrol or 184bhp diesel sixes and 286 bhp 4.4 litre V8 option. Has become THE urban battlewagon to be seen in, with huge, intimidating road presence. Better than a Range Rover, Discovery or Mercedes ML. 4.4 came first; 3.0 petrol in Spring 2001 priced from £33,000; diesel summer 2001 similarly priced; 347bhp X5 4.6iS in UK late 2001 capable of 0–60 in 6.5 seconds and 150mph, at a higher than anticipated price of £54,000. Capable off road as well as on the road. Improved unlimited mileage two year full manufacturer warranty followed by one year full dealer warranty from November 2001, making total three year unlimited mileage warranty. BMW, Toyota and Ford jointly suffered the fewest breakdowns attended by German ADAC during 2001.

What's bad: 4.4 priced from a high £46,300 and far from economical. Pre November 2001 2nd and 3rd year dealer warranty required expensive top-up to be comprehensive. On road handling of 3.0 petrol model not as good as arch rival Lexus RX300. Feels top-heavy. 3.0 can use any petrol from 87Ron to German 99Ron but only develops 231bhp on 98Ron +, so best to run it on Shell Optimax. Diesel doesn't get the massive twin tailpipes of petrol models and isn't as economical as you would expect. Options can hugely inflate the price paid for a new one.

What to watch out for: Build date shown on engine compartment label on top of front nearside wheelarch. Otherwise too soon to say. Reports of blown turbos on 530Ds may also apply to X5 3.0Ds.

Recalls: 31/1/2001: Build dates 21/9/2000–19/1/2001 Check for possibility that steering column joint was not assembled correctly. 16/11/2001: cars built 11/11/2000–30/9/2001 recalled because fault with radiator fan motor could lead electrics to overload, fan motor to fail and a small electrical fire to result.

Z1 Roadster (1986 to 1991)

What's good: Classic from day one. Groovy drop down doors. Sophisticated multi-link rear suspension. 12ft 10in long by 5ft 6in wide and weighed 1,338kg. Old iron block, single belt cam 171 bhp BMW six. Only 8,093 built.

What's bad: LHD only. Many imported used from Germany so difficult to check history, and may be clocked. 'Old' single cam 325i engine needs regular cambelt changes, can suffer cracking of cylinder head. Panels hard to replace. Prices still hover around £20,000. From April 2002 BMW started to phase out production of official replacement parts for cars over 10 years old.

What to watch out for: Badly fitting panels hiding old accident damage. Make sure the door mechanisms work properly. Cambelts need replacing every 3 years or 36,000 miles.

Recalls: 1998: all Z1s recalled to fit new radiator cap.

Z3 Roadster (1997 to 2003)

What's good: Very compact. Snug cockpit. Doesn't buffet badly up to 80 mph. 140 bhp 1.9 auto available. 190 bhp 2.8 litre six replaced by new 231 bhp 3.0 litre six in Spring 2000. 321 bhp 3.2 litre 'M' version almost too powerful. American built. New small engine range from Spring 1999, with 115 bhp 1.9 litre 'four' and 150 bhp 2.0 litre 'six', then 170bhp 2.2 litre six. Improved unlimited mileage two year full manufacturer warranty followed by one year full dealer warranty from November 2001, making total three year unlimited mileage warranty. BMW, Toyota and Ford jointly suffered the fewest breakdowns attended by German ADAC during 2001. BMW had sixth lowest average cost in warranty claims for cars up to 10 years old in 2002 Warranty Direct index

What's bad: 115 bhp and 140 bhp 1.9 litre fours not really enough except for cruisers. No clever roof like the SLK. Not very sporty to drive. Soft-tops can leak. Optional hardtops offer poor seal for side windows – modification kit available from early 1999. Z3 'M' coupe may be fast but is aesthetically hideous. Pre-November 2001 3 year warranty required expensive top up to be comprehensive in 2nd and 3rd years.

What to watch out for: Build date from 2001 shown on engine compartment label on top of front nearside wheelarch. Many RHDs were personally imported to avoid long delivery dates and don't have UK 3-year dealer warranty. 2.8s imported from other markets may have vulnerable Nickasil-lined bores rather than steel-lined bores. Check fuel tank for damaged from bottoming out (very expensive to replace). Front suspension lower ball joints and inner bushes wear, but are comparatively cheap to replace. Service light indicator can easily be re-set, so a paid invoice is the only guarantee of a recent service. Check toolkit is all there.

Z4 (from Spring 2003)

What's good: Re-styled, re-suspended Z car should handle much better than present offering. The one to have will be the 3.0i with BMW's 231bhp 3.0 litre straight six and six-speed manual gearbox, giving it a top speed of 155mph. Next down is a 192bhp 2.5 straight six which will do 146mph. Optional SSG sequential manual gearbox available on both. Will also be a 143bhp 2.0 litre Brit-built four in autumn 2003 and maybe a 3.2 litre 345bhp M engine. New car has perfect 50;50 weight distribution. Run flat tyres are standard, leaving 260 litres of boot space capable of taking two golf bags. Also has pushbotton 'Dynamic Drive Control' allowing driver to select sportier response from accelerator and steering. 'Fade-free' high performance brakes. DSC III traction control. Electric folding soft-top with glass rear window. 2.5 to cost from £28,000 in UK; 2.0 to cost about £25,000.

What's bad: The Americans and the Germans get it first (from Autumn 2002).

What to watch out for: Too soon to say.

Z8 Roadster (from 2000)

What's good: Very fast 400 bhp V8 'retro' roadster, as driven by James Bond in limited production at BMW's Dingolfing plant. Improved unlimited mileage two year full manufacturer warranty followed by one year full dealer warranty from November 2001, making total three year unlimited mileage warranty. BMW, Toyota and Ford jointly suffered the fewest breakdowns attended by German ADAC during 2001.

What's bad: Expensive. Likely to blow your hairpiece off.

What to watch out for: Build date from 2001 shown on engine compartment label on top of front nearside wheelarch. Otherwise too soon to say.

Recalls: 16/11/2001: cars built 11/11/2000–30/9/2001 recalled because fault with radiator fan motor could lead electrics to overload, fan motor to fail and a small electrical fire to result.

BRISTOL

Blenheim 3S

What's good: The ultimate gentleman's carriage.

Bristol has now been building bespoke motor cars and the occasional racer for 55 years. Its new model, the Blenheim 3S is a sportier but no less refined version of the Blenheim 3, which continues in production.

S model differentiated by 16 inch five spoke alloy sports wheels. Larger section, lower profile tyres are fitted and the rear track has been widened by two inches for improved stability. Lower part of rear body subtly widened to disguise track increase and four low restriction exhaust outlets visible below the rear valence. Six additional standard colours: Le Mans Green, Goodwood Blue, Cambridge Grey, Sahara Gold, Jet Black and Copper Beech are available.

Four-piston front brake callipers and a brake servo system offering improved pedal feel. Stiffer front anti-roll bar is combined with adjustable dampers offers revised ratio of bump-to-rebound damping for better body control. Firmness of the power steering can be tailored during vehicle build to suit the taste of the individual owner. To help assure satisfactory average speeds on long Continental trips, the petrol tank has twin fillers which allow it to be topped from either side of the car at the first pump to become available.

Interior changes for the Blenheim 3S are subtle. By arranging the leather seat pleating to run vertically instead of horizontally, the lateral support has been enhanced without incurring any unsightly creases in the Connolly leather. Elegantly curved mahogany door cappings and waist rails with walnut veneered facings make a welcome return with the benefit of safety breakaway mountings, along with a matching veneered wood air conditioning control panel. Tooled leather Bristol motifs appear on the front seat backs as well as contrasting leather piping for the Wilton carpets. Extra soundproofing and a revised exhaust mounting arrangement add a further degree of running refinement.

S model is a serious high performance motorcar. Bristol's already powerful V8 has been given better breathing to release more of its potential. A redesigned inlet manifold with straighter passages takes extra air which is ingested by specially ported big-valve cylinder heads. Complementing these improvements is a recalibrated engine control system and a low restriction exhaust with larger catalysts placed closer to the engine for quicker warm-up. A 3.06:1 performance rear axle ratio is fitted as standard. This new TS4 series engine has its operating range extended by 500 rpm for the enjoyment of the enthusiast yet nothing is lost in terms of sweetness, silence or efficiency during normal motoring. When the need arises, however, there is no mistaking the Ss immediate response and muscular authority.

Zero to 60mph in the new car takes just 5.4 seconds and its top speed on the autobahn is best described as "adequate".

More online at www.bristolcars.co.uk

What's bad: Expensive, but a car as bespoke as this has to be.

What to watch out for: Too soon to say.

CADILLAC

CTS (from late 2002)

What's good: New Euro-Cadillac powered by same British-built 3.2 litre V6 as Omega. Engine develops 220bhp at 6,000rpm and 295Nm torque at 3,400rpm. Unusual 54 degree angle between cylinder banks. To be offered with a 5-speed manual or 5-speed automatic transmission. Also cheaper 182bhp 2.6 litre version.

What's bad: Too soon to say.

What to watch out for: Too soon to say.

Seville STS (from 1998)

What's good: Big, squat car with reasonably restrained styling. Loaded with kit. Looks best in black. Very comfortable. Powerful, low-maintenance 305 bhp 4.6 litre V8. Not bad to drive, with strong acceleration, decent steering 'feel', good handling, nicely calculated traction control and anti-skid. Brilliant Bose stereo system (possibly the best standard in-car system available). EC fuel consumption: 13.7/27.2/19.9, so 20 mpg possible. Automatic parking brake release. 3-year, 60,000–mile warranty with 24–hour assistance. Electrically folding door mirrors.

What's bad: Severe tyre roar. Looks a bit like a larger Rover 800 4–door. Variable-ratio steering loses 'feel' on very tight corners. Some trim not up to the standards of a luxurious European car. Garish chromed alloys. Indicator switch on the right of the column.

What to watch out for: Nearside suspension damage by drivers not able to judge the width. Possibility of having previously been owned by undesirable people with enemies.

CHEVROLET

Blazer 4.3

What's good: LHD American 4x4 SUV, slightly smaller than the Ford Explorer, briefly offered in the UK by GM, usually with a five on the floor manual transmission rather than 4-speed autobox. 4.3 litre V6.

What's bad: Spares are all going to have to come air-freight from the States.

What to watch out for: Sorry, not enough known.

Camaro (from 1999)

What's good: Relatively cheap starter price of £17,950 for 3.8 litre V6 auto. 3.8 convertibles from £21,500. But 284 bhp 6-speed 5.7 Z28 a much hunkier choice at £22,725 and can be surprisingly economical, with 23 mpg obtained by Sunday *Telegraph*'s Neil Lyndon.

What's bad: 5-speed manual box adds £1,000 to price of V6. Crude, cheapskate interiors. LHD only. Difficult to see out of and to park.

What to watch out for: Parking dings and dongs. Lack of proper servicing.

Corvette (1999 to 2001)

What's good: Really quick and relatively cheap at prices from £36,705 on the road. (Convertible dearer at £40,605.) 345 bhp and 356 lb ft torque give over 170 mph and 0–60 in 5.3 seconds. Surprisingly economical with over 20 mpg easy to achieve. 385 bhp ZO6 model from 2000 gives 4–second 0–60.

What's bad: Six-speed manual box costs an extra £1,150. LHD only. Withdrawn from UK market in late 2001 due to lack of demand (only 44 sold Jan-August 2001).

What to watch out for: Parking scratches and cracks in fibreglass body. Lack of proper servicing.

CHRYSLER

Crossfire (from 2003)

What's good: Concept car turned production reality. To be built in Europe by Karmann of Osnabruck from 2003 and to reach UK late 2003. Will have longitudinal 18 valve 3.2 litre V6 developing 215bhp and 310Nm (229 lb ft) torque fed through 5-speed autobox or 6-speed manual to rear wheels. Length: 4059mm (160 ins); width: 1750mm (69 ins); height: 1288mm (51 ins); weight: 1361kg (3050 lbs); ABS. ESP. traction control, rear wheel drive with double wishbone front suspension and five link independent rear suspension.

More online at www.chrysler.co.uk

What's bad: Too soon to say.

What to watch out for: Too soon to say.

Jeep Cherokee (1993 to 2001)

What's good: Powerful yet simple 184bhp 4.0 litre pushrod straight six. European 114bhp VM 2.5 litre turbodiesel. Or 122bhp petrol four. Fairly compact at 13ft 11in long and 5ft 10in wide. Much lower than Discovery and Range Rover so better in multi-story carparks. Facelifted and updated in April 1997. 4.0 litre can be converted to run on LPG, but make sure you choose the right converter. 2.5 petrol manual has a useful towing weight of 3,150kg; diesel 2,500kg.

What's bad: 4.0 six automatic only in the UK (manual available in other markets). 2.5 litre four cylinder petrol engine noisy and far from effortless. The model was on the LHD market for many years before it came to the UK. Small luggage area, especially with spare wheel in place. Spare wheel creates a rear blind spot. Have been automatic gearbox and transfer case problems. Lots came onto the market all at once, part-exchanged for Voyagers. Headlamp self-levelling motors cost £265 + VAT a side and are an MOT requirement. Have been aircon evaporator failures at 2 to 4 years old. £1,000 job to put right. 12th from Bottom in 144 car 2002 JD Power/*What Car?* Customer Satisfaction Survey of V and W reg. cars.

What to watch out for: Automatic transmission problems (where fitted). Old LHD imports undermining RHD values. If buying an import, make sure it had four-wheel-drive (they didn't all have). Look for oil leaks from gearbox, transfer case and axles. Check steering box mounting carefully. Check tyres for uneven wear. Check electrics such as headlamp self-levelling motors. Cylinder head problems with VM diesels up to 1997. Make sure aircon blows freezing cold.

Recalls: 1997 (January 1993–1997 model year RHD; 19,200 cars): check for stress fractures around steering box mounting. 1997: 567 cars built before Sept '96 recalled due to possibility of 'inadvertent deployment of airbags'. 1998: further recall over steering box mounting problem. 2/8/2000: 651 Cherokees recalled because airbag warning light and or airbags may deploy without warning. Airbag control unit to be replaced with modified type. Check coolant level and look under oil cap of diesel for mayonnaise indicating head problems.

Jeep Cherokee (2002 on)

What's good: Cute retro looking Jeep Cherokee with new, lighter 211bhp 3.7 litre V6 petrol with 235lb ft torque at 3,800rpm driven through automatic transmission. Zero to 60 of 10.5 seconds, tops speed 112mph, combined consumption 19.3mpg, CO_2 output 347g/km. Length: 4,496mm, width: 1,819mm, height: 1,866mm; weight: 1,867kg; towing weight: 2,250kg. Also new 143bhp 2.5 litre common rail diesel engine putting out 253 lb ft (343Nm) torque at 2,000 rpm. 145bhp 2.4 litre petrol four from January 2002, priced £17,815. Useful 10 inches (244mm) ground clearance. Price of 3.7: £23,145 as from October 2001 UK launch.

What's bad: Very heavy. Excessive fuel consumption and huge C02 output will not favour this car for company drivers. Reports that the new Cherokee is prone to roll over after a magazine tester managed to roll one during a simulated sudden avoidance test. Achieved an average three star 71%rating for crash safety in 2002

NCAP tests, with very poor pedestrian safety.
What to watch out for: Too soon to say.

Jeep Grand Cherokee (1994 to 1999)

What's good: See Cherokee. 15ft 1in long by 7ft 4in wide and weighing in from 1,820kg. 174bhp 4.0 Limited auto had impressive towing weight of 3,500kg. Slightly more room inside than Cherokee. First imports were 5.2 litre V8s with 212 bhp in LHD and auto only. 174bhp 4.0 litre RHD straight sixes came in January 1996 followed by a 114 bhp VM-powered 2.5 diesel in February 1997. 5.7 litre 237 bhp V8 from October 1997, still LHD auto only. American 'luxury' interiors.

What's bad: Still comparatively small inside. Old LHD 'special order' 5,216cc (212 bhp) and 5,899cc (237 bhp) V8 s very 'American'. Isolate the driver from what's going on. Only do 13–26 mpg. V8 values likely to fall heavily as fuel taxes increase. Lack of crumple zones means it can be severely damaged by hard impacts at speeds as low as 5 mph. Headlamp self-levelling motors cost £265 + VAT a side and are an MOT requirement. Spate of aircon evaporator failures at 2 to 4 years old. £1,000 job to put right. 162 reports in USA of automatic transmission changing from Park to Reverse unintentionally. Chrysler denies there is a problem. Per Automotive Online 14–9–2001. Joint 10th from Bottom with Chrysler Voyager in 144 car 2002 JD Power/*What Car?* Customer Satisfaction Survey of V and W reg. cars.

What to watch out for: See Cherokee. Possible head problems with VW diesel. Make sure aircon blows cold.

Recalls: 1997: 2,536 cars recalled due to danger of fire from a short circuit in heated seat wiring. February 2002: Recall in Germany (apparently worldwide) of 316,000 Grand Cherokees build 1993–1998 due to an automatic transmission problem.

Jeep Grand Cherokee (1999 on)

What's good: Restyled, re-shelled Grand Cherokee. 15ft 1in long by 7ft 4in wide. 4.7 weighs 1,975kg and tows 3,500kg. Slightly more room inside than Cherokee. Range includes RHD 4.7 litre 217 bhp V8 from spring 1999. New 5-cylinder 3.1 litre VM turbodiesel with 283 lb ft torque for Y2K. VM diesel replaced by much better 5 cylinder 2.7 litre Mercedes common rail diesel (same as ML 270CDI) from February 2002.

What's bad: Still comparatively small inside. Grille looks like the frightening central heating furnace in 'Home Alone'. Spate of aircon evaporator failures at 2 to 4 years old. £1,000 job to put right. Joint 10th from Bottom with Chrysler Voyager in 144 car 2002 JD Power/*What Car?* Customer Satisfaction Survey of V and W reg. cars.

What to watch out for: See Cherokee. Make sure aircon blows freezing cold.

Jeep Wrangler (1993 on)

What's good: Powerful but simple 174bhp 4.0 litre six cylinder engines, or less powerful 117bhp 2.5 litre four. Sixes usually automatic, but 5-speed manual available. Fours all manual. 12ft 9in long by 5ft 8in wide. 2,500kg towing weight. Completely revised in May 1997, round headlights replaced square eyes; coil springs replaced leaf springs. Still a fashion accessory. Demi Moore's chosen mount in 'St Elmo's Fire' and the car in which Alicia Silverstone memorably failed her driver's test in 'Clueless'. Can get manual box with 4.0 litre six.

What's bad: 2.5 litre four cylinder petrol engine noisy, but comes with a manual shifter. On road handling not great. Older, leaf sprung examples with PAS are pretty horrible to drive. Standard weather equipment is not up to much and a fibreglass hardtop with fibreglass doors is highly advised for winter driving.

What to watch out for: Damage from off-roading. Carefully check front axle swivel joints for pitting and oil leaks.

Recalls: February 2002: Recall in Germany (apparently worldwide) of 268,700 Wranglers due to a parking brake problem.

Neon (1996 to 1999)

What's good: Well-equipped. 14ft 4in long by 5ft 7in wide. 1,996cc four had 131bhp. 5-speed manual or 3-speed autobox at no extra cost. Good features such as electrically folding door mirrors very helpful in multi-story carparks. ABS and aircon standard on LX. Reasonably priced by UK standards. Good paint finish, especially metallics. 3-year warranty. Chain-driven camshafts. 115bhp base 1.8 engine available in base spec LE from 1998 to 1999.

What's bad: Coarse engine. Autobox has only three speeds but better suited to engine than manual. Not as fuel efficient as a Mondeo. Huge diameter rear coil 'bedsprings' intrude into boot space. Rear backrests flop down crudely onto squabs. Seating material and interior plastics a bit iffy and more suited to a £7,000 car, which the Neon is in the USA. Reports of cylinder head gasket failure at around three years old. Possible problem with the front wheel universal joints and gaiters if excessive lock has been used. Spate of aircon evaporator failures at 2 to 4 years old. £1,000 job to put right. Have also been some expensive autobox failures and cost of repair can now exceed value of the car.

What to watch out for: Kerbing damage. Damage to the mirror mechanisms (£350+ to replace). Tears in seat trim, especially flimsy backs of front seats. Check coolant level and look under oil cap for emulsified oil indicating head gasket failure. Check front driveshaft gaiters for splits as UJs can wear out very rapidly if grease is lost. Make sure aircon blows freezing cold.

Neon II (from 1999)

What's good: Good looking, well-equipped and reasonably priced from £10,995 OTR with standard aircon, standard electrically folding door mirrors and standard 3-year warranty. 14ft 5in long by 5ft 7in wide. 131 bhp twin cam 16v 2.0 litre engine now smoother. £13,495 LX model loaded with goodies such as leather interior trim, wood trim, cruise control (with auto), 15in alloys, ABS and Thatcham Category-2 immobiliser. Optional no-extra-cost auto (4 speed from 2001MY). Chain-driven camshafts. 150bhp R/T version, 5-speed manual only, from April 2001.

What's bad: Autobox still had just three speeds at launch, but has had the Euro spec four speed box from 2001 model year. Spate of aircon evaporator failures at 2 to 4 years old. £1,000 job to put right.

What to watch out for: See original Neon. Make sure aircon blows freezing cold.

PT Cruiser (from 2000)

What's good: Brave, retro-styled estate car from the people who brought you the Prowler and are now in league with Mercedes Benz. Based on the new Neon with better rear suspension, stronger chain-cam 140 bhp engine and practical interior that can even take surf boards. A bigger success than the new Beetle in the USA. Short throw 5-speed manual or 4-speed auto. Practical with big, strong, impact absorbing black bumpers, removable rear seats, three proper rear belts and plenty of luggage space. Decent ride and handling. All models have a/c and six speaker radio/cassette/CD player. UK prices from £14,995, but Euro sourced £15,995 Touring models discounted to £14,295. List of improvements for 2002 include optional 'Autostick' 4-speed automatic transmission at £800 extra, new colours, a Mercedes 2.2 CRD chain-cam diesel engine with 121bhp and 300Nm (221 lb ft) torque which does 0–60 in 11.8 seconds and 114mph. Huge fun. Latest model is Street Cruiser Series 1 in Inca Gold, with 16 inch chrome wheels and pearl beige leather interior, listed at £17,775 for the manual and £18,575 with Autostick electric clutch. (Manual C02: 196g/km; auto: 232g/km). 2.2 CRD much torquier than standard petrol 2.0 litre: goes and cruises better. See road test of petrol model online at www. honestjohn.co.uk.

What's bad: Not everyone will go for the styling. Long waiting list could be replaced by oversupply (already building 180,000 a year in Mexico and planning to build 310,000 a year once Austrian factory comes on line). European sales slowed down over 2001. Handling seems fine at first on smooth roads but can get a bit ragged on difficult corners. Performance hampered a bit by the weight of the body and petrol model only does 28mpg. Retro styling might actually date in a few years time. Tough black plastic bumpers discarded in favour of silly colour coded bumpers for 2002. CRD diesel prices start at a huge £17,495.

What to watch out for: Too soon to say.

Sebring Cabrio

What's good: Chrysler is importing fifty of its good-looking Sebring Cabrio soft-tops priced £22,995, which isn't bad for big, modern, front-wheel drive 200bhp, reasonably fuel efficient American drop-top. The huge spec includes a 200bhp quad cam 2,736cc V6 giving 193lb ft (262N) torque at 4,300rpm; 41TE four-speed overdrive autobox; 131 mph top speed; 26.6mpg combined fuel economy (34.4mpg extra urban); air-con; cruise; PAS; central locking; electric windows; electric drop top; tilt steering wheel; front fogs; solar glass; power antenna; cloth drop top; speed sensitive wipers; two front airbags; parking brake interlock; remote keyless entry; sentry key immobiliser; leather low-back bucket seats with driver lumbar support; six-way power driver's seat; front seat map pocket; back lit white instrument cluster; walnut burl trim; full length floor console with four cupholders and two bins; locking glove box; day/night rearview mirror; illuminated entry; illuminated vanity mirrors; AM/FM radio cassette and CD player; 150 watt infinity speakers; leather steering wheel and gearknob; power socket; glass rear window with defroster; mini computer with compass and temperature gauge; 205/60R x 16 tyres; 12 spoke alloy wheels; compact spare wheel plus full size alloy spare wheel (choose which you take with you); headlamp levelling system; headlamp washers; and headlamp 'see you home' delay. Dimensions are: length 4,921mm (16 ft 2in), width 1,763mm (5ft 10in); height 1,398mm (4ft 7ins). The boot (trunk) is apparently huge. Warranty is 3 years or 60,000 miles.

More online at www.chryslerjeep.co.uk

What's bad: Left-hand drive. Accommodation is for four, not five.

What to watch out for: Too soon to say.

Voyager (1997 to 2001)

What's good: Very good looking, very 'big' MPV from the company that has made more MPVs than anyone else. 15ft 6in x 6ft 4in (Grand Voyager 16ft 8in long). Rear seat rolls out on castors. 114bhp 2.5 litre VM turbodiesel does 30 mpg and has plenty of torque to pull the vast Grand Voyager body along. Excellent cruise control. 2.0 litre 131bhp engines are chain-cam, same as Neon. 3.3 V6 has 156bhp, 4-speed auto only.

What's bad: Inconvenient 2–2–3 seating arrangement with back three seats on a single bench which is heavy to remove. 2.0 litre 131 bhp Neon engine with manual box not really man enough (3.3 litre autos more suited to the job). Terrible roadholding and handling on tight turns. Poor two-star performer in NCAP crash tests (0 points front impact; 14 points side impact). More than its fair share of electrical gremlins. Spate of aircon evaporator failures at 2 to 4 years old. £1,000 job to put right. Screen venting system can fail on 1997 examples and readers have been quoted up to £1,800 to put it right. Joint 10th from Bottom in 144 car 2002 JD Power/*What Car?* Customer Satisfaction Survey of V and W reg. cars.

What to watch out for: Damage from heavy use and uncontrolled children. School-run kerbing damage by drivers used to Cherokees. Make sure aircon blows freezing cold. Check screen vents on 1997 and 1998 models and if not working DO NOT BUY THE VEHICLE (see above).

Recalls: 1998: voluntary European recall of old (squarer shape) model due to possible problems with rear door latches. 2000: 15,567 UK-market current-shape vehicles recalled because excessively long parking brake cable leads to cable stretch, making brake very difficult to apply. Announced Radio 5 News 3/5/2000. Wordwide recall of 3.3 litre model affecting 1,400,000 vehicles built between 1996 and 1999 to check for fuel pipes leaking in extremely hot weather which has led to a spate of vehicle fires. 26/11/2001: 18,000 Voyagers built 1/8/1997 to 31/8/2000 recalled because parking brake self-adjusting mechanism may "become out of range or fail to engage" leading vehicle to roll away if not left in gear. Lockup clip to be installed.

Voyager (from 2001)

What's good: Revised Voyager for 2001. Voyager is 4,803mm long, 1,997mm wide and 1,749mm high. Grand Voyager is 5,094mm long and offers much more luggage space. All are more spacious than before with better handling and stronger body structures for better crash safety. New engines include a 2,499cc chain-driven twin-cam petrol four with 142bhp and 167 lb ft (226Nm) torque at 4,000 rpm (manual only); a 3,301cc petrol V6 with 172bhp and 210lb ft (285Nm) torque at 4,000 rpm (automatic only); and a 2,500cc twin-cam diesel four with 140bhp at 4,000 rpm and 230 lb ft (312Nm) torque at 1,800rpm (manual only). Prices from £18,495 on the road for the 2.4SE manual to £28,995 for the 3.3 Limited. Cheapest diesel is the 2.5CRD at £19,695. Usual three year warranty applies.

What's bad: Gearbox problem with diesel models. Inappropriate ratios. Difficulty engaging gears. Baulking when changing up. Modified gearboxes apparently being made ready, but supply still delayed at 10/9/2001.

What to watch out for: Too soon to say.

Recalls: Likely to be a recall of diesel models for gearboxes to be replaced.

CITROEN

2CV (to 1990)

What's good: Good fun in its day, especially on empty summer country roads and in and around holiday resorts. Easy to appreciate the design. You can still have a laugh in them. 2CV experts say that all since the early 70s are happy on unleaded. 12ft 7in long by 4ft 10in wide and weighed just 560kg. 602cc engine, Group 1 insurance and 45–50mpg economy.

What's bad: A mere 26bhp pulled it along. It's had its day. Dreadful to drive in town and to park in multi-storeys. Can suffer severe chassis rust. Body also rusts, especially around fresh-air ventilator. Jobs like brakes very expensive (drive-shafts have to come off to replace front discs). Some 'beardy' and 'girlie' owners tend to neglect servicing or do it on the cheap. So flimsy, a crash in one is a terrifying thought.

What to watch out for: Chassis rot (galvanised chassis available, but expensive). Smoking engines. Clocking (oh, yes). Loose underbonnet heater ducts. Ripped tops (but cheap to replace). Last of the line were built in Portugal and build quality of these was poor.

AX (1987 to 1997)

What's good: Chirpy, light to drive, economical. Cheap to run. 11ft 7in long by 5ft 1in wide and weighed from just 668kg. 58bhp 1.5 litre iron block diesel engine can be very long-lived if well maintained with regular oil, coolant, injector and cambelt changes. Also delivers 55–60 mpg. Front door pockets designed to take 2–litre bottles of wine. Other engines were 45bhp 1.0; 55bhp 1.1; 65bhp, 85bhp and 100bhp 1.4s; and an alloy block 53bhp 1.4 diesel.

What's bad: Very light build, so not good in a crash (especially early ones). Offset twisted-spine driving position and big feet can cover more than one pedal at the same time. Fall-apart interior trim.

Reports of premature bore wear on 1.5 diesels could be due to worn injectors washing out the bores.

What to watch out for: Any body rot will significantly weaken fairly feeble structure. Thin body panels easily dented. Worn engines start to rattle. Oil leaks are common. Smoking usually caused by more than just valve stem oil seals. Make sure the heater is not leaking. Also check that brakes stop the car straight and true.

Berlingo Multispace (from 1998)

What's good: Originally designed as a van on the ZX/306 floorpan with Peugeot 405 estate car rear suspension. 13ft 6in long by 5ft 7in wide. Lots of good design points. Decent ride quality. Launched in UK in summer 1998 as Multispace with full-length electric fun-roof, bright colours and 1.8 litre 8-valve engine giving 100 mph. Relaunched spring 1999 at lower prices from £10,830 OTR with 1.4i engine. Sunroof, aircon, 1.8i or 1.9D engines now all extra-cost options. Further price cut down to £8,995 in spring 2000 for the 1.9XUD 3–door due to competition from the Renault Kangoo Combi. Relaunched for third time in summer 2000 as the Multispace Forte, now with twin rear sliding side doors, three three-point rear belts, Multiplex wiring and cubbyholes everywhere including the rear floor from £9,495 for the 1.4i and £9,750 for the 1.9D. Handles well for a van (though not as much fun to drive as the Polo Caddy Combi). Excellent for gardeners, people with dogs and the elderly due to ease of ingress and egress. Sensibly priced Brotherwood conversion available for transporting the disabled in dignity. Price of perky new 1.4i Forte with aircon cut to bargain £8,995 on 30/09/2000. Three year, 60,000 mile warranty announced 24/10/2000. Forte 1.9Ds advertised by Citroën at £8,745 after £500 cashback in Summer 2001. By December 2001, 110bhp 1.6 16vs were the best value at £9,495. 2.0 HDI finally arrived February 2002 from £9,760 after £500 cashback. Has 90bhp, top speed is 98mph, and 60mph comes up in around 12.7 seconds. Combined fuel consumption is 47.9mpg and CO_2 emissions 155g/km, putting it in the £130pa VED bracket. Very highly recommended for the non status conscious. Run-out old 1.9 diesel cut to £7,995 for just four days at end of April 2002. June 2002, Citroën cashback brought price of 2.0HDI 90 down to £8,995. Top value for money for anyone with a small business or into dogs, kids or doing up houses. HDI 90 at £8,995 highly recommended.

More, and latest offers, online at www.citroen.co.uk

What's bad: It's a van-based car, not a car-based van. 1998–2000 pre 'Forte' models only had three doors. Brakes aren't as good as you would expect on a car. Clutch a bit sharp on 1.4i and gearchange positive, but a bit obstructive. Carries no status at all. Trying to use the washers when the pipes are frozen blows a 5 amp fuse for about half the Multiplex wiring, so make sure there are spare 5 amp fuses in the fusebox lid; if not, buy some. Also one report of instruments intermittently failing to register on Multiplex wired Forte models.

What to watch out for: As these kombis get older they may suffer the same rear suspension pivot wear as Peugeot 405 estates.

Recalls: 1/2/2000 (Sept/Oct 1999 build only): brake servo valve may fail, leading to loss of servo assistance. Inspect and possibly replace brake servo valve.

BX (1983 to 1993)

What's good: Excellent ride and handling. 13ft 10in long by 5ft 5in wide. Light weight for its size from 900kg. Well designed. 62–72bhp 1.4 was under-powered, but XU-engined cars okay. Excellent estate. 71bhp 1.9D or 90bhp 1.7TD with PAS are the obvious choices. 1.9D will do 100 mph and 50 mpg. 160bhp Gate 16v was the ultimate BX. Height-adjustable suspension allows 'stilt effect' for floods or rough going. There was a very quick 16v version. 4x4 likely to become troublesome. Plastic bonnet and boot on all but last few years' production are light and don't rust. Very few rust traps in the car. Suspension spheres easy and cheap to replace.

What's bad: Getting old. Not all 1980s BXs had PAS. Very light build quality. Brake pipes go. Many independent servicing dealers have moved on from BXs now.

What to watch out for: Clocking (there are plenty of BX diesels around with well over 200,000 miles under their wheels). Make all standard XU engine cambelt, cambelt end seal, coolant and cylinder head gasket checks. Clutch cables can pull through bulkhead. Make sure the brake pipes have been replaced (replacements were better protected and longer lasting). Plastic ends of car can hide rust underneath. The last BXs had steel bonnets.

C2 (from early 2003)

What's good: New basic small 3 door Citroën to replace the Saxo and sit under the 5 door C3. Similar engine range, but starting lower with basic £5,500 1.0 litre and rising to 137bhp 2.0 litre. Launch date: autumn 2002; UK sales from early 2003.

More, and latest offers, online at www.citroen.co.uk

What's bad: Too soon to say.

What to watch out for: Too soon to say.

C3 (from 2002)

What's good: New small car from Citroën launched early 2002 in 5–door format. Dimensions of the 5–door: length 3,815mm (12 ft 6in); width 1,670mm (5 ft 6in); height: 1,520mm (5ft 0in). (Shorter, but four inches higher than the new Ford Fiesta.) Luggage volume is 305 litres to the parcel shelf with the rear seats up (slightly greater than the new Fiesta) with a clever modular floor to keep things in place.

Five different engines. Most interesting are the two new PSA/Ford 1,399cc aluminium block, common rail direct-injected HDI diesels. Power output of the 8 valve HDI is 70bhp with 150Nm (111 lb ft) torque. Power output of the 16 valve HDI coming later is 92bhp with 200Nm (148 lb ft) torque. With 65bhp per litre, this is the most efficient engine available in cars of the C3ft s size. 1.4 HDI 70bhp emits just 110g/km CO_2 and qualifies for £80pa VED from April 2002. 1.4 HDI 92bhp launched June 2002. Does 65.7mpg combined, emits 112g/km CO_2 (£80pa VED), gets to 60 in 11.4 seconds and goes on to 110mph.

The 1.1 litre petrol engine develops 61bhp at 5,500rpm and 94Nm (69 lb ft) torque at 3,400rpm. The 1.4i petrol engine develops 75bhp at 5,500rpm and 120Nm (89 lb ft) torque at 3,400rpm.

While the 1.6i 16v puts out 110bhp at 5,750rpm with 147Nm (108 lb ft) torque at 4,000 rpm. Optional with the 1.4 engine is the AL4 auto-adaptive automatic transmission featuring three operating programmes with the option of manual sequential shift override.

Standard equipment on all models includes electric power steering, ABS with EBD, six airbags, Multiplex wiring, two gloveboxes, dash 12v socket, passenger and driver's seat under-drawers, height and reach adjustable steering wheel, height adjustable driver's seat, central locking and 60/40 split rear seat. Options include brake assist with automatic hazard warning lights; a large electric glass sunroof; manual or automatic air-conditioning; electronic park assist; and a 'Child Pack' of a special mirror for watching children in the back seat, electric de-activation of the rear child locks, 12 volt rear socket for games machines and folding trays on the backs of the front seats. 1.6i 16v 5-speed Sensodrive from November 2002 is an electric clutch manual with steering wheel paddle shifters.

1.4 HDI is the best to drive.

More online at www.citroen.co.uk

What's bad: Some of the dashboard trim is a bit flimsy. Lacks rear seat legroom and headroom compared to Yaris, Jazz, Polo, Fiesta, etc. 1.4 auto not a great drive. All C3 engines, including HDIs, are belt cam, not chain cam like the Yaris.

What to watch out for: Far too soon to say.

C4 (from 2003)

What's good: Radically styled new car due to replace the boring looking Xsara in 2003. Very French, like the new Renaults. Should please Citroën fans. Airdream concept is a showcar taster of the look.

More, and latest offers, online at www.citroen.co.uk

What's bad: Too soon to say.

What to watch out for: Too soon to say.

C5 (from 2001)

What's good: Citroën hatchback replaced the Xantia from April 2001. Larger car with much more interior space. Price range is around £14,500 to around £21,000, but very heavily discounted. Underneath it is based on PSA's new Platform 3 and incorporates Hydractive 3, Citroën's latest version of its active hydropneumatic suspension system which automatically lowers the car at speed and requires no scheduled maintenance for the first five years. Engine range begins with 112bhp 1.8 litre and 2.0 litre 136bhp fours. Also a 2.0 litre 143bhp Hpi petrol engine, a 210bhp 3.0 litre V6 petrol and a powerful 2.2 litre Hdi diese1. This impressive new motor puts out 136bhp at a low 4,000 rpm coupled with 234 lb ft torque (317 Nm) at 2,000 rpm. Dimensions are: length 4,618mm (15 feet 2 inches) width 1,770mm (5 feet 10 inches); height: 1,476mm (4 feet 10 inches); luggage capacity (rear seats up): 456 litres. Galvanized body. Three year mechanical warranty. 15 foot 10 inch estate version launched at Geneva Motor Show on 27th February uses hydractive suspension to lower the rear for easier loading. Estate is by far the best C5. 3–piece bumpers cheap to replace. For more details, dimensions and driving impressions of C5 hatchbacks and estates models, see the two road tests at www.honestjohn.co.uk. 235bhp V6 C5 Carlsson sequential automatic Estate with 240 lb ft torque shown at Frankfurt in September 2001. 2.0HDI Estate voted Caravan Club Towcar of 2001 in £16,501–£20,000 class. Xsara 2.2HDI hatchback was second. Good four star score in 2001 NCAP crash tests. Some very good new car deals offered on UK supplied C5s. By June 2002 Citroën was offering cashbacks on C5 1.8 LXs with a/c bringing the price down to £11,995. HDI 90s £12,995.

More, and latest offers, online at www.citroen.co.uk

What's bad: Bland looks compared to Mondeo and Laguna. Hatchbacks known to Back Roomers as 'Mr Kipling cars' (see The Back Room – the online forum at www.honestjohn.co.uk). No rear wiper. New 2.2 HDI not brilliantly economical with combined figure of 44.1mpg and many complaints of much poorer economy from users. Not as enjoyable to drive as the Xantia. Open hatchback can deposit water into load area in wet and windy conditions. Self levelling suspension ECU can go wrong. Reports of problems with electronic low oil level warning system on 2.2HDI. Lots of problems reported with gearchanges of automatics, apparently curable by an ECU software upgrade.

What to watch out for: Faults emerging include rattle from rear suspension. This is now acknowledged by Citroën UK and fixed by applying balance weights. Also both manual and automatic transmission problems, fixed under warranty (software upgrade for autobox). Check that the various settings for the self-levelling suspension actually work. If they don't it could indicate an ECU fault. Report of tail-end of laden estate car twitching/leaping about at higher speeds, especially during windy weather. (Apparently the Hyperactive 3 PLUS suspension versions are much improved.) Headlights cut-out intermittently then re-illuminate later.

Recalls: Late 2001: PSA TSB issued to check all common-rail to injector unions on HDIs for leaks. February 2002: PSA TSB: if customer complains of rattle from rear suspension, fit repair kit of balance weights which cures it. News from Germany 6–4–2002 that Citroën is recalling 100,000 C5 estates to rectify up to 18 different faults.

C8 MPV (from Autumn 2002)

What's good: Second generation Citroën/FIAT/Peugeot MPV made its debut at the Geneva Motor Show March 2002. All are longer, taller and wider than the models they replace. Citroën's is called simply the C8 and matches this with seating for up to eight passengers. Features include automatic electric sliding rear side doors with really neat brushed alloy handles; sliding rear seats fitted with the Quickfix patented anchorage system for easy moving and removal; a huge number of storage compartments and cubby holes; air conditioning offering up to four independent climate zones (like the new MB E Class); the option of three electric tilt/slide sunroofs; foldaway mirror to enable the driver to keep an eye on passengers. The dashboard has a central instrument display, like the Picasso, Yaris and new Nissan Primera, and a seven inch information display monitor can be included. Engine range includes the 2.0 litre 110bhp HDI; the 2.0 litre 138bhp 16v petrol;

the 2.2 litre 136bhp HDI; a brand new 2.2 litre 160bhp 16v petrol and a 3.0 litre 208bhp petrol V6. Transmission options are Citroën's sequential auto adaptive automatic or a five-speed manual. Safety equipment includes strong, reinforced body; electronic stability programme; ABS with EBD; six airbags; automatic low tyre pressure warning; and electronic parking assistance. All 7 passengers get a three-point belt with belt for centre row centre passenger built into seat back.

More, and latest offers, online at www.citroen.co.uk

What's bad: Too soon to say.

What to watch out for: Too soon to say.

Pluriel (from early 2003)

What's good: Citroën's wacky but practical convertible-coupe-pick-up show car now scheduled to become a production reality in 2003, before 3–door C2. Should be fun, for sensible money.

More, and latest offers, online at www.citroen.co.uk

What's bad: Too soon to say.

What to watch out for: Too soon to say.

Saxo (1997 to 2003)

What's good: Bigger, better, stronger AX. 12ft 2in long by 5ft 3in wide and weighing from 805kg. Quite refined. 1.1 is very economical. 125bhp 1.6 VTS very quick. Seem to be pretty good and relatively problem-free for a Citroën. Good value by UK standards. 58bhp 1.5 diesel does 55 mpg. Autumn 1999 facelift includes galvanised panels, now with 12-year no-perforation warranty. Most now have PAS apart from 1.1 base models. SXs have switchable passenger airbags. 60bhp 1.1i LPG version available in Europe. Starter prices dropped to under £5,995 in spring 2000, including driver's airbag and radio/cassette. 1.6 VTR got boost to 100bhp for 2001 and now gets to 60 in 9.4 seconds for just £8,995. Saxo First got power boost from 1.0 litre to 1.1 litres and 60bhp for same low list price of £5,995. Three year, 60,000 mile warranty announced October 2000.

More, and latest offers, online at www.citroen.co.uk

What's bad: Twisted spine from offset driving position and big feet can hit more than one pedal at the same time. 3-speed 1.6 automatic replaced by 3-speed 1.4 auto. Can suffer mechanical problems and unsympathetic dealers. Only two stars in Euro NCAP crash tests. ECU problems beginning to be reported. Reports of premature bore wear on iron block 1.5Ds could be due to dirty or worn injectors washing out the bores. Saxo VTS can suffer same problem of water ingress to gearbox after driving through floodwater as Xantia and Synergie. Some VTRs are fitted with alloy wheels with no hole in the centre which makes balancing them difficult and expensive. S and T platers 14th from bottom in 2001 *Top Gear*/J.D. Power Customer Satisfaction Survey. In June 2001 Citroën was rated by Motor Warranty Direct as Britain's 3rd worst out of 22 marques for warranty claims (check online at www.warrantydirect.co.uk) 16th from bottom for reliability in *Auto Express* 2002 reader survey of 100 models.

'Free' insurance now only for 22–80 year olds.

What to watch out for: Two years free insurance made them attractive to 17-year-olds who may have crashed them. See Peugeot 106 for what to watch out for on VTR and VTS.

Recalls: 1997: faulty driver's seat catch on 3–door model. 1/2/2000 (Sept/Oct 1999 build only): brake servo valve may fail, leading to loss of servo assistance. Inspect and possibly replace brake servo valve. 28/2/01: Build 1/1/2001–31/1/2001: Possibility that brake relay lever may be faulty. recall to replace relay lever. 11/5/2001: 2000 Build 5–door models only: Lower fixing bolt of adjustable upper anchorage of LH front seat belt may not be to specification. Recall to replace bolts. 16/5/2001: Build date: January 2001, VIN VF7S*****57426214 to VF7S*****57436943: Front disc brake calliper bolts may not be to correct spec and may fail. Recall to replace calliper bolts. 8/8/2001: 484 1.6 VTRs built 1/1/2001–28/2/2002 recalled because defect in rear brake calliper may cause parking brake efficiency to be reduced. Check and replace calliper if necessary.

Synergie (1995 to 2002)

What's good: Good, well-planned, bright walk-through interior with dash-mounted gearshift. Nice trim colours. Compact for an 7/8 seater at 14ft 7in long by 6ft wide and easy to park. Sliding doors easy to get in and out of in tight parking spaces. Excellent, economical 110 bhp HDI diesel engine from autumn 1999. Achieved a good four star rating for crash safety in 2002 NCAP tests. Similar Peugeot 806 was a Three-Star performer in NCAP crash tests (7 points front impact; 15 points side impact). 12-year body warranty from September 1999. Three year, 60,000 mile warranty announced October 2000.

What's bad: Doesn't handle as well as Galaxy family. No automatics. Centre rear passenger only gets a lap belt. Flood water ingress to the gearbox is a problem, causing the box to seize. Rod through bock failures in 1997 and 1998 XUDTs. In June 2001 Citroën was rated by Motor Warranty Direct as Britain's 3rd worst out of 22 marques for warranty claims (check online at www.warrantydirect.co.uk) To be replaced by C7 in Spring 2002.

What to watch out for: Some may be ex-rental or ex-taxi. Make sure sliding side doors open smoothly and don't stick. Check for uneven front tyre wear. Look for signs of having been overloaded. May have done a few Calais beer runs.

Recalls: 1996 (Sept '95–Oct '95 build): Check airbag trigger. March '99–April '99 build Synergies with ABS only: possibility of air in brake fluid. March '98–July '98 build: handbrake ratchet could fail. Late 2001: PSA TSB issued to check all common-rail to injector unions on HDIs for leaks.

Xantia (1993 to 2000)

What's good: Good looking, 'different' hatchbacks and estates with excellent front-end grip, safe handling, fine ride quality out of town plus the ability to raise themselves on their suspension to clear obstacles and to sink down to the ground if required. Good rear legroom. Length 14ft 7in, width 5ft 9in, weight from 1,170kg. Estates have three lap/diagonal rear belts. Suspension never goes baggy. Suspension spheres quick, easy and cheap to replace.

112bhp 16 valve 1.8 and 135bhp 2.0 litre engines from N reg. on quite sporty but can use a bit of oil in valve stem lubrication. 150bhp turbocharged 8v Activa had fantastic handling and roadholding. 194bhp 3.0 V6 was a bit overkill for this market. Facelift Feb '98 with 3–piece bumpers. Turbo-diesel automatic from Spring '98 a good cruiser. New HDI diesel engine from October 1998 best fuel miser in-CLASS. 12-year body warranty from September 1999. Not dear second-hand.

What's bad: Hydraulic pumps can still go. ABS computers fail. Parts of more complex VSX and Activa suspension can stick. Average performance in NCAP crash tests. TD auto a bit high geared for town work (lingers in 2nd or 3rd). Clutch cable connector prone to breaking at the pedal end and, it's a long, tedious and expensive job to put right. Rate of depreciation can take you by surprise. Hatchbacks of Xantia estates apt to leak through wiper spindle seal. Very heavy depreciation and difficult to sell. Early 'K' and 'L' reg. Xantias fetching as little as £500 at auction. Flood water ingress to the gearbox is a problem, causing the box to seize. Faulty ABS sensors can lead to short front brake disc life. Cat heat shield can trap moisture which can lead to rust on a car driven short distances from cold. 17th from bottom for reliability in *Auto Express* 2002 reader survey of 100 models.

What to watch out for: LX non-ABS models are the best used buy because there's less to go wrong. ABS computers are a common problem. Check spare wheel is in its underboot cradle and not nicked. Look for smoke from diesels – may be curable with a dose of injector cleaner and a new air filter. 1.6s likely to wear out first. If fitted with aircon, make sure it blows cold. If 2.0 litre petrol engine knocks, don't buy the car (see XM for reason).

Recalls: 1994 (May 1993–Oct 1994): Recall for parking brake modification to force drivers to apply it properly. 2001 (May 1993–August 1994): Recall of Xantias with electric sunroofs because electrics can short out leading to total failure of all electrics, stopping the car. Late 2001: PSA TSB issued to check all common-rail to injector unions on HDIs for leaks. 5/11/2001: 4134 Xantia 1.8i 16vs built 1/1/1995 to 31/12/96 recalled because timing belt may fail before 72,000 miles. Belt to be replaced.

XM (1990 to 2000)

What's good: Excellent ride and handling once you get to 'feel through' the steering to the front wheels. 15ft 5in long by 6ft 7in wide (including mirrors). Estate 16ft 3in long. Weighed from 1,500kg. 110bhp 2.1TD can be very economical and give quick journey times at 40 mpg. 130bhp 2.5TD altogether more powerful, less economical. 1994 Mk II brought much higher-quality electrics. Best petrol engine is the 150 bhp 8 valve 2.0 litre turbo. Estates are very spacious and comfortable. Rock bottom used prices.

What's bad: Riddled with niggly problems and rattles prior to 'M' reg. Mark IIs from 'M' reg. much better. Mk I V6 24v fast but not a success. Horrible American-style foot-operated parking brake. In June 2001 Citroën was rated by Motor Warranty Direct as Britain's 3rd worst out of 22 marques for warranty claims (check online at www.warrantydirect.co.uk)

What to watch out for: Where to start? Clutch problems (best replaced at a Citroën dealer), slurry automatics due to neglected ATF changes, dodgy electrics mainly due to poor contacts (solved on Mk II), ABS computer can give up, ABS pump will rust up inside if hydraulic fluid not changed frequently. Uneven tyre wear can mean serious chassis problems. Hard ride and excessive roll means suspension links have seized up. Brakes eat pads and discs will eventually wear. Make sure aircon blows cold. Listen for knocking from engines of 2.0 litre models (both 8v and 16v) due to design of piston skirts. If fault developed early, pistons were replaced FOC, but only when knocking became excessive.

Xsara (1997 to 2003)

What's good: Bigger, more refined ZX. 13ft 8in long by 5ft 7in wide and weighing from 1,030kg. Much improved safety features. Ingenious (patented) side-impact protection. 3–Star above-average performance in NCAP crash testing. Good 1.8 litre 16-valve engine. Excellent ride quality and bump absorption. Sharp turn-in with enhanced rear steer effect (very little understeer). 2.0 litre 167 bhp coupe seriously quick and a fine, safe handler. Estates better than 5–door hatchbacks, with lots of room, better handling and no sacrifice in ride quality. Evergreen XUTD still good. New HDI diesel from early 1999, first with 90bhp; later with 110bhp. Three-piece bumpers cheap to replace. 12-year body warranty from September 1999. Major facelift in autumn 2000 made it much better looking, but slightly reminiscent of defunct Ford Scorpio. New 110 bhp 1.6 16v engine replaced old 1.6 and 1.8. SX with a/c and abs costs £11,995 after £1,000 cashback. Three year 60,000 mile mechanical warranty announced 24/10/2000. New 137bhp 2.0 litre 16 valve engine available in coupe, 5–door and estate car bodies. Still a family car that offers good handling and driving pleasure. HDI 110 with 10.3 second 0–60, 54mpg and £110pa VED launched in May 2001 at £12,350 for the hatchback and £13,150 for the estate. Automatic gearbox option available on both at an extra £1,020. HDI 110 voted Caravan Club Towcar of 2001 in up to £13,500 class.

More, and latest offers, online at www.citroen.co.uk

What's bad: Nondescript looks of 5–door and coupe. Instrument bezel can reflect in screen. Only two three-point rear seatbelts. Model for model, lacks the equipment of equivalent Astras. Depreciates more quickly than class average. ECU problems starting to be reported. Rod through bock failures in 1997 and 1998 XUDTs. In June 2001 Citroën was rated by Motor Warranty Direct as Britain's 3rd worst out of 22 marques for warranty claims (check online at www.warrantydirect.co.uk) Xsara to be replaced by radical new C4 in 2002.

What to watch out for: Check spare wheel is in its underboot cradle and not nicked.

Recalls: 1998: 14,000 owners of cars registered Sep '97–Feb '98 notified that may be a delay in airbag inflating in an accident. Also possibility of faulty seatbelt pretensioner. 2000: 1.8i models built April '97–May '98: possibility of underbonnet fuel leak. 1/2/2000 (Sept/Oct 1999 build only): brake servo valve may fail, leading to loss of servo assistance. Inspect and possibly replace brake servo valve. 12/6/2000: VIN VF7N*****367694 to VF7N*****367779626: passenger airbag 'off' switch may not de-activate airbag. If switch defective, to be replaced. 25/9/2000: 3,648 Xsaras built 7/2000–9/2000 recalled because front suspension ball joint clamp bolt hold may have been incorrectly machined leading to disengagement of the ball joint. Pivots replaced of necessity. 20/11/2000: 1,314 Xsara diesels built in 1999/2000 recalled due to possibility of failure of brake vacuum pump dog drive leading to loss of power assistance to brakes. Drive dog to be replaced on all Xsara diesels fitted with Magneti Marelli vacuum pumps. Late 2001: PSA TSB issued to check all common-rail to injector unions on HDIs for leaks.

Xsara Picasso (from 2000)

What's good: Xsara-based and by far the best looking of the new 5–seater MPVs. Also one of the best handling and most car-like to drive, with very little roll understeer. Excellent ride quality. Electro-galvanised body with 12-year warranty. Three full sized rear seats, each with its own lap/diagonal safety belt. 14ft long by 5ft 9in wide and weighing from 1,240kg. 90 bhp 1.6i petrol, 115 bhp 1.8i 16v petrol, or 90 bhp 2.0 litre HDI. 1.8i will do over 60 mph in 2nd gear, but relaxed HDI engine suits the car best, can easily do 50 mpg and is a brilliant motorway cruiser. 'Walk through' cabin allowing the driver to get out kerb-side or attend to a child in the rear seat. Masses of back seat room. Huge boot. Optional full-length electric canvas sunroof. Three year, 60,000 mile dealer warranty announced 24/10/2000. Launch prices from £13,600 petrol and from £15,000 diesel. LX 2.0 HDI 90 advertised by Citroën at £12,950 after £800 cashback in Summer 2001; down to £11,195 after £1,770 cashback by June 2002. Very good 2001 four star NCAP crash safety rating announced 28/3/2001. Users website: www.CitroënPicasso.org.uk Recommended.

More, and latest offers, online at www.citroen.co.uk

What's bad: Front window pillars can slightly obscure front three-quarter vision. Aircon £650 extra on base-spec LX models. A really tricky road will show up its handling limits, but still impressive for a mini MPV. Some problems reported with Multiplex wiring. Some elderly drivers unable to ignore windscreen reflections.

What to watch out for: Too soon to say. Make sure all the electrics work, especially the dash functions.

Recalls: 25/9/2000: 3,648 Xsaras and Picassos built 7/2000–9/2000 recalled because front suspension ball joint clamp bolt hold may have been incorrectly machined leading to disengagement of the ball joint.

Pivots replaced if necessary. Late 2001: PSA TSB issued to check all common-rail to injector unions on HDIs for leaks. March 2002: All 70,000 RHD Picassos sold in UK recalled to check/replace circlip which holds brake pedal pin in place (source: '*Autocar*' 20/3/2002). May 2002: 4,000 UK Picasso HDIs recalled (24,000 worldwide)starting with VIN 392XXXX. Problem with a turbocharger pipe which can lead to erratic performance and/or excessive smoking.

ZX (1992 to 1998)

What's good: Excellent ride and handling combination, second only to Peugeot 306. 13ft 4in long by 5ft 7in wide and weighing from a light 945kg. Comfortable and absorbs bumps well. 1.4 TU engines and 1.9XU diesels are the best buys. All capable of 150,000 miles plus if properly looked after. 130bhp 2.0 Volcane was quick; 155bhp 16v should have been quicker still. 92bhp 1.9 turbodiesel could also be made to shift a bit. Non-turbo XUD capable of 50 mpg. Sensible nearside-only electric door mirror. Bargain basement prices now.

What's bad: 1.6 is a bit of a camel, 1.8 less so. 155bhp 2.0 16v had strange power delivery and throttle delay, making old 130bhp Volcane feel nicer to drive. Turbo XUD not that economical – can drop to as little as 36 mpg. Boot not much bigger than Peugeot 205. Early front brake problems cured by modified callipers. Brake warning light very sensitive to low brake fluid level. If this happens with a diesel, which has a brake vacuum pump, disappearing brake fluid could leave you with no brakes. Brake master cylinders themselves also fail. Cambelts and camshaft end seals must be changed every 3 years and 36,000 miles. Coolant must be changed every two years to avoid cylinder head gasket problems. (Coolant is difficult to change without getting air-locks.) Radiators apt to fail every 3 years or so. Petrol models may have cat converter MOT test problems. Always difficult to sell and becoming increasingly so. Transmission oil cooler of automatic can perforate, letting in radiator coolant which wrecks the transmission. Rod through bock failures in 1997 and 1998 XUDTs. In June 2001 Citroën was rated by Motor Warranty Direct as Britain's 3rd worst out of 22 marques for warranty claims (check online at www.warrantydirect.co.uk)

What to watch out for: See above. 'J' reg. ZXs could suffer front brake calliper problems cured by fitting later callipers (this will have been done to most of them). Some reports of sticking handbrakes, easily checked by seeing how easy the car is to push. Early Avantage diesels lacked power steering, as did early Avantage diesel estates which came out long after the hatch got PAS. 16v noisy, not really that quick and best avoided. Upholstery tears easily and is difficult to repair. Make sure all the electrics work. Insist on new MOT, especially if car is post-August 1992 and fitted with a cat. Check spare wheel is in its underboot cradle and not nicked. Look for engine oil leaks, gearbox oil leaks, coolant leaks from radiator and heater matrix, brake fluid leaks from rear brakes.

In summary (with thanks to David W. in The Back Room – the online forum at www.honestjohn.co.uk):

- Timing belt at 50,000ml intervals, tensioner at every other belt change.
- Water pump may be needed at second or third belt change.
- Coolant should be changed two yearly.
- Heater matrixs do go anything after 100,000mls. They are a fair job having a trade time to change from 7–10hrs. At £50/hr plus the matrix you can get up to a major bill.
- Change brake fluid two yearly.
- Front discs may be needed every 50,000mls.
- Rear brake cylinders (on drum models) may fail after 60,000mls.
- Handbrake cables can fail after 80,000mls.
- Front suspension bushes are often needed after 60,000mls.
- Diesel fuel filter housing cover can distort giving rise to air leaks; easy/cheap to cure.
- Glowplugs perhaps needed every 75,000mls
- Diesel fast idle "waxstat" often sticks in slow or fast position after 75,000mls.....easy/cheap to replace.
- Tailgate lock solenoid assy can fail after 100,000mls...easy to replace.

Recalls: 1994 (mostly Volcane, May 1992–Oct 1992, and 16v 1992–1994): Brake pipe chafing. 1996 ('facelift' model from June 1994): faulty seatbelt pretensioners and, on cars so fitted, faulty airbag sensors.

DAEWOO

Espero (1995 to 1997)

What's good: Lots and lots of car for the money. Even better used value than the Nexia and much better looking. 15ft 2in long by 5ft 8in wide and weighing 1,103 to 1,165kg. 90bhp 1.5, 95bhp 1.8 and 105bhp 2.0. 1.8 CDi has standard aircon which will always make it a good summertime seller. Makes a perfect replacement for those who mourn the passing of the Montego saloon. May have some of its original 3-year warranty left. Not my cup of tea, but cheap with most used examples under £1,000.

What's bad: Called the 'despairer' in the trade. Interior trim not as good as exterior of car. May suffer premature front tyre wear. Not great at fuel economy. Aircon has been known to pack up. Rapidly depreciated once 3-year warranties and service contracts came to an end, though some owners managed to extend them for 5 years.

What to watch out for: Why bother with base spec 90 bhp 1.5GLXi when 95 bhp 1.8CDi is only a few hundred pounds more? Esperos struggled to sell at first, many went onto rental fleets where they could have suffered damage to front suspension. As a second-hand buy they have been popular as minicabs, so watch out for clocking when buying third-hand. If it hasn't been serviced on time, why not? (The first three years' routine services were included in the price.) Make sure the ABS works properly as this is expensive to replace. Check under oil filler cap for emulsion as expansion tank pipe has been known to blow off leading to overheating and warped cylinder head. Bonnet catches break, so you have to ask yourself how long it has been broken and how long it is since anyone looked underneath. Central locking can play up. Make sure aircon blows cold. Timing belt and GF50 tensioner pulley replacement at 40k miles or 4 years whichever comes first is critical.

Recalls: 3/7/2000: All 22,266 Esperos sold 1995–1997 recalled to replace seatbelt buckles.

Kalos (from October 2002)

What's good: New Fiesta sized supermini to rival Honda Jazz, VW Polo, new SEAT Ibiza, Vauxhall Corsa, new Nissan Micra, Toyota Yaris, Citroën C3 and Peugeot 206 as well as the new Fiesta in a very crowded sector of the market. To have 1.2, 1.4 and 1.6 litre engines. Now that GM has taken over Daewoo, launch is likely to go ahead.

What's bad: Too soon to say.

What to watch out for: Too soon to say.

Korando 4x4 (from March 1999)

What's good: See Ssangyong Korando. Daewoo took over from March 1999.

What's bad: See Ssangyong Korando.

What to watch out for: See Ssangyong Korando.

Lanos (from 1997)

What's good: Rover 200–sized: 13ft 4in long by 5ft 6in wide and weighing from 1,000kg. 3–door hatch, 5–door hatch or 4 door saloon. Lots of standard features, including power steering, twin airbags, three years routine servicing included in price. Better value than a Rover 200. Decent colours and paint. Doesn't look naff and cheapskate. 74 bhp 1.4 or 105 bhp 1.6. £10,700 I.6 comes with standard ABS, aircon, electric mirrors and electric windows. Sold quite well to private market until doubts began to emerge about Daewoo's future. Average performance in NCAP crash tests. A cheap second-hand buy.

What's bad: A bit nondescript. Not particularly nice to drive. Interiors not great. Smaller than Nexia, so less space for rear passengers and luggage. Trim rattles, wind noise, poor mpg. R reg. 1.6s down to £1,500 at auction by mid 2001 due to doubts about company's future. One complaint of rear parking brake shoes binding and burning out without the warning light showing. Running problems with 1.6 engine.

What to watch out for: A reasonable new-car buy for a certain type of owner. Questionable used-car buy because why would anyone sell it before they had used up the three-year deal? Used Lanos at Daewoo 'Motor Shows' likely to be ex-rental. Timing belt and GF50 tensioner pulley replacement at 40k miles or 4 years whichever comes first is critical. Don't buy a 1.6 without extensive test driving to make sure it runs properly.

Leganza (from 1997)

What's good: Bigger than the Espero and almost in the Galant/Passat size category, but much cheaper and in UK terms a 'new car bargain'. 15ft 4in long by 5ft 10in wide and weighing from 1,325kg. Loaded with kit, including ABS, aircon, electric windows, height-adjustable seats. £13,800 SX better value than £15,000 CDX. Smooth 132bhp 2.0 litre engines. New car Daewoo Deal includes three-year warranty and servicing. Daewoo's best car so far. Smooth engines praised. Now very good value for money as a second hand buy.

What's bad: Not the world's greatest driver's car, but how you judge it depends on what you're used to. Came bottom of the list in USA Insurance Industry crash tests.

What to watch out for: Collapse of servicing network. Timing belt and GF50 tensioner pulley replacement at 40k miles or 4 years whichever comes first is critical.

Matiz (from 1998)

What's good: Tiny and cute. Styled by Giugiaro from scratch and much better looking than Move, Wagon R or ATOZ. Just 11ft 6in long by 4ft 11in wide and only 778kg. Sensible, eco-friendly city car or suburban runabout. Excellent for the school run. Not bad value with full Daewoo 3-year servicing and warranty package. Handles well enough given its obvious limitations. Tiny size makes it easy to park. Outsells Fiat Seicento in Italy. Reasonable Three-Star rating in Euro NCAP crash tests. Facelifted inside and out for 2001. Hold their value very well. Price cut to £5,995 summer 2001. £600 cashback kept this offer going from April 2002.

What's bad: 796cc 50 bhp 3-cylinder engine not quite up to motorway travel. Rolled over on high-speed reverse-turn by *Autocar* magazine. Trim quality not brilliant. Terrible Neil Lyndon road test. report in *Sunday Telegraph* on 4/10/98. More powerful version seen testing at over 100mph was shelved, possibly for stability or crash worthiness reasons.

What to watch out for: Proper Daewoo/Halfords service history. Collapse of servicing network. Timing belt and GF50 tensioner pulley replacement at 40k miles or 4 years whichever comes first is critical.

Recalls: 18/7/2000: 4,837 Matiz models recalled due to possibility of corrosion in fuel filter which could lead to a fuel leak. Fuel filter to be replaced with modified type.

Musso 4x4 (from March 1999)

What's good: See Ssangyong Musso. Daewoo took over using Daewoo corporate grille from March 1999.

What's bad: See Ssangyong Musso.

What to watch out for: See Ssangyong Musso.

Nexia (1995 to 1997)

What's good: Based on the old (pre-1991) Astra with 1.5 litre 75 bhp and 90 bhp GM engines. 3–door hatch, 5–door hatch, or 4–door saloon. 13ft 11in long by 5ft 5in wide (4–door 14ft 8in long). Weighs 1,068kg to 1,138kg. Lots of kit as standard, including power steering and ABS on even the most basic cars. Aircon was a buyer-tempting standard fit from May 1996. 4-speed auto optional from October 1995. 75bhp single cam 1.5 or 90bhp twin cam 1.5. 5-speed manuals with optional 4 speed auto. Used models very cheap now for the age and specification.

What's bad: New cars were priced to include the Daewoo Deal, so initially lost value very quickly (bounced back up once the public realised what value they were). Poor ride and handling by late 1990s standards. ABS is a desirable feature, but a very expensive MOT failure when it goes wrong. The booted version looks hideous. Poor build quality. Can suffer electrical problems. Heavy tyre wear.

Sudden failure of GF50 plastic timing belt tensioner pulleys. Reports of bulkhead failure.

What to watch out for: Needs frequent brake fluid changes to prevent damage to ABS. Watch out for kerbing damage. Expect trim troubles, particularly driver's door seal. Creaks and rattles are normal from ageing design. May have been bought by elderly people with no previous experience of PAS. Popular with Motability lessees, so may be holes where cars have been adapted. Collapse of servicing network. Timing belt and GF50 tensioner pulley replacement at 40k miles or 4 years whichever comes first is critical.

Recalls: 1997 (to May '95): check engine bay wiring harness routing (helpline: 0800 060606). 3/7/2000: all cars built from 1995 to 1997 recalled to check seatbelt buckles and replace if necessary.

Nubira (from 1997)

What's good: Second generation Daewoo, sized between old Nexia and Espero. British designed. Usual Daewoo Deal benefits. 1.6 litre twin-cam 90 bhp engine or 2.0 litre twin-cam 132 bhp quite powerful for car's size. Available as saloon or useful, reasonable looking estate. 14ft 8in long by 5ft 7in wide (estate 14ft 10in long). Weighs 1,153 to 1,282kg. Two engines: 105bhp 1.6 or 132bhp 2.0. Standard ABS and aircon across the range. Sensibly priced by UK standards when Daewoo Deal is taken into consideration. Sold well in UK. Bigger headlight facelift in Spring 1999. Decent ICE. Cheap second hand.

What's bad: Engines a bit coarse. Estate car load area suffers from rear suspension intrusion. Wind noise. Reports of bulkhead failure.

What to watch out for: Not a bad new car buy for those not seeking the ultimate in refinement and handling. Used Nubiras at Daewoo 'Motor Shows' likely to be ex-rental, so check carefully for careless driver or accident damage. Watch out for uneven front tyre wear from kerbed and bent front suspension. Collapse of servicing network. Timing belt and GF50 tensioner pulley replacement at 40k miles or 4 years whichever comes first is critical.

Recalls: 19–6–2001: 3000 Nubira CDX models recalled due to possible fault with the fuel filter. 30 minutes work required to be carried out "while you wait" replacing rigid fuel filter and fuel line with flexible line. Freefone helpline 0800 060606. Also a TSB to fix a fault in the air-con system due to a faulty pressure relief valve which also damages the chiller plate.

Rexton 4x4 (from 2002 in S. Korea)

What's good: Built by Daewoo's Ssangyong factory to replace Musso as Daewoo's big 4x4. Engine choice: 138bhp 2.3 litre four, 118bhp 2.9 litre five cylinder MB diesel or 180bhp 3.2 litre six cylinder MB diesel.

What's bad: Another big, heavy tarmac-crunching 4x4. May not come to the UK.

What to watch out for: Too soon to say.

Tacuma (from 2000)

What's good: Daweoo's Scenic-sized mini MPV. 1.6 litre, 1.8 litre or 2.0 litre petrol engines. Standard c/a, aircon, ABS. Driver's seat has height adjustment and lumbar support. Front passenger seat swivels. Plenty of room inside. 4-speed auto option on 2.0CDX. Underseat drawers and picnic tables in the front seat backs. Rides and handles quite well. Plenty of in car entertainment available for the kids in the back seats. Quality better than previous Daewoos.

What's bad: Not the best looking small MPV and that's putting it kindly. High rear load sill. Not cheap with 1.8SE listed at Daewoo Deal price of £12,495 and 2.0CDX at £13,495 (1.6 from £11,000). Parcel shelf cannot be removed without first folding the rear seats forward. Centre rear belt just a lap belt.

What to watch out for: Collapse of original servicing network. Timing belt and GF50 tensioner pulley replacement at 40k miles or 4 years whichever comes first is critical. 1.6s seem to have developed ECU problems and do not run properly.

DAIHATSU

Applause (1992 to 1996)

What's good: Looks like a 3–box saloon, but is really a hatchback. Can be reliable, efficient and good value but has no image whatsoever. People may wonder what it is, but won't bother to ask. All had 1.6 litre engines: 91 bhp with carb; 105 bhp with injection. PAS always standard. Cheap now.

What's bad: Old before its time. Very light 'feel-free' power steering, soggy ride, uninspiring plastic trim. Body parts likely to become hard to get.

What to watch out for: Worn steering and tyres and kerbed front suspension due to lightness of steering. Needs new timing belt every 3 years. 2nd gear can get noisy. Emulsified oil from short runs leads to premature camshaft, cam follower wear. Injected models have rear discs which may be rusty from lack of use.

Charade (1987 to 1993)

What's good: Good looking. 993cc three-cylinder 99 bhp GTti very quick and lots of fun to drive. 52 bhp Charade 1.0 CXs decent enough pre-cat superminis. PAS was available from September 1990 in CX Special and 2-speed autos. 1.3 litre 16v four-cylinder 75 bhp pre-cat engines were more robust. 89 bhp 'cat' engine launched July 1991. 1.3s had 3-speed rather than 2-speed auto. Ultra-economical 3-cylinder 993cc 46 bhp turbodiesel.

What's bad: Light build now that the cars are getting old. Two-speed auto struggles. Plasticky interior and not great to drive. Ride and handling of all but GTti not quite up to the mark. Most diesels kicked off their lives with driving schools.

What to watch out for: GTti very likely to have been thrashed. All models likely to be showing their age by now, could have some rust which will weaken an already light structure. GTti needs expert servicing – can't be done by the bloke with the lock-up round the corner. Only buy GTti from enthusiastic owners who have changed the oil every 3,000 miles. Timing belts need replacing every 3 years. Watch out for uneven tyre wear on all models and excessive tyre scrub on GTti.

Charade (from 1993)

What's good: Much more highly rated than previous model. Grew up with base engine now an 84 bhp 1.3 litre catalysed four. Also an 88 bhp 1.5, a 105 bhp 1.6 and, from February 1997, a 97 bhp 1.3 Gate with lowered suspension, ABS and alloys. All light and easy to drive. All got drivers airbags from January 1988.

What's bad: Not much boot space and still has poor ride quality.

What to watch out for: Lasts quite well. But check carefully for short-run syndrome ('mayonnaise' under the oil filler and a rusty rear silencer). GTis need regular brake fluid changes. Airbag may have gone off for no reason and the steering wheel trim panel simply stuck back on.

Copen (from 2002 in Japan)

What's good: Tiny roadster 3,395mm (11ft 2in)long filling gap left by Suzuki Cappuccino and Honda Beat and also nibbling into Street Ka and SEAT Tango territory. Has huge plus of a hardtop that folds into the boot like an MB SLK and Peugeot 206CC. Sits on much modified Cuore platform. Has 65bhp 660cc turbo engine. 5-speed manual or 4-speed pushbutton auto. From just £8,000 in Japan.

What's bad: If it comes to UK will be much dearer than in Japan.

What to watch out for: Lets see if the grey import boys can get the cars through enhanced SVA.

Cuore (from 1997)

What's good: Replaced Mira. Little screamer of an engine. Prices start at £5,995 for three-door 'Start' model, rise to £9,750 for turbocharged all-wheel-drive 660cc Cuore Avanzato TR-XX R4. Standard model useful for school run. Reliable and frugal on fuel. Easy to steer and park. Slow depreciator in both percentage terms and money terms. Extensively revised for 2002. Prices now start at £5,995 on the road for the three-door 1.0 E, and this includes three years servicing, three years roadside recovery, and three years unlimited mileage warranty.

The three-cylinder twin cam 12 valve engine now develops 55PS at 5,200rpm and 83Nm (65.1 lb ft) torque at 3,600rpm. Top speed is 87mph, 0–60 takes a quite quick 12.5 seconds, combined consumption is 55.4mpg and CO_2 emissions are 124g/km (£100 VED). Fifth gear ratio is now stretched to 21.7mph per 1,000 rpm making the car a much better motorway cruiser than before. An automatic version is also available.

More online at www.daihatsu.co.uk

What's bad: Handling and drivability ok, but nothing special. Manual transmission whines. Fared badly in German TUV/*Auto Bild* front offset crash tests.

What to watch out for: Front suspension damage and excessive tyre wear. Make sure brake servo is assisting the brakes. Uneven tyre wear on souped-up Avanzato. Supermarket carpark dings and dents. Emulsified oil under the oil filler cap a sure sign of short-run syndrome. Check for tears and damage to trim.

Recalls: 10/10/2001: Cuore models built 1/1/1998–31/12/1999 recalled because headlights and horn could fail due to a wiring fault.

Fourtrak (from 1985)

What's good: The Yorkshire farmer's favourite. Tough as horsemeat. Very good at towing. Independent model from July 1993 by far the best. 2.0 litre 87–90 bhp engine lasted from Jan '89 to July '93, otherwise all diesel. Slow 72 bhp non-turbo 2.8 from Jan '89–July '93; 90 bhp turbo from Jan '90 to July '93; 101 bhp turbo 2.8 TDS from July '93 also has automatically freewheeling front hubs. Power then cut to 97 bhp from March '96 to meet new emissions regs. Lots of special editions include 'Timberline'. 'Anjou' and 'Riviera'. Discovery-style side-facing jump seats in back okay for short trips.

What's bad: Since it's a farmer's car, it has probably seen some hard use by farmers. Pre-'Independent' models have harsh ride from two solid axles. Disadvantage of only three doors makes getting into the mid-row seats difficult.

What to watch out for: What's it been towing? If it has a tow hook, check transmission carefully. Give it a really thorough 4x4 check. Expect bodywork, suspension, axle, steering, exhaust and general underside damage, as these cars are rarely bought by townies. Look for oil smoke from worn turbo bearings, burned-out turbo oil seals.

Grand Move (1997 to 2000)

What's good: Applause-based tall estate car (not really an MPV). Grand Move+ well equipped with standard aircon, and relatively well priced by UK standards. Lots of armrests and cupholders. Optional 4-speed auto. 1.5 litre 88 bhp engine. All seats recline flat to form double bed. 'Secret' compartment for valuables. A niche model appealing to an elderly niche market which wants upright seats, cupholders and reclining seats for Sunday outings. Facelifted in October 1998 and got 1,590cc 90bhp engine with 5-speed manual or 4-speed autobox.

What's bad: Awkward looks. Uninspiring to drive. Many sold via Motability Finance took a long time to get re-housed via the auctions.

What to watch out for: See Applause. Last ones came on an X reg.

Mira (1993 to 1995)

What's good: Cheap, updated Domino a useful school-run special. Reliable and frugal on fuel.

What's bad: Not happy on motorways. Very light build. Not exactly built to last.

What to watch out for: High mileage would be quite unusual. Kerbing could damage structure as well as front suspension. Look for dings and dents and especially rust, as this will seriously weaken an already weak structure. Emulsified oil under the oil filler cap a sure sign of short-run syndrome. As long as exhaust not smoking white, this should be curable with a flush and oil change. Oil is best changed every six months, but make sure it hasn't been left to more than a year. Timing belt needs changing every 3 years.

Move (from 1997)

What's good: Low centre of gravity means it handled surprisingly well in the *Daily Telegraph* 'slalom' test. Little screamer of an engine. More fun to drive than bigger Suzuki Wagon R. Restyled for 1999 model year.

What's bad: Originally cost less than £4,000 in Japan. Looks like a phone box on wheels. Feels like it's made out of Bacofoil (don't have an accident in one). Not much room inside. Large glass area and lots of bare metal means it suffers severe condensation in winter. Though road wheels are tiny, still has a 'space saver' spare.

What to watch out for: Any damage likely to be obvious, but a kerbing or serious potholing could damage the structure as well as the suspension. Has a timing belt which will need to be changed every 3 years or so.

Naked

What's good: Curious retro basic hatchback shown at Birmingham Motor Show in autumn 2000 may come to the UK at a very low price.

What's bad: too soon to say.

What to watch out for: Too soon to say.

Sirion (from 1998)

What's good: Cheap, decently built, small 5–door hatchback with three-year warranty. Lots of safety kit and reasonable three star rating in Euro NCAP crash tests (but see TUV test results). Optional four-speed autobox. Revised range from October 2000 priced from £7,495 for 1.0E included quite quick uprated 100bhp 1,299cc Toyota engined versions from £8,995 (F Speed auto £9,995). Drive with a light foot and 1.0E can be very economical. Drive hard and the 1.3 does 112mph, with 60 coming up in just 9.5 seconds. Range updated June 2002, including new entry level 1.0EL automatic or 1.3EL manual each at £7,995, new four wheel drive '4trak' at £9,995 and new 110bhp Rally 2 and Rally 4 models with top speed of

115mph and 0–60 of 7.9 seconds. With low CO_2 of 134g/km, strong performance and 60mph potential on the motorway the £7,995 1.3EL makes a lot of sense.

What's bad: Peculiar looking and, not surprisingly, the trade calls it the 'Silly-one'. 3-cylinder 989cc 54 bhp engine needs working hard to deliver acceptable performance. Lightweight construction did not do well in German TUV/*Auto Bild* front offset crash tests.

What to watch out for: Complaints about original model from *Telegraph* readers include coolant leaks, poor panel alignment, clutch cable failures, frequent failure of front nearside suspension strut and rust on the tailgate around the chrome handle. Make sure the car has proper franchise service history.

Recalls: 17/1/2000 (April/May 1998 build: 902 cars): horn and headlights could fail due to bad connection. Connectors to be replaced. 10/10/2001: Further recall for same reason.

Sportrak (1989 to 1998)

What's good: Cheap, niche, short wheelbase 4x4 with 94 bhp 1.6 litre petrol engines. 12ft 5in long by 5. 4in wide and weighing 1,175kg. Hood, hardtop or both, depending on model.

What's bad: Not much room in the back. Hard top components hard to store and quite a job to remove. Not really strong enough for serious off-roading. Some of the trim is a bit flimsy. Very hard ride, not very stable at speed and slow on the road.

What to watch out for: Probably has seen some off-road use, most likely launching sailing dinghies. Do all the usual 4x4 checks and have a good look for rust from salt water.

Taruna

What's good: Smart-looking grown-up Terios with two-wheel-drive 1.6 litre engine and seats for seven by virtue of two jump seats facing each other in the extreme rear. So far seems to be Indonesian market only.

What's bad: Not available in UK.

What to watch out for: Any imports likely to be tough to get through SVA as will lack UK safety belts, heating and de-misting system, etc.

Terios (from 1998)

What's good: Titchy but tall and narrow 4x4. 82 bhp 1,296cc engine, 5-speed gearbox and 4-speed auto option. Terios+ has alloys, aircon, passenger airbag and electric front windows. Very capable off road and one of the lightest 4x4s you can buy, which helps enormously in snow. Starting prices under £10,000. Late models have same 85bhp 1,298cc Toyota Yaris engine as YRV.

What's bad: Some people might think it looks a bit silly.

What to watch out for: Unlikely to have seen hard off-road use, but sold by same dealers who sell Fourtrak so could have gone to a farmer's kids.

YRV (from 2001)

What's good: Attractively styled small five door hatchback from March 2001. Standard engine is a 1,298cc twin cam four developing 86bhp and 88.5 lb ft torque, as in the updated Sirion. Daihatsu's F-speed automatic transmission also available. Emissions are 145g/km CO_2 for the manual and 156g/km for the auto, qualifying the manual for £100pa VED. An important fitting for this type of car is abs with electronic brake force distribution on all but the base model. UK list prices include a three year unlimited mileage warranty. Reasonable alternative to the Toyota Yaris, but doesn't handle as well. F speed button automatic works fine as long as you remember to switch it on using the dash mounted button. Cut price, cut spec YRV Radical at £7,995 and new YRV 4trak four wheel drive at £10,995 from July 2001, Also 5 year unlimited mileage warranty on Premium and F-speed models. A 140bhp turbocharged version already on sale in Japan may eventually arrive in the UK.

What's bad: Has been a problem of F-speed transmission oil coolers failing, leading to transmission fluid contamination by engine coolant and failure of the box.

What to watch out for: Too soon to say.

ECOVEC

Merlin

What's good: Amazing single seater three wheeler coupe powered by an all new range of water-cooled V-Twin engines of between 749cc and 1,198cc. 1,200 develops 100bhp, does 60mpg and takes the car to 100mph. All-up weight is just 900lbs so can be driven on a B1 motorcycle licence. Due to arrive in the UK in 2001. Projected price £10,999. Visit the website at www.corbinmotors.com

What's bad: Only for one. Derbyshire based importer Ecovec has "ceased trading".

What to watch out for: Too soon to say.

Sparrow

What's good: American-built extraordinary plastic-bodied single seater electric car. Has a top speed of 70mph and a range of 40–60 miles, making it ideal for cross-city commuting. Battery charger is on board so only needs to be connected to a power supply. Takes 3 hours for a full charge costing about 50p. Price £5,999. CD player and electric windows. Visit the website at www.corbinmotors.com

What's bad: Odd, but would have made sense had there not been a generator fault which proved impossible to fix. Derbyshire based Ecovec "ceased trading".

What to watch out for: Too soon to say.

FERRARI

456M (from 1993)

What's good: Big, powerful 5.5 litre 442bhp genuine four-seater coupe. Strong performance of 0–60 in under 5 seconds and top speed of 186mph. The original 437bhp 456 Gt has been around since 1993 and second-hand examples can be bought for as little as £50,000. Excellent independents such as DK engineering can look after it for more affordable buckets of cash than official Ferrari dealers. 456M means manual 6-speed, which it MUST be. Fitted luggage can be purchased to go with it.

What's bad: The wonderful, old fashioned, gated Ferrari gearchange is getting a bit old-fashioned. Dimply dashboard trim looks like an old lady's thighs. Feels a bit flat compared to 550 Maranello. Other potential problems are fuel consumption and losing your licence in the UK.

What to watch out for: Accident damage. Cars stolen from another country. Anything remotely dodgy about the car's history, stay well away.

Recalls: 17–12–98: Barrel nuts of fuel hoses could be over-tightened causing fuel leaks. Hoses and barrel nuts to be replaced and tightened correctly. 9–8–99: connection from brake fluid reservoir to master cylinder may fail. Replacement connector to be fitted. 23/7/2001: 23 456s and 550s built 1/1/2001 to 31/12/2001 (VINs ending 3276 to 4683) recalled for parking brake ratchet to be replaced.

550 Maranello (Sep 1996 to Jul 2002)

What's good: Fabulous front-engined coupe with all of 485bhp from its 5.5 litre V12. 0–60 in 4.1 seconds, a top speed of 199mph. Reaches 170mph with indecent ease and easily capable of lapping the Millbrook 2–mile bowl at 180. Remarkably unflustered and docile in traffic. Feels immensely strong. Probably the best supercar you can buy.

What's bad: Just two seats. Quite a big car. Gobbles fuel. Replaced in Summer 2002 by even more powerful 575M.

What to watch out for: Accident damage. Stolen imports. If there is anything strange or unexplained about the car, trust your gut feelings and walk away.

Recalls: 21–9–98: Insufficient clamping may lead to engine compartment fuel leak and risk of fire. Fuel lines to be replaced and correctly clamped. 11–12–98: Damage to inner hydraulic seals of steering rack through driver using too much lock will lead to loss of steering power assistance. Steering rack and oil cooler to be replaced. 23/7/2001: 23 550s built 1/1/2001 to 31/12/2001 (VINs ending 3276 to 4683) recalled for parking brake ratchet to be replaced. 20/11/2001: possibility that bolt locating inserts fitted to mag wheels may crack if excessive force applied. Original mag wheel rims to be replaced with aluminium rims that do not have inserts. Also new wheel bolts to be fitted.

575M Maranello (from Summer 2002)

What's good: 575M Maranello officially launched at Geneva on 5th March and on sale in UK from summer 2002. Instead of the gated manual six-speed shift, the 575M can be fitted with an electro-hydraulic F1 control unit at the rear of the car. The driver has the option of changing gear by fingertip paddle shifts on the steering wheel, or by selecting 'auto' and leaving changes to the transmission electronics which can be set to operate in 'normal' or 'sport' modes. Power unit of the 575M has been stretched to 5,750cc and develops 379kW (515bhp) at 7,250rpm and 589Nm (434 lb ft) torque at 5,250rpm. Adaptive suspension offers 'sport' or 'comfort' settings. The braking has been uprated. Weight distribution is a perfect 50:50 front to rear. Belts are now full harness. And the seats offer more side support for spirited driving. Top speed is quoted at 202mph (yes, 202 mph), 0–60 takes less than four seconds, combined fuel consumption is 12.97mpg (yes, 12.97 mpg), CO_2 output 499g/km. Prices are £154,350 for the six-speed gated manual and £160,845 for the F1.

More online at www.ferrari.co.uk

What's bad: Fuel consumption and CO_2.

What to watch out for: Speed cameras.

F355 (1994 to 1999)

What's good: Stunning looks. Stunning performance. Stunning handling. Low depreciation. Jeremy Clarkson bought one with his own money so it must be really special. Option of sequential gearshift controlled by buttons on steering wheel.

What's bad: Brakes aren't as good as some race drivers expected. Enormously high maintenance costs whether you use the car or not. Frequent timing belt replacement essential.

What to watch out for: Repaired accident damage. Lack of maintenance (very common among little-used supercars). Flat battery. Rusted discs. Seized handbrakes. Any sign of emulsion in the engine oil. Clutch cables go (Jeremy's did). Badly worn tyres (from 'track days'). Needs new timing belts every 12,000 miles – job costs £1,000–plus.

Recalls: 23–4–96: Steering rack retaining bracket may loosen. To be replaced by better quality bracket. 23–7–97: Fuel line retaining bolts my split leading to duel leakage. 10–6–98: Installation of hood mechanism in 355 Spider may lead to a bolt puncturing the fuel tank. To be checked and bolt re-aligned (fuel tank replaced if necessary). 27–1–98: Water hose clamp may chafe on fuel line. To be re-aligned. 3–2–98 (repeat of 23–7–97 recall): Fuel tank retaining nuts may split leading to fuel leakage. Fuel lined to be replaced. 30–9–98 Throttle pedal pivot may snap. Pivots to be replaced. 9–8–99: Connection from brake fluid reservoir to master cylinder may fail. Replacement connection to be fitted.

F360 Modena (1999 on)

What's good: Brilliant sportscar. Even better than 355. 400 bhp at 8,000 rpm and 275 lb ft at 4,750 rpm. Top speed over 180mph. Out-pointed all other cars at *Autocar* magazine's 1999 handling day at Oulton Park. 360 Spider and Spider F1 from October 2000. F1 has sequential gearshift controlled by buttons on steering wheel.

What's bad: One of the few cars selling at a significant premium in 1999 and still very hard to get in 2002. High CO_2 at 395g/km may be more severely penalised by VED in the future.

What to watch out for: See 355.

Recalls: 10/2/2000: 115 cars built in 1999 recalled because screws retaining the airbag ECU may not be long enough. To be replaced with longer screws; 18/2/2000: 125 cars built 1999–2000 may suffer from ABS ECU problem increasing bias to rear brakes. ECU software to be upgraded. 26/4/2000: 27 cars built 1999–2000 to fit American-standard fuel tank side protection plates to make tank less vulnerable in a side impact accident. 20/10/2000: 188 360 models recalled because fixing bolts holding starter ring to clutch may fracture causing severe damage to clutch bellhousing. Ring gear and fixing bolts of affected vehicles to be replaced. 26/4/2001: Build 1/1/1999–31/12/2000: Build, VIN: ZFFYR51C000114014 to ZFFYR51B0001119149EBD warning light may fail to illuminate if there is a fault. Dashboard ECU and software to be updated. 30/7/2001: Four 360 Spiders, VINs ending 0799, 0801, 2025 and 2026 recalled to replace door striker retaining plates which could break leading doors to open at speed.

F60 Enzo (from late 2002)

What's good: Ultimate track day and rich poser's Ferrari. Engine is a 650bhp 6.0 litre V12 with 485lb ft torque. Top speed quoted at 217mph; 0–100kph 3.6 seconds, so 0–60 must be in about 3.3. Six speeds, F1 pushbutton shift and no clutch pedal. Economical, though, at 12.3mpg on the combined cycle. Will it fit your stables? Dimensions are 4,8702mm by 2,035mm by 1,147mm high. Weighs 1.365kg.

What's bad: Price tag has now risen to £500,000. Health and Safety Inspectors are now starting to look at Track Days.

What to watch out for: Paying Tom Hartley too much of a premium to get one.

Older model recalls

Recalls: 23/7/2001: "Various models" of Ferraris built 1/1/1967 to 31/12/1998 recalled because incorrect tightening of engine oil filter with insufficiently compliant 'O' ring could lead to a serious oil leak and fire risk. New type of oil filter to be fitted: part no. 191993.

FIAT

Barchetta (from 1995)

What's good: Cute, 1,800cc twin-cam, front-wheel-drive sportscar with some nice design touches. Useful 130bhp. 12ft 10in long by 5ft 5in wide and weighing 1,060kg. Drives quite well. FIAT had 2nd lowest average cost in warranty claims for cars up to 10 years old in 2002 Warranty Direct index, check online at www.performanceindex.co.uk

What's bad: Left-hand-drive only. Most will have been personally imported from Europe where they can cost as little as £10,000 new. FIAT/Alfa joint worst for breakdowns attended by German ADAC during 2001.

What to watch out for: Imports with the wrong lights and speedos being re-sold as UK-market cars at UK prices. Make sure it has its 'Red Key'.

Recalls: 1999: problem of sticking control valve for engine variable valve timing-makes engine sound like a diesel. Announced on BBC 'Watchdog' 21/1/99.

Bravo and Brava (1995 to late 2001)

What's good: Bravo (3–door) styling. Brava (5–door) practicality. Bravo 13ft 2in by 5ft 9in and weighting 1,000kg to 1,190kg. Brava 13ft 9in by 5ft 8in and weighing 1,040kg to 1,180kg. Good, sharp steering. Easy to use dash-top radio/cassette. Excellent, fully-adjustable seats and steering wheels throughout the range (designed by Professor Mark Porter's Ergonomics Group at Loughborough University). Engines are 1.4 with 80bhp; 1.2 16v (from December 1998) with 86bhp; 1.6 with 103bhp; 1.8 with 113bhp; 2.0 five cylinder with 147bhp; 1.9 diesel with 75bhp, 100bhp and 105bhp. 5-cylinder HGT is a powerful, well-balanced 'hot hatch'. Used prices came down sharply in 1998/99. Diesel Bravas well priced at 6 months old with 12,000–16,000 miles. Even better range of metallic colours than Punto. 'Ink Black' and 'Juvarra

Ivory' best of the lot. FIAT had 2nd lowest average cost in warranty claims for cars up to 10 years old in 2002 Warranty Direct index, check online at www.performanceindex.co.uk

What's bad: Many UK cars begin their lives on rental fleets. First thing that breaks is the cassette lid. Bravos (three-door) were about £1,000 dearer than more practical (five-door) Bravas in 1999, but difference fell to much less by 2002. Bravas can be affected by side winds. Two-Star below-average performance in NCAP crash tests. Small number of cars have suffered from faulty engine speed sensor leading to erratic running and cut-outs. Timing belt changes on 5-cylinder HGTs are a very expensive, engine-out job and all Bravos/Bravas MUST have a timing belt and tensioner change every 3 years or 36,000 miles whichever comes first. Need frequent oil changes to avoid carbon build up in oil feed pipe to camshaft. Came joint bottom with Marea in 2001 ADAC list 2001 of cars which break down most on German autobahns. Problems with plastic thermostat housing on earlier models which lead to localised overheating not picked up by temperature sensor and may result in head gasket failure. S and T plate Bravo 11th from bottom in 2001 *Top Gear*/J.D. Power Customer Satisfaction Survey. See website: www.fiatbravo.org.uk FIAT/Alfa joint worst for breakdowns attended by German ADAC during 2001. Replaced by Stilo early 2002. 7th from Bottom of 100 models for reliability in *Auto Express* 2002 survey. Bravo 5th from Bottom, Brava 13th from Bottom in 144 car 2002 JD Power/*What Car?* Customer Satisfaction Survey of V and W reg. cars.

What to watch out for: Make sure it comes with the original 'Red Key'. Check cassette lid not broken. Silly damage from careless renters and their kids. Check aircon on cars where fitted. Check operation of electric sunroof and windows where fitted. Reports of premature HT lead failure which could, in turn, spike the catalytic converter. Bonnet catches break (see Tipo). Plastic timing belt tensioner pulley can shatter without warning. Make sure timing belt and tensioner have been changed within last 3 years/36,000 miles. Trim starts to creak and rattle. Check everything electrical. Check carefully for signs of overheating, such as emulsified oil under oil cap (see above).

Recalls: 1997 (1996–97 build: 17,000 cars): petrol may contaminate brake vacuum diaphragm leading to loss of power assistance to brakes. 1998: Bravo/Brava 1.4 and 1.6 with ABS built before Oct '97: check for chafing of brake hoses.

Cinquecento (1993 to 1998)

What's good: Tiny four seater with minimal boot. 10ft 7in long by 4ft 11in wide and weighing 710kg to 735kg. 899cc pushrod engine with 41bhp and 1,108cc 'Fire' engine with 54bhp. Cinquecento Sporting 1.1 engine from Punto 55 is by far the best and the most likely to get some proper exercise. FIAT had 2nd lowest average cost in warranty claims for cars up to 10 years old in 2002 Warranty Direct index, check online at www.performanceindex.co.uk

What's bad: No power steering. Nasty gearchange on 900. 'Space saver' emergency wheel not liked by Brits. Polish build quality. Not as practical as the Panda. Cinquecento 900s have the old 899cc pushrod engine which can suffer premature rocker shaft wear due to emulsified oil and insufficiently frequent oil changes. Rear window can break if you shut the hatch from one side. Gearboxes also prone to failure. FIAT/Alfa joint worst for breakdowns attended by German ADAC during 2001.

What to watch out for: Lack of maintenance and 'short-run syndrome' typical of city cars. Ticking tappets. Duff cats. Signs of careless driving by inexperienced youngsters. Check trim for damage. Check for cylinder head gasket failure on 1.1 Fire engines. Make sure it has its 'Red Key'. Make sure fuel tank not rusty (see recalls). Report of metal fatigue in the clutch driven plate. Check clutch take-up and gearchange quality carefully.

Recalls: Recall to replace rusted fuel tanks FOC, but only notified to the first owner of the car or via FIAT dealers.

Cinquecento (from late 2002)

What's good: 3–door smart new small car to sell from around £5,500.

What's bad: Polish build quality. This project is now thought to have been canned and replaced by more sophisticated new Seicento due September 2003.

What to watch out for: Too soon to say.

Coupe (1995 to 2000)

What's good: Great-looking coupe, first with twin-cam 2.0 litre 4-cylinder 16v injected or turbo engines, then with stronger 2.0 litre 5-cylinder 20 valve injected or turbo engines from November 1996. Six-speed gearbox from 2000. Lots of nice design touches such as body colour painted dash and alloy fuel filler cap. 13ft 11in long by 5ft 9in wide and weighing 1,250kg to 1,320kg. 1,995cc four had 142 bhp or 200bhp with turbo; 1,998cc five had 147bhp or a solid 220bhp with turbo.

What's bad: Back seat is only suitable for dwarfs and pre-teen children. Quality/assembly problems. As with a Ferrari, timing belt changes of 5 cylinder cars are an engine-out job and can cost as much as £1,300. Has same plastic timing belt tensioner problem as other FIATs with same engine. Belt and tensioner need to be replaced every 3 years or 36,000 miles whichever comes first without fail. Condensation from parking brake cable can get into parking brake drums leading to the linings disintegrating and the debris from this seizing up the real calliper pins. Should be possible to clean it off, but some dealers specify expensive new callipers. Dropped from range in spring 2000. S and T platers 15th from bottom in 2001 *Top Gear*/J.D. Power Customer Satisfaction Survey. FIAT/Alfa joint worst for breakdowns attended by German ADAC during 2001.

What to watch out for: Signs of being driven hard or badly. Avoid any cars with kerbed wheels. Make sure it has its 'Red Key'.

Doblo (from 2001)

What's good: Utility estate designed to look like one. Boot space floor to parcel shelf is a huge 750 litres and folding the back seats releases a cavernous 3,000 litres (200 litres more than the Berlingo and 400 litres more than the Kangoo). Relatively compact at

4,160mm long, 1,710mm wide and 1,800mm high (13ft 8ins x 5ft 7ins x 5ft 10ins). Power steering with just 2.2 turns lock to lock and a tight turning circle of 10.5 metres help make manoeuvring stress free. 700mm (27.5 inch) wide sliding rear side doors and high rear seats make it easier for the elderly or disabled to get in and out. At 1,245mm (4ft 1ins) high and 1,231mm (4ft 0.5ins) wide the rear door aperture is also bigger than the Berlingo, Partner and Kangoo. The rear load sill is just 21 inches from the ground. Engine choice of a 65bhp 1,242cc petrol which delivers 75lb ft (102Nm) torque at 3,500rpm or a 63bhp 1,910cc IDI diesel which churns out 87lb ft (118Nm) torque at 2,500rpm. The petrol model has a top speed of 88mph, gets to sixty in 17.5 seconds, emits 183g/km CO_2 (£140pa VED) and manages a combined consumption of 36.7mpg. The original diesel also does 88mph, but takes about 19.5 seconds to get to sixty, emits 191g/km CO_2 (£160pa VED) and squeezes 39.2 miles out of a gallon on the combined cycle. Air-conditioning (optional on SX, standard on ELX) increases the CO_2 output of the diesel to 204g/km. Remote central locking, height-adjustable steering wheel, height adjustable drivers seat with adjustable lumbar support, dash-mounted gear stick, two dashboard accessory power points, driver and passenger airbags are standard on all models. ELX models have five three-point seatbelts, alloy wheels and air conditioning. Air-conditioning is optional on the SX at £651, and ABS with EBD are optional extras on both models at £564.Prices are: 1.2 petrol SX: £8,694.65; 1.9D diesel SX: £8,949,65; 1.9 diesel ELX: £9,995. Independent tests say it handles well. Uprated diesel announced February 2002 with 1.9 litre JTD common rail injected engine developing 100bhp and 201Nm (148 lb ft) torque at 1,500rpm. This gets to 60mph in just over 12 seconds, goes on to 104mph and emits 168g/km CO_2, which pulls it back to the £150pa VED bracket. Combined fuel consumption is 44.1mpg. Load capacity remains a class leading 3.2 to 3.8 cubic metres, payload weight is 625kg and for an extra £176.25 payload weight can be increased to 850kg. Prices start at £9,585 for the SX, rising to £10,629 for the ELX which has body coloured bumpers and a lifting tailgate instead of twin rear doors. Prices for 1.2 litre petrol engined Doblo utilities start at £8,695. A long list of optional extra includes air conditioning at

£651, ABS at £564 and reverse parking sensors at £117.50. Curiously, Doblo Cargo vans are much more expensive, ranging from £10,074 for the 1.2 petrol to £11,895 for the SX JTD, though VAT on these is usually reclaimable by VAT registered businesses.

More online at www.fiat.co.uk

What's bad: 1.2 petrol 63bhp diesel versions very slow.

What to watch out for: Nothing has come up yet.

Ecobasic (stillborn)

What's good: A true car of the future. Plastic panels on a space frame. 1.2 litre 61bhp direct injected diesel engine and 5 speed Selaspeed autoclutched gearbox giving up to 94mpg, 100mph and 0–60 in 13 seconds. Weighs less than 750kilos; emits just 80 g/km CO_2. Could sell for around £4,000.

What's bad: Project shelved in 2001 due to EU crash safety regulations.

What to watch out for: Nothing, since it's not happening.

Marea (1997 to 2002)

What's good: As Bravo/Brava. Replaced Tempra. Useful 'Weekend' estate. Saloon 14ft 5in by 5ft 8in; estate 14ft 8in long. Weighed from 1,140kg. Same engine line-up as Bravo/Brava, but starting at 1.6 and going up to a tremendous 125 bhp 2,307cc 5 cylinder diesel followed by an even better 130 bhp JTD shared with the Alfa 156. Handles well. Used 5 year old examples going for buttons now, but estates aren't quite as cheap. FIAT had 2nd lowest average cost in warranty claims for cars up to 10 years old in 2002 Warranty Direct index, check online at www.performanceindex.co.uk

What's bad: Ugly. Lousy build quality. Problems not easily put right by dealers, themselves thin on the ground. Timing belt changes on 5-cylinder cars are a very expensive, engine-out job and all Mareas MUST have a timing belt and tensioner change every 3 years or 36,000 miles whichever comes first. Came joint bottom with Bravo and Brava in 2001 ADAC list 2001 of cars which break down most on German autobahns. 9th from Bottom in 144 car 2002 JD

Power/*What Car?* Customer Satisfaction Survey of V and W reg. cars.

What to watch out for: As Bravo/Brava. Make sure it has its 'Red Key'.

Recalls: 1998: 1.6 16v, non-ABS: check for chafing of brake hoses; 1999: 1.8, 2.0 and 1.9TDS (1993–96 build): front coil springs

Multipla (2000 to 2005)

What's good: Bravo-based, but shorter, built on a spaceframe. Just 13ft 1in long but 6ft 2in wide. Petrol weighs 1,300kg; diesel 1,370kg. Six seats in two rows of three, all with proper three-point belts. Funky interior styling. Dashboard gearshift, so no obstructions in the floor. Excellent 105 bhp 1.9JTD engine pulled it to 115 mph on the Millbrook test bowl, so must be more aerodynamic than it looks. 103 bhp 1.6 16v has very good steering, handles much better than diesel and can be thrown around like a hot hatch. Twin lens mirrors make it easy to judge kerbs for parking. Bright range of colours. Has become a fashion item. Integrated rev counter and other improvements from 2001 MY, including power boost of diesel to 110bhp. Minor front and rear facelift July 2002 with lower rear load lip.

What's bad: Controversial looks. Diesel suffers roll understeer on tight bends (petrol doesn't). A long step up to the seats and down from them for the elderly or infirm (much easier from a high kerb). Petrol model is short-geared and gets noisy at around 80 mph. Lots of niggling faults, especially with alarm/immobiliser. Poor performance in TUV/*Auto Bild* front offset crash test. Worst mini MPV score of all of 56% in Euro NCAP 2001 crash safety tests (but FIAT now claims to have modified it to achieve a four star score). Some of the trim is a bit cheap: rubbery plastic on ashtray peels off. Petrol engined model lacks the splash undertray of the diesel and in really bad wet and salty road conditions the engine can ingest water and self destruct. One-piece exhausts of petrol models (from car back)have a fairly limited life and cost £275 for the part alone to replace. FIAT/Alfa joint worst for breakdowns attended by German ADAC during 2001. Major restyle due in July 2005.

What to watch out for: Make sure everything works and exhaust not blowing.

Palio Weekend (stillborn for UK)

What's good: FIAT's 'World Car', code name 178, marketed in Europe at sub-Punto prices and planned to come to the UK in useful RHD 103 bhp 1.6 litre estate car form at a price level of around £8,000–£8,500. To be updated for World markets in 2003.

What's bad: Never happened. Design not up to new Punto standards and quality levels not brilliant. FIAT/Alfa joint worst for breakdowns attended by German ADAC during 2001. Production of 178 Palio now to be phased out in Brazil and Argentina later in the decade, though production will continue to the end of the decade in emerging markets.

What to watch out for: Too soon to say.

Panda (1984 to 2003)

What's good: Simple, practical, cheap car. 11ft 2in long by 4ft 11in wide and weighing from 700kg. 999cc 'Fire' engines go on and on. 4x4 was best lightweight 4x4 of the lot (I found a 4x4 Fire that had done 210,000 miles, then the guy's neighbour turned up with one that had done 215,000 miles). Engines were 903cc pushrod with 45bhp; 769cc 'Fire' with 34bhp; or 999cc Fire with 45bhp to 50bhp. Still being made in 2002, but, sadly, with the 899cc pushrod Seicento engine rather than the ohc 'Fire' engine. Sell for £3,500 new in Italy. Cheap to buy and cheap insurance. Part-galvanised from 1990. 1000cc FIRE engines are non-interference if the timing belt snaps (valves don't hit pistons).

What's bad: Pre-1990s Pandas rusted badly from new and even 90s models rust in the doors. 'Old' pushrod 903cc engine should be avoided. Selecta troublesome and expensive to fix. Can suffer cold-starting problems. Clutch cables snap. Wheel bearings go. Suspension bushes wear. With the FIRE engine, if the engine cuts out when hot, will restart after about 10 mins, then last another couple of miles, the reason could be that the cable insulation cracks and shorts inside the distributor from the magnetic pickup to the ignition module. Results in no spark. Happens on cars from late E reg. onwards. Pre mod distributors had red & green cables which never gave a problem. If the FIRE engine suffers from flat performance, the vacuum advance/retard units on the distributor has failed. Units can purchased separately from Fiat for about £12. If the FIRE engine suffers from fast idle, very weak mixture the reason is Weber carbs designed in Germany. These suffer from air leaks, hence fast idle and weak mixture. Fitting repair kit risky! Best by new from FIAT (£110 + VAT). Weber charges a lot more. LHD only Panda now due for replacement by new Seicento in September 2003.

What to watch out for: Rust. Fall-apart trim. Don't pay extra for low mileage. Many low mileage cars serviced once every two years or worse. Look for wear in 4x4 drivetrain. Bounce the car on its suspension to make sure shocks are still absorbing. 'Mayonnaise' under oil filler denotes life of short runs, never properly warmed up. Oil leaks common. Timing chain gets noisy on 903cc pushrod engine (not recommended). Make sure timing belt changed recently on 'Fire' engines. Check tyres for uneven wear. Any clunks selecting 'drive' on the Selecta should be avoided like the plague. Look for rust in the back corners of the non-galvanised side doors.

Punto (1994 to 1999)

What's good: The best-designed small car in the world in its day and a worthy 'Car of the Year' award winner. 12ft 4in long by 5ft 5in wide and weighing from 850kg. Excellent upright seating. 4–door SX and ELX versions have height-adjustable seats and steering wheels and are easy cars for the elderly to get in and out of. Best of the range are basic 1,108cc '55ft (bhp) or 1,242cc '60ft three-door models with sunroofs, or 1,242 '85ft SX 5–doors with standard PAS. Was also a '75ft (bhp) 1.2, a '90ft (bhp) 1.6, a 56bhp '60ft diesel and a 72bhp 'TDS' diesel. Galvanised bodies won't rust unless accident-damaged. Were cheap 'nearly new' because most started their lives on rental fleets. Amazing range of bright and attractive metallic colours, best of which is 'Rialto' blue (adds £200 to the used price). 60S does over 40 mpg. Recommended new, and now a good value first car for youngsters which is also relatively cheap to insure. FIAT had 2nd lowest average cost in warranty claims for cars up to 10 years old in 2002 Warranty Direct index, check online at www.performanceindex.co.uk

What's bad: Choppy ride quality. Handling and roadholding not as good as the latest Fiestas. 90 Sporting has mismatched engine. 'Space saver' emergency wheel not liked by Brits. Rear brake adjusters a bit gimpy, as with Uno. Selecta CVT auto is excellent in both theory and practice, but can become troublesome. Diesels not brilliant. Bonnet releases break (see Uno). Hydraulic clutch slave cylinder may develop a leak. High number of cylinder head gasket failures being registered. Franchised dealers thin on the ground and not always helpful. Isolated report of front suspension wishbone collapse. If heater matrix fails it may leak onto the ECU immobilising the car. Electric sunroofs prone to failure. Possibility of brake master cylinder seal reversing itself leading to momentary but total loss of braking. Seal then flips back and braking is normal. FIAT dealers have renewed master cylinders when the problem was reported by owners. Seems to have been a spate of sumps rusting through on four year old Puntos. FIAT/Alfa joint worst for breakdowns attended by German ADAC during 2001. 12th from Bottom of 100 models for reliability in *Auto Express* 2002 survey.

What to watch out for: Accident damage. Silly damage from careless renters and their kids. Rear suspension arm bushes wear and are expensive to replace (check for uneven rear tyre wear). If test driving a Selecta, make sure the electromagnetic clutch is 100% (there should be no jerk when you put the lever in 'drive', no jerk when you drive away, and no 'creep' at idle). Make sure it has its 'Red Key' and that all keys work (problem emerging over mismatched keys and lost codes at FIAT HQ). Check for cylinder head gasket failure. Make sure that the fuel pump is not leaking (new pump: £159 + VAT + fitting.)If the car has an electric sunroof, make sure it works as FIAT dealers charge £600 for a replacement.

Recalls: 1998 (March '97–Nov '97 build): Faulty seatbelt pretensioner. 1/8/2001: 77,166 Mk 1 Puntos built 1/1/1993 to 31/12/1996 (VINs ending 0010087 to 6023643)recalled to check for corroded brake pipe, replace as necessary and apply corrosion protection to remaining pipes. 17/8/2001: 3,055 Mk 1 Puntos built 1/1/1994 to 31/12/1995 recalled because water ingress to driver and passenger airbag ECU can set them off. Water protection to be fitted to ECU. Source: reader 22–9–2001: Possible secret TSB to renew brake master cylinders if owners report sudden loss of brakes (see 'What's Bad').

Punto II (1999 to 2005)

What's good: FIAT improved the Punto in every area where the old model was criticised. The current car has a sharp 'designer' look that could tempt Polo buyers, and one of the best driving environments of any small car. New torsion beam rear suspension helps handling and comfort and eliminates the bearing wear problem of the old model. Galvanized bodies won't rust. Amazing range of bright and attractive metallic colours. 12ft 6in long by 4ft 5in wide and 860kg to 975kg. All models from 60S up have height-adjustable steering wheel, drivers seat with lumbar support and dual assist electric power steering. (Can select ultra light for City use.) Plenty of headroom. Engines now: 60 bhp 1.2 8v; 80 bhp 1.2 16v; 130 bhp 1.7 16v; 60 bhp 1.9 diesel; 80 bhp 1.9 JTD common rail diesel. 6-speed manual box available with 80 bhp 1.2 in 'Sporting' model. 'Speedgear' CVT available with 7 speeds and 80 bhp 1.2 or 6 speeds and 60 bhp 1.2. Witty 'Spirito di Punto' advertising campaign. Four-Star NCAP crash safety rating. Three proper three-point rear seatbelts standard in HLX spec and above; £75 extra in base models. 'Red Key' security system abandoned, which makes buying second-hand easier. Range updated May 2002, starting with lead-in £6,499 Mia and range proper beginning with £6,999 Active 3–door. 60bhp Active diesel 3–door: £7,499. FIAT had 2nd lowest average cost in warranty claims for cars up to 10 years old in 2002 Warranty Direct index, check online at www.performanceindex.co.uk Not due for replacement by new car (code named project 199) until September 2005.

What's bad: 'Space saver' emergency wheel not liked by Brits. Interior not quite as roomy as old model, but has stowage pockets

335

everywhere and lots of brilliant design features that bring a smile. Indicator stalk unpleasant to use and does not always self-cancel. Dual mode power steering gives electric power to column rather than rack, and in 'City' mode feels almost frighteningly light. 7-speed CVT may seem to have too many gears, and constant gearchanging slows acceleration. Doubts remain over longevity of CVT. Thick rear pillars make reversing 3 door more difficult. Headlights don't give out much light, and integrated foglights are a £400 extra. Reports of wrong size pistons having been fitted to 80bhp 1.2 engines. 12th from Bottom of 100 models for reliability in *Auto Express* 2002 survey.

What to watch out for: Signs of water ingress (wet carpets). Problems with the electric power steering and steering column (the column is directly driven by an electric motor) on Puntos built between 12–2–2001 and 18–5–2001. See Recalls. If buying a 'new' or 'nearly new' Punto check with your FIAT dealer that the bearing bush has been replaced.

Recalls: 26/7/2000: 2,016 Puntos with air conditioning built 8/1999–7/2000 recalled because fuel vapour recirculation pipe might foul against a/c compressor resulting in risk of fire. Recirculation pipe to be repositioned away from compressor. 31/5/2001: Faulty batch of bearing bushes fitted to the top section of powered steering columns of Puntos and Punto vans built between 1–2–2001 and 28–5–2001. Affects 21,112 cars. Fit new steering column if bearing found to be cracked. December 2001: TSB dealer fix for juddering wipers caused by too much grease on the contacts of the wiper relay.

Punto MPV (from March 2004)

What's good: Mini B-MPV on Punto floorpan now due to go on sale in March 2004. Features rear sliding doors and pillarless construction for ease of entry and egress.

What's bad: Too soon to say.

What to watch out for: Too soon to say.

Seicento (1998 to 2003)

What's good: Replaced Cinquecento in Spring 1998. Much cuter, with optional PAS and optional Citymatic autoclutch. 10ft 11in long by 5ft wide and weighing 730kg to 735kg. Base 899cc pushrod engine with 39bhp or 1,108 cc ohc 'Fire' engine with 54bhp. The best older model is the SX-based 'En Suite' from September 1999V which has a bigger, longer-lasting 1,108cc 'Fire' engine, standard PAS and aircon. Cosmetic facelift in autumn 2000. No Red Key problems. As from October 2000 facelift, all UK-market Seicentos were powered by 54 bhp 1,108cc multipoint injected 'Fire' engine with standard electric power steering. FIAT had 2nd lowest average cost in warranty claims for cars up to 10 years old in 2002 Warranty Direct index, check online at www.performanceindex.co.uk

What's bad: Many used models still have 899cc version of old Fiat 903cc pushrod engine which is apt to develop rocker shaft wear. Only two stars in Euro NCAP tests. FIAT/Alfa joint worst for breakdowns attended by German ADAC during 2001. Replacement now due September 2003.

What to watch out for: As Cinquecento, except they don't have Red Keys. Check for cylinder head gasket failures.

Seicento (from 2003)

What's good: New 5–door Seicento, maybe with new name, to replace both Panda and Seicento from September 2003. May have option of new small diesel engine and probably marks the end for the Polish built Panda which still sells about 10,000 a year in Italy. Replaces Ecobasic and also thought to replace new Cinquecento.

What's bad: Too soon to say.

What to watch out for: Too soon to say.

Stilo (from February 2002)

What's good: New models code named Project 192 replaced Bravo and Brava. Built on new 'C' platform with engines from a 1.2 litre four with 80bhp to a 2.4 litre five with 170bhp. Like the Bravo and Brava the 3–door and 5–door Stilo models are very different cars from each other. The 3–door is rakish and sporty, the driver sits lower down and the appeal is generally younger. The 5–door is more practical. Both models are 1,760mm wide, but the 3–door is 4,180mm (13ft 9in) long and 1,460mm high while the 5–door is 4,250mm (13ft 11in) long and 1,760mm high.

As with mini MPVs in the same market sector, the five-door Stilo has been designed to be easy to get into and out of with plenty of room inside and a high driving position that ensures a feeling of control. The front passenger seat tilts right forward, and the rear seats slide, recline and tilt independently enabling the interior to be adapted to changing individual needs. This basic versatility is complemented by a ski flap, various storage compartments with flaps, a child seat built into the rear seat, and a front seat that folds down to form a table to accommodate long loads or act as a work surface. Airline-type folding tables pull down from the front seat squab so that children can draw or adult passengers can write or work on a laptop. There are three roomy closed compartments on the facia (one of them is cooled on cars with air conditioning), and both front and rear armrests contain interior compartments. There's a roomy container under both front seats (if they are mechanically adjusted), generous pouches and five cup-holders. Both 3–door and 5–door Stilos share all the latest safety equipment, including up to eight airbags, six of which are standard equipment, three rear head restraints and three 3–point rear seatbelts There are disc brakes on all four wheels, and ABS anti-lock braking with EBD and ASR is standard.

The Stilo range went sale in February 2002 with four petrol engine options, together with two common rail direct injection turbodiesel (JTD) engines, ranging from 80–170 bhp, driving through 5 or 6-speed gearboxes, and a Selespeed sequential transmission.

Entry level Stilos are well equipped and come with ABS anti-lock braking with Brake Assist, remote control central locking, six airbags, built-in front fog lights and body coloured bumpers all as standard. Optional features will include sliding rear seats, adaptive cruise control, the CONNECT Infotelematic system with voice commands for the phone, a voice memo and WAP internet access, rear side airbags, a louvred sunroof and an MP3 music player.

Pricing rationale is that for any engine capacity increment, say from 1.2 16v to 1.6 16v, a customer will be charged £500; for a trim level upgrade £1,000; and to go from a 3–door to a 5–door version will cost £500. Selespeed transmission costs £800. This simple building block approach means that customers will be able to assemble the cost of the car they want and, once in possession of the entry level price, it is a simple matter to arrive at the price of any Stilo version.

More online at www.fiat.co.uk

What's bad: The market doesn't seem to be taking to it big-time, which might turn to the buyers advantage if FIAT is forced to discount or launder the cars into nearly-news via the rental fleets.

What to watch out for: Too soon to say.

SUV (from March 2004)

What's good: A small four wheel drive FIAT SUV is apparently still on the schedule for launch in March 2004.

What's bad: Too soon to say.

What to watch out for: Too soon to say.

Tempra (1990 to 1996)

What's good: The saloon and estate ('Weekend') versions of the Tipo. Saloon: 14ft 4in long; estate 14ft 9in long. Same engine line-up as Tipo. FIAT had 2nd lowest average cost in warranty claims for cars up to 10 years old in 2002 Warranty Direct index, check online at www.performanceindex.co.uk

What's bad: See Tipo. Not as good looking or as well designed as the Tipo. FIAT/Alfa joint worst for breakdowns attended by German ADAC during 2001.

What to watch out for: See Tipo.

Tipo (1988 to 1995)

What's good: Nicknamed the 'Teapot' in the trade: Brilliant, practical design, more roomy inside than any other car in its class before or since. Just 13ft long but 5ft 7in wide and weighing a solid 965kg to 1,150kg. Original engine range began with 72bhp carbed 1.4, 83bhp carbed 1.6, 57bhp 1.7 diesel and 92bhp 1.9 TD, which was the performance model. 1.8 from September 1990 had 110bhp. Power of 1.4 cut in 1992 to 71bhp with single point injection and cat; 1.6 down to 765bhp. Cheap to buy. Electro-galvanised bodies won't rust unless accident damaged and badly repaired. Evocative 142bhp 1,995cc 'Sedicivalvole' (16-valve) from January 1992 a bargain performance buy. Also a 115bhp 2.0 litre. 1.9 TD quick, economical and cheap to buy once the miles pile on. Most Tipos now selling for banger money. FIAT had 2nd lowest average cost in warranty claims for cars up to 10 years old in 2002 Warranty Direct index, check online at www.performanceindex.co.uk

What's bad: Shape and design qualities not generally appreciated. Dodgy cost-saving digital dash on early 'DGT' versions. 1.6 not much quicker than 1.4. 1.8 not a good engine. Most 1.4ies began their lives on rental fleets. Some reports of non-galvanised subframes rusting prematurely. FIAT/Alfa joint worst for breakdowns attended by German ADAC during 2001.

What to watch out for: Leaks between cam carrier and cylinder head of modular 1.4 and 1.6 engines. Also cylinder head gasket failure common. All need coolant changed every two years, particularly iron-block, alloy-headed diesel. Electrics develop problems. Make sure all the lights work. All-too-easy to cross the threads in the alloy head when replacing spark plugs. Bonnet catch cable release mechanism breaks, begging the question of how long it's been since anyone looked underneath.

Ulysse (1995 to 2002)

What's good: As Citroën Synergie. Has PSA XUD diesel rather than Fiat engine. Early models now cheap for a 7 seater. FIAT had 2nd lowest average cost in warranty claims for cars up to 10 years old in 2002 Warranty Direct index, check online at www. performanceindex.co.uk

What's bad: As Citroën Synergie. S and T platers 5th from bottom in 2001 *Top Gear*/J.D. Power Customer Satisfaction Survey. To be replaced with a new model in Spring 2002. FIAT/Alfa joint worst for breakdowns attended by German ADAC during 2001.

What to watch out for: As Citroën Synergie.

Recalls: 1996 (Sept '95–Oct '95 build): Check airbag trigger. March '99–April '99 build Ulysses with ABS only: possibility of air in brake fluid. March '98–July '98 build: handbrake ratchet could fail.

Ulysse replacement (from 2002)

What's good: New 7 seater MPV on same floorpan as new Citroën C8 and Peugeot 807. Due to be launched autumn 2002. See Citroën C8 and Peugeot 807.

What's bad: Nothing known.

What to watch out for: Too soon to say.

Uno (1983 to 1994)

What's good: Boxy, sensible, practical design also stylish in its day. 12ft 1in long by 5ft 1in wide. Some panels galvanised from 1990 when all acquired plastic hatchback. Early engines were 903cc pushrod with 45bhp; 1,116cc '60ft with 58bhp, 1,299cc '70ft with 65bhp, 1,697cc 60DS diesel with 60bhp and rip-snorting 1,299cc Turbo ie with 105bhp. Later 999cc 45bhp 'Fire' engine good for 200,000 miles plus with proper maintenance. 57bhp 1,108cc 60S also good. 1,372cc 72bhp '70ft engine was same as Tipo. Good range of bright metallic colours. Uno 1.0 'Start' models were well equipped and great bargains. Low insurance and bargain basement used prices means rust-free examples make good sense for youngsters. Part-galvanised from 1990 facelift which includes non-rusting plastic tailgate. 1000cc FIRE engines are non-interference if the timing belt snaps (valves don't hit pistons). FIAT had 2nd lowest average cost in warranty claims for cars up to 10 years old in 2002 Warranty Direct index, check online at www. performanceindex.co.uk

What's bad: Avoid the 903cc 'Uno 45ft engine (the timing chain and valve gear rattle and it's well past its sell-by date). Be extremely careful buying a Turbo (if you can find one) as the engine was very easily hopped up to give much more power and 'boy raced' to death. Unos look like refrigerators in white. Many started their UK lives on rental fleets. Privately owned Unos that are used for shopping and the school run never warm up, contaminate their oil and suffer premature engine wear. If the car suffers from crashing from rear suspension, replace rear upper shock absorber mounts. About £12 from FIAT. Problems with rear drum brake adjustors. FIAT/Alfa joint worst for breakdowns attended by German ADAC during 2001.

What to watch out for: Rust by the bucketload in pre-1990 facelift models. Duff catalytic converters. Kerbing damage. Bonnet catch cable releases break, so you have to ask yourself how long it has been broken and how long since anyone looked underneath. Selecta best avoided due to potentially expensive problems.

FORD

Cougar (1998 to 2000)

What's good: Sharp-suited Mondeo coupe with Mondeo 2.0 litre and 2.5 litre engines. 15ft 5in long by 5ft 10in wide and weighing 1,291kg to 1,342kg. Good looking and different. Low wind noise. 2.5 V6 recovers lost speed extremely well. Handles and holds the road nicely without much understeer. Effective 'eyeball' vents. Sensible boot. Fold-down rear seats ideal for golf clubs. Rear-view mirror well placed for motorways and heavy traffic. Sounds a bit like an Alfa 156 2.5 V6. 30 mpg possible from 2.5 litre; 36–plus from 2.0. 4-speed auto available, but not a very good one. Most V6s were 2,544cc, but last shrunk slightly to Mondeo II/Jag X Type 2,495cc. BMW, Toyota and Ford jointly suffered the fewest breakdowns attended by German ADAC during 2001. Ford had 3rd lowest cost in warranty claims for cars up to 10 years old in 2002 Warranty Direct index, check online at www.performanceindex.co.uk

What's bad: Hopeless rear headroom. Harsh, crashy ride. Quite a few rattles, even when new. Console straight out of Mondeo. 2.5 V6 lacks low-down torque and needs to be revved for maximum effect (redline only starts at 7,000 rpm). Short-range tank only good for 300 miles at a push. Odometer under-reads by 2%. Fairly heavy tyre wear on 2.5 V6. 215/50 16 tyres are specifically made for the Cougar by Pirelli and Michelin and cost £130 to £190 each. Oil pump problem causes frothing and oil starvation at top of 2,544cc V6. Some cars have had two engines replaced under warranty for this reason. Withdrawn from UK market due to poor sales of just 12,000 in two years (Daily Mirror 21/11/2000). 8th from Bottom in 144 car 2002 JD Power/*What Car?* Customer Satisfaction Survey of V and W reg. cars. Parts are going to become an increasing problem, particularly trim and body parts. Door mirrors are 'snap-off', not sprung.

What to watch out for: Damaged panels and trim which may become difficult to obtain replacements for.

Recalls: Cars Built Sept-Nov '98 recalled in October 1999 to cure possible failure of door latches. 1/5/2001: Build 1/1/1999 to

18/9/2000 recalled because battery cable may be misrouted and or loose connection to alternator B+ stud which could lead to electrical short. B+ stud to be checked and battery cable routing to be checked. 8/5/2001: Build 6/12/1997 to 31/8/1998: Brass rather than bronze terminal in brake lamp switch jumper harness could lead to malfunction of brake lamp switch. Jumper harness to be replaced on all vehicles and brake lamp switches to be replaced if overheated. 8/10/2001: recall of 32,665 Mondeos and Cougars built 1/11/1999 to 1/5/2000 because parking brake ratchet can lose a tooth. Lever ratchet assembly to be replaced. 15/10/2001: 24 US spec Cougars in UK built 1/12/1997 to 31/5/1998 recalled because heater blower resistor connector blades can damage wiring harness leading to arcing and overheating of the connector.

Escort (1983 to 1990)

What's good: Popular. 13ft long by 5ft 5in wide and weighing from a light 765kg. 3–door and 5–door hatchbacks and estates. Two door convertibles. Big engine range over the years included 1,117 ohv 53bhp; 1,297cc ohv 59bhp; 1,295cc ohc 69bhp; 1,392cc ohc 74bhp; 1,597cc ohc 90bhp, 105bhp (XR3), 115bhp (XR3i) and 132bhp (RS 1600 turbo). 54bhp 1.6 diesels; 60bhp 1.8 diesels. Cheap. Now selling for buttons. Don't pay more unless you find a cherished, well-preserved XR3i, RS 1600 turbo or convertible.

What's bad: Old. Rust badly underneath and fail the MOT on structural corrosion which isn't worth attempting to repair. CVH engines choke themselves to death with black sludge.

What to watch out for: Crash repaired, cloned, clocked, stolen in their thousands. An Escort bought in 1998 may have been stolen and ringed ten years ago and never been noticed. Often fail the MOT on structural rust.

Escort (1990 to 2000)

What's good: Popular. Bland, but not bad looking. 13ft 4in long by 5ft 7in wide and weighting 980 to 1,100kg. 3–door hatch, 5–door hatch and estate and two door cabrio from 1990. Handling and roadholding improved through the car's model life. Oval grille from October 1992 for 1993 model year and 'wide mouth' cars from 1995 model year on are by far the best. Almost all of these later models from LX up have power steering. Best model is probably a post-1995 1.6iLX, and most late cars had aircon. Engine range began with 72bhp 1.4 and 90bhp 1.6 CVHs (lifted to 107bhp for the cabrio) or 59bhp diesels. 103bhp twin-cam Zetec E 1.8 from 1992 (option of up to 130bhp for XR3i and XR3i/Si cabrio). Four wheel drive Escort Cosworth arrived in 1992 with two litre turbocharged engine putting out 223bhp in standard form. 59bhp 1.8 diesels continued. 89bhp 1.6 Zetec engine arrived January 1994 along with 148bhp RS2000. New front from January 1995. Ford had 3rd lowest cost in warranty claims for cars up to 10 years old in 2002 Warranty Direct index, check online at www.performanceindex.co.uk

What's bad: Had a terrible start. Early cars were a disgrace with awful handling, terrible steering and suspect bodyshells which rotted in the bulkhead and around the rear window. Early diesels had overstrength valve springs which caused them to snap their cambelts. Early Zetec engines from 1992 suffered sticky valves (see Mondeo). Rear suspension trailing arms up to 1995 were too weak and twist when they're not supposed to. Mid-life 'oval grille' facelift looks terrible and dated almost immediately. Fuse boxes rust out. Two-Star below-average performance in 1999 NCAP secondary safety tests. Close to bottom in 'R' reg. JD Power Customer Satisfaction Survey. On Zetec E petrol engines, several reports of timing belt tensioner pulley heating up and shattering after 5–6 years and 60–80,000 miles. Essential to replace the pulley at the same time as the belt. 14th from Bottom of 100 models for reliability in *Auto Express* 2002 survey. 14th from Bottom in 144 car 2002 JD Power/*What Car?* Customer Satisfaction Survey of V and W reg. cars.

What to watch out for: Bodged rust repairs on early cars. Clocked mega-mile ex-fleet cars. Inadequate 'home servicing'. Poor quality aftermarket parts – especially brake parts. Check for uneven tyre wear due to suspension damage from kerbing. Electrics may play up (check for damp and/or rusting inside fusebox). Rear suspension arms flex too much and may weaken as a result (16-valves were strengthened with rear anti-roll bar). Some 1992/93 Escorts came out of the factory with misaligned front suspension which caused the insides of the front tyres to wear excessively. Diesels should have had nylon timing belt idler replaced with a steel idler. These should both have been sorted out 'in service', but if the car was maintained 'in house' by a fleet or by a private owner, it may not have been done. Some fleets reckon on just 60,000 miles for Zetec timing belts and idler pulleys. CVT automatic is prone to problems and is best avoided.

Recalls: 1994 (1.3 and 1.4CFi-92 VIN NE, NL, NY, NS, NT; 93 VIN PJ, PU, PM, PP, PB, PR, PA, PG, PC, PK): electrical check. 1995 (VIN: SE): brake lights may not work. 1995 (Escort diesels: VIN: SY, SS, ST): brake vacuum pump may not create enough vacuum for servo. 1995 (VIN: SE, SL): loose rear brake cylinders. 1995 (VIN: SC, SK, SD): possible damage to seatbelt webbing. 1998 Escorts with passenger airbags built Aug '96–Feb '98: passenger airbag may go off while car is stationary.

Explorer (1997 to 2001)

What's good: Starred along with the other dinosaurs in 'Jurassic Park'. American alternative to the Range Rover and Jeep Grand Cherokee.15ft 8in long by 6ft 5in wide and weighing in at 2,008kg. 204bhp 4.0 litre V6 gives decent motorway cruising and adequate performance. Towing weight of 2,55okg makes them quite a good towcar for people with twin-wheel 20ft caravans. Under £10,000 on used market from early 2000, much less now. Ford had 3rd lowest cost in warranty claims for cars up to 10 years old in 2002 Warranty Direct index, check online at www.performanceindex.co.uk

What's bad: Oversized and over here. Not as well rust-proofed in body cavities as you might expect. Fuel consumption difficult to justify. Major scandal over Firestone Tyres blowing out when wrongly inflated. Suffered from jamming electronic throttle, caused by electronic interference to the cruise control giving maximum engine revs. If this happens to you, knock the selector into neutral and switch off the engine as soon as you have stopped. Once the car is out of its 3 year or 60,000 mile warranty repairs can be frequent and expensive. Common to need new front wishbone balljoints at three years old (MOT failure point) and these cost £500, so book an early first MOT that falls within the 3 year warranty. Also if the engine oil is less than perfectly clean, the oil feed to the timing chain tensioners can block leading to noise when the engine is first started each day. Eventually the tensioners break and replacement is a £2,000 engine out job. S and T platers 9th from bottom in 2001 *Top Gear* J.D. Power Customer Satisfaction Survey. The August/September 2001 UK tyre recall only provided for replacement tyres if Firestone Wilderness A/T tyres are still fitted to the vehicle. Retrospective claims are not being met.

What to watch out for: More of a suburban status symbol than a serious off-roader. Look for damage due to underestimated vehicle size. Check front wishbone ball joints and listen for timing chain rattles (see above).

Recalls: Oil pump recall notice issued January 1998. Bonnet latch recall issued 2000. Explorer TSBs include curing a transmission shudder. Warning in May 1998 that accelerator may be jammed open by the driver's floormat. This turned out to be a fault with the cruise control which, while switched off, can receive an electronic signal giving maximum revs. 14/3/2000: tailgate lift cylinder brackets may weaken. Strengthening plates to be fitted. Only 5 UK imports built 1/4/93 to 17/2/95 affected. 10/8/2000 Firestone Wilderness, ATX and ATX II tyres fitted to some Explorers recalled for free replacement regardless of age and wear. 22/01/2001: Build dates 1/1/1995 to 31/10/1996 recalled because front stabiliser links may break. Both links to be replaced with stronger links. 5/3/2001: Build dates 29/5/1996 to 18/9/198 recalled because accelerator pedal may stick at idle or become unprogressive in action after vehicle has been parked. Revised throttle body to be fitted. By September 2001 replacement Goodyear tyres for the Firestone recall were beginning to arrive in quantity, tel: 0845 841 1111.

(From desktop.com news 5–10–2001): The US Department of Transportation's National Highway Traffic Safety Administration (NHTSA) has ordered the recall of an estimated 3.5 million Firestone Wilderness AT tyres installed on Ford Explorer and

Mercury Mountaineer SUVs, and to a lesser extent on Ford Ranger compact pickup trucks. The NHTSA identified the tyres as sizes P235/75R15 and P255/70R16 manufactured by Firestone prior to May 1998 that were either supplied to Ford as original equipment or were sold as replacement tyres. Firestone has agreed to recall the tyres and offer replacements to consumers at no extra cost.

In August 2000, Firestone determined that a safety-related defect existed in all Firestone P235/75R15 ATX tyres and in Wilderness AT tyres of that size manufactured at its Decatur, Illinois plant, and recalled those tyres. Since then, NHTSA's Office of Defects Investigation (ODI) has been conducting an extensive investigation to determine whether other Wilderness tyres, beyond those recalled by Firestone, contain a safety-related defect, and whether they should be recalled.

NHTSA, which ordered the recall yesterday, said it had discovered 68 more fatalities connected to Firestone tyre tread separation failures, raising the total to 271. Twenty-five of the newly reported deaths and about 50 of the more than 800 injuries involved the newly recalled tyres. The tread separations at issue in the NHTSA's investigation reduce the ability of a driver to control the vehicle, particularly where the failure occurs on a rear tyre and at high speeds, and can lead to a crash. The likelihood of such a crash, and of injuries or fatalities, is far greater when the tread separation occurs on an SUV than when it occurs on a pickup truck. Claims and complaint data indicate that a tread separation on an Explorer is no more likely to lead to a crash than on other SUVs, the NHTSA concluded.

The agency's decision seems to support Ford's claim that Firestone tyres are to blame for the worst vehicle safety scandal in decades. But Bridgestone/Firestone still says its products are safe and that the problem is due to a design flaw with the steering on the Explorer. (Various sources) (05/10/01)

Explorer (from 2001)

What's good: New Ford Explorer now with up to seven forward-facing seats, rearmost of which fold into the floor when not wanted. Has options of 210bhp 4.0 litre V6 with 255 lb ft (346Nm) torque at 4,000 rpm and 5-speed autobox giving a top speed of over 100mph and a 0–60 of 8.9 seconds; 5.0 V8 with 215bhp and 288 lb ft (390Nm) torque and common rail diesel engine. Reported to drive, ride and brake much better than the old Explorer on the road. No Firestone Wilderness tyres to be fitted.

What's bad: Fuel consumption of 18–24mpg and see Recalls. Decision announced December 2001 that the Explorer is not to be imported to the UK. (It would be in competition with Ford's Premier Division Range Rover.)

What to watch out for: See Recalls.

Recalls: 2001 American Recall to replace exploding back windows. 2001 second American recall to check for cuts in tyres caused during building of vehicles.

Fiesta (1977 to 1989)

What's good: Low insurance groups. Cheap and simple. 'Valencia' pushrod engines are long-lasting so long as the cars get driven. Spares cheap and second-hand parts plentiful. 11ft 8in long by 5ft 2in wide and weighing from 700kg to 800kg. 957 had 40bhp; 1,117 had 53bhp; 1.3 CVH had 69bhp; 1.4 CVH had 74bhp; 1.6 CVH in XR2 had 96bhp. Also a 54bhp 1.6 diesel. CTX auto could be reliable in '84–'89 cars.

What's bad: Old and rust-prone. Too light. 'Square front' (pre-1984 model year) extremely rust-prone, particularly front inner wings just above strut top mountings. A rust-weakened light car is a disaster waiting to happen, particularly with young people aboard. 'Round front' 1984–89 Fiesta had improved anti-rust treatment, but all these cars are so old now they need checking carefully. 1.3 and 1.4 CVH engines best avoided as prone to oil sludge.

What to watch out for: Rust. 'Short-run syndrome', because many were used for shopping by elderly ladies and never got properly warmed up. A 10-year-old Fiesta with 25,000 miles will be close to needing a new engine and clutch. On the other hand a white socks and back-to-front baseball cap XR2 might have been surprisingly well cared for apart from huge holes in the parcel shelf for oversize speakers.

Recalls: (None known 1994–98, but check seatbelt inertia reels.)

Fiesta (1989 to 1995)

What's good: A bigger, better Fiesta with more than a hint of the Peugeot 205 about it. 12ft 3in long by 5ft 3in wide and weighing 770kg to 895kg. The cheapest, most basic ones seem to be the best. 999cc had 45bhp; 1,118cc had 54bhp; 1,297cc ohv had 60bhp; 1,382cc CVH had 75bhp; 1,596cc CVH had 90bhp or 110bhp as XR2i or even 133bhp as Fiesta RS Turbo. Diesel now 1,753cc with 60bhp. Some later 1.3s had power steering. Pre-cat 1.0 litre cars cheap to buy, insure and run. (Continued as Fiesta Classic to Jan 1997.) Ford had 3rd lowest cost in warranty claims for cars up to 10 years old in 2002 Warranty Direct index, check online at www.performanceindex.co.uk

What's bad: Roadholding and handling a far cry from 205ft s higher standards. Fiestas suffered badly from catalysation in 1992. 1.1s and 1.3s from this date on were almost unbelievably slow and suffer from oil emulsification problems, over-rich running, premature rocker shaft wear, cam follower wear and a variety of other ailments. Catalysed 1.1s probably best avoided. CTX autoboxes became troublesome due to oil leak. On 1.1 and 1.3 pushrod engines spark plugs may either have corroded into the head or been over tightened (taper fit) which means head removal to drill them out. Bodies rust quite badly in places.

What to watch out for: Front suspension bushes wear and suspension likely to have been 'kerbed'. Be very wary of uneven front tyre wear. Brake discs don't last long and can start to judder after 20,000 miles. CVHs need regular timing belt changes. Timing chains of 1.1 and 1.3 pushrod engines can start to rattle. Engines suffer badly from sludging up due to short-run syndrome and insufficiently frequent oil changes. More than its fair share of recalls, so satisfy yourself that the recall work has been carried out. Make sure nylon timing belt idler gear in diesel engine has been replaced with a steel idler. 1.4CVHs with ECUs may suffer starting and running problems due to loose flywheel sensor connector. Rust can seriously weaken the base of the centre door pillar of 5–door cars. Also check for severe rust in the nearside back wing in the corner under the petrol cap and in the front valence. If 1300 pushrod engine is tappety it probably needs a new set of cam followers, which isn't a quick and easy job on a pushrod engine. If 1300 pushrod engine is tappety it probably needs a new set of cam followers which isn't a quick and easy job.

Recalls: 1995 (VIN: SK, SD): Tyres may be incorrectly fitted. 1995 (VIN: SE): Brake lights may not work. 1995 (Fiesta diesels: VIN: SIGHS, ST): Brake vacuum pump may not create enough vacuum for servo. 1996: (March 1989F-Sept 1990H build): Check for possibility of front seatbelt inertia reel locking mechanism failure.

Fiesta (1995 to 1999)

What's good: Same size as before with new front. Zippy 74bhp 1.25 and 89bhp 1.4 Zetec 'S' engines. Nice power steering. Vastly improved chassis offering excellent ride, handling and roadholding. Good fun to drive. Came out well in NCAP crash tests. Favourable insurance ratings due to reduced damageability and improved reparability. BMW, Toyota and Ford jointly suffered the fewest breakdowns attended by German ADAC during 2001. Ford had 3rd lowest cost in warranty claims for cars up to 10 years old in 2002 Warranty Direct index, check online at www. performanceindex.co.uk

What's bad: 1.3 'Endura' pushrod engines starting to show their age. Cabin lower and not as roomy as Punto, Ibiza, Polo. Water ingress via ventilation system. Starting to get reports of piston ring failures on 1.4 Zetec 'S' engines. The oil burned as a result may also wreck the catalytic converter. On Endura 1.3 pushrod engines Spark plugs may either have corroded into the head or been over tightened (taper fit) which means head removal to drill them out. Report with photographic evidence of cam follower wear on 1.3 pushrod engine. The pins which hold the foot pedals in place may fall out, leaving the driver unable to brake or declutch. Tend to get through front discs and pads very rapidly. Either replace front pads at 18,000–20,000 miles or expect to have to replace discs every

25,000 miles. May simply need calliper pins cleaning and lubricating.

What to watch out for: Have been a number of recalls. Double recall over front brake pipes because original recall failed to remedy the problem. Make sure these have been carried out. A wet carpet may mean failure of the bulkhead sealant. Check for high oil consumption, smoky exhaust on 1.4 Zetec S. Check front discs if you can and budget for replacement. If 1300 pushrod engine is tappety it probably needs a new set of cam followers, which isn't a quick and easy job on a pushrod engine. Since 95MY handling improvements, front suspension bushes have been prone to wear so if the front suspension clonks this is probably why.

Recalls: 1995 (VIN SE): Brake lights may not work. 1995 diesel (VIN SY, SS, ST): Brake vacuum pump may not create enough vacuum for servo. 1996 (Fiesta and Courier van, 1996 model year; 47,500 cars): Check for faulty piston seal in hydraulic clutch master cylinder. Check for contamination of brake fluid and incorrect front brake hose routing. 1997 (5–door models built Oct '95–May '96): may have faulty rear door latches. Also TSB 107 concerning complaints about noisy alternator drive-belt of diesel model causing battery discharge. Modified parts to be fitted (was not always done). 1998 (July 1995–June 1996 build-67,000 cars): Possibility of brake failure due to front brake pipe chafing on bracket. Modified pipe and bracket to be fitted to both front brakes. (Repeat brake pipe recall announced on radio 12/2/98). Fiestas with ABS (Mar '98–Sep '98): Brake master cylinder may fail. Fiestas with passenger airbags built Aug '96–Feb '97: passenger airbag may go off while car is stationary.

Fiesta (2000 to 2002)

What's good: New face to old favourite. 104 bhp Zetec S 1.6 is fun and makes this a good substitute for the old Peugeot 205GTi. Drives as well as the previous version, with really sharp handling. 74bhp turbodiesel from October 2000. Reasonable Three-Star rating in Euro NCAP crash tests. BMW, Toyota and Ford jointly suffered the fewest breakdowns attended by German ADAC during 2001.

What's bad: An old favourite, as basic bodyshell dates back to 1989, and was replaced by new model in 2002. Not much more than a '2+2ft . De-motivated workforce, all facing redundancy at Dagenham plant for final year's production 2000–2002. (New Fiesta to built at Cologne.)The pins which hold the foot pedals in place may fall out, leaving the driver unable to brake or declutch. Several reports that the 1.25 engine has become much coarser in this latest version, apparently due to changes to meet the latest emissions regulations. On Endura 1.3 pushrod engines Spark plugs may either have corroded into the head or been over tightened (taper fit) which means head removal to drill them out. Further brake failures have occurred.

What to watch out for: See 1995–1999 Fiesta. Since 1995 handling improvements, front suspension bushes have been prone to wear so if the front suspension clonks this is probably why.

Recalls: See Fiesta 1995–1999.

Fiesta (2002 on)

What's good: All-new Fiesta launched at September 2001 Frankfurt Motor Show. Looks very much like a slightly smaller Focus, but with a less radical rear-end treatment. Handles nicely enough. Dimensions of 5–door are: length 3,917mm (12 ft 10in); width 1,683mm (5 ft 6in); height: 1,417mm (4ft 8in). Luggage volume is 284 litres to the parcel shelf with the rear seats up. Four engines available at launch: New PSA sourced 1,399cc Duratorq TDCi aluminium block, common rail direct-injected diesel. Power output is 68ps at 4,000rpm with 160Nm (118 lb ft) torque at 1,750rpm. 0–60 is quoted at 14.5 seconds, top speed 102mph, Euro combined mpg 62.8 and CO_2 emissions 119g/km (£110pa VED). This engine meets Euro III emissions limits. Next, 1,388cc Duratec 16v which is a development of 1.4 16v Zetec S engine in older Fiesta and Focus. Power output is 80ps at 5,700rpm with 127Nm (94 lb ft) torque at 3,500rpm. 0–60 quoted at 13.2 seconds, top speed 103mph, Euro combined mpg 46.3 and CO_2 emissions 146g/km (£100pa VED). This engine meets Euro IV emissions limits. Next, 1,596cc Duratec 16v which is a development of 1.6 16v Zetec S engine in the current Fiesta, Puma and Focus. Power output is 100ps at 6,000rpm with

143Nm (105 lb ft) torque at 4,000rpm. 0–60 quoted at 10.5 seconds, top speed 115mph, Euro combined mpg 42.8 and CO_2 emissions 158g/km (£120pa VED). This engine meets Euro IV emissions limits.

Finally, the 1,297cc Duratec 8v derived from ancient pushrod Valencia engine. Power output 68ps at 5,000rpm with 108Nm (80 lb ft) torque at 2,800rpm. 0–60 is quoted at 15.7 seconds, top speed 99mph, Euro combined mpg 48.7 and CO_2 emissions 139g/km (£100pa VED). This engine also meets Euro IV emissions limits. Future engines may include a three cylinder 1.1 litre turbocharged direct-injection petrol engine shown in the concept Fiesta Fusion mini MPV at Frankfurt 2001. This engine weighs just 100kg, yet puts out 110bhp and a useful 118lb ft torque (160Nm) at 1,800rpm. Fusion concept car also had a five speed gearbox with electric clutch. (See separate entry for Fiesta Fusion UAV.) Standard equipment on all five-door Fiestas will include ABS with EBD, height adjustable driver and passenger seats, twin dual stage front airbags, five three-point seatbelts, decoupling pedals to protect the driver's feet in a severe impact, a passive anti-theft system, and a spare wheel stowed inside the boot rather than slung under it. Standard tyres will be 175/65R14 which helps ride comfort. Side airbags, side curtain bags, perimeter alarm system and remote central locking are available either as standard or as extras depending on model. Rear suspension is twist beam with compact spring damper units developed from system used on the current Fiesta and Puma rather than the 'Control Blade' rear suspension used on the Focus. Prices from £8,495 for 1.3 pushrod Duratec Finesse to £11,195 for 1.6i Ghia. 3–door due early 2003, range topped by 2.0 litre ST150 with 7.0 second 0–60 and 135mph plus top speed.

More online at www.ford.co.uk

What's bad: Not built in the UK. 1.25 Zetec S engine not in line-up. Though handling is good, trim level very basic and ordinary compared to Toyota Yaris, Honda Jazz, VW Polo or even Citroën C3. 1.4 Zetec S lacks sparkle. Even 1.4 diesel seems less enthusiastic in the Fiesta than in the Citroën C3 and not to the standard set by the Yaris D-4D.

What to watch out for: Too soon to say.

Focus (1998 to 2004)

What's good: 1998 'Car of the Year', and cars in its class come no better. Brave all-new styling. Different from the mainstream. 13ft 7in long by 6ft 7in wide (including mirrors) and weighing 1,074kg to 1,240kg. Proper independent 'control blade' rear suspension. Excellent roadholding and handling and ride quality combination on 15in wheels fitted with 195/60 tyres. Plenty of leg and headroom inside. Good seats. Multi-adjustable steering wheel. Nice deep door pockets. Close gearbox ratios and precise shift quality (60 mph at 6,500 rpm in 2nd in a 1.6). Galvanized body with 12-year anti-perforation warranty. Joint top of the class for secondary safety in NCAP tests. Has rightly appealed to the public as well as the fleets and residuals better than any previous mainstream Ford. 74bhp 1.4 and 99bhp 1.6 16-valve Zetec 'S' engines; same 113bhp 1.8 litre and 128bhp 2.0 litre 16-valve Zetec 'E' engines as Mondeo. Same 89bhp turbodiesel. You get the feeling that everything has been very carefully thought through. Three year warranty on Focuses sold by UK Ford dealers from November 2000. Until the new Mondeo, the best Ford ever built. Finally becoming popular in Germany among a population deeply cynical of Fords which is at last realising it's a better car than the Golf Mk IV. Focus 'Black' special edition launched Summer 2001. £12,495 price includes 1.6 engine, 15in alloys, mesh grille, Panther Black metallic paint, air-conditioning, black leather seats, 6000 series radio/CD and Quickclear front screen. Facelift for 2002. For 2002 the Focus got an optional common rail TDCi development of its 1,753cc diesel developing 115PS (113.4bhp) and 184.4lb ft (250Nm) torque at 1,850rpm. This gives it a 0–60 of 10.5 seconds, a top speed of 120mph, a combined economy figure of 51.4mpg and a CO_2 output of 145g/km. Prices start at £14,595 for the five door LX. Focus ST170 arrived March 200 £15,995. Engine is Ford's 1,988cc belt-driven twin-cam Zetec/Duratec modified to deliver 127kW (170bhp) at 7,000rpm and 196Nm (145 lb ft) torque from 2,500 to 5,500rpm. Power is fed through a Getrag twin-shaft six-speed gearbox (like VAG's), offering 0–60 in 7.9 seconds, a top speed of 134mph, a combined fuel consumption of 31.0mpg and CO_2 emissions of 218g/km. Emissions conform to Euro 4. Excellent handling. BMW, Toyota and Ford jointly suffered the fewest breakdowns attended by German ADAC during 2001. Best accolade of all, in April 2002 the German TUV announced that the Ford Focus was the car with the least problems over a three year period. Ford had 3rd lowest cost in warranty claims for cars up to 10 years old in 2002 Warranty Direct index, check online at www.performanceindex.co.uk Highly recommended.

More online at www.ford.co.uk

What's bad: Sharp edges of rear hatch. Bonnet opened by key-lock in grille badge which could be vulnerable to road salt. ABS, aircon etc. all extra, bundled in £500 'extras' packs. 1.6 is overgeared at 23.35 mph/1,000 rpm (3,000 rpm = 70 mph and 6,500 rpm would equal 152 mph) which gives flat performance at motorway speeds. Original diesel is ancient 1,753cc with vulnerable fuel pump to camshaft belt drive that needs replacing every 36,000 miles. Estate not as good looking as hatchback. Saloon is plain ugly and depreciates more heavily than the hatch. 1.6 with Mazda 4-speed automatic initially proved to be a disaster due to ATF leaks between transmission and engine (see recalls about this). Now fixed and proving to be reliable (no reports of any failures at all during 2001/2002). Some late 'W' and early 'X' reg. 2.0 litre Focuses were fitted with Mondeo inlet manifolds and sometimes refuse to drop below 2,500 rpm. The pins which hold the foot pedals in place may fall out, leaving the driver unable to brake or declutch. Rear silencers can rot through in two years. Contacts in rear number plate light can rust up. Can suffer water leaks at rear through vertical light clusters and light contacts can rust up causing current drains. Rear window wiper action on T to W reg. cars causes movement of the glass, scraping the paint in the base of the rear window V which is a natural rust trap. (Rust occurs even though the shell is supposed to be electro galvanizes.) Sharp front edge of parcel shelf can chafe back seat material. Some cars have a protective strip over the parcel shelf edge. Others don't. Strangely delayed launch of new TDCi diesel engine, which is belt cam, not chain cam like the Mondeo TDCi. 1.4 and 1.6 models can have a problem cause by spark plug interference with their GEM (Generic Electronic Module). This controls instrument cluster, interior lights,

FORD

rear heated screen timer, front wiper intermittent, central locking, airbag, reverse lamps, rear wiper, trip computer, etc. The cure is to realign the cylinder head temperature wiring and cable tie it to the engine. Report in *Autocar* 10/4/2002 that USA NHTSA had received a number of reports of burns from airbag pyrotechnics ('*Autocar*' 10–4–2002).

What to watch out for: See Recalls. Some fleets reckon on just 60,000 miles for Zetec E timing belts and idler pulleys. 35,000 miles still max for diesel timing belts. On estates and other models not fitted with plastic sill protectors, look for stone damage and possible rusting at rear bottom edge of front wheel arches. Corrosion can start in hatchback at the sharp point in the recess for the rear screen. Look for flaked paint here. Listen for rumbly rear wheel bearings, especially on estates.

Recalls: TSB 3/1999 'Knocking noise when braking' and involves a different torque setting on one of the lower suspension arm bolts. It also states a new bolt and nut should be fitted, and notes that care must be taken to assemble the washers in the correct order, and that the torque should be applied to the bolt and not the nut. 61,000 cars built Sept '98–Mar '99 recalled in July 1999 for better waterproofing of alternators to prevent short circuits. Announced *Daily Telegraph* 16/7/99. Cars built Sept-Nov '98 recalled in October '99 to cure possible failure of door latches. TSB 52/1999 entitled 'Rattle or knocking noise from front suspension over rough surfaces' and involves too much freeplay between the spring and upper seat, This is rectified by the fitting of a rubber insulator between the spring and mount. 2000: rear light bulb holders rust around the bulbs. New rear light fittings are installed under a Technical Service Bulletin if a rear bulb fails. (Discovered 28/2/2000.) 101,000 Focuses recalled: 1.8 litre and 2.0 litre Zetec E-engined Focuses recalled because oil filler cap can come adrift and oil then be blown out over engine. Wiring harnesses also to be checked for correct routing. ECUs of 1.6 litre Zetec S to be re-programmed if engines suffer from intermittent loss of power. (Announced *Daily Telegraph* 18/3/2000.) TSB 40/2000 entitled 'knocking noises from engine bay under load changes is a misalignment between the engine rear mount and bracket.

Rectified by fitting new components. TSB issued to Ford agents to replace the rear hubs of Focus models fitted with rear disc brakes when in for a service due to snapping of the wheel studs. (Announced 25/4/2000): defect in ECU of Saarlouis and Valencia cars built March 1999 could cause inadvertent deployment of airbags and seatbelt pre-tensioners. 30/5/2000: all Focus automatics recalled because excessive crankshaft end float may allow torque converter to contact crankshaft position sensor leading engine to cut out. Revised crankshaft thrust bearing and new crankshaft position sensor to be fitted. (Unknown date) 2.0 litre Focus models recalled for brake master cylinder to be replaced. 2001: diesels checked under Ford TSB system for possible air leaks into the fuel system. TSB on 1.8 and 2.0 Zetec engines which suffer from stalling suggests that Power Control Module may need recalibrating using 'FDS2000ft diagnostic equipment (source: The Back Room, the online forum at www.honestjohn.co.uk, 21–9–2001). Another TSB on 1.6s that if engine cuts out to replace clutch switch bracket.

Focus (from 2004)

What's good: Next generation Focus, also to provide its C1 floorpan for Volvo S50/V50/C50, will follow Focus C1 MPV. Will be fitted with Ford's Intelligent Protection system and aim for a 5 star NCAP crash safety rating. Engines to start with 1.6 twin cam as current Focus, plus new 1.6 and 1.8 litre petrol engines with variable valve timing and new 1.6 and 2.0 TDCi diesels with up to 135bhp and up to 300lb ft torque. Will be variations all the way up to a 300bhp four wheel drive 160mph Cosworth.

What's bad: Too soon to say.

What to watch out for: Too soon to say.

Focus MPV (from August 2003)

What's good: Paris Show launch in Autumn 2002 on longer wheelbase C1 chassis which allows room for 7 seats. Will be fitted with Ford's Intelligent Protection system and aim for a 5 star NCAP crash safety rating. Engines to start with 1.6 twin cam as current

Focus, plus new 1.6 and 1.8 litre petrol engines with variable valve timing and new 1.6 and 2.0 TDCi diesels with up to 135bhp and up to 300lb ft torque.

What's bad: Too soon to say.

What to watch out for: Too soon to say.

Fusion UAV (from August 2002)

What's good: Fiesta-based Fusion 'Urban Activity Vehicle' on sale in UK from late 2002. Longer, wider and taller than the Fiesta, it is also more versatile. The interior is very attractive with folding 60/40 split rear seat backs and a flat folding front passenger seat allowing the transportation of longer items. The rear load floor is flush with the hatchback sill. Dimensions are: length 4,020 mm (13ft 2in); width 1,708mm (5 ft 7in); height: 1,503mm (4ft 11in). Luggage volume is 337 litres to the parcel shelf with the rear seats up. Three engines:

PSA sourced 1,399cc Duratorq TDCi aluminium block, common rail direct-injected diesel. Power output is 68ps at 4,000rpm with 160Nm (118 lb ft) torque at 1,750rpm. 0–60 is quoted at 15.1 seconds, top speed 99mph, Target Euro combined mpg 64.2 and CO_2 emissions 119g/km (£110pa VED). This engine meets Euro III emissions limits.

1,388cc Duratec 16v petrol. Power output is 80ps at 5,700rpm with 124Nm (91 lb ft) torque at 3,500rpm. 0–60: 13.3 seconds, top speed 102mph, Target Euro combined mpg 43.5 and CO_2 emissions 156g/km (£120pa VED). This engine meets Euro IV emissions limits.

1,596cc Duratec 16v petrol. Power output 100ps at 6,000rpm with 146Nm (108 lb ft) torque at 4,000rpm. 0–60: 10.5 seconds, top speed 111mph, Euro combined mpg 42.8 and CO_2 emissions 158g/km (£120pa VED). This engine meets Euro IV emissions limits.

Standard equipment includes ABS with EBD, height adjustable driver and passenger seats, twin dual-stage front airbags, five three-point seatbelts, decoupling pedals to protect the driver's feet in a severe impact, a passive anti-theft system, and a spare wheel stowed inside the boot rather than slung under it. Standard tyres 195/60R15 (as suggested in the original car by car posting) which is a reasonable compromise between handling and pot-hole protection. Side airbags, side curtain bags, perimeter alarm system and remote central locking are available either as standard or as extras.

More online at www.ford.co.uk

What's bad: No hatch latch on the hatch itself. You have to open it remotely. Up against the Honda Jazz and the Vauxhall Meriva.

What to watch out for: Too soon to say.

Galaxy (1995 to 2003)

What's good: Good styling, low wind noise, decent handling, nice to drive. Up to seven proper seats. 15ft 2in long by 7ft wide and weighing from 1,585kg. 89bhp TDI 90 takes 10,000 miles to run-in, then goes quite well and delivers 38 mpg fuel economy. Aldo 109bhp TDI 110 from November 1997 and 113bhp TDI 115 with six-speed VW gearbox from August 2000 facelift. Base engine was old 113bhp twin chain cam 1,998cc four from Sierra, with 143bhp 1,295cc version from February 1999. Big engine is VW's 172bhp VR6 with standard 5-speed manual, but often fitted with 4 speed autobox. Similar VW Sharan was a Three-Star performer in NCAP crash tests (6 points front impact; 15 points side impact). 'New Edge' face for 2001, on sale in UK from September 2000. See also SEAT Alhambra and VW Sharan. User's website: www.FordGalaxy.org.uk Ford had 3rd lowest cost in warranty claims for cars up to 10 years old in 2002 Warranty Direct index, check online at www.performanceindex.co.uk

What's bad: Hard to park. 2.8 VR6 okay in manual form but VR6 autos guzzle fuel. You have to open the doors to turn the GL's front seats right round. Lots of quality problems. On early models, water can enter car via ventilation, soak the underfloor and get into the ECU which controls the electric windows and alarm system. On later models, this ECU has been moved. Aircon vulnerable to front end shunts. Also shifted in later models. TDIs can blow turbos and catalytic converters. Have also been manual gearbox problems with TDIs. Came last in 'P' reg. J.D. Power Customer Satisfaction Survey, but by 'R' reg. had improved.

Ford dealers unable to work on latest Galaxy 2.8 automatic with the "Tiptronic AG5in gearbox as it is purely VW and they do not have VAG diagnostic equipment. Pre 1999MY key-lock immobiliser models suffer same security design fault as Passats, A4s and early Golf Mk IVs. Thieves can pop out the lock barrel then use the same screwdriver to turn lock so all the windows open and alarm sensors are disabled. On early Galaxy 2000MY the two rear seats are very difficult to put upright and to remove. The padding was increased in the foam for 2000 models, made them harder to tumble over (or impossible). Problems emerging of stretched timing chains on VR6s and chains actually breaking at around 90,000 miles. Air mass meters on TDI 110s can suffer failure through corrosion.

What to watch out for: Make sure 7–seaters are genuine seven-seaters with rearmost area heating and not just 5–seaters with two extra seats clipped in. Make sure recall work carried out.

Recalls: 1996 (April '96–July '96): check for overheating of brake system. 1996 (2–litre with air-conditioning -Jan '95–Feb '96): air conditioning compressor may seize up. 1997 (built Jan '96–Apr '97): check optional child seats. 13/1/2000: 80,000 Galaxys, Alhambras and Sharans VIN TV000001 to YV509825 recalled to check for contamination of brake fluid through master cylinder vent. Brake master cylinders of older cars to be replaced. 23/5/2001: Build dates 1/1/1994 to 5/11/1999 2.0 litre and 2.3 litre petrol models with a/c: when engine rocks the fuel feed and return line may hit the a/c low pressure suction pipe, eventually leading to abraded fuel lines. Fuel lines to be inspected and replaced as necessary and spacer clips to be fitted to all.

Granada/Scorpio (1985 to 1998)

What's good: Big, soft, comfortable, overgrown Sierra hatchback. 15ft 3in long by 5ft 10in wide (saloon: 15ft 7in; estate 5ft 10in long) and weighing from 1,185kg to 1,362kg. Big engine range began with 1,796 single ohc carb engine with 89bhp complemented by 1,993cc single ohc engine at 104bhp with a carb and 107 to 113bhp with injection; 130bhp 2,394cc injected V6 and 148bhp 2,792cc injected V6. 69bhp Peugeot 2.5 diesel engine also available. In March 1989, 1,998cc twin chain cam 123bhp four replaced 1,993cc single cammer; V6 grew to 2,933cc and 150bhp. Cosworth chain driven overhead cam 2.9 V6 came along in 1991 with 193bhp. 2.0 litre twin-cam petrol is reasonably economical. Cosworth 24v V6 is quick. Controversial facelift occurred in January 1995. All models now 15ft 10in long saloons and all named Scorpio. Engine range: same 114bhp 2.0; more powerful twin cam 2.0 at 134bhp; 2.3 litre version with 145bhp; 148bhp pushrod 2.9 V6; 208bhp 2.9 Cosworth and 123bhp 2.5 turbodiesel. Very useful website for sorting out problems: www.fordscorpio.co.uk BMW, Toyota and Ford jointly suffered the fewest breakdowns attended by German ADAC during 2001. Website now has special section for air-conditioning problems: www.fordscorpio.co.uk/aircon.htm

What's bad: Hideous facelift in 1995 and hatchback dropped from range. Dropped entirely from Ford line-up in April 1998. Autobox problems common from 60,000 miles. ECU problems common, leading to catalytic converter problems. Fuseboxes vulnerable and contacts rust. Standard ABS costs a fortune to fix. Timing chain of 24v only lasts 60,000 miles. Cracked heads and oil leaks on two litre twin-cams. Ford had 3rd lowest cost in warranty claims for cars up to 10 years old in 2002 Warranty Direct index, check online at www.performanceindex.co.uk

What to watch out for: Oil leaks caused by cracked head on 2.0 litre 16v. Smoking V6s. ABS failure. ECU failure. Fusebox failure. Cat failure. Alternator failure on 2.5TDs (instead of 120 amp alternators, some Turbodiesel models were fitted with 75 amp alternators which are not up to the job and cost £900 to replace with 120 amp units). 24-valve needs a new timing chain and associated tensioners every 60,000 miles. Autoboxes only last 60,000–80,000 miles. Clocking rife on these cars. Avoid 4x4. Check footwells for damp because a leaking heater matrix costs £500 to replace.

Recalls: 1996 (Aug '94–Jul '96): check for sticking throttle due to corrosion by road salt. 1996 (Feb '96–March '96): rear axle mounting may loosen. 1997: TSB 21: replace 75 amp alternators with 120 amp alternators on 2.5 litre Turbodiesel models. 1997: TSB 186/97: On 2.5TD replace PCM and two vacuum switches which cause engine to overfuel, sooting and damaging the MAF. 1998

Scorpios with passenger airbags built Aug '96–Feb '98: passenger airbag may go off while car is stationary.

KA, KA², KA³ (from 1996)

What's good: Like it or lump it styling. Small size: 11ft 10in by 6ft wide (inc mirrors) and weighing 871kg. Flexible edges good for parking bumps. Good ride comfort. Great handling. With PAS, nice to drive, easy to park. Aircon available. Promise of £12,000 1.6 Zetec 'Street Ka' roadster (see separate entry). Base model Ka now with PAS reduced to £5,995. Reasonable Three-Star rating in Euro NCAP crash tests. Ka Sun Collection from March 2001 with big electric folding canvas sunroof at a steep £8,560 on the road. 'Free' insurance offers. BMW, Toyota and Ford jointly suffered the fewest breakdowns attended by German ADAC during 2001. Ford had 3rd lowest cost in warranty claims for cars up to 10 years old in 2002 Warranty Direct index, check online at www. performanceindex.co.uk

More online at www.ford.co.uk

What's bad: 59nhp Endura E 1.3 pushrod engine very long in the tooth, apt to emulsify oil, block oilways and develop rocker shaft trouble. Non case-hardened cam followers wear away making engine very tappety. Not much space in the back. Doors unprotected from parking damage. Have been complaints of over-servoed brakes. May suffer engine idle flare between gearchanges (see TSB below). Spark plugs may either have corroded into the head or been over tightened (taper fit) which means head removal to drill them out. The pins which hold the foot pedals in place may fall out, leaving the driver unable to brake or declutch. Ka 2s and Ka 3s can suffer from corrosion of the door wiring loom connectors, leading to electric window and central locking failures. Cost of replacing the wiring can amount to £300 for parts plus up to a full day's labour. Either replace front pads at 18,000–20,000 miles or expect to have to replace discs every 25,000 miles. Reports of reverse gear selector forks shearing.

What to watch out for: Flaking paint. Suspension damage from kerbing. Hidden damage underneath deformable ends. Kids sweets, etc., stuck to carpet and seats. Aircon much better than an aftermarket sunroof, but can develop problems (see Ka Sun Collection in What's Good). Make sure remote central locking and electric window winders work properly (see 'What's Bad'). Beware of emulsified oil under oil filler cap. If the engine is tappety it probably needs a new set of cam followers, which isn't a quick and easy job on a pushrod engine. Front suspension bushes have been prone to wear so if the front suspension clonks this is probably why.

Recalls: 1998 Kas with ABS (Mar '98–Sep '98): Brake master cylinder may fail. 2000: TSB issued to replace throttle position sensor and connector if revs fail to decrease on lift off when upchanging. TSB issued advising dealers to use copper grease on spark plugs to aid removal. Mention Technical Service Bulletin (TSB) 095/200 entitled 'Engine Idle Flare during Gear Changes', as this sounds like it could be the problem. It involves the replacement of the throttle position sensor (FPS) and wiring to it. It looks as though it is simply replaced and the wires spliced to the existing loom. Time taken/charge should be 0.3 hours. Rumours of Summer 2001 TSB over problems with a/c pump. Stage 1 tighten auxiliary belt. Stage 2 if that does not work replace pump.

Maverick (1993 to 1997)

What's good: Nissan Terrano II with Ford badge. SWB 13ft 5in by 5ft 8in wide and weighing from 1,620kg to 1,850kg. Reasonably effective off-road. LWB 5–door model has 7–seat option. High driving position. All on strong ladder frame chassis. High- and low-range gears. 2,389cc OHC four had 122bhp; 2,663cc turbodiesel had 98bhp, boosted in July 1996 to 123bhp. This is the best engine to go for. GLS 7 seater best body because it also came with air-conditioning. Had a 3-year dealer warranty to match Nissan's for Terrano II. BMW, Toyota and Ford jointly suffered the fewest breakdowns attended by German ADAC during 2001.

What's bad: 4x4 on-road handling. Dropped from Ford line up in April 1998 along with Scorpio. 3–door very high and narrow looking, so not bought by suburbanites as a style statement.

What to watch out for: Make all usual 4x4 hard usage checks, especially if fitted with a tow hook. Tends to suffer premature wheel bearing wear. TD needs oil changes at least every 5,000 miles to protect turbo from coking up and rest of engine from burned out oil. Be very wary of blue oil smoke from burned out turbo oil seals.

Recalls: 1995 (Maverick with Michelin 215/80 R15 tyres-VIN: PM, PP, PB, PR, PA, PG, PK, PD, PE, RL, RY, RS, RT, RJ, RV, RM, RP, RB, RA): tyres may lose pressure. 19/7/2000: 4,898 Terrano IIs built 1995–1997 recalled because metal brake pipe linking front brake circuit to rear pressure regulation valve may chafe on floorpan, eventually leading to brake fluid leak. Vehicles to be inspected and pipes either repositioned or replaced if worn.

Maverick II (from 2001)

What's good: New Maverick signed off before Ford decided to buy Land Rover. 14ft 5in long by 6ft 7in wide and weighing 1,440kg to 1,530kg. More of a tarmac than an off-road 4x4. Monocoque, chassisless construction. Whereas the old Maverick was developed jointly with Nissan and built in Spain, this is an all new Ford/Mazda co-production built at Mazda's Hofu plant in Japan and a much more refined, road-friendly vehicle with a unitary body rather than separate chassis. Fully independent suspension front and rear rather than solid axles, rack and pinion steering, MacPherson strut front suspension, Control-Trac II automatic 4x4 system and ABS with Electronic Brakeforce Distribution. Already well proven, having been launched as the Ford Escape in the USA in August 2000 and selling 75,000 units in its first three months. Car-like to drive and handles well with none of the top-heaviness of some of the opposition.

Towing weights: 1,500kg for the 2.0 litre manual and 1,700kg for the 3.0 V6 automatic – enough to pull a sizeable trailer, twin horsebox or caravan.

Dimensions: length 4,415mm; width including mirrors 2,018mm; width (mirrors folded) 1,825mm; height (without roof bars) 1,626 mm (including roof bars) 1,755mm. Loading capacity rear seats up and to sill height is 490 litres; rear seats folded and to roof: 1,830 litres. Maximum cargo height is 991mm and maximum width between rear wheel arches is 1,032mm.

Performance: 2.0 litre Zetec 124bhp @ 5,300rpm and 129 lb ft (175Nm) torque @ 4,500rpm. 0 to 60 comes up in 11.8 seconds, top speed is 103mph, combined fuel consumption 28.8mpg and CO_2 emissions 234 grams per km. The 3.0 litre V6 develops 197bhp @ 6,000rpm and 195 lb ft (265Nm) torque @ 4,750rpm. 0 to 60 takes 9.8 seconds, top speed is 112mph, combined fuel consumption 22.1mpg and CO_2 emissions 305 grams per km (which could mean expensive VED in years to come).

Launch on-the-road prices are £17,995 for the 2.0 Zetec and £20,995 for the 3.0 V6 automatic. Air-conditioning, alloy wheels, adjustable roof rack, dual front airbags and side airbags are standard on all models while the 3.0V6 also comes with standard cruise control, CD player and leather seat trim. Did well in '*Autocar*' off-road test (issue 12–9–2001), beating Freelander TD4.

More online at www.ford.co.uk

What's bad: Interior plastics criticised in first independent reports. Did badly in American IIHS and NCAP crash tests. Airbag failed to inflate in American test. Some drivers may not like the column mounted auto shifter of the 3.0 V6 auto (I found it no problem at all). 2.0 litre a bit underpowered, but the only way to get a manual gearbox. Towing weight not as high as the 2,000kg of a Freelander TD4 or X-Trail DI.

What to watch out for: Too soon to say.

Mondeo (1993 to 2000)

What's good: Decent build, decent handling, tremendous 'feelgood factor', multi-adjustable steering (in, out, up, down). 14ft 8in long by 6ft 4in wide and weighing from 1,235kg to 1,375kg. 4–door saloon, 5–door hatchback or longer 15ft 2in estate. 89bhp 1.6 Zetec E; 113bhp 1.8 Zetec E; 128bhp 2.0 Zetec E; 87bhp 1.7 diesel; 168bhp 2.5 V6. ST24 from January 1999 had 202bhp. Hugely improved from 1997 model year facelift, which made the 5–door much better looking than rather dowdy 93K-96N original; three lap/diagonal rear belts now standard. Faults virtually all eliminated from '97 model year and 2.0LX can offer 40 mpg economy. Very strong bodyshell at the front. Comparatively good performance in NCAP crash tests. Easy and cheap to repair body damage. 1997 MY on is sensational used value for money and highly recommended. BMW, Toyota and Ford jointly suffered the fewest breakdowns attended by German ADAC during 2001. Enthusiasts and problem solving website: www.fordmondeo.org

What's bad: Lacks spaces for oddments such as mobile phones inside cockpit. Subframe needs dismantling to change the clutch, making it a £500–£600 job. Incorrect reassembly leads to tracking problems. Sticking valves on pre-1997 1.6s, 1.8s and 2.0s run short distances on cheap petrol (most have now been cured by 'in-service' mods which cause engine to use a bit more oil.) 2.0 litre is still a bit coarse and boomy and gear ratios are for town rather than open road use. Engine management problems on 2.5 24v V6 can burn out catalytic converters (the car has three). 1.8 diesel engine very antiquated. ST 200 has very short gears and traction problems. Question-mark over longevity of front wishbone bushes on V6 – even post-97MY version. Suspension bags out after 120,000 miles. Reports of early front coil spring failures on 'R' and 'S' reg. cars, now also coming in on earlier cars. Report of £500 diesel injector pumps "only" lasting 100,000 miles, but this could be due to the lack of lubricity of the fuel being used. Reports of driveshaft failures on the last of the Mk I 'W' and 'X' reg. Mondeos. Seems the driveshaft UJ boot clips were wrongly fitted, allowing water ingress to the UJs causing them to fail. Free replacement for affected cars. Chrome comes off the smart 12 spoke wheels fitted to some high spec Mondeos at the time of the 97MY facelift. Screenwasher pumps apt to clog up. The simple cure is to use a bamboo cane or similar to give the reservoir a stir, but better to flush the reservoir out with a fairly high pressure hose and get rid of the gunk in there. Also make sure screenwash pipes have not become trapped or kinked in bonnet hinge. Reports of 2nd gear band breaking up in 4-speed autobox, contaminating the ATF and requiring the box to be rebuilt.

What to watch out for: Slipping clutch. Baggy suspension. A bang on a speed bump can knock out the otherwise well protected catalytic converter on 4-cylinder cars. Infamous 'pulling to the left' caused by kerbing damage, by worn track control arm bushes, by misaligned reassembly of front subframe after clutch replacement or by failure to re-track properly after replacing track control arms. Look for uneven tyre wear (outer shoulder wear normal). Early (1993) Mondeos prone to starter motor failure. If ABS fitted, make sure light goes out after 3 seconds or new pump or ECU may be needed. Shafts of front electric window winder mechanism can go: make sure both work. More than its fair share of recalls. The Mondeo is a bigger, heavier, wider car than the Sierra. May not fit your garage. If automatic, make sure shifts are smooth and check ATF which should be red, not black. Timing belts on diesels only good for 3 years or 36,000 miles. Reports of shorting out of resistors to heater/ventilator fan motor of 1996 and 1997 build cars. (Repair/replacement kit: '97BG18A336AA...1 056972) Resistors situated upper RH side of passenger footwell. If you smell an electrical fire, this is the first place to look for the source. On Zetec E petrol engines, several reports of timing belt tensioner pulley heating up and shattering after 5–6 years and 60–80,000 miles. Essential to replace the pulley at the same time as the belt.

Alarm sensors under the rear windows of V6 Ghia estates can suffer water ingress leading to electrical short and flat battery.

Recalls: 1994 (92 VIN NY, NS, NT; 93 VIN PJ, PU, PM, PP, PB, PR, PA, PG, PC, PK, PD, PE; 94 VIN RL, RY, RS, RT, RJ, RU, RM): headlamp failure. 1995 (Mondeo diesels: VIN: SY, SS, ST): brake vacuum pump may not create enough vacuum for servo. 1995: fuel pipe. 1995: (VIN: RP, RB, RR): static sparks may occur when refuelling. 1996: free recall (per *What Car?* 9/96, p. 132) to sort out problem of sticking valves – work will usually be carried out when car is in for a routine service. 1996 (1996 model year with hydraulic clutch – excluding V6): check, replace if necessary clutch master cylinder/slave cylinder. Check front brake callipers. 1997: (24v built 1/8/94–14/6/96; 9,000 cars): free official recall to replace catalytic converter closest to exhaust manifold. 1998 Mondeos with passenger airbags built Aug '96–Feb '97: passenger airbag may go off while car is stationary. Ford Mondeo V6 with ABS (Dec '97–Jan '98): ABS system may fail. TSB 47/1997: Procedure and parts to correct hot weather pinking of 1.8s. October 1999: Mondeos built Sept-Nov 1998 recalled to cure possible failure of door latches. TSB issued to replace door light switches of cars built 8/96 to 11/98 as can cause current leakdown and alarm problems. 2000: Mondeos built June '95–Sept '97 recalled to check for chafing of front seatbelt webbing. 30/5/2000: 160,376 Mondeos without ABS built 2/1/96 to 7/8/98 recalled to replace rear brake pressure limiting valve which may corrode and leak. 2001 TSB to add section of damper pipe to power steering of 1999 cars to prevent clonking from steering when negotiating uneven surfaces. 8/10/2001: recall of 32,665 Mondeos and Cougars built 1/11/1999 to 1/5/2000 because parking brake ratchet can lose a tooth. Lever ratchet assembly to be replaced. 2001 TSB to fit 24v V6 models with larger air intake pipe to cure tendency for engine to hunt when idling.

Mondeo II (from 2000)

What's good: Bigger than the already big 1993–2000 Mondeo, and now a Scorpio sized 15ft 6in long by 6ft 4in wide (estate: 15ft 9in long). More roomy inside. Better handling from Focus-like 'control blade' rear suspension. 'New Edge' styling. Estate car even bigger inside than E-Class Mercedes. Engine range includes new 125 bhp 1.8 litre Duratec HE petrol, new 143 bhp 2.0 litre Duratec HE petrol; 168 bhp 2.5 litre Duratec V6 and 113 bhp 156g/km CO_2 2.0 litre chain-cam 16v direct injected Duratorq diesel engine. The new petrol engines already meet Euro 2005 emissions limits. Smallest wheel/tyre combination is 16in with 205/55 R16 tyres, going up to 17in and 18in wheels. UK list prices: £14,595 for 1.8iLX and £15,095 for 2.0iLX both with a/c, alloy wheels, three year warranty and 12 year anti-corrosion warranty. On your first drive of the car it immediately feels fantastic. Then it gets better. V6 Zetec S launched at £19,095 (note that 10 spoke alloys much better looking than 5 spoke.) 4x4 version of estate with higher ground clearance on the way. 2.0 litre 217bhp 150mph V6 ST220 from May 2002. New 128bhp 2.0 litre chain-cam 16v common rail direct injected TDCi diesel with 243lb ft (329Nm)torque finally arrived in UK from December 2001. Its 0–60 is 9.6 seconds, top speed 124mph, combined economy 47.9mpg and CO_2 output 156g/km. Prices start at £16,145 for the four or five door LX. The Mondeo II pips even the Passat at its own game and is now becoming popular in Germany. Looks best in silver or metallic grey. Four star performance in 2001 and 2002 NCAP crash safety tests and did particularly well in side impact test. BMW, Toyota and Ford jointly suffered the fewest breakdowns attended by German ADAC during 2001. Hot ST220 in 2002 powered by de-tuned 217bhp version of Jaguar Duratec V6. New 5-speed 'Durashift 5–tronic' autobox for V6 and TDCi 130 announced at Brussels Motor Show, priced £1,500 v/s £1,000 for standard 4-speed autobox. Enthusiasts and problem solving website: www.fordmondeo.org Mondeo II range. Highly recommended.

What's bad: Criticised for "unstable body structure" in 2001 NCAP test, despite four star score. Still seems to lack space for oddments inside cockpit. Reports of poor 35mpg economy from stop-gap 2.0 litre 115bhp DI engine. 2.0 DI diesel engine also prone to flat spots and surging. On early LX and Zetecs the bottom of the seat is not very friendly to the coccyx. Also uncomfortable for heavier drivers because the plastic pins holding the moulded padding in place can actually protrude through to the seat face. Later models much improved.

What to watch out for: Too soon to say.

Recalls: 29/12/2000: 2,500 2001 model year Mondeos recalled to have side airbag trigger electronics replaced. (Source Daily Mirror 29/12/2000.)16/7/2001: Warning sent out to owners about correct operation of handbrake: press brake pedal firmly; while brake pedal pressed, pull handbrake lever up to its fullest extent keeping finger off the ratchet button. Always park an automatic in 'P'. 21/8/2001: 5,595 2001 model year Mondeos built October 2000 to July 2001 fitted with cruise control recalled because water ingress can corrode the electrics leading to failure to switch off. May 2002: 60,000 Mondeos built January to November 2001 recalled for parking brake ratchet to be adjusted.

Orion (1983 to 1993)

What's good: As for equivalent Escort, but with a boot. Oval grille on Post September 1990 shape came in during October 1992 for 1993MY. Ford had 3rd lowest cost in warranty claims for cars up to 10 years old in 2002 Warranty Direct index, check online at www.performanceindex.co.uk

What's bad: As for equivalent Escort. Diesels more likely to have once been taxis. Orion name dropped in 1993 in favour of 'Escort 4–door' – which helped to boost 'Escort' sales figures.

What to watch out for: As for equivalent Escort.

Recalls: As for equivalent Escort.

Probe (1994 to 1998)

What's good: First fruit of Ford's gradual buying into Mazda. Launched in the USA in 1992. 15ft 1in long by 5ft 10in wide and weighing 1,215kg to 1,280kg. Essentially a re-styled Mazda MX6 with the same smooth and revvy quad-cam 163 bhp V6, but also offered with a 2.0 litre 128 bhp four from the 626. Only started to sell once it dropped to a sensible price on the used market and actually bounced back for a year or so. BMW, Toyota and Ford jointly suffered the fewest breakdowns attended by German ADAC during 2001. Probes are cheap now.

What's bad: A model Ford would prefer to forget. Huge and variable panel gaps. Not enough rear legroom. Harsh ride. Far too expensive new. A Ford dealer even tried to pre-interest the trade with a UK 'K' registered 3,000–mile LHD 24v. Between December 1992 and January 1993 it dropped from a top 'bid' of £14,800 to £12,700, clearly showing that an original list price of £19,350 was pie in the sky.

What to watch out for: Accident damage. And the sort of deterioration that results from sitting around unsold in compounds (rusty discs, rusty exhaust, flat battery, aircon shot, etc.). 2.0 litre can suffer expensive ignition igniter problems (£700) so best avoided. V6 may need a new timing belt.

Recalls: 2000: Probes built Jan '95–Oct '96: fuel vapours may escape from tank.

Puma (1997 to 2001)

What's good: Highly rated, brilliant handling, Fiesta-based coupe. 13ft long by 6ft wide. Yamaha-developed 125 bhp 1.7 litre Zetec S engine supplemented by 90 bhp 1.4 Zetec S in February 1998 and 153 bhp 'Racing' in early 2000. 1.4 replaced by 99bhp 1.6 in Spring 2001. 'Racing' Puma offered outstanding grip and 'race car feel' for those prepared to fork out £20k plus. Trade Sales of Slough were selling 1.7s with Lux pack (including aircon) for £10,999 in July 2001. BMW, Toyota and Ford jointly suffered the fewest breakdowns attended by German ADAC during 2001. Ford had 3rd lowest cost in warranty claims for cars up to 10 years old in 2002 Warranty Direct index, check online at www.performanceindex.co.uk Final edition was the Puma Thunder.

What's bad: Production ceased at end of 2001, though stockpiled cars continue to be sold into 2002. Could suffer similar brake problems to Fiesta. Long-term life of special bore linings of 1.7 unknown in day-to-day use, though no problems to date. Misfiring 1.7 litre engine may be due to weeping core plugs leaking coolant onto spark plugs.

What to watch out for: Possibility of having been thrashed. Check the oil level as well as the oil colour of 1.7s. 5,000–mile oil changes far more sensible than Ford recommended 10,000–mile intervals. Don't switch to fully synthetic oil without written approval from Ford as this may affect bore liners. Kerbing will throw out critical front suspension alignment. Uneven front tyre wear should put you on your guard. Don't pay too much just to get one. Front suspension bushes have been prone to wear so if the front suspension clonks this is probably why.

Recalls: 1998 (built Mar '98–Sep '98): 4,500 Pumas recalled to have brake master cylinder replaced.

Sierra and Sapphire (1982 to 1993)

What's good: All independently sprung successor to the Cortina, sold as 'man and machine in perfect harmony. 14ft 5in long by 5ft 6in wide and weighing 969kg to 1,194kg. Estates were 14ft 9in long and saloons (called Sapphires, from March 1987) 14ft 8in long.

Multitude of different engine, gearbox, drive system and trim combinations, including a rate 3–door hatchback with 1.3 and 1.6 engines also used for the Sierra Cosworth. 1,294cc CVH had 60bhp; 1,593cc Pinto had 73bhp; 1,597cc CVH EMAX had 75bhp; 1,796cc CVH had 89bhp; 1,993cc single cam carb had 101bhp; 1,993cc single cam injection had 115bhp; 1,998cc twin cam carb from August 1989 had 107bhp; 1,998cc twin cam injection had 123 to 125 bhp; 1,993cc twin cam Cosworth Turbos had 204bhp; 2,933cc V6 had 150bhp. Early 2.0 litre 4-speed versions were fast cars with 9–second 0–60 and 120 mph max. Last of the line 124bhp GT was a good model, but best to avoid catalysed versions. XR 4x4s had later Cosworth four wheel drive system with 125bhp four or 150bhp V6. Very cheap now. No need to pay more than £500 for any apart from Cosworth.

What's bad: Front suspension wears out and makes it terrible to drive. Sierras are one of the few cars better bought after accident repairs to the front which can make them feel new again. But make sure damage has not crumpled transmission tunnel, severely weakening the shell. All are now getting old and tired and were never supposed to last 10 years-plus. Many have done huge mileages and the clocks may not be showing it.

What to watch out for: Every single trick in the book. Clockers. Cloners. Cut 'n' Shuts. Rust traps in doors. Warped front discs. Cracked heads and oil leaks on two litre twin-cams. If the steering feels unusually horrible the front suspension reaction arm bushes have gone. Treat all 4x4s and Cosworths with particular suspicion. 2x4s are apt to snap the front transfer case to final drive driveshaft. Rust badly in the doors. This is just the tip of the iceberg, so check everything.

StreetKa from 2003

What's good: Ford's £12,000 Ka based roadster due to hit the UK market in early 2003 using the 1.6 litre 103bhp Zetec S engine from the Fiesta and Focus. May also have option of 125bhp 1.7 from Puma. Very attractive and bound to sell well at this price level.

What's bad: Too soon to say

What to watch out for: Too soon to say.

Think City (in UK from 2002)

What's good: Ford's contribution to the urban environment. Small, two seater plastic bodied car 9ft 10 ins long (2,990mm) first seen at 1999 Frankfurt Motor Show. Reaches 30mph in 7 seconds and has a top speed of 56mph. Power is from 19 NiCd batteries and range is 53 miles. Fully recharging takes around 8 hours and costs 38p; 80% recharging 4–6 hours. Has a driver's airbag and acquitted itself well in US crash tests. On trial with London businesses from September 2001. Free parking in London and free recharging at special sites in Westminster. Zero rated VED. Exempt from London congestion charges. Could become the ideal London commuter car for those living within 30 miles of the centre. Websites: www.thinkmobility.com and www.thinkaboutlondon.co.uk

What's bad: Not on public sale in the UK until mid 2002. Doubts about whether Ford seriously wants to sell the Think or whether it is really a 'Think Green' publicity stunt.

What to watch out for: Too soon to say.

Thunderbird (from 2001)

What's good: Lovely retro cruiser on lines of '57 T-Bird but with S Type Jag underpinnings, decent 5-speed autobox and 255bhp V8. Drives really nicely up to 120mph: smooth, quiet, soaks up the bumps and also handles quite well. A better boulevard cruiser than the new Mercedes 500SL because power take-up is smoother and nicer. Long queue in the USA at US list of £24,000, but UK suppliers can get you one ESVA approved and UK registered for £44,000.

What's bad: Pay the UK premium and you won't see your money back.

What to watch out for: Too soon to say.

Tourneo Connect (from August 2002)

What's good: Ford's Berlingo type kombi utility version of its new Connect mini-Transit. SWB 4,278mm x 1,795mm wide (excluding mirrors) x 1,814mm high and weighing 1,540kg. LWB 4,525mm x 1,795mm x 1,981mm with GVW of 2,340kg. Has a hugely capacious rear (load length 1,583–1,830mm rear seats up to 1,760–2,007mm rear seats folded to 2,467–2,714mm front seat folded; all 1,409mm wide) with twin sliding side doors and a rear seat for three. Uniquely, on the Tourneo, this is 60/40 split-folding for even greater versatility. Stylishly good looking and car-like to drive compared with other kombi utilities. 5 stud wheels and reinforced tyres for heavy load carrying. Optional fold-flat front passenger seat for maximum load length and additional cube, or four-way adjustable seat with underseat stowage for improved comfort and security. As well as being fully removable, the rear seat backrests fold flat, and the seat folds fully forward and stows vertically.

Security features include a 'lock-in-latch' system, first used on the full-size Ford Transit. Also has security-shielded wiring, key-operated bonnet lock and the latest generation of Ford's Passive Anti-Theft System (PATS) which prevents hot wiring. Safety equipment includes driver, passenger and side airbags, and anti-lock brakes. Assembled at Ford's new, state-of-the-art Kocaeli plant near Izmit, Turkey, along with the full-size Transit van and new Transit Connect. Engines: 1.8 Zetec E (now called 'Duratec') with 115PS and 160Nm torque at 4,400rpm; 1.8 Duratorq TDdi with 75PS and 175NM torque at 1,800rpm; 1.8 Duratorq TDCi with 90PS and 220Nm torque at 1,700rpm.

More online at www.fordvans.co.uk

What's bad: Too soon to say.

What to watch out for: Too soon to say.

HINDUSTAN

Ambassador

What's good: Basically an Indian built 1957 Morris Oxford with a catalysed 1.8 litre Isuzu engine. Heavy and cumbersome, but interesting to lovers of nostalgia. Some now used as mini cabs in London and share driving characteristics with the FX4 taxi.

What's bad: Became a nightmare for the importer, Fullbore Motors of Fulham and ultimately sent the firm into liquidation. What started as a good idea became entangled in European Type Approval and emissions regulations. This meant the change of engine from the old, Indian built 1,500cc 'B' Series pushrod engine to the Isuzu, the price escalated from £6,000 to £10,000, then, because the cars had to be virtually re-built before they could be sold in the UK, the price rose to around £12,000 at which there were very few takers.

What to watch out for: You'll have to get your spare parts from the Morris Oxford Motor Club or from India. Will rust quite badly due to the poor quality of the welding and the steel.

HONDA

Accord (1985 to 1989)

What's good: Well regarded 4–door saloon and 3–door Aerodeck hatchback. Saloon 14ft 7in long by 5ft 6in wide and weighing 980kg to 1,185kg. Aerodeck hatch 14ft 4in long by 5ft 7in wide and weighing 1,075kg to 1,135kg. 100bhp 1.8; 106bhp 2.0; 122bhp 2.0i; and 137bhp 2.0i 16 valve. 5-speed manual or 4-speed automatic. Was also a 14ft 4in coupe with 114bhp 2.0 engine or 148bhp 2.0i 16v. Many have remained totally reliable, even at 16 years old.

What's bad: Starting to rust and once it gets hold this can be bad. A/C was filled with old type R34 refrigerant which is now unobtainable. Replacing with CFC free refrigerant often leads to leaks.

What to watch out for: Rust, particularly around the window frames because if it's taken hold there the car is a write-off. If fitted with a/c and you're paying good money, then make sure the a/c works or repairing it could cost you more than the car.

Accord (1989 to 1993)

What's good: Extremely well regarded, reliable Japanese-built saloon cars give ten years fault-free service as long as serviced on time. 15ft 4in long by 5ft 7in wide and weighing 1,225kg to 1,355kg. 112bhp from 2.0 16v carb engine, 135bhp from 2.0i 16v; 148bhp from 2.2i. Badged Acura, have been the USA's top selling car. Healthy 135 bhp 2.0 litre catalysed down to 131 bhp from December 1991, but 2.2 remained Alternative 148 bhp. Excellent four-speed autoboxes. Beautifully built. From April 1991 was also an American assembled 148bhp 2.2i 'Aerodeck' estate 15ft 5in long and 1,430kg which carried on alongside the next generation Japanese built Accord saloon until June 1994.

What's bad: Steering a bit light. Bonded windscreens very difficult to replace and this usually leads to scratches, rust and water ingress around screen area. Sheet metal not as thick as German cars. An intermittent fault which causes the engine to cut out may be nothing more than a failed ignition amplifier. A replacement part costs £50 and some RAC patrolmen actually carry them. Air conditioning filled with the old CFC refrigerant, supplies of which have now dried up. Replacing with new CFC free gas can lead to leaks.

What to watch out for: Tend to be entirely trouble free as long as serviced on time. Check screen area and rear wheel arches for rust. Make sure aircon blows cold. Aircon may still contain environmentally unfriendly R12 refrigerant. Needs to be recharged with CFC-free 134A refrigerant and this may lead to weeping seals. Look for uneven tyre wear as a result of kerbing. Check under oil cap for emulsified oil due to short runs from cold starts – also likely to have rotted out rear silencer box.

Accord (from early 2003)

What's good: New Accord due early 2003 as 4–door saloon only with estate to come later. 2.0 litre 160bhp and 2.3 litre 180bhp VTEC 4-cylinder engines, plus Type R with 240bhp. Also 2.2 litre Honda-built common rail Euro 4 diesel with 140bhp and 250lb ft torque.

What's bad: No longer British built.

What to watch out for: Too soon to say.

Accord UK (1993 to 1998)

What's good: Accord saloons built in Swindon which also formed the basis of the Rover 600. 15ft 4in long by 5ft 8in wide and weighing 1,300kg to 1,400kg. Smooth Swindon built engines: 113 bhp 1.8 from March '96; 129 bhp 2.0 from May '93; 148 bhp 2.2iVTEC from March '96; 156 bhp 2.3iSR from October '93 to March '96. Also sold with Rover's 104bhp 1,994cc diesel from 1996 to 1998. Decent roadholding and handling, especially 2.2 and 2.3. Excellent four-speed autoboxes. Two-year warranty grew to three. In June 2001 Honda was rated by Motor Warranty Direct as Britain's

4th most claim-free used marque (check online at www.warrantydirect.co.uk)15th from top of 100 models for reliability in *Auto Express* 2002 survey. Recommended.

What's bad: Steering a bit light. Exhaust rear silencer boxes rot out on low mileage 'short run' examples. Electric front windows have a habit of popping out of runners. New 1999 model instantly 'dates' a 98R old model.

What to watch out for: Tend to be entirely trouble-free as long as serviced on time with regular changes of coolant and brake fluid. Look for stone and screen chips on the quicker versions. Make sure electric front windows work properly and are not sluggish. Look for rust bubbling through just behind each rear wheel arch. This is a big panel in short supply, so the problem is very expensive to remedy. Check for emulsified oil under the oil cap of 2.3i engines as this could indicate a cracked cylinder head which is £2k to replace.

Recalls: May 2002: contact point in ignition can fail at speed causing a stall in cars built 1997 to 1998 (*Auto Express* 30/5/2002).

Accord UK (1998 to 2003)

What's good: Re-engineered and rebodied Swindon Accord. Shorter at 15ft 1in by 5ft 9in but heavier, weighing 1,405kg to 1,460kg. Very well received and a good alternative to the VW Passat. 5–door hatch supplemented 4–door saloon from Summer 1999. 136 bhp 1.8 and 146 bhp 2.0 powerful enough. Fire-breathing 210 bhp Type R very fast indeed and an excellent handler with the best pedal set I've ever driven. Rover-engined diesel now dropped from line-up. Three-year warranty. Four-Star performance in NCAP crash safety tests. Most reliable car in 2001 Fleet News Survey of 620,000 fleet cars mostly under 3 years old. 15th from top of 100 models for reliability in *Auto Express* 2002 survey.

What's bad: Reports of problems with manual gearboxes. Serious problem with the printed circuit boards that control the automatic load compensating headlamp beam adjusters of Type Rs which may become the subject of a safety recall. New Accord due Summer 2003.

What to watch out for: Too soon to say.

Recalls: 2000: Accords built July '98–July '99: check for sticking throttle. 2001: Safety recall to check brakes. TSBs to fir plastic sleeve to doorlocks to cure a rattle and to check tension of ancillaries belt because too much can wear out the water pump bearings. May 2002: contact point in ignition can fail at speed causing a stall in cars built 1997 to 2000 (*Auto Express* 30/5/2002).

Accord USA (1994 to 1997)

What's good: Good-looking American built 'Aerodeck' 5–door estate cars and two-door coupes, badged Acura in the States. Aerodecks 15ft 8in long by 5ft 10in wide and weighing 1,385kg to 1,440kg. High specification includes aircon. 131–145 bhp 2.0 litre engine, 148 bhp 2.2 litre (same as Shuttle). Two-year warranty grew to three. In June 2001 Honda was rated by Motor Warranty Direct as Britain's 4th most claim-free used marque (check online at www.warrantydirect.co.uk)15th from top of 100 models for reliability in *Auto Express* 2002 survey.

What's bad: Load area of Aerodeck compromised by suspension intrusion. Honda servicing can work out expensive.

What to watch out for: Aircon needs recharging every three years with CFC-free 134A refrigerant. Must have regular servicing to remain reliable.

Recalls: 2000: Aircon wiring may chafe and short-circuit.

Accord USA Coupe (from 1998)

What's good: New American-built coupe from summer 1998 with choice of 145 bhp four-cylinder engine man/auto or 197 bhp V6 auto only. 15ft 8in long by 5ft 10in wide and V6 weighs 1,470kg. Understated good looks. Three-year warranty. Full five seater with three three-point rear seatbelts. 15th from top of 100 models for reliability in *Auto Express* 2002 survey.

What's bad: A bit too 'American' for some European tastes.

What to watch out for: Nothing yet, and they've been around for four years. No wonder owners like them.

Recalls: May 2002: contact point in ignition can fail at speed causing a stall in cars built 1997 to 2000 (*Auto Express* 30/5/2002).

Beat (1990 to 1995)

What's good: Tiny 656cc 64bhp three-cylinder 'K' class sportscar from Japan, introduced in 1990 and production of which ended in 1995. Has a cult following. Revs to 8,000rpm. LCD stereo. Zebra striped seats. Available on the used grey market from around £2,500 to £7,000 for a top example.

What's bad: You need to find a specialist to look after it and they are few and far between. Because of this, some cars may not have been properly serviced.

What to watch out for: Excessive oil consumption (check exhaust gas colour carefully). Minor damage because parts can be difficult to source.

Civic (1987 to 1991)

What's good: Slightly longer than previous model, offered as 3-door hatchback or 4 door saloon. 12ft 6in long by 5ft 4in wide (saloon 13ft long); weighed 830 to 885kg. Engines were 75bhp 1,343cc; 90bhp 1,396cc; 128bhp 1,590cc and, from 1990 to 1991, the first 1.6 VTEC with 148bhp. Nice looking. Mechanical parts last well.

What's bad: Now starting to rust, some quite badly. Spares becoming harder to get.

What to watch out for: Rust and MOT failures due to damaged hard to get parts such as rear light lenses.

Civic Coupe USA (from 1994)

What's good: 2-door coupes, launched as 100 bhp 1.5s in February 1994 and ran through to January 1996. Then relaunched in January 1996 as LS with same goggle-eyed front as Japanese Civics with 103 bhp 1.6 or SR with 123 bhp 1.6, ABS and alloys. 14ft 8in long by 5ft 8in wide. 4-speed auto optional. Aircon optional from June '97.

Praised for much softer ride than other Civics. Reasonable rear head and legroom. In June 2001 Honda was rated by Motor Warranty Direct as Britain's 4th most claim-free used marque. Eighth most reliable car in 2001 Fleet News Survey of 620,000 fleet cars mostly under 3 years old. (check online at www.warrantydirect.co.uk) 10th from top for reliability in *Auto Express* 2002 survey.

What's bad: Not much.

What to watch out for: Same as Japanese Civics.

Civic hybrid 4-door (from 2003)

What's good: Logical development of the Insight in the Japanese/American Civic 4–door body. Power unit is the smaller 1.3 i-DSI engine optional in Japan in the Jazz. This is married to a 10kW electric motor. The combination gives torque equivalent to a 1.6 litre engine, 100mph top speed, 0–60 in around 13 seconds and 60mpg economy potential in mixed motoring.

What's bad: Hybrids don't offer the best economy in stop-start city use.

What to watch out for: Battery life.

Civic Japan (1991 to 1996)

What's good: 3–door hatchback with split tailgate or 4–door saloon. Hatch 13ft 5in by 5ft 7in and weighing from 925kg. Impressive engines: 74 bhp 1.3; 89 bhp 1.5; 123 bhp 1.6 and 158 bhp VTi. 4-speed autos available on 89 bhp 1.5 and 123 bhp 1.6. In June 2001 Honda was rated by Motor Warranty Direct as Britain's 4th most claim-free used marque (check online at www.warrantydirect.co.uk)

What's bad: Very small luggage area in split tailgate hatch. Saloon not as roomy inside as exterior dimensions suggest because roofline is quite low. Honda servicing is usually pricy. Ride not very smooth. Suits the small rather than the tall.

What to watch out for: Needs to have been regularly serviced, preferably with six-monthly oil changes. VTECs must have clean oil and are particularly vulnerable to extended service intervals.

Recalls: 1994: Honda Civic 3–door, 4–door, CRX automatics: auto gear indicator may show wrong transmission mode.

Civic Japan (from 1996)

What's good: Restyled, slightly bigger, quieter Civics. 3–door hatchback now 13ft 9in long by 5ft 8in wide; 4–door saloon 14ft 8in by 5ft 8in. Weights from 1,168kg. 3–door now has conventional hatchback and more luggage space. Engine range now 90 bhp 1.4, 114 bhp 1.5, 116 bhp 1.6, 158 bhp VTi. Normal 4-speed auto or option of CVT auto in 116 bhp 1.6ES 3–door only. Two-year warranty grew to three. In June 2001 Honda was rated by Motor Warranty Direct as Britain's 4th most claim-free used marque. Eighth most reliable car in 2001 Fleet News Survey of 620,000 fleet cars mostly under 3 years old. (check online at www.warrantydirect.co.uk) 10th from top for reliability in *Auto Express* 2002 survey.

What's bad: Average NCAP crash test results. Goggle-eyed restyle not wholly successful. 3–door side doors very long, so difficult to emerge in tight parking spaces with any dignity.

What to watch out for: The last thing you want to see in a Honda is dirty oil on the dipstick.

Civic Shuttle (1984 to 1991)

What's good: Useful, upright, Civic based estate car. Almost what we now call a mini MPV. Original 1984 to 1988 version was 13ft 1in long and 5ft 5in wide with an 85bhp 1,488cc engine, 5 speed gearbox and optional 4 speed auto. 1988 to 1991 version was bigger and much prettier. Now 31ft 6in long and 5ft 6in wide with 90bhp 1,396cc engine, 5 speed gearbox and optional 4 speed auto. Also a 4x4 version from 1985 to 1990, originally with the 90bhp 1.4, but with a 116bhp 1.6 from April 1998. That's obviously the one to have if you can find one. Sill look smart and contemporary.

What's bad: Getting old now. Spares can be hard to find, especially body parts.

What to watch out for: Usual Civic mechanical checks and check all hard to replace screen glass and light lenses, etc., for MOT failure damage. Rust first seems to occur in the backs of the rear wheel arches, but older models could be very rusty.

Civic UK (1995 to late 2000)

What's good: 'Swindon' 5–door hatchbacks and estate on floorpan shared with Rover 400. 14ft 2in long by 5ft 7in long and from 1,075kg. 89 bhp 1.4, 89 bhp 1.5 VTEC-E, 111 bhp 1.6 from '95–'97; 112 bhp 1.5 VTEC, 114 bhp 1.6 and rip roaring 167 bhp 1.8 VTEC from '97 on. Smooth 4-speed autos. 1.5 VTEC-E was capable of 45–50 mpg, but at a price. Very nicely built, under-bonnet looks like Honda motorcycle high tech. 1.5 VTEC-E replaced by 85 bhp Rover 2.0 DI engine in May 1997. Aerodeck 5–door estate from February 1998. Average performance in 1998 NCAP safety tests. Two-year warranty grew to three. In June 2001 Honda was rated by Motor Warranty Direct as Britain's 4th most claim-free used marque. Eighth most reliable car in 2001 Fleet News Survey of 620,000 fleet cars mostly under 3 years old. (check online at www.warrantydirect.co.uk) 10th from top for reliability in *Auto Express* 2002 survey.

What's bad: 1.5 VTEC-E sometimes seen at head of long traffic queue as elderly driver tries to keep in economy range. 5–door range did not sell as well as Honda might have hoped as was still some anti-Japanese ill-feeling and 'True Brits' went for the Rover equivalents.

What to watch out for: Quite a few 1.5 VTEC-Es were laundered into second-hand cars via the rental fleets. All 'Swindon Civics' appreciate frequent servicing and clean oil. Some complaints of poor reverse gear selection, so check this on test drive.

Recalls: 20/5/2000: 1999 and 2000 MY: 12,711 1.4s and 1.5s not fitted with ABS may suffer failure of brake proportion control valve leading to instability when braking. Part to be replaced with modified unit. 3/11/2000: 2,327 5–door Civics built 10/3/1999 to 10/10/2000 recalled because of possibility of breakage of rear suspension lower arm bolts. Bolts to be replaced. 1/7/2001: 3,694 Swindon Civics built 27/11/2000 to 24/4/2001 recalled because brake pedal and clutch pedal lock pins may be incorrectly installed. Check and re-install as necessary. 5/7/2001: 4,601 Swindon Civics built up to 4/12/2000 recalled because screw clips on filler tube connecting filler pipe to tank may not be correctly installed and could result in a leak in a severe impact. Check and re-install as necessary. May 2002: contact point in ignition can fail at speed causing a stall in cars built 1997 to 2000 (*Auto Express* 30/5/2002).

Civic UK (from 2001)

What's good: Radical, good looking and stylish new 5–door 'Swindon' Civic hatchback launched at September 2000 Paris Motor Show and sold in UK from January 2001. 14ft 1in long by 5ft 7in wide (3–door 13ft 7in long) and weighing from 1,200kg. Dash-mounted gearchange, flat floor and very spacious 'walk through' interior ideal for mothers with babies and small children. Front seats recline fully into single beds if required. Fascia-mounted gearstick. New 90 bhp 1.4 litre non-VTEC and 110 bhp 1.6 litre VTEC-II engines. Already meet Euro 2005 emissions limits. 5-speed manual or 4-speed automatic options in all but base 1.4iS. Electric power steering, ABS with electronic brake distribution and air conditioning in all models. Achieved five stars in American National Highway Traffic Safety Administration tests and four stars in Euro NCAP crash tests. Also got the highest pedestrian impact safety score ever recorded. 2–door coupe from April 2001 and 3–door hatch followed in September 2001 priced £1,000 less model for model than 5–door. Range now includes a sensational six-speed 200 bhp 3–door Type R priced at a reasonable £15,995 (a/c a £800 extra on this). Three year, 90,000 mile manufacturer warranty. Deservedly becoming very popular. 60mpg, 100bhp twin-cam common rail diesel launched at September 2001 Frankfurt Show, in UK from early 2002. CO_2 just 134g/km. Badged 1.7CTDi, the new engine features high pressure common rail injection and variable injector nozzles. Power output is 100bhp at 4,400rpm and torque 220Nm (162 lb ft) at 1,800rpm. This takes the 3–door model to 60mph in just over 11 seconds and on to a top speed of 113mph. Combined fuel consumption is an excellent 57.7mpg and CO_2 emissions 134g/km which easily qualifies for the lowest £110pa VED bracket for diesel cars. Prices from £12,995 for 3–dr SE and from £13,495 for 5–dr S. A/c standard on all diesels. On UK sale May 2002. Eighth most reliable car in 2001 Fleet News Survey of 620,000 fleet cars mostly under 3 years old. 10th from top for reliability in *Auto Express* 2002 survey. Base model 1.4iE 3–door cut to £9,995 in April 2002. 1.4i Vision 3–door with a/c £9,995 from June 2002; Vision 1.4 5–door with a/c £10,995; Vision 1.6 auto 5–door with a/c £11,995.

What's bad: 1.6 can be a bit noisy on the motorway due to harmonics of its flat floor (1.4 seemed to be better). Doesn't handle in the same sporty fashion as the Ford Focus. Body not electro galvanized so only has a six year no perforation warranty. Otherwise too soon to say. To keep the price down to £15,995, air-conditioning is an £800 extra on the Type R. Attractive 3–door models have consoles so lack the walk through practicality of the 5–doors.

What to watch out for: Too soon to say.

Recalls: 7/6/2001: (affects 9,000 cars Worldwide): Make sure circlip on brake pedal pivot is properly positioned to hold the clevis pin in place. Make sure clip holding fuel filler pipe to tank has been tightened sufficiently.

Concerto (1989 to 1994)

What's good: Basically the same as Rover 200/400 without Rover K Series engines. 14ft long by 5ft 7in wide (4–door saloon 14ft 6in long). Smooth Honda engines: Pre-cat 88 bhp 1.4; 106 bhp 1.6; 130 bhp twin cam 1.6 to August 1991. Post-cat 89 bhp 1.5; 110 bhp 1.6; 121 bhp 1.6i-16 from August 1991. Twin-cam 16-valve cars were quick. Smooth 4-speed autos. Decent UK build quality formerly from Rover, latterly from new Swindon factory. 'Blaise' run-out 1.6i-16v well liked.

What's bad: Old cars now, past their design life. Same body problems as old Rover 200. Honda engines require more maintenance than Rovers. Honda dealer labour rates can be high. Expensive ignition igniters tend to go at 50,000–60,000 miles and resulting misfire could hot-spot the cat. Relatively expensive to service and repair. The cost of a new ABS unit can be more than the car is worth.

What to watch out for: Serious rust around windscreen under rubber surround. Rusty sunroof surrounds. Frequent oil changes important

– vital with twin-cam 16-valve cars. Ignition igniter problem. High incidence of ABS pump failures when the brake fluid had not been changed regularly.

CRV (1997 to 2002)

What's good: Very good 'supermarket' 4x4. 14ft 10in by 5ft 9in. Rear drive only cuts in when front wheels slip. More car like to drive than other 1990s 'multi activity vehicles'. Lots of useful knick-knacks. Cheaper and better than equivalent Land Rover Freelander. Honda three-year 90,000 mile warranty. 11th from top in 'R' reg. J.D. Power Customer Satisfaction Survey. Power increased from 125bhp to 147bhp from March 1999. In June 2001 Honda was rated by Motor Warranty Direct as Britain's 4th most claim-free used marque. UK models briefly built at Swindon late 2000 to early 2001 when UK production stopped to make way for new lines being installed at the factory. Continued to be built in Japan. 6th from top for reliability in *Auto Express* 2002 survey.(check online at www.warrantydirect.co.uk)

What's bad: Low towing limit of 1,200kg. You can't drive at more than 40 mph with the centre sunroof open unless you also open a few windows or fit a Clim Air deflector. The seats are lower than in a Freelander, which is fine if you have a long back, but not if you're little and want to look over the tops of hedges. Replacement model improved on the existing package rather than changed it. Low towing limit of 1,500kg.

What to watch out for: Signs of severe usage. Tow hooks (what's it been towing?) – can indicate wear in both front and rear clutches. But this is the most suburban-friendly 4x4 of the lot and therefore the least likely to have led a hard life.

Recalls: May 2002: contact point in ignition can fail at speed causing a stall in cars built 1997 to 2000 (*Auto Express* 30/5/2002).

CRV II (from 2002)

What's good: Familiar shape, even though the entire vehicle is brand new. Length: 14ft 11.5in (15ft with hard spare wheel cover);

Width: 5ft 10in; Height: 1,710mm. British built in Swindon plant. New 2.0 litre VTEC engine tuned for torque rather than out and out power. The result is 148bhp at 6,500rpm and 192Nm (142lb ft) torque at 4,000rpm. But the variable valve timing means there is bags of torque at low revs too, making this superbly sweet engine very strong between 30 to 80 in third, and 10 to 55 in second. Honda's World Car flat-floor platform means that the CRV automatic now has a proper walk-through cabin. With its meaty handbrake on the dash and 'four on the tree' gear lever there is nothing to stop you sliding across to get out of the nearside or paying a visit to the kids in the back seat. (Manual not so handy because gear lever sprouts from floor.) Rear seats recline or slide backwards and forwards to give 527 to 628 litres of loadspace behind them, or fold up to free up 952 litres. All three back seats have proper three-point safety belts. With its new ultra stiff body shell, Honda expected and got a four star result in the NCAP crash tests, together with the best rating of any SUV of three stars for pedestrian safety. Honda's hydraulic Dual Pump four wheel drive system does the same job as before. In most conditions drive is to the front wheels only, but if the system detects any slippage at the front, it engages a clutch to the rear wheels. This works very well in wet grass, mud and snow, and also in the wet on mountain hairpins where the rear wheels clutch in and push the car around the corner without it scrabbling for grip.

Old model was 6th from top for reliability in *Auto Express* 2002 survey.

More online at www.honda.co.uk

What's bad: Low towing limit of 1,500kg. Nissan X-Trail 2.2DI Sport 6-speed makes a better case for itself.

What to watch out for: Too soon to say.

CRX (1992 to 1998)

What's good: In 1992 the CRX became a two seater convertible 13ft 2in long by 5ft 7in wide rather than a 2+2 coupe. There was a 123bhp 1.6 with 5 speed manual or 4 speed automatic gearboxes, or a hot 158bhp 1.6 VTi VTEC version. Normally the roof panel has to be manually removed, but the top VTi had an electric mechanism that automatically lifted then stored the hardtop in the boot. Still very popular and a good little car.

What's bad: Not much. Honda servicing can be steep. Can go through discs and pads a bit quickly. VTi only to February 1995, though 123bhp 1.6 continued to February 1998.

What to watch out for: Mainly front suspension damage from careless parking and accident damage, especially with VTis. Compression of VTi should be carefully checked because these engines rev and a previous owner may have revved the nuts off the one you're about to buy. Check condition of discs and adjust price paid if they need replacing. Make sure the ABS is functioning correctly on a VTi, because a malfunction is an MOT failure and it could cost you a fortune to put it right. Getting a bit old now, so check carefully for rust. If fitted, a/c may have old CFC refrigerant or been recharged with new non-CFC refrigerant and leaked, so make sure it works.

HRV (from 1999)

What's good: Be-spoilered suburban style wagon with part-time four-wheel-drive. 3–door: 13ft 2in long by 5ft 7in wide, weighing 1,200kg and capable of towing 1,200kg. Cheaper than CRV with smaller 1.6 engine offering 104 or 123 bhp. 4x4 5–door version added from spring 2000 together with two-wheel-drive version of 3–door. 5–door is 13ft 6in long. Two-wheel-drive 123 bhp version is quite fast with 10.8–second 0–60. Much better than a Vitara. Improvements for 2002 model year include CVT option, new look interior and Type-T mesh grille. 11th from top of 100 models for reliability in *Auto Express* 2002 survey.

What's bad: Not hugely roomy.

What to watch out for: Nothing significant so far.

Insight (from 2000)

What's good: Aluminium-bodied two-seater aerodynamic hybrid coupe reminiscent of Le Mans Panhard DB endurance racers. 1.0

litre 3 -cylinder VTEC engine offering 76 ps supplemented by 10 kW brushless DC electric motor. Very high geared, yet surprisingly quick and good to drive with 11.5–second 0–60 and 112 mph top speed. Ultra low CO_2 emissions of just 80 g/km and 83 mpg capability mean VED dropped to just £60pa from April 2002 and London Congestion Charge exempt. Government subsidy drops £16,960 list price to £15,960. Started appearing at auction in 2002 and bidding to £10,000.

What's bad: Two seats only, plus luggage shelf and luggage cubby hole at rear. Lease only to Jan 2001, £16k from then on. High insurance premiums due to high cost of repairs.

What to watch out for: Too soon to say.

Integra (1986 to 2000)

What's good: Two completely different cars. 1986 to 1989 was a low-roof five door hatchback, like the Mazda 323 F Type, 14ft 3in long by 5ft 6in wide and weighing 945kg to 1,030kg. Had 85bhp 1.5 with 5-speed manual or 4-speed auto, or, from March 1986, a 125bhp twin-cam 1.6, 5-speed manual only. Name continued in Japan on a two door coupe which finally reached UK in January 1998 fitted with a 'Fast and Furious', red-hot 188bhp 1.8 VTEC. 145mph and 0–60 on 6.5 seconds. This is huge fun to drive.

What's bad: The old Integra is now a bit old and spares, especially body parts, are hard to find.

What to watch out for: Grey imports of earlier non Type R Integra coupes posing as Integra Rs. Also make obvious checks on genuine Integra Rs as a lot of them have seen time at track days and Bedford Autodrome even had a small fleet. Independently imported Integra Type Rs are highly likely to have been heavily modified, so you will need to find a specialist who knows them and the mods to look after it.

Jazz (from Feb 2002)

What's good: The first giant step forward in small car design since the original 1959 Mini. Entirely new one box model on sale in

Japan from June 2001. Already Japan's best seller by December 2001. Replaced the lacklustre Logo and arrived in the UK early in 2002, providing stiff competition for the new Ford Fiesta, new VW Polo, new SEAT Ibiza, Skoda Fabia, Citroën C3, new Nissan Micra, Renault Clio, Vauxhall Corsa, Toyota Yaris and Daihatsu YRV. Features new chain-cam 1,339cc 8 valve 1–DSI engine technology. (Dual and Sequential Ignition System comprises two spark plugs per cylinder in a compact combustion chamber where sequential ignition results in low CO_2 emissions and excellent fuel economy.) Dimensions are: length 3,830mm (12 ft 7in: 3in shorter than the new Fiesta); width 1,675mm (5 ft 6in) -1,878mm mirror tip to mirror tip); height: 1,525mm (5ft 0in). Despite its compact dimensions, the one box cab forward design make it look quite big. Luggage volume is 353 litres to the parcel shelf with the rear seats up (more than the Fiesta) and a huge 1,323 litres with the seats down. The chain cam engine puts out 61kW (82bhp) at 5,700rpm and 119Nm (88 lb ft) torque at a low 2,800 rpm. Combined economy is 49.6mpg and CO_2 output 134g/km, well within the £100 a year VED grade. The engine is optimised for ordinary 95Ron Premium unleaded petrol. Insurance is a low Group 3E. Mounting the fuel tank in the centre of the car and using a new H-shaped torsion beam rear axle allows for an unusually low cabin floor. The short nose also allows more interior space which is equivalent to many C sector sized cars. Honda expects the car to achieve a four star NCAP crash safety rating. The 2/3 + 1/3 split rear seats can each be fully folded into the floor with headrests in place, providing a completely flat loadspace 1,740mm (5ft 9in) long. And by sliding the front passenger seat fully forward, then completely reclining it, objects as long as 2,400mm (7ft 10in) will fit. The versatile rear seat squabs can also be tipped up and locked against the seat backs creating a central luggage area ideal for a dog to be carried. The height of this area from floor to ceiling is 1,280mm (4ft 2in), enough for small children to stand up and change clothes after an afternoon on the beach. Prices: £8,995. £10,295 and £11,295. Order yours early for March 02 reg. CVT-7 from August 2002 at £900 extra has seven steering wheel paddle shift selectable ratios. Much liked by readers who have bought one. Now also available with a well-integrated body colour side-protection strip. Voted *Auto Express* 2002 Car of the Year. Available from July 2002 in wider choice of colours including Iris Red (pink); Orchid Yellow, Clover Green, Ice Blue metallic and Nighthawk Black pearl. Recommended.

More online at www.honda.co.uk

What's bad: Steering a bit sticky and dead in the straight-ahead position. Though Jazz handling and grip is good, the new Fiesta, Polo and Yaris are all a bit better in these respects.

What to watch out for: All the readers who bought one and wrote back are very happy.

Legend (from 1991)

What's good: A one-time Quentin Willson favourite: four-door saloon or plush two-door coupe. Grew up once it shook off Rover 800 association, first with 201 bhp 3.2 V6, then with 202 bhp 3.5 V6 from June 1996. The big Legend is 16ft 4in long by 6ft wide. In June 2001 Honda was rated by Motor Warranty Direct as Britain's 4th most claim-free used marque (check online at www.warrantydirect.co.uk)

What's bad: Any problems tend to be expensive.

What to watch out for: Treat like a Lexus, so must have full dealer service history with frequent ATF, brake fluid, coolant, aircon refrigerant changes. Check carefully for any signs of uneven tyre wear. Look for oil leaks on ground where car has been standing. Give it some heavy braking on the test drive to check for warped discs caused by drivers holding the car on the brakes after a heavy stop.

Recalls: 2000: Legend saloons and coupes built 1996 to 1999: automatic gearbox fault leading to selector slipping into 'Park'. Cars built in 1996 and 1997: steering ball joints could separate.

Logo (2000 to 2001)

What's good: Worthy, perpendicular small three-door hatchback sold in Europe for more than a year finally reached UK in Y2K. 12ft 3in long by 5ft 5in wide and weighing 950kg. 1,343cc 64 bhp engine with 80 lb ft torque and 5 speed manual or CVT auto. Deep-section tyres give fairly good ride quality. Also manual-only diesel version in Europe. Did reasonably well in German TUV/*Auto Bild* front offset crash tests. Three-Star NCAP 2000 crash safety rating. ABS and aircon standard on official UK market cars. SE version replaced S version in July 2000. Additional kit includes rev counter, white-on-black dials, LCD odometer, 2–spoke sports steering wheel, black interior trim, black door mirrors and body coloured bumpers. Prices cut to £8,995 for manual and £9,895 for CVT auto in September 2000. Further price cut to £7,995 for SE manual from 5/10/2000, still including a/c.

What's bad: Styling isn't exactly inspired. Ridiculous launch list price of £9,495 and replacement SE even dearer. Criticised for 'gutless' and 'rough' 1.3 engine, 'lifeless' steering and 'too much body roll'. Already three years into its model life when launched in the UK. Quietly dropped from the UK market after all stocks were sold in January 2001. Replaced by vastly better Jazz.

What to watch out for: Too soon to say.

NSX (from 1992)

What's good: Surprisingly civilised supercar. 14ft 7in long by 6ft wide and weighing 1,410kg. As easy to drive as a Honda Civic, but has storming VTEC V6 with 271 bhp that sounds wonderful. Early 5-speed models did not have standard PAS and were better for it (optional PAS was electric). Aircon standard, naturally. Auto optional. Targa came along in July '95 with standard PAS and optional F-Matic auto or six-speed manual. Engine grew to 3,179cc in Feb 1998 giving 276hp and more torque. Far more reliable and easy to live with on a day-to-day basis than a Ferrari. Revamped again for 2002: 276b, 220lb ft torque; top speed 168mph; 0–60 in 5.5 seconds; combined economy 22.8mpg. In June 2001 Honda was rated by Motor Warranty Direct as Britain's 4th most claim-free used marque (check online at www.warrantydirect.co.uk)

What's bad: Tends to understeer quite a lot rather than catch you out with snap-oversteer. Power-steered cars lack steering feel. Eats rear tyres (6,000–8,000 miles), but price of these has now come down.

What to watch out for: Must have full dealer service history with super-clean fully synthetic oil, frequent ATF, brake fluid, coolant, aircon refrigerant changes. Check carefully for any signs of uneven tyre wear. Alloy suspension is vulnerable to off road (or off track) excursions and pot hole damage.

Prelude (1983 to 1992)

What's good: Nice looking, airy wedge-shaped 2+2 coupe with sloping bonnet and retracting headlights. 14ft 1in long by 5ft 6in wide. First engines (1983–1987)were 1,829cc with 102–106bhp plus 5-speed manual or four speed autobox. 1,958cc 137bhp engine 1985–1987. Lower power 1,958cc 114bhp EX model and higher power 1,958cc 147bhp 2.0i-16–4WS from 1987. Reliable and can still look good.

What's bad: They rust out in the rear wings. Body parts now very hard to get.

What to watch out for: Rust. If 4ws, make very sure the four wheel steering system is working properly by looking for unevenly work tyres.

Prelude (1992 to 1996)

What's good: Old Prelude turned from a glassy coupe into a more serious looking car altogether. 14ft 7in long by 5ft 6in wide. Nice shark-nose 'mini XJS' styling. Useful range of engines include 131 bhp 2.0 litre; 158 bhp 2.3 and 183 bhp 2.2 VTEC. VTEC is the enthusiast's choice, but they're all good.

What's bad: Honda maintenance is expensive, particularly VTEC. Aircon may play up (best serviced and recharged with CFC-free 134A refrigerant by an aircon specialist who knows what he's doing). Not much room in the back seat. Paint may flake, particularly silver.

What to watch out for: Rusty or damaged exhausts and blown cats. Look for mismatched paint and check if due to flaking or accident damage. Check for kerbed alloys, uneven tyre wear, suspension damage. If 4ws, make sure the system is tracking properly by looking for even tyre wear.

Prelude (1996 to 2000)

What's good: American styling not as interesting or original as predecessor. 14ft 4in long by 5ft 6in wide. 132 bhp 2.0 litre or strong 185 bhp 2.2 VTi. 4-speed auto has 'Tiptronic'-type manual control. Motegi-kitted 132 bhp 2.0 and 183 bhp 2.2 from summer 1998. Aircon standard on all. One of the few cars the look of which is improved by lowered suspension and a factory body kit. Best colour: dark metallic blue. 13th from top in 'R' reg. J.D. Power Customer Satisfaction Survey. In June 2001 Honda was rated by Motor Warranty Direct as Britain's 4th most claim-free used marque (check online at www.warrantydirect.co.uk) 7th from top for reliability in *Auto Express* 2002 survey.

What's bad: Autobox manual control the wrong way round (should be back for upshifts and forward for downshifts to match laws of physics). Production ended in June 2000.

What to watch out for: Watch out for kerbing damage to big alloys and front suspension. Check for uneven tyre wear. Engine oil should be clean. Honda dealer service record should be complete.

Recalls: Cars built in 1997 and 1998: steering ball joints could separate. May 2002: contact point in ignition can fail at speed causing a stall in cars built 1997 to 2000 (*Auto Express* 30/5/2002).

S2000 (from 1999)

What's good: Two-seater roadster with astonishing 2.0 litre 237 bhp VTi engine that revs to 9,000 rpm allied to six-speed box. Has track car performance if you use the revs. Electric roof goes up and down in seconds. Revisions including glass rear window from February 2002. Achieved an excellent four star rating for crash safety in 2002 NCAP tests.

What's bad: Doesn't have track car handling, so you feel a bit nervous about using the power on the road. Torque output doesn't match power output, so gears need to be used. Plastic back window up to February 2002.

What to watch out for: Kerb damage from over-exuberant drivers. Plastic rear window dates car as before Feb 2002, whatever the reg. date.

Recalls: 26/5/2000: June-December 1999 build: seatbelt webbing could become trapped between seat back and roof cover and fail to tension properly. Modified roof cover to be fitted. 24/11/2000: 1,426 S2000 models built 29/6/1999 to 21/4/2000 recalled because seat belt webbing may lock in the retracted position. Locking mechanisms of both belts to be replaced.

Shuttle MPV (1995 to 2000)

What's good: The most reliable MPV. 15ft 7in long by 5ft 10in wide and 1,535kg. Air conditioning standard. Excellent, obedient four-speed autobox with good column shift as standard. Powerful 2,156cc 150 bhp engine also standard (grew to 2,258cc from early 1998). Handles very well for an MPV. Called the 'Odyssey' in the USA where it is far and away the most reliable MPV of the lot. Late-model LS offered with seven seats at new low £18,000 price, sometimes discounted as low as a real bargain £15,000. Rear pair of seats fold away into the floor. Not too juicy (25–28 mpg). Looks more like a big car than a van. Top MPV and sixth from top overall in 'R' reg. J.D. Power Customer Satisfaction Survey. In June 2001 Honda was rated by Motor Warranty Direct as Britain's 4th most claim-free used marque (check online at www.warrantydirect.co.uk) Can be under £6,000 at auction for a high mileage 'R' reg. Recommended.

What's bad: Not as versatile as Galaxy/Alhambra/Sharan or Renault Espace. Lap belt only for centre mid-row seat. Sadly, dropped in April 2000 because new, larger Odyssey being built for USA and Civic based 7 seater Stream for the UK.

What to watch out for: Look for a proper Honda service history. Buy on basis of current £18,000 LS model rather than previous, overpriced £24,000 six-seater ES. Aircon needs servicing and recharging every two years with CFC-free 134a refrigerant – costs around £150. Make sure ABS light goes out because a new ABS pump is £1,400 and this is one potential problem area that is emerging with the earliest Shuttles.

Recalls: Shuttles built in 1997 and 1998: steering ball joints could separate.

Stream 2001 (from 2002)

What's good: New 7–seater MPV 15ft long by 6ft 4in wide based on the 2001 Honda Civic platform but with bigger engines including a 125bhp 1.7 litre VTEC and a 156bhp 2.0 litre VTEC, giving a 0–60 of 9.2 seconds and a top speed of 130mph. 5-speed manual gearbox with dash mounted lever or new 5-speed sequential automatic. Effectively replaces the old, larger Shuttle. Road testers praised the steering, roadholding and handling as better than any other MPV until the advent of the Peugeot 307SW. Four star NCAP crash safety rating and three star pedestrian safety rating: highest of all small MPVs. Fantastic Honda reliability.

What's bad: Rearmost row of seats unsuitable for all but small children making the car effectively a '5+2ft rather than a 7 seater. These seats are also very difficult to access as the centre seats need to be slid forward. Cannot compete against the Zafira and Avensis Verso for versatility.

What to watch out for: Too soon to say.

HYUNDAI

Accent (1994 to 1999)

What's good: Replaced Pony X2 and a much better car with something akin to sporty handling. 'Coupe' was 13ft 5in long by 5ft 4in wide and weight 930kg. Also a 5–door hatch and 4–door saloon. Engines include 83 bhp 1.3, 87 bhp 1.5 or, from Jan '97, a 98 bhp 1.5. PAS standard on 1.5s. 4-speed auto optional on 1.5 saloon and 5–door hatch. Quite well screwed together and value for money. Proper three-year warranties. Good reputation for reliability and helpful, inexpensive dealers. Came top in *Which?* Y2k reliability survey. Run-out models sold for less than £6,000 new.

What's bad: Comparatively poor 1.5–Star NCAP crash test results. Base 1.3s don't have PAS. Dumpy looks. Styling of front valance is dubious. Replaced by new Accent for 2000 model year.

What to watch out for: Some did go onto leasing, rental and particularly Motability fleets. If less than three years old, make sure has not disqualified itself from 3-year warranty. With older cars watch out for same inadequate or incompetent kerbside home servicing as Pony. Front tyres tend to wear badly. Must have cambelt changes every 3 years or 36,000 miles.

Recalls: 1998 (built 1994–1997): possibility of road salt corrosion to front coil spring causing spring to damage tyre.

Accent (from 2000)

What's good: New model looks 'all new' and takes the car up half a class – bigger than a supermini, but smaller than a Focus/Golf. Now 13ft 9in long by 5ft 6in wide and weighing from 1,040kg. Slots into Hyundai/Kia range between Kia Pride and Kia Shuma. 3–door hatch, 5–door hatch and 4–door saloon. 1.3 manual has 55 bhp; 1.3 auto has 63 bhp; and 1.5 man/auto has 65 bhp with 97 lb ft torque. All models now have PAS. All autos 4-speed. All can do over 100 mph. Average fuel consumption: 36.22 mpg to 44.14 mpg. Good ride quality. Twin airbags. All have PAS. Owners of previous model consulted about improvements. Price competitive, from £6,799. Small family-business dealers. Very reliable. 82bhp 1.5 litre common-rail turbodiesel launched July 2002 at £9,295. Performance figures are: top speed 106mph, 0 – 60 in 13.7 seconds, combined economy 51.4mpg; and CO_2 emissions 145g/km (£110 VED). Torque is 184Nm (136 lb ft) at 2,200rpm. Insurance is a low Group 4A. Three year UNLIMITED MILEAGE manufacturer warranty. Equipment of diesel includes driver and passenger airbags, five speed manual gearbox, central locking, electric front and rear windows and power steering, but a/c is not on the list.

More online at www.hyundai-car.co.uk

What's bad: Grille styling won't appeal to everyone. Handling is not inspiring, but typical owners don't want it to be.

What to watch out for: Too soon to say.

Amica (from 2000)

What's good: New tall and short 5–door hatch on ATOZ platform, but radically different and lower priced. 11ft 6in long by 4ft 11in wide and around 850kg. 55 bhp 1.0 litre 4-cylinder timing belt engine from ATOZ with 5-speed manual gearbox. First cars had 3-speed auto option; 4-speed auto introduced summer 2000. £5,999 for Si, or £7,799 for SE with PAS, a/c, electric front windows and central locking. PAS just £199 extra on base model. Auto £699 extra. Decent-sized boot. Full-sized 'spare'. Brilliant for the school run. Should share Three-Star NCAP crash safety rating of ATOZ. Voted 7th equal from Top in 144 car 2002 JD Power/*What Car?* Customer Satisfaction Survey of V and W reg. cars. Price of base model cut to £5,495 in April 2002.

What's bad: A/c heat exchanger right at the front is a bit vulnerable to road salt and stone or parking damage. Best to avoid 3-speed auto.

What to watch out for: The readers who buy them seem to like them. No reports of any problems.

ATOZ (1998 to 2000)

What's good: Quite good, tall, 5-door micro competed against Daewoo Matiz. Name springs from 'A to Z'. 11ft 6in long by 4ft 11in wide and around 825kg. Power steering and three-year unlimited mileage warranty standard in price cut to £5,799 in May 2000. But £7,947 bought 'Plus' model with PAS, air-conditioning, driver's airbag, alloys and central locking. 3-speed auto option. Makes much more sense for the school run than a Grand Cherokee. Fits tiny parking spaces or a short, narrow, pre-war garage. 55 bhp, 90 mph and 45 mpg. Three-Star NCAP crash safety rating.

What's bad: Not exactly a style statement. Snobs driving their offspring to school in Grand Cherokees will look down their noses at you. Build quality a bit light. Looks like a wardrobe on castors. Costs just £4,750 in Spain. Automatic only has three speeds. UK imports discontinued in favour of Amica in late 2000.

What to watch out for: Kerbing damage. Damage to thin body panels. Damage to trim by children. But in general owners seem to be happy.

Coupe (1996 to 2002)

What's good: If the Lantra is 'the curvy car', then this is 'the swoopy coupe'. The first incarnation was good looking and a lot of coupe for the money. 14ft 3in long by 5ft 8in wide and around 1,200kg. 112 bhp 1.6 the entry level at a reasonable £14,000. 137 bhp 2.0 litre a more serious car with standard alloys. Aircon optional on 1.6 and 2.0i; standard on 2.0iSE which also comes with leather seats. FI has big alloys and low-profile tyres. Will impress those who don't know what it is and is not a bad car in its own right. 130 mph plus. Handles nicely. Sells very well. Re-styled Y2k model has better sound-proofing and re-tuned, pleasant-sounding exhaust. Priced from £12,999 for the 1.6i. 19th from top of 100 models for reliability in *Auto Express* 2002 survey.

What's bad: OTT launch advertising campaign compared the look of it to a Ferrari. Will not confer quite the same status on driver as a 3-Series, a Corrado, a Celica or even a Prelude. Year 2000 front-end restyle is not to everyone's taste.

What to watch out for: Cars that are flash for not much cash can be prime candidates for the repo man, so used examples may be without service books and some of the keys, and definitely warrant an HPI check. Still young enough to want to see full dealer service history.

Coupe (from 2002)

What's good: All new, much better looking Hyundai Coupe replaced wart-fronted bobble-eyed 2000–2001 model. Choice of 1.6 or 2.0 litre fours and a 2.7 litre V6 with H-matic automatic or 6-speed manual gearbox. 1.6 down in power to 105bhp, 2.0 still has 137bhp, 2.7 V6 has 171bhp giving it a top speed of 136mph. Five-speed manual, six-speed manual or four-speed auto. In UK from Feb 2002 at prices from £14k to £20k. 1.6 delayed to Summer 2002. V6 version highly praised in '*Autocar*' first drive. Dimensions are: length 4,395mm (14 ft 5in); width 1,760mm (5 ft 9in); height: 1,330mm (4ft 4in). Two engines available at launch in early 2002. 2.7 litre V6 develops 171bhp at 6,000rpm and 181 lb ft (245Nm) torque at 4,000 rpm. Zero to 60 takes 7.9 seconds and top speed is 136mph. Transmission options are either a six-speed manual or a four-speed H-tronic automatic. Tyres are 215/45 R17. Also 1,975cc four with 137bhp at 6,000rpm and 133lb ft (180Nm) torque at 4,500rpm. Zero to 60 takes 9.1 seconds and top speed is 126mph. Transmission options are 5-speed manual or four-speed H-tronic automatic. Tyres are 205/55 R16s. 1.6 is now down in power to 105bhp at 5,800rpm, while torque is 106 lb ft (144Nm). Zero to 60 takes 11.6 seconds and top speed 114mph. Only the 5-speed manual with the 1.6.

Standard kit on all models includes: twin front and side airbags, ABS, electric windows and mirrors, seat belt pre-tensioners, front fog lamps, six speaker radio/CD player, air-conditioning, leather gearknob and steering wheel, alloy wheels and engine immobiliser. In addition, the 2.0 and 2.7 will have keyless entry and alarm, cruise control, leather seats and a sunroof. Will steal potential sales from Alfa 147, Alfa GTV, Peugeot 406 Coupe, Renault Megane Coupe, Toyota Celica, Vauxhall Astra Coupe, VW Beetle, VW Golf

Gate. Old model 19th from top of 100 models for reliability in *Auto Express* 2002 survey.

More online at www.hyundai-car.co.uk

What's bad: Doesn't go anywhere in the snob stakes except among people who don't know what it is and merely see it as a very good looking car.

What to watch out for: Too soon to say.

Elantra (from March 2001)

What's good: Elantra saloon and hatchback replaced Lantra model from March 2001. Hatchback 14ft 9in long by 5ft 8in wide and weighing from 1,244kg. Engines are a 106bhp 1.6 which takes the car to 113mph and a 139bhp 2.0 which reaches 128mph and reaches 60mph in 9.1 seconds. ABS, air conditioning, three three-point rear seatbelts and driver and passenger airbags are standard across the range, while the 2.0 litre CDX model has traction control, cruise control, climate control and leather seats. On the road prices which include a three year warranty are: 1.6Si five-door £10,999; 1.6Gsi four or five-door £12,199; 2.0CDX four or five-door £13,999. 111bhp 2.0 litre diesel from February 2002. Torque is 235Nm (173lb ft) at 2,000 rpm, 0–60 takes 11.4 seconds, top speed is 118mph, combined consumption is 44.1mpg and CO_2 emissions 169g/km (£150pa VED). Standard features are driver, passenger and side airbags; ABS with EBD; air-conditioning; electric front windows and four speaker CD/radio. GSi versions also come with electric rear windows; keyless entry; six speaker CD/radio; electric tilt/slide sunroof and electric door mirrors. CDX models have in addition traction control, leather seat trim and climate control. Prices are TD Si: £11,999; TD GSi: £13,199; TD CDX: £14,999.

More online at www.Hyundai-car.co.uk

What's bad: Three star score in 2001 NCAP Crash Tests, otherwise too soon to say

What to watch out for: Too soon to say

Galloper (from 1991 to 2001)

What's good: The old LWB 1986–1991 Shogun 7 seater, which continued to by built by Hyundai in South Korea as the Galloper to late 1991. 15ft 1in long by 5ft 6in wide, weighing around 1,650kg. 4 cylinder 2,477cc 98bhp intercooled turbodiesel. Parts for 1985 to 1991 Shogun may fit. Also some commonality of mechanical parts with L200 4x4 pick-ups. Tough and low priced.

What's bad: LHD only in Europe and doesn't seem to have been independently imported as RHD.

What to watch out for: Have been some mechanical problems caused by poor PDIs.

Getz (from Autumn 2002)

What's good: New tall and small hatchback in UK from autumn 2002. Platform comes from Clio sports concept car. Dimensions are: 3,800mm x 1,660mm x 1,485mm. High roofline provides airy and roomy interior. Three or five doors. Engines all four cylinder: 1,078cc 12 valve with 62bhp at 5,500rpm and 91Nm torque at 3,500rpm. This gets it to sixty in 15.4 seconds and on to a top speed of 91mph; 1,345cc 12 valve with 82bhp at 5,500rpm and 114Nm torque at 4,000rpm. It dashes to sixty in 12.6 seconds and on to 103 mph; 1,599cc 16 valve with 105bhp at 5,800rpm and 143Nm torque at 3,000rpm. It hits sixty in 10.9 seconds and races away to 113mph. Finally, coming in 2003, is a 1,493cc 12 valve common rail diesel offering 80bhp at 4,000rpm and stumping up 170Nm torque at 2,000rpm. Performance of this is sixty in 13.7 seconds, topping out at 106mph. Safety well covered with ABS with EBD, front seatbelt pretensioners, front and front side airbags and three three-point rear seatbelts. Price range: from around £7,000.

   More online at www.hyundai-car.co.uk

What's bad: Crowded market.

What to watch out for: Too soon to say.

Lantra (1991 to 1995)

What's good: Not bad Orion-sized four-door with Mitsubishi-derived power trains. 14ft 5in long by 5ft 6in wide and weighing from 1,130kg. 84 bhp 1.5, 112 bhp manual 1.6, 104 bhp 1.6 auto, 124 bhp 1.8. All had standard PAS. 1.6CDi and all 1.8s had standard aircon. 1.8CDi got standard ABS from October '93.

What's bad: Danger of being seduced by high spec of CD version. This is a reasonable car, but it's no BMW.

What to watch out for: Must have regular cambelt changes every 3 years or 36,000 miles. ABS needs frequent brake fluid changes. Aircon needs recharging with CFC-free 134A refrigerant every 3 years.

Recalls: 1996 (1991–1996): check for fracture of rear suspension bolt.

Lantra (1995 to 2000)

What's good: Quite nicely styled saloon or 5–door estate. 14ft 6in long by 5ft 7in wide and weighing from 1,100kg. Grown-up engine range of 112 bhp 1.6, 126 bhp 1.8 or 137 bhp 2.0 litre. PAS standard on all; ABS either standard or optional. Aircon standard on CDs; optional on 1.8Si and 1.6s. 16th from top in 'R' reg. J.D. Power Customer Satisfaction Survey, just ahead of BMW 3–Series. 25th from top of 100 models for reliability in *Auto Express* 2002 survey. Prices from £8,999 for 1.6i, including 3-year warranty.

What's bad: Advertised as 'the curvy car', which was an odd way to attract customers. Dealers try to sell them as more upmarket than they are.

What to watch out for: Must have regular cambelt changes every 3 years or 36,000 miles. If still less than 3 years old, make sure has been regularly serviced and still qualifies for warranty.

Matrix (from October 2001)

What's good: Smart, European-designed 5–seater MPV based on the Elantra platform went on sale in the UK late 2001. 102bhp 1.6 GSi with 104lb ft (141Nm) torque is £10,999 in GSi trim; twin-cam three cylinder 89bhp 1.5 TD GSi with 136lb ft (182Nm) torque is £11,799 in GSi trim; and 121bhp 1.8 CDX with 119lb ft (161Nm) torque is £12,199. 1.6 petrol engine with manual or automatic transmission; others manual only. At overall length of 4,025mm Hyundai reckons that Matrix is shortest mini MPV on the market. Width is 1,740mm and height, 1,625mm. Versatility enhanced by a 60/40 split sliding and double-folding rear seat.

More online at www.Hyundai-car.co.uk

What's bad: It only just pips the Mitsubishi Space Star for shortest mini MPV as that is 4,030mm. Diesel reviled by Jeremy Clarkson, Sunday Times, 2–6–2002. 0–60 apparently takes 18 seconds.

What to watch out for: Too soon to say

Pony X2 (1990 to 1994)

What's good: Cheap and fairly reliable if properly serviced. 13ft 4in by 5ft 3in and from 915kg. 1.3 litre had 72 bhp; 1.5 had 83 bhp. 1.5 has PAS. Not overly complicated so not too much to go wrong. Banger money now.

What's bad: Ugly. Cheap trim. Sunroofs leak. Power outputs of both engines fell sharply when catalysed from August 1992. 'Pony and trap' is Cockney rhyming slang for 'crap'. Automatic gearboxes can start to give trouble after 6–7 years.

What to watch out for: Inadequate or incompetent kerbside home servicing. Could have sat around for a long time before being first registered. Cheap when new, so very cheap by now.

S Coupe (1990 to 1995)

What's good: Four seater coupe 13ft 10in long by 5ft 4in wide; weight 977kg. At first had an 83bhp 1,468cc ex-Mitsubishi engine. Restyled October 1992 and fitted with Hyundai's own 'Alpha' 12 valve catalysed 1,495cc engine with 87bhp in standard form and 114bhp with turbo. Reliable.

What's bad: Not very exciting to look at. Apparently fairly bland to drive. Now 7–12 years old so may not be as reliable as when newer. Parts may get to be a problem.

What to watch out for: Obviously you're not going to pay too much for one, are you? The original cars are now down to £500 or less. Even a good early 1995 turbo shouldn't set you back more than £2,000 tops.

Santa Fe (from 2001)

What's good: Hyundai's new Sports Utility, a five door 4x4 with a choice of 143bhp 2.4 litre or 177bhp 2.7 litre V6 engines and a 115bhp 2.0 litre common rail diesel. The 2.4 has a manual five-speed gearbox, while the 2.7 has an H-tronic automatic offering manual over-ride. Equipment includes driver and passenger airbags, ABS with EBD, air conditioning, and a rear hatchback window which can be opened separately to accommodate long loads such as surfboards. The 2.7 also has leather covered seats. On the road prices, including a three year warranty, are £15,999 for the 2.4, £16,999 for the 2.0 diesel and £17,999 for the 2.7 automatic. Length: 14ft 9in; width: 6ft . Good reports.

More online at www.Hyundai-car.co.uk

What's bad: Strangely organic styling. You either like the look or you don't.

What to watch out for: No reports of any problems yet.

Sonata (1992 to 1994)

What's good: First front wheel drive Sonata with 126bhp or 136bhp 1,997cc twin cam four cylinder engine, 5-speed manual or 4-speed autobox. 15ft 4in long; 5ft 9in wide. Very reliable.

What's bad: Big and bland. Spares hard to get (if you ever need them).

What to watch out for: MOT failure as result of damaged hard to get part such as a rear light lens. Big, cheap and reliable so quite likely to have been minicabbed.

Sonata (1994 to 2001)

What's good: Biggish cheap car, at first with four headlights and oval grille. Reliable enough. 15ft 4in by 5ft 9in. Surprise restyle in

September 1996 gave it a new begrilled nose but 2.0 litre dropped in power to 123 bhp. Became 15ft 10in long by 5ft 10in wide. 1994–96 2.0 litre had a reasonable 136 bhp. 5-speed manual or 4-speed auto. ABS standard on 2.0CD and 3.0 litre. CDs and V6s also have aircon, while V6 offers cruise control and leather. Revised again in June 1998 when V6 went down in size to 2,493cc, but up in power to 160 bhp. 2.0 litre fours also back up to 136 bhp. Still not the subject of any rave reviews. Facelifted for 2001 with double lens headlights. £12,995 132bhp 2.0 offers 122mph, 0–60 in 12.5 seconds, 29.7mpg combined and 228g/km CO_2. £17,000 172bhp 2.7KV6 gives 138mph, 0–60 in 9.5 seconds, 26.4mpg combined, 256g/km CO_2.

What's bad: Ride and handling of pre-2001 model not up to European standards for the class. Power of 2.0 litre dropped to 122 bhp after the 1995 re-style. 3.0 litre V6 only ever had 143 bhp and a sluggish autobox. 2001 model essentially the same but more expensive than the KIA Magentis. Timing belt and tensioner need to be replaced together: a £340 job even at Halfords. Car must then not be started for 15 minutes or timing will slip out.

What to watch out for: Though it may be out of warranty, you still want to see a proper dealer service history showing regular brake fluid, ATF, coolant, timing belt and aircon refrigerant changes. Don't buy an ex-taxi that's been serviced on the taxi rank.

Sonata (from Jan 2002)

What's good: New Sonata with similar peanut shell headlamp treatment to new C Class Mercedes. Bags of standard equipment including ABS, a/c, CD, sunroof, alloy wheels. electric mirrors, dual front and side airbags. 2.7 V6 also has H-tronic autobox, traction control, climate control, cruise control, Multi CD with autochanger, electric memory seats and leather trim. Size is 4,727mm long, 1,820mm wide; 1,422mm high. 2.0 puts out 136bhp, gets to 60 in 13 seconds, does 121mph; 2.7 has 160bhp, gets to 60 in 9.5 seconds, does 131mph. Prices: 2.0CDX manual: £14,499; 2.0CDX auto: £15,499; 2.7 V6 auto: £17,499.

What's bad: Doesn't do anything the KIA Magentis doesn't do for less. Depreciation likely to be high.

What to watch out for: Too soon to say.

TB (from September 2002)

What's good: Attractive and practical new supermini from Hyundai. Single cam 1.1 petrol four, twin-cam 1.3 and 1.6, or a 1.5 litre common rail turbodiesel. Three or five door format. Optional electrically controlled 4-speed autobox on 1.3 or 1.6. Re-named for UK market.

What's bad: Too soon to say.

What to watch out for: Too soon to say.

Terracan (from 2001)

What's good: Tough, chassis-framed 4x4. Engine options are a 98bhp 2.5 litre petrol, a 3.5 litre V6 petrol and a 150bhp 2.9 litre common-rail turbodiesel, top speed 106mph. Standard equipment includes ABS with electronic brake force distribution, driver and passenger airbags, variable ratio steering; the option of manual or automatic transmission; and the option of either part-time four-wheel-drive with electric shift transfer or full-time four-wheel-drive. Dimensions are: length: 4,710mm; width: 1,860mm; height: 1,790mm. Replaces Galloper to meet requirements of people who need a serious off-roader, leaving Santa Fe for those who like the looks of a 4x4 but rarely venture off the tarmac.

More online at www.Hyundai-car.co.uk

What's bad: Criticised as being unrefined and thirsty (particularly V6) and being introduced to a market sector that is shrinking in favour of more road-friendly 4x4s. No decision yet reached as to whether the Terracan will be marketed in the UK.

What to watch out for: Too soon to say.

Trajet MPV (from 2000)

What's good: 7–seater launched June 2000 priced from £15,500. 15ft 5in long by 6ft wide and 1,900kg. 133 bhp 2.0 litre 4-cylinder plus a 111bhp 2.0 litre common rail direct-injected diesel with 188lb ft (255Nm) torque from June 2001, priced at £16,499. (mpg 37.2 combined) Seats in 2–3–2 pattern; all five rear seats individually removable. A/c, ABS, Electronic Brake Distribution (important on an MPV), CD and two de-powered airbags all standard. 30 mpg economy possible from 2.0 litre. Plenty of equipment including underseat trays; map, bottle and pen holders; four reading lights; luggage net, etc. 168bhp 2.7 litre V6 announced for 2001 giving top speed of 120mph and 0–60 of 11.5 seconds at an on the road price of £19,999. Towing capacity of this version is 1,950kg assuming driver only on board. 4-speed autobox no extra cost on V6. Trajet V6 cut to £18,545 in April 2002.

What's bad: Rather anonymous. Yet another 7–seat MPV, curiously from the same company that builds the Kia Sedona, but a more refined, more car-like vehicle.

What to watch out for: Too soon to say.

XG30 (from 2000)

What's good: Hyundai's big car, slightly larger than MB E-Class and BMW 5–Series (16ft long by 6ft wide), but smaller than S-Class, with 3.0 litre 192 bhp V6 and 5-speed 'Tiptronic'-type auto offering 9.3 second 0–60, 140 mph top speed and Euromix economy of 26.4 mpg. Soft ride with very quiet cruising: two qualities much sought after by many owner-drivers. Handling is reasonable in the circumstances. ABS, aircon, alloys, lots of kit and lots of car for £20,999. Three-year warranty. Facelift autumn 2002. Should appeal to people who mourn the passing of the Granada/Scorpio and a much better car than either.

What's bad: Front-drive chassis tramps badly at the front when pushed hard on tight corners (though, of course, the car isn't likely to be driven in a manner that exposes this).

What to watch out for: Very heavy first year depreciation of more than 50%, so don't buy until 12–15 months old. Then it will be a LOT of car for the money.

ISUZU

Trooper (1987 to 1992)

What's good: Square, 'honest' and quite well-thought-of 4x4s with petrol or diesel engines and short 3–door(13ft 4in) or long 5–door (14ft 4in) bodies and the option of 7 seats in the 5–door. Engines: 2,254cc 109 bhp petrol four; 2,559cc 111 bhp petrol four; 2,238cc ohc 74 bhp diesel four to Jan 1988, then much better 2,771cc 95 bhp TD from Jan 1988. 'Duty' pack offered better kit and, from Jan 1988, a limited slip diff.

What's bad: Were around on other World markets from around 1984. They do rust, quite badly. Older ones are likely to have had a hard life and may well be simply worn out.

What to watch out for: Rust, signs of hard usage such as a battered floor, scrubs on bodywork, oil leaks from powertrain, inadequate servicing, broken springs, shocked out shocks, uneven tyre wear, excessive smoke from turbodiesel, crunchy gearchange. Make sure four-wheel-drive engages properly. Some reports of cracks developing in cylinder heads of petrol models. The car could easily be an older 'grey import' offering no means of checking on its past.

Trooper (1992 to 1998)

What's good: 3.1 litre 113 bhp TD or 3.2 litre 174 bhp petrol V6 in two wheelbases – short with 3 doors (13ft 6in) or long with 5 doors (14ft 11in) and the option of 7 seats. 3-year warranty. 'Duty' pack took trim up one stage from basic. 'Citation' takes it up another stage.

What's bad: Brick-like styling. The last two years worth sat around for a long time waiting to be sold which delayed the UK launch of the new model. Not quite as reliable as you might expect, possibly due to long wait for a buyer. Re-incarnated (disastrously) as the Vauxhall Monterey.

What to watch out for: Rust, signs of hard usage such as a battered floor, scrubs on bodywork, oil leaks from powertrain, inadequate servicing, broken springs, shocked out shocks, uneven tyre wear, smoke from diesel's turbo, crunchy gearchange. Make sure four-wheel-drive engages properly. If it has a tow hook, what has it been towing – and where? Could have been pulling a livestock trailer over a Welsh mountain. Not quite the same 'green welly' appeal as a Discovery or a Shogun, so more likely to have been a working vehicle.

Trooper (from 1998)

What's good: New 3.0 litre four cylinder 159 bhp twin-cam 16-valve direct-injected common rail diesel engine gives stump-pulling 246 ft lb torque at just 2,000 rpm. Combined fuel consumption figure of 31.6 very good for this type of vehicle. Also a 215 bhp 3.5 litre petrol V6. Same sizes as before: SWB: 13ft 6in long;, LWB: 14ft 11in long. Usefully high towing weight of 3,300kg.

What's bad: Essentially, the old body with a more rounded front – and we had to wait for it while stocks of the slow-selling old model got shifted. First common rail DI in the UK, so first test of individual electronically controlled injectors. Seems to be a problem with the injector seals which results in fuel oil getting into the engine lubricating oil, leading the engine to run on its crankcase oil and making it impossible to stop.

What to watch out for: Reports of drive-train whine and vibration and an admitted gearbox defect on 1999MY Troopers. Has a high towing weight, so could have been towing a huge hamburger stand.

Recalls: Defective gearboxes have been replaced FOC under warranty.

JAGUAR

S-Type (from 1999)

What's good: New 'small' Jaguar with design cues from 1960s Mk II. Actually far from small at 15ft 11in long by 6ft wide and weighing from 1,628kg. Began with choice of 240 bhp 3.0 Duratec V6 or 280 bhp 4.0 Jaguar V8 engines. Manual (V6 only) or Ford auto. CATS option of adaptive damping and 17in wheels worth having. Prices started at £26,700 OTR. Good to drive, with immense charm, enough steering feel, decent handling and good ride quality. A success from day one. Six-cylinder manual model the recommended choice. Steering, gearchange and engine management system all improved by early 2001. See road test of £30,600 S-Type 3.0 V6 Sport manual at www.honestjohn.co.uk S and T reg. cars came a good 17th in 2001 *Top Gear*/JD Power Customer Satisfaction Survey, ahead of the Toyota Corolla. Strong residual values. From January 2002, six-speed automatic 4.2 supercharged S-Type R with huge 541Nm (399lb ft) at 3,500rpm; sixty mph comes up in just 5.3 seconds, top speed limited to 155mph. On the road price is £47,400, combined fuel consumption 22.5mpg and C02 output 314g/km which means a hefty company car BIK tax bill of £6,636 pa for a 40% taxpayer. At the other end of the scale, Jaguar also launched a more BIK friendly 201bhp 2.5 litre V6 engine which, with five-speed manual box pumps out 229g/km and with a retail price of £24,950 means a BIK bill of £2,794. Still no slouch, the S-Type 2.5 gets to sixty in 8.2 seconds, goes on to 142mph and stretches each gallon 29.6 miles in the combined cycle. Other new offerings are a 2.5 V6 six-speed automatic, a 240bhp 3.0 V6 five-speed manual or six-speed automatic and a 300bhp unsupercharged 4.2V8. On the road prices are £28,900, £29,950, £31,400 and £36,000 respectively. 3 year unlimited mileage warranty on all new Jags sold by UK Jag dealers from 24-1-2002. 3.0V6 manual and 4.2V8 6-speed auto recommended.

Much more online at www.jaguar.co.uk

What's bad: No limited slip diff, so apt to rely on traction control instead. Outclassed in handling, roadholding and safety by W211 E Class Mercedes. Automatic 'J' change of older 5-speed autobox can be sloppy and apt to drop a gear unasked when you're halfway round a corner. Early V6 manuals criticised for baulky gearchange and too revvy engine management system. Second-hand prices still higher than same age XJ8s. 'Hushed up' problem of V8 blocks becoming porous after 50,000–60,000 miles, losing compression and being replaced without question by Jaguar. Whining of Type R's Eaton supercharger sounds great to start with but can become wearing on the driver.

What to watch out for: Lumpy feeling V8 engine is a sign of the V8 engine problem above.

Recalls: 4/10/2000: 2,109 S Types built 5/200 to 7/2000 recalled because part in front seatbelt buckles not to standard and may release the belt when subject to load. All buckles assemblies between production dates to be replaced. 23/11/2000: 18,062 S Types built 1/1999 to 9/2000 recalled because first thread of the ball stud in the front suspension lower ball joint could fracture leading to separation of the lower control arm from the knuckle leading to limited steering control. Ball joints to be checked and vertical links to be replaced if necessary.

X-Type (from 2001)

What's good: Engine range began with 195bhp 2,495cc Duratec V6 offering 180lb ft torque at 3,000rpm and 231bhp 2,968cc Duratec V6 with 210lb ft torque at 3,000rpm. Five speed manual and five speed automatic transmissions available with both engines. Performance of 2.5 manual is 0–60mph in 7.9 seconds, 140mph top speed, combined mpg of 29.5 and CO_2 emissions of 234g/km which puts cars registered from 1st March into the £155pa VED bracket. 3.0 manual gets to 60 in 6.6 seconds, goes on to 146mph, delivers a combined mpg of 27.5 and emits 244g/km CO_2 which puts it in the same £155pa VED bracket. On the Road List Prices, which include three year warranty, are: 2.5 V6: £22,000; 2.5 V6 Sport: £24,000; 2.5 V6 SE: £24,750; 3.0 V6 Sport: £25,500; 3.0 V6 SE: £26,250. Air-Conditioning, ABS, Alloy Wheels and All-Round

Airbags standard on all models. Automatic Transmission is an extra £1,250, Dynamic Stability Control an extra £480, and Rear Parking Sensors an extra £310. '*Autocar*' magazine scoop in issue 13/12/2000 showed 330bhp 155mph X-Type R to rival BMW M3, delayed by Ford cutbacks. Softish suspension allows car to handle really well without taking it into Mitsubishi Evo VI territory. 2.5 is smoother and sweeter than 3.0 litre but very obviously lacks the power of its bigger-engined brother. Manuals much better than automatics. But this is good car which is bound to be hugely successful. 2.1 litre front-drive only version from £19,995 from March 2002 puts out 156PS at 6,800rpm and 145lb ft torque at 4,100rpm. 0–60 8.9 seconds, top speed 130mph, combined consumption 20.7mpg and CO_2 output 219g/km which gives it a BIK % of 26%m costing a 40% taxpayer £2,080 for 2002–2003. 3 year UNLIMITED MILEAGE warranty on all new Jags sold by UK Jag dealers from 24–1–2002. Recognises when child seat fitted to front passenger seat and de-activates the airbag. Achieved an excellent four star rating for crash safety in 2002 NCAP tests.

More online at www.X-TYPE.com

What's bad: Over-enthusiastic traction control system can temporarily lock a wheel.

What to watch out for: Problems starting to emerge include drive train drone on four wheel drive manuals, erratic slow running in traffic with poor engine response from low revs and lights dimming (both main and dipped beam)for no apparent reason.

XJ6 and XJR (1994 to 1997)

What's good: 300 Series gained an impressive reputation for reliability both on the fleets and in private hands. Better even than Mercedes or BMW. Well liked by owners. 216 bhp 3.2 litre straight six; 245 bhp 4.0 straight six; 322 bhp 4.0 litre supercharged straight six. 5-speed manual or 'J-change' 4-speed ZF automatic. XJR has much stronger, better Mercedes 600 autobox. Standard length 16ft 4in long by 6ft 7in wide and weighing from 1,880kg. Long wheelbase 16ft 10in long. Three-year 60,000–mile warranty.

What's bad: A glut of these were p/xd for XJ8s by status seekers when the XJ8 came out and prices fell. They climbed back up once the market realised how good the sixes were.

What to watch out for: Less than pristine examples are worth a lot less – pay no more than 'Parker's Guide' Fair prices for scruffy XJs. Also check the spec, because you don't want a standard model with cloth seats and no aircon unless it's really cheap. Still new enough to insist on a proper Jag franchise or Jag specialist service record. Bodies may flex and crack windscreens. Alloys oxidise easily. Rear bumper protector falls off. Check all electrics, particularly the dashboard computer. Feel the discs for lipping or scoring and watch out for uneven braking on the test drive. Brake judder may be due to drivers sitting on the brakes after a hard stop which causes localised overheating and warps the discs. For older cars, see tips for previous model XJ 40 above.

XJ6 SIII (1979 to 1986)

What's good: Last of the classic 'feline' shape XJ6 and prices of good late examples have been rising. 3.4 had 162bhp; 4.2 had 205 bhp; 5.3 V12 had 299 bhp and carried on alongside XJ40 to September 1989. 16ft 3in long by 5ft 10in wide and weighing around 1,850kg.

What's bad: Old cars now with old car problems. Autobox is just a three speeder which makes these cars juicy and hard work on the motorway. The dashboard is a mess. Rust may have set in. Ropey examples are rock bottom.

What to watch out for: Buy carefully from an expert specialist such as Robert Hughes (01932 858381) to avoid pitfalls. The coolant needs to have been changed every two years without fail or the block will sludge up at the back, overheat, blow its head gasket and possibly warp its cylinder head. Rust first appears under rear valance, under the front wings behind the headlamps and along the top of the wing seam. Use a magnet. Otherwise, see XJ40 below and be very wary if the car overheats.

XJ6 XJ40 (1986 to 1994)

What's good: Less likely to have build faults than previous Jaguars.

16ft 4in long by 6ft 7in wide and around 1,750kg. Quiet and quick, nice ambience inside a Sovereign. Non-cat 3.6 has 221 bhp. Catted 3.2 AJ6 has 200 bhp. Pre-cat 4.0 has 235 bhp, sinking to 205 bhp with cat. 4.0 XJR has 248 bhp. Catalysed 5.3 V12 has 264 bhp. All should take unleaded. Car has nice ambience inside. Demand exceeded supply when new, so in 1986 and 1987 these cars sold for silly premiums.

What's bad: Styling the most boring of any XJ. Lack of steering 'feel'. Too low for some. Not as much rear legroom as length implies. 165 bhp 2.9 litre version best avoided unless really cheap (less than £1,000).

What to watch out for: Must have leather seats (or at least leather seat facings) – a £750 trimming job. Aircon more desirable than sunroof. Make sure aircon blows cold. Good news if has been recharged with CFC-free 134A refrigerant instead of old R12 and the seals aren't leaking. Will rust – the first place is around number plate lights in the boot lid, but if there's rust in the wings, sills and inside the boot, walk away. Light reflectors also let in water and rust. Listen for timing chain rattle – a sign of age and insufficiently frequent oil changes. The coolant needs to have been changed every two years without fail or the block will sludge up at the back, overheat, blow its head gasket and possibly warp its cylinder head. If the brake fluid isn't changed every two years, the ABS pump could rust up inside, so make sure the ABS light goes on when you switch on and goes off again a few seconds after start-up. Check all electrics. Check for uneven tyre wear signifying suspension or steering damage. If tyres are worn, they're costly to replace. Listen for clonking from the rear axle on gearchanges, which should be smooth. Manuals are rare and early ones had a clutch problem, but all should have been sorted by now. If fitted with self-levelling suspension, make sure it self-levels. Try and feel the discs for scoring, lipping and wear. Brake callipers can seize and are expensive, so be very suspicious of uneven braking on test drive.

XJ6, XJ8, XJR (from Feb 2003)

What's good: All new aluminium bodied XJ range, to kick off with a 240bhp V6 XJ6 with Jag's new six-speed ZF autobox. To weigh in at a light 1,630kg and get to 60 in 7.3 seconds. XJR to have 400bhp and 408 lb ft torque.

What's bad: Looks are a mixture of X type and XJ.

What to watch out for: Too soon to say.

XJ8 and XJR8 (1997 to 2003)

What's good: Same car as 300 Series with new 240 bhp 3.2 V8, new 290 bhp 4.0 V8 and stonking 370 bhp supercharged 4.0 V8. 5-speed automatic (Mercedes box on XJR8). 16ft 6in long by 5ft 11in wide and weighing from 1,710kg due to lighter engines. Climate control on all models. Three-year 60,000–mile warranty. XJR 100 launched summer 2001 to mark Sir William Lyons Centenary, priced at £58,935. New six-speed ZF automatic gearbox to replace five speed Ford or Mercedes boxes from mid 2002. 3 year UNLIMITED MILEAGE warranty on all new Jags sold by UK Jag dealers from 24–1–2002. 4th top in the 'R' reg. J.D. Power Customer Satisfaction Survey. 7th in 2001 *Top Gear*/JD Power Customer Satisfaction Survey of S and T reg. cars. 3rd Top in 144 car 2002 JD Power/*What Car?* Customer Satisfaction Survey of V and W reg. cars.

What's bad: Painted front bumper looks organic and is easy to scratch. No means of checking 5-speed ZF autobox oil level or refilling it. Jaguar says 'sealed for life', but no oil changes could mean a 'life' of just 10 years. No manual option. Whine of Eaton supercharger of XJR8 can become irritating, but you only hear it when you boot the car heavily. 'Hushed up' problem of early V8 blocks becoming porous after 50,000–60,000 miles, losing compression and being replaced without question by Jaguar.

What to watch out for: Must have a full Jaguar dealer service history (without it, you lose the 3-year warranty) and must be immaculate to command top money. If the engine feels lumpy, it's a sign of the engine problem described above.

Recalls: Jaguar XJ8 (July-October 1997: 11,221 cars): may suffer sudden deceleration due to weak retention bracket on accelerator cable. Extra clip 'costing pennies' solves the problem. (Announced on radio 7/2/98.)

XJS 3.6 AND 4.0 (1983 to 1995)

What's good: 3.6s didn't have cats and did have 225 bhp. Roll-bar cabrio from 1986–87 was stiffer than later convertible. 4.0 had 223bhp. Convertible 4.0 litre from 1992 was much better looking. Rare option of a 5-speed manual instead of 4-speed autobox. 15ft 8in long by 5ft 11in wide and from 1,660kg.

What's bad: Early 1986–87 AJ6 3.6s don't like unleaded and had dodgy engine management systems. 4.0 litre came with a cat so, despite an extra 390cc, is down on power slightly to 223 bhp.

What to watch out for: Fairly apt to suffer front suspension and steering damage, so check this carefully. Any signs of uneven tyre wear – either avoid the car or budget for a big bill. The coolant needs to have been changed every two years without fail or the block will sludge up at the back, overheat, blow its head gasket and possibly warp its cylinder head. Check that standard aircon blows cold. Good news if has been recharged with CFC-free 134A refrigerant instead of old R12 and seals aren't leaking. Look for rust in the flying buttresses at the back, sills and wheelarches. Otherwise, see XJ40 above.

XJS V12 (1975 to 1995)

What's good: Monster 5.3 litre 299 bhp lost 20 bhp to catalyser, but 6.0 litre V12 from May 1993 was back up to 308 bhp. Only a few early versions were manual. Rest automatic only and all are oilwell emptiers. 6.0 litre pre-cat XJRS from Sept '89 had 318 bhp, boosted to 333 bhp in October 1991. Convertibles the most desirable. 15ft 8in long by 5ft 11in wide and weighing from 1,770kg. Can be very reliable, but see below.

What's bad: Ask yourself if you really need all this power in a soft car with overlight power steering which lacks 'feel'. I know of two XJS single-car accidents within half a mile of each other on the same stretch of road.

What to watch out for: The rearmost pair of spark plugs are hidden by plumbing, take hours of dismantling to get at and consequently are rarely changed. Contrary to the horror stories, these big, unstressed V12s can be very reliable and trouble-free if treated and maintained with respect. This means 3,000–mile or six-month fully synthetic oil changes (no later), annual transmission oil changes, new brake fluid and coolant every two years without fail. Fairly apt to suffer front suspension and steering damage, so check this carefully. Any signs of uneven tyre wear – either avoid the car or budget for a big bill. Otherwise, see comments on XJS 3.6/40 and XJ40. If it overheats it's going to be trouble, so leave it alone. A/c on older cars had old CFC gas, now unobtainable. Re-filling with non CFC refrigerant may cause leaks through incompatibility of lubricant.

XK8 and XKR (from 1996)

What's good: Much better looking, more 'Jaguar-like' than XJS. 15ft 7in long by 6ft 7in wide and from 1,640kg (coupe) to 1,750kg (convertible). Tried and tested styling seen before on Aston Martin DB7. Convertible looks lovely. Says you're rich, British and proud of it. 290 bhp in standard form. Supercharged XKR has 370 bhp and 387 lb ft (525Nm) torque, plus better Mercedes autobox – and there is an XKR convertible. 0–60 in 5.2 seconds. Three-year 60,000–mile warranty. 370bhp XJR 100 launched summer 2001 to mark Sir William Lyons Centenary, priced at £69,950 for the coupe and £74,950 for the convertible. 3 year UNLIMITED MILEAGE warranty on all new Jags sold by UK Jag dealers from 24–1–2002. £20k gets you a reasonable used convertible these days.

What's bad: May suffer from infuriating build quality problems. No easy means of checking 5-speed autobox oil level or refilling it. Jaguar says 'sealed for life', but no oil changes mean a 'life' of 10 years tops. (XKR has a stronger Mercedes box.) Whine of Eaton supercharger pf XKR sounds great at first, but can end up getting on your nerves. Don't handle as well as saloons, mainly because you can't see out as well. These cars gulp gas, of course. Rear passengers need to be legless. 'Hushed up' problem of early V8 blocks becoming porous after 50,000–60,000 miles, losing compression and being replaced without question by Jaguar.

What to watch out for: Vital to buy the right trim combination – the 'Classic' rather than the 'Sport' or the base model. Lumpy feeling engine is a sign of the problem above.

Recalls: 1997: rear suspension. 1998 (July-October 1997 build-11,221 cars): may suffer sudden deceleration due to weak retention bracket on accelerator cable. Extra clip 'costing pennies' solves the problem. (Announced on radio 7/2/98.)

JENSEN

C-V8 (stillborn)

What's good: Coupe version of S-V8, was due to be launched late 2001 at prices slightly higher than the £39,650 of the Jensen S-V8. See Jensen S-V8, but was stillborn. Website: www.jensen-motors.com

What's bad: Jensen workforce laid off July 2002. Looking to relocate to S. Africa.

What to watch out for: Too soon to say.

S-V8 (????)

What's good: Marque revived as a two-seater sports car with front end styling reminiscent of the C-V8. Powerful 32-valve 4.6 litre 316 bhp Ford engine also delivers 316 lb ft torque. 5-speed manual box. Priced at £39,650 + £675 on the road charges, a comfortable alternative to an AC Mk IV or a TVR. Extensive list of luxurious extras. Website: www.jensen-motors.com

What's bad: Have never seen one on the road. Jensen workforce laid off July 2002. Looking to relocate to S. Africa.

What to watch out for: Too soon to say.

KIA

Carens (from 2000)

What's good: Strangely styled multi-purpose estate car based on Kia Shuma. 110 bhp 1.8 litre engine. Five seats in two rows or six seats in three rows. Prices start at less than £10k. ABS and aircon standard on more expensive GSX. 3 year or 60,000 mile manufacturer warranty extended to 100,000 miles for all cars sold from 1st January 2002. Optional 4 or 5 year warranty. Gets a facelift for 2002.

What's bad: Just look at it. Six-seater has no boot space and rearmost seats are for children only.

What to watch out for: Too soon to say.

Clarus (2000 to 2001)

What's good: Mondeo-sized 4–door saloon and estate, but much cheaper. 15ft 6in long by5ft 10in wide. 116 bhp 1.8 litre SX priced close to Chrysler Neon at £10,995; 133 bhp 2.0 litre Executive top model with a/c, alloys, ABS and leather just £13,495, or £14,295 with 4-speed autobox. Station wagon also available with huge lights set high in rear 'D' pillars. Standard 3-year warranty.

What's bad: Zero image. Replaced by KIA Magentis in Summer 2001.

What to watch out for: Too soon to say.

Joice

What's good: 7–seater 'carlike' MPV. 2.0 litre 139 bhp engine. Standard ABS. Based on Kia Shuma. 110 bhp 1.8 litre engine. Standard 3-year warranty.

What's bad: Utilitarian external looks. Did not officially come to UK.

What to watch out for: Too soon to say.

Magentis (from mid 2001)

What's good: The biggest new car bargain currently available in the UK. A 166bhp 2.5 litre KV6 saloon for just £12,995 on the road. 15ft 6in long and 6ft wide with an interior volume of 2,832 litres and a boot capacity of 386 litres. Standard equipment includes 4 sensor ABS with Electronic Brakeforce Distribution, air-conditioning, alloy wheels, front fog lights, CD player, remote control central locking, a useful 60/40 split folding rear seat and 5mph impact-sustaining bumpers. Sports H-Matic automatic transmission is a £1,000 option. Combined fuel consumption figure for the manual is 28.2mpg with CO_2 emissions of 237g/km (£155 VED); for the automatic the figures are 25.9mpg and 257 g/km (£155 VED). Prices are £12,995 on the road for the LX manual; £13,995 for the LX automatic; and £15,995 for the more luxurious, leather trimmed SE automatic. All prices include KIA's three year 60,000 mile warranty and three year recovery/assistance package. Replaces the KIA Clarus. 3 year or 60,000 mile manufacturer warranty extended to 100,000 miles for all cars sold from 1st January 2002. Optional 4 or 5 year warranty. Drives well with a lovely engine note.

More online at www.kia.co.uk

What's bad: Doesn't handle as well as a Mondeo. Chromed plastic radiator grille is garish and naff. Interior plastics have an unpleasant smell.

What to watch out for: No problems reported.

Mentor (1996 to 1999)

What's good: Quite well made and quite reliable. 13ft 11in long by 5ft 7in wide and from 1,053kg. 80bhp 1.5 or 80bhp 1.6 with more torque. 5-speed manual of 4 speed automatic. Owners seem to like them. Available as 4–door saloon or 5–door hatch.

What's bad: Zero image, completely ordinary, fairly small 4–door saloon (slightly smaller than an Orion) or 5–door hatch. Lacks specification (sun roofs are cheap aftermarket 'pop-up' add-ons). Strange engine line-up on earlier models. 1.5 litre had 80 bhp and 88 ft. lbs torque; 1.6 litre had 79 bhp and 92 ft. lbs torque. But peak power and torque figures closer in rev range on 1.6.

What to watch out for: Hard to match damaged body panels. Likely to have been privately owned by the over-50s and frequently parked facing the sea.

Mentor (from mid 2001)

What's good: Re-launched Mentor saloon at low prices from £8,995 in Summer 2001. At 4,510mm the new Mentor is 15mm longer than contemporary Vauxhall Vectra. Power comes from a twin-cam 1,594cc 16 valve engine giving a top speed of 115mph and a 0–60 of 11.5 seconds. Combined consumption is 35.3mpg and CO_2 emissions 190g/km (£155 VED). Automatic tops out at 109mph, gets to 60 in 13.4 seconds, does 33.6mpg on the combined cycle and emits 198 g/km CO_2 (also £155 VED). Standard kit on the £8,995 L includes twin airbags, central locking, electric front and rear windows, seatbelt pre-tensioners and 14 inch wheels. £10,200 LX also has ABS, air-conditioning, electric mirrors and height and lumbar adjustable driver's seat. Automatic was a NO COST option on both. All prices were on the road including KIA's three year 60,000 mile warranty and three year recovery package. 3 year or 60,000 mile manufacturer warranty extended to 100,000 miles for all cars sold from 1st January 2002. Optional 4 or 5 year warranty.
What's bad: Standard, rather bland South Korean car.
What to watch out for: Nothing reported.

Mentor II/Shuma (1999 to 2002)

What's good: 4–door saloon and 5–door hatch, more modern and much better looking than previous model. 1.5 litre 88 bhp and 1.8 litre 110 bhp engines. Mentor II saloon has more restrained styling. Shuma 'Fastback' goes for twin headlight look. Optional 4-speed auto. Three-year mechanical and six-year body warranties. Low prices (from £8,500 OTR). Shuma hatch continues but new Mentor from Summer 2001.
What's bad: Mentor II replaced in Summer 2001. Shuma replaced by Shuma II in February 2002. Model line-up and dates are very confusing.
What to watch out for: Too soon to say.

Pride (1991 to 2000)

What's good: Old Mazda 121 re-incarnated and built in South Korea with three or five doors and even as a small estate. 11ft 3in to 11ft 10in long. From 765kg. Helped KIA establish UK foothold. 1.1 had 53bhp; 1.3 had 64bhp. Dropped in January 1999, but 1,324cc model relaunched at lower price in summer 1999 after company taken over by Hyundai. Standard 3-year warranty.

What's bad: Old design. UK never got estate car version. Reports of repeated wheel bearing failures. Re-launched model only lasted to July 2000.

What to watch out for: Uneven tyre wear signifies worn front suspension bushes. Catted versions may have problems. Treat only as a cheap buy offering decent reliability.

Rio (from Summer 2001)

What's good: New Focus-sized 5–door 1.3 litre (74 bhp) and 1.5 litre (97 bhp) semi-estate car launched in Korea in December 1999, and in Europe at the 2000 Geneva Show. 13ft 10in long by 5ft 6in wide and from 900kg. Came to UK Summer 2001 at very low prices from £5,995 for base 1.3. Top speed of 1.5 111mph and 0–60 in 10.6 seconds (1.5 auto 96mph and 0–60 in 13.9 seconds). 3 year or 60,000 mile manufacturer warranty extended to 100,000 miles for all cars sold from 1st January 2002. Optional 4 or 5 year warranty. Lots of car for little money.

What's bad: Not one for enthusiasts. Bland, feel-free steering and very average handling. Rubbery manual gearchange. Not as much rear legroom as you'd expect. Doesn't come with USA 10 year 100,000 mile warranty.

What to watch out for: Nothing reported so far.

Roadster (stillborn)

What's good: Effectively a re-working of the much sought after front-wheel-drive Lotus Elan, now with less powerful 136 bhp 1.8 litre engine. Standard 3 year warranty.

What's bad: Not quite the car it looks to be. Top speed only 123 mph with 0–60 in 9 seconds. Never officially came to UK. Victim of KIA's 1998 take-over by Hyundai.

What to watch out for: Too soon to say.

Sedona (from 1999)

What's good: Big, heavy, very popular Voyager-sized 7–seater MPV with sliding side doors and either a 126 bhp 2.9 litre 16-valve TDI diesel engine with 249 lb ft torque or a 165 bhp 3.0 litre petrol V6 with 164 lb ft torque. 16ft 1in long, 6ft 3in wide and weighing in from 1,671kg to a hefty 1,963kg. Top speed of manual V6 is 116 mph with 13.5–second 0–60; diesel does 105mph with 17–second 0–60 and 34.03 mpg. Autobox available with both engines but is slower. 'Slide through' driving compartment with dash-mounted gearlever. Centre row seats of LS version swivel to face rear seats. Aircon standard in LS. RS base models priced from £14,000. Not bad looking out on the road. Selling very well. Standard 3-year warranty. Facelift, easily removable seats and new 143bhp common rail diesel from October 2001 + free bicycle will all Sedonas sold. 3 year or 60,000 mile manufacturer warranty extended to 100,000 miles for all cars sold from 1st January 2002. Optional 4 or 5 year warranty. Good safety ratings in American National Highway Traffic Safety Administration tests.

More online at www.kia.co.uk

What's bad: Inconvenient 2–2–3 seating arrangement with back three seats on a single bench up to 2001MY (separately folding and removable from 2002MY). A bit slow for the power outputs. Very truck-like to drive and understeers heavily.

What to watch out for: Too soon to say.

Shuma II (from Feb 2002)

What's good: New-look Shuma II 5–door hatchback with new interior and prices from just £8,995. This buys the 1.6L, which has the sweeter of the two engines. Its 1,594cc twin-cam four puts out 75kw (100bhp) at 5,500rpm and 144Nm (106 lb ft) torque at 4,500rpm. With a kerb weight of 1,189kg, this is adequate, pulling the car to 60mph in 11.5 seconds and on to a top speed of 115mph. Combined economy is 35.3 mpg and CO_2 emissions 190g/km (£160pa VED). The slightly more gruff 1,793cc 1.8LX delivers 84kw (113bhp) at 5,600rpm and 157Nm (116 lb ft) torque at 4,500rpm. Weighing only slightly more at 1,206kg, it gets to 60mph in a respectable 9.7 seconds and goes on to 126mph. Combined economy is 31.4 mpg and CO_2 emissions 214g/km (£160pa VED). Makes sense for retired private buyers as a smart, ultra-reliable family hatchback that doesn't look too mainstream for very sensible money. Specification of 1.6L includes twin de-powered airbags, ABS with EBD, front seatbelt pretensioners with load limiters, electric windows front and rear, electric door mirrors, cabin dust filter, remote central locking, 60:40 split folding rear seat, height-adjustable steering wheel, height and lumbar adjustable driver's seat. The 1.8LX at £10,350 has the additions of air-conditioning, body colour rear boot spoiler, leather steering wheel and gearknob, metallic grain centre fascia and instrument panel and parking distance sensors. This is also available with a four speed automatic transmission at £11,100. Performance figures of the auto are 0–60 in 12.0 seconds, top speed 119 mph, combined mpg 28.8, CO_2/km 232 (£160 VED). Top model is the 1.8SE at £11,850 which also has leather seat facings, front fog lamps, 14 inch alloy wheels (with alloy spare) and a single CD player. All come with KIA's three year unlimited mileage warranty with three year's pan European roadside assistance and a six year no perforation body warranty.

More online at www.kia.co.uk

What's bad: Only two lap/diagonal rear belts with just a lap strap in the centre. Handling and roadholding will not appeal to enthusiasts.

What to watch out for: Too soon to say.

Sorrento SUV (from late 2002)

What's good: 4x4 SUV 4,570mm (15ft) long by 1,885mm (6ft 2in) wide by 1,735mm (5ft 8in) high to compete against X-Trail, Freelander, CRV and RAV-4. Standard 5–door 5–seat body, lift-up rear window (as on CRV), high/low range, centre diff lock, ABS, auto option. Engines are 143bhp 2.5 diesel with 323Nm (238 lb ft) torque at 2,000rpm or 3.5 litre V6. Prices from £17,500 to £21,000. Reported to drive well. Diesel does 32.2mpg on combined cycle and should tow 2,500kg. The market place needs another SUV as good as the Nissan X-Trail.

What's bad: Too soon to say.

What to watch out for: Too soon to say.

Sportage (1995 on)

What's good: Cheap alternative to Vitara, Rav4, Honda CRV and Land Rover Freelander. 13ft 11in long by 5ft 8in wide. Lively enough, with 128 bhp and 88 bhp turbodiesel. Re-launched summer 1999 to include longer wheelbase version five-door and a retro-styled short-wheelbase 'Sportage classic' as well as the standard SWB three-door. Standard 3-year warranty.

What's bad: Not exactly sophisticated. Or very roomy. Not as good as any of the expensive alternatives. Can be troublesome and, when they are, the dealers may not be very good at putting them right. S and T platers 6th from bottom in 2001 *Top Gear*/J.D. Power Customer Satisfaction Survey. Consistent 6th from bottom in 144 car 2002 JD Power/*What Car?* Customer Satisfaction Survey of V and W reg. cars.

What to watch out for: Evidence of off-road use. Has the upholstery been 'crocodiled' (eaten by dogs)? Better to buy a town car than a country car.

Recalls: (None known 1994–98, but some cars have been riddled with faults.)

LADA

Niva (1978 to 1997)

What's good: Lada's 4x4. Dates back to the 1970s, but quite good if your need is for a tough, basic 4x4. 12ft 2in long by 5ft 6in wide and 1,210kg to 1,550kg. 79bhp 1.6 engine. 5-speed gearbox with high and low range transfer box. Usual Lada full tool kit supplied. Reasonably competent off road. Latest cars have Suzuki-like front. Some have been fitted with aftermarket PSA XUD diesel engine. Should be next to nothing cheap.

What's bad: Very noisy, slow, thirsty and dated. Quite a small cabin (looks like a Fiat 127 on stilts). Trim not up to the job. Horrible to drive on the road (swaps ends in the wet). Obstructive gearbox.

What to watch out for: Make all the usual working 4x4 checks as these aren't bought for status and are bound to have been hammered off road. Look for leaking gaskets and seals in the axles, gearbox and transfer case. Check the hub bearings and steering bushes carefully. Look for rock damage to sump and axles. Expect the seat trim to have fallen apart. Expect some rust. If there are holes on the surface panels, check the structure very carefully with an old screwdriver. Be highly suspicious of fresh underseal.

Riva (1983 to 1997)

What's good: Based on 1960s Fiat 124. 13ft 4in long by 5ft 3in wide and around 1,050kg. Last ones had 1,452cc 72bhp catalysed engine. Very tough. They gave you a full set of tools to fix it when it went wrong. Kids don't steal them for joy rides. Made infamous by Maureen and Dave Rees from 'Driving School'. Owners display their own brand of inverted snobbery. Quite a few 'catless' cars legally took advantage of extended 'cat' deadline. Estate cars make the best sense. Dealers and parts specialists can be 'salt of the earth'. Should all be well under £100.

What's bad: Appalling build quality. Very basic. Noisy, thirsty, dated and lumpy to drive (nothing like a real Fiat 124). Spare parts supply not guaranteed to last indefinitely. Factory infiltrated by the Russian Mafia. Post-August 1992 models fitted with cats have severe trouble passing MOT advanced emissions systems test.

What to watch out for: Where do you start? Conscientious owners look after them properly. People who buy them for £100 at an auction, don't bother to maintain them and simply run them into the ground. Listen for signs of big ends going. Expect some gearbox whine, but not too much. Unscrew a spark plug to see if it's burning oil. Trim may have fallen apart of its own accord under the inevitable seat covers. Electrics play up (fusebox shorts, distributor wears out). If you're paying the full £100, make sure the tools are all there.

Samara (1984 to 1996)

What's good: Engines and gearboxes not that bad. 1,099cc had 53bhp; 1,288cc had 65bhp; 1,499cc had 75bhp. 13ft 2in x 6ft 2in (inc mirrors) and from 900kg. Three or four door hatchback or 4 door saloon. Body reasonably robust. Cheap.

What's bad: Usual dreadful Lada build quality. Slothful suspension. Horrible handling. Rickety ride. Terrible trim. Eccentric electrics. May not pass MOT 'advanced emission control system' test.

What to watch out for: Depends who's had it before (see Riva). Check all electrics. 'Reverse-turn test' driveshaft joints for clonks.

LAMBORGHINI

Murcielago (from 2001)

What's good: Audi now owns and runs Lamborghini and this was its September 11th 2001 Frankfurt show stopper. The new car has a 6,192cc V12 putting out an awesome 571bhp at 7,500rpm and 479 lb ft, enough to propel it from zero to 60 in 3.6 seconds and on to a top speed of more than 205mph. Will it fit your motor house? Length: 4,580mm; width: 2,045mm; height: 2,665mm.

What's bad: Where do you find to drive a car like this?

What to watch out for: Speed cameras.

LANCIA

Dedra (1990 to 1995)

What's good: Mostly galvanised Tipo/Tempra-based Lancia saloon, so won't rust like a Beta. 165 bhp 2.0 turbo is a bit of a tyre shredder, but will give BMW 318i drivers a nasty shock. 2.0ie has 120 bhp which sank to 115 bhp with cat. SE has automatic suspension control. 1.8ie has 110 bhp – down to 107 bhp with cat; 1.6ie has 90 bhp, down to 80 bhp with cat. Good ride quality, decent handling. Alcantara trim is nice, but not everyone likes the colours. These cars are cheap and can be bargains.

What's bad: Ugly, especially from rear. Dated. Body parts hard to source. When did you last see one of these on the road?

What to watch out for: Check for uneven and excessive front tyre wear (especially turbo) – may be suspension damage. Heater may be u/s. Look for exhaust smoke from turbo oil seals. Satisfy yourself that performance of turbo is up to the mark. Check all electrics (of course). Expect the odd oil leak, especially from gasket between two-piece head and cam carrier. Need regular 35,000–40,000 mile timing belt changes.

Delta HF and Integrale (1987 to 1995)

What's good: Integrale has sensational performance. 165 bhp 8v HF from May '87 to Dec '87; 185 bhp 8v Integrale from Feb '88 to March '89; 196 bhp 16v from Sep '89 to Jan '92. Special order only last of the line 210 bhp Evo 2 from Jan '92 is a collector's item and if kept immaculate will hold its value. Late models had swish leather and Alcantara interiors.

What's bad: Integrale was left-hand-drive only. May be an expensive performance car, but is still based on the Delta which itself is based on the Fiat Ritmo/Strada. So will rust. Will have iffy electrics (dash, rear wash-wipe, heated rear screen, central locking. electric door mirrors). Expensive to keep in good shape.

What to watch out for: First, decide if you want a competition car for rallies or track days, or a flash road car with air and leather. A used competition car will have had offs and will have suffered damage. Uneven tyre wear could be due to suspension misalignment, suspension damage or a distorted shell and is a big job to set up correctly. Timing belts must be changed every 36,000 miles or 3 years, whichever comes first. Brake fluid needs changing every year on ABS systems. Coolant needs changing every two years. Look for coolant and oil leaks. Don't buy one that smokes. Check the condition of the very expensive brake discs. You really need an Integrale specialist to go over one of these for you. Check for cracks developing at the stress points in the bodyshells.

Thema (1985 to 1989)

What's good: Decent handling, decent performance. The 8.32 of 1988 even had a 215 bhp Ferrari V8 engine, but the 165 bhp 2.0 Turbo is probably the best performance buy. Normal 8-valve 2.0 litre 120 bhp, 2.8 V6 150 bhp. Lots of room inside cabin. Big boot. (See Thema from 1989.)

What's bad: An old car now. Tainted by Lancia's UK reputation for unreliability and rust and not entirely immune from either.

What to watch out for: Urgently need new timing belts every 3 years or 36,000 miles. Benefits from fully synthetic oil with regular changes (particularly 8.32 and Turbo). 8.32 often low mileage and doesn't take well to sitting around. Will need expensive timing belt change before you drive it anywhere (this work could cost £1,000). Look for mayo under oil cap – usually indicates cylinder head problems. Check turbo exhaust for oil smoke. Gearbox synchromesh gets worn. Do a reverse-turn driveshaft test and listen for clonking. Check condition of discs. Check all electrics – some are bound to be u/s so use your judgement and adjust your price. Rattles and squeaks are normal. Do look for rust. If front tyre wear uneven, look carefully for signs of accident or suspension damage.

Thema (1989 to 1994)

What's good: Range rationalised from 1989. 2.0 litre 16-valve now has 150 bhp; turbo 185 bhp. Turbo SE best Thema ever on sale in UK, though Italians had an estate car version and a diesel. Cats from August 1992 strangely brought yet another power hike: to 155 bhp and 205 bhp. To help curb torque steer, Turbo got Viscodrive diff. Late models are a lot of car for not much money.

What's bad: Lancia's poor UK reputation robs a good car of the status it deserved. Turbo has high insurance group. Market doesn't like them. No Lancia dealers, just specialists. Increasingly hard to get parts.

What to watch out for: As '85–'89, but exclude notes about 8.32. Smoky exhaust, excessive oil consumption may be turbo, may be valve stem seals.

Y10 (1985 to 1992)

What's good: Fiat Panda-based upmarket mini. Range included excellent, long-lived 45 bhp 999cc 'Fire' engine, 55 bhp ohc 1,049cc Brazil engine; 85 bhp 1,049cc Turbo Brazil, 57 bhp 1,108cc 'Fire' engine and 1,301cc ohc from Strada with multipoint injection giving 78 bhp to GTie. 1,108cc 55 bhp 'Selectronic' CVT auto also available. Size always a benefit for parking. GTie best model. The first car with suede-like Alcantara trim.

What's bad: Rust, rust, rust, citycar abuse, handling abilities strictly limited. Parts hard to get, so hardly any of these cars left on UK roads.

What to watch out for: Look for oil and coolant leaks, accident damage, rust, damaged trim.

LEXUS

GS300 (1993 to 1998)

What's good: Beautifully built and quite good looking with plenty of road presence. 15ft 5in long by 5ft 11in wide. Smooth, 209 bhp six-cylinder engines. Warranty lasted 3 years and 100,000 miles.

What's bad: Steering, handling, roadholding and ride quality not up to BMW standards (over-light steering and can snap into oversteer). Not as much space inside as length suggests. Will not endow drivers with the status of a Mercedes E-Class. Sport model best looking but doesn't drive as well as it looks.

What to watch out for: Full Lexus service history. Evidence of having been carelessly driven by people with business rather than driving on their minds. Suspension damage from kerbing.

Recalls: June 1999: all GS300s built July '95–July '97 recalled to replace potentially faulty suspension links.

GS300 (from 1998)

What's good: VVT engine gives more power (219 bhp); 5-speed auto helps to use it. Longer wheelbase give more room inside. Now 15ft 10in long, but new shape makes it look shorter. Weighs 1,665kg. Double wishbone suspension improves handling and roadholding. Traction Control and Vehicle Stability Control help keep drivers out of trouble while they're on the phone. 3-year, 100,000–mile warranty. S and T reg. cars came third in 2001 *Top Gear*/JD Power Customer Satisfaction Survey.

What's bad: In dubious taste. Chopping off the front and the back did not improve the looks of this car.

What to watch out for: Full Lexus service history.

GS430 (from 2001)

What's good: Smaller GS300 body with LS430 engine. 283bhp 4.3 litre engine makes this car very quick with 0–60 of just over six seconds. Priced at £36,995.

What's bad: See GS300.

What to watch out for: See GS300.

GX470 (from 2003)

What's good: For the North American market only, the new Lexus GX470 will be positioned between the RX300 and the premium-luxury LX470 SUVs in size, price and capability. The V8–powered GX470 arrives in Lexus dealerships in North America in January 2003 with an annual sales target that exceeding 20,000 units. No plans for the Lexus GX470 to enter the European market. Based on a new global SUV platform, the Lexus GX470 will combine the luxury specification and workmanship of a Lexus saloon with full-time four-wheel drive, high-tech suspension for responsive handling and a smooth ride, plus the company's latest safety technology. This new SUV includes seating for up to eight and a factory-installed DVD rear-seat entertainment system. The GX470, available with five-speed automatic transmission, will share the 4.7 litre V8 engine producing 235 horsepower and 320lb ft of torque (preliminary figure) and full-time four-wheel drive system from the larger LX470 model. The full complement of dynamic handling technology includes anti-lock brakes (ABS), Active TRAC (traction control), Brake Assist, Vehicle Stability Control (VSC) and Electronic Brake Force Distribution (EBD). A new Downhill Assist Control (DAC) system will provide additional control for off-road driving on steep descents. Passive safety features include dual front and side airbag supplemental restraint systems and side curtain airbags.

What's bad: LHD only. Not coming to Europe so we don't get it apart from via enterprising independent importers.

What to watch out for: Personal import only.

IS300 (from 2001)

What's good: Answers criticism of lack of power of original 153bhp IS200. Has 5-speed autobox with steering wheel pushbutton controls. Engine is a 2,997cc straight six VVT-i. Develops 211bhp at 5,800rpm and 212lb ft (288Nm) torque at 3,800rpm. Gets the IS300 to sixty in 8.2 seconds and on to a top speed of 143mph. Combined fuel consumption figure of the saloon is 26.1mpg with CO_2 output of 256g/km (SportCross 25.2mpg and 265g/km). For company drivers, CO_2 outputs give a tax base of 33% for the saloon and 35% for the SportCross, but because the cars have very high levels of standard kit, including leather seats, BIK tax is lower than similarly equipped competitors. Insurance group is a reasonable 15E. IS300 saloon dimensions are length 4,400mm, width 1,725mm, height 1,405mm. Boot luggage capacity is 400 litres and towing limit is 1,200kg. SportCross dimensions are length 4,505mm; width 1,725mm, height 1,430mm. Boot luggage capacity under the luggage cover is 360 litres, plus 36 litres in side boxes, expanding to 1,046 litres with the rear seats down. Towing limit is also 1,200kg. Full climate control air conditioning system standard on both models. An additional Foot/Demist mode has been added. Tyre size is 215/45 ZR17. New eight-speaker audio system is integrated into the centre console and includes an in-dash six-disc CD changer. For safety and convenience, audio equipment controls have been simplified for ease of operation. As with other Lexus models, the IS300 saloon and SportCross are backed by a three year/ 60,000 miles warranty, three year paint and 12 year anti-perforation warranty. Prices: £26,700 for the attractive saloon or £28,450 for the SportCross.

More online at www.lexus.co.uk

What's bad: No six-speeder. No UK manual option at all.

What to watch out for: Too soon to say.

IS200 (from 1999)

What's good: Toyota's answer to the BMW 3–Series and Audi A4. Fresh, 'clean sheet' styling. 14ft 5in long by 5ft 8in wide and from 1,350kg. Promising 153 bhp twin-cam 24v 2.0 litre straight six. Six-speed manual gearbox has rifle-bolt precision (four speed auto optional). Rear-wheel-drive with proper rear drive handling. Interesting instruments. Big 17in alloy wheels. Much sharper steering than other Lexus models. Sport has traction control, which is a mixed blessing for keen drivers. Three three-point rear seatbelts. Prices start at £20,500. S and T reg. cars came fifth in 2001 *Top Gear*/JD Power Customer Satisfaction Survey. Third most reliable car in 2001 Fleet News Survey of 620,000 fleet cars mostly under 3 years old. 5th top for reliability in *Auto Express* 2002 survey. 2nd Top in 144 car 2002 JD Power/*What Car?* Customer Satisfaction Survey of V and W reg. cars. Holds its value very well. Recommended.

What's bad: Needs to be revved to perform, otherwise doesn't feel powerful enough. Auto can be sluggish at times. Complaints of alloy wheels suffering from pitting as a result of salt on UK roads. 800 wheels returned to Japan Many and replaced under warranty. The first Lexus LS400s had the same problem. Some complaints of clutch judder on 6-speed IS200s not cured by repeated replacement clutches. Can lead to gearbox problems. High used prices (only a problem if you're buying used).

What to watch out for: See above problem areas. Check gearbox and clutch action carefully before buying a manual.

LS400 (1990 to 2000)

What's good: World's most refined V8. Effortless acceleration. Brilliant, fully controllable, utterly obedient 5-speed autobox from Oct '97 (4-speed before, and 3-speed to October '94). Unobtrusive traction and stability control system. As luxurious, reliable and trouble-free as you'd expect of an S-Class competitor built by Toyota. 16ft 5in long by 6ft wide and from 1,765kg. 3-year, 100,000–mile warranty. Quentin Willson reckons they're fantastic buys at over 100,000 miles. He has no trouble with them. Trade generally approves of quality levels, particularly trim and switchgear. Lexus servicing seems to be top notch. Pre-August 1992 cars can legally be 'de-catted' for better performance and economy (talk to BBR on 01280 702389). 241 bhp 3-speed auto Jan '90–Oct

'94; 260 bhp 4-speed auto Oct '94–Oct '97; 280 bhp 5-speed auto from Oct '97. S and T reg. cars came first in 2001 *Top Gear*/JD Power Customer Satisfaction Survey.

What's bad: Lack of steering 'feel' (even the Cadillac Seville STS is better in this respect). Pre-1995 model-year cars could suffer from engine surging. Limo 'stretchers' not happy about the thickness of the body panels. Lacquer coating on early-model alloy wheels peels off, allowing them to oxidise badly. A new set of tyres and a complete exhaust system costs the wrong side of £2,500.

What to watch out for: Underservicing. Some busy company directors run these cars very hard as mobile offices, clock up 75,000 miles a year, don't always have time to get services done on time. Check 'cats' (£610 each) Buy young with high mileage rather than old with low mileage. Toyota GB says: make sure the car has a full Lexus service history, that the automatic transmission fluid and filter have been changed every year, that the shocks and suspension are okay, that the timing belts have been changed at 60,000–mile intervals and that there is no excess wear on the rear discs through misuse of the parking brake. Check the exhaust system carefully (see above).

Recalls: (Unknown date)Cars built July 1995–July 1997, possible separation of the lower ball joint, this affects 2230 cars. (Unknown date) Cars built 1992–1994, possible failure of suspension ball joint, affecting 1298 cars (Unknown date)possibility that the vehicle stability control (VSC), can operate wrongly when a call is being received on a mobile phone that is near the console box, if this should happen the brakes might activate without prior notice. 1998 (April '95–June '96 build): Risk of underbonnet fire due to faulty wiring.

LS430 (from 2001)

What's good: 'All new' large Lexus with new 4.3 litre 282bhp Variable Valve Timing V8 priced at £49,950 on the road or £53,950 for 'Premium Pack' version. 16ft 5in long by 6ft wide, with 4,293cc B8 putting out 280bhp. Top speed 155mph; 0–60 in 6.7 seconds; combined economy figure: 23.5mpg (31.7mpg possible cruising at

75mph); CO_2 emissions: 289g/km. 5-speed automatic box. Navigation system standard. 'Premium Pack' includes self-levelling air suspension, multi-function wood and leather steering wheel, individual controls for rear compartment air-conditioning, electrically operated reclining rear seats with memory functions and, get this, "electric vibro-massaging rear seats".

What's bad: Ostentatious rather than a genuinely good looker, otherwise too soon to say.

What to watch out for: Too soon to say.

RX300 (from 2001)

What's good: UK market name for the 4x4 version of the Harrier which has been around in other markets for some time now. 15ft long by 6ft wide and from 1,790kg. Transverse, belt-cam 201 bhp, 208 lb ft torque 2,995cc 24 valve V6 engine. 4-speed autobox. 0–60 in 9 seconds; top speed 112mph; EC Urban fuel consumption 15.9mpg. A/c standard on all. List priced at £28,950 and £32,550 for SE. Reasonably compact. Handles very well indeed for a 4x4 – on a par with the new Ford Maverick – and really good to drive. Better steering than a Lexus GS or LX. Good ride comfort on sensible 70 profile tyres. Seemed better to drive on a difficult road than a BMW X5 3.0 and rides over road humps with aplomb.

What's bad: The two-wheel drive option available in other markets with a lower ride height might have made sense in the UK. Did badly in '*Autocar*' off road test (see issue 12–9–2001). Some of the trim is a bit cheap and nasty, particularly the cupholders between the seats. Lowish towing weight of just 2,000kg.

What to watch out for: Beware of paying too much for 'personally imported' Harriers, etc. posing as the genuine UK Lexus RX300 (these sell 75,000 a year in the USA). A 99V 4x4 Harrier with all the kit and negligible mileage sold for just £16,125 at auction on 1/12/2000. And if you're knowingly buying an import, check the spec very carefully. It could be a 2.0 litre four cylinder version and not even have four-wheel drive.

SC430 (from 2001)

What's good: Luxurious new two seater from Lexus to compete with the Mercedes SL. Has an SLK and new SL-like retractable hardtop that folds up or down in a matter of seconds. Two tiny child seats in the back. Top speed from revised 278bhp LS430 engine is 150mph; 0 to 60 6.4 seconds. UK list price £50,850.

What's bad: Does 'SC' stand for 'Scorpio'? The front looks very like the defunct Ford. Not actually in the UK until Summer 2001. Steering, handling, roadholding, ride quality and body flexing all heavily criticised by '*Autocar*' magazine 22/8/2001. Car as a whole, especially its hard 'run flat' tyres panned by Jeremy Clarkson in the *Sun* on 7/12/2001 and *The Sunday Times* 9/12/2001. Seems to have lost the battle against the new Merc SL before it even started.

What to watch out for: Paying a premium.

Soarer coupe

What's good: Luxurious, Ford Thunderbird like coupe with the Lexus LS400 running gear. Sporty version has a 2.5 litre twin turbo straight six. Quite a lot of car for the money these days.

What's bad: Not officially a 'Lexus' in the UK at least. All are private imports and some may have been registered on dodgy MOTs before the need for a proper SVA test. Can look like a lot of car for the money, but can also be ten years old. Alloys apt to become scabrous and possibly porous too, so that will be the reason for a flat tyre.

What to watch out for: Dodgy spec and possibly even stolen imports. Make sure a/c runs cold and is gas tight. May still be filled with old CFC gas.

LIGIER

Ambra County Diesel (from 1999)

What's good: Tiny French two-seater micro hatchback built at the rate of 300 a week imported by Reliant since 1999. County is basic model with two-cylinder 505cc Lombardini diesel engine developing 6.5bhp giving 50 mph and up to 85 mpg. Simple, exposed belt CVT transmission. Electric windows and stereo. Alloy wheels and RHD standard in UK. Under the weight limit, so can be driven on a B1 motorcycle licence from the age of 17. Euro Type-Approved. Base models have been on offer at £4,995. July 2002 base price: £5,276 on the road.

What's bad: Slow acceleration of diesel will take a bit of getting used to but petrol version is a fair bit quicker.

What to watch out for: Too soon to say.

Ambra GLX Fi and D (from Jan 2001)

What's good: Facelifted Ambra from January 2001, offered with 15bhp 505cc petrol engine or 6.5bhp diesel. Simple open wheel CVT automatic. 8ft 1in long, 4ft 7in wide and, of course, under the 550kg B1 weight limit. Petrol up to 70mph and up to 65mpg. Diesel up to 50mph and up to 85mpg. Petrol listed at £6,826 on the road; diesel listed at £5,776 OTR.

What's bad: Small, still slow, and not rock bottom cheap.

What to watch out for: Trucks.

Be Up

What's good: Bizarre two seater minimalist resort car by Giugiaro Design. Powered by 505cc 4 stroke twin cylinder petrol engine developing 21bhp with open belt CVT transmission and can be driven on a B1 motorcycle licence from the age of 17.

What's bad: It rains in the UK. Have not seen one on the road.

What to watch out for: People will certainly see you coming.

LOTUS

Elan (1989 to 1992; 1994 to 1995)

What's good: Fine handling front-drive sports car with excellent grip. 12ft 6in long by 6ft 2@ wide and weighing around 1,000kg. An instant 'classic' despite KIA lookalike with not quite the same dynamics. Non-turbo Isuzu engine has 130 bhp. Turbos have 165 bhp pre-cat, down to 155 bhp with twin cats when re-launched as S2 in June 1994. Engines and gearboxes tough and reliable. Held its value well for years.

What's bad: Eats front tyres. Promotes heavy wear of front driveshaft joints, bushes and bearings. Fizzy electrics. Hoods leak. Hard driven, underserviced turbos will smoke. Red examples can develop a paint problem. 80,000 mile H reg. SE turbos selling for £6,000 to £7,000 in 2002.

What to watch out for: Repaired accident damage. Smoking turbos. Kerbed alloys. Front suspension, hubs and driveshaft wear. Need to see evidence of proper servicing, in particular frequent fully-synthetic oil changes.

Elise (1996 to 2000)

What's good: Gorgeous, mouthwatering little road racer in the mould of the Porsche RSK and Elva BMW. Brilliant, ultra-lightweight chassis design and construction. 12ft 3in long and weighing only 690kg. Only 120bhp, but Tremendous handling and grip best checked out under instruction at a race circuit 'track day'. 111S from March 1999 had 143bhp. Facelifted with new targa top and uprated standard engine from October 2000. Last of the original shape hold their value better than new shape.

More online at www.lotuscars.co.uk

What's bad: Not enough power in standard 118 bhp form for the track, but BBR (01280 702389) does an Interceptor 2000 for better mid-range grunt. 'Sport' version's 190 bhp almost too much for the road. Minimal weather protection. Not a 'girlie townie' fashion accessory. Not for wimps. Expect roof to leak. Snap oversteer in the wet hard to predict and catch on first acquaintance, especially on slicks in the wet. 2001 facelift not nearly as attractive as original car. S and T platers 17th from bottom in 2001 *Top Gear*/J.D. Power Customer Satisfaction Survey. Head gasket failure common because very low coolant capacity of engine means small leaks rapidly lead to overheating. Weakest point is water heated inlet manifold gasket.

What to watch out for: Typical track day 'off' damage underneath, bent suspension, crunched ends. Cat damage from misfiring off rev-limiter. Won't pass advanced emissions test at first MOT if cat has been removed.

Recalls: Lotus modified the rudimentary soft top in Spring 1998 because owners complained of leaks. Daft, really. You just don't buy an Elise as an everyday car. 10/3/2000 recall of all Elise 111S models built before 1/2/2000 to fit electromagnetic interference shield to prevent interference causing misfires. 9/2/2001: Elise 111S models built 1/9/1999 to 31/8/2001 recalled because continual driving with a misfire could lead to excessive exhaust heat and a fire. Ignition system to be modified and exhaust mountings changed. 9/2/2001: Elise and Exige models built 1/10/1999 to 31/1/2001 recalled because hose connecting a spigot on the filler neck to the fuel tank top surface may be of incorrect material and may tear. Modified breather hoses to be fitted. 16/6/2001: Elise models built Sept 1998 to Jan 1999 recalled because rack bars of steering racks were not heat treated correctly and may wear prematurely. Steering racks to be replaced as necessary.

Elise (from October 2000)

What's good: Facelifted with new targa top and uprated standard engine from October 2000. Now 12ft 5in long by 5ft 8in wide and weighing 756kg. In May 2002 new variant called Elise 111 got power hike to 156bhp, 0–60 dropped to 5.3 seconds and top speed went up to 132mph. Priced at £25,999, but options such as a/c, hardtop and leather can take it over £30k. Exige version from April 2000 had 177bhp, same length and width and weighed 780kg.

More online at www.lotuscars.co.uk

What's bad: Last of the original shape hold their value better than new shape. Can now set you back Porsche Boxter money, which is too much.

What to watch out for: Track day 'offs' damage.

Esprit SE/S4/S4S/Sport 300/V8 (1987 on)

What's good: 'James Bond' submarine car still listed. (Original Esprit launched in 1976. SE launched in 1987.) In the 'junior supercar' league, light in weight with 264 bhp (S4) or 300 bhp turbocharged engines (S4S). Excellent handling and roadholding. Sport 300 is a lightweight 300 bhp car. 3,506cc V8 has 349 bhp. At £49,950 the V8 GT. Esprit V8 facelifted for 2002, still with 350bhp and 295lb ft (400Nm) torque, top speed 175mph, 0–60 in 4.8 seconds, combined consumption 21.24mpg. Price now £49,995. 2002 measurements are 14ft 8in long by 6ft 6in wide, with the 349bhp V8SE weighing in at 1,380kg.

More online at www.lotuscars.co.uk

What's bad: Four-cylinder Lotus engines became stretched to the limit. Poor gearchange. 'Lie down' seats. Apt to go wrong quite a lot. Still looks like a kit car inside.

What to watch out for: This car really needs expert and frequent attention. If it hasn't been checked over at least every six months, leave it alone. You don't want to hear any rattles from the engine, especially the timing belt tensioner. Look for smoke from turbo, oil leaks, fizzy electrics, leaking heater matrix, inoperative aircon, hotspotted cats. If 1992K or later, make sure it has passed a recent advanced emissions test.

Recalls: 1998: 200 V8 models recalled for new timing belt, idler pulley bearings, new clutch and 5th gear locknut, cost to Lotus at least £1,500 per car. Also check rear alloy wheels for hairline cracks.

Excel (1985 to 1991)

What's good: A Lotus with four seats. 15ft 5in long by 5ft 11in wide and 1,136kg. Had 2,174cc four with 180bhp. 4-speed automatic option from October 1986, Decent handling, fast, reasonably economical and quite reliable in the right hands. Last model Jan to August 1991 was called the Celebration.

What's bad: Collector's car jokes still apply (you have to collect the bits that drop off). Fiercely defended by club members. Screen surround comes adrift. Trim comes unstuck. Needs to be revved to perform (not a town car). If you don't know these cars you need to find someone local who does.

What to watch out for: Make sure no leaks from heater matrix and that air conditioning works. Needs frequent correct maintenance by experts, not the bloke under the arches (unless he is a Lotus genius). May have been 'owner serviced' so make sure it's been done properly by cross-examining the owner. Fully synthetic oil preferred.

LAND ROVER

Defender

What's good: Fantastic off road capability. Simple, flat alloy panels easy to replace. Diesels now come with same 122PS TD5 engine as Discovery TD5. 'Black' edition for urban warriors launched Canary Wharf Motor Expo on 10th June 2002. Comes either as a 90 station wagon or 110 double cab for £24,995 and includes leather trim, single slot CD, aircon, alloy wheels, chequer plate trim on wingtops and body sides (like Lara Croft's Landy), "chrome detailing on the instrument bezels and alloy knobs for the gear transfer boxes", ABS and four wheel electronic traction control.

Owners' online bulletin board: www.landrover.org/wwwboard/wwwboard.html

What's bad: Nicknamed the 'Deafener'. Very crude (for fresh air ventilation, open a flap under the windscreen and get it direct). Very noisy. Reports of crankshaft, gearbox and transfer case misalignment and failed wheel bearings. For those seeking traditional Land Rover virtues, take a look at Santana. Land Rover had joint highest average cost in warranty claims for cars up to 10 years old in 2002 Warranty Direct index

What to watch out for:

Recalls: May 2002: 13,000 Defenders built September 1998 to April 2001 recalled to check condition of front brake hoses which can chafe on suspension struts. Chafed pipes to be replaced.

Discovery (1989 to 1998)

What's good: High driving position good for sightseeing. Outstandingly competent and comfortable off-road. Diesels are surprisingly economical with 30 mpg on the cards. Autobox goes well with the four-cylinder diesel. Seven-seat versatility (though the two back jump seats are not suitable for long journeys). 14ft 8in long by 5ft 11in wide and weighing from 2,000kg, which is more than the 'Classic' shape Range Rover. TDi had 111bhp to July 1995, then 120bhp; 3.9 V8 had 180bhp. 5-speed manual or 4-speed automatic, both with low range.

Owners' online bulletin board: www.landrover.org/wwwboard/wwwboard.html

What's bad: Build problems went from bad to worse in the transition from 200 to 300 model. Very ponderous on the road due to high centre of gravity. Dangerous to carry anything on the roof. Generally poor build quality. Post-1993 '300 Series' manual gearbox has better change but suffers severe input shaft wear (can be alleviated by high-tech gearbox lubricants). 300 TDi engines also prone to timing belt failure after 40,000 miles. Kits are available to extend timing belt life, but fitting them is a long job. V8s guzzle fuel. Avoid the underpowered 2.0 litre 16v 'MPi' model. Lack of crumple zones mean it can be expensively damaged by hard impacts at speeds as low as 5 mph. In June 2001 Land Rover was rated by Motor Warranty Direct as Britain's 2nd worst out of 22 marques for warranty claims (check online at www.warrantydirect.co.uk) Suggested oil to help prevent problems with the notorious 300 manual gearbox is: Morris LODEXOL MTF APIGL4 FULLY SYNTHETIC TRANSMISSION FLUID. Up to 1,500 Discoverys put off the road in 2002 because an immobiliser part 'Spider Unit', Land Rover part No ARM 4889 become virtually impossible to obtain. LandRover had joint highest average cost in warranty claims for cars up to 10 years old in 2002 Warranty Direct index

What to watch out for: Signs of severe usage. Tow hooks (what's it been towing? It's rated to 3.4 tons). Underbody 'off-roading' damage. Leaks from axles, transmission, transfer case. Worn suspension and steering bushes. Worn and noisy gearboxes (especially post-1993 '300 Series'). Rust where steel chassis touches alloy body panels. 5-door models worth much more than 3-doors. If it's a TDi 300, has the timing belt modification been carried out? Check the trim carefully as dashboards of post-'94 models can warp. 6th from Bottom of 100 models for reliability in *Auto Express* 2002 survey.

Recalls: 1995 (VIN LJ163104 to LJ172980 and LJ501920 to LJ504252): check seatbelts. 1997 (April '95–July '96: 22,723

vehicles): possibility of failure of RHS front door latch. 1998: (build Jan '94–Mar '97): airbag may go off involuntarily. 1998 TSB dated 25/3/98 warned dealers of timing belt failure due to misalignment of belt and pulleys on 300TDi's up to VIN WA748935 and gave procedures for repair under warranty if warranty conditions apply. TWO RECALLS 3/4/2001: Build 1/1/1998 to 31/12/2000, VINs XA410482 to 1A452817 and XA220000 to 1A299999: Recall 1 (automatics only): Water may migrate up gearbox breather pipe and corrode park lock mechanism leading it to fail to lock properly. Gearbox breather pipe to be re-routed and affected gearboxes to be repaired. Recall 2: High pressure hose of Active Cornering Enhancement system not fitted with anti vibration attenuator may fracture. Where attenuator not fitted, high pressure hoses to be replaced.

Discovery (1998 to mid 2002)

What's good: Revised, more expensive, slightly longer model from October 1998 with new 136bhp 'TD5ft 5-cylinder direct injected diesel engine, up to seven forward-facing seats and much better road handling than the old model. Same high driving position good for sightseeing. Outstandingly competent and comfortable off-road. Price of entry level Discovery E TD5 cut to £21,995. Facelift Summer 2002 (see separate entry). Unlimited mileage 3-year warranty on all new Discoverys sold by official UK dealers from 1–3–2002.

Owners' online bulletin board: www.landrover.org/wwwboard/wwwboard.html

What's bad: Appalling catalogue of build problems – worse even than 300 model. Sometimes delivered with wrong spec. Hard to distinguish visually from old model, so the neighbours may not realise you've got the new one. Fuel consumption of TD5 around 17% worse than previous four-cylinder diesel. 6th from Bottom of 100 models for reliability in *Auto Express* 2002 survey. Joint 16th from Bottom in 144 car 2002 JD Power/*What Car?* Customer Satisfaction Survey of V and W reg. cars. Facelifted with 700 improvements in Spring 2002. LandRover had joint highest average cost in warranty claims for cars up to 10 years old in 2002 Warranty Direct index

What to watch out for: See old model.

Recalls: October 1999: all 9,296 new model Discoverys sold to date recalled because of a problem with the ABS brakes. Ten minutes' work required on car. March 2000 recall of vehicles built July-Dec 1999: Active Cornering Enhancement system could malfunction due to pipes fracturing. New pipes to be fitted. June 2000 recall of 11,000 TD5s built between September 1998 and June 1999 because flywheel of manual versions could fail. Further recall of V8s because engine idler pulley could fragment throwing drive belt off and leading to loss of cooling, power steering. TWO RECALLS 3/4/2001: Build 1/1/1998 to 31/12/2000, VINs XA410482 to 1A452817 and XA220000 to 1A299999: Recall 1 (automatics only): Water may migrate up gearbox breather pipe and corrode park lock mechanism leading it to fail to lock properly. Gearbox breather pipe to be re-routed and affected gearboxes to be repaired. Recall 2: High pressure hose of Active Cornering Enhancement system not fitted with anti vibration attenuator may fracture. Where attenuator not fitted, high pressure hoses to be replaced.

Discovery (from mid 2002)

What's good: Extensive facelift distinguished by new lights and 700 improvements for 2003, on sale from 1–6–2002. 2003MY Disco has option of centre diff lock making it better off road and suspension and braking improvements making it better on road. US buyers get 225bhp 4.6 V8, but biggest UK engine is 182bhp 4.0 V8. Most sold with 136bhp 2.5 TD5. Petrol models apparently to get Jaguar V8s late in 2002.

What's bad: Fingers crossed that the faults have been fixed.

What to watch out for: Too soon to say.

Freelander (1997 on)

What's good: Good styling. Comfortable. Likeable. Plenty of room for four or five passengers. Kids enjoy the high back seat. Proper three-point centre belt in 5–door. Useful underfloor lockable cubby-safe. Hill descent control works well. The more you drive it the more you like it. SWB 14ft 5in long; LWB 14ft 7in long. From 1,480kg. Originally with 118bhp 1.8 litre K Series petrol engine of 96bhp 2.0 Rover L Series diesel. Longer 3-year warranty inclusive from spring 1998. Fairly damage-proof at the front because even the wings are plastic. 175bhp/177lb ft 2.5 litre KV6 and 110bhp/192lb ft 2.0 litre BMW TD4 diesel with Steptronic automatic options on both finally arrived in Autumn 2000. TD4 does 102mph and 0–60 in 13.2 seconds, a useful improvement on the slow old Rover diesel. Still depreciates less than a mass-market estate car. 2001 list prices from £15,995 for 1.8, from £17,195 for TD4 and from £21,595 for KV6. TD4 5–door recommended. Unlimited mileage 3-year warranty on all new Freelanders sold by official UK dealers from 1–3–2002. Owners' online bulletin board: www.landrover.org/wwwboard/wwwboard.html

What's bad: The main problem is that Nissan's X-Trail 2.2DI Sport 6-speed is better in every respect. TD4s had to get hold of due to supply problems with BMW engines. Initial promise of high quality build not met. Lots of niggly failures. Also failures of hill descent control, driveshafts and gearboxes and blocked ventilation slots (Sunday Times 6/3/99). More ponderous than Honda CRV, Toyota RAV-4 and X-Trail and more expensive than CRV. Not as economical as expected, but Rover diesel can average 35 mpg at a 70 mph cruise. Become increasingly expensive with Freelander 50th 5–door diesel listed at £24,995. Several recalls. Many owners taking a hit, getting out and getting into fault-free Honda CRVs, RAV-4s and X-Trails. Low profile tyres fitted to 'Millennium' model Freelanders aren't up to suburban kerb mounting, which is the main off road activity of these vehicles. S and T platers 16th from bottom in 2001 *Top Gear*/J.D. Power Customer Satisfaction Survey. In June 2001 Land Rover was rated by Motor Warranty Direct as Britain's 2nd worst out of 22 marques for warranty claims (check online at www.warrantydirect.co.uk)To prevent cylinder head warping and cylinder head gasket failure, all 1.8 and 2.5 litre K Series engines need their head to sump stretch bolts re-torquing periodically (does not apply to diesels which are not K Series). One (only one) report so far of total engine failure of the KV6. One report of failure of rear axle at 47,000 miles, apparently not unique. Several reports of Steptronic gearbox problems on the KV6. 2nd bottom of 100 models for reliability in *Auto Express* 2002 survey. 7th from Bottom in 144 car 2002 JD Power/*What Car?* Customer Satisfaction Survey of V and W reg. cars. LandRover had joint highest average cost in warranty claims for cars up to 10 years old in 2002 Warranty Direct index

What to watch out for: Signs of severe usage. Tow hooks (what's it been towing? Neither the 1.8 nor the diesel is really powerful enough). Underside damage. Drivetrain leaks. Make sure everything works, especially the 'hill descent control', if fitted. Reports of accelerator of 1.8 petrol models sticking and leading to accidents. Reports of gearbox failures. Check clutch operation carefully as off road driving can lead them to fail in as little as 20,000 miles due to lack of a low range first gear.

Recalls: TSBs (Technical Service Bulletins) over some part-time four-wheel-drive clutch systems failing due to fluid leaks and replaced 'in service' by Land Rover dealers. Official November 1998 recall (build dates June '97–June '98) to check welding on joints of rear suspension arms. 1999: official note to owners to reduce tyre pressures from 2.1 bar to 1.8 bar when not fully loaded, to increase tyre life. 22/10/2001: 68,838 Freelanders from 1/10/1997 launch to 28/2/2001 recalled to check and replace parking brake ratchet if necessary. Further 12,286 built 1/8/2000 to 30/11/2000 recalled because wiring harness can chafe against fuse box putting out headlights, engine management, cooling fans, fuel pump, ignition circuit, a/c, abs and hdc. Further 4,391 3–door Freelanders built 1/8/2000 to 31/2/2002 recalled to check latches of folding front seats and replace as necessary. Feb/March 2002: Apparent recall of TD4 Steptronic automatics to correct fuel lifter pump/fuel pump relay fault.

Range Rover 'Classic' (1970 to 1995)

What's good: 'Classic' Range Rover, warts and all. Some people still love them. 4-cylinder 90bhp 2,343cc diesels the most economical (later models from October 1989 had 2.5 litre 119bhp VM diesels, then from November 1992 111bhp 2.5 litre Land Rover TDI diesels). Old carburettor 3,528cc V8s to October 1989 had only 130bhp; 3,947cc V8s from October 1989 had 185bhp; 4,278cc V8 from October 1992 had 200bhp. 14ft 8in long by 5ft 10in wide and from 1,724kg to 2,150ky for 15ft 3in Vogue LSE. Unrivalled cross country performance until the replacement model arrived. Final metallic-blue 25 individually numbered '25th Anniversary' models the most valuable.

Owners' online bulletin board: www.landrover.org/wwwboard/wwwboard.html

What's bad: V-8s guzzle petrol. Misfires destroy 'cats'. Litany of quality problems which may or may not have been sorted by the previous owner. The three-door CSK (Cyril Spencer King) was an interesting aberration – not wanted at 2–3 years old, but might develop a cult classic following in years to come if kept clean. Air suspension fitted to LSE and Vogue SE can be troublesome. In June 2001 Land Rover was rated by Motor Warranty Direct as Britain's 2nd worst out of 22 marques for warranty claims (check online at www.warrantydirect.co.uk) LandRover had joint highest average cost in warranty claims for cars up to 10 years old in 2002 Warranty Direct index

What to watch out for: Signs of severe usage. Check suspension bushes for wear. Steering box may be worn. Look for oil leaks from gearbox, transfer case and axles. Make sure rear axle breather not blocked. Make sure VM diesel not suffering from cracked cylinder heads (white smoke from exhaust; mayonnaise under oil cap). Sludge on dipstick is really bad news – a walk-away fault because it means the oil has rarely been changed. Look for dog damage to leather seats and trim. Scuff marks and trim damage from shooting trips. Alloy parts of body won't rot, but steel parts and chassis do, particularly at the back, and electrolyticly corrode where the steel and alloy meet. Check Boge rear suspension unit. Avoid cars with specialist, heavy duty tow bars (may have been pulling a 6–ton yacht or, worse still, a mobile hamburger stand). Try to buy town cars rather than country cars. May be reliable, but you can still expect niggling faults.

Recalls: 1998: (Jan '94–Mar '97 build): airbag may go off inadvertently.

Range Rover (1994 to 2002)

What's good: Undeniable road presence. Far less vague on the road than the old model. 225bhp 4.6HE is a powerful car. All are brilliant off the road, soak up the bumps and are the most comfortable way to travel cross-country. Slow 134bhp BMW six cylinder diesel comes into its own off road, but has been chipped for more power. Other engine is 190bhp 4.0 V8. Dimensions: 15ft 6in long by 6ft 2in wide and 2,090kg to 2,115kg.

Owners' online bulletin board: www.landrover.org/wwwboard/wwwboard.html

What's bad: Appalling catalogue of build problems. Water ingress into ECU will stop the car. BMW-powered diesel version is ridiculously slow on the road – especially in automatic form. 4.6HE drinks petrol, may be hit by future 'guzzler' taxes. 4.0 V8 a bit less juicy. 4.6HE loses value fast. Heavy duty prices of £53,000 for the 4.6 Vogue, £57,500 for the 30th Anniversary (30 years ago a Range Rover was £2,000) and £64,495 for the Holland & Holland (no shotguns included). S and T platers 19th from bottom in 2001 *Top Gear*/J.D. Power Customer Satisfaction Survey. In June 2001 Land Rover was rated by Motor Warranty Direct as Britain's 2nd worst out of 22 marques for warranty claims (check online at www.warrantydirect.co.uk) Complaints of collapsing rear air suspension on late examples. Reports both from *Telegraph* readers and from the trade of over-bored 4.6 V8 engines developing porous bore liners, costing from £1,800 (trade price) to £3,600 (punter price) to put right. Further reports of camshaft failures on 4.0 litre V8s. LandRover had joint highest average cost in warranty claims for cars up to 10 years old in 2002 Warranty Direct index

What to watch out for: Avoid the 4.6. Signs of severe usage. Tow hooks (what's it been towing?). Listen for transmission noise on manual versions. Make sure all gearbox functions work (manual and automatic). Look for oil leaks from axles, gearbox and transfer case. Look for dog damage to leather seats and trim. Scuff marks and trim damage from shooting trips. Check all electrics. Make sure wheels will come off as the alloy wheels have a habit of corroding to the hubs. If paying dealer prices, make sure it comes with a full service history. See 5/12/2000 Recall notice below. This has resulted in some cooling systems becoming over-pressurised resulting in total engine failure. Further problem on 4.6s of coolant loss through block porosity (see above), so check for lack of coolant.

Recalls: 1995 (VIN LP311035 to LP312917): ABS braking hose may fail. 1998 V8: cooling system hoses found to be failing. 2000: June '94–August '98 build: automatic gearbox fluid can seep out and spill onto hot exhaust creating fire risk. V8 models built June '98–Sept '99 may lose power steering. 5/12/2000: 15,767 Range Rover V8s recalled because of possibility of premature failure of cooling system hoses and throttle body heater gasket. Expelled coolant allowed to remain on hot engine components could result in the evaporation of the water content and leave an artificially high concentration level of anti-freeze which is both corrosive and inflammable. Affected vehicles to be recalled to replace cooling system hoses and throttle body heater gasket. TWO RECALLS 3/4/2001: Build 1/1/1998 to 31/12/2000, VINs XA410482 to 1A452817 and XA220000 to 1A299999: Recall 1 (automatics only): Water may migrate up gearbox breather pipe and corrode park lock mechanism leading it to fail to lock properly. Gearbox breather pipe to be re-routed and affected gearboxes to be repaired. Recall 2: High pressure hose of Active Cornering Enhancement system not fitted with anti vibration attenuator may fracture. Where attenuator not fitted, high pressure hoses to be replaced.

Range Rover (from 2002)

What's good: New Range Rover on sale from February 2002. Engines are a BMW 288bhp 4.4 litre V8 with 325lb ft (440Nm torque)or a BMW 184bhp 3.0 litre straight-six turbodiesel. The interior is both luxurious and stylishly modern with an architectural theme, unlike that of any of its competitors. Automatic only. Unlimited mileage 3-year warranty on all new Range Rovers sold by official UK dealers from official sale date of

15–3–2002. Much more competent off road than the BMW X5. Achieved an excellent four star rating for crash safety in 2002 NCAP tests but a very poor one for pedestrian safety.

More at dedicated website: www.rangerover.landrover.com

Owners' online bulletin board: www.landrover.org/wwwboard/wwwboard.html

What's bad: Massively overweight at 2,440kg. Now up against the BMW X5, Porsche Cayenne, Volvo XC90 and VW Touareg. s well as the Toyota LandCruiser Amazon.

What to watch out for: Too soon to say.

MARCOS

Mantis and Manta Ray

What's good: 352 bhp 4.6 litre Rover Buick V8 with hefty 330 lb ft torque gives 4.1–second 0–60 capability. Well developed, safe, precise handling. At £43,995 a very serious alternative to a TVR. New Manta Ray range with engines from 2.0 litres and prices from £32,500 launched at 1998 Motor Show. Taken over by Dutch firm Eurotech in June 2000.

What's bad: Basic shape was launched in 1964. Has a lie-down seating position, poor rearward visibility, only the pedal carrier adjusts, heavy but very tight gearchange gate.

What to watch out for: Second-hand needs an expert check.

MASERATI

3200GT (2000 to 2002)

What's good: Dubbed by *Autocar* magazine Best Maserati for 20 years it's also Maserati's best seller in the UK. 3,217cc twin turbo V8 puts out 370bhp at 6,000rpm and 352lb ft torque at 4,500rpm. Top speed 160mph for the four-speed auto; 175mph for the six-speed manual, and very comfortable even at these speeds. Has a wonderful engine note. 0–60 around six seconds. Praised for excellent brakes. Decent amount of room in the back for a couple of kids, or for two adults on a short journey. Manual priced at £60,575 on the road; automatic £62,950. Best to go for the manual. Auto puts out a very high 422 CO_2/km. 3200 Assetto Corso launched June 2001 has many detail improvements to chassis and brakes at £65,950 for the six-speed manual and £67,950 for the four-speed automatic.

What's bad: Criticised by press for firm ride and old fashioned 4-speed BTR autobox. Change quality of Getrag six-speed box varies from car to car.

What to watch out for: See Recalls. If this work hasn't been done, it will be very expensive.

Recalls: 20/10/2001: 374 cars built 1999 to 2000 recalled because brake fluid reservoir supply hoses may contaminate the fluid causing degradation of various seals, leading to leakage of fluid and loss of braking efficiency. Reservoir supply hoses, brake master cylinder, ABS/ABR hydraulic control unit all to be replaced.

4200 GT Coupe (from May 2002)

What's good: Replacement for 3200GT from May 2002. 390bhp 4,244cc non-turbo V8. Prices are £59,950 for the six-speed manual GT and £62,950 for the paddle-shift Cambiocorsa. Optional 'Skyhook' electronic suspension control highly recommended at an extra £990 and most British drivers will probably also opt for the extra cost spare wheel at £420. With a top speed of 285kph

(177mph), the 4.2 Coupe also offers a 0–60 of 4.5 seconds, a standing 400metres in 13 seconds and a standing kilometre in 23.5 seconds. Gear speeds are: 1st: 45mph; 2nd: 69mph; 3rd: 92mph; 4th: 117mph; 5th: 144mph; 6th: 177mph. Alarmingly, reverse is good for 58mph. Ferrari motoring for half the price. Even less online from www.trade-sales.co.uk which was offering them for £49,999 in June 2002.

More online at www.maserati.co.uk

What's bad: Hard to find comfortable seating position. Jumps about a bit at speed. Manual gearchange of rear-mounted box not as good as old front mounted Getrag.

What to watch out for: Too soon to say.

Spyder 4.2 (from 2002)

What's good: Shorter, two-seater spyder version of 3200GT with new non-turbo 4,244cc V8 engine putting out 390bhp at 7,000rpm and 333lb ft torque at 5,500rpm. Length 4,303mm, width 1,822mm, height 1,3055mm, fuel tank capacity 88 litres. Six speed manual transmission or six speed electric clutch 'Cambiocorsa' box with steering wheel paddle controls. Zero to sixty in 4.8 seconds. Tops out at 170mph. On sale in UK from April 2002 at £65,750 for the manual and £68,750 for the Cambiocorsa. Top speed of 176 mph and a zero to 60 mph 4.9 seconds. Styled by Giorgetto Giugiaro. The Cambiocorsa transmission has four specific modes: Normal, Sport, Auto and Low Grip. These modes are linked to the electronic traction control system and, where fitted, the variable 'Skyhook' suspension setting option. This allows the driver to select the optimum combination of transmission, suspension and traction settings to match conditions and driving requirements. Standard equipment includes 18–inch 15–spoke alloy wheels, electronic traction control, a powerful Bosch 5.3 anti-lock braking system and a fully automatic powered hood in lightweight fabric, which folds into a separate compartment with no intrusion on boot space. Inside, the Spyder has a full leather interior, air conditioning, remote central locking, powered seats with two memory settings on the driver's side, power lumbar seat adjustment and an electronic 'info centre' with a 5.8–inch colour display for climate, audio and trip computer controls.

More online at www.maserati.co.uk

What's bad: Fuel consumption heavy at 9.9mpg around town and 15.2mpg combined, but can manage 22mpg cruising. High CO_2 output of 430g/km likely to be penalised in the future. Has been criticised for some degree of scuttle shake. Only a two seater.

What to watch out for: Too soon to say.

Recalls: May 2002: recall on LHD Spyders only to sort PAS problem which could cause an engine compartment fire (UK RHDs not affected).

MAYBACH

Maybach Type 12 (from late 2002)

What's good: Revival of the old Maybach name embodied in the ultimate luxurious limousine costing upwards of £230,000 and on sale in Europe from October 2002. The new car has a relatively modest capacity V12 engine of 5,513cc, but with twin spark ignition and twin turbochargers it develops a staggering 405kW (550bhp) at 5,250 rpm and a mammoth 900Nm (664 lb ft) torque at 2,300rpm. The standard £230,000 Maybach 57 is 5,720mm long (18 ft 9 ins) and the £268,000 long wheel-base 62 is 6,160mm (20 ft 3 ins). The rear seats of the LWB recline fully into individual aircraft-style beds and rear passengers are cosseted with every luxury including television with a DVD player and Dolby 'surround sound'. Cars can be customised to individual wishes via a personal customer liaison officer. £50,000 deposits taken in Spring 2002 for UK delivery of RHDs in Spring 2003.

More online at www.mercedes-benz.co.uk

What's bad: If you have to ask the price you can't afford it. For long distance travel an aircraft or helicopter usually makes more sense.

What to watch out for: Tight corners.

MAZDA

121 (1988 to 1991)

What's good: Short (11ft 5in), tall and light at 725kg. 1,138cc 56bhp engine with 5-speed gearbox, or 1,324cc 65bhp with 5-speeds. Optional full length electric sunroof cheered it up. All were pre-cat. Lived on as the Kia Pride.

What's bad: Old now. Even though it's a Mazda, it looks like a Kia Pride. Front suspension bushes wear. Carburettor engine can give trouble.

What to watch out for: Treat only as a cheap, fairly reliable buy. Almost all were scrapped in Japan years ago.

121 (1991 to 1995)

What's good: Cute oddball with amazing headroom and fun looks. 12ft 6in long by 5ft 5in wide and weighing 861kg. Later model specification (from April 1993) of manual gearbox, power steering and full-length sun roof by far the best. 1,324cc 74 bhp engine identical to stronger-selling 323. Sold well in Holland where Mazda was seen as an interesting brand with popular quirky advertising. May have scarcity value in years to come. Mazda had lowest average cost in warranty claims for cars up to 10 years old in 2002 Warranty Direct index, check online at www.performanceindex.co.uk

What's bad: Derided by motoring press and simply failed to sell in the UK. Feb 1991 to April '93 UK models had silly spec of 4-speed automatic gearbox, but no power steering and no sun roof. So few UK sales that body spares situation is not promising in years to come.

What to watch out for: You have to ask yourself what sort of person would buy one. Look for eccentric modifications and evidence of bad driving, such as kerbing. Make sure the electric sunroof works properly and has no tears.

121 (from 1996)

What's good: 3 year warranty, otherwise see Fiesta. 1.3 pushrod, 1.8 diesel or 1.25 16v Zetec S engine. Mazda had lowest average cost and Ford third lowest average cost in warranty claims for cars up to 10 years old in 2002 Warranty Direct index, check online at www.performanceindex.co.uk

What's bad: Really a Fiesta, built at Dagenham. More popular in Holland than in the UK due to Mazda's excellent advertising there. Most seem to have had the old 1.3 pushrod engine.

What to watch out for: See Fiesta

Recalls: 1996 (1996 model year): Check for faulty piston seal in hydraulic clutch master cylinder. Check for contamination of brake fluid and incorrect front brake hose routing. 1997 (5–door models built Dec '95–May '96): may have faulty rear door latches. 1998 (Dec '95–Jun '96 Build): possibility of brake failure due to front brake pipe chafing on bracket. Modified pipe and bracket to be fitted to both front brakes.

2 (from late 2002 or early 2003)

What's good: Based on new Fiesta but with new 1.5 Mazda engine as well as PSA 1.4 common rail direct injected diesel.

What's bad: Too soon to say.

What to watch out for: Too soon to say.

3 (from 2003)

What's good: New mid-size Mazda to replace 323 on same floorpan as next Focus.

What's bad: Too soon to say.

What to watch out for: Too soon to say.

323 (1989 to 1991)

What's good: Beautifully built and attractive. Low-roofed 5–door F-Type hatchback more of a 5–door coupe. 14ft long by 5ft 6in wide. Neat 4–door saloon 13ft 9in by 5ft 5in tends to appeal more to the elderly. All under 1,000kg. Sweet engines, all 16-valve. (1,324cc 75 bhp carb; 1,598cc 87 bhp carb; 1,840cc 140 bhp twin-cam injection.) Sensationally reliable. Typically Japanese slick gearchanges. Automatic choke problems of pre-October 1989 323s was solved for this model. SE Exec models very well equipped. I owned one for 6 months and still saw a profit.

What's bad: Immensely complicated model range of 3–door hatchbacks, 5–door hatchbacks, 4–door saloons and 5–door estates. Handling and roadholding not quite to UK tastes. Very light power steering. Not immune to snapped timing belts. Excellent factory paint finish can be hard to match. Average ventilation on saloon is poor on F-Type hatchback, which is prone to misting up. Not much room in the back seat of F-Types.

What to watch out for: Make sure car has been regularly serviced, at least every 6,000 miles. Damaged trim is expensive to replace. Make sure all the electrics work. F-Types may have suffered parking damage due to poor rearward visibility.

323 (1991 to 1994)

What's good: All got fuel injection, as from May 1991, same bodies as before. general good points as 1989 to 1991. F Type was a sort of four-door hatchback coupe. Mazda had lowest average cost in warranty claims for cars up to 10 years old in 2002 Warranty Direct index, check online at www.performanceindex.co.uk

What's bad: All got catalytic converters. Power outputs now 74 bhp from 1.3, 89 bhp from 1.6, but just 129 bhp from 1.8. General bad points, as 1989 to 1991, but no carburettor worries.

What to watch out for: Make sure car has been regularly serviced, at least every 6,000 miles. Damaged trim is expensive to replace. Make sure all the electrics work. F-Types may have suffered parking damage due to poor rearward visibility.

323 (1994 to 1995)

What's good: Re-styled range introduced in August 1994. F-type 5–door hatchback became even more coupe-like. 13ft 11in by 5ft

7in and now from 1,115kg. Unusual, but attractive. New 1,489cc 89 bhp engine replaced 1.6. 146 bhp V6 from Xedos 6 introduced to top of the range 323F models. V6 very good looking on its bigger wheels. Service miles extended to 9,000, but still better to stick to 6,000. Mazda had lowest average cost in warranty claims for cars up to 10 years old in 2002 Warranty Direct index, check online at www.performanceindex.co.uk

What's bad: An odd period for the 323 with only a handful of a new 3–door hatchbacks and very pretty 4–door saloons imported and no estates. Power output of 1.8 dropped to 115 bhp.

What to watch out for: Make sure car has been regularly serviced. Damaged trim is expensive to replace. Make sure all the electrics work. Uneven tyre wear may be evidence of kerbing. Paint is hard to match and a giveaway of accident damage. Make sure the central locking works on all the doors. If you buy a 'glassback' 3–door or the pretty 4–door, be aware that body panels will probably have to come from Mazda's HQ in Brussels, and any RHD bits from Japan. Check complex quad cam 24v V6 carefully. Smoke could mean any one of 24 valve stem seals. Timing belt failure means disaster and replacing the belt is expensive. Recent reports of aircon compressor failures (look for seeming seals) and ABS failures, so make sure the ABS light comes on then goes out.

323 (1995 to 1998)

What's good: Range shrunk to just one body, the 323F, until 1997, when a new 1.3 hatchback and a new 1.5 saloon both appeared. Some of 3-year warranty may remain. 20th from top in 'R' reg. J.D. Power Customer Satisfaction Survey. Mazda was rated by Motor Warranty Direct as Britain's most claim-free marque (check online at www.warrantydirect.co.uk) 12th from top of 100 models for reliability in *Auto Express* 2002 survey. Mazda had lowest average cost in warranty claims for cars up to 10 years old in 2002 Warranty Direct index, check online at www.performanceindex.co.uk

What's bad: 3–door hatchback and pretty 4–door saloon disappeared from range from 1995–1997. New model range arrived late 1998/early 1999. 'F' model name dropped, but concept of the car remained similar.

What to watch out for: As above. Some 1995 cars suffered from a faulty batch of clutches. Check complex quad cam 24v V6 carefully. Smoke could mean any one of 24 valve stem seals. Timing belt failure means disaster and replacing the belt is expensive.

Recalls: 1997: 'Mystique' special edition based on 323F 1.5LXi may have loose wheel nuts on spare wheel.

323 (October 1998 to 2003)

What's good: Back to just one body, but a new five-door hatchback b, bigger inside. 13ft 9in by 5ft 7in and weighing from 1,072kg. Initially a bit bland, still with low roofline. Looks improved enormously by dropped suspension and a range of smart alloy wheels. Flat cornering from 'Diagonal Roll Axis' suspension. Clever interior touches such as a front passenger seat that folds to become a table, and split, fully folding back seats. Engines: 1,324cc 75 bhp/80 lb ft torque; 1,498cc 87 bhp/97lb ft torque; 1,840cc 114/118 lb ft torque. Range topping Sport introduced Spring 1999 at £16,320. 1,998cc diesel develops 99bhp at 4,000rpm and 162 lb ft torque at 1,800rpm. Combined economy 55.4mpg and CO_2 149g/km which qualifies for £110pa VED. Mazda was rated by Motor Warranty Direct as Britain's most claim-free marque (check online at www.warrantydirect.co.uk) 12th from top of 100 models for reliability in *Auto Express* 2002 survey. Mazda had lowest average cost in warranty claims for cars up to 10 years old in 2002 Warranty Direct index, check online at www.performanceindex.co.uk

What's bad: Needs alloy wheels to look good.

What to watch out for: No problems reported apart from one recall, below.

Recalls: 19,799 323s and Premacys built to 30/6/2001 recalled because rivets securing fuel tank heatshield may corrode and break leaving the heatshield to rattle.

6 (from Spring 2002)

What's good: Launched at the 2001 Tokyo Motor Show, this is Mazda's Hofu built replacement for the 626. At 4,745mm long (15ft 7ins) it's a long car up against the Mondeo and Vectra. Big boots also feature at 500 litres for the saloon and 490 for the hatchback. The new car it has 'control blade' independent rear suspension similar to the Ford Focus. Driving and handling thought to be best in class. Also enjoys some new engine technology. Follow-over engines include Mazda's 118bhp 1.8 litre and 139bhp 2.0 litre units. The new petrol engine is a 2.3 litre chain-cam balancer-shaft four which develops 164bhp. Plus a pair of new 2.0 litre direct-injected diesels which pump out 118 or 134bhp and a serious 220lb ft (298Nm) torque at 2,000rpm. New crash safety engineering channels front rear and side impact forces into three H-shaped sections of body structure which Mazda engineers have dubbed 'Triple-H'. Dual-stage front airbags and side curtain bags also feature. Hatchbacks, four door saloons and estate bodies all available in UK from Summer 2002 will all be available. Very price competitive, starting at £13,495 for 118bhp 1.8, £14,995 for 2.0 and £17,995 for 2.3. 2.3 does 133mph,with 8.6 second 0–60, 33mpg combined and 212g/km CO_2. Low prices and excellent reputation for reliability mean strong residual values are predicted. Bolt-on front panels make it easy to repair. Insurance groups: 1.8: 7E; 2.0: 9E; 2.3: 13E. Sport Wagon estate and 121ps common rail diesel from September 2002. Sport Wagons start at £15,595 for 121ps 2.0 petrol; diesels start at £14,595. Expect to see a lot more of the Mazda 6 than you did of the previous 626.

More online at www.mazda.co.uk

What's bad: Too soon to say, but on Japanese market for 6 months before it reached UK so should be no teething troubles.

What to watch out for: Too soon to say.

626 (1987 to 1991)

What's good: Long, slim looking saloons, 5–door hatchbacks and two door coupes 14ft 10in by 5ft 7in including mirrors and weighing from 1,090kg. Engine choice included 90bhp 1.8 carb,

108bhp 2.0 carb and strong 146bhp 2.0 Gate injected. Gate could be had a four wheel steer. Also, from 1990 to 1991, a 2.2 litre 114bhp GLX four wheel drive. Seem to last quite well and can remain reasonably rust-free.

What's bad: Carburettor engines get to be troublesome and four wheel steer can be a nightmare to track properly. Spares starting to be difficult to obtain.

What to watch out for: Rust, rough running (carb problem), uneven tyre wear of four wheel steer. Beware of short MOTs and broken light lenses because it can be a long haul to find second-hand parts. Don't pay more than banger money.

626 (1992 to 1997)

What's good: Nicely styled 5–door, with amazing built-in rear boot spoiler. 15ft 5in long by 5ft 9in wide and weighing from 1,150kg. Briefly available as 'GT' (Feb '92–Dec '94) with full-on 165 bhp 2.5 litre V-6 from MX6, but not many were imported. Normal engines were an 1,840cc four with 105bhp, a 1,991cc four with 115bhp; 1,991cc four with 138bhp; or a 1,998cc 75bhp Comprex supercharged diesel. Mazda was rated by Motor Warranty Direct as Britain's most claim-free marque (check online at www.warrantydirect.co.uk) Mazda had lowest average cost in warranty claims for cars up to 10 years old in 2002 Warranty Direct index, check online at www.performanceindex.co.uk

What's bad: 4–door less inspiring, but still well liked. Comprex supercharged 2.0 litre diesel not a success – only lasted from May '94 to Oct '95. Body damage extremely difficult to repair, particularly to rear of 5–door hatchback. Paint quality virtually impossible to match. No estate cars except carryovers with older body.

What to watch out for: Repaired accident damage. Uneven tyre wear from kerbed suspension. Check complex quad cam 24v V6 of GT carefully. Smoke could mean any one of 24 valve stem seals. Timing belt failure means disaster and replacing the belt is expensive.

Recalls: 1997: 'Mystique' special edition based on 626 1.8LXi may have loose wheel nuts on spare wheel.

626 (1997 to 1999)

What's good: Same Mazda qualities of good build, excellent reliability, superb paint finish. Now shorter at 15ft long by 5ft 7in wide and slightly heavier at from 1,216kg. Useful engine range of 89 bhp 1.8, 113 bhp 2.0 litre and 134 bhp 2.0 litre GSi. Aircon standard throughout. Three three-point rear seatbelts. Estate car back in range. 19th from top in 'R' reg. J.D. Power Customer Satisfaction Survey. S and T reg. cars came 13th from top in 2001 *Top Gear*/JD Power Customer Satisfaction Survey. Mazda was rated by Motor Warranty Direct as Britain's most claim-free used marque (check online at www.warrantydirect.co.uk) 2nd top for reliability in *Auto Express* 2002 survey. 11th from Top in 144 car 2002 JD Power/*What Car?* Customer Satisfaction Survey of V and W reg. cars. Mazda had lowest average cost in warranty claims for cars up to 10 years old in 2002 Warranty Direct index, check online at www.performanceindex.co.uk

What's bad: Very 'ordinary'-looking 5–door hatchbacks and 4–door saloons.

What to watch out for: Make sure has full Mazda service history or warranty could be void. See Recalls, particularly timing belt tensioner recall.

Recalls: 1998 (Nov '96–May '97 build): Possibility of timing belt failure leading to total loss of engine power and power assistance to steering and brakes; 626 diesel (to May '98 build): Faulty fuel injector may stall engine. July 2000: further recall of 5,431 petrol-engined 626s built May '97–November '97 to inspect the spring of the timing belt tensioner. Inspection/replacement takes 1.6 hours. Helpline: 0800 387942. 1/8/2000: 5,431 626 models built 5/97 to 11/97 recalled because spring in timing belt tensioner may fail leading engine to suddenly lose power. Timing belt tensioners to be replaced. 5/3/2001: 648 diesel engined 626s built 1/5/1998 to 31/8/1999 recalled because camshaft drive belt may break and cause engine to stop suddenly. Timing belts to be replaced.

626 (2000 to 2002)

What's good: New-look 626 with corporate pentagonal grille. Engines: 100 bhp 1.8 and 122 bhp 2.0 litre petrol, plus 2.0 litre direct injected diesel. Diesel develops 99bhp at 4,000rpm and 162lb ft torque at 1,800 rpm. Combined fuel consumption 54.3mpg and CO_2 output 152g/km. ABS and a/c standard. Very reliable. 3-year warranty. Mazda was rated by Motor Warranty Direct as Britain's most claim-free used marque (check online at www. warrantydirect.co.uk) 2nd top for reliability in *Auto Express* 2002 survey. 11th from Top in 144 car 2002 JD Power/*What Car?* Customer Satisfaction Survey of V and W reg. cars.

What's bad: Nice enough looking, but you hardly ever see any.

What to watch out for: Nothing reported.

Demio (from 1998)

What's good: Neat and versatile small boxy estate, with sliding, folding and reclining rear seats that can be turned into a bed. 12ft 6in by 5ft 6in and weighing 950kg. 72 bhp 1,324 cc engine. 3-year warranty. A bit more substantial than the Move/Wagon R/ATOZ/Matiz brigade, initially with mini front bull bar. Five carbon dioxide absorbing trees were planted for every car sold to achieve first year "carbon neutrality". Facelift launched at Y2K Geneva Motor Show with much improved handling, from a reasonable £9,000 in UK (a £1,500 price cut) and option of 1.5 litre 75 bhp automatic. New version quite nimble and nice to drive. Mazda was rated by Motor Warranty Direct as Britain's most claim-free used marque (check online at www.warrantydirect.co.uk) Mazda had lowest average cost in warranty claims for cars up to 10 years old in 2002 Warranty Direct index, check online at www.performanceindex.co.uk

What's bad: Criticised for lack of things like internally adjustable door mirrors. Original version slow and stodgy to drive. Also consider the bigger £9,995 Colt Space Star.

What to watch out for: Secondhand 'school run' damage.

MPV (from 2000)

What's good: Third of Mazda's family of MPVs, but this one has 7 seats and is 626–based. 15ft 7in long by 6ft wide and weighing

1,631kg. Separately controllable front and rear aircon, twin sliding side doors, comfortable, well-equipped with good luggage space behind the third row. 1,991cc engine with 121 bhp and 129 lb ft torque, plus 5-speed gearbox. Pedigree comes from ten years of Japanese/American Mazda MPVs. UK launch at 1999 London Motor Show. Price cut from £19,800 to £16,995. Mazda was rated by Motor Warranty Direct as Britain's most claim-free used marque (check online at www.warrantydirect.co.uk) Power hike in June 2002 when new 2.3 litre 134bhp replaced old 2.0 litre at price of £18,495, also joined by 2.0 litre 134bhp common rail diesel at £19,995. Mazda had lowest average cost in warranty claims for cars up to 10 years old in 2002 Warranty Direct index, check online at www.performanceindex.co.uk

What's bad: No auto option. Didn't sell at original price: only 72 were sold in UK in 2001.

What to watch out for: Too soon to say.

MX3 (1991 to 1998)

What's good: Very sweet 1,846cc 134 bhp 24v V6. Electric roof. Oddball but inoffensive styling. Mazda was rated by Motor Warranty Direct as Britain's most claim-free used marque (check online at www.warrantydirect.co.uk) Mazda had lowest average cost in warranty claims for cars up to 10 years old in 2002 Warranty Direct index, check online at www.performanceindex.co.uk

What's bad: 1,598cc 88 bhp automatic much less impressive. Back seat strictly for small children. Power of V6 dropped to 128 bhp in August 1994. Complexity of quad cam 24v V6 makes it expensive to service once the miles and age pile on.

What to watch out for: Don't buy at the 80,000–mile mark unless it has had a timing belt change. Look for a proper Mazda history. Don't pay a 'coupe premium' price without it. Check if it's a personal import with a Eunos badge and, if so, pay less. If a V6, check the engine very carefully, especially timing belt replacement. If a V6 is smoking the reason could be any one of 24 valve stem seals.

Recalls: 1994: MX3 1.6 & 1.8 (build March '92–Aug '94: VIN JMZ

EC13** 00100001–00113020): front suspension coil may fail and puncture tyre. 25/4/2000: front springs of 108 cars built May/June 1995 may rust and fail. Springs to be replaced.

MX5 (1989 to 1998)

What's good: Sweet, neat, 'back to basics' sportscar. The best small, affordable sports car ever made. Twin-cam 16-valve 114bhp 1.6 and 130bhp 1.8 engines. 1.6ft s uncatted at first and rare 150bhp 1.6 BBR Turbo. 5-speed gearboxes. (Autos only on independently imported Eunos Roadsters and Miatas. Nice 'works' hard-top. Hood opens with one hand from driver's seat. Mazda was rated by Motor Warranty Direct as Britain's most claim-free used marque (check online at www.warrantydirect.co.uk)8th from top for reliability in *Auto Express* 2002 survey. 17th equal from Top in 144 car 2002 JD Power/*What Car?* Customer Satisfaction Survey of V and W reg. cars. Mazda had lowest average cost in warranty claims for cars up to 10 years old in 2002 Warranty Direct index, check online at www.performanceindex.co.uk

What's bad: Cheaper to build than a 323 but sells for a lot more money. Lots of dodgy second-hand Eunos Roadster imports about. Catalysed 1.6i engine from April 1995 not powerful enough (just 88 bhp, as against 114 bhp for previous 1.6, 130 bhp for 1.8 and 150 bhp for 1.6 BBR Turbo): PAS not always fitted (enthusiasts prefer non PAS; girl drivers won't buy without it). All Mk 1s had plastic rear windows.

What to watch out for: Uncertificated Eunos Roadsters imported by traders after May 1998 could not legally be registered, so any Eunos Roadster might be a 'clone'. MX5s are sports cars, so could have been thrashed. Fashion accessory MX5s may not have been serviced properly. SVA 'kits' available to get imports through SVA, but non-SVA Japanese parts may then be put back. Check speed ratings on tyres (Japan has a 55 mph limit.) Series 1 headlight motors go. Uneven tyre wear probably signifies accident damage. Ageing MX5s can rust in the sills. Jap market Eunos Roadsters were not rustproofed from new.

Recalls: 7/12/2000: 135 Jasper Conran Limited Edition MX5s recalled because driver's floormat my interfere with throttle pedal causing throttle to stick open. Mat to be replaced with modified mat.

MX5 (from 1998)

What's good: Revised in spring 1998 with heated glass rear window, fixed headlights, bigger boot that now takes two bags of golf clubs. 1.8 recommended. Further facelift in UK spring 2001. The best-selling sportscar ever built. Power upped and prices dropped for 2002 model year. 110bhp 1.6 stays at £14,995 (undercutting the quicker MGF 1.6 by £500), gets to sixty in 9.5 seconds and does 120mph. Combined fuel consumption is 34.9mpg. 1.8s all get a power boost to 146bhp at 7,000rpm and a torque hike to 124lb ft (168Nm) at 5,000rpm. The base five speeder costs £15,495 (same as the MGF 1.6), gets to sixty in 8.2 seconds and goes on to 127mph. Combined fuel consumption is 32.5mpg. With a six-speed gearbox, 16 inch alloy wheels and 205/45R16 tyres, the £17,495 1.8 Sport now gets to sixty in 8.1 seconds and goes on to 130mph. Combined fuel consumption is 31.7mpg. And to complete the range you can now get a UK official automatic MX5 1.8. Performance is severely compromised, though, with a zero to sixty of 10.7 seconds and a top speed of 118mph. Price is £16,495 and combined consumption 29.8mpg. 8th from top for reliability in *Auto Express* 2002 survey. 17th equal from Top in 144 car 2002 JD Power/*What Car?* Customer Satisfaction Survey of V and W reg. cars. Even in 2002, the 6-speed 1.8 Sport is still the definitive small, reliable, sportscar. Mazda was rated by Motor Warranty Direct as Britain's most claim-free used marque (check online at www.warrantydirect.co.uk)Achieved a good 74% four star rating for crash safety in 2002 NCAP tests. Mazda had lowest average cost in warranty claims for cars up to 10 years old in 2002 Warranty Direct index, check online at www.performanceindex.co.uk

More online at www.mazda.co.uk

What's bad: Still a good drive, but not as comfortable as an MGTF and less fun to chuck around than an MGTF or an MR2.

What to watch out for: Uncertificated Eunos Roadsters imported by traders after May 1998 could not legally be registered, so any Eunos Roadster might be a 'clone'. MX5s are sports cars, so could have been thrashed. Fashion accessory MX5s may not have been serviced properly. SVA 'kits' available to get imports through SVA, but non-SVA Japanese parts may then be put back. Check speed ratings on tyres (Japan has a 55 mph limit.)

Recalls: 7/12/2000: 135 Jasper Conran Limited Edition MX5s recalled because driver's floormat my interfere with throttle pedal causing throttle to stick open. Mat to be replaced with modified mat.

MX6 (1992 to 1998)

What's good: Interesting looks. Lovely 2.5 litre 24v 165 bhp V6. Decent American build quality. Automatic and aircon optional. Mazda was rated by Motor Warranty Direct as Britain's most claim-free used marque (check online at www.warrantydirect.co.uk). Online self-help group: www.mx6.com

What's bad: Looks not universally liked (looks a bit like an old Opel Manta). Chassis not nearly as good as engine and gearbox. 2.0 litre Xedos 6 V6 fitted in some European markets and a 2.0 V6s has been found under the bonnet of at least one RHD MX6. Needs a timing belt and tensioner change at least every 60,000 miles.

What to watch out for: All that glass means it gets hot in summer, so aircon highly desirable. Check tyres for uneven wear – may be maladjustment or may signify suspension damage. Check complex quad cam 24v V6 carefully. Smoke could mean any one of 24 valve stem seals. Timing belt failure can mean disaster and replacing the belt is a 3 hour job. Check which engine the car has because some RHD imports have 2.0 litre Xedos 6 engine.

Premacy (from 2000)

What's good: Mini MPV based on mix of 323 and 626 components from the same mould as the Colt Space Star. 14ft 1in long by 5ft 7in wide and from 1,330kg. Good to drive, practical and versatile. Scenic-like, separately reclinable, foldable and removable rear seats.

Front passenger seat folds to form a table or support for long loads. 99 bhp and 113 bhp 1.8 litre petrol or 89 bhp 2.0 litre turbodiesel. A/c standard on all and electronic brake force distribution, which can be much needed on a short boxy car braking heavily. Starting price cut to £12,900 in spring 2000. 1.8 and diesel supplemented by 130bhp 2.0 litre with 171Nm torque from November 2001. Prices of 2.0 litre from £14,495 for GSi to £15,495 for Sport. GSi also available with 4-speed autobox at £15,495. Mazda was rated by Motor Warranty Direct as Britain's most claim-free used marque (check online at www.warrantydirect.co.uk) Mazda had lowest average cost in warranty claims for cars up to 10 years old in 2002 Warranty Direct index, check online at www.performanceindex.co.uk Massively more reliable than a Renault Megane Scenic.

What's bad: Average three star NCAP crash safety rating announced 28/3/2001, but very good three stars for pedestrian safety. Nothing else so far.

What to watch out for: Nothing so far.

Recalls: 19,799 323s and Premacys built to 30/6/2001 recalled because rivets securing fuel tank heatshield may corrode and break leaving the heatshield to rattle.

RX7 (1989 to 1992)

What's good: Attractive Porsche 944 lookalike with 200 bhp turbocharged rotary engine. Good looking cabriolet with well fitting power top.

What's bad: Needs specialist maintenance.

What to watch out for: Engine must idle smoothly (rough idle sure sign of rotor tip wear). Make sure no smoke. Uneven tyre wear signifies accident damage. Must see a record of specialist maintenance even if not all done by Mazda dealers.

RX7 Twin-Turbo (1992 to 2002)

What's good: Sensational looking retro minimalist classic. Searing 'junior supercar' performance from 237 bhp engine. 0–60 in six seconds and 160mph top speed. Quick steering. In the same league as a Porsche 911 C2 or a Porsche 968 of the same age. Better looking than either. Can be uprated to 280 bhp. UK imports revived in late 2001 by Mazda dealer TW White. Last imported RX7s have 265bhp and vestigial rear seats. The price is £29,950. More online from www.twwhiteandsons.co.uk Mazda had lowest average cost in warranty claims for cars up to 10 years old in 2002 Warranty Direct index, check online at www.performanceindex.co.uk

What's bad: Power had to be restricted to get through EU emissions laws. Not enough 'feel' in the quick steering. Heavy fuel consumption. Originally, UK spec strictly a two-seater and back seats in TW White imports are tiny. Needs expert specialist maintenance.

What to watch out for: Evidence of proper, regular specialist maintenance, with regular changes of all fluids. Worth having an MOT cat test done even if not due, to check for excess hydrocarbons which could mean that the rotor seals are wearing out. Don't buy without getting the car properly checked by an expert in the model, even if the inspection costs you £250. There are a few dodgy grey imports about that won't pass a proper UK MOT emissions test. (Rear seats mean it's definitely an import.) If buying a used grey imported RX7, check it out online at www.bimta.com

RX8 (from 2003)

What's good: Four seater 250bhp rotary engined coupé to go into production. Has a similar transmission tunnel backbone design to the previous RX7 twin turbo. It remains rear wheel drive. And with its very small engine set slightly lower and further back it has perfect 50:50 weight distribution. New RENESIS rotary engine develops 250bhp at 8,500rmp and 162 lb ft (220Nm) torque at a similarly high 7,500rpm. Apparently to be priced from £26,000.

More online at www.mazda.co.uk

What's bad: It's been a long time coming.

What to watch out for: Too soon to say.

Tribute SUV (from 2001)

What's good: New 'Sports Utility Vehicle' from Mazda/Ford with choice of 3.0 litre V6 or 2.0 litre four. Five-door, double opening tailgate with hinged window, 50/40 split folding rear seat, standard ABS, four wheel drive on demand and a three year 60,000 mile warranty. On sale in UK early 2001. The same vehicle as the new Ford Maverick.

What's bad: Did badly in American IIHS and NCAP crash tests. Airbag failed to inflate in American test. Not as good looking as Maverick II.

What to watch out for: Too soon to say.

Xedos 6 (1992 to 1998)

What's good: Beautiful looking car. Really stunning. Could have been the prototype for a new small Jaguar – with Mazda reliability. 15ft 3in long by 5ft 7in wide and from 1,142kg. Sensationally smooth, free-revving 146bhp 2.0 litre quad cam 24-valve engine (which powered Ford's Mondeo Touring Cars). Mirror-like thick lacquer over paint has to be baked on while the car is rotating on a rotisserie. Suspension and handling much improved from 'N' reg. on. Mazda was rated by Motor Warranty Direct as Britain's most claim-free used marque (check online at www.warrantydirect.co.uk) Mazda had lowest average cost in warranty claims for cars up to 10 years old in 2002 Warranty Direct index, check online at www.performanceindex.co.uk

What's bad: Early suspension not up to the engine or the sporty looks. Really just a 626 with strut braces. Difficult to feel what's going on through the steering. Very hard to match the original paint quality, particularly metallics, so don't think a £300 bonnet respray will work. MX5–engined 114bhp 1.6 four is underpowered.

What to watch out for: Early UK SEs did not have aircon, just an aircon button with a sticker over it, so make sure aircon blows cold. (Aircon standard on SE from 'N' reg. on.) Look for clean oil on the dipstick and evidence it has been changed regularly. Any mayonnaise under the oil cap, leave the car alone. First jobs: change coolant and brake fluid. Check for uneven tyre wear. Check complex quad cam 24v V6 carefully. Smoke could mean any one of 24 valve stem seals. Timing belt failure means disaster and replacing the belt is expensive.

Recalls: 1994 (VIN JMZ CA1***01100001–01119137): engine may stop without warning. 1997 (built March '92 to Aug '94): suspension coil may break and puncture tyre.

Xedos 9 (1994 to 1999)

What's good: Bigger Xedos 6 with MX6/626GT 168 bhp V6 engine. 15ft 10in long by 5ft 7in wide and from 1,546kg. Loaded with kit. Aircon, sunroof, ABS, 4-speed autobox all standard. Leather and walnut trim standard from June 1996. Tasty new alloy wheels and lowered suspension from 1997 transform the car and make it an eye-catcher. Brought huge handling and roadholding benefits. Supercharged 208 bhp Miller Cycle 2.3 litre V6 from 1999 makes it an even better car offering surprising 35 mpg economy potential. Mazda was rated by Motor Warranty Direct as Britain's most claim-free used marque (check online at www.warrantydirect.co.uk) Mazda had lowest average cost in warranty claims for cars up to 10 years old in 2002 Warranty Direct index, check online at www.performanceindex.co.uk

What's bad: Not the same stunning looker as the Xedos 6 – until it got those new alloys in 1997.

What to watch out for: Make sure has full Mazda service history so warranty is still valid. 97 model onward the one to go for second-hand. Be very wary of uneven tyre wear. Check complex quad cam 24v V6 carefully. Smoke could mean any one of 24 valve stem seals. Timing belt failure means disaster and replacing the belt is expensive.

MCC

Smart (from 1998)

What's good: Handy 8ft 1in long by 5ft wide and weighing from 720kg. Quite powerful 599cc 44bhp to 54bhp petrol engines coupled to six-speed sequential autoboxes. Much faster than other microcars. And, of course, has city style which other micros lack. Euro Type-Approved. 799cc CDI diesel from autumn 1999 has 41 bhp, 74lb ft, does 85 mph and 85 mpg – and, at 90 g/km, has ultra-low carbon dioxide output. Convertible version from early spring 2000. Low chassis sports roadster on the way. Four seater planned. Also mean-looking 70 bhp Brabus version for under £10,000. Did well in German TUV/*Auto Bild* front offside crash test. Three-Star NCAP crash safety rating. Official imports by MBUK from October 2000, tel: 0800 037 9966. Official Smart Centres now at Chiswick (0870 2400 944); Piccadilly, London (0870 240 940); Brentford Service Centre (0870 2400 942); Milton Keynes (0870 2400 950); Birmingham (0870 2400 960); and Manchester (0870 2400 963). Summer 2001 facelift brought a power boost from 54bhp to 61bhp for the Smart & Pulse plus better front suspension. Official combined consumption 57.6mpg; CO_2 emissions 118g/km. RHD due early November 2001. RHD Prices: 44bhp Smart & Pure: £6,295; 61bhp Smart & Pulse: £7,295; 54bhp Smart & Passion: £7,995; 54bhp Smart & Passin City Cabriolet £9,995.

Daimler Chrysler showed a hybrid concept version of the MCC Smart at Frankfurt in September 2001. Dubbed the Smart Hyper (hybrid and performance) this combines a diesel engine with electric motor drive to offer extra economy and performance. Fuel consumption is less than 3 litres of diesel per 100 kilometres in the new European driving cycle (NEDC), which corresponds to CO_2 emissions of less than 80 g/km. The system allows spontaneous starting when the combustion engine is shut off (automatic start-stop system). The electric drive bridges the time needed for starting and torque build-up. As well as this, it compensates the traction interruption caused by the system during gear shifting. At low speeds it can drive the car on its own.

Like the Citroën Dynalto, driving performance also benefits from the electrical energy which is supplied to the drivetrain in addition to the engine power. The car accelerates from zero to 60mph in just 17.4 seconds, two seconds less than the Smart CDI.

More online at www.thesmart.co.uk

What's bad: Gearbox and accelerator can take some getting used to. LHD only up to eqrly 2002. Two seats only. Definitely doesn't handle like a hot hatch, though handling can be hugely improved by fitting wide wheels and tyres to the front. Official imports of City Cabrio disappointingly expensive at £9,360 on the road. No official imports of Smart CDI diesel yet scheduled.

What to watch out for: With first generation Smarts, take care on corners, or fit wider front wheels and tyres.

Recalls: May 2000: Official recall by Daimler Chrysler via DVLA records on all 602 MCC Smarts imported in 1998 and 1999 to uprate part of the stability control system software, to check the front axle ball joints for water ingress and corrosion and to check the throttle pedal module. Any replacements free of charge wherever the car was purchased.

Smart 5-door (from 2004)

What's good: 5–door version of Smart with conventional one piece hatchback seen cold weather testing in Sweden. Designed for LHD or RHD and due UK late 2004 at prices from around £8,500. 3,650mm long. New engines may include 1.0 and 1.4 litre four cylinder diesels and 1.3 and 1.5 litre direct injection petrol engines. May also be a Hyper-drive diesel/electric version. Will also form the basis of Mitsubishi's next Colt. Both to be built at Mitsubishi's Nedcar plant at Born in Holland.

What's bad: Too soon to say.

What to watch out for: Too soon to say.

Smart RHD (from October 2001)

What's good: RHD Smarts are priced from £6,295 to £9,995 on the road with a three year 25,000 mile warranty. £6,295 gets you the 44bhp Smart & Pure; £7,295 buys the 61bhp Smart & Pulse; £7,995 puts you into the 54bhp Smart & Passion, while £9,995 gets you behind the wheel of the 54bhp Smart City Cabrio. All come with 'Softip' semi-automatic sequential six-speed transmissions. Passion and City Cabrio versions also have a fully automatic pre-programmed 'Softouch' mode. Air-conditioning is standard on Passion and City Cabrio models, optional on the Pulse. Alloy wheels are a no cost option on Pulse, Passion and City Cabrio. Whichever version, combined fuel consumption is 57.6mpg using the 'Softip' semi-automatic and CO_2 emissions are 118g/km.

Length is 2,500mm (8ft 3ins); width is 1,593mm (5ft 3ins); height is 1,549mm (5ft 1inch); and kerb weight is 720kg. With front suspension improvements further refined, Handling is much better than the original LHD Smarts. UK petrol engined Smarts emit 118g/km CO_2, so qualify for £70pa VED from April 2002. Latest big improvement from June 2002 is the £300 option of steering wheel push button gearchanges which makes driving the car a lot easier. More, and to buy one on the net, visit www.thesmart.co.uk

What's bad: Choppy ride. Softip transmission takes a while to master, but better than Softouch programmed automatic. Gear changes are slow either way, but slowest in fully automatic mode.

What to watch out for: Parallel imports sold as UK market cars.

Recalls: None on RHD Smarts so far.

MERCEDES

190 W201 Diesels (1983 to 1993)

What's good: The most economical 190s, if driven with economy in mind. 14ft 6in long by 5. 6in wide and from 1,110kg. 190D 2.0 had 72bhp; 190D 2.5 had 90bhp. 5-speed manual or 4-speed automatic boxes. Usual long list of options, including steel sunroof, alloy wheels, electric windows, a/c, radio, etc.

What's bad: Slow and dreadfully boring. None more so than 72 bhp 2.0 litre diesel automatic. 5-cylinder 90 bhp 2.5 is better. UK did not get turbodiesel engines.

What to watch out for: Clocking especially, otherwise see 190.

190/190E 1.8/2.0 (1983 to 1993)

What's good: Build quality, solidity, door latching system. 14ft 7in long by 5. 6in wide and from 1,080kg. Takes age and mileage very well indeed if properly maintained. 1989 model-year facelift brought more legroom in back. Hard, flat seats like those of W123 are longest-lasting seats I know. Good autoboxes. 190 2.0 carb engine has 90 bhp, 1.8 injection 113 bhp, 2.0 injection 122 bhp. Was a 136 bhp 2.3 injection in Europe, LHD only. Better built than C Class which followed.

What's bad: Hard, flat seats not comfortable for everyone. 'Simplex' timing chains on pre-1989 model-year cars prone to snap at around 60,000 miles. Some facelift cars (with lower body side-moulding) used up old stocks of 'Simplex' engines. Tinny boot lid. Clumsy manual gearbox.

What to watch out for: If buying an 'F' or 'G' four-cylinder 190 or 190E, open the oil filler cap and look at timing chain underneath. Single link = 'Simplex'; Double link = 'Duplex'. If buying high mileage, make sure service records show 5,000–mile oil changes. 190s more than 10 years old may have started to rust. Clonking autoboxes. Noisy rear axles. Power steering leaks. Kerb damage to front suspension (look for uneven tyre wear). Clocking of these cars is rife so a full service history with receipts and old MOTs tells you a lot more than that the car has been properly serviced.

190E 2.3/2.5 16v (1985 to 1993)

What's good: The 'hot' 190 2.3 has 187 bhp; 2.5 has 197 bhp, rising to 204 bhp from September 1990. Autobox available with 2.5 16v.
What's bad: Manual gearboxes not the best.
What to watch out for: Clocking. Uneven tyre wear a particularly bad sign on this one as could have been crashed. Otherwise, see 190/190E 1.8/2.0.

190E 2.6 W201 (1986 to 1993)

What's good: This simple, smooth and brawny 160 bhp chain cam engine is the best of the W201 190s. 14ft 7in long by 5ft 6in wide and weighing 1,200kg. 130 mph performance, 28 mpg and no running out of breath when overtaking. Ideal when mated to autobox. Properly maintained, can run well over 12 years and 300,000 miles without serious engine or gearbox problems. Recommended (if you can find a good one). Still worth paying £3,000 for the best.
What's bad: Getting old now. See 190.
What to watch out for: Could have been clocked, or odometer may simply have broken at around 160,000 miles (make sure it's working on your test drive). Will need new valve stem seals each 120,000 miles (a £120 job at a specialist, but much more at a Mercedes dealer). See 190 1.8 and 2.0 litre for other checks. Id a/c fitted make sure it works, has been regassed with CFC free refrigerant and has no leaks.

A-Class (from 1998)

What's good: Brilliant packaging. 11ft 9in long by 6ft 4in wide and weighing from 1,095kg. Choice of 82bhp 1.4 or 102bhp 1.6 litre petrol engines, 95bhp 1.7 litre common-rail direct-injected diesel or 125 bhp 1.9. Manual, clutchless manual or automatic gearchanges all 5-speed. Various trim options. Interesting full-length sliding sunroof. Double-skin floor lifts passengers into safer position in side impacts. Four-Star performance in 1999 NCAP crash safety tests. Loaded with anti-skid, anti-roll-over technology. Prior to Audi A2, the most status you could buy at its length. Modifications for Spring 2001 include 'S' Class quality trim, better seats, new traction control system, a parcel shelf instead of retractable luggage cover and new 75bhp and 95bhp CDI diesels capable of combined mpg figures of up to 59mpg. 2001 models are identified by new rear door handle housed in an oval-shaped flap and a new front. Stretched model seven inches longer also available from June 2001 (see A-Class LWB) 3 year mechanical warranty and 30 year Mobilo roadside assistance + anti corrosion warranty. MB was rated by Motor Warranty Direct as Britain's 2nd most claim-free used marque (check online at www.warrantydirect.co.uk)A210 Evo arrived February 2002 with 2,084cc 140bhp engine offering 0–60 in 7.9 seconds, 127mph top speed, 35.8mpg combined and 190g/km CO_2. SWB prices from £18,990. Mercedes had fifth lowest average cost in warranty claims for cars up to 10 years old in 2002 Warranty Direct index, check online at www.performanceindex.co.uk

What's bad: Not as well built as you expect from Mercedes. Convoluted right hand wheel to left hand rack steering column robs steering of feel. Wipers are also designed for LHD and cannot be altered, leaving an unwiped strip down the right hand side of the screen. Ride quality far from brilliant. Still suffers from top-heavy 'roll understeer' on tight, adversely cambered corners. Essential to pay full attention on the motorway or can swap lanes. Long step up or down from seats for elderly or infirm unless parked against a high kerb. Expensive. Mega expensive service costs, for example £446.96 for a two year 20,000 mile 'B' service of an A160 in Swindon. Lots of drivers have trouble with the keyfob immobiliser control. There have also been alarm system faults, water leaks, problems with anti roll bar links and faulty air flow sensors. Another widespread problem is fractured fuel filler pipes leading the rear of the car to fill with petrol if the tank is over-filled. Reports of failures of rear trailing arm control arm bushes on early A Class, initially benefiting from a 50% goodwill payment on what

484

is a £330 job using a standard repair kit, which tends to indicate some awareness of the problem by the manufacturer. Reports of manual gearbox failure. New A Class due in 2004.

What to watch out for: Doubts beginning to emerge over clutch life of semi-automatic with 170CDI diesel engine. Two reports of slippage after 40,000 miles received within a week of each other; another soon after; yet another of failure after just 21,000 miles. Anti-roll bar links on early models prone to problems and may need replacing with the modified links of later models. Also take great care to check the car's stability electronics before buying. A140 Classics will be coming off Easy Rent-a-Car fleet in large numbers.

Recalls: 27/4/2001: 4,106 cars built 1/9/2000 to 31/1/2001 recalled because brake master cylinder may malfunction in extreme cold and only apply half of split braking system. Master cylinder to be replaced.

A-Class LWB (from 2001)

What's good: Stretched A-Class launched as a mini MPV on sale in UK from June 2001. Seven inches longer at 12ft 5in stretched from the B pillar back. Offers 1,930 litres of interior space. With rear seats removed has 1,530 litres of loadspace. Longer wheelbase means it handles better than the short wheelbase A Class, but still has some unusual handling characteristics. For other A Class improvements from June 2001, see A Class. EU4 compliant emissions. A210 Evo arrived February 2002 with 2,084cc 140bhp engine offering 0–60 in 7.9 seconds, 127mph top speed, 35.8mpg combined and 190g/km CO_2. LWB prices from £19,890.

What's bad: See A Class. Mega expensive service costs, for example £446.96 for a two year 20,000 mile 'B' service of an A160 in Swindon. New A Class due in 2004.

What to watch out for: Too soon to say.

C-Class W202 (1993 to 2000)

What's good: Galvanised body has 30-year warranty. 14ft 8in long by 5ft 8in wide and from 1,350kg. Extensive range of engines offer something for everyone. Start with 122 bhp C180, 136 bhp C200, 150 bhp C220 four, 148 bhp C230 four, 193 bhp C230 Kompressor, 170 bhp twin-spark C240 V6, 193 bhp C280 straight six, 280 bhp C36AMG; 94 bhp C220D, 113 bhp C250D and 150 bhp C250TD. C250TD is a very good diesel, replaced by new 125 bhp/221 lb ft C220 CDI common rail indirect injected diesel. Estates are smart and offer more status than saloons. 5-speed autos standard from 1997. Top model, 4.3 litre 40 valve 310 bhp V8 C43 lists at £47,640 and originally sold for over list, as did 218 bhp 320 CLK coupe and convertible. Progressive spec upgrades over the years. S and T reg. cars came 11th in 2001 *Top Gear*/JD Power Customer Satisfaction Survey. MB was rated by Motor Warranty Direct as Britain's 2nd most claim-free used marque (check online at www.warrantydirect.co.uk) Mercedes had fifth lowest average cost in warranty claims for cars up to 10 years old in 2002 Warranty Direct index, check online at www.performanceindex.co.uk

What's bad: Early build quality not up to scratch and headlamps poor (much improved later). Not as good to drive as 190E or E-Class. Steering over light and lacking in feel. C180 classic manuals without sunroofs or aircon don't hold their value in the way Mercedes owners expect. Average performance in NCAP crash tests. Huge overs paid by snobs to get hold of CLK coupes and convertibles did not feed through into used values. C180, C200 and C220 seems to be unusually prone to premature failure of the catalytic converter, leading to an £800 repair bill. Reports of cylinder head stretch bolts failing on four-cylinder engines, with replacement a 'head-off' job. Up to 1999, C180s had a low-rated battery and alternator that wasn't up to a life of short runs. Glow plugs of C250TD can fail after about 3 years and 50,000 miles. Cost £300–£400 to replace due to amount of dismantling involved. Modest 240V6 has huge engine oil capacity of 8 litres.

What to watch out for: Chip lots of price off if the car is scruffy (a good way to get a cheap, long-lasting car you would have damaged yourself over the years). Glut of cancelled Far East export orders hit used values hard in 1998. C180 classic manuals without sunroofs became very hard to sell. Make sure wiper mechanism works because it's prone to failure and costs £800 to replace. Cat failure also likely to set you back £800. Oil leaks from cylinder head a sign of stretch bolt problem. Beware of cancelled export order 1995–1997 C-Class sold in UK as new when they were up to 3 years old. Check paint very carefully for starring on later South African built cars. If C250TD is a poor starter, may be due to glow plug problem above.

Recalls: 1996: Check for sticking bonnet catch and safety catch which may lead bonnet to fly open. 8/5/2001: Build dates 1/9/1995 to 31/12/1996: high humidity may cause corrosion of trigger mechanism leading to airbag inflating. Airbags to be replaced.

C-Class W203 (from 2000)

What's good: Complete new range launched September 2000 starting with 4–door saloon and later including 3–door hatchback and 5–door estate. Pretty 4–door saloon looks exactly like a small S-Class. Galvanised body with 30-year warranty. Engines are 129 bhp 2.0 litre four; 163 bhp 2.0 litre supercharged four; 170 bhp 2.6 V6; 218 bhp 3.2 V6; 143 bhp 2.2 CDI four-cylinder; and 170 bhp 2.7 CDI five-cylinder. Gearboxes either a six-speed manual, five-speed fully automatic or five speed Sequentronic semi-automatic. 220CDI offers 45 mpg potential. Three lap/diagonal rear belts, a/c, driver and passenger airbags plus side bags and window bags and cruise control with 'Speedtronic' speed limiter standard throughout the range. Now has rack and pinion steering and polycarbonate headlight lenses. Decent sized boot. Electric folding door mirrors incorporate indicator repeaters. Optional 'Command' voice-activated telephone, navigation system and sound system. Later developments to include new direct-injected petrol engines from 125 bhp to 200 bhp and a CVT auto. 354bhp C32 AMG launched at Detroit Show in January 2001. Estate version and coupe from Summer 2001. Estate with punchy 170bhp 2.7 litre CDI and Sequentronic box is almost as quick as 3.2 V6 fully automatic. Excellent score of 31 points in 2001 Euro NCAP crash safety tests. See road test of estate and coupe at www.honestjohn.co.uk Price cuts in June 2002 bring lead in prices to £18,795 for the 180 Classic Sport Coupe, £19,995 for the 180

Classic saloon and £20,945 for the 180 Classic estate. Classic SE spec upgrades also announced at £1,645 more and you now need this to get air-conditioning. You still get ABS (anti-lock brakes) with BAS (Brake Assist); alarm and immobiliser; electric heated mirrors; ESP (Electronic Stability Program) with ASR traction control; six airbags (two front, two side and window-bags); four electric windows; four seat belt pre-tensioners; multi-function steering wheel; partial electric seats and remote central locking all still feature as standard on every car. A single CD player in place of cassette remains a no cost option. To get Automatic Climate Control on the Classic Saloon and Estate you have to move up to the Classic SE at an extra £1,645, starting at £21,640 for the 180 saloon and £22,590 for the 180 estate. You also get alloy wheels; CD player; five-speed automatic transmission (with Speedtronic cruise control and speed limiter); and leather-trimmed steering wheel and gear shift. SE pack also available on five and six cylinder C Class models, with Sequentronic transmissions a no cost option on all Classic SE models, where available. For the first time, a C 320 Classic SE will became available, costing £29,200 (Saloon) and £30,150 (Estate). Top model is £43,740 C32AMG with 349bhp and 332lb ft torque. Revisions lead to excellent five star Euro NCAP award for C Class range in 2002 tests. New 1,796cc supercharged balancer shaft engines in Sports Coupe and Estates from July 2002 and in saloons from September 2002. '180K' engine develops 143bhp, emits 175g/km and gets the car t0 139mph; '200K' engine develops 163bhp; 230K engine develops 192bhp, but this is for Sports Coupe only. Saloon and estate retain 2.4 V6. No price change for the new engines.

More online at www.mercedes-benz.co.uk

What's bad: Indicator stalk on RHD models is clumsy and difficult to use. Six-speed manual box can be a bit notchy with smaller engines. Autobox quadrant markings on wrong side for RHD. Steering better than old C-Class but still over-light and lacking in road feel. Ride quality of 'Classic' base model far from brilliant. 163 bhp 200K a bit boomy. Definitely not as good to drive as equivalent 3–Series. Sold out to end of 2000, but expected to sell 22,000 units in UK in 2001. Supply problem in Autumn 2001 due to a strike at the South African factory from which all RHD UK market C Class Mercedes are normally sourced. Can suffer from suspension misalignment and aggravated tyre wear. It's a good idea to have all four wheels laser-aligned to be sure. Other build quality niggles include faulty turbo oil seals on diesels, badly fitted door seals, faulty earth to heated read window. Modest 240V6 has huge engine oil capacity of 8 litres. June 2002 price cuts also meant specification cuts so you have to be careful buying these cars used as a Mercedes without aircon is as easy to re-sell as snow in Antarctica.

What to watch out for: South African build quality niggles. Check paint very carefully for starring, particularly solid colours. Consumers Association members have reported minor rattles and electrical faults. Six speed manual gearbox has sometimes given trouble on other MB models fitted with it. Go through the exact spec with a fine tooth comb as imports and now even UK sourced cars may not have the spec you are expecting. Has also been one report of accelerated suspension bush wear problems due to the dire state of Britain's road and its unique traffic calming/harming measures.

Recalls: December 2001: German Police C Class with steel wheels have all been recalled because the wheel nuts have unfastened themselves in use.

CL 420–600 (1996 to 2000)

What's good: Monster coupes based on S Class. 420 has 4,196cc 279bhp V8; 500 has 4,973cc 320bhp V8; 600 has 5,987cc 394bhp V12. Replaced by stunning new CL in Summer 2000. Mercedes had fifth lowest average cost in warranty claims for cars up to 10 years old in 2002 Warranty Direct index, check online at www.performanceindex.co.uk

What's bad: Slab-sided, hideously ugly. Tells people that you used to be rich, but can't afford the new CL.

What to watch out for: Too wide for some streets.

CL 500, CL55 (from Summer 2000)

What's good: Stunning big new coupe based on S Class. Standard CL500 has 306bhp 4,933cc V8, gets to 60 in 6 seconds, top speed limited to 155. CL500 AMG has 354bhp 5,439cc V8.

What's bad: Extravagant, but it does tell everyone you've arrived.

What to watch out for: Thieves. Nothing else yet.

CLK W202 (June 1997 to July 2002)

What's good: Coupe version of C Class effectively replaced the old E Class coupes. 136bhp 2.0 litre four followed by supercharged 163bhp 200K in June 2000; supercharged 193bhp 2.3 litre four; 218bhp 3.2 V6; and, from August 1999 Merc's 275bhp 4.3V8 or 242bhp 5.4 litre AMG 55 V8. Six speed manual option on 200K. First cabrios: 230K and 320 in June 1998. Big overs were paid to get one of these at the time. 430 cabrio came along in August 1999. Mercedes had fifth lowest average cost in warranty claims for cars up to 10 years old in 2002 Warranty Direct index, check online at www.performanceindex.co.uk

What's bad: See C Class. Huge overs paid by snobs to get hold of CLK coupes and convertibles did not feed through into used values.

What to watch out for: See C Class. Don't buy a scruffy one unless you can get it for thousands under book.

CLK W203 (from June 2002)

What's good: Stunning new pillarless CLK coupe on sale in UK from June 2002 and based con current much better handling C Class. Strong range of engines with outputs from 163bhp to 367bhp. Base engine is four cylinder supercharged 200K with 163bhp. Next up is 240 V6 (actually now 2.6 litres) with 170bhp. Next after that, the 320 V6 with a slight power reduction to 218bhp. And, for the first time in a CLK, the 170bhp 270CDI diesel will also be available, offering a combined economy figure of 42.2 mpg. Top engines are 500E V8 with 306bhp and 500E AMG with 476bhp. The 500 E gets to 60mph in under 6 seconds and the AMG in under 5 with a top speed of around 195mph probably limited to 155. All come in either Elegance or Avantgarde trim at the same price.

More online at www.mercedes-benz.co.uk

What's bad: Too soon to say. Much more competition, so unlikely to be the same long waiting list as there was for the previous CLK at launch.

What to watch out for: Too soon to say.

E-Class W123 (1976 to 1985)

What's good: Succeeded the square-cut W114/115. 15ft 6in by 5ft 10in and weighing from 1,340kg. The last beautifully-built working-class Mercedes. Solid as a rock. I've seen them with 350,000 miles still looking almost like new. The seats don't sag. 136bhp 230E the most popular. 72bhp 240D slow, but goes on for ever. 5-cylinder 88bhp 300D slightly faster, with similar longevity, less likely to have been a taxi. 185bhp 280E fastest. Handsome, useful estates.

What's bad: Old cars now. They do rust and diffs do go. Don't take well to unleaded. Must have 3,000–mile oil changes and a new timing chain every 60,000 miles or 5 years whichever comes first. 1984–85 230Es tried to go unleaded and suffered premature valve guide wear. Slow changing manuals best avoided. Don't buy without a sunroof. Avoid the 250 six-cylinder engine because its badly engineered. An all new engine for a 280E is £6,000.

What to watch out for: Most of the good ones were bought up by 'private hire' and minicab operations who will have serviced them pragmatically but run up a mega mileage and don't let them go until they're knackered. If the big bumpers are damaged it means a heavy impact which may have deformed the structure. Find out when the Simplex timing chain of 4-cylinder engines was last changed. Listen for rattles and look for oil smoke signifying valve guide wear. Listen for noisy, clonky rear axle. Bounce the rear suspension to make sure shocks still absorb. Estate car rear shocks are very expensive. Look for oil leaks underneath.

E-Class W124 Estates (1985 to 1996)

What's good: Estate cars come no better. Strong, reliable, comfortable, well-built, safe with more floor-to-window loadspace than any Volvo. 6-cylinder 300E and 5-cylinder 300D best older engines. 280 and 320 24v best newer engines. Last three years production has smaller radiator grille introduced in August 1993. Mercedes had fifth lowest average cost in warranty claims for cars up to 10 years old in 2002 Warranty Direct index, check online at www.performanceindex.co.uk

What's bad: 200s are underpowered, especially automatics. 230TE autos with aircon struggle with a full load. (See W124 saloons.) Cats from September 1990 when power dropped from 136bhp to 132bhp. 16 valve 220 engine from August 1993 had 150bhp.

What to watch out for: Very important to check the rear suspension as replacement shocks are expensive. Has it been towing? 200TEs and 230TE autos aren't really powerful enough to tow a caravan, so will be well worn if they have been trying. Engine and autobox may have overheated. The electric tailgate closer is vulnerable to failure and expensive to replace. Otherwise see W124 saloons. Head gaskets on the 104 series six cylinder engines had poor manufacturing tolerances and tend to go when the mileage approaches 100k, if not before (has been seen it on a 70k car). Signs are oil at front and rear of cylinder head joint. This is a £1500 job. The engine wiring loom breaks down through heat and exposes the wires. Symptoms as you are varied. This is £450 for the loom plus fitting. For more to look for see W124 E Class saloons.

Recalls: 1995: passenger Footrest. 1996: airbag may inflate on wrong side. 13/10/2000: 15,105 E Class VIN A000043 to A313828 built late 1994 to 1994 recalled because insufficiently tightened PAS steering damper screw could result in fluid loss. In extreme circumstances this could ignite on a hot exhaust manifold. Torque of steering damper screw to be checked and damper O ring seals to be replaced if leaking. 8/5/2001: Build dates 1/9/1995 to 31/12/1996: high humidity may cause corrosion of trigger mechanism leading to airbag inflating. Airbags to be replaced.

E-Class W124 Saloons and Coupes

What's good: Strong, reliable, comfortable, well-built, safe. Bigger, more modern car than W123. Best compromise engine in older models is the 170bhp six-cylinder 12-valve 260E (not available in UK estates). Best in newer models is the 197bhp 24-valve 280E. 260E is rare in the UK because large numbers were exported second-hand to Malaysia, Thailand and Singapore in the mid-1990s. Awesome LHD only 326bhp 500E, briefly officially available in UK from 1991 to 1992, had ASR self-levelling suspension and protruding 8Jx16 wheels. Mercedes had fifth lowest average cost in warranty claims for cars up to 10 years old in 2002 Warranty Direct index, check online at www.performanceindex.co.uk

What's bad: Lots of quality problems when the model was launched. Four-cylinder 200E and 230E had valve trouble running on unleaded and can still wear out their valve stems in the guides. Six-cylinder 300 12 valve and 300 24 valve engines sometimes prone to cracking of the cylinder head. 'Simplex' timing chains not replaced by 'Duplex' chains on 4-cylinder engines until 1988 (see 190). American-style foot parking brake on automatics. Manual gearchange slow and not very pleasant. Reports of cylinder head stretch bolts failing on later four-cylinder engines (200, 220) with replacement a 'head-off' job.

What to watch out for: Built to cover high mileages and many did, but may not show it. Listen for noises from top of engine, look for oil smoke in exhaust. Simplex timing chains on older 200E and 230E last only 60,000 miles and require 3,000–mile engine oil changes. No such problems with later Duplex chains or with 260E, 300E, 300E 24v, 320E 24v. Look for oil in the coolant, low coolant and emulsified oil under the oil filler cap of six cylinder models (could signify cracked head). Head gaskets on the 104 Series six cylinder engines had poor manufacturing tolerances and tend to go when the mileage approaches 100k, if not before (has been seen it on a 70k car). Signs are oil at front and rear of cylinder head joint. This is a £1500 job. The engine wiring loom breaks down through heat and exposes the wires. Symptoms are varied. This is £450 for the loom plus fitting. Check for uneven tyre wear (kerbed suspension, worn steering or merely adjustment needed). Brake hard and check for judder (front discs may be warped). Look for oil leaks underneath. Avoid 4–Matic unless you really need a large four-wheel-drive saloon car. Make sure autobox works in 'sport' (if fitted), feel for 'slip', check colour of ATF (should be dark red), listen for diff rumble. Make sure ABS light goes on and off when it should (brake fluid changes may have been missed). Ask to see a proper service history, if not by a Mercedes dealer, then by a competent specialist. Oil leaks from cylinder heads of four cylinder engines a sign of the stretch bolt problem. Some cancelled export order W124s still being sold as new in 2000 when 5 years old.

Recalls: 1995: passenger Footrest. 1996: airbag may inflate on wrong side. 13/10/2000: 15,105 E Class VIN A000043 to A313828 built late 1994 to 1994 recalled because insufficiently tightened PAS steering damper screw could result in fluid loss. In extreme circumstances this could ignite on a hot exhaust manifold. Torque of steering damper screw to be checked and damper O ring seals to be replaced if leaking. 8/5/2001: Build dates 1/9/1995 to 31/12/1996: high humidity may cause corrosion of trigger mechanism leading to airbag inflating. Airbags to be replaced.

E-Class W210 (1995 to 2002)

What's good: Good-looking cars with slightly better ride and handling than W124. Engines range from 2.0 litre 136 bhp four through straight sixes and V6s to 280 bhp E430 V8. Very useful 177 bhp 300 Turbodiesel goes well with reasonable economy, replaced by 195 bhp 320CDI with massive 350 lb ft torque. 125 bhp 220CDI boosted to 143 bhp and 232 lb ft. Estate cars particularly elegant. Top model 5.5 litre 40-valve 354 bhp V8 E55 competes head on against Jag XJR8. 1995–1999 models got Three-Star NCAP crash test rating (marked down for distortion of pedal box). 2000 models onwards were modified and achieved a Four-Star NCAP rating. 220CDI or 320CDI 5-speed auto recommended. S and T reg. cars came eighth in 2001 *Top Gear*/JD Power Customer Satisfaction Survey. Conflicts with *Telegraph* readers experiences, but MB was rated by Motor Warranty Direct as Britain's 2nd most claim-free used marque (check online at www.warrantydirect.co.uk) High mileage 3 year old W210 230E Elegance models with 5-speed autobox (MUST be 5-speed) sought after for export to Far East and periodically fetch big money at auction. W210 voted 7th equal from Top in 144 car 2002 JD Power/*What Car?* Customer Satisfaction Survey of V and W reg. cars. Mercedes had fifth lowest average cost in warranty claims for cars up to 10 years old in 2002 Warranty Direct index, check online at www.performanceindex.co.uk

What's bad: These are expensive cars. Old 5-cylinder 113 bhp E250D slow, but would be the taxi driver's choice. Standard 'Brake Assist' caused lots of problems which took Mercedes years to sort out. Reports of cylinder head stretch bolts failing on four-cylinder engines, with replacement a 'head-off' job. 1995 to 1997 cars have had paint and rust problems, particularly around the numberplate area on the bootlid in the bottoms of doors and now developing in the front wings. This is well known in Germany. Daimler Chrysler has now admitted to another rust problem on all W210 E Class up to June 2001 build – apparently due to using stretched steel construction. Affects areas around door window seals and suspension mounting points. May be a problem with the engine mounts of the E320CDI. Complaints of water ingress leading to corrosion damage of ventilation system blower motor. Modest 240V6 has huge engine oil capacity of 8 litres. Replacement much better E-Class arrived mid 2002.

What to watch out for: Cancelled Far East export orders found their way back to the UK at mammoth discounts. Make sure any car you buy from a non-Mercedes dealer is properly certificated with either an EU Certificate of Conformity or UK SVA. Oil leaks from cylinder head a sign of the stretch bolt problem on 200s. Beware of cancelled export order 1995–1997 W210 E-Class sold in UK as new when they were up to 3 years old. An 'R' reg. could be a 1995 car.

Recalls: 1995: passenger Footrest. 1996: airbag may inflate on wrong side. 2000: 1997–build cars recalled to have both sills re-treated with cavity rust-proofing. 8/5/2001: Build dates 1/9/1995 to 31/12/1996: high humidity may cause corrosion of trigger mechanism leading to airbag inflating. Airbags to be replaced. September 2001: Recall of 1996 build E210s for steering damper screw leak fault (recall No. 1827) which affected late W124s. Lost fluid could cause underbonnet fire.

E-Class W211 (from August 2002)

What's good: The W211 E500 is probably the finest car you can buy in the real world in 2002. Truly "engineered like no other car in the World" and marks MB getting back to its core values. As Mercedes says, "Everything we know in one car". Incredibly strong. Incredibly safe. Incredibly advanced. And stunningly good to drive. Underneath is four-link front suspension and multi-link rear suspension built mainly of aluminium like the BMW 5 Series and latest Audis. Optional dual stage AIRMATIC (standard on E500), as the S Class, using electronically controlled springing and damping. Vast amount of electronic technology that make the car almost impossible to crash. The first W211s in the UK have five different engine options: three petrol and two diesel. Base petrol engine is the E240, a 2.6 litre 177bhp V6. The 6-speed manual does 148mph and gets to 60mph in 8.6 seconds. Next up is the familiar E320 3.2 litre 224bhp V6, which g auto only which does 155mph and gets to 60mph in 7.5 seconds. This is slightly more economical than the E240 manual or auto. Top of the range is the E500, a 5.0 litre 306bhp V8, which reaches 164mph and gets to 60mph in 5.8 seconds. Diesels are the 2.2 litre four cylinder balancer shaft 150bhp E220CDI, which gets to 60 in 9.8 seconds, goes on to 138mph and delivers 44.8mpg (177g/km CO_2) and the 2.7 litre five cylinder 177bhp E270CDI, which is good for 144mph and zero to sixty in 8.7 seconds. A supercharged 200K four will come later, as will the six cylinder 320CDI and a supercharged 470bhp 200mph E55 AMG V8. Six-speed manual gearboxes from the C Class and SLK are standard on the E200K, E220CDI and E270CDI, with the option of MB's excellent 'Tipfunction' 5-speed auto. E240, E320CDI, E320 and E500 come with 5-speed auto as standard. Will also be a 200mph 0–60 in 4.5 seconds supercharged E55 AMG at less than £60,000. Expecting Five star performance in NCAP crash tests. Full road test at wwww.honestjohn.co.uk Whole range from E220CDI auto upwards very highly recommended.

More online at www.mercedes-benz.co.uk

What's bad: Rear seat not as wide as previous E class and centre rear seat not comfortable.

What to watch out for: Too soon to say.

M-Class (from 1998)

What's good: MB's 4x4 much in evidence around places like Weybridge, Surrey (famed for 4x4s that never do any more off-roading than climbing the kerb outside Cullens). 3,199cc six - cylinder engine or 4,256cc V8. Standard autobox. 430 model does 0–60 in under 8 seconds and runs to 130 mph, which is comfortably better than a Range Rover 4.6 and at £43,390, a lot less money. Five-cylinder 270CDI model a comparative bargain at prices starting from £29,000 for the six-speed manual or £30,500 for the more powerful auto. The only M-Class capable of 30 mpg plus. MB was rated by Motor Warranty Direct as Britain's 2nd most claim-free used marque (check online at www.warrantydirect.co.uk) Comprehensively facelifted for Autumn 2001 with 292bhp ML 500 replacing the ML 430 and 347bhp ML 55 AMG on offer. Mercedes had fifth lowest average cost in warranty claims for cars up to 10 years old in 2002 Warranty Direct index, check online at www.performanceindex.co.uk

What's bad: Getting eclipsed in the snob stakes by the BMW X5. American build quality not quite up to Stuttgart's. Very tall, so take care on corners. Hideous optional external rear wheel carrier that blots out rearward vision from the interior mirror. Nothing like as good as a Range Rover off-road. Quite a few complaints from *Telegraph* readers about the inability of MB dealers to rectify faults. Isolated complaints of failures of 6-speed manual gearboxes fitted to 270CDI.

What to watch out for: Highly unlikely damage from off-roading. Highly likely damage from kerbs, but most are fitted with ultrasonic reversing aids so parking damage will be minimal.

Recalls: 4/2/2000: driver's seatbelt may unbuckle. To be replaced with modified buckle. 30/4/2001 ML320 engines converted to gas fuelling may exceed permitted rpm leading automatic gearbox to shift into neutral. Control box to be fitted to switch fuel to petrol at over 5,500 rpm.

S-Class W126 (1983 to 1991)

What's good: Good looking, carved from solid Mercedes from the same box as the W123. Big cars 16ft long (SEL 17ft long) b6ft wide and weighing 1,520kg to 1,810kg. 1Engines range from 185 bhp twin cam 12-valve 280 six, through 188bhp 300SE (from 1986), 204bhp 380SE V8, 218bhp 420SE(from 1986) and 231bhp 500SE to 300 bhp 560 V8. You can still get a good one with 10 years useful life left in it. SEL means long wheelbase with more rear legroom. Electric reclining rear seats were a £9,000 option in the 560SEL.

What's bad: 280SE and 300SE not significantly more economical than the smaller V8s. All these cars like petrol.

What to watch out for: When checking a V8, take off the top of the air filter plenum chamber and look for oil. If there's oil in there, the car needs a £12,000 new engine. Listen for timing chain rattle, signifying infrequent oil changes. Don't want to hear any coarseness from the engine, transmission, diff or rumbles from the wheel bearings. Look for uneven tyre wear – could signify suspension wear. Small dinks and donks in the bodywork cost an arm and a leg to fix properly. Remember, these cars only go on forever if frequently and expensively maintained. Cut back on the maintenance and they will break, leaving you with bills for more than the value of the car. Could have been clocked – especially if on its 2nd or 3rd owner.

S-Class W140 (1991 to 1999)

What's good: Sensible engine range from 190 bhp S280 through 228 bhp S300, 286 bhp S420, 308 bhp S500 and awesome 408 bhp S600 (power on this cut back to 389 bhp in October 1992). MB was rated by Motor Warranty Direct as Britain's 2nd most claim-free used marque (check online at www.warrantydirect.co.uk) Mercedes had fifth lowest average cost in warranty claims for cars up to 10 years old in 2002 Warranty Direct index, check online at www.performanceindex.co.uk

What's bad: All these cars are just a bit too big. European mid-90s slump left a lot of 'S'-Class unsold – sitting outside in Baltic Sea dockside compounds which won't have done them much good. Used prices go up and down like a lift in a department store. All were slow sellers in the UK, particularly in 1997–98. Official UK sales hit by diverted RHD Far East exports at up to £17,000 less.

What to watch out for: Can be a huge amount of car for the money if bought right. Tyres are enormous, wear heavily and are very expensive, so budget for this.

Recalls: 1997 (1995–96 build): may lose brake fluid from hose. 8/5/2001: Build dates 1/9/1995 to 31/12/1996: high humidity may cause corrosion of trigger mechanism leading to airbag inflating. Airbags to be replaced.

S-Class W220 (from 1999)

What's good: Galvanised body has 30-year warranty and car carries 30-year MB Mobilo roadside assistance. Nice looking, beautifully built, unaggressively styled big cars. Sensible engine range from S280 through To S600. Smaller 280 and 320 are V6s. Rack and pinion steering gives good road feel and makes the cars much better to drive then 140 Series without sacrificing ride comfort. Excellent 'Tipfunction' side-flick manual control over 5-speed automatic. S320 V6 is just about adequate. 430 V8 probably the best compromise. Nothing better as a quiet, refined 140 mph Autobahn cruiser. Straight-six S320CDI diesel arrived in UK in Spring 2000 with 197 bhp and 347lb ft torque giving 143 mph or 35 mpg. V8 S400 CDI has 247 bhp and a staggering 414 lb ft giving 155mph or 30mpg. Not unreasonably priced for what you get. Probably the best car in the world from 1999 to 2001 after which it is only supplanted by the new W211 E500. Recommended. S and T reg. cars came 19th in 2001 *Top Gear*/JD Power Customer Satisfaction Survey. Mercedes had fifth lowest average cost in warranty claims for cars up to 10 years old in 2002 Warranty Direct index, check online at www.performanceindex.co.uk

What's bad: As length and weight increases from S280 to S600L, handling qualities deteriorate. Not a lot of boot space for such a big car. Huge options list can increase new price considerably, and spec needs to be checked carefully when buying second hand. Vulgar £554 walnut/leather optional steering wheel not nice to hold. There may be a problem with the engine mounts of the S320CDI diesel and has been criticism of false alarms from dashboard oil light.

What to watch out for: Niggling build-quality problems. Make sure every electric/electronic gizmo works as it should. If it's an import you don't get the same warranty so should allow for that and lower resale values in what you pay.

Recalls: 8/8/2000: 780 new S Class built 1/2000 to 5/2000 recalled because a short circuit could result in the heater blower motor regulator overheating which could lead to charring and smouldering. Blower motor regulator units to be replaced.

SL (from April 2002)

What's good: In response to the official launch of the Lexus SC430, Daimler-Chrysler pulled the wraps off its stunning new SL. This, too, has folding aluminium hard top, like that of the SLK, Peugeot 206CC and Lexus SC430. Engines are a 306bhp V8 for the SL500, in the UK from April 2002, followed later in 2002 by the SL55 AMG. A 3.2 litre V6 will arrive by the end of 2002 and finally an awesome bi-turbo V12 in mid 2003. The most status you can buy in a car. (For the ultimate version see SL 55 AMG.)Price announced 12–2–2002: SL500: £67,790.

What's bad: 1,400 UK allocation for 2002 sold out, so if you want one before mid 2003 and haven't made a firm order with a deposit you'll have to pay a premium to get one. Talk to Tom Hartley Senior or Tom Hartley Junior on 01283 762762; linked website www.tomhartley.com

Be aware of the need for personal security when driving one of these cars, as everyone will think you are rich.

What to watch out for: Too soon to say.

SL 55 AMG (from Summer 2002)

What's good: Worth covering as a separate model because this is bound to become THE most desired car in the World. Same electric folding hardtop as lesser 2002 SLs, but under the bonnet lurks a supercharged 5.5 litre V8 putting out 493bhp and a monster 700Nm (515 lb ft) torque from 2,650 to 4,500rpm. Zero to 60 takes just 4.5 seconds and unrestricted top speed over 200mph, though electronically limited to 155mph. The engine even conforms to EU-4 emissions standards, but only gives 14.2mpg in the combined cycle. Price announced 12–2–2002: £89,040. FORGET FERRARIS, ROLLS ROYCES AND NEW RANGE ROVERS. THIS IS THE MOST STATUS YOU CAN BUY IN A CAR.

What's bad: Likely to command premiums of £20,000 or so for the first year. Talk to Tom Hartley Senior or Tom Hartley Junior on 01283 762762; linked website www.tomhartley.com

Be aware that this car tells everyone you are rich and makes you a target.

What to watch out for: Too soon to say.

SL W107 (1971 to 1989)

What's good: Roadsters originally bought by movie stars, nouveaux riches and pools winners, had very long model life from 1971 to 1989. 14ft 5in long by 5ft 10in wide. Six-cylinder engines more economical and cheaper to repair than V8s. A lady in Weybridge used to drive her pet parrot around in one. It just sat there on a box in the passenger seat chattering away.

What's bad: I call these 'ribside' roadsters from the Fiat Panda-like ribbing along the sides. To some eyes, they are really ugly and look like oversized fairground dodgem cars. But other people like them and there is still some status attached to driving one around with the top down. Unlikely ever to be as 'classic' as previous model 230SL, 250SL, 280SL 'Pagoda Top' and light years behind the 50s to early 60s 300SL.

What to watch out for: Fell into the wrong hands in those middle years between being old cars and becoming 'classics'. Lots driven by rich women, some of whom bounce them off kerbs, so check for uneven tyre wear signifying suspension damage. Be very wary of 'customised' SLs with oversize alloys, vulgar body kits and white leather steering wheels. If it has aircon, make sure the aircon blows cold. Faulty ABS means a very expensive MOT failure. Make sure the power hood works properly and has no tears. Must have had 3,000–mile fully synthetic oil changes. Take the air filter top off and look for oil in the plenum chamber underneath. If you find any, walk away sharpish.

SL W129 (1989 to 2001)

What's good: Vastly better looking than previous SL. 14ft 10in by 6ft wide. Six-cylinder cars probably the most sensible. 300 12-valve: 190 bhp; 280 12-valve 193 bhp; 300 24v 231 bhp, 320 24v also 231 bhp, pre-cat 500 V8 326 bhp, catalysed 500 from Sept '90 down to 308 bhp, then power up again to 315 bhp from May '95; 600 V12 has 389 bhp; AMG SL60 is a bored-out 5,956cc 381 bhp V8 handles better than 600SL. All these cars came with a standard, lift-off hardtop which is a two person job to remove. MB was rated by Motor Warranty Direct as Britain's 2nd most claim-free used marque (check online at www.warrantydirect.co.uk) Mercedes had fifth lowest average cost in warranty claims for cars up to 10 years old in 2002 Warranty Direct index, check online at www.performanceindex.co.uk

What's bad: Splodgy fat car handling. Autobox apt to change gear on corners when you don't want it to. Vastly better replacement with electric folding hard top arrived early 2002 (and promptly sold out).

What to watch out for: Lots of iffy cars with doubtful pasts in the trade: LHD to RHD conversions. Clones. Cancelled Far East Export orders. Check carefully for repaired body damage. Look for rust at the bottom rear sides of the hard top. Make sure the aircon blows cold. Don't buy with the hardtop fitted and no chance to check out the hood operation and the hood itself for mould or tears. Really need 3,000–mile fully synthetic oil changes.

Recalls: 8/5/2001: Build dates 1/9/1995 to 31/12/1996: high humidity may cause corrosion of trigger mechanism leading to airbag inflating. Airbags to be replaced. 27/4/2001: Build dates 1/1/1993 to 31/12/1996: end of exhaust may break from silencer causing heat damage to rear of car. Rear silencer to be replaced with one of stainless steel if this has not already been done.

SLK (1996 to 2004)

What's good: Beautifully engineered electrically folding hard-top. High build quality. Galvanised body has 30-year warranty. Revised for Y2K with three engine options: 163 bhp 200K, 193 bhp 230K and

218 bhp 320 V6, and either a six-speed manual of five-speed autobox. Now a much better, sportier car than the original UK 230K auto, with 200Ks more reasonably priced, from £26,390. 320 six-speed goes like a real sports car at last and gets up to 120 mph very quickly. MB was rated by Motor Warranty Direct as Britain's 2nd most claim-free used marque (check online at www.warrantydirect.co.uk) Achieved an excellent four star rating for crash safety in 2002 NCAP tests. Mercedes had fifth lowest average cost in warranty claims for cars up to 10 years old in 2002 Warranty Direct index, check online at www.performanceindex.co.uk

What's bad: Silly premiums paid for the first few years cars on UK roads. Offset driving position. 'Kiddy car' looks from side and rear. Original official UK imports were automatic 2.3 'Kompressor' only, so more a two-seat roadster than a 'sports car'. Autobox changes gear on corners when you don't want it to (manual obviously doesn't). Some problems reported with the 5-speed autobox. Steering is old-fashioned recirculating ball. Not much boot space. Older 230K models devalued by arrival of new range. Isolated complaints of failures of 6-speed manual gearboxes. Problems starting to emerge with sensors of folding roof mechanisms if not used regularly. Replacement due 2004; prototypes already seen testing.

What to watch out for: Sellers may try to base used prices on premium price paid rather than market value. LHD 2.0 litre manual 'personal imports' can be a better bet at £12,500 v/s £25,000 for RHD 2.3 auto. Make sure the roof opens and shuts properly.

SLK 32 AMG (from August 2001)

What's good: Effectively a new high performance supercharged model of the SLK boasting all of 354bhp and 332 lb ft torque giving the car a 0–60 of 5.1 seconds, yet capable of running on 95Ron premium unleaded petrol. 17in wheels with 225 tyres on the front and 245s on the back. Comes with 5-speed 'Speedshift' selectable automatic transmission. The most status you can buy in a car. Achieved an excellent four star rating for crash safety in 2002 NCAP tests. More information online at www.mercedes-benz.co.uk

What's bad: Insurance premiums likely to be stiff, otherwise too soon to say.

What to watch out for: Nothing reported.

SLR-Maclaren (from Spring 2003)

What's good: Mad Maclaren Mercedes for rich people for whom even a 200mph SL55 AMG isn't enough. To have 580bhp supercharged V8 developed from 493bhp SL55 V8. To weigh a low 1,420kg. Expected performance of 0–60 in 4 seconds, 0–100 in 10 seconds, top speed over 200mph, price £180,000.

What's bad: If the SL55 AMG is the ultimate status symbol, this tells the elite you're one of them.

What to watch out for: Where you drive with the top down and where you leave the car because you and it are bound to be targets.

V-Class (from 1996)

What's good: Based on the smart Vito van. 2.2 litre common rail direct-injected diesel is powerful and economical. Lap/diagonal seatbelts for everyone in 7–seater version. Most have just six big seats, all fully removable. Seats themselves lightened for 2001 model from 39kg to 28kg, making them easier to handle. List prices cut to £23,230 to £29,280. All covered by 3 year mechanical warranty and 30 year Mobilo warranty giving 30 years roadside assistance and a 30 year guarantee against perforation by corrosion. Mercedes had fifth lowest average cost in warranty claims for cars up to 10 years old in 2002 Warranty Direct index, check online at www.performanceindex.co.uk

What's bad: V' stands for Vito van with rear side windows, but can't really stand the move up-market and loses buckets of value over the first two years. Many only had 6 seats. Bits drop off. Sliding side door mechanism fails. Van-like to drive. S and T platers 2nd from bottom in 2001 *Top Gear*/J.D. Power Customer Satisfaction Survey.

What to watch out for: Dings and dents. Check all trim carefully inside and out. Watch for signs of hard usage. Drive-shaft boots prone to failure (MOT failure point, but worth checking or the UJs will lose their lubrication and replacement drive-shafts are expensive).

Recalls: 1999 V-Class and Vito van (1996–98 build): tread may separate from tyres.

Vaneo (from 2002)

What's good: Stretched A-Class 4.2 metres long with voluminous rear (3,000 litres) and removable kombi-style second row of seats aimed at families and small businesses and tradesmen who want one vehicle for both work and domestic use. 3rd row of child seats offered as an optional extra, making it a 7 seater. Lots of other useful options including a slide-out luggage compartment floor to aid loading. Will have ESP. Brake Assist and the sandwich floor design of the A Class, but should be inherently more stable due to its longer wheelbase. Launched at Frankfurt Motor Show 13th-23rd September 2001. 75bhp 1.6 and 125bhp 1.9 litre petrol engines or 1.7 litre CDI with 75bhp or 91bhp. Arrived UK with RHD in May 2002. Prices from £14,500. World's tallest tail-lights.

What's bad: News from Germany in April 2002 that the launch date was put back due to build quality problems which MB wanted to rectify before the Vaneo went on sale. Starter prices are £5,500 more than a Berlingo Multispace Forte HDI 90 on offer at £9,000 which some people might find had to justify for a vehicle actually names the 'Vaneo'.

What to watch out for: Too soon to say.

MG

MG TF from 2002

What's good: Comprehensively revamped and re-named MGF. Peter Stevens designed front similar to MG X80, all new suspension, more power throughout the range and masses of detail improvements. Power outputs go up as per model designations, starting with the 1.6 litre MGTF 115 and rising through the 1.8 litre MFTF 120 Stepspeed and 1.8 litre MGTF 135 to the 1.8 litre VVC MGTF 160. New suspension includes a multi-link rear axle with "precise kinematics control", coil springs instead of interconnected Hydragas spheres, and solid mounted subframes for improved response. Detail improvements include a greater choice of paint colours, interior trims and optional hood colours (but no mention of a glass rear screen).Debut at the Brussels Motor Show on January 15, 2002. On sale in the UK in February 2002 at prices from around £15,750. Excellent, confidence-inspiring roadholding and handling, good brakes, enough performance from 160.

More online at www.rovergroup.co.uk

What's bad: Still no glass rear window. Cheap feeling dashboard trim. Head gasket failure common on K series four cylinder engines because very low coolant capacity of engine means small leaks rapidly lead to overheating. Weakest point is water heated inlet manifold gasket.

What to watch out for: Too soon to say.

MG ZR (from June 2001)

What's good: Rover 25 based ZR160 boasts the same 160bhp VVC engine as the MGF Trophy 160, with a 0–60 of 7.4 seconds and a top end of 131mph. List price is a reasonable £14,345. MG ZRs with smaller, less powerful engines are 1.4 101bhp ZR105 at £9,995 and 1.8 115bhp ZR120. LPG ZR 120 from July 2002 at an extra £2,195 awaiting Powershift certification which may result in up to 70% rebate.

What's bad: See Rover 25. Head gasket failure common on K series four cylinder engines because very low coolant capacity of engine means small leaks rapidly lead to overheating. Weakest point is water heated inlet manifold gasket.

What to watch out for: See Rover 25.

MG ZS (from June 2001)

What's good: Rover 45 based ZS180 has a 177bhp version of Rover's 2.5 litre KV6 to propel it to 60 in 7.3 seconds then on to a top whack of 139 for a list price of £16,395. Handling praised by '*Autocar*' magazine issue 11–7–2001. ZS120 with 115bhp 1.8 K Series engine from £12,495. LPG ZS 120 from July 2002 at an extra £2,195 awaiting Powershift certification which may result in up to 70% rebate.

What's bad: See Rover 45. Head gasket failure common on K series four cylinder engines because very low coolant capacity of engine means small leaks rapidly lead to overheating. Weakest point is water heated inlet manifold gasket.

What to watch out for: See Rover 45.

MG ZT (from June 2001)

What's good: Rover 75 based ZT190 has 2.5 litre KV6 boosted to 190bhp, getting the heavier car to 60 in 7.8 seconds and on to 141mph, which is easily handled by the much improved 75 chassis. Combined economy figure 28.7mpg; Group 15 insurance. ZT190 priced at £21,095. Less powerful MG ZTs from £18,595. Basic chassis of Longbridge built Rover 75 much improved over original Cowley built car. 158bhp ZT160 also available. Rear drive V8 ZT 260 and LPG ZT due summer 2002. BIK Tax beating diesel versions launched August 2002. Saloon gets to 0–60mph in 11.0 secs, goes from 30–50mph in 4th in 8.1 seconds and has a top speed of 120mph. Combined economy is 48.8mpg and CO_2 emissions 163g/km for the manual and 190g/km for the automatic. CO_2 based BIK base rates are 18% and 23% respectively, so with list prices starting at £18,795 and £20,205, 40% BIK tax liability begins at £1,353 and £1,859. MG also announced standard fitment of a slightly more pliant suspension set-up, with a sports suspension option.

What's bad: See Rover 75. Head gasket failure common on K series four cylinder engines because very low coolant capacity of engine means small leaks rapidly lead to overheating. Weakest point is water heated inlet manifold gasket.

What to watch out for: See Rover 75

Recalls: July 2002 recall of 13,000 Rover 75 and MG ZT models due to concerns about front coil spring breakage in cold and high corrosion operating conditions. Front coil springs to be replaced.

MGF (1995 to 2002)

What's good: The car MG enthusiasts had been clamouring for and, true to their words, they bought it in droves. 118 bhp 1.8 or 143 bhp 1.8 VVC. BBR (01280 702389) does a cheap tweak to improve mid-range performance of both engines. Works hard-top looks made for the car. Clever 'crush' boxes built into front bumpers protect the structure of the car in low-speed impacts. Excellent brakes. Plenty of boot space front and rear. Easy to get in and out through wide opening doors. Three years warranty and servicing included from 6/10/2000. Range brightened up considerably in March 2001 with announcement of £15,500 112bhp 1.6i with standard alloys and rip-snorting £21,000 160bhp Trophy SE models. See range road test at www.honestjohn.co.uk.

What's bad: More of a modern MGB than an MGA or Midget. Early MGFs suffered a lot of quality problems, most serious of which was a leaking top, windscreen and bootlid, but fixes were quickly found (park the wrong way on an incline, though, and the soft top may still leak). Suspension and suspension subframe misalignment is more serious. Plastic back window. Started to lose value quite heavily by 1999. Steptronic auto not very good in this car and has horrible, naff and nasty plastic model kit steering wheel buttons. Possibility of camshaft sprocket coming adrift on VVC. According to MG Rover the reason for this is a typing error in the workshop manual which gives the wrong torque setting for the camshaft retaining bolt. The factory and Rover dealers know the correct setting, but independents may go by the manual and get it wrong. Cylinder head and head gasket failures quite common on modular 'K' series engines fitted to all MGFs. S and T platers 10th from bottom in 2001 *Top Gear*/J.D. Power Customer Satisfaction Survey. Second worst after FIAT/Alfa for breakdowns attended by German ADAC during 2001. Head gasket failure common on K series four cylinder engines because very low coolant capacity of engine means small leaks rapidly lead to overheating. Weakest point is water heated inlet manifold gasket. 11th from Bottom of 100 models for reliability in *Auto Express* 2002 survey. Replaced by much improved steel-spring MGTF early 2002.

What to watch out for: The MGF bulletin board (online at www.ipl.co.uk/cgi-bin/forum/MG/sub69/cmtlist.html) is a useful means by which owners can swap information about faults. First look for uneven tyre wear which signifies misaligned suspension or suspension subframes. Then silly things, like a bent cable from the exhaust manifold lambda probe can lose its insulation on the hot pipes, short out and stop the car. British Racing Green paint chips easily on flexible front. Have a good look under the carpets for rust caused by water from leaking hoods. Look under the car for damaged coolant pipes from front radiator to mid-engine (loss of coolant will lead to head gasket problems and possible cracking or warping of the head). Also look for mayonnaise under the oil filler cap. Full dealer service history essential or 'in service' mods may not have been made and a serious mistake may have been made over the camshaft retaining bolt torque setting. Flexible under-engine exhaust joint gives up (like Cavalier diesel) and rattles. It's in unit with rear silencer and the section costs £380. Gear linkages can be troublesome so check for clean changes on test drive. Hard tops are £1,450 – worth remembering if car has not got one. If buying an MGF with a hard top fitted, take it off and check the hood for damage. Immobiliser frequency can suffer interference. The clutch and brake pedals share the same mounting shaft and the clutch pedal can interfere with the brake light switch.

Recalls: Boot and windscreen seals carried out as 'in-service' modifications. No official recalls known 1995–98. 1998: 20,000

MGFs recalled to check for snagging of drivers seatbelt webbing. 10/12/2001: 7,010 MGFs built September 2000 to September 2001 recalled because short circuit in wiring harness may set off seatbelt pretensioners when ignition is switched on. Additional sleeve to be fitted to wiring harness.

X80 (from Summer 2002)

What's good: New £50,000 160mph 2+2 coupe based on the Qvale Mangusta, to have a 4.6 litre V8 delivering 260bhp to 385bhp, manual or automatic transmissions, coupe or roadster bodies. Launch Summer 2002.

Latest news online at www.mg-rover.com

What's bad: Too soon to say.

What to watch out for: Too soon to say.

ZT XPower 385 (from Summer 2002)

What's good: 385bhp rear-drive version of the Rover 75 based MG ZT to be called the MG ZT XPower 385. Torque is a mammoth 385lb ft (522Nm) fed through a six-speed manual box, zero to 60 is predicted at less than 5 seconds, top speed will be 175mph and the price will be around £40,000. A Touring version will also be available when the car goes on sale in summer, 2002, together with a softer 260bhp version.

More online at www.mg-rover.com

What's bad: Not exactly politically correct but gives the brand excitement and glamour.

What to watch out for: Too soon to say.

MICROCAR

Virgo (from 1999)

What's good: French two-seater micro hatchback. Has two-cylinder 505cc Lombardini petrol or diesel engines giving up to 68 mph and up to 78 mpg. Simple, exposed-belt Variomatic transmission. Electric windows and stereo. Fibreglass rather than polycarbonate body. Under the weight limit, so can be driven on a motorcycle licence. Euro Type-Approved. From £6,402 on the road. Three-year warranty on engine.

What's bad: Slow acceleration of diesel.

What to watch out for: Too soon to say.

MINI

Cabrio (from Spring 2004)

What's good: German developed cabrio based on MINI One, MINI Cooper and MINI Cooper S due in UK Spring 2004. Extensive strengthening will make it much heavier than MINI at around 1,250kg, so performance will be down. Might be offered both as a convertible and with a removable hard top but no hood.

What's bad: Pix have shown cars with hood sitting on top of back like old Beetle and Golf, and with stowed hood fully concealed, but can't offer both a boot and seats for four people with the hood invisibly stowed.

What to watch out for: Premiums for the first cars.

Cooper (from 2001)

What's good: BMW's MINI brand shown at the 2000 Motor Show and on sale from July 2001. Great to sit in with retro dials and switchgear, good seats, straight-ahead seating position, adjustable steering column. CHAIN CAM Brazil built engines is 115 bhp 16v 1.6. (See separate entry for 163bhp MINI Cooper S.) Cooper has 15in alloy wheels. Prices from £11,600 with deliveries from September 2001. Very desirable indeed in the right colour. Unlimited mileage two year full manufacturer warranty followed by one year full dealer warranty from November 2001, making total three year unlimited mileage warranty. Paint warranty also extended from 12 months to 24 months. 'TLC' five year or 50,000 mile servicing package for just £100 is an essential add-on. John Cooper garage converted 'Works' MINI Cooper from December 2001 with 131bhp and 119lb ft (162Nm) torque give 0–60 in 8.5 seconds and tops out at 127mph. Priced at £14,100. Controlled second-hand programme launched March 2002 called 'MINI Cherished'. Offers used buyers a complete package of at least 12 months unlimited mileage warranty and Europe-wide emergency service, plus accident management throughout the car's life. Most

Cherished MINIs will come with the remainder of their £100 five-year MINI tlc service pack. All will get a full service prior to sale (if a service is due within 4,000 miles), a thorough multi-point check and road test, a fresh MOT if over 3 years old and an independent history and mileage check. Also a commitment that if any demonstrable fault is found within 30 days or 1,000 miles which can't be fixed then the car will be replaced like for like. Will benefit first owners of MINIs by protecting their investment. Achieved an excellent four star rating for crash safety in 2002 NCAP tests. See road test at www.honestjohn.co.uk

Highly recommended. The most fun car there is.

More online at www.mini.co.uk

What's bad: Not how the original Mini was conceived, but offers more accessible fun than any other production car. Not much room in the back seat (but was there ever in a Mini?) Jiggly ride, worse with Sports Suspension Plus. Doesn't look right in all colours. Faults emerging include pulling to the left (despite alignment checks), dashboard rattles and faulty fuel gauges ('*Autocar*' 10–10–2001). Extras can add thousands to the price. Batteries flattened by a batch of single CD players which do not switch off by the ignition. Other electrical glitches with central locking system. Cat converter is low slung, so best to avoid driving off roading as crud and grass can get trapped between the cat and its heat shield. Report of several MINIs hydraulicing due to ingesting shallow flood water. Further reports of problems with airbags. Reports of gearbox failures.

What to watch out for: Avoid the colour yellow like the plague. It makes the MINI look like a hideous mess of mismatched panels, especially with stuck-on chrome bumper trims. Avoid 17in wheels. Avoid Sports Suspension Plus pack on MINI Cooper (better on standard Sports Suspension with 15in wheels). Independent imports without £100 tlc service package will cost you an extra £500 in servicing. Massive used MINI price confusion because the cost of extras could easily add £4,000 to the price of the car. Some cars have the right extras. Others don't.

Recalls: All new MINIs recalled "due to danger of static electricity causing fires while re-fuelling" (Announced LBC radio news p.m. 3/9/2001). Seems that special paint used to earth the filler neck wears away when filler nozzles are inserted. January 2002 recall to replace the non-switching off CD players which flattened the batteries of early build MINIs.

Cooper S (from Summer 2002)

What's good: Supercharged MINI Cooper S with 163bhp. Together with a six-speed gearbox, gets it from zero to sixty in around seven seconds and on to a top speed of 135mph. Fuel consumption need not suffer unless you boot it hard as a combined figure of 33.6mpg has been recorded for the 1,140kg car. Torque is 155lb ft (210Nm) at 4,000rpm, with at least 124lb ft (179Nm) available between 2,500 and 6,500rpm. Main external differences between the Cooper S and the standard Cooper are a front bonnet air-scoop, and big sixteen-inch or seventeen-inch wheels (the original Mini had to make do with ten-inch wheels). Run-flat 195/55 R16 tyres or optional 205/45 R17 tyres remove the need for a 'spare' wheel, allowing progress to continue for up to 90 miles at up to 50mph. Electro-hydraulic rack and pinion power steering offers a direct 2.5 turns lock to lock. Automatic Stability Control and Traction Control (ASC + T) is standard. Dynamic Stability Control (DSC) will be an option. Expect prices between £15,000 and £16,000. Unlimited mileage two year full manufacturer warranty followed by one year full dealer warranty, making total three year unlimited mileage warranty, plus 24 month paint warranty. First reports are hugely enthusiastic, but recommend 16in rather than better looking 17in wheels as ride is unacceptably hard on 17in. 200bhp John Cooper 'Works' garage conversion eventually expected. Achieved an excellent four star rating for crash safety in 2002 NCAP tests.

More online at www.mini.co.uk

What's bad: Demand is so high that will sell for considerable premiums on base £14,500 price tag. Avoid yellow.

What to watch out for: Go for 16in rather than better looking 17in wheels as ride is unacceptably hard on 17in.

MINI One (from 2001)

What's good: BMW's MINI shown at the 2000 Motor Show and taking orders from July 2001. Great to sit in with retro dials and switchgear, good seats, straight-ahead seating position, adjustable steering column. CHAIN CAM Brazil built engine is 90 bhp 8-valve 1.6. Deliveries from September 2001. Very desirable indeed in the right colour. Unlimited mileage two year full manufacturer warranty followed by one year full dealer warranty from November 2001, making total three year unlimited mileage warranty. Paint warranty also extended from 12 months to 24 months. 'tlc' five year or 50,000 mile servicing package for just £100 is an essential add-on. MINI One to get Toyota's New 75bhp, 123lb ft torque chain-cam 1,364cc D4–D diesel from late 2002. Expect 12.9 second 0–60, 106mph top speed, 64.2mpg combined economy and 117g/km CO_2 output. Controlled second-hand programme launched March 2002 called 'MINI Cherished'. Offers used buyers a complete package of at least 12 months unlimited mileage warranty and Europe-wide emergency service, plus accident management throughout the car's life. Most Cherished MINIs will come with the remainder of their £100 five-year MINI tlc service pack. All will get a full service prior to sale (if a service is due within 4,000 miles), a thorough multi-point check and road test, a fresh MOT if over 3 years old and an independent history and mileage check. Also a commitment that if any demonstrable fault is found within 30 days or 1,000 miles which can't be fixed then the car will be replaced like for like. Will benefit first owners of MINIs by protecting their investment. Achieved an excellent four star rating for crash safety in 2002 NCAP tests.

Highly recommended. The most fun car there is.

More online at www.mini.co.uk

What's bad: Not how the original Mini was conceived, but offers more accessible fun than any other production car. Not much room in the back seat (but was there ever in a Mini?) Jiggly ride on optional Sports Suspension. Doesn't look right in all colours. Faults emerging include pulling to the left (despite alignment checks), dashboard rattles and faulty fuel gauges ('*Autocar*' 10–10–2001). Extras can add thousands to the price. Batteries flattened by a batch of single CD players which do not switch off by the ignition. Other electrical glitches with central locking system. Cat converter is low slung, so best to avoid driving off roading as crud and grass can get trapped between the cat and its heat shield. Report of several MINIs hydraulicing due to ingesting shallow flood water. Further reports of problems with airbags. Reports of gearbox failures.

What to watch out for: Avoid the colour yellow like the plague. It makes the MINI look like a hideous mess of mismatched panels, especially with stuck-on chrome bumper trims. Independent imports without £100 tlc service package will cost you an extra £500 in servicing. Massive used MINI price confusion because the cost of extras could easily add £4,000 to the price of the car. Some cars have the right extras. Others don't.

Recalls: All new MINIs recalled "due to danger of static electricity causing fires while re-fuelling" (Announced LBC radio news p.m. 3/9/2001). Seems that special paint used to earth the filler neck wears away when filler nozzles are inserted. January 2002 recall to replace the non-switching off CD players which flattened the batteries of early build MINIs.

MITSUBISHI

3000GT (1992 to 2000)

What's good: Mitsubishi GTO, Dodge Eagle Talon 282bhp V6 twin turbo four wheel drive, four wheel steer 160mph coupe with 5.6 second 0–60. Quite big at 15 ft long and more than 6ft wide and no lightweight at 1,740kg. Facelifted in October 1994 and August 1995. Six-speed manual gearbox from August 1996. Navigation system from September 1998.

What's bad: Around in other markets such as Japan (RHD) and USA (LHD) fore several years before it came to the UK, which is why you see G and H reg. independent imports at auction.

What to watch out for: The cheap ones will be independent imports and may be the non turbo 225bhp SR. Starter price is around £3,000 for an old one. Unless you're prepared to gamble, these cars need a thorough professional check by someone who knows them inside out.

Airtek 4x4 (from April 2003)

What's good: Lancer based 'crossover' mid-size SUV/estate car based on US Outlander model due in Europe with revised suspension, 2.0 litre and 2.4 litre GDI engines and different name.

What's bad: Too soon to say.

What to watch out for: Too soon to say.

Carisma (1995 to 2004)

What's good: Decent engines, especially 1.8GDI which gives 40 mpg plus economy or strong acceleration from 125 bhp – but not both at the same time. Painless to drive and own. Excellent three-year unlimited mileage warranty. Designed for low servicing costs. Facelifted summer 1999 with new beak-like front. In June 2001 Mitsubishi was rated by Motor Warranty Direct as Britain's 5th most claim-free used marque (check online at www.warrantydirect.co.uk)

1,870cc DI-D direct injected diesel introduced March 2002 with 100bhp, 158lb ft torque, 0–60 in 11.5 seconds, top speed 118mph, CO_2 emissions 146g/km and prices from £10,995. BIK tax payable 2002/2003 just £435.40 at 22% or £791.64 at 40%. 17th from top of 100 models for reliability in *Auto Express* 2002 survey.

What's bad: Bland Nedcar Eurobox, more Orion- than Mondeo-sized. Not great to drive. Diesel version much slower and not much more economical than petrol GDI. Cheap and nasty welds holding front side window frames onto doors.

What to watch out for: Ex-fleet cars may have been abused by drivers. Steering could have suffered damage from kerbing. If you smell petrol, it could be that the in-tank fuel pump retaining cap ring has shattered. Was a recall but did not reach all early Carisma owners. Drive-shaft gaiters prone to leaking grease. Have been reports of valve gear failure in 1.8GDI engines fitted to Volvo S40s and V40s, possibly due to dirty oil.

Recalls: Unknown date: recall of early Carismas to correct a fault with the plastic in tank fuel pump cap ring which could shatter.

Challenger /Shogun Sport (from 1998)

What's good: 4x4 pick-up-based 5–seater cut-price alternative to the long wheelbase Shogun, with Shogun's 'old' 2.5 diesel and 3.0 V6 petrol engines plus independent front suspension. Tough and should last well. Improved for 2000 model year with option of INVECS II four speed autobox. Re-named Shogun Sport. Got the new L200ft s uprated Step III 2.5 diesel engine from mid November 2001, which brought it a 16% power boost and a 5% improvement in economy. Revised 4-cylinder in-line 2.5 litre turbo-diesel engine delivers 177 lb ft (240Nm) torque at 2,000 rpm thanks to long-stroke design and twin-scroll turbo with intercooler. 'Silent Shaft' technology makes it smoother than usual diesels. Variable nozzle turbocharger also boosts top-end power by a healthy 16%, which has resulted in an improved power output of 114 bhp at 4,000 rpm (previously 98 bhp at 4,000rpm). The 2.5 engine gives an Extra Urban fuel consumption figure of 31.4 mpg (Equippe model), an increase of over 5%. The 3.0 V6 ECI-MULTI Step III engine delivers

168bhp at 5,000 rpm and 188 lb ft (255Nm) torque at 4,500 rpm, and an Extra Urban fuel consumption figure of 28.5mpg (Equippe manual model) but 168bhp v.s 174bhp in order to meet Euro III regs. Other specification changes for 2002 include; electrically folding door mirrors, improved security by means of additional door lock shielding, a more luxurious 'soft-feel' seat trim, and the addition of EBD (Electronic Brakeforce Distribution) to the ABS braking system on Equippe and Elegance models. Three trim levels: Classic, Equippe or Elegance, with prices starting at £19,000 for the 2.5 TD Classic, ranging to £24,495 for the 3.0 litre V6 Elegance petrol model with automatic transmission. CO_2 tax band D.

More online at www.mitsubishi-cars.co.uk

What's bad: Ride and handling not up to new monocoque Shogun.
What to watch out for: Evidence of heavy off-road use or heavy towing.

Colt (1989 to 1992)

What's good: Pleasingly-styled along same lines as larger Galant and Lancer 4–door and 5–door. Better looking than Lancer. Engines: 1,298cc 68 bhp; 1,468cc, 74 bhp; 1,596cc, 123 bhp Gate 16v grew to 1,836cc and 134 bhp in April 1990 putting it firmly in the Golf GTI 16v league. All models run on standard premium unleaded.
What's bad: Service costs and parts prices, particularly body parts.
What to watch out for: Rust in the seams and floor pan. Skimped, independent servicing after 3-year warranty ran out.
Recalls: 1996 (1991–1994 build): check for loss of brake fluid.

Colt (1992 to 1996)

What's good: Quite a pretty car which lived on as the Proton Compact when Mitsubishi restyled the Colt in 1996. 1,298cc 74 bhp; 1,597cc 111 bhp; 1,834cc twin-cam 138 bhp. Very well built. In June 2001 Mitsubishi was rated by Motor Warranty Direct as Britain's 5th most claim-free used marque (check online at www.warrantydirect.co.uk)
What's bad: Only one small three-door body-style, more supermini-

sized than Escort-sized. If body parts are hard to get, try a Proton dealer.

What to watch out for: Skimped, independent servicing after 3-year warranty ran out. Tappety engines. Badly shifting autobox. Uneven tyre wear signifies kerb damage, possibly strained PAS rack. Could need a cambelt change.

Recalls: 1996 (1991–1994 build): check for loss of brake fluid.

Colt (1996 to 2004)

What's good: Smooth 88 bhp 1.6 engine feels more powerful (more like the 111 bhp it used to have). Gives excellent combination of performance and up to 42 mpg. Other engine option: 74 bhp 1,298cc. Decent steering, ride and handling. Beautifully built. In June 2001 Mitsubishi was rated by Motor Warranty Direct as Britain's 5th most claim-free used marque (check online at www.warrantydirect.co.uk).

What's bad: Only one small three-door body-style, more supermini-sized than Escort-sized. Not very space efficient and not as neat looking as previous model. Mirage bodykit ugly and rear spoiler not car-wash proof. Not much back seat room. Shorter people find restricted rear visibility makes it difficult to reverse. Getting very long in the tooth compared to the opposition.

What to watch out for: Must have been dealer serviced to retain warranty. Aircon was a very expensive dealer aftermarket extra.

Recalls: 1997 (June-August 1997 build): 213 cars found to have sticking brake booster valve. 6/11/2000: 4,249 Colts built 1996–1999 recalled because crankshaft pulley securing bolt may not have been torqued correctly and may loosen or break leading to detachment of pulley. All engines up to YD2145 remove pulley securing bolt, increase the depth of thread in the crankshaft by 5mm, check for damage and renew if necessary. Lubricate threads, refit and tighten to specified torque. Engines from YD2146 on: remove pulley securing bolt, examine for damage and renew if necessary, lubricate threads, refit and tighten to specified torque.

Colt CZ2 (from late 2003)

What's good: Mitsubishi's new joint venture, now with Daimler Chrysler (company called MDC) to be built at the Born plant in Holland along with the 5–door MCC Smart. Code name NCC (New Compact Car). German built Mitsubishi designed MDC 1.1 and 1.3 direct injected petrol engines, plus a diesel. Due late 2003. Likely to cost from around £9,000.

What's bad: Too soon to say.

What to watch out for: Too soon to say.

FTO (1996 to 2000)

What's good: Looks like a 3/4 size Aston Martin DB7 and now backed by the UK Mitsubishi service network. Front wheel drive. GS model has 1,834cc 125bhp four cylinder engine giving 0–60 in 9.2 seconds and topping out at 125mph. GR and GX have 1,999cc 170bhp V6 giving 0–60 in 7.9 seconds and 136mph. GPX and GPR have 1,999cc 200bhp MIVEC V6 giving 0–60 in 7 seconds and 142mph. Mitsubishi's own Red Zebra scheme means you can now buy selected used Japanese imports with franchised dealer peace of mind. In June 2001 Mitsubishi was rated by Motor Warranty Direct as Britain's 5th most claim-free used marque (check online at www.warrantydirect.co.uk)

What's bad: As they come off the boat from Japan numerous mods are needed for the cars to run properly on UK petrol and meet UK/EU Type Approval regs. A good outfit to sort the car out is Protech, tel: 01179 861611. Now out of production.

What to watch out for: Mainly watch out you're not buying a GS for GPX MIVEC money. Make sure the car is properly UK SVA certificated, or has at least been sorted by a specialist such as Protech.

Galant (1988 to 1993)

What's good: Quite good looking and well equipped. GLSI an early beneficiary of ABS. Much improved by Diamond Option Pack. Wood trim packs also help. Normal models very reliable.

521

What's bad: 4WD/4WS model too complicated to make a sound second-hand buy. Diesel engine only available briefly in 1989. Parts for major repairs are expensive.

What to watch out for: If fitted with ABS, make sure warning light goes out and that it works. Check for aircon and, if fitted, make sure it delivers cold air. Independent servicing once warranty ran out may have been skimped. Water pumps go (check expansion tank level and check under oil cap for mayonnaise indicating a cooked engine and cylinder head trouble). Power steering pump or rack may leak fluid. Engines wrecked by timing belt failure, so best changed every 36,000 miles or every three years. Uneven tyre wear on 4WD/4WS could signify suspension problems which cost a fortune to put right. Getting old now, so check carefully for rust.

Galant (1993 to 1997)

What's good: Better looking, slightly bigger Galant, still in Mondeo/Vectra class. 125bhp 1.8 16v and 135bhp 2.9 16v four cylinder engines. 4 speed auto option on 2.0. Or 147bhp 2.0 V6 manual or auto and 168bhp 2.5 V6 four wheel drive with four wheel steer, 5 speed manual only. In June 2001 Mitsubishi was rated by Motor Warranty Direct as Britain's 5th most claim-free used marque (check online at www.warrantydirect.co.uk)

What's bad: 2.5 V6 four-wheel-drive with four-wheel steer a bit too complex to be a sensible second-hand buy.

What to watch out for: See 1989–93.

Recalls: 1994/1995 models (2,000 UK cars): possible fault with brake booster. (Announced August 2000. Owners to be contacted later.) 22/1/2001: Possibility that fuel tank upper panel and baffle plate not correctly welded leading to crack in the weld and fuel leaks. To be inspected and tanks replaced if leaking, otherwise protector plate to be fitted. 12/7/2001: 5,207 Galants built 1/1/1993 to 31/12/1996 recalled because water and dirt may get into lower arm ball joint leading to premature wear. Lower ball joints to be inspected and replaced if necessary.

Galant (from 1997)

What's good: Grew from being Mercedes C-Class size to Mercedes E-Class size. Saloon or estate (made Sigma redundant.) Very Japanese, but very striking styling. By UK standards, quite good value. 161bhp 2.5 litre V6 automatic estate is a big, heavy, luxurious car. Usual excellent three-year unlimited mileage warranty. Three three-point rear seatbelts from 1998 model year. Smallest engine now 134bhp 2.0 litre 16v four. 147bhp 2.4 GDI engine from October 1999. Amazing VR4 estate has 280 bhp, four-wheel drive, 'Tiptronic'-type auto, anti-yaw control, and is both quick and safe. In June 2001 Mitsubishi was rated by Motor Warranty Direct as Britain's 5th most claim-free used marque (check online at www.warrantydirect.co.uk)20th from top of 100 models for reliability in *Auto Express* 2002 survey.

What's bad: Quite hard to judge the front when parking. More suspension 'clonks' than a BMW. Don't hold their value as well as a Mercedes or BMW. Mix of officially imported and grey imported VR4s. Only pay grey price for a grey.

What to watch out for: Minor body damage could mean a major repair bill.

Recalls: Mitsubishi Galant 2.4GDI (264 cars in UK): possible fault with brake booster. August 2000 official recall. 24/8/2000: 1,921 Galants and Spacewagons built 1998–1999 recalled because nipple of brake booster vacuum hose may become choked with combustion products from engine causing reduced braking efficiency. Nipple to be relocated away from source of combustion products.

L200

What's good: Very good looking pick-up, most popular with four-door twin-cab and four wheel drive. Has Mitsubishi's evergreen 2,477cc turbo intercooled 4 cylinder diesel developing 98bhp at 4,000rpm and 177lb ft torque at 2,000rpm giving top speed of 88mph. Even twin cab has payload of more than 1 tonne which qualifies it to be treated as a commercial vehicle for VAT purposes. Cut price Trojan diesel four-wheel-drive twin-cab version at pre-

VAT prices from £13,995 on the road. Standard kit includes part-time four-wheel-drive, power steering, electric front and rear windows, electronic immobiliser, side protector mouldings, headlamp washers, rear cabguard frame and load-hooks. Trojan III, priced at £14,495 + VAT does away with the cabguard frame and load hooks and instead is fitted with alloy wheels, colour-keyed front bumper, side steps, wheelarch extensions, two-tone paint, electric heated door mirrors and central locking. At £15,495 + VAT, Trojan IV has in addition a leather steering wheel and gearshift knob, driver and passenger airbags, ABS and air-con. Further spec changes, price cuts of up to £1,551 and new Step III engines in November 1991. Revised engine still delivers 177 lb ft (240Nm) torque at 2,000 rpm. 'Silent Shaft' technology makes it smoother than usual diesels. Variable nozzle turbocharger boosts top-end power by a healthy 16% to 114 bhp at 4,000 rpm. 2002 line-up consists of 2WD and 4WD Single Cab Pick-Up, L200 Double Cab GL 2.5 TD, L200 Double Cab 4–Life 2.5 TD, and the third generation Animal Cab which will be introduced early in 2002. Price reductions range from £585 to £1,551. Prices are: 2WD Single Cab £9,995 + VAT; 4WD Single Cab £12,395 + VAT; 4WD Double Cab GL £14,495 + VAT; 4WD Double Cab 4–Life £15,995 + VAT. All new range meet the Euro III emissions regulations.

More online at www.mitsubishi.co.uk

What's bad: A truck, but a good looking nice truck that's not bad to drive. At time of writing could qualify as a van with £500 BIK liability, but not in every tax area and moves are afoot to close this 'loophole'.

What to watch out for: Most have been and still are sold as independent imports, so be very wary of what you pay for what.

Lancer (1988 to 1992)

What's good: Essentially a slightly stretched Colt with either a 4–door saloon or 5–door hatchback body. Looks very much like a shrunken Galant. Engines: 1,298cc 68 bhp; 1,468cc, 74 bhp; 1,596cc, 123 bhp Gate 16v grew to 1,836cc and 134 bhp in April 1990. Also, just to complicate matters, a 1,755cc 95 bhp engine for the GLXi with four-wheel drive. All models run on standard premium unleaded.

What's bad: Not much rear legroom for a four-door saloon. Looks a bit truncated. GLXi had an (unnecessary) catalytic converter. Lancers dropped from official UK line-up from 1992. Next generation Japanese Lancer became Proton Persona. Body parts very difficult to obtain.

What to watch out for: Rust in the seams and floor pan. Skimped, independent servicing after 3-year warranty ran out. Uneven tyre wear may signify suspension damage or misalignment on four-wheel-drive model. Very hard to re-set and get right.

Recalls: 1996 (1991–1994 build): check for loss of brake fluid.

Lancer (from late 2003)

What's good: Japanese Lancer may come to Europe to replace Carisma.

What's bad: Too soon to say.

What to watch out for: Too soon to say.

Lancer Estate (2000 to 2002)

What's good: 1,600cc 111bhp 5–door air-conditioned, Australian built estate launched in UK at a bargain price of £10,995 complete with 3-year warranty. 14 ft long; 5ft 7in wide. Some specialists cut the price back to an incredible £8,995. A real bargain.

What's bad: Can't think of anything.

What to watch out for: No complaints at all.

Lancer Evo (1996 to 2001)

What's good: Hat-trick, three wins in a row Tommi Makinen World Rally car, officially imported by Mitsubishi joint venture with Ralliart. £31,000 280 bhp EVO VI reckoned to be better than the best Imprezas, and GSR450 has 450 bhp. EVO VI does 0–60 in 5 seconds and tops out at 150 mph at 7,000 rpm in 5th. Incredible anti-yaw control means it always corners flat. In the hands of a good driver it's probably the fastest road car for UK driving conditions. Very safe as well as enormous fun to drive. So good it flatters the driver. Apart from on a motorway or dual carriageway virtually nothing could outrun one. Cut-price stripped out EVO V1 RSX loses aircon, anti-lock brakes and anti-yaw control but sold for £25,995 OTR. New EVO VII on sale in UK from September 2001 is based on Japanese Lancer Cedia model (see separate entry).

What's bad: Most UK cars weren't officially imported. Older Japanese grey imports start rusting in as little as three years. Specifications of grey imports may be all over the place, so tread very carefully. Could be problems with Enhanced Single Vehicle Approval from August 2001. Mitsubishi and Ralliart parted company in early 2002.

What to watch out for: Accident damage and hidden suspension damage.

Recalls: Apparent suspension recall notified to owners, but by February 2001 parts to rectify had still not arrived from Japan. 27/7/2001: 156 Lancer Evo IV and V models built 20/12/1996 to 17/7/1998 recalled because ECU of Active Yaw Control may be incorrectly programmed causing clutches in torque transfer diff to remain disengaged when the engine starts leading to damage to the rear diff. ECU to be replaced.

Lancer Evo VII (from late 2001)

What's good: Effectively, in real world conditions, the Evo VII 300 is probably the fastest point to point car in the UK. Two EVO VIIs are available: the RS II 276 bhp model which has Active Yaw Control and Recaro seats and is priced at £29,995. But there is also a 300bhp version of the same car called the EVO VII 300 priced at £31,495. Both do over 150mph, but whereas the 276 gets to sixty in 4.4 seconds, the 300 does it in 4.0 dead. In addition to the enhancements to the power unit and exhaust system, the Evo VII 300 has a carbon fibre dash and switch panels, carbon fibre gear knob and carbon fibre rear spoiler end plates. The work on the Evo VII 300 is undertaken by Mitsubishi Motors own UK preparation centre at Portbury, Bristol. The handling and roadholding of these cars is literally unbelievable, and that's what puts them ahead of any roadgoing Ferrari or even the quickest motorbikes. They will catch anything and nothing will stay with them.

More online at www.mitsubishi-cars.co.uk

What's bad: It will lead you into temptation and you could very easily lose your licence as a result.

What to watch out for: Damage from over-revved engines and kerbing.

Shogun (1991 to 1999)

What's good: Big, but not 'aggressive' looking. Better on the road than a Discovery or Range Rover. 3-year unlimited mileage warranty from new. Useful 139bhp 3.0 litre V6 replaced by 205bhp 3.5 litre 24v V6 in February 1994. 98bhp 2.5 turbodiesel replaced by 123bhp TD in 5–door from February 1994, but lived on in the swb 3–door Shogun. Auto available. 5–door is a full seven-seater, but driver's rear vision badly restricted. 5–door is a big vehicle 15 ft 6ins long and 5ft 10in wide. Curious 'bitty' facelift as from autumn 1997 Motor Show. In June 2001 Mitsubishi was rated by Motor Warranty Direct as Britain's 5th most claim-free used marque (check online at www.warrantydirect.co.uk)

What's bad: Don't buy for economy. Even the 2.8 litre diesel in the 5–door body is pushed to better 22 mpg and the 2.5 diesel is not really powerful enough. 3.0 litre V6s even more thirsty. Diesels are a bit slow. Gearboxes are the first bits to break. Timing belt of V6 drives water pump, so seizure of water pump wrecks engine.

What to watch out for: Eventually, they do rust and it's important to check all the points where the body meets the chassis. Listen for transmission whine (used replacement gear and transfer boxes are available from API, tel: 0500 830530). Make all usual 4x4 checks: underbody damage; grumbling wheel bearings; suspension alignment; if it's been towing, what has it been towing? Steering arm balljoints go, but are fairly cheap to replace and easy to get at. Quite a few 'exported' to BFPO squaddies and re-imported tax-free. Make sure it's a real UK-market Shogun and not a 'Pajero' or 'Montero' badged as one. Pay less for Pajeros and Monteros.

Recalls: 1996: (1991–1994 build): check for loss of brake fluid. 27/9/2000: 278 Shoguns built in 1994 recalled because brake fluid may seep from front hoses. Hoses to be replaced. 17th April 2002: '*Autocar*' report that 60,000 Shoguns and Pajeros built 1989–1999 recalled to replace steering components, failure of which could result in loss of control. UK recall includes private imports.

Shogun (from 1999)

What's good: Still obviously a Shogun, but now more rounded looking with monocoque shell. New '4M41ft 3.2 litre 16-valve direct injected diesel replaces underpowered old 2.8, offering 173 bhp and 282 lb ft torque. 217 bhp/257 lb ft 3.5 litre GDI V6 replaces thirsty old 24v V6. Suspension now independent both front and rear which improves on road ride comfort and handling enormously. Improved water pump on V6 to help prevent engine failures. Cut price Classic model from October 2000 with 3.2 DI-D engine and 3–door or 5–door bodies from £22,995.

What's bad: Nothing yet.

What to watch out for: Beware of grey imports and RHD Pajeros stolen in another country. The Pajero is Europe's most stolen and unrecovered vehicle.

Recalls: 2001 recall on 8,800 2001 build Shoguns/Pajeros to replace faulty brake amplifier.

Shogun Pinin (from 1999)

What's good: Cute 'shrunken Shogun' designed to compete with Vitara. 120 bhp 1.8 litre GDI engine helps economy. 5-speed manual or 4-speed auto options. Not bad to drive short distances on road in two-wheel drive. Short overhangs, selectable four-wheel drive, high/low-range gears, centre diff lock and light weight make it very capable off-road. By far the best junior 4x4 off road. 2.0 litre 5–door version also available from January 2001 at prices from £15,995 on the road with Mitsubishi's bulletproof 3 year warranty. ABS and EBS standard on this model. New 2.0 litre GDI engine develops 127bhp at 5,000 rpm and 140 lb ft torque at 3,500 rpm.

Top speed 106mph, 0–60 10.6 seconds v/s max 104 mph and 0–60 10.0 seconds for 1.8 GDI Pinin 3–door. 2.0 GDI introduced in 3–door as Shogun Pinin Mirage in October 2001 priced at £13,995 for the manual or £14,995 for the auto, both with standard ABS + EBD and two-tone bodywork. Other Shogun Pinin prices start at £12,495 for the 1.8 GDI 3–door Classic and run through to £17,995 for the top of the range 2.0 GDI 5–door Elegance with automatic transmission.

More online at www.mitsubishi-cars.co.uk

What's bad: Not as quick as RAV 4 on the road and tiring to drive long distances. Limited interior space. Not much luggage space behind rear seats of 3–door version. Quite severe rust problems reported even on apparently new cars, possible due to quality of steel used in Italy to build the car.

What to watch out for: Evidence of heavy off-road use.

Recalls: 18/12/2000: 1,488 Shogun Pinins built 1999–2000 recalled due to possibility that a condenser may come away from the circuit board due to a wiring breakage resulting in the engine stopping or becoming difficult to start. Silicone to be applied to the condenser to act as a vibration damper to counteract shocks transmitted from the suspension to the circuit board.

Sigma (1991 to 1996)

What's good: Two cars: Japanese-built high-tech 202 bhp 24-valve 3.0 litre V6 'executive' saloon or Australian-built 168 bhp 12-valve 3.0 litre V6 estate which came later in Feb '93. Both front-wheel-drive, both capable of over 130 mph and saloon capable of over 140. Engines sound wonderful. Steering a bit too light. Manual option on estate, but not saloon. Aircon standard on saloon, optional on estate. In June 2001 Mitsubishi was rated by Motor Warranty Direct as Britain's 5th most claim-free used marque (check online at www.warrantydirect.co.uk)

What's bad: 202 bhp Sigma saloon too complicated for long-term reliability at more than three years old. Lots of gewgaws to go wrong. Body parts and light lenses can be hard to get.

What to watch out for: Make sure estate has aircon. Check for damage in load area from loads and dogs. If it's had a towbar, what has it been towing? Look for skimped independent servicing once warranty ran out. Especially important to look for things like body damage and MOT failure cracked light lenses because of difficulty getting replacements.

Recalls: 1996: (1991–1994 build): check for loss of brake fluid.

Space Runner (1992 to 1998)

What's good: Strange looking, but very practical car. Rear seat comes right out leaving large cube of space. Excellent 3-speed plus overdrive automatic gives 35 mpg. Neat handling. Good performance from 121 bhp 16-valve 1.8 litre engine. Upright driving position. Optional aircon does not hurt fuel consumption unduly. Excellent vehicle for the disabled. 3-year unlimited mileage warranty. In June 2001 Mitsubishi was rated by Motor Warranty Direct as Britain's 5th most claim-free used marque (check online at www.warrantydirect.co.uk)

What's bad: Rear seat in one piece and heavy. Needs optional £35 rear bumper protector to avoid scuff marks. Only one (left hand side) sliding rear door. Comparatively high used prices due to usefulness and scarcity. Replaced in UK at end of 1998 by new Carisma-based Space Star. (We didn't get new Japanese market Space Runner.) Regular timing belt changes essential.

What to watch out for: Check sliding door mechanism. Timing belts need changing regularly or engines destroy themselves. Have a good sniff for lingering doggy smells. Check for damage form clumsy wheelchair ramp modifications. Servicing may have been skimped after 3-year warranty period.

Space Runner (from 1999)

What's good: Japanese market new Space Runner seen at European Motor Shows with twin rear sliding side doors, engines up to 2.4GDI and even a rip-snorting Evo version.

What's bad: Did not officially come to the UK, but Red Zebra dealers may be able to offer used Japanese imports.

What to watch out for: No UK parts stocks, so parts have to come from Japan.

Space Star (1998 -to 2002)

What's good: Carisma-based, Netherlands built 5–door mini MPV to compete against Scenic. Had 85 bhp 1.3 Colt engine or 125 bhp 1.8 GDI at launch. 3-year, unlimited mileage warranty. Versatile rear seats can be double-folded, slid forwards or reclined. Three proper three-point rear seatbelts. Prices from just £9,995 OTR. Auto option from October 2000. New 96bhp 1.6 engine gives top speed of 112mph and combined consumption of 39.2. 'Mirage' 1.6 from Summer 2001 has alloys, central locking, front electric windows, radio/cassette, driver and passenger airbags, metallic silver paint, colour coded bumpers and alloy dashboard trim all for £10,695. Mirage also available with 81bhp 1.3 engine for £9,995. Facelift plus 101bhp diesel and GDI engine options due September/October 2002.

What's bad: Average three star NCAP crash safety rating announced 28/3/2001. 1.3 will tug a family of four along at a reasonable pace, but economy suffers. Not powerful enough for five adults and their luggage. For this you need the 1.6 or the 1.8GDi.

What to watch out for: Nothing yet.

Space Star II (from 2002)

What's good: Launched Summer 2002. Looks very similar, but under the skin this is a new Space Star. Huge suspension improvements turn it into a positive handler, much better than Scenic and Picasso. New 1.6 petrol engine, automatic option and new Renault block/Mitsubishi head 101bhp 1.9DI-D common rail diesel which offers strong performance. Prices still start at £9,995 for 1.3. DI-D diesel will start at £11,995. Diesel models have ABS.

What's bad: Too soon to say.

What to watch out for: Too soon to say.

Space Wagon (1984 to 1991)

What's good: The original Space Wagon, often used as taxis and capable of running to 300,000 miles within the three year unlimited mileage warranty. 1,755cc 90bhp petrol engine with 5 speed manual or 3 speed autobox. Briefly supplemented by 1,795cc 74bhp turbodiesel from November 1985 to September 1989. Seven seats. Compact size of 14ft long by 5ft 5ins wide.

What's bad: Old now and likely to have covered a Starship Enterprise mileage.

What to watch out for: Clocking, rust, lack of oil changes and when was the timing belt and tensioner last changed?

Space Wagon (1991 to 1999)

What's good: Car-sized seven-seater (14ft 9ins long, 5ft 7ins wide). Not as high as other MPVs. More car-like to drive. 121 bhp 1.8 litre engine replaced by 131 bhp 2.0 litre in August 1992 ('K' reg. onwards). 3 speed plus overdrive 4th automatic option. 80bhp 2.0 litre turbodiesel briefly available from January 1995 to March 1996. In June 2001 Mitsubishi was rated by Motor Warranty Direct as Britain's 5th most claim-free used marque (check online at www.warrantydirect.co.uk)

What's bad: Rearmost seat slopes forwards, not very comfortable for adults. Heavier than Space Runner, so doesn't handle as well and not as much fun to drive.

What to watch out for: Timing belts need changing regularly or engines destroy themselves. May have been mini-cabbed and run up huge mileage under 3-year warranty. Servicing may have been skimped after first three years. Check for uneven tyre wear. Cable gearchange of manual can become sloppy. Also quite a few grey imports knocking around, so satisfy yourself as to proper UK spec unless offered extremely cheaply.

Recalls: 24/8/2000: 1,921 Galants and Spacewagons built 1998–1999 recalled because nipple of brake booster vacuum hose may become choked with combustion products from engine causing reduced braking efficiency. Nipple to be relocated away from source of combustion products.

Space Wagon (1999 on)

What's good: Bigger than its predecessor (15 ft long and 6ft wide), now with 145 bhp 2.4 litre four-cylinder GDI engine and option of cheaper 2.0 litre engine. 5 speed manual or 4 speed auto. All have dash mounted gearlever and very useful 'walk through' cab design enabling the driver to get out kerbside or walk between the front seats to reach a child in the rear. Prices cut from December 2001, with fresh deliveries from February 2002. Base 2.0 litre model at £15,995 develops 131bhp at 6,000rmp and 175Nm (129lb ft) torque at 4,500rpm, averages 29.7 mpg and emits 225g/km CO_2. 2.4GDI at £17,995 develops 145bhp at 5,700rpm and 212Nm (156lb ft) torque at 3,500rpm, averages 28.0 mpg and emits 242g/km CO_2. Both have ABS, EBD, 15in locking alloy wheels, manual air-conditioning and roof rails.

More online at www.mitsubishi-cars.co.uk

What's bad: New model only a Three-Star performer in NCAP crash tests (4 points front impact; 15 points side impact).

What to watch out for: As predecessor, but will still be under the 3-year warranty, so will have been properly dealer serviced.

Recalls: Mitsubishi Space Wagon 2.4GDI (1,657 cars in UK): possible fault with brake booster. August 2000 official recall.. 24/8/2000: 1,921 Galants and Spacewagons built 1998–1999 recalled because nipple of brake booster vacuum hose may become choked with combustion products from engine causing reduced braking efficiency. Nipple to be relocated away from source of combustion products. 18/5/2001: Worldwide recall of all 250,000 new shape Space Wagons to check for cracks around fuel tank mounting plates. 31/10/2001: 2,801 Space Wagons and Space Runners built 1/1/1998 to 31/12/2001 recalled because fuel tank upper panel may suffer stress fatigue. If there are any cracks in the tank, the tank is to be replaced.

MORGAN

4/4

What's good: Traditional Morgan looks and sliding pillar front suspension with 1,796cc 115bhp Rover K Series engine putting out 120lb/ft (160Nm) torque. Light weight of 868kg, five speed gearbox and combined consumption of 34.53 make it surprisingly economical. Length: 3,890mm (12ft 9ins); width: 1,500mm (4ft 9ins). New Junair paint-shop means much wider range of colours, better quality finish and shorter delivery dates, now down to less than two years and as little as 13 months for new orders. Le Mans '62 special launched June 2002 with a specially-developed hard top, unique Morgan Racing Green finish, and racing trim throughout. The 4/4 version costs £27,500.

More online at www.morgan-motor.co.uk

What's bad: Hard ride. Uncomfortable driving position. Low ground clearance. Draughty hood. Front end hops about all over the place. Sports car motoring like it used to be.

What to watch out for: See Rover 25 and 45 for engine.

Aero 8

What's good: Morgan Motor Company (MMC) has secured European Whole Vehicle Type approval for its new Aero 8 supercar. The first completely new Morgan car for 60 years, the Aero8 features an advanced bonded aluminium chassis and a specially-developed 4,398cc 32 valve BMW V8 which puts out 286bhp and 324lb ft (440Nm) torque through six speed gearbox giving this 1,000kg car serious performance potential. Zero to 60 in about 4.5 seconds. Tops out at 160mph. Combined consumption 22.8mpg. Emissions 295g/km. Length: 4,120mm (13ft 6ins); width: 1,770mm 5ft 10ins.). New Junair paint-shop means much wider range of colours, better quality finish and shorter delivery dates, now down to less than two years and as little as 13 months for new orders.

More online at www.morgan-motor.co.uk

What's bad: Controversial retro/modern looks.
What to watch out for: Too soon to say.

Plus 8

What's good: 4.0 litre aluminium Rover V8 pumps out a conservative 190bhp and 225lb ft (305Nm) torque. 5-speed gearbox and low kerb weight of 940kg. Length: 3,960mm (13 ft); width: 1,630mm (5 ft 4 ins). New Junair paint-shop means much wider range of colours, better quality finish and shorter delivery dates, now down to less than two years and as little as 13 months for new orders. Le Mans '62 special launched June 2002 with a specially-developed hard top, unique Morgan Racing Green finish, and racing trim throughout priced at £39,900.

More online at www.morgan-motor.co.uk

What's bad: Hard ride. Low ground clearance. 30 year model life due to end soon.
What to watch out for: If buying used, have the car checked by a Morgan specialist.

NISSAN

100NX (1992 to 1995)

What's good: Small Sunny based targa topped coupe with twin removable glass panel roof. Seats two adults and two kids. 1,597cc catalysed 16 valve engine pumps out 89bhp. 4 speed auto optional. Power increased to 101bhp from February 1993. Limited edition 'Pacific' model in June 1995. Used to hold its value well because was much loved by its fans. Timing chain rather than timing belt engine.
What's bad: Odd looking and neither practical not sporty, but some people love them.
What to watch out for: Same twin timing chain engine as Primera, Sunny and Almera 1.6. Needs clean oil.

200SX (1994 to 2001)

What's good: Transformed by new body from October 1994. Squat, well-proportioned, almost Italian looks. Very tasty. 1996 facelift made it even better. 197 bhp 2.0 litre turbo four not bad either. Manual or automatic. Usually with leather and aircon. Rear drive handling. Better ride than previous version. More room inside, especially back seats.
What's bad: Not as sharp to drive as previous model. (But still inclined to swap ends in the wet.)
What to watch out for: Oddball grey imports not to proper spec with 55 mph limited Japanese tyres, and wipers that lift off the screen at 70 mph. Must have been serviced zealously, with extra oil changes to protect the turbo bearings. Synthetic oil a wise move.

300SX (1990 to 1994)

What's good: Very serious twin-turbo 280 bhp junior supercar, killed off by European emissions legislation. 'Full on' manuals or 'Mr Softy' autos, usually with leather and air. Squat shape 14ft 10in long by 5ft 11in wide and a substantial 1,580kg. Very comfortable.

Goes like stink and handles surprisingly well. 5-speed manual or 4-speed auto.

What's bad: Rear three-quarter vision not good. Handbrake a long way back. To drive, the manual is best, but buy an auto.

What to watch out for: Grey imports without the twin turbos and other important items of kit. Greys have less rust-proofing so tin worm is also a problem with these cars. Noisy engines. Exhaust smoke (turbo oil seals), dirty oil, lack of maintenance. Look for uneven tyre wear – may be simple misalignment, may have been 'sausaged'. Manual boxes and clutches lead a hard life and boxes are mega expensive to replace. Cars which have been sitting require a full recommission or you'll be in for all sorts of problems. Tyres may have 'flat-spotted', discs rusted, exhaust rotted (especially rear silencer boxes). Targa roof panels may leak – not easy to get new seals for them. Power steering may have sprung a leak.

350Z (from 2004)

What's good: New two seater 'Z car' with 287bhp 3,498cc V6 pumping out 274lb ft torque through a six-speed gearbox. 4,308mm long by 1,816mm wide by 1,318mm high and weighing in at 1,440kg. Factory figures are 150mph and 0–60 in 6 seconds, but they have to be better than this. Should be in UK early 2004 at from £24,000. First reports are that it offers a great drive with bags of power and grip.

What's bad: Hideous protruding door handles that look like something on a kitchen unit. Not enough life in the steering.

What to watch out for: Too soon to say.

Almera (1995 to 2000)

What's good: Tough. Strong, chain-driven twin-cam engines. Decent handling, good to drive, good ride quality, good roadholding. 143 bhp Gate (launched 1996) is a good 'hot hatch'. Four-door saloon version by far the best looking and has three three-point rear belts. 18th from top of 100 models for reliability in *Auto Express* 2002 survey.

What's bad: Hopeless styling of original hatchbacks. Some 1.4 litre models have very mean equipment levels. Diesels are slow. We pay about twice as much for them as they do in Japan. Comparatively poor performance of hatchback in 1999 NCAP secondary safety crash tests.

What to watch out for: Make sure engine has clean oil and that coolant has been changed every two years (a messy, but necessary, service job, often neglected). Engines have two timing chains so if any rattles in this department, don't buy. Expect noises from multi-link suspension – often cured by spraying with WD40.

Recalls: 1998 (Dec '97–May '98 BUILD): inertia reel seatbelts may not lock on impact.

Almera (from 2000)

What's good: New Almera from early 2000. Has more exaggerated 'beaked front' look than new Primera. 5–door hatch does away with 'D' pillar side windows and looks much better for it. 1.5 and 1.8 litre petrol engines. New 2.2 litre direct injected diesel. British built at Sunderland alongside Micra and Primera. Very good 30 point four star NCAP crash safety rating announced 28/3/2001, actually beat the Volvo S80. Much prettier saloon version from June 2001 at prices from £11,065 including air-conditioning. 18th from top of 100 models for reliability in *Auto Express* 2002 survey.

What's bad: Nothing much so far.

What to watch out for: Too soon to say.

Almera Tino (2000 on)

What's good: New, good looking Scenic-sized MPV first seen at the Barcelona Motor Show in May 1999, being built by Nissan Motor Iberica in Barcelona. Three lap/diagonal rear seatbelts. Power-trains include reliable 2.0 litre Sunderland-built 136 bhp chain-cam 16v engine with Nissan's Japanese-made torque converter CVT. Very good four star NCAP crash safety rating announced 28/3/2001. 18th from top of 100 models for reliability in *Auto Express* 2002 survey.

What's bad: Less good two star NCAP rating for pedestrian safety.

Torque converter robs CVT of instant response. Wipers set for Left Hand Drive.

What to watch out for: Problems reported by the Consumers Association include faulty exhausts, rattles from rear seats (recall for this: see below), faulty airbag warning light, stuck petrol gauge, noisy clutch.

Recalls: 1/12/2000: 761 Almera Tinos built 5/2000 to 9/2000 recalled because side airbag satellite sensor may be incorrectly programmed and side bags may not deploy during a side impact. Sensors to be re-programmed. 1,015 Tinos built 5/2000 t0 8/2000 recalled because pins which locate centre rear seat hinge may not have been installed correctly which could lead to the hinge failing under load. Rear seat hinges to be replaced where found to be defective (explains Consumers Association "rattles from rear seats".

Bluebird (1984 to 1990)

What's good: This is the front wheel drive Bluebird, later examples of which were UK built at Sunderland. Available as a four door saloon, a five door hatchback or a five door estate car. Introduced with 90bhp overhead cam 1,809cc engines, the same block but turbocharged to 135bhp, or a 105 bhp 1,973cc ohc unit. 3 speed auto optional on 1.8; 4 speed auto optional on turbo and 2.0. Facelift and 82bhp 1.6 introduced in March 1986, plus new 1,796cc engine with 88bhp. I.8 turbo and 2.0 continued as before. 2.0 'Executive' introduced in October 1989 with 115bhp and ran to the end in September 1990 when the range was replaced by the Primera. Always solid and reliable. Name used on later Sunnys in Indonesia and there is a 460 strong 'Bluebird' taxi fleet on Bali.

What's bad: Old cars now. Some would say "stolid" and reliable. Banger territory, but previously a great favourite among min-cabbers, though almost all Bluebirds this happened to will have died. Very little underbody protection until 1985, which is why you rarely see a pre '85 on the road any more. These cars also had dodgy carbs and are generally not recommended unless you're paying a fiver to end the car's life on a banger racing circuit. Pre 1996 Bluebirds also had poor cooling systems which were apt to silt up.

What to watch out for: Only go for a post March 1986 Bluebird if you're planning to run it. Check brakes and suspension carefully. Look for signs it's been a family car rather than a mini cab. If you're looking at a turbo, it's getting a bit old for a performance car, so check turbo oil seals by getting someone to follow behind on your test drive looking for puffs of black smoke. Also check the discs themselves and adjust what you pay if they are lipped or scored. (But, of course, you're not going to be paying much anyway.)

Maxima (1989 to 1994)

What's good: Code name Series OOHJ30 four door saloons with 170 bhp 3.0 litre V6 engines and four speed autoboxes. 15ft 8in long by 5ft 9in wide and weighing 1,275kg.

What's bad: A bit nondescript. Getting old now. Parts hard to get, especially body parts and light lenses.

What to watch out for: Rust. Short MOTs.

Maxima QX (1994 to 1999)

What's good: Large front wheel drive saloon with chain cam V6 engines. 15ft 8in long by 5ft 102 wide and weighing 1,335kg to 1,385kg. 1,995cc V6 has 138bhp; 2,988cc V6 has 191bhp. 5 speed manual available on smaller engine, otherwise 4-speed auto. Extremely reliable and a good high mileage buy as long as the oil has been kept clean.

What's bad: A bit soft and slushy to drive. Some spares may take a while to come through.

What to watch out for: No problems reported.

Maxima QX (From October 2000)

What's good: Nissan's new large car designed to compete against the Omega and supply an alternative to the defunct Scorpio. 16ft 2in long by 5ft 10in wide. Chain cam V6 engines from a 130bho 2.0 litre V6 to a 200bhp 3.0 litre V6. List prices from £20,700 to £27,400. Manual option on 2.0 litre, otherwise all automatic.

Loaded with goodies such as climate control. Three proper lap/diagonal seatbelts in the back. Three year warranty. Should be as reliable as the previous Maxima QX.

What's bad: Nothing has come up.

What to watch out for: No feedback.

Micra (1983 to 1992)

What's good: Small hatchbacks 12ft 4in long by 5ft 1in wide and weighing from just 660kg. Engines were 988cc with 50bhp or 1,235cc with 60bhp. Amazingly reliable until they get old. Could be run on a shoestring. Cambelt replacement is a cheap £60 job, but best to replace camshaft end seal and water pump at the same time. API can supply good quality second-hand replacement engines for £455 plus VAT (0500 830530).

What's bad: Bodies start to rattle after 4 years. Very light build makes occupants vulnerable in a crash. Scratches rust quickly. Cambelts need to be replaced regularly and camshaft end seals at the same time. Waterpumps eventually go and either snap the cambelt or lead to severe overheating which can wreck the engine. Fuel pump diaphragms fail, leaking neat petrol into the oil sump leading to severe engine wear and possibly even an explosion. Failed engines not worth replacing now, even at API's low prices.

What to watch out for: Far too many suffer from neglected servicing and 'short run syndrome'. Elderly owners simply forgot to service them. Mayonnaise under oil filler cap may be condensation, but mayonnaise under the radiator cap is a sign of a head problem. If the engine overheats on the test drive, its cylinder head is warped. Requires coolant replacement with special Nissan coolant (or Trigard) every two years or engine will corrode internally. After high mileage, will start to burn oil and need either new valve stem seals or a replacement engine. If engine has been replaced or reconditioned it may be dodgy. Any 'rumbling' from the bottom of the engine is likely to be the water pump about to fail (allow £150–£200 for new water pump, timing belt, camshaft end seal). A smell of petrol under the bonnet usually signifies fuel pump failure (allow £100 for new fuel pump plus oil and filter change). None worth more than £250.

Recalls: Early Micras from 1985–87 recalled for gearbox oil loss fault. Oil fed its way up the speedo cable and dripped onto the pedals. Many Micras did not come back for the modification.

Micra (1992 to 2003)

What's good: Jewel-like 16-valve chain-cam engines; 1.0 with 53bhp and 1.3 with 75bhp. 12ft 2in long by 5ft 2in wide and weighing from 775kg. Broadened the market for the Micra, making it a young person's car as well as an old person's. Well built, in Sunderland. Sensible parts prices (cats are £200). Special pre-facelift 1998 run out 1.0 litre model had CVT and power steering. Restyled in 1998. 1,275cc '1.3ft engine increased to 1,348cc in July 2000, with increase in power from 75 ps to 82 ps and torque from 76 lb ft to 80 lb ft at 2,800 rpm. 16th from top of 100 models for reliability in *Auto Express* 2002 survey. Joint 20th from Top in 144 car 2002 JD Power/*What Car?* Customer Satisfaction Survey of V and W reg. cars.

What's bad: Cute 'blobby' styling works for some, not for others. Most did not have power steering. Average performance in NCAP crash tests. Must have 6–monthly oil changes to avoid timing chain trouble. Japanese 'March' models look the same but many parts are not interchangeable. Can suffer from poor starting in damp conditions due to susceptibility of the spark plugs to condensation. Poor starting can also be caused by the wrong temperature sensor which leads the combustion chambers to flood and the ECU to shut down the engine to prevent spiking the catalytic converter. To be replaced by new car on same platform as new Renault Clio in early 2003.

What to watch out for: Clocking. Dirty oil. Must have clean oil. If the timing chain rattles and the car is out of warranty, leave it alone. You could be in for a £400–£500 tensioner replacement job. May have suspension damage from kerbing – most likely and most damaging on power steered cars. Clutches of early cars don't last, but most will by now have been replaced. Previously reliable CVT has started to develop the same electromechanical clutch problems as Puntos. If it thumps when you move the lever to drive, or if the lever is hard to move, leave the car alone. Front chassis cross-member may fail due to rust(the metal strut below and in front of the radiator). The rust results in MOT failure and cost £208 to replace the part, most of it labour. Cross-member itself costs £55. Check rest of underneath carefully for rust.

Recalls: 1994 (Sep 92–June 94 VIN 000001–237783): floor may crack next to handbrake.

Micra (from 2003)

What's good: New Sunderland built Micra to rival new Fiesta, new Polo, new Citroën C3, Toyota Yaris, Vauxhall Corsa, Honda Jazz and new SEAT Ibiza, due early 2003. Will be built on the same floorpan as the next generation Renault Clio, but with Nissan petrol engines and perhaps Renault's new 1.5 diesel. Revealed as a concept car at the September 2001 Frankfurt Motor Show. Still blobby, but much fresher than current Micra.

What's bad: Statement made by Shiro Nakamura at Frankfurt motor show that not due to reach the UK market until 2003.

What to watch out for: Too soon to say.

Navara (from 2002)

What's good: Big, brawny and surprisingly good to drive. Power of 2.5Di upped to 133PS in late 2001, making them the most powerful 4x4 diesel pick-ups in the UK. 133PS is developed at 3,600rpm and 304Nm (224lb ft) torque is developed at 2,000rpm. As well as being useful for caravan and trailer towing this has raised the maximum braked trailer weight to 3,000kg. Prices start at £12,600 + VAT for the basic single cab 4x4 pick-up, rising through £12,850 + VAT for the King Cab and £14,450 + VAT for the Double Cab to £16,100 + VAT for the Navara Double Cab. This comes complete with 16in four spoke alloys, chrome side steps, choice of Shiraz metallic red or Blade Silver paint, four speaker CD radio, ABS and air-conditioning. Truckman tops from £810 to £1,690 + VAT.

More online at www.nissan.co.uk

What's bad: Too soon to say.

What to watch out for: If buying an import, make sure you're getting UK spec and make especially sure you're getting the 133PS engine.

Patrol (1983 to 1992)

What's good: Tough, basic 4x4 in short and long wheelbase of 13ft 4in or 15ft 5in. Petrol engines were four cylinder 2,753cc four with 120bhp and just a four speed manual gearbox to July 1986 when it acquired five speeds. Engine great to 2,962cc and 135bhp in September 1989. Diesels began with 95bhp 3,246cc six with four speed box to January 1984; five speeds thereafter. Engine shrunk to 2,826cc and 92bhp in September 1989. Big and brutal, but seems to go on forever.

What's bad: Fairly crude. Not very comfortable.

What to watch out for: Rust in body and chassis rails. Check what it's been towing.

Patrol GR (from 1992)

What's good: Big, tough, brawny 4x4s. Replaced earlier 2.8/3.0 litre petrol and 2.8/3.2 litre diesel models. 170bhp 4,169cc petrol six with auto option in LWB bodies from 1992 to 1995. 4,169cc 123bhp diesel in SWB and LWB bodies from 1993 to 1995. Replaced by 111bhp 2.8 six cylinder diesels in SWB and LWB bodies from 1995 to 2000. Power upped to 130bhp in 1998. Replaced by 156bhp 3.0 four cylinder engine in swb and lwb bodies in May 2000. LWB is 16ft 5 ins long, 6 ft 4 ins wide with kerb weight 2,335 and maximum towing weight of 3,500kg. 2002 prices are swb 3–door SE: £23,355; lwb 5–dr SE+: £29,755; lwb 5–dr auto: £31,255.

What's bad: Big and ugly.

What to watch out for: Clocking of Patrols which have been used for extensive towing. Driveline strain from towing big, heavy hamburger stalls.

Prairie (1989 to 1992)

What's good: Replaced box-like 1983–89 Prairie, still Sunny-based, but now with up to seven seats. 14ft 4in long by 5ft 6in wide and 1,190kg to 1,320kg. 102bhp 1,973cc Bluebird engine. Much liked by mobility converters because the design allows a drop-down floor ramp and slightly raised rear roof so electric wheelchairs can drive straight in. Was also a 4x4 version.

What's bad: No nicer to drive than old Prairie due to vague steering and body roll.

What to watch out for: Rust, sticking sliding side doors, suspension wear from overloading, dog-eaten upholstery, gears difficult to select, uneven tyre wear. Engine needs regular timing belt changes.

Primera (1990 to 1996)

What's good: Well built saloons, hatchbacks and estates, from 14ft 5in long by 5ft 7in wide and weighing from 1,075kg. 1.6 16v carb had 95bhp; 2.0i 16v injection started with 121bhp, 2.0 GT had 150bhp. 75bhp 2.0 belt cam diesel from June 1992. Catalysation pulled power of 1.6 down to 90bhp in January 1992, then multipoint injection pulled it up to 102bhp in January 1993. 2.0 down to 116bhp, then up to 123bhp. Unbreakable chain-cam engines on 2.0 litre petrol but not diesel. 2.0 litre twin cam petrol engine very punchy. Decent ride/handling combination. Very good (Sunderland) build quality. Big boot. 2.0 litre petrol models are the best buy among 1990–96 upper-medium-size cars. Recommended.

What's bad: Not a great 'looker'. Steering a bit light on Mk I models. Gearbox a bit weak and won't stand abuse. Complex rear suspension develops squeaks and rattles (easily cured with a spray of WD 40). Non-turbo diesels are slow and have timing belts rather than chains. Shielding makes it very difficult to drain the block to change the coolant (best changed every 3 years to prevent internal engine corrosion). Two timing chains in 1.6 engine are one too many, but still no record of problems from them unless oil changes neglected.

What to watch out for: Clocking. Evidence of lack of oil changes (black sludge on the dipstick) and lack of coolant changes (highly likely due to difficulty of job). Uneven tyre wear will mean front suspension damage from kerbing or wear in suspension bushes. Squeaking multi-link rear suspension has a lot of bushes to replace. Rear silencer boxes rust out rapidly even on 25,000–mile-a-year cars. High incidence of hydraulic clutch and starter motor failure on 'N' reg. Primeras. Could have been mini cabbed. Older cars now starting to rust. First place seems to be the tops of the rear wheel arches.

Recalls: 1995 (VIN 000001 to 472213): front brake hoses may chafe. 1997 (June '96–Feb '97 build): fuel vapour may leak from tank.

Primera II (1996 to 1999)

What's good: New look Primera had same dimensions of 14ft 5in long by 5ft 7in wide and same weight from 1,075kg. Engines also the same, but diesel now up to 89bhp. Unbreakable chain-cam engines on 2.0 litre petrol but not diesel. Drivetrain feels exactly the same as previous model. But steering slightly better and roadholding from new rear suspension is astonishing. Very good build quality. Big boot. Comparatively good performance in NCAP crash tests.

What's bad: Not a great 'looker' compared to the rest of the class. Gearbox still a bit weak and won't stand abuse. Still difficult to drain the block to change the coolant (best changed every 3 years to prevent internal engine corrosion). Still two timing chains in 1.6 engine. Delays in supply of spare parts can put cars off the road for three months. Possible premature wear in the pivots of the windscreen wiper mechanism at around 40K miles allowing the arm to move forwards in the well, so touching the rear edge of the bonnet. Opening and slamming shut the bonnet in this condition would cause the bonnet edge to foul the arm with damage to both.

What to watch out for: Clocking. Evidence of lack of oil changes (black sludge on the dipstick). Uneven tyre wear and front suspension damage from kerbing.

Recalls: 1997 (June '96–Feb '97 build): fuel vapour may leak from tank.

Primera III (1999 to 2002)

What's good: New sheetmetal from September 1999 turned the Primera from an excellent car let down by nondescript looks into a real polariser of tastes. Now 14ft 10in long by 5ft 8in wide (estate 15ft long) and weighing from 1.235kg. New flexible 1,769cc 114 bhp engine develops 111 lb ft torque from 2,400–4,800 rpm. New 'Hypertronic' CVT transmission is the first CVT with a 2.0 litre engine. CVT offered with six-ratio electronic manual hold. By far the best to drive is the 138 bhp 2.0i 16v Sport manual. Tenth most reliable car in 2001 Fleet News Survey of 620,000 fleet cars mostly under 3 years old.

What's bad: Do you like the way it looks? Do your neighbours like the way it looks? Different models have different suspension set-ups, some not as good as previous model. Torque converter makes CVT slow to accelerate. Due to be replaced early 2002. Complaint of rust on the tailgate of a brand new car and laminate peeling off alloy wheels of same car.

What to watch out for: Nothing new seems to have come up. See previous Primera II.

Primera IV (from 2002)

What's good: Futuristic new Primera based on the Fusion concept seen at motorshows last year. A 'first' is the built-in closed circuit TV camera in its rear number plate surround. This is linked to the TV screen on the central instrument pod and, instead of aiding rear-parking by coloured lights or bleepers, actually lets you see what is directly behind the car. Since this could save a child's life it has to be worth having. All Primera IV models from SE up get the system. Naturally enough, a tail-eye view isn't all it does. It also displays information for the audio, malfunction warnings, communication, satnav system and climate control. Six buttons change the display according to the function selected, with two large circular switches for the main ones and a joystick for the navigation system. All well thought through and intuitive. Primera IV saloons and estates available in S, SE or SVE trim from March 2002. Engine choice includes a 116PS 1.8 with five-speed manual or automatic transmission: a 140PS 2.0 with Nissan's M-CVT automatic which also offers manual ratio selection; and a 126bhp 2.2 turbodiesel with six-speed manual box promises healthy performance with 50mpg economy. Five door hatchbacks and a six-speed manual version of the 140PS 2.0 followed in summer 2002. 2.2 DI six-speed is good to drive and promises fantastic economy from its ultra-tall top gear which gives nearly 37mph per 1,000rpm.

More online at www.Nissan.co.uk

What's bad: Handling of 1.8 SVE is far from brilliant and engine lacks power. Using TV screen alone to reverse can be disorientating. (There have been a few bumps.)

What to watch out for: Too soon to say.

QX (1994 to 2000)

What's good: Nissan's big front-drive saloon with smooth 1995cc 138bhp V6 and 5 speed manual of 4 speed automatic gearbox. Also 3.0SE model with 191bhp 2,988cc V6 and 4-speed autobox from 1995 to 2000.

What's bad: Big, bland, not many sold so, even though the model is recent, spares are becoming increasingly difficult to get.

What to watch out for: Things like cracked light lenses and other difficult to replace minor parts.

S-Cargo (1988 to 1991)

What's good: Cute, jokey Sunny 1.5 automatic based delivery van that has stood the test of time remarkably well. Can have porthole rear sides and back seat. Plastic protruding wheelarch protectors shrug odd scuffs. Pre-cat, not no problems there. RHD, as in Japan.

What's bad: Lots have been used as publicity vehicles so may have several coats of paint as various liveries were painted over.

What to watch out for: Getting spares is tricky but not impossible. Beware high mileage, hacked-about examples for too much money. There are plenty of very good ones about.

Serena (1993 to 2000)

What's good: Tall, narrow MPV, fits a normal car-size parking space. 14ft 2in long by 5ft 8in wide and from 1,385kg. Rear-wheel drive (though specials were made with front- or four-wheel drive). 2.0 litre 126 bhp Primera engined SGX models with independent rear suspension and aircon by far the best. Other engines were 95bhp chain cam 1.6; 66bhp 2.0 diesel and 74bhp 2.3 diesel. SLX and 'Excursion' models have standard aircon from May '97. The cheapest 7–8 seater. Reliable. Timing chains on petrol models. Three-Star performer in NCAP crash tests (5 points front impact; 16 points side impact).

What's bad: A step back from the 89–92 Prairie. Crude, commercial van-based design, built in Spain. Vile pig of a thing to drive. 66 bhp 2.0 litre and 74 bhp 2.3 litre diesels plain awful, with horrible droning jerky drive-train like a pre-war double-decker bus. S and T platers 8th from bottom in 2001 *Top Gear*/J.D. Power Customer Satisfaction Survey.

What to watch out for: Likely to have been airport taxis and to have covered more miles than on the clock. Some had two side doors; some had only one. Check for excessive smoke from diesels (dirty injectors or air filter). With its two timing chains, 1.6 petrol needs to have had regular oil changes. Electric windows stick.

Skyline GT-R (1989 to 2002)

What's good: Phenomenal four-wheel-drive junior supercar that looks like a tricked-up coupe. Astonishing performance and handling. Three different generations of GT-R among unofficial imports: R32 (1989–1994); R33 (1995–1998); and R34 (1999 on). Also V-Spec models. Have been chipped in Japan to more than 1,000 bhp, but standard conservatively estimated 280 bhp (more like a true 320 bhp) is plenty.

What's bad: Very limited official UK imports (and performance limited to get through SVA).

What to watch out for: Lots of grey imports about dating back to the early 1990s, so make sure you know what you're getting. Check for uneven tyre wear and for pulling to either side on a flat road.

Extremely complex suspension and drivetrain difficult to get parts for, to repair and to set up. Make sure the car is a GT-R and not either a rear-drive-only R33 GT-S or, worse still, an ordinary Skyline which could be eleven years old.

Stagea (from late 2002)

What's good: New large rear-wheel-drive estate car to compete with Volvo V70 and MB E Class. To have 210bhp 2.5 litre and 250bhp 3.0 litre V6 petrol engines. 500 litres of boot space with rear seats up.
What's bad: Too soon to say.
What to watch out for: Too soon to say.

Sunny (1986 to 1991)

What's good: Easy to drive. 13ft 11in long by 5ft 6in wide and from 990kg. Strong, long lasting 1,270cc 60bhp and 84bhp 1,597cc engines. (Grew to 1,392cc with 82bhp and 1,597cc with 94bhp in March 1989). ZX with fuel injected 1,809cc 125bhp from July 1989 to 1991. 1,681cc 55bhp diesel from 1986 to 1991. Can be cheap to run and home maintenance is possible with Haynes manual no 1378. Can last well if looked after.
What's bad: Hideous styling. Uninvolving to drive. Thin sheet metal rusts quickly if paint is broken. Not built to last.
What to watch out for: Skimped or incompetent home maintenance. Rust (especially structural rust underneath). Oil smoke denoting either bore wear or worn valve stem seals. Suspension damage from kerbing by elderly owners (most likely with 1.6 litre power-steered cars). Likely to have been mini cabbed. Diesel almost certain to have been cabbed. Diesel needs regular timing belt changes.

Sunny (1991 to 1995)

What's good: Better looking than previous model. Reliable, easy to drive, reasonable build and decent equipment levels. 143 bhp 2.0e Gate is quick

What's bad: Nondescript 'Golf clone' styling, with excessive rear overhang for a car of this type. Apart from Gate, uninvolving to drive. 'K' reg. 'carb and cat' combination is troublesome.

What to watch out for: Carry out reverse turn test for driveshaft clonks. Look for oil leaks. Check for uneven front tyre wear signifying suspension misalignment or damage from kerbing by elderly owners. Never pay extra for ultra-low mileage. Look for front end damage on Gate from falling off the road. Best cars will have a full service history with oil changes every six months and coolant and brake fluid changes every two years, but most will have been serviced once a year if the owner remembered. Vital to see a recent MOT emissions check on K reg. 'carb and cat' cars as they are very difficult to get through this test.

Terrano II (from 1993)

What's good: Unbreakable, simple, old-fashioned 4x4 with high/low range, etc. Vastly improved in July 1996, especially 2.7 litre diesel which gained intercooler and 25 more bhp. (This is the same engine as most London taxis.) 5–door LWB versions can have 7 seats. Carried on when Ford pulled the plug on the Maverick. Option of 3.0 litre engine, itself with auto option from early 2002. 2002 SWB prices from £17,395 for 2.7 SWB and from £19,995 for 7 seater LWB.

What's bad: Tall and narrow, so you have to be careful on corners and better not pile stuff on the roof. Jerky on-road ride – partly due to suspension, partly to driveline. Spanish build quality not 100% up to the mark, especially trim items. 3.0DI SVE auto isn't exactly cheap at £25,295.

What to watch out for: Quite likely to have been off-roaded, especially if registered in a country area. Farmers cars will have seen some work, though remember farmers drive to preserve their vehicles – it's the off-road enthusiasts who break them. Look for weeping seals, noisy hubs, clonky driveshafts, driveshaft 'lash', noisy gearbox or transfer case, oil leaks from engine and drive-train. Smoke from diesel may indicate that turbo oil seals have failed.

Recalls: 1995 (with Michelin 215/80 R15 tyres: VIN 200000 to 242699): tyres may lose pressure.

X-Trail (from 2001)

What's good: Immensely likeable new Nissan 4x4 aimed at Freelander, CRV, RAV-4 market and new Maverick. Impresses by its honesty. Front drive with selectable four wheel drive and centre diff lock. Familiar 2.0 litre twin-cam Primera engine for UK or 2.2 diesel. Up to 276bhp available in Japan. Arrived UK October 2001. Big advantage of totally flat floor with rear seats folded, ideal for dogs and as a working vehicle. Dimensions are: length 4,510mm (14 ft 10in); width 1,765mm (6 ft 3in); height (without roof spoiler): 1,675mm (5ft 6in). Luggage volume is 350 litres to the parcel shelf or 410 litres to window sill level with the rear seats up. Torque converter CVT automatic option on the petrol engine only. This is the 1,998cc 16 valve twin-cam developing 138bhp at 6,000rpm and 142 lb ft (192Nm) torque at 4,000rpm. This gets to sixty in 11.0 seconds, tops out at 110mph, does 30.4mpg on the combined cycle and emits 221g/km CO_2. (Auto: 12.8 secs, 101mph; 28.2mpg; 237g/km CO_2.) Kerb weight of the manual is 1,415kg and maximum braked trailer weight is 1,500kg. The 2,184cc direct-injected external chain cam diesel puts out 112bhp at 4,000rpm and 199lb ft (270Nm) torque at 2,000rpm. It manages sixty in 13.4 seconds, reaches 103mph, does 39.2mpg on the combined cycle and emits 190g/km CO_2. (35–36mpg is genuinely realistic.) Kerb weight is 1,525kg and maximum braked trailer weight a useful 2,000kg. Standard equipment on all models includes triple-mode four-wheel-drive controlled by press-button; disc brakes front and rear; ABS with EBD and brake assist; twin front airbag;, anti-hijack remote central locking; and a ski/snowboard flap in the centre of the rear seat. Sport models gain the additions of wipe-clean dimpled upholstery; side airbags; automatic climate control; two can drinks cooler; six-speaker CD/radio; 16 inch alloy wheels and a roof spoiler that takes the overall height up to 1,750mm (5ft 10ins). SE+ spec adds leather covered seats, steering wheel rim and gearknob; electric folding door mirrors; adjustable armrest; steering wheel mounted audio controls and a six CD autochanger. Prices are: 2.0 S £16,750; 2.2Di S £17,750; 2.0 Sport £17,995; 2.2Di Sport £18,995; 2.0 SE+ £19,895; 2.2Di SE+ £20,895. BIK tax for 2002–2003 will be based on 26% of the petrol model's list price and 23% of the diesel's list price. 2.2 6–speed is also better than any of the competition off road. By far the best mid size 4x4 and a pleasure to drive. Highly recommended.

More online at www.nissan.co.uk

What's bad: 2001 MY Sport models had cheap, garish Clarion single slot CD, cassette player radio that cheapens the interior. (This was dropped in favour of a CD multi-player in early 2002.)

What to watch out for: Too soon to say.

NOBLE

M12 GTO (from 2000)

What's good: Brilliant British-built supercar based on extensive racing experience. Has twin turbo 2.5 litre Ford/Jaguar Duratec V6 putting out 310bhp and 320lb ft torque 155mph, which gets it to 60 in 3.9 seconds, to 100 in 9.4 seconds and on to short-geared 165. The ideal track day car. Can manage 19.5mpg on the combined cycle. List price £45,110. Factory telephone number: 01455 844052.

What's bad: Getting one: very limited production and huge demand. No traction control of any sort, so does require skill to drive quickly.

What to watch out for: A very heavy price premium if buying used. Damage from track day offs. Out of alignment suspension.

PERODUA

Kelisa (from 2002)

What's good: Boasts a mass of improvements over the Nippa including the 55PS 3-cylinder twin-cam 12-valve 989cc engine from the Kenari and also the Kenari's power steering. It may be tiny, but it has five doors, five gears, driver and passenger airbags, side impact protection, seat belt pretensioners, child locks in the rear doors, engine immobiliser, folding rear seat and tailgate wash/wipe all as standard for just £5,425. There is also a deluxe GX version at £5,925 on the road with a year's VED and a three speed automatic EZ at £6,745. All prices include a two year 24,000 mile manufacturer warranty. An excellent car for the elderly, combining small size with low price and low running costs. Dimensions of the 5–door are: length 3,480mm (11 ft 5in); width 1,490mm (4 ft 11in), and the turning circle is just 8.6 metres (28ft 2in) so no problems getting it into the garage. Weight is a mere 760kg. Insurance is Group 3A and they don't come much cheaper than that. Power output is 55PS at 5,200rpm with 88.3Nm (65 lb ft) torque at 3,600rpm. 0–60 is quoted at 14.8 seconds, top speed is 88 mph, Euro combined mpg 64.2 and CO_2 emissions 121g/km (£100pa VED). 0–60 of the 3-speed automatic is 17.2 seconds, top speed 87mph, Euro combined mpg 48.7 and CO_2 emissions 253g/km (£120pa VED). In addition to the standard equipment of the EX model, the GX and EZ have electric front windows, central door locking, front cup holders, coin holders, two tone cloth upholstery, body colour bumpers and the option of metallic paint at no extra cost. Goes well, handles well and is good fun to drive. Narrowness will appeal to people with narrow driveways and garages.

More online at www.perodua-uk.com

What's bad: Only 36 dealers countrywide, but that's an improvement on before.

What to watch out for: Too soon to say.

Kenari (from 2001)

What's good: New in the UK from 2001 and basically the old Daihatsu Move with a new, much cuter Far East retro front. Has a 989cc 3 cylinder twin-cam engine developing 55bhp and 66 lb ft (88.3 Nm) torque. So is faster than the old Move and should be an absolute riot to drive. Low CO_2 emissions at 136g/km. Combined fuel consumption figure: 50.4mpg. Priced from just £5,800 for the GX manual and £6,600 for the EZ automatic (both plus £125 VED and registration tax). Power steering standard, 2 year 24,000 mile warranty and a 6 year body warranty.

What's bad: The foot or so of air over your head helps handling but makes the Move (on which the Kenari is based) feel like a shed to drive. Very thin sheetmetal and lots of glass means lots of condensation in winter.

What to watch out for: Doggy smells inside used examples.

Recalls: 1/8/2001: 520 Kenaris built 1/9/2000 to 31/5/2001 recalled because incorrect operation of airbag warning lamp could lead to no pre-warning of a fault and could lead to bag inflating. Meter assemblies to be replaced.

Nippa (1997 to 2002)

What's good: Strong Sterling exchange rates against the Malaysian Ringit enabled the importer to offer its EX model as low as £4,495, including a two-year 24,000–mile warranty but plus VED and registration tax. For the UK, that's cheap. Has same responsive 42 bhp 850cc three-cylinder engine as Daihatsu Mira, Cuore and Move. Sells well in North East England, but brilliant for cities, shopping, suburbia and the school run.

What's bad: Very small. Very basic. Very simple little car. Very Limited cornering abilities and uninspiring to drive. For £4,495 you don't get a radio (can't have everything). Called a 'Prodder' in the trade.

What to watch out for: If previously owned by an elderly person, may have suffered heavy clutch wear and over-revving when cold. Younger owners may also have revved the nuts off them trying to find some performance.

PEUGEOT

007 (from 2005)

What's good: 5–door £5,000 basic car joint venture between PSA and Toyota. Likely to have 1.0 to 1.1 litre petrol engines and 1.0 to 1.4 litre diesels. Aiming for very high volumes of 200,000 a year in Europe alone.

What's bad: Has to meet ever more stringent safety requirements which killed off the FIAT Ecobasic, so trim and goodies will be minimal to keep the price down.

What to watch out for: Too soon to say.

106 (1991 to 2002)

What's good: All handle well. Stronger (and actually heavier) than bigger 205. Revised and facelifted range from June 1996 includes hot 120 bhp Gate 16v generally reckoned to handle better than equivalent Saxo. 3-year warranty from January 2000. 60bhp 1.1 litre Independence model with sunroof, metallic paint and a year's insurance (for 22–80 year olds) included at a bargain at £6,495 as from June 2001.

What's bad: Twisted-spine offset driving position and big feet can hit more than one pedal at the same time. Tall people just don't fit. Automatics have only 3 speeds. Reports of premature bore wear on iron block 1.5Ds could be due to dirty or worn injectors washing out the bores. Also see Citroën Saxo which is virtually the same car. Report of chafing of wiring for seatbelt pretensioners and airbag by the seat mechanism. 5th from Bottom of 100 models for reliability in *Auto Express* 2002 survey. 19th from Bottom in 144 car 2002 JD Power/*What Car?* Customer Satisfaction Survey of V and W reg. cars.

What to watch out for: Check spare wheel is in its underboot cradle and not nicked. Front suspension wear. Oil leaks. Needs frequent timing belt changes. 1.5 diesels need regular servicing and regular coolant replacement – are especially heavy on front tyres. Check for falling-off-the-road damage to Gate 16v. 16vs tend to blow their cats when run against rev limiter.

Recalls: 1997 (March-Nov '96 build: 15,821 cars): ignition switch harness may foul on steering column. 1/2/2000: possibility that brake servo valve may not operate correctly resulting in loss of servo assistance. 18,405 cars recalled for inspection and possible replacement of brake servo valve. 21/2/1001: On 2000 106s brake pedal relay lever may fracture leading to loss of brakes. Relay levers to be replaced (See Citroën Saxo).

107 (from late 2002)

What's good: New small car, same length as 106 but taller, like a cross between a 206 and a Honda Logo so has more space inside. Big innovation is sliding side doors making it easier to get in and out in tight parking spaces such as multi-story carparks and domestic garages. Will have new 1.4HDI diesel engines, plus a direct injected three cylinder 1.2. Built on same PAS 'Platform One' as Citroën C2. Star of 2002 Paris Motor Show.

What's bad: Too soon to say.

What to watch out for: Too soon to say.

205 (1983 to 1997)

What's good: The definitive 1980s hatchback. Brilliant 'wheel in each corner' design, no space wasted anywhere and great looking. Also no rust traps. It's rare to see a rusty 205 except at the leading edge of the roof and door bottoms. Excellent ride and handling combination. Light weight, from 740kg for 1.0XE to 850kg for 1.6GTi. Gate models very throttle sensitive with lift-off oversteer available on demand. Sold 5.3 million. Later post-1988 'TU' sub-1.4 engines better than early small engines which still had their gearboxes in the sump. Diesels capable of 50 mpg and late versions came with power steering. Clever cantilever folding front seats of three-door bodies give good access to rear seat. I've done 950 miles in a day in a 1.6 Gate without even a twinge of backache.

What's bad: Very light build, so vulnerable in accidents – especially at the back. Small front discs of early diesels lead to heavy pad wear. Single front reservoir of pre-86 cars could lead to problems with rear wash/wipe. Valve stem seals of GTis give out at around 60,000 miles. Cambelts and camshaft end seals of all XUs must be changed every 3 years and 36,000 miles. Coolant of diesels must be changed every two years to avoid cylinder head gasket problems. No underbody rust traps, but superficial rust a problem on early cars.

What to watch out for: Check spare wheel is in its underboot cradle and not nicked. Front suspension wear (205s and 306s tend to 'lean' on the front suspension and are particularly vulnerable to kerb damage). Oil burning petrol engines needing new valve stem seals (allow £120). Crash damage and rust in doors, window surrounds and brake pipes. Rusty rear discs on 1.9 GTis.

206 Coupe Cabriolet (from 2000)

What's good: Stylish, folding hardtop 2.0 litre Coupe Cabriolet arrived October 2000. 1.6 litre followed December 2000. Automatic 1.6 litre Coupe Cabriolet from late June 2001. High UK list prices of £16,000 for 2.0; £14,530 for 1.6 and £15,430 for 1.6 auto undercut by independent importers.

What's bad: 2+2, not a full four-seater. Have been problems with the roof mechanism and autobox of 1.6 auto. Otherwise, see 206.

What to watch out for: Make sure roof opens and shuts properly. Check origin carefully as may be an import and may not have Peugeot 3 year warranty. Also see 206.

Recalls: 15/1/2001: On 384 cars, front stub axle lower ball joint fixing may have been incorrectly machines, leading to separation of stub axle from ball joint and lower suspension arm. Cars to be checked and stub axles replaced where necessary. 12/11/2001: Limited recall of 84 206s fitted with wrong part in the airbag module. April 2002: German recall of 206CCs due to a problem with the roof motor.

206 hatchback (from 1998)

What's good: Interesting new 3– or 5–door supermini sized between 106 and 306. 60 bhp 1.1, 75 bhp 1.4 and 90 bhp 1.6 petrol engines from 106, but new 70 bhp 1,868cc DW8 diesel based on XUD. PAS and height adjustable steering column standard. Same excellent 306 suspension. 136 bhp 2.0 litre 16v Gate, 90 bhp HDI diesel and 1.4 litre automatic all came later. More roomy inside than new Clio. 500 a day built in Coventry. Image promoted by 300 bhp WRC rally version. Well thought out inside with options such as a folding passenger seat that turns into a desk. 3-year warranty from January 2000. Price-cuts down to £8,795 for 'Look' special edition in Spring 2000 included PAS, aircon and 1 year's insurance. Very Good Four-Star rating in Euro NCAP crash tests. Sporty 110bhp 1.6XSi priced at £11,695 and ultra economical 63mpg 2.0HDi eco priced at £9,845 both launched February 2001. Haynes manual now available. 68bhp PSA/Ford 1.4 litre HDI engine available from January 2002, gets to 60 in 15 seconds, top speed 104.3mph, combined consumption 65.7mpg, CO_2 112g/km (£80pa VED) and priced from £8,995 for 3 door HDI Style. Three three point rear belts from June 2002 and lots of spec upgrades through the range.

What's bad: Not quite the style classic the 205 and 306 were (styled in-house by computer, not by Pininfarina). Mixed reactions from journalists to handling qualities, but Quentin Willson liked it and the model has been very successful. Emergency wheel still slung underneath the boot floor. Reports of side airbags going off for no reason. Reports of water getting into electric door locking control box of late 1998/early 1999 build cars. Easy DIY replacement using Haynes manual, saves typical £55 garage labour cost (part alone £75). (Peugeot Customer Services will sometimes pay for the job.) Water gets in through bonnet vent and plenum chamber underneath is not well drained so drips are carried in through vents in the control box. Also wets the carpet and leads to steaming up in winter. Repeat of Peugeot 106 problem of sudden losses of power caused by faulty throttle position sensing potentiometer seems to re-occur on some 206 1.4s. If driven through floodwater, gearbox can suffer from water ingress via breather. Technical problems with automatic gearboxes on 1.4s led to many orders being cancelled in early 2001. Reports of severely rusted exhaust systems on GTis after just 12 months. External factory fitted sunroof prone to rattles for which Peugeot has no cure. 19th from bottom for reliability in *Auto Express* 2002 reader survey of 100 models.

What to watch out for: Misfiring problem with 1,150cc models could lead to spiked catalytic converters (see 'Recalls'). Make sure central locking system works (see above). Reports of 1,150cc 206s still being sold with faulty ECUs and a shortage of chips to repair them in March 2001.

Recalls: 1,150 cc models only, 1,000 cars affected: TSB issued in spring 2000 to replace ignition coil pack, leads and plugs owning to misfire, but correction packs only supplied at rate of 20 a month. 1/2/2000: possibility that brake servo valve may not operate correctly resulting in loss of servo assistance. 18,405 cars recalled for inspection and possible replacement of brake servo valve. 19/9/2000: 1,415 206s fitted with side airbags recalled because they may unintentionally deploy. Side airbag control units to be replaced. 15/1/2001: On 384 cars, front stub axle lower ball joint fixing may have been incorrectly machines, leading to separation of stub axle from ball joint and lower suspension arm. Cars to be checked and stub axles replaced where necessary. 12/11/2001: Limited recall of 84 206s fitted with wrong part in the airbag module.

206 SW (from May 2002)

What's good: British-built 206 SW on sale in May 2002 at prices starting from a UK competitive £8,995. The SW is 193mm longer than the 206 hatchback with the extra length all at the back to provide greater load capacity. This is 480 litres with the rear seats up. A handy touch is the rear window glass which, as on the Citroën C5 estate, can be opened independently of the tailgate for dropping small items into the load area. Rear seats are split-folding 60/40 and all three have lap/diagonal seatbelts. Five engines are available; four from launch. The 1.1 puts out 60bhp at 5,500rpm and 70 lb ft torque at 2,700rpm. Top speed is just short of 100mph, 0–60 takes 15.5 seconds, combined consumption is 43.5mpg and

CO_2 output is 156g/km. The 1.4 develops 75bhp at 5,500rpm and 90 lb ft torque at 2,800rpm. It has a top speed of 107mph, a 0–60 of 13.0 seconds, combined consumption slightly better than the 1.1 at 44.1mpg and CO_2 output also better at 153g/km.

The 1.6 offers 110bhp at 5,800rpm and 110 lb ft torque at 4,000rpm. It does 121mph, gets to 60 in 10.6 seconds, does 42.2mpg in the combined cycle and emits 159g/km CO_2. The 2.0HDI pumps out 90bhp at 4,000 rpm and 154 lb ft torque at 1,900rpm. It tops out at 114mph, reaches 60 in 11.5 seconds, stretches a gallon 55.4 miles in the combined cycle and emits 138g/km CO_2. New PSA 1,399cc aluminium block, common rail direct-injected diesel will not be available in the SW until October 2002.

More online at www.peugeot.co.uk

What's bad: Possible quality problems. See Peugeot 206.

What to watch out for: See Peugeot 206.

207 (from 2004)

What's good: Good looking successor to Peugeot 206, to be built on stretched PSA 'Platform One' with same family of engines as 107, from 65bhp 3 cylinder 1.2 petrol direct injection to 150bhp 2.0 petrol. 1.4HDI likely to be a popular engine choice.

What's bad: Too soon to say.

What to watch out for: Too soon to say.

306 (1993 to 2001)

What's good: Excellent ride and handling combination and a joy to drive. Best in class until Focus came along. 90bhp 1.6 TU is a decent petrol engine for a family car – very nicely balanced. 167 bhp 2.0 litre GTi-6 is track-car quick with roadholding and handling to match, plus a six-speed gearbox. All capable of 150,000–plus miles if properly looked after. Non-turbo XUD can do 50 mpg. D-Turbo surprisingly quick. Three-Star 'above average' performance in NCAP crash tests. 3-year warranty from January 2000. Sedan saloon (from 1994) has a rear screen wiper. 306 cabriolets (from 1994) and estate cars (from 1996) continued after the launch of the 307.

What's bad: High used values due to prettiness of body. 1.8 8-valve XU petrol is the worst engine and many were fitted with the wrong ECU chip leading to failed emissions tests. Autobox not recommended. Cambelts and camshaft end seals must be changed every 3 years and 36,000 miles. Coolant of diesels must be changed every two years to avoid cylinder head gasket problems. Like Citroën ZX, can have cat converter test problems. Build quality a bit 'light'. Easy to fluff 2nd to 3rd gearchange on GTi-6. Clutch cable of RHD cars is routed close to the exhaust, which dries out the lubrication and prevents the self-adjuster working properly which leads to premature clutch failure. (Thanks to Mike Brewer of Channel 4ft s 'Driven' for this snippet.) Contacts fail in remote keys leading to rapid discharge of batteries. Reports of failure of rear disc brake callipers. Reports of engine compartment fuse box short out on diesel almost leading to engine compartment fires (see Recalls). Spate of conrod failures on 1998 R and S reg. 1.9 XUTD diesels: too many to attribute merely to running with low oil levels.

What to watch out for: See above. Front suspension bush wear (205s and 306s tend to 'lean' on the front suspension and are vulnerable to kerb damage. They also suffer badly from road hump damage). Oil burning petrol engines needing new valve stem seals (allow £120). Not all diesels have PAS and all need it. Check spare wheel is in its underboot cradle and not nicked. If fitted with low profile tyres, check for tyre and rim damage. If fitted with aircon, make sure it works properly. Some reports of fuel line failure on petrol cars, cured by reinforced pipes. If car has rear discs, check callipers for fluid leaks. Check for stiff clutch, as cable may need replacing. 13th from Bottom of 100 models for reliability in *Auto Express* 2002 survey.

Recalls: 1995: Check accelerator cable. 1996 (July 1993–February 1996 bulld-150,000 cars): underbonnet wiring may chafe leading to short circuit and fire. 1997: possible starter motor fault on 1996 model cars. Free replacement. 1997 (Feb-May '97 build: 2,060 cars): incorrect brake compensator fitted. 1998: (Sep '97–Oct '97 BUILD): steering wheel hub may crack; (Nov '97–Apr '98 build): front suspension may collapse. May 1999: R reg. 1.8 and 2.0 litre petrol engined models recalled for reinforced fuel lines to be fitted. 2000:

1.9TD October '98 build: front brake pipes may chafe. All March '98–build 306 models: steering rack bolts could crack if overtightened during assembly. March '99–April '99 build 306s with ABS only: possibility of air in brake fluid. 1/2/2000: possibility that brake servo valve may not operate correctly resulting in loss of servo assistance. 18,405 cars recalled for inspection and possible replacement of brake servo valve. Technical Information Circular No 1555 issued in 2000 re airbag warning light flashing then remaining on. Remove both front seats, carry out repairs to harness connectors, replace seats and clear fault from ECU. 3/10/2000: 4,898 306s and Partner vans recalled because of chance of incorrect machining of front stub axles which could lead to excessive wear and possibility of lower ball joint collapsing. Vehicles to be checked and front stub axles to be replaced if necessary. 2/1/2001: 96 cars were fitted with incorrect LH driveshafts which could separate from gearbox on a sharp bend or during excessive suspension deflection. Correct spec driveshafts to be fitted. 2/1/2001: on 7,853 diesel 306s brake vacuum pump pin may fail due to excessive wear losing power assistance to brakes. Replacement pins to be fitted. 2/1/2001: on 2,409 306s possibility that an open circuit could occur in front seatbelt pretensioner harness connector leading to flashing of airbag warning light. Pretensioner harnesses top be replaced. 29/10/2001: 7,593 1.8 16v 306s and 406s recalled for timing belts to be replaced as could fail before 72,000 mile 'life'. 12/11/2001: Limited recall of 61 306s to check seatbelt mounting bolts. Late 2001: TSB issued to check all common-rail to injector unions on HDIs for leaks.

307 (from 2001)

What's good: Combines elements of 206 with mini MPV headroom and soon became very popular. Five basic spec levels: Style, Rapier, LX, GLX and XSi with choice of seven interiors and five ambiences which together provide around 79 different combinations of interior finish including colour co-ordinated dashboards. Engines are 1.4 litre petrol, giving 75bhp at 5,500rpm, 0–60 in 14.2 seconds and combined mpg of 42.2; a 1.6 litre 16v petrol giving 110bhp at

5,800rpm, 0–60 in 10.6 seconds and combined mpg of 39.2; a 2.0 litre 16 valve petrol giving 138bhp at 6,000rpm, 0–60 in 8.9 seconds and combined mpg of 35.8; and a 2.0 litre HDI diesel giving 90bhp at 4,000rpm, 0–60 of 12.4 seconds and combined mpg of 54.3. All 307s have six airbags: front, side and curtain; ABS with electronic brake force distribution and emergency brake assist; active anti-whiplash front seat head restraints; three three-point rear seatbelts; large front and rear storage bins with storage drawers under the front seats; air conditioned gloveboxes to cool drinks on most models; and a choice of 14 exterior paint finishes. Anti theft measures include reinforced lock cowlings inside the doors, an emergency door lock button on the dash and automatic locking of the boot as soon as the car exceeds 6mph after start-up. Generally good to drive. On the road prices, which include a three year part manufacturer part dealer warranty, start at £10,860 for the three door 1.4i Style, rising to £15,560 for the 5–door 2.0Xsi. Other price examples are £12,460 for the 1.6i 16v 3–door Rapier with air-conditioning and £14,560 for the 90bhp 2.0HDI GLX 5–door with air-conditioning. SW labelled station wagon from Summer 2002. 307 2.0 HDI 110bhp diesel models with FAP particulate filters use 54.3mpg in the combined cycle and emit 138g/km CO_2, which should keep them in the lowest £110 VED category for diesels for years to come. A 0–60 of 10.6 seconds and top speed of 119mph is more than adequate. Prices are: 307 2.0HDi 110 GLX 5–door is £16,060 on the road, the D-Turbo 3–door is £16,160 and the D-Turbo 5–door is £16,660. Also new is a 1.6 16v AL4 4-speed automatic at prices from £13,510 for the LX. A 70bhp 1.4 litre HDI from December 2001 gets to 60 in 16.3 seconds, tops out at 102mph, delivers 62.8mpg and emits 120g/km CO_2, priced from £11,560 for 3–door Style. Voted 'European Car of The Year 2002ft in November 2001. Good four star score in 2001 NCAP crash tests. BIK beating 5–door HDI 110 Rapier launched May 2002 at £14,160 does 119mph, gets to 60 in 10.6 seconds, averages 54.3mpg on the combined cycle and emits 138g/km CO_2. Spec includes a/c, alloy wheels, ABS with EBD, ESP, electric front windows and mirrors and a six-speaker radio/CD player. 307 Coupe Cabrio with folding hardtop like 206CC due in 2003.

More online at www.peugeot.co.uk

What's bad: Mini MPV attributes do not extend to a flat floor and no centre console as in the much better packaged Honda Civic. Doesn't shift the goal posts set by the Ford Focus. Problems developing include trip computer failures, steering column stalk malfunctions, splits in seat covers and rattles. Complaints of poor ride quality even on 1.6 version. ECU problem with HDIs is causing flat spots and hesitation. A permanent cure seems to be slow in coming through. Shocking 4th from Bottom of 100 models for reliability in *Auto Express* 2002 survey.

What to watch out for: See above.

Recalls: Late 2001: TSB issued to check all common-rail to injector unions on HDIs for leaks. July 2002: Recall for ignition switch failures.

307 SW (from April 2002)

What's good: Having given the 307 MPV looks but zero MPV practicality, Peugeot's ace was a stunning 307 station wagon with a full complement of up to seven forward-facing seats, each with their own three-point seat-belts. The rear five seats all double-fold or remove. A third of the car's total body area is made of glass making it very light and airy inside. (All 307s come with a huge athermic glass sunroof which reflects the sun's rays and standard air conditioning). Engine choice starts with the 90BHP 2.0 HDI, rising through the 110bhp 1.6 16v, and 110bhp 2.0 HDI, to the 136bhp 2.0 16v. Good looks and seven properly belted seats will sell this car. Prices from £13,660 for five seat 1.6, and from £13,990 for seven seat 1.6. On sale from April 2002. Nice to drive. Very good to drive. The best handling seven seater you can buy.

More online at www.peugeot.co.uk

What's bad: Rear seats are optional extras at £165 each, but rearmost seatbelts are standard. Otherwise, see 2306 hatchback which, sadly, was 4th from Bottom of 100 models for reliability in *Auto Express* 2002 survey.

What to watch out for: See 306 hatchback.

309 (1986 to 1993)

What's good: Not as bad as it looks. Stretched 205 floorpan gives good combination of ride and handling, plus decent-sized square-shaped boot. Old 'suitcase' pre-TU engines (they need to be unpacked before you can work on them) good for 170,000 miles. Later TU and larger XU engines also long lasting if oil and belts changed regularly. Diesels were the best of their day. The 130bhp 309GTi 1.9 outhandled the Golf Gate Mk II and many thought it a better (though flimsier) car. High back seats of 3–door Gate give back seat passengers a good view. Clever levers next to handbrake open rear windows. Rare and desirable LHD only 309 Gate 16v once favoured by French professional racing drivers and a good trackday car.

What's bad: Its looks. Truly dreadful British styling (Peugeot's only departure from Pininfarina between 1959 and 1998). Was supposed to be a successor to the awful American Chrysler Horizon. To see what good looks could do for basically the same car, read Peugeot 306. Getting to be an old car now.

What to watch out for: TU and XU cambelts and cambelt end-seals need changing every 35,000–40,000 miles whatever the handbook tells you, especially now these cars are getting older. Mk I (high boot sill) rear hatchbacks are leak-prone and this may have led to rusting of boot floor. GTis tend to start smoking at around 60,000 miles, but all they usually need are new valve stem seals.

405 (1988 to 1996)

What's good: Fine Pininfarina styling. All handle and ride well. Practical estate cars. Narrow enough to fit most garages. At least one diesel model has done more than 600,000 miles. Like 205, rust traps are designed out, so these cars don't rust badly. Huge range of engines over the years from rare 75bhp 1.4 through 92bhp 1.6, 103bhp 1.8, 110 and 125bhp 1.9s, 160bhp twin-cam MI 16s, 71 and 92bhp 1.7 to 1.9 litre diesels.

What's bad: Light build. So any rust in seams will seriously weaken structure. Rusty brake pipes common on early examples but all should have been replaced with coated pipes by now. Not all had power steering and all need it. Aircon system on GTX models prone to problems. Early 'plip key' immobiliser system was a joke because it was easy to unplug inside the centre console. Little things like failed heater thermostatic controls can cost £500 to replace which is usually more than the car is now worth. Trim does not take a hammering.

What to watch out for: Check spare wheel is in its underboot cradle and not nicked. Look for front suspension wear. Rear suspension pivots also wear, particularly on estate cars and can cost more to replace than the car is worth. Rusted brake pipes are an MOT failure point (later models had coated brake pipes). Many diesels were taxis so look for the signs. Clocking of diesels is rife. Run diesels with dipstick out to check for excessive fumes from worn engine. Check for mayonnaise under oil cap signifying head gasket problems. All 405s, petrol or diesel, need a cambelt and camshaft end seal change every 3 years and 36,000 miles. Early carburettor petrol cars suffered from fuel vaporisation. All XU engines can suffer premature bore and big end wear if the oil has not been changed regularly. Look for fluid leaks from power steering rack and pump, clonky driveshafts, seeping gearbox driveshaft oil seals, worn bushes in external gearshift mechanism. A heavy clutch could either mean the clutch is on the way out or the cable is binding.

Recalls: 1995 (1995 model year to VIN 71339513): airbag may fail to inflate in an accident. 1996 (Sept '93–May '95 build): check for seepage of fuel from feed pipe.

406 (from 1996)

What's good: Bigger 'classier' car than the 405. Useful estates from Feb 1997 with 7 seat 'Family' option from Nov 1997. Spare wheel now inside boot. Excellent ride and handling compromise. Powerful and economical 110bhp 2.1TD. New class-leading 110bhp 2.0 litre HDI diesel engine from October 1998. Petrol engines from 112bhp 1.8 to 194bhp V6. Three lap and diagonal rear belts. 7–seater estate. Spare wheel now in boot floor well. Facelifted in March 1999. 3-year warranty from January 2000. New 2.2 litre 160 bhp SRi from July 2000. New 2.2 litre 136bhp HDI with particulate filter from March 2001 at prices from £19,390.

2.0–litre 143bhp HPi petrol engine from September 2001 offers top speed of 130 mph and 0–60 mph in 10.3 seconds with combined consumption of 37.6mpg and low 177g/km CO_2 putting it in £140pa VED bracket and also a low BIK tax base. Also a 2.0–litre, 110 bhp HDI automatic GLX, GTX and Executive models. Top speed is 117 mph, combined fuel consumption 43.5mpg and CO_2 output 173g/km. 2.2HDi GTX estate voted Caravan Club Towcar of the Year 2002 due to its impressive torque delivery.

More online at www.peugeot.co.uk

What's bad: Still only a three star performer in 2001 NCAP crash safety tests, despite improvements since 1997. Build still feels a bit light. 2.1TD is a nightmare for mechanics to work on. Average performance in NCAP crash tests. Have received a well-above-average number of complaints from owners. Spate of starter motor failures on 2.1TD model. Starting to get reports of radiators failing after 3 years. Combined rear discs and parking brake drums apt to give trouble after 3–4 years. Rear discs more prone than average to rusting. Replacement of discs/drums, pads and parking brake shoes is a £450 job. Can suffer coolant loss from hoses or rad which can lead to damage from overheating. Reports of front coil springs collapsing on 2.1TDs causing loss of control and the cars to crash. Spate of electrical problems: speedos and all sorts of failures on cars fitted with satnav.

What to watch out for: Small dings in sheetmetal. ECU problems not sorted out in 96N/96P reg. cars. Wrong chips fitted to ECUs on first year's production may or may not have been replaced (an MOT emissions test should tell you). 'Clonking' (likely to be wear in anti-roll bar bushes). Clocking of diesels (has it been a taxi?). Oil consumption of 1.8i and 2.0i 16v petrol engines. Aircon system prone to problems. Look for leaks: coolant, power steering fluid, gearbox oil, engine oil. If looking at a 406 with a lot of toys, such as satnav, make absolutely sure that everything works.

Recalls: 1996 (1.8i and 2.0i petrol): Free upgrade of engine management chip if owner complains of 'rough' running, flat spots and lack of power on hills. 1997 (Nov '95–Apr '96 build: 13,412 cars): ignition switch harness may foul on steering column.

1997 (Feb '97 build: 333 cars) incorrect front subframe mountings. 1998: 'Low level recall' no XKG to replace timing belts and tensioners of 1.8litre XU7JP4 engines at 36,000 miles. 2000: check alloy wheels as damage could lead to fractures. 1/2/2000: possibility that brake servo valve may not operate correctly resulting in loss of servo assistance. 18,405 cars recalled for inspection and possible replacement of brake servo valve. 1/2/2000: 487 cars: possibility that brake pedal assembly nuts may work loose. Nuts to be tightened and lost nuts to be replaced. 19/1/2001: Incorrect specification rear suspension arm pivot fixing bolts could fail under arduous operating conditions, possibly resulting in rear wheel locking. Pivot fixing bolts to be examined and replaced as necessary. 3/8/2001: Limited recall of 195 406s because brake servo vacuum pipe may become damaged due to chafing on wiring harness leading to loss of brake servo assistance. 29/10/2001: 7,593 1.8 16v 306s and 406s recalled for timing belts to be replaced as could fail before 72,000 mile 'life'. Late 2001 to March 2002: TSB issued to check all common-rail to injector unions on HDIs for leaks.

406 Coupe (from 1997)

What's good: Jawdropping Pininfarina styling. One of the best looking cars in the world – better looking than more expensive Volvo C70 and Mercedes CLK. A truly beautiful car. Plenty of room for four passengers. Big boot. Air-conditioning a more sensible option than sunroof. 2.0 litre versions go and handle like a sports car – much better than 406 saloon. 3.0 litre V6 has four-pot Brembo front brake callipers. Hold their value reasonably well. 3-year warranty from January 2000. 136bhp 2.2 HDi diesel version with 235lb ft (315Nm) torque and 129mph top speed from June 2001 qualifies for 18% list price BIK tax base. New 160bhp 2.2 16v petrol engine from April 2002 replaces 2.0 litre. Develops an extra 23lb ft torque, gets to 60 in 9 seconds, goes on to 135mph, does 32.1mpg on the combined cycle and emits 210g/km CO_2. Prices are £20,995 for the S and £23,495 for the more luxurious SE.

What's bad: Steering and handling of 3.0 litre V6 not as sharp or as sporty as 2.0/2.2 litre 16v. Could suffer same aircon system problems as saloon and estate. Can suffer coolant loss from hoses or rad which can lead to damage from overheating.

What to watch out for: The 2.0 litre engines are easily chipped and power can be anything from standard 135 bhp up to 155 bhp. They don't have the low back pressure tubular exhaust manifold of the 167/180 bhp GTi-6, though. Oil consumption may be quite high. 3.0 autos may suffer from warped discs due to owners holding them in gear on the brakes. Look for leaks: coolant, power steering fluid, gearbox oil, engine oil.

Recalls: See 406 saloon.

407 (from late 2002)

What's good: 406 replacement on same floorpan as Citroën C5, but with conventional suspension. Same range of petrol and diesel engines, plus a new 2.7 litre V6 TDI built as a joint venture between PSA and Ford.

What's bad: Too soon to say.

What to watch out for: Too soon to say.

505 Family estate (1982 to 1992)

What's good: Big rear drive estate car with seven forward-facing seats. 16ft long. Base engine 1,971cc 96bhp four, but there were also 100bhp and 108bhp versions of this engine, a 2,165cc 130bhp Gate, a 63bhp 2.3 diesel (same engine that powered the original Sierra diesel), and a 76 bhp 2,498cc diesel and a 95bhp turbodiesel.

What's bad: Getting old now, most will have covered starship mileages, spares becoming increasingly difficult to source.

What to watch out for: Rust, excess smoke from diesels and anything likely to lead to an MOT failure.

605 (1989 to 1999)

What's good: Big car with the best rear legroom in its class. V6s handle very well and can be thrown about like a 205GTi. 2.1TD is economical and a relaxed long-distance cruiser. Build quality much improved after January 1995 facelift. 1990–94 SVE 24-valve had 200 bhp and was a seriously fast car. 170 bhp 12-valve V6 not a bad compromise. 150 bhp 2.0 8v turbo not a bad engine. Can be very cheap to buy.

What's bad: Overlight power steering. Riddled with build-quality and electrical problems. The UK market never took to it. 2.1TD very hard to work on. Manual gearboxes a bit weak for V6 engines. 16-valve 2.0 litre engines had ECU problems. 2.1TD auto more suited to long distance than town work. Rock bottom residual values. K reg. cars going for less than £400 in Summer 2001, but MOT repairs could easily cost three times that.

What to watch out for: Most 2.1TD covered mega mileages, so may have been taxis, may have been clocked. Check all electrics. Make sure aircon blows cold. Make sure petrol catalytic converters aren't hot spotted. (Put it through an advanced emissions test.) If manual, satisfy yourself that clutch and gearbox are in good health. ABS prone to failure and cost of repairing may be more than the car is worth.

Recalls: (None known 1994–96–but that's surprising.)

607 (from 2000)

What's good: Peugeot's new big car starting with new 2.2 litre 160 bhp 'four' at around £22,995 and rising to £31,995 for the 210 bhp 3.0 V6 SE auto. Also a new 2.2 litre HDI from £24,295, the first diesel with a particulate trap exhaust system. 3-year warranty should help put minds at rest. Achieved a good four star rating for crash safety in 2002 NCAP tests.

What's bad: Severe lift-off oversteer problem in 'Elk avoidance' test delayed the launch but made sure the car is properly sorted. Might be doomed by the lack of success of the 605, so expect huge depreciation. Motors for electric drivers seats leave little space for padding in the squab and make the seats hard and uncomfortable.

What to watch out for: Not enough feedback to say.

806 MPV (1995 to Autumn 2002)

What's good: Same well-planned, reasonably compact MPV as the Citroën Synergie, with the same PSA engines, including new HDI 110 bhp from August 1999. Three-Star performer in NCAP crash tests (7 points front impact; 15 points side impact). 3-year warranty from January 2000. Earliest 7–seaters now in £5,000 bracket.

What's bad: See Citroën Synergie. To be replaced by new 807 in autumn 2002.

What to watch out for: See Citroën Synergie.

Recalls: 1996 (Sept '95–Oct '95 build): Check airbag trigger. March '99–April '99 build 806s with ABS only: possibility of air in brake fluid. March '98–July '98 build: handbrake ratchet could fail. 19/9/2001: Limited recall of 109 806s with ABS because of risk of internal cracking in the brake pipe unions. Four way brake pipe unions to be replaced. Late 2001: TSB issued to check all common-rail to injector unions on HDIs for leaks.

807 MPV (from Autumn 2002)

What's good: Second generation Citroën/FIAT/Peugeot MPV made its debut at the Geneva Motor Show March 2002. All are longer, taller and wider than the models they replace. Peugeot's is called the 807. Features include automatic electric sliding rear side doors; sliding rear seats fitted with the Quickfix patented anchorage system for easy moving and removal; a huge number of storage compartments and cubby holes; air conditioning offering up to four independent climate zones (like the new MB E Class); the option of three electric tilt/slide sunroofs; foldaway mirror to enable the driver to keep an eye on passengers. The dashboard has a central instrument display, like the Picasso, Yaris and new Nissan Primera, and a seven inch information display monitor can be included. Engine range includes the 2.0 litre 110bhp HDI; the 2.0 litre 138bhp 16v petrol; the 2.2 litre 136bhp HDI; a brand new 2.2 litre 160bhp 16v petrol and a 3.0 litre 208bhp petrol V6. Transmission options are Citroën's sequential auto adaptive automatic or a five-speed manual. Safety equipment includes strong, reinforced body; electronic stability programme; ABS with

EBD; six airbags; automatic low tyre pressure warning; and electronic parking assistance. All 7 passengers get a three-point belt with belt for centre row centre passenger built into seat back.

More online at www.peugeot.co.uk

What's bad: Too soon to say.

What to watch out for: Too soon to say.

Partner Combi (from mid 2001)

What's good: Exactly the same vehicle as the excellent Citroën Berlingo Multispace Forte. Same choice of 75bhp 1.4 litre petrol engine at £9,095 on the road, or 70bhp 1.9 litre XUD diesel at £9,360 on the road. CO2 emissions are 168g/km (£140 VED) and 181g/km (£150 VED); combined fuel consumption 40mpg and 41mpg. Standard features include two huge sliding rear side doors and a gigantic, washing machine swallowing hatchback; drivers airbag, side impact beams, seatbelt pre-tensioners, engine immobiliser, remote central door locking; three-point seatbelts for all three rear passengers; Isofix mountings for two child seats. Does nothing the Citroën Berlingo Multispace doesn't do, but if you live nearer to a Peugeot dealer than a Citroën dealer it's the obvious choice. 3 year warranty. Partner Combi Quicksilver from £9,645 has multi-purpose roof with five overhead fixed glass panels, roof mounted air vents and rood storage compartments.

More online at www.peugeot.co.uk

What's bad: See Citroën Berlingo Multispace.

What to watch out for: See Citroën Berlingo Multispace. As these cars get older they may suffer the same rear suspension pivot wear as Peugeot 405 estates.

PORSCHE

911 930 (1983 to 1989)

What's good: Some say the last 'classic' 911. Galvanised body pants. Engine size up from previous 2,994cc and 204bhp to 2,164cc and 231bhp. Carrera Sport had tea-tray rear spoiler. Properly looked after, it will last for ever. Easier to work on and cheaper to service than '89–'93 964.

What's bad: Can be a handful in the wrong hands, particularly the 300 bhp 3.3 Turbo. Very likely to have seen a few 'track days'.

What to watch out for: Signs of accident damage (suspiciously new-looking rear wing stays); clutch slip (a new clutch is a £2,000 engine-out job); exhaust system (as expensive as a clutch); oil cooler (expensive). Feel the discs for ridges, wear and shouldering. Make sure callipers aren't sticking at the back. Find a good local independent Porsche specialist to inspect the car and give it a compression test before you buy it. Once you own the car, take it in for regular servicing at least every 6 months even if you hardly use it.

911 C2 and C4 964 (1989 to 1993)

What's good: Engine size now up to 3,600cc with more power than previous 911 (250 bhp v/s 231 bhp). A great drive with far more controllable and exploitable oversteer than bar talk would have you believe. Nothing to be scared of at all. C2 preferable to four-wheel-drive C4. 260 bhp Carrera RS Lightweight the pick of the bunch. Recommended.

What's bad: Idiots still crash them on the road. All have catalytic converters. 320 bhp Turbos are for experienced racing drivers only. Very likely to have seen a few 'track days'. More expensive to service than previous 911 due to twin cam multivalve heads.

What to watch out for: If they fall off the road, C2s still tend to do it arse-first. So check the back end very carefully. New stays inside the rear wings are a sure sign of damage repairs, as are rear reflectors full of condensation (once the car has been smacked, they're difficult to seal). C4s, on the other hand, go straight on, so you need to check the fronts of these. You need to see a full and consistent service history from a Porsche dealer or respected Porsche specialist with no major gaps during which it might have been stolen or awaiting a rebuild. Proper histories also make clocking more difficult. A duff clutch is an engine-out £2,000 job to replace. Town-driven cars may wear out their oil stem seals – not easy to replace on a quad cam flat six (don't buy without a compression test). Exhaust systems and heat exchangers still expensive. Feel the brake discs for scoring and lipping through the wheels (when they're cool, of course). Make sure pop-up rear spoiler works. Targa is the least desirable. Check the seals roof very carefully for leaks and the floorpan for water damage and rust as a result of leaks.

Recalls: 1996 (1989–1993 build): 54,000 cars worldwide recalled (2,966 in UK) to check universal joint in steering column which may fail. Early signs are noises or free play in the system.

911 C2 and C4 993 (1993 to 1997)

What's good: The last incarnation of the flat six, air-cooled 911 and also the cleanest looking. Still 3,600cc, but power output 272 bhp from December '93 to October '95; 285 bhp from then on.

What's bad: Monster 408 bhp four-wheel-drive Turbo not a very nice drive. All 911s still have floor-hinged pedals. Very likely to have seen a few 'track days'.

What to watch out for: See above, see 911–964. You're still likely to be investing upwards of £15,000 so pay a Porsche expert to inspect it for you.

Recalls: 1996 (1993 build): 54,000 cars worldwide recalled (2,966 in UK) to check universal joint in steering column which may fail. Early signs are noises or free play in the system.

911 C2, C4, Turbo 996 (from 1997)

What's good: Top-hinged pedals at last. 300 bhp 3.4 litre engine. Lighter, more powerful 360 bhp GT3 with adjustable suspension by far the best. Substantial UK price cuts in May 2000. Incredible, 414bhp 190mph Turbo. C2 and C4 revised again with 3.6 litre Variocam engine developing 315bhp for September 2001. Top speed 177mph, 0–60 4.8 seconds, prices from £55,950.

What's bad: Watercooling has proven to be a mixed blessing with lots of engines mixing their oil and water and needing to be replaced. Wet-sump 996s can suffer oil starvation when driven hard round corners. Can lead to problems with road as well as race cars. (Dry-sump GT3 and GT3–based Turbo not affected.) Surprising amount of understeer. Four-wheel-drive versions have a very noisy drivetrain. Desirable new turbos selling at substantial premiums.

What to watch out for: Major Warning. Any mayonnaise-like emulsion or scum in the radiator header tank or under the oil filler cap, don't touch the car. It probably needs a new engine. Check rear brake discs carefully as they tend to rust on cars not subjected to regular hard braking.

Recalls: Porsche 911/996 Carrera (1998 MY 996 model: 540 UK cars): wrong size pulley fitted driving ancillaries drive belt which may slip affecting PAS, brakes, water pump and alternator (announced 3/6/98). Porsche 911/996 Carrera 4: 1,179 RHD Carrera 4s built between October 1998 and April 2000 recalled to correct software fault which affects fuel gauge reading (*Auto Express* issue 598). 6/2/2001: FIVE recalls of 996 Turbo announced: 1: to replace fuel pump wiring harness due to poor electrical connection in original. 2: to replace coolant line spring clamp band with screw type hose clip because original could chafe the fuel return line. 3: fit anti chafing sheath to engine compartment fuel line to prevent it coming into contact with the air intake pipe. 4: fit protective sheaf to wiring harness in area of oil filter console to prevent harness being chafed by oil filter. 5: secure hydraulic clutch line with an extra bracket to prevent it leaking at its connection with the slave cylinder due to vibration.

928 (1977 to 1995)

What's good: Sporty, reliable alternative to the Jaguar XJS V12 and to a Mercedes SL. Kids seats in the back will also take small adults for short distances. Manuals more satisfying to drive, but autobox less likely to give trouble. High quality German engineering. Original 4,474cc V8 had 240 bhp. Final incarnation had grown to 5,399cc V8 with 340 bhp.

What's bad: A new engine will set you back £12,000. A clutch and gearbox rebuild could hit you for £6,000. Catalysed exhaust systems are also a fortune. Early 3-speed automatics aren't the iron fist in a velvet glove like the later cars. Need to inflate a space saver spare tyre if you get a puncture.

What to watch out for: Don't buy unless from a Porsche dealer or after an inspection by an independent Porsche specialist. Automatics go through brake pads and discs. Feel the brake discs for scoring and lipping through the wheels (when they're cool, of course). Don't buy town-driven cruisers.

944 (1982 to 1993)

What's good: A grown-up 924 with a proper Porsche engine rather than the Audi engine out of a VW LT van. 2.5 had 163 bhp from August '82 to Sept '88; 2.7 had 165 bhp from Sept '88 to June '89. 2.5S16v had 190 bhp from Sept '86 to June '88; 2.5 Turbo had 220 bhp from Jan '86 to Sept '88, then 250 bhp to May '92. 3.0 S2 had 221 bhp from Jan '89 to May '92.

What's bad: Strong acceleration likely to have been used. Many were stolen. Likely to have seen time on 'track days' and could have come off the track. Confusing engine range, but 221 bhp S2 the best overall. 165 bhp 3-speed autos are comparatively slow.

What to watch out for: Getting old now and may have fallen into the hands of abusers unable or unwilling to afford proper maintenance. This doesn't have to be Porsche dealer, but does have to be a respected Porsche specialist who knows what he's doing. (Visit the bloke who maintained it and see how many Porsches he's working on that day.) Has two timing belts (one for the balancer shaft) and periodic re-tensioning of these is critical. Needs a new chain between the two cams plus tensioner every 70,000–80,000 miles (particularly if oil changes have been pushed). If engine vibrates, the hydraulic engine mounting may have failed and needs replacing.

968 (1992 to 1995)

What's good: Very punchy 240 bhp 3.0 litre 4-cylinder twin balancer shaft engine more powerful than 231 bhp 1983–89 911. 6-speed manual gearbox. Near-perfect balance. Brilliant rear-wheel-drive handling. Stripped-out 'Club Sport' model for purists. Became a 'classic' as soon as it went out of production. Will do 160 mph 'on the clock'. Recommended.

What's bad: Will probably have seen a few track days on race tracks. (Club Sport models definitely will have – no point in the car otherwise). 4-speed Tiptronic cabriolet comparatively slow. Cabriolet hoods attract envy slashes. Rear axle pinions fail (see below).

What to watch out for: Check carefully, preferably by professionals, that it has not been thrashed and crashed. HPI or AA/Experian check will make sure it's not on VCAR, but if crashed on a circuit would not have been insured anyway. Make sure the clutch still has plenty of life left in it. Look out for damaged alloys (could be from kerbs, could have had an off.) Cat could be blown from running against rev limiter. Like 944, has two timing belts (one for the balancer shafts) and periodic re-tensioning of these is critical. Needs a new chain between the two cams plus tensioner every 70,000–80,000 miles (particularly if oil changes have been pushed). If engine vibrates, the hydraulic engine mounting may have failed and needs replacing. Noise from rear means it is suffering from rear axle pinion failure which costs £1,200–£1,500 to put right. More about this online at http://members.rennlist.org/martin

Boxster and Boxter S (from 1996)

What's good: Of the original MB SLK, BMW Z3 and Boxster, the Boxster is the best of the bunch. Some echoes of old RSK. Original 2,480cc Boxster had 204 bhp. Engine grew to 2,867cc and 220 bhp in August 1999. But 3,179cc 252 bhp Boxster S also from August 1999 stole sales from standard 911 cabrio. Substantial UK price cuts in May 2000. Facelift in 2001 and 320 bhp 2.7 Turbo set to arrive. Very good to drive with such high limits of adhesion most drivers will never find them. 4th top for reliability in *Auto Express* 2002 survey. Revamp in 2002 brought an extra 8bhp (2.9 now 228bhp with 192 lb ft torque; Boxter S 260bhp with 229lb ft torque) and finally a glass rear window which makes 2002 upgrade easy to identify. Boxter S now lists at £38,450. which isn't bad for an ultra-reliable 165mph sportscar you can use every day.

What's bad: Takes a while to learn and fully exploit the car's handling, especially the more powerful Boxster S. Still selling for 'overs' in 2000. Engine is completely concealed behind difficult-to-remove panels (owner drivers aren't supposed to touch it). You check the oil and water and top them up from the boot. Standard model could do with a bit more power, which it got in the 'S' version. Even small out-of-warranty problems can be very expensive due to inaccessibility of engine. Plastic rear window until 2002 revamp.

What to watch out for: Must have fully stamped up Porsche dealer service history, preferably itemised bills as well. Any mayonnaise-like emulsion or scum in the radiator header tank or under the oil filler cap, don't touch the car. It probably needs a new engine. (Difficult to check with a Boxster because oil and water fillers are remote and engine cover cannot easily be removed.)

Recalls: 1998: 9574 cars recalled to replace steering lock assembly because of faulty ignition switches. 2692 Tiptronics recalled because gear selector bearing sleeves could seize up over time.

Cayenne (from 2003)

What's good: Porsche's BMW X5 and Range Rover rival 4x4. Range now rationalised to two models: the 4.5 litre 340bhp S, which does 0–60 in 7 seconds and gets to 150mph for £60,000; and the 450bhp Turbo which does 0–60 in 5.4 seconds and goes on to 165mph for £80,000. Later may be a 240bhp V6 and a diesel.

What's bad: Another tarmac crunching, fuel guzzling big 4x4.

What to watch out for: Too soon to say.

GT1, GT2, GT3

What's good: Special 911s based on current 996. GT1 has 544bhp 3.2 motor; GT2 has 456bhp; GT3 has 350bhp 3.6. Ceramic disc brakes.

What's bad: Limited editions: GT2 just 300 cars.

What to watch out for: Police speed traps. Track day damage.

PROTON

Compact (1995 to 2000)

What's good: The previous model Mitsubishi Colt hatchback with a Persona front. Re-named Satria. Good engines. Decent handling. Autumn 1999 cuts brought prices down to from £6,750 with alloy wheeled 1.6 litre 'Spectrum' model at £9,999, 133 bhp 1.8 coupe at £12,499 and fine handling Lotus-developed Gate at £14,524. Re-named 'Satria' from 2000. (See Satria.)

What's bad: Just a bit cramped. See Mitsubishi Colt.

What to watch out for: As Persona.

Recalls: 1996 (from October 1995 build): fuel pump can allow fuel to leak when tank is brimmed. 1997 (July-August '97 build: 1,797 cars): Mitsubishi sourced brake booster valve may stick. 1998 (13in wheels only Aug '97–Aug '98 build): Front tyres may lose pressure. 1/5/2001: faulty starter motor relay may cause starter motor to operate independently of ignition switch. Starter motor relays to be replaced.

Impian (from July 2001)

What's good: All new Proton designed medium saloon in UK from July 2001. Mitsubishi derived 102bhp 1.6 litre engine with 103 lb ft (140Nm) torque and later option of a twin-cam 1.8 litre Renault engine. Strong body/chassis structure. Lotus tuned suspension. ABS, traction control and four airbags all standard. Combined consumption of 1.6 is 42.2 mpg. CO_2 output is 161 g/km (£120pa VED) for the manual and 214g/km (£155pa VED) for the automatic. Top speed 110mph. 0 to 60 12.0 seconds. Insurance Group 10. Length: 4,465mm; width 1,740mm. ABS, traction control and three three-point rear seatbelts all standard. Price £12,000 (manual); £13,000 (automatic).

What's bad: Criticised for poor engine refinement and poor quality trim. No more than a three star 53% performance in 2002 NCAP crash tests.

What to watch out for: Too soon to say.

MPI (1989 to 1997)

What's good: Reliable with good first-owner warranty package. Very cheap. Based on an old mid- 80s Mitsubishi Lancer with 1,298cc 68–78bhp or 1,468 75–89bhp Mitsubishi motors. 4 door or 'aeroback' hatchback. Quite light 923 to 950kg weight.

What's bad: Hideously ugly and irredeemably naff. Had some of the most ridiculous wheeltrims ever seen on a car.

What to watch out for: Rear suspension can collapse. Highly likely to have been mini-cabbed at the bottom end of the market. Old ones mostly owner-serviced or simply neglected.

Perdana

What's good: Malaysia's economic recovery has allowed the launch of its larger car with looks a bit like those of the Toyota Camry. 2.0 litre V6 with auto, a/c, leather, etc. for around £16,000.

What's bad: Criticised for restless ride and uninvolving handling at launch. Undercut in price by Kia Magentis at £12,995.

What to watch out for: Likely to depreciate quickly from list, so should be a serious bargain second-hand.

Persona (1993 to 2000)

What's good: Really a Mitsubishi Lancer model which never reached the UK, but which, when highly modified, was hugely successful in international rallying. Quite good to drive with perky 1,600cc engine. Light years ahead of ancient Lancer-based Proton MPI. Prices from £7,750 for 1.3LSi, rising via 2.0TDi diesel at £11,024 to 1.8 EXi at £11,524. Re-named 'Wira' from 2000.

What's bad: Slightly unfinished, undeveloped feel to gearchange and interior. Rattles.

What to watch out for: Trim doesn't wear well. Rattles become more pronounced. Cambelts need changing regularly. Could have been cabbed. 1/5/2001: faulty starter motor relay may cause starter motor to operate independently of ignition switch. Starter motor relays to be replaced.

Recalls: 1997 (July-August '97 build: 1,797 cars): Mitsubishi sourced brake booster valve may stick. 1998 (13 wheels only Aug '97–Aug '98 build): front tyres may lose pressure.

Satria (from 2000)

What's good: New name for Compact. See Compact for range. Fine handling Lotus-developed Gate at £14,524. Satria 1.5 Sport with Gti bodykit £9,299 from July 2001.

What's bad: Detailing of Gate a bit fussy and 'boy racerish'.

What to watch out for: As Persona.

Recalls: 17/10/2001: 271 Satria GTis recalled because front suspension stabiliser bar may break. Stabiliser bar to be replaced.

Waja ('Impian' from 2001)

What's good: Code name 'XG'. Malaysian name for the Impian in the UK. Good looking Mondeo-sized car due in UK early 2001. Mitsubishi 1.6 litre and Renault 1.8 litre 16 valve engines. CNG version for Malaysia. Sauber-Petronas high performance 1.8 engine due later. Big boot. Well equipped. Three three-point seatbelts in the back. Suspension developed by Lotus. Re-named 'Impian' before UK launch (see Proton Impian).

What's bad: Too soon to say.

What to watch out for: Too soon to say.

Wira (from 2000)

What's good: See Persona. Prices cut to from £8,999 for 1.6Exi from October 2000. Three year warranty and six year powertrain guarantee continue.

What's bad: See Persona

What to watch out for: See Persona

RELIANT

Scimitar

What's good: Reliant name Scimitar to return soon on a very pretty modified version of the former De La Chapelle roadster. 2.0 litre Peugeot engines develop 135bhp and 167bhp. Also a PSA 3.0 V6 with 200bhp. Model with 167bhp should do 0–60 in 6 seconds and go on to 140mph.

What's bad: Too soon to say.

What to watch out for: Too soon to say.

RENAULT

19 (1988 to 996)

What's good: 1.4s surprisingly trouble-free. You can reckon on 8–9 years and 90,000–100,000 miles before they start to get expensive. Even the catalytic converters can last 9 years and 90,000 miles. Diesels are rough but tough with good economy. 16-valve models are screamers and were one of the 'cars to have' in the mid-90s.

What's bad: Dull looks before the beak-like facelift. Autos can give up at around 60,000 miles. In June 2001 Renault was rated by Motor Warranty Direct as Britain's joint 4th worst out of 22 marques for used car warranty claims (check online at www.warrantydirect.co.uk)

What to watch out for: If the paint has faded, it may come up with Mer polish. Torn seat trim difficult to do much about unless you call a local car upholsterer (Yellow Pages). Switches break. Non-PAS have heavy helms. Autobox the first bit to break. Likely to be rust under plastic window sill trims. Rear shocks eventually punch their way through their towers.

Recalls: 1994 (Renault 19 Phase II-Apr 92–Mar 94): faulty seatbelt pretensioners and bonnet catch.

21 (1986 to 1994)

What's good: Cheap. 175 bhp Turbo and Turbo Quadra were flyers in their day. Comfortable enough but, apart from enthusiasts for the turbo, the market is not really interested unless the cars are seriously cheap.

What's bad: Cheap, flimsy build. Quite a few parts are hard to get, such as rear discs for turbos and TXis. 19 model tended to be much stronger, better built and more reliable. Dashboards expensive to remove to replace bulbs or heater matrix. Automatics often troublesome.

What to watch out for: Have to be cheap to be worth buying. Check all electrics carefully. Look for uneven front tyre wear. Check coolant for mayonnaise (blown head gasket). If has ABS, make sure it works. Sniff for fishy smell – a sure sign of a failed heater matrix (putting this right may cost more than the car is worth).

21 Savanna (1986 to 1995)

What's good: Estates have option of seven forward-facing seats with reasonable luggage space behind. Diesels are economical, but diesel range was complicated: 67 bhp 2,068cc non-turbo from Jan-Sept 1989; 65 bhp 1,870cc non-turbo from Sept '89–Oct 95; 88 bhp 2,068cc turbo from Jan '89–Oct '90 and then again from Nov '93–Oct '95.

What's bad: Two completely different drivetrains: 1.7 petrol engines were transverse, but everything else was longitudinal, overhanging the front wheels. Lousy ventilation – particularly bad for rearmost passengers on long hot summer journeys. Not cheap to repair. Dashboards expensive to remove to replace bulbs or heater matrix. Automatics can be troublesome. Mild steel retaining straps of plastic fuel tank rust through. In June 2001 Renault was rated by Motor Warranty Direct as Britain's joint 4th worst out of 22 marques for used car warranty claims (check online at www.warrantydirect.co.uk)

What to watch out for: Repaired accident damage (high used values made them worth repairing for a while). Rust. Family and dog damage. Torn upholstery. Sagging suspension. Don't buy one that's been towing because seven occupied seats and a caravan is just too much. Sniff for the fishy smell which means the heater matrix is leaking and you are in for a stiff replacement bill. Look under the back and check that fuel tank retaining straps are not about to rust through and drop off, depositing the tank on the street with dire consequences.

25 (1984 to 1992)

What's good: Much loved by owners and many have clocked up 300,000–plus miles. Can be extremely cheap. 1,995cc 4 cylinder engines with 103bhp, 120bhp and 140bhp; 2,165cc 4 cylinder engines with 123bhp and 126bhp; 2,664cc V6 with 144 bhp; 2,849cc V6 with 153bhp and 160bhp; 2,458cc V6 turbo with 182bhp. 5-speed manual boxes; 3 and 4 speed autoboxes.

What's bad: Automatic gearbox can give trouble. Heater matrix may fail. Huge labour cost in removing dashboard to replace heater matrix, or minor failures such as warning or dash light bulbs. V6 not a specially good engine and guzzles petrol. Turbos too old to remain reliable. Automatics can be troublesome.

What to watch out for: May have covered more miles than indicated on odometer. Make sure ABS is okay (pump not as dear as some at £660, but ECU is another £460 plus VAT). Check all electrics (even the dashboard bulbs give up). Check auto especially carefully (some 25s go through three of four in a lifetime). PAS pump or rack may leak (common old Renault problem). Try to feel discs for scoring, lipping or wear. Fishy smell inside and condensation on screen usually indicates failure of heater matrix, many of which were poorly made. You could easily buy a 25 for £750 than have to spend £2,000 on it immediately. Buy only from a careful, appreciative, enthusiastic owner who's had it for years. Definitely not a backstreet buy.

Recalls: (None known 1994–98 but autobox a well known problem area.)

5 Supercinq (1987 to 1996)

What's good: Simple, old car, quite rightly kept in production as the 60 bhp 1.4 Campus until March 1996. 11ft 9in long and 5ft 2in wide. Light at 725 to 740kg. Cheap.

What's bad: Shows its age. Can be very difficult to get through MOT advanced emissions test after 5–6 years. Work can cost as much as £2,000 which is far more than the car is worth and consequently the model is dying out. In June 2001 Renault was rated by Motor Warranty Direct as Britain's joint 4th worst out of 22 marques for used car warranty claims (check online at www.warrantydirect.co.uk)

What to watch out for: May suffer cat converter problems. Don't buy without a recent MOT certificate and emissions pass printout.

Recalls: 1995 (Campus 1.4: VIN C4070510214892 to C4070511788781): car may pull to left when braking.

Avantime (from 2002)

What's good: Avant Garde MPV 'Town Coupe' with two wide side doors, pillarless side windows and plush seats for just four on an Espace floorpan. Powered by either a 165bhp 2.0 turbo four cylinder petrol engine or a 210bhp 3.0 litre V6. V6 came first with a six-speed manual gearbox offering a 138mph top speed, 8.4 second zero to 60, combined mpg of 25 and CO_2 output of 266g/km. High, MPV and 4x4 like driving position. On sale in UK from 16th May 2002 at £24,050 for 165bhp 2.0 Turbo, £27,050 for 210bhp 6-speed 3.0V6 and £28,450 for 2.0V6 auto.

What's bad: Pointless. Rear seats criticised as uncomfortable. 5-speed autobox in Laguna V6 criticised by *'What Car?'* August 2001 issue for lumpy full throttle changes, slow kickdown and slack throttle response, and no four cylinder Laguna automatics to be built until February 2002. These problems could be the reason for no automatic option on the first Avantimes. I can't imagine why anyone would buy one.

What to watch out for: Too soon to say.

Clio (1991 to 1998)

What's good: Amazingly quiet at town speeds. Decent ride quality. 12ft 2in long by 6ft wide (inc mirrors) and weighing from 825kg. Hot and red hot Clio 1.8 16v and 2.0 Clio Williams. Engines start with old pushrod 49 bhp 1,108cc ohv in 1992 'Night and Day' special. Rise through 60 bhp 1,171 single point injected and 1,149cc multipoint injected OHCs, 75 bhp 1,390cc OHCs, 110 bhp 1.8s to 137 bhp 1.8 16v and 150 bhp 2.0 16v Clio Williams. Also a 65 bhp 1,870cc diesel. PAS widely available from 1.4s up. 4-speed auto became 3-speed auto in 1.4s from Jan 1996. Facelift with new grille from March 1994. Second facelift with bigger headlights and high level brake light from May 1996.

What's bad: Nicole-Papa advertising saga became boring marketing speak, despite the presence of Estelle Skornak. Average performance in NCAP crash tests. Watch out for kerbing damage, especially on power-steered Clios. Some automatics have been prone to surging – cured by replacing faulty inlet manifold gaskets. June 2001 Renault was rated by Motor Warranty Direct as Britain's joint 4th worst out of 22 marques for used car warranty claims (check online at www.warrantydirect.co.uk) 18th from bottom for reliability in *Auto Express* 2002 reader survey of 100 models.

What to watch out for: 4-speed autobox cooling system (oil cooler within the water radiator) can cause problems. Kerbing damage to front suspension. 1998: (June '97–Nov '97 build): possibility of inadvertent deployment of airbags. 2000: may lose brake servo assistance. High incidence of automatic transmission failures. On 1,149cc D7F engines it is essential to change the timing belt, tensioners and the water pump every 3 years of 36,000 miles (whichever comes first).

Recalls: 27/9/2001: News from The Back Room, the online forum at www.honestjohn.co.uk, of a recall of R reg. Clios because the throttle cable can snap.

Clio (1998 to late 2003)

What's good: Pleasingly 'different' with cute protruding bottom. Looks good on the streets and definitely has cred. High spec includes electro-hydraulic power steering, sunroof and driver's airbag. Famous 'Size Matters' TV campaign. 172 bhp Sport Clio launched in spring 2000 is very quick, a bundle of fun to drive and one of the best junior hot hatches. Very good Four-Star rating in Euro NCAP crash tests. Mad mid-engined Clio RenaultSport V6 24v from October 2000. Three year, 60,000 mile warranty from October 2000. Plastic front wings deform and shrug off minor impacts. To get a 'nose job' in autumn 2001. Facelift July 2001 and new 1.5 litre diesel engine. 80bhp 110mph version of 1.5dCi arrived March 2002. Has very low CO_2 output of 110g/km, combined consumption of 67.3mpg and prices to start at £10,995. Both Clio 1.5 diesels qualify for £80pa VED from April 2002. Clio 172 Cup model due July 2002; new V6 due late 2002.

What's bad: Renault build quality. Complaints of seat material fraying. To be replaced with new car on same platform as new Nissan Micra in late 2003. Some automatics have been prone to surging – cured by replacing faulty inlet manifold gaskets. Various other engine problems. June 2001 Renault was rated by Motor Warranty Direct as Britain's joint 4th worst out of 22 marques for used car warranty claims (check online at www.warrantydirect.co.uk). 18th from bottom for reliability in *Auto Express* 2002 reader survey of 100 models.

What to watch out for: See above and expect kerbing damage, easily spotted by damaged protruding plastic wheeltrims. Continued high incidence of automatic transmission failures. On 1,149cc D7F engines it is essential to change the timing belt, tensioners and the water pump every 3 years of 36,000 miles (whichever comes first).

Recalls: 21/2/2000: 29,000 cars built Jan '99 to Nov '99: possibility that brake servo valve may malfunction resulting in loss of servo assistance. Valve to be inspected and replaced if necessary. 24/8/2001: 10,588 Clios built 1/1/1998 to 28/12/1998 recalled because accelerator cable may break. Modified cable to be fitted. 7/12/2001: 897 Clios built 27/7/2000 to 29/7 2000 recalled because one of the four airbag securing bolts could be missing. Missing bolts to be replaced. January 2001: TSB on 1.2 16v models to solve a fuelling problem by re-mapping the ECU.

Clio (from late 2003)

What's good: All new Clio on same floorpan as new Micra, with Renault look but much more restrained styling than Megane and Vel Satis. Ultra low CO_2 and very economical 1.5 litre diesel engines.

What's bad: Too soon to say.

What to watch out for: Too soon to say.

Espace (1985 to 1997)

What's good: Immensely practical design. Individual seat removal system much copied and only bettered by new Espace. Easy to see out of and to park. Early models up to the first (1991) facelift handled nicely. Nevertheless, your best bet is the facelifted 2.1 litre turbodiesel. Clutches will last 3 years and 120,000 miles in mostly motorway use. Engines can run up to 200,000 miles with few problems.

What's bad: Strange relationship between driver's seat and accelerator pedal leads to ankle cramp, so aftermarket cruise control is a good idea. There was a recall over a wiring loom problem. Trim is a bit flimsy, not up to hard family use. Automatic transmissions have a history of problems. Be very careful driving the diesel in standing water as apt to suck it up and blow its cylinder head off. Serious reliability problems reported by ADAC (the German breakdown organisation) in its 2001 report. In June 2001 Renault was rated by Motor Warranty Direct as Britain's joint 4th worst out of 22 marques for used car warranty claims (check online at www.warrantydirect.co.uk)

What to watch out for: Clocked ex-taxis. Dodgy electrics. Chipped or cracked windscreens (expensive to replace). Wear in front and rear suspension from carrying heavy loads. Clonking driveshafts. Wear in gearshift linkage. Clutch wear (can last up to 120,000 miles, but depends on usage). Leaking or groaning power steering. Duff cats in post-1991 facelift model. Automatics best avoided. Make sure 2.1TD has received regular oil changes. Pull the dipstick and look for clean oil in all petrol versions, especially the V6. Look for mayonnaise under the oil filler cap, signifying cylinder head problems. Family damage from baby's bottles, food, sweets, felt-tip pens, dogs, etc. Check that seat locking mechanisms aren't damaged ⋅ from misunderstandings. Fishy smell inside and condensation on screen usually indicates failure of heater matrix, many of which were poorly made. Make sure the heater works on all speed settings, not just maximum (a common fault). Make sure recall work has been carried out.

Recalls: 1995 (2.1TD built 3/93–6/94). install fuse in preheater wiring circuit, re-route wiring away from main loom and install clip to keep it away from loom to prevent risk of insulation damage. 1996 (Espaces-on original tyres built March '91–Oct '92): check for separation of tyre tread.

Espace (1997 to 2002)

What's good: Revamp of the original design put it back at the top of the class again. Now transverse-engined like Laguna. No other

MPV has such a versatile seating arrangement. Longer-bodied Grande Espace overcomes lack of luggage space with seven aboard. Best buys should have been the diesels (air intakes now in mirror assemblies). Four-Star performer and the best MPV in NCAP crash test (11 points front impact; 16 points side impact). Three year 60,000 mile UK warranty from October 2000. New 130bhp 2.2 litre direct injected common rail dCi diesel from Laguna II became available in March 2001 from £21,350. Diesels hold their values better than most other MPVs.

What's bad: Have heard of one wiring fire, which was a recall problem on the previous model diesels. Have been problems with the older 2.2 diesel engine (crankshaft thrust bearings dropping out is one). Quite a lot of niggling problems. Whole dashboard needs to come out to replace a single dashboard bulb. Serious reliability problems reported by ADAC (the German breakdown organisation) in its 2001 report. In June 2001 Renault was rated by Motor Warranty Direct as Britain's joint 4th worst out of 22 marques for used car warranty claims (check online at www.warrantydirect.co.uk). 3rd from Bottom in 144 car 2002 JD Power/*What Car?* Customer Satisfaction Survey of V and W reg. cars. Great in theory, but not recommended.

What to watch out for: Chipped or cracked windscreens (it's a lot of glass). Family damage from baby's bottles, food, sweets, felt-tip pens, dogs, etc. Make sure the seat locking mechanisms aren't damaged. Before buying one of these, make sure everything works as it should: ABS warning light, automatic transmission, a/c, electrics. On diesel, listen for flywheel noises which could be first sign that crankshaft thrust washers have dropped out.

Recalls: 2000: March '99–August '99 build: fuel could be ignited by heat from exhaust. 18/4/2000: 1,000 diesel engined cars built February to April 2000 may be fitted with defective brake vacuum pumps. 2001 TSB to replace Exhaust Gas Recirculation valves on 2000 model 2.2 litre diesel engines. 28/2/2001: Build daters 17/7/2000–20/9/2000: rear wheel brake calliper fastenings may shear leading to callipers becoming loose on the stub axles. Original fastenings to be replaced with modified type with lock washers.

Espace (late 2002 on)

What's good: Radical new Espace with new Renault corporate look established on Avantime and Vel Satis, to be launched late 2002. Three year UK warranty.

What's bad: Too soon to say.

What to watch out for: Too soon to say.

Kangoo Combi (1999 to 2004)

What's good: Renault's answer to the Citroën Berlingo Multispace – with two more doors and a lower price. 75 bhp 1.4 litre 8-valve petrol or 65 bhp 1.9 litre non-turbo diesel. Prices from a very sensible £9,500 OTR which includes PAS and metallic paint. RXE versions (£1,000 extra) have passenger airbag, three three-point rear seatbelts and front driving lights. Extremely sensible. Brilliant doggy wagon. Three year 60,000 mile warranty from October 2000. 2002 Model Year improvements include 75bhp 1.2 litre engine from Clio, 95bhp 1.6 16v petrol and 95bhp 1.9dCi diesel. 4x4 Kombi Trekka arrived early 2002 at £10,995 and has to be the ultimate doggy wagon. This buys you the petrol version. Diesel is £11,995. All Trekkas with alloys and met paint.

What's bad: Fairly basic and certainly not for the status conscious – unless, of course, the Kangoo Combi becomes trendy. Driving experience inferior to Citroën Berlingo. Watch out for trapped fingers in those sliding rear doors. Kangoo's sliding side doors forced PSA to follow suit.

What to watch out for: Nothing significant as yet.

Recalls: 21/2/2000: 29,000 cars built Jan '99 to Nov '99: possibility that brake servo valve may malfunction resulting in loss of servo assistance. Valve to be inspected and replaced if necessary. 4/10/2000: 25,000 Kangoos, including 200 UK market Kombis fitted with Kleber tyres recalled because tyres can suddenly deflate. December 2000 (official 26/1/2001) 14,054 Kangoos recalled for modifications to the sensor which controls seatbelt pretensioners and airbags.

Kangoo II (from 2004)

What's good: New Kangoo to keep up with new kombi utilities from GM, Opel and Ford.

What's bad: Too soon to say.

What to watch out for: Too soon to say.

Laguna (1994 to 2001)

What's good: Three clever lap and diagonal rear seatbelts fitted from Jan '95 (third belt retracts into offside 'D' pillar). New 110 bhp 1.6 16v and 120 bhp 1.8 16v engines from spring 1998. 2.0 litre twin-cam 149 bhp RTi 16v also good. Roomy inside, comfortable ride, big boot. Non-turbo 2.2 12-valve diesels make good taxis as are pleasant to drive in heavy traffic. But 115 bhp TD better still. All better-built than old 21. New 194 bhp 2,946cc Peugeot-powered V6 from October 1997 much better than previous Laguna V6. Estate cars have masses of loadspace, but 7–seater option is rear-facing and folds to the side rather than into the floor. Comparatively good performance in NCAP crash tests. But so many problems likely I can't recommend the Laguna 1 as a second-hand buy.

What's bad: 85 bhp 2.2 diesels sluggish on the open road. Long-backed drivers find themselves sitting too close to the top of the huge windscreen. Old 95 bhp 1.8 and 115 bhp 2.0 litre 8-valve engines outclassed. Old 170 bhp 2,963 cc V6 not a very good package. Poor quality electrics lead to all manner of irritating failures, including alternator and the auto gearbox multi-function switch. More than its fair share of recalls. Power steering failure common. Heater matrixes fail in the welds. Dashboards expensive to remove to replace bulbs or heater matrix. Automatics troublesome (front drive clutch drum splits). Manual gearboxes subject to bearing failure after 6–7 years and 60–80,000 miles. Timing belt of diesel drives the water pump and these have been known to seize at as little as 59,200 miles and two years old, stripping the teeth off the belt and causing £1,100 worth of engine damage. In June 2001 started to get reports of noisy front dampers on 2000W reg. Lagunas due to faulty batch of dampers. Getting reports of failed hatchback locks. Immobiliser keys have rolling codes, can't be coded by locksmiths and cost £120 to replace at Renault dealers. In June 2001 Renault was rated by Motor Warranty Direct as Britain's joint 4th worst out of 22 marques for used car warranty claims (check online at www.warrantydirect.co.uk).

What to watch out for: Look for leaking power steering on all Lagunas. Check for 'clonking' from wear in front anti-roll bar bushes. 2.2 litre diesels could have been cabbed and clocked. Check tyres for uneven wear denoting crash damage, suspension damage or simple misalignment. Check automatic transmission fluid for signs of overheating (will be black instead of dark red). Need cambelt changes every 35,000–40,000 miles (ex-fleet cars may be on borrowed time). Try to feel the brake discs as these may need replacing. If aircon fitted, make sure it blows cold. Fishy smell inside and condensation on screen usually indicates failure of heater matrix, many of which were poorly made. Damp under carpets may be due to this or failed damp-proof membranes inside doors. Make sure keyfob transmitter was replaced under free recall. Pulling to one side or the other may be due to failing front coil springs.

Recalls: 1996 (May '94–Aug '94 build): Automatic transmission may lock up. 1996 (Jul '94–Dec '94 build): Airbag warning light may be faulty. 1996 (April '96–Aug '96 build): Fuel injection system computer may be faulty. 1997 (April-August '96 build: 12,494 cars): Engine ECU may malfunction causing exhaust manifold to overheat and set fire to bulkhead insulation. 1998: failed heater matrixes replaced FOC. 1998: 'plip' key transmitters can go out of sequence due to static or fiddling with them in the pocket. Improved 'plip' key transmitters now available free of charge to Laguna owners. (Per BBC 'Watchdog' 12/2/98) 1998: 17,000 cars recalled due to possibility of inadvertent deployment of airbags. Cambelt tensioner on diesel engines may lead to premature cambelt failure. To be checked as a TSB item at services. 2000: July 1998 build only: driveshaft CV may fail and affect steering. All Lagunas: possible sudden failure of gear selectors. 12/1/2000: 4,422 F9Q diesel engined cars built Dec '98 to May '99: brake vacuum pump may leak allowing oil to enter the brake servo resulting in loss of servo assistance to the brakes. Magnetti Marelli brake vacuum pumps to be replaced; servos to be inspected for oil ingress and replaced if necessary. 21/2/2000: 29,000 cars built Jan '99 to Nov '99: possibility that brake servo valve may malfunction resulting in loss of servo assistance. Valve to be inspected and replaced if necessary. 18/4/2000: 1,000 diesel-engined cars built February to April 2000 may be fitted with defective brake vacuum pumps. Sympathetic FOC replacement of rear door damp proof membranes on Lagunas up to 5 years old.

Laguna II (from 2001)

What's good: New Laguna launched September 2000 Paris Show to compete with new Citroën C5, new Mondeo and new Vectra. Extremely good looking. Novel keyless entry and starting system easy to get used to. Engine line-up includes 110 bhp 1.6 litre 16v; 123 bhp 1.8 litre 16v; 140 bhp 2.0. litre 'IDE'; 210 bhp 3.0 litre V6; 105 bhp 1.9 litre dCi diesel; 135 bhp 2.2 litre dCi diesel. The Sport Tourer estate car is very good looking. Three year, 60,000 mile UK warranty. Plastic front wings deform and shrug off minor impacts. Much better to drive than old Laguna. Excellent, top-of-the-class Five Star NCAP crash safety rating announced 28/3/2001. 150ps 2.2 litre common rail diesel on sale in Germany from 1st January 2002 and UK from February at prices from £19,450. Has 236 lb ft torque and emits 170g/km CO_2.

What's bad: Not quite as good as the new Mondeo, but a better cruiser at 70–80mph and has a slightly better ride. Worrying number of gimmicks from a company not known for high quality electrics. Complex specification variations led to delivery delays of cars built to order in Spring and Summer 2001. Problems with automatic transmissions for four cylinder cars have led to a statement "none will be built until February 2002in. 5-speed automatic in V6 heavily criticised by '*What Car?*' magazine August 2001 issue for lumpy full throttle changes, slow kickdowns and slack throttle response. Could be the reason why the first Avantimes were manual only. In five months and 3,000 miles, one reader's Y reg. Sport Tourer has required two new gearboxes, one new driveshaft, one new drivers side electric window motor and repairs to the hand-brake. Other readers have suffered problems with the ambitious electronic gizmos, heating system failures, airbag failures, seat comfort and a lack of availability of essential spare parts. Radio aerial in rear side glass of Sports Tourer gives poor radio reception in parts of Britain. 'Which' magazine has highlighted problems with ECUs of all Laguna II petrol engines from 1.6 to 3.0 litre and is urging Renault to recall them.

What to watch out for: See 'What's Bad'. Has been one reader report of a good DCI with 22,000 trouble-free miles, but still best to stay away from this model until Renault gets the bugs out. Don't buy the a nearly new example at auction as it may well be a reject car.

Recalls: 19/9/01: Limited recall of 223 Sport Tourers fitted with towing balls to fit reinforcement to towing ball mounting panel otherwise it may flex and crack. w/c 17/12/2001: All Laguna IIs built before September 2001 recalled for clips to be fitted preventing accelerator from wedging under carpet jamming throttle open. 2002: All Laguna II 1.6s recalled because fault in ECU software means engine can stall when a/c is switched on.

Megane (1996 to late 2002)

What's good: Sweet, precise handling. Economical diesel. Even more economical TDI from May 1998. Joint top of the class for secondary safety in NCAP crash testing. Galvanised body has 12-year warranty. New, much better 110bhp 1.6 litre 16-valve engine from Summer 1999. Booted 'Classic' saloon. Three year, 60,000 mile warranty from October 2000.

What's bad: Silly things go wrong, such as flywheel sensor cable connector failure which immobilises the car. 8-valve 1.4s and 1.6s a bit underpowered. 'Classic' saloon not the best looking car in the World. Coupe pointless except as a basis for the smart cabrio. Engine has to come out to replace the clutch. Several *Telegraph* readers reported needing a replacement engine around 8,000 miles. 1.6 8-valve engine prone to head gasket failure. Heater matrixes may also fail and cost £350 to replace if the car does not have a/c or £600 if it does. Automatics give trouble (front drive clutch drum splits). One report of digital odometer failure requiring a new instrument cluster, but Renault paid most of the cost even though the car was two years old. Report of a/c bracket failing due to corrosion causing unit to puncture radiator matrix leaving owner with a £900 bill. In June 2001 Renault was rated by Motor Warranty Direct as Britain's joint 4th worst out of 22 marques for used car warranty claims (check online at www.warrantydirect.co.uk) 20th from bottom for reliability in *Auto Express* 2002 reader survey of 100 models. Renault has admitted to a cold running problem with some 1.4 and 1.6 16v engines which run over lean on start up to reduce CO_2 output and as a result run roughly. Sharp edge of engine soundproofing cover of diesel can cut through fuel pump wiring loom. Replacement available from Renault dealers. Radically restyled new Megane with Vel Satis look due to be launched in Spring 2002.

What to watch out for: Kerbing damage, strange electrical faults. To check for head gasket failure on 1.6 8v look under oil cap for 'mayonnaise'. (Low-mileage cars had head gaskets replaced FOC under a Renault 'Tech Note'.) A 'fishy' smell inside the car and damp under the carpets is usually a symptom of heater matrix failure.

Recalls: 1997 (Megane and Scenic July-Sept '97 build): 7,434 cars found to have potentially defective braking system. 2000: July 1998 build only: driveshaft CV may fail and affect steering. 12/1/2000: 4,422 F9Q diesel engined cars built Dec '98 to May '99: brake vacuum pump may leak allowing oil to enter the brake servo resulting in loss of servo assistance to the brakes. Magnetti Marelli brake vacuum pumps to be replaced; servos to be inspected for oil ingress and replaced if necessary. 18/4/2000: 1,000 diesel engined cars built February to April 2000 may be fitted with defective brake vacuum pumps. 17/8/2001: 761 Megane Coupes and Cabrios built 15/9/1999 to 8/2/2001 recalled because may suffer from fuel leakage of fuel injection pipes; 761 2.0 litre coupes and cabrios recalled because may be a faulty connection between the coil and HT leads causing connector to overheat; 761 coupes recalled because EGR pipe may fail causing the car to hesitate on acceleration; 761 coupes and cabrios recalled because camshaft sensor may fail and cause engine to cut out. 14/12/2001: 3,586 Meganes and Scenics fitted with F9Q 732/740 engines and dCi engines recall because of risk of diesel return pipe rubbing against the alternator leading to risk of leakage from high pressure pipes. Reposition/replace chafing pipes and check unions for correct tightness.

Megane Coupe and Cabrio

What's good: Strange looking coupe, but good looking cabrio, many offered at big discounts both by independent importers and Renault franchises. Two-door coupe and 'Roadster' cabrio originally available with 90 bhp 1.6 or 150 bhp 2.0 litre 16v engines. Later 1.6 16v has 110 bhp.
What's bad: See Megane.
What to watch out for: See Megane.
Recalls: See Megane. Additionally: 17/8/2001: 761 Megane Coupes and Cabrios built 15/9/1999 to 8/2/2001 recalled because may suffer from fuel leakage of fuel injection pipes; 761 2.0 litre coupes and cabrios recalled because may be a faulty connection between the coil and HT leads causing connector to overheat; 761 coupes recalled because EGR pipe may fail causing the car to hesitate on acceleration; 761 coupes and cabrios recalled because camshaft sensor may fail and cause engine to cut out.

Megane II (from October 2002)

What's good: Radical new Megane with Patrick le Quement styling along the lines of the Avantime and Vel Satis. Launch at European Motor Shows autumn 2002, UK sales from October 2002; prices from £10,500. Engine line up to include 61mpg 80bhp 1.5 dCi diesel; 100bhp 1.5dCi; 120bhp 1.9dCi and 140bhp dCi. Petrol engines start with 98bhp 1.4 that does 42.2mog combined, a 41mpg 115bhp 1.6, a 136bhp 2.0 litre, going all the way up to a 2.0 litre 200bhp RenaultSport turbo. Cabrio to have folding hardtop like Peugeot 206CC. Same card entry and button start as Laguna II. Does look good. Official photos and more details from 2nd July 2002 online at www.newmegane.co.uk

What's bad: Worry about those Renault electrics. *Autocar* says that the rear styling has resulted in a loss of boot space, down to 330 litres.

What to watch out for: Too soon to say.

RenaultSport Spyder (1997 to 1998)

What's good: Very basic road and track sports car launched by Renault just before Lotus launched the Elise. Had Clio Williams 1,998cc 150bhp twin cam engine mounted transversely in the back, like the Elise. A windscreen was an option. Quite light at 930kg but Elise much lighter at 756kg. There was a racing series for them in 1997/1998. Production ended September 1998. LHD or RHD. A few around on the used market and at auction from £11,000 or so.

What's bad: Apparently doesn't handle as well as the Elise.

What to watch out for: Highly likely to have seen circuit use at some time in its life. Make sure cat isn't spiked by engine running against limiter. Look for damage from comings off. Hard to price, but be careful not to pay too much.

Safrane (1992 on)

What's good: Very comfortable with cosseting ride and excellent rear legroom. Revised and facelifted in October 1996. Volvo-engined 2.5 litre 5-cylinder automatic capable of covering immense distances at high average speeds. Reasonable fuel consumption. Low used prices.

What's bad: Electronic autobox problems on pre-1996 facelift versions expensive to fix. ECU problems with pre-facelift V6. Lose value quickly. Jerky cruise control. Dashboards expensive to remove to replace bulbs or heater matrix which is prone to leaks. In June 2001 Renault was rated by Motor Warranty Direct as Britain's joint 4th worst out of 22 marques for used car warranty claims (check online at www.warrantydirect.co.uk).

What to watch out for: Clonky autobox. Duff cats. Make sure aircon blows cold. Check all electrics. Hard ride signifies failure of top model's variable suspension. Fishy smell inside and condensation on screen usually indicates failure of heater matrix, many of which were poorly made.

Recalls: 1994 (Dec 91–Mar 94 build): heat shield required to protect fuel tank from exhaust. 1996 (May '94–Aug '94 build): automatic transmission may lock up. 1996 (Jul '94–Dec '94 build): airbag warning light may be faulty. 21/2/2000: 29,000 cars built Jan '99 to Nov '99: possibility that brake servo valve may malfunction resulting in loss of servo assistance.

Scenic (1997 to 2003)

What's good: By far the most popular Megane. Sensible, practical, without being in the least dull. Brilliantly planned, versatile interior with lots of cubbyholes and strong, two-level rear parcel shelf. Three three-point rear belts. Huge square-shaped boot. Economical diesel. Even more economical TDI from mid-1998. Galvanised body has 12-year warranty. Refreshed from October 1999 with a new front, new 95 bhp 1.4, 110 bhp 1.6 and 140 bhp 2.0 litre engines and 35 different models. 1.6 16v reckoned to be the best of the bunch. Three year, 60,000 mile warranty from October 2000. Facelifted model has plastic front wings which deform and shrug off minor impacts. Very good 29 point four star NCAP crash safety rating announced 28/3/2001.

What's bad: Less good two star NCAP pedestrian safety rating. Loses out to later Citroën Xsara Picasso which has wider centre rear seat, more room inside and is even better planned. Automatic gearbox failures increasing in 2002 (front drive clutch drum splits). 1.6 8v and 1.6 16v are underpowered. Non-electric sunroofs don't slide and serve as no more than pop-up vents. Needs aircon. Clutch replacement is expensive. Don't try to carry things on the roof. Comparatively poor performance in TUV/*Auto Bild* offset crash test. Flywheel sensor connection may fail, immobilising car. Reports of wiring loom failures due to poor insulation (an old Renault bugbear)and engine management system problems. 1.6 8v prone to head gasket failure. (Low-mileage cars had head gaskets replaced FOC under a Renault 'Tech Note'.) One report of manual gearbox mounting bolt failing on a 1.6 16v Alize. Bolt replaced by "a modified part". 'Sporty' facelifted 2.0 litre 16v criticised for harsh suspension and unsporty steering. A/c condensers are vulnerable to stone damage. The plastic front wings of facelift models change shape, leaving gaps around the headlights. Problem of leaking sunroofs on facelift Scenics due to kinked drainage channels. If the car suffers any small faults with electric sunroof mechanism, Renault dealers have been known to quote £700 for an entirely new pair of sunroofs. Water penetration of the spark plug coil units of the 1.6 16v can put it out of action. Problem with springs on RX4 but only a sliding scale of goodwill from Renault on cars not under UK warranty. In June 2001 Renault was rated by Motor Warranty Direct as Britain's joint 4th worst out of 22 marques for used car warranty claims (check online at www.warrantydirect.co.uk) 20th from bottom for reliability in *Auto Express* 2002 reader survey of 100 models. High number of complaints from *Telegraph* readers and honestjohn website visitors. Great concept let down by poor quality. Not recommended.

What to watch out for: Check gearbox carefully, whether manual or auto. PAS rack may spring a leak. To check for head gasket failure on 1.6 8v look under oil cap for 'mayonnaise'. Also look for kerbing damage, electrical faults, stained seats, unspeakable smells left by incontinent babies, 'fishy' smell denoting leaking heater matrix. If sunroofs are fitted, check them. If fitted with a/c, make sure it blows cold.

Recalls: 1997 (Megane and Scenic July-Sept '97 build): 7,434 cars found to have potentially defective braking system. 1998: (June '97–Sep '97 build): roof bars may fail under load. Replacements redesigned and sourced from a different manufacturer. 2000: July 1998 build only: driveshaft CV may fail and affect steering. 12/1/2000: 4,422 F9Q diesel-engined cars built Dec '98–May '99: brake vacuum pump may leak allowing oil to enter the brake servo resulting in loss of servo assistance to the brakes. Magnetti Marelli brake vacuum pumps to be replaced; servos to be inspected for oil ingress and replaced if necessary. 18/4/2000: 1,000 diesel-engined cars built Feb-April 2000 may be fitted with defective brake vacuum pumps. 14/12/2001: 3,586 Meganes and Scenics fitted with F9Q 732/740 engines and dCi engines recall because of risk of diesel return pipe rubbing against the alternator leading to risk of leakage from high pressure pipes. Reposition/replace chafing pipes and check unions for correct tightness.

Scenic II (from late 2003)

What's good: Slightly bigger, much better 5 or 7 seater Scenic with watered down Renault family styling. Scenic Grande will be 4,234mm long; seats in 2–3–2 layout; rearmost five all separately removable. Drivetrain will combine Renault and Nissan technology and include Nissan CVT and six speed manual transmissions, hopefully putting an end to Renault autobox problems.

What's bad: Will Renault build quality have improved?

What to watch out for: Build quality niggles.

Twingo (1995 to 2004)

What's good: Great design, practical and fun. Looks like Kermit the frog. Sliding rear seat (like Citroën ZX) gives choice of bootspace or rear legroom. Transmission options of: 5-speed manual; 5-speed electric clutch 'Easy' or 3-speed 'Matic'. Electro-hydraulic PAS also became available in 1996. Latest airbagged version did reasonably well in German TUV front offset crash tests. All new 5–door 'one box' Twingo due in 2003 and will be sold with RHD in UK.

Sales, parts and service, online at www.twingo.co.uk, or tel: 01766 770203.

What's bad: LHD only. Never officially sold in the UK. Lots about with unconverted digital speedos and right-dipping headlamps which dazzle oncoming drivers and may fail the UK MOT. (Daffyd Williams does a speedo mod for £99 which converts the French speedos to mph, tel: 01766 770203.) In June 2001 Renault was rated by Motor Warranty Direct as Britain's joint 4th worst out of 22 marques for used car warranty claims (check online at www.warrantydirect.co.uk)

What to watch out for: Second-generation multipoint injected 60 bhp 1,149cc D7F engines much better than older single-point injected 1,171cc engines. But on 1,149cc D7F engines it is essential to change the timing belt, tensioners and the water pump every 3 years or 36,000 miles (whichever comes first).

Recalls: June 2000: 14,000 2nd generation Twingo 2s recalled to correct fault which can lead to premature triggering of airbag. 18/9/2000: three Twingos recalled for same reason. Airbag computer to be replaced.

Twingo II (from 2004)

What's good: All new Twingo to sit beneath Clio, now slated for 2004

What's bad: Too soon to say.

What to watch out for: Too soon to say.

Vel Satis (from 2002)

What's good: New, big, luxurious four door car from Renault, seen at Motor Shows through 2001 and on sale in UK from Spring 2002. Makes much more sense than Avantime. 165bhp 2.0 litre turbocharged petrol manual does 131 mph, 0–60 in 9.4 seconds, puts out 243g/km C02. 245bhp 3.0 V6 petrol auto does 147mph, 0–60 in 8 seconds, puts out 275g/km CO_2. 150bhp 2.2 diesel does 125mph, 0–60 in 10.6 seconds, puts out 188g/km CO_2. 180bhp 3.0 V6 diesel auto does 131mph, 0–60 in 10.2 seconds, puts out 232g/km CO_2. Prices: £20,730 for 2.0 turbo Expression to £30,255 for 3.0DCi Initiale auto. Curiously un-carlike to drive, but not unpleasant. Impossible to tell that the diesel is a diesel. Likely to make a good chauffeur private-hire car.

What's bad: UK sales delayed from January 2002 to Spring 2002. A very different driving experience from almost anything else. Will appeal to some, but won't appeal to everyone.

What to watch out for: Too soon to say.

ROVER

100 (1995 to 1998)

What's good: Restyled Rover Metro. CVT auto one of the best and still has a small market. Killed off in early 1998.

What's bad: Past its 'sell by' date. Poor performance in NCAP crash tests. No power steering option and steering very heavy when wide tyres are fitted. 'K' Series engine inlet manifold 'O' rings tend to perish between 25–30,000 miles. Head gasket failure common because very low coolant capacity of engine means small leaks rapidly lead to overheating. Weakest point is water heated inlet manifold gasket. Rear wheel arches highly prone to corrosion.

What to watch out for: As Rover Metro. As Citroën AX and Saxo for possible problems with 1.5 diesel engine. First places to look for rust and filler are the rear wheel arches.

200 (1995 to 1999)

What's good: Compact. Good looking. Low wind noise at speed. Stainless steel kickplate 'Rover' image. All good performers for their engine size apart from 1.1 and 1.4 8-valve. Vi, fitted with MGF VVC engine tremendously quick and also very economical. Perky 1.6 CVT automatic offers instant acceleration out of side roads. 1.1 replaced Rover 100 as a sub-£10,000 offering. All have three three-point rear belts. One of the few cars offering warm air to the feet and fresh air to the face at the same time. Timing belts of L Series diesels apparently do last the scheduled 5 years or 84,000 miles.

What's bad: Slow, over-light steering spoils all models, including Vi. Not quite out of Rover build-quality problems. CVT could be too 'instant' for some elderly drivers not used to automatics. 'K' Series engine inlet manifold 'O' rings tend to perish between 25–30,000 miles. Possibility of camshaft coming adrift on 1.8 Vi. Crankshaft sensor cable is too short on some cars and may pull out of the connector, immobilising the car. Head gasket failure common because very low coolant capacity of engine means small leaks rapidly lead to overheating. Weakest point is water heated inlet manifold gasket. Many trim parts not being made and consequently unavailable. 15th from bottom for reliability in *Auto Express* 2002 reader survey of 100 models. 20th from Bottom in 144 car 2002 JD Power/*What Car?* Customer Satisfaction Survey of V and W reg. cars. **What to watch out for:** Variable gearshift quality. Different models have different linkages, but a hollow pin wears and may drop out. No big deal since a replacement costs just 6p. 'K' Series cylinder heads have been known to become porous and their head gaskets to fail (look for mayo under oil cap). Timing belt replacement on K Series essential every 35,000–40,000 miles or every 3–4 years. Back Room advice (from the online forum at www.honestjohn.co.uk) from expert David Lacey on buying a Rover 200 diesel: "Watch out for oil leaks from the oil pump area, coolant leaks from the thermostat housing at the front of the engine, cracked/broken/ missing underbelly acoustic trays (Expensive), cambelt and fuel pump belt change at 84000 miles. Check that the radio and remote control on the steering wheel works and also check that you receive TWO sets of keys with TWO remote controls as the key will be useless to start the engine on its own without the remote. Another remote will cost about £80."

200 and 400 (1989 to 1996)

What's good: Product of Honda/Rover marriage and first to use 'K' series modular engines (really a Honda Concerto). English 'feelgood' factor from stainless steel kick-plates, bits of wood fillet in the dash and doors. Honda 1.6 engine is the best engine, often wedded to smooth Honda autobox. From July 1997, 400 'Tourer' estate could be had with 109 bhp 1.6 K' Series engine and CVT transmission or 143 bhp 1.8 litre VVC 'K' Series engine and manual box. (Continued as Cabrio and Tourer to 1999.)

What's bad: Diesels are pretty terrible. PSA XUD engines at their noisiest and least refined. Gearbox/clutch problems can occur relatively early. 220s seem to develop all sorts of problems. Turbos best avoided. Distributor ignition igniter of Honda 1.6 can fail at about 50,000 miles and might lead to catalytic converter damage. Rover 'K' Series modular engines not as reliable, particularly pre-'K'

reg. monopoint injected versions. Cylinder head problems not uncommon and stretch bolts can stretch. Rover 2.0 litre M16 engine least reliable; later T16 from 'K' reg. on (badged 'ROVER' on cam cover) more reliable, but even T16 apt to coke up its valves if run on cheap petrol with inadequate detergent content. Honda-engined 216 and 416 models starting to prove very expensive to service and repair at Rover dealers. High incidence of ABS failure on cars so fitted. Another problem is a leaking gearbox input shaft oil seal. This is symptomised by oil leaks and slipping clutch (due to oil contamination). Cause: input shaft bearing of gearbox worn leading to excessive movement on the seal. Difficult to source secondhand gearbox. Head gasket failure common because very low coolant capacity of engine means small leaks rapidly lead to overheating. Weakest point is water heated inlet manifold gasket. Many trim parts not being made and consequently unavailable. 15th from bottom for reliability in *Auto Express* 2002 reader survey of 100 models.
What to watch out for: Premature clutch wear. Noisy gearboxes. Clonking suspension. Cooling system leaks. Hidden rust around windscreen. Visible rust at top of hatch and around hinges. Coolant leaks from corroded coolant rail at back of engine (coolant should be changed every 2–3 years). Look under oil cap for mayonnaise – sure sign of distorted or cracked cylinder head. ECU faults causing misfires. Excessive oil consumption. Diesel turbo hose can rub on front bulkhead. No power steering (if PAS, look for leaks at the pump). Make sure cambelt has been changed. Allow £160 for new distributor ignition igniter for Honda 1.6. Front anti-roll bar drop links rattle, but cheap to replace. Clonks from rear could be trailing arm bushes which are £200 a side to replace, or one of the roof support bars come unstuck. Rear silencer box rots inside out quickly. If fitted with ABS, the pump may fail if the brake fluid has not been changed often enough. A smell of petrol may indicate a rusted and leaking petrol tank – especially on 'N' reg. cars. If car has ABS, make sure the warning light goes on and off as per the handbook.

213 and 116 4-door (1984 to 1989)
What's good: Second product of Honda/BL co-operative ventures

after the Triumph Acclaim. This is a Honda Civic/Ballade based small 4–door saloon 13ft 7in long by 5ft 4in wide and weighing from 840kg. Honda 72bhp 1,342cc engine with 5-speed manual of Honda 3-speed auto from 1985. Also from 1985 an 1,598cc Montego engined version with 85bhp or 103bhp in injected VDP and Vitesse applications. The VDP could be had with a 3 speed automatic. The Vitesse was reasonably quick. Quite a lot of these cars still on the road.

What's bad: No power steering option, even on the VDP. Rover engine can suffer the usual problems.

What to watch out for: If buying as a banger, the Honda engine is the one to go for. Though they seem to resist rust quite well, if it has taken a hold there is nothing you can do about it, so treat as terminal. The first places to look are round the rear wheel arches and round the window frames. Any damp inside the car and it's likely to be due to a rusted through window frame.

25 (from 1999)

What's good: Good looking, successfully re-thought Rover 200, aimed at the younger market, now with faster, meatier steering, more sporty suspension, much more sensible pricing and, importantly, a three-year warranty. Prices cut to from £8,495 for 84bhp 1.4i with three years servicing included as from October 2000. Basic 1.1i announced from April 2001 at £7,995 on the road. New 'Steptronic' ECVT has more controlled take-off than old 200 CVT and works really well in town or out. 150bhp Gti replaces VI as top of the range at a reasonable £13,495. 103 bhp 1.4Si is now as much fun to drive as a Fiesta Zetec or Focus with an excellent set of gear ratios giving 60 mph plus in 2nd. Ventilation system allows cool face/warm feet. Ex-rental one year old 25 1.6iL 5–doors with alloys and sunroofs are bargains at around £7,500. January 2001: Launch of Impression specials. 84bhp 1.4 litre 25 Impression 3–door has drivers airbag, stereo radio cassette, anti-theft alarm and immobiliser, power steering, height adjustable steering wheel, tinted glass, 15 inch Octet alloy wheels and remote central locking for £8,675 on the road. (5–door £9,175). Slightly up spec is the 25

1.4 Impression S which also has air-conditioning, electric front windows and a CD tuner (3–dr: £9,595; 5–dr £10,095). Timing belts of L Series diesels apparently do last the scheduled 5 years or 84,000 miles. Spirit and Spirit S specials from July 2002 (Spirit S have a/c). **What's bad:** Three star score in 2001 NCAP crash tests. Fascia a bit old fashioned. Light-coloured dash tops reflect badly in windscreen. Irritating 'twist-stalk' for wipers and lights. Electric window switches on centre console. A/c rarely fitted. Steptronic upshift and downshift is the wrong way round. 'K' Series engine inlet manifold 'O' rings tend to perish between 25–30,000 miles. Re-named MG ZR in Summer 2001. Head gasket failure common because very low coolant capacity of engine means small leaks rapidly lead to overheating. Weakest point is water heated inlet manifold gasket.
What to watch out for: As 200.

400 (1995 to 1999)

What's good: Honda 'Swindon Civic' in tweed suit, but mostly with Rover's own 'K' Series engines and (Rover claims) better ride and handling. Automatic retains Honda's 1.6 engine and autobox with engine in front of passenger rather than driver. Available as 5–door hatch or good-looking 4–door saloon (not many good looking saloons in this class). Falling sales led to cut prices in 1998 with a 1.4Si 16v with alloys selling for £12,000 OTR. One of the few cars offering warm air to the feet and fresh air to the face at the same time. Timing belts of L Series diesels apparently do last the scheduled 5 years or 84,000 miles.
What's bad: If it's been owned by an elderly person, may be three years old and not yet run-in. 'K' Series engine inlet manifold 'O' rings tend to perish between 25–30,000 miles. T16 2.0 litre engine apt to coke up its valves if run on cheap petrol with inadequate detergent content. Head gasket failure common because very low coolant capacity of engine means small leaks rapidly lead to overheating. Weakest point is water heated inlet manifold gasket. Many trim parts not being made and consequently unavailable.
What to watch out for: 'K' Series cylinder heads have been known to

crack and their head gaskets to fail (look for mayonnaise under oil filler cap). Timing belt replacement essential on K series every 35,000–40,000 miles or every 3–4 years. Front suspension bushes tend to wear. T16 2.0 litre engine apt to coke up its valves if run on cheap petrol with inadequate detergent content. A smell of petrol may indicate a rusted and leaking petrol tank – especially on 'N' reg. cars (applies to both 'old' and 'new' 'N' reg. 400s).

Recalls: 1996: driver's seat lock does not always click into place properly. May mean seat slides when car is being driven. Most likely on cars with several drivers where seat is moved to and fro.

45 (from 1999)

What's good: Progressively improved so the newer the better. Engine range includes a 2.0 litre KV6 mated to the 'Steptronic' CVT automatic. New three-year warranty. Prices cut to from £9,995 for 103bhp 1.4IE 5–door to £17,095 for V6 Connoisseur. Amazing, diesel-like economy. *Autocar* averaged 41.8 mpg in its road test 45 1.6 (issue 8/3/2000). One of the few cars offering warm air to the feet and fresh air to the face at the same time. January 2001: Launch of Impression specials: the 103bhp 1.4 litre 45 Impression has air-conditioning, ABS, four airbags, alarm with immobiliser, CD tuner, electric windows and electric mirrors for £11,495, while the 45 1.4 Impression S has in addition 15 inch Fission alloy wheels, rear spoiler, front fogs and a leather steering wheel and gearknob for £12,095. Impression S specs are also available on 1.6 109ps 45s, 1.8 117bhp 43s and 101 bhp 2.0TD 45s at prices from £12,695 to £14,695. Timing belts of L Series diesels apparently do last the scheduled 5 years or 84,000 miles.

Reincarnation as MG ZS 180 with 2.5 KV6 has had good reviews. LPG version of 45 1.8 from July 2002 at an extra £2,195 awaiting Powershift certification which may result in up to 70% rebate. Spirit and Spirit S specials from July 2002 (all 45 Spirits have a/c).

What's bad: Testers originally thought the steering too light and the ride to soft but these have since been improved. 'K' Series engine inlet manifold 'O' rings tend to perish between 25–30,000 miles. Head gasket failure common on K series four cylinder engines because very low coolant capacity of engine means small leaks rapidly lead to overheating. Weakest point is water heated inlet manifold gasket.

What to watch out for: As Rover 'new' 400.

600 (1993 to 1999)

What's good: The most reliable mid 1990s Rover (really a Honda Accord). Nice-looking car. Wood, leather and stainless steel kickplate image. 156 bhp 2.3 litre Honda engine by far the best. Chassis also greatly improved on 2.3s. All manuals have good gearchanges and 129 bhp Honda 2.0 litre engines are smooth and economical. 113 bhp 1.8 is an 1,850cc multipoint injected Honda engine, not a Rover 'K'. Automatics by Honda. Good metallic paint colours, such as Nightfire Red, Caribbean Blue. Generally quite a good, cheap second-hand buy. Timing belts of L Series diesels apparently do last the scheduled 5 years or 84,000 miles.

What's bad: Understeery handling, over-light steering on all but 2.3. Ride quality not up to luxurious image. Body mods over Honda Accord were difficult to assemble and can lead to premature rust, especially in rear inner wings. 620Ti Turbo with Rover 'T' Series engines apt to blow gaskets. Average performance in NCAP crash tests. Production ended in 1999, but still on 'Glass's Guide's' new car price lists in Summer 2000 so watch out for late registrations.

What to watch out for: Check everything electrical (windows, roof, mirrors, seats, etc.). Look for rust bubbling through just behind each rear wheel arch. This is a big panel in short supply, so the problem is very expensive to remedy. Will run to high mileages (150k plus) so might be clocked. A 50,000–miler should not have excessive paint and windscreen chips, front number plate should be original. Avoid the 'ti' petrol turbo model as was plagued with oil seal problems. Ignition igniter on Honda engines can fail and is expensive to replace. Rover direct-injected 'T' Series diesels okay, but only gain about 7 mpg on the petrol 2.0 litre. Exhaust rear boxes blow on low-mileage 'short-run' cars. A 'V' or 'W' reg. will have been sitting around for months before it was registered. Check for emulsified oil under the oil filler caps of 2.3i engines as this could indicate a cracked cylinder head which is £2k to replace.

611

Recalls: 1996 (built between 12/94 and 12/95): check to ensure steering rack mounting bolts are secure-symptom of problem: stiff steering.

75 (from 1999)

What's good: Replaced both 600 and 800. Very good looking with styling cues from 1950s Rover P4. Looks a bit like a Rolls Seraph from the back, and sits in the market exactly where P4s did between 1955 and 1965. Nice retro-look cream oval dial instruments. 1.8 litre 120 bhp K Series four; 2.0 litre 150 bhp KV6, 2.5 litre 175 bhp KV6, or pleasant, quiet and torquey 2.0 litre 115 bhp BMW common rail direct-injected diesel. All front-wheel-drive. JATCO 5-speed automatic or Getrag 5-speed manual. Softish, cosseting ride quality. Not a sports saloon, but still handles fairly well. Good sized but fairly shallow boot. Excellent cool face/warm feet ventilation system. Prices now from £16,494 including three year warranty. 'Tourer' estate car and shift to production at Longbridge in Spring 2001 brought across-the-range handling improvements. S and T reg. cars came an excellent sixth in 2001 *Top Gear*/JD Power Customer Satisfaction Survey. Very good score or 30 points in Euro NCAP crash safety tests. Has now been successfully developed into MGZT with 180bhp front wheel drive and up to 385bhp rear wheel drive. LPG version of 75 1.8 from July 2002 at an extra £2,195 awaiting Powershift certification which may result in up to 70% rebate. The 75 model has settled down into the market very well indeed. BIK tax beating 150PS turbocharged version from August 2002. 215Nm (159 lb ft) torque and low CO_2 rating of 193g/km for both saloon and Tourer qualifies it for a BIK tax base of 20% of the list price, which works out at £3,659 for the 1.8T Classic and means a 40% taxpayer will fork out £1,463.60 a year. The 1.8T gets to 60mph in 9.1 seconds, from 30–50 in 7.1 seconds and from 50–70 in 7.4 seconds. The torque allows the higher 3.9:1 final drive of the 2.5litre to be used, giving 22.6mph per 1,000rpm in 5th and a 130mph top speed for the saloon. Official combined consumption is 35.3mpg. Tyres are 195/65 15s giving much better ride quality than low profiles. Recommended.
What's bad: The badly-timed debacles over the future of Rover which marred its launch, and the fiasco of March to May 2000. Driving

position and handling at speed not in same class as Mondeo. Rear-seat passengers feel confined. Suspension clonks. Susceptible to strong side winds. Not easy to reverse. Hazard light switch hard to find. Diesel could do with the full 150bhp power output of the same engine in the BMW 320D, or even the old 320D 136bhp, and is particularly slow with the 5-speed autobox. Head gasket failure common on 1.8 petrol engines because very low coolant capacity of engine means small leaks rapidly lead to overheating. Weakest point is water heated inlet manifold gasket. No reported disasters like those of the KV6 in the 800. Have been problems obtaining body parts.

What to watch out for: Parking dings in easily damaged slab-side doors. A nice surprise is that Longbridge cars are better built with better handling. The easy way to distinguish a Longbridge (MG Rover) built 75 from a Oxford (BMW) built 75 is that Longbridge 75s have body colour sills and Oxford built cars have black sills. All Longbridge cars are fully EOBD compliant (3 oxygen sensors).

Recalls: 13/3/2000. 8,550 cars VIN RJ 001242 to RJ 127623 built between Feb '98 and Oct '99 recalled to correct crankshaft position sender fault which could cause the engine to cut out, announced Radio 4 News 10/3/2000. Sensors to be replaced with modified units. July 2002 recall of 13,000 Rover 75 and MG ZT models due to concerns about front coil spring breakage in cold and high corrosion operating conditions. Front coil springs to be replaced.

75 Vanden Plas (from 2002)

What's good: Stretched VDP version with 200mm more legroom in the back. The 75 Vanden Plas is modified by specialist coachbuilders S. MacNeillie & Son Ltd. Comes in Connoisseur trim level only, with the 130kW (177PS) 2.5 KV6 which develops 240Nm (177 lb ft) torque, mated to the standard 5-speed JATCO automatic transmission. Price £27,995 with metallic paint. Armour plating and bulletproof glass are, of course, extra. Smart move by Rover because there aren't any 'British' alternatives and Government and 'British' industry captains will be obliged to be seen in it, which in turn gets Rover excellent publicity.

More online at www.mg-rover.com

What's bad: Too soon to say.
What to watch out for: Too soon to say.

800 (1986 to 1999)

What's good: Cheap big cars that don't look cheap. Wood, leather, etc. on Sterling models and decent trim levels generally. High-revving 2.0 litre 16-valve engines. Smooth Honda 2.7 litre V6s. (Early Honda 2.5 and later 2.5 KV6 less highly regarded.) T16 2.0 litre engine better regarded than earlier M16. 2.5 VM diesel option. 138bhp 2.0 SLi is the best model to go for.

What's bad: Clonky front suspension. Cambelts of 2.0 litre M16 engines (pre-1991 facelift) need replacing every 3 years or 36,000 miles and must be correctly tensioned. Water pumps fail, leading to distorted cylinder heads. Brake callipers seize. Power steering pumps of early cars pack up. Depreciate rapidly. Even T16 apt to coke up its valves if run on cheap petrol with inadequate detergent content. Individual cylinder heads on VM diesel may crack. Production ended in April 1999, but still on 'Glass's Guide' new car price lists in July 2000. Cylinder heads of early 2.5 litre KV6s highly prone to failure. Very low trade prices reflect KV6 problems. Bottom of 100 models for reliability in *Auto Express* 2002 survey. 2nd Bottom in 144 car 2002 JD Power/*What Car?* Customer Satisfaction Survey of V and W reg. cars.

What to watch out for: Front suspension can deteriorate alarmingly. Rust in seams, sills and particularly around all windows. Iffy electrics. Head gasket problems from failure to replace antifreeze every 2–3 years. ECU problems. Duff cats in catted facelift model. Earlier M16 valves can burn out on unleaded petrol (a very quiet engine is a bad sign). Look for white exhaust, mayonnaise under oil cap signifying head failure on diesels. Pay no more than £500 for a pre-facelift 820, however good it may look. Make sure aircon blows cold if fitted. A 'V' or 'W' reg. will have been sitting around for months before it was registered. Early 2.5 litre KV6s highly prone to cylinder head gasket and cylinder head failures, so check very carefully for mayonnaise and any signs of overheating. Best to avoid an 800 2.5KV6 entirely.

Recalls: 1994 (VIN RS 100001–117697 and RS 150000 to 187439): front seatbelt security. 21/1/2000: 956 825 diesels VIN RS 230976 to RS 260898 recalled because while engine is performing a pre-determined self-diagnosis the engine could stall. Modified ECU to be fitted.

Metro (1990 to 1995)

What's good: Decent new 'K' series 1.1 and 1.4 engines. End-on gearbox and up to 5-speeds at last. Front-end rust traps largely eliminated. Better built than Austin Metro and generally reliable. Simple CVT auto worked well – far less troublesome than Ford and Fiat CVTs. Comfortable. I've done 450 miles in a day in a Metro CVT. Decent fuel consumption. Iron block 1.4 TUD diesel engine comes from Citroën AX and Peugeot 106.

What's bad: Cramped cabin due to bigger, more luxurious seats. Heavy, non-power-assisted steering – the wider the tyres the heavier it is. Diesel very slow and not that economical if worked hard. Still rust-prone in seams. Head gasket failure common because very low coolant capacity of engine means small leaks rapidly lead to overheating. Weakest point is water heated inlet manifold gasket.

What to watch out for: Oil leaks from engine. Cracked cylinder heads (look for mayo under oil cap). Head gasket leaks due to stretched or re-used stretch bolts which go all the way to the sump. Tappety noises. Abused 16-valve versions. Kerbed alloy wheels (suspect suspension damage). Many still went to driving schools. Some were built long before they were UK registered. Rear wheel studs come loose from hubs. If twin-cam 16v K series suffers cabin boom at idle the engine mount is worn at the timing belt end(not enough rubber). Replacement mounts £48 + VAT. Check rear wheel arches for rust or bodge.

TCV

What's good: The shape of things to come from MG Rover. May replace 45 model if MG Rover can find another company to provide the platform.

What's bad: Too soon to say.

What to watch out for: Too soon to say.

ROLLS ROYCE

Corniche (1971 to 1995)

What's good: Amazingly long model life. Big, heavy and iconic convertible with 6,750cc GM derived carburetted pushrod V8. 17 feet long. 6 feet wide. Much improved from 1977 with general Shadow II mods. Speed control and dual level a/c from 1978. Bosch fuel injection and ABS from 1987. Listed as Corniche II in late 1987, then as Corniche III from 1989. Cat converter optional from 1990. 4-speed autobox, glass rear screen and listed as Corniche IV from 1992. More power (engine now built by Cosworth), 5-speed autobox and adaptive suspension from 1993.

What's bad: Heavy and juicy. Expensive to maintain. Will rust.

What to watch out for: Plenty of mutton dressed as lamb about, so best to have the car inspected by an independent Rolls Royce expert.

Corniche convertible (from 2000)

What's good: Back again with new body and 325bhp 6,750cc Cosworth V8.

What's bad: You get at least 420bhp in the equivalent Bentley Azure convertible.

What to watch out for: Choose your parking places very carefully.

Silver Seraph (1998 on)

What's good: The Rolls Royce version of the Bentley Arnage. Smoother BMW 5.3 litre V12 engine pumps out 322 bhp through five-speed auto in similar very British body

What's bad: As Arnage.

What to watch out for: As Arnage.

Recalls: 1999: possible wiring fault in heated seat circuit.

Silver Spirit and Silver Spur (1980 to 1999

What's good: Plutocrat's car. Like driving along in a mobile gentlemen's' club. Poshest colour is a dark browny green. Gradually improved over the years with injection and ABS in October 1986, automatic ride control in 1987, four- rather than three-speed autobox in September 1991. Cats came in during June 1990, but were initially a no-cost option. Company taken over by VW in spring 1998 and then sold to BMW. Starting production again in new factory at Goodwood in 2002.

What's bad: Stink of cigar smoke clings to the headlining. 9 mpg in town. Likely be hit hard by engine-size or carbon dioxide-based annual taxation. Resentful drivers don't let you out of side roads, particularly during recessions. Apt to get vandalised with rusty nails or keys while parked. White or cream tells the public it's a wedding hire car, or has been. Daft RR defensive habit of not giving power outputs. (1993 Silver Spur had 226 bhp and 340 ft lb torque; 1994 Flying Spur turbo had 360 bhp and 552 ft lb torque.)

What to watch out for: Must have a proper Rolls Royce dealer or Rolls Royce specialist history. The Cosworth-built engine is an old fashioned pushrod V8, so you don't want to hear ticking tappets or see any blue smoke from the exhaust pipe. Make sure the suspension is not unduly wallowy. Check expensive tyres for tread depth and uneven wear. Make sure aircon blows cold. Good Rolls Royces have a patina and aura about them. Bad ones make you feel uneasy. Best to have the car inspected by a different Rolls Royce specialist from the one who's selling it.

Recalls: 1997: 29 left-hand drive cars found to have potentially defective braking system. 18/4/2001: (Corniche) fuel vapour could escape from leak detection pump, collect in body cavity and ignite. Fuel tank venting system to be modified.

SAAB

9–3 (1998 to 2002)

What's good: Steering, handling and roadholding all improved over previous same-shape 900. Even better with 17in wheels and Michelin Pilot tyres. 115 bhp 2.2 litre direct injected diesel particularly good to drive – better than 2.0 litre petrol. 225 bhp 2.3 litre HOT Viggen from March 1999. Very impressive safety features include a full set of five 3–point belts, two airbags and excellent side-impact protection. Clever anti-whiplash head restraints. Rear boot sill has been lowered to make it more like the old 900 and you can used the rear bumper to sit on. 2.0 litre eco turbo engine replaced 2.3i for 1999 model year. Four-Star NCAP crash safety rating due to excellent side impact protection but much less satisfactory front offset impact protection due to bulkhead inherited from 900. In late October 2000, power of the 2.2TiD diesel was increased to 125bhp and torque to 206lb ft at a very low 1,500 rpm, giving 0–60 in 10 seconds and combined cycle fuel economy of 45.6mpg.

What's bad: Still has bulkhead mounted steering rack like Cavalier. Scuttle-shake of popular convertible can still set your teeth rattling. Turbo a bit vicious. Diesel needs to be kept on the boil (above 1,900 rpm) so not too good for caravan towing. Some GM 2.2 litre DI diesels use a lot of engine oil.

What to watch out for: Timing chains of 4-cylinder Saab engines need clean oil or can give problems at around 60,000 miles. (No timing chain problems yet reported on GM 2.2 litre diesel.) Clean oil also essential for turbo life. Turbos best run on fully synthetic oil once run-in. Reports of injector seal failure in 2.2 diesels leading to fuel oil leaking into sump oil.

Recalls: 2000: 9–3 models built August '97 to July '99: front seats may move during heavy braking. 2001: TSB to replace ECU on older 9–3 Viggen models free of charge. 8/10/2001: 1,625 9–3s built 1/8/2001 to 31/8/2001 recalled because nuts securing track rod ends to steering swivel members may not have been sufficiently tightened, resulting in track rod end becoming loose. Nuts to be tightened to correct torque.

9–3 (from September 2002)

What's good: Virtually all new. Sits on the Epsilon floorpan developed jointly by SAAB and GM. Structure is more than twice as torsionally stiff as the old Cavalier-based car. Suspension is MacPherson strut at the front and multi-link independent at the rear, mounted on subframes by rubber bushes which are laterally stiff for good steering response but longitudinally compliant for good ride comfort and isolation of road noise from the cabin. For the first time on a SAAB, the rear provides passive rear wheel steer to reduce understeer and sharpen steering response. ABS, EBD, ESP, CBC and TCS all standard kit. New petrol engines all lightweight aluminium turbocharged 2.0 litre chain-cammers, but badged 1.8t, 2.0t and 2.0T to differentiate their SAAB Trionic 8 managed power outputs. Transmissions are also new: 5-speed manual for the 1.8t and 2.0t; 6-speed manual for the 2.0T and 5-speed automatic for all three. Auto available with optional 'Sentronic' steering wheel paddle shift from Jan 2003. 2.2 diesel and 5-speed manual box carries over. Communications systems are Bluetooth enabled so mobile phones, PDAs and notebook computers need no physical connection to the integrated car system. SAAB's own satnav system is optional or pre-fitted according to spec level. Specs are: 'Linear, which sits on 15 alloys and has fabric upholstery with anthracite trim; 'Arc', which comes on 16 alloys with leather upholstery and polar wood trim; 'Vector', which has 17 alloys and sports leather/textile upholstery with matt chrome trim; and the flagship 'Aero' with lowered sports suspension and 210bhp turbo engine only (arrives Jan 2003). Safety features include improved SAAB Active Head restraints, load limiting seatbelts, dual stage front airbags, seat-mounted side airbags and side curtain airbags.

A huge improvement over the old 9–3. Recommended.

More online at www.saab.co.uk

What's bad: 6-speed gearchange too rubbery.

What to watch out for: Too soon to say

9–5 (from 1997)

What's good: SAAB's 'big' car loaded with safety features. Nothing quirky about this one. 170 bhp 2.3 eco turbo, 150 bhp 2.0 eco turbo and 200 bhp 3.0V6 auto. 2.0 litre much improved compared to 9000 series. Most people find the seats very comfortable. Should both be capable of over 30 mpg. 2.3HOT Aero from September 1999 has 230 bhp. Four-Star 31 point NCAP crash test rating and best of all 'executive cars'(second only overall to new Renault Laguna). Super-safe estate version from early 1999 usurps Volvo as probably the safest estate car you can buy. Year 2000 model achieve highest ever NCAP crash safety score of 91% overall. 14th from top in 'R' reg. J.D. Power Customer Satisfaction Survey. 'New' SAAB 9–5 from October 2001 with option of General Motors new 3.0 litre 176bhp common rail turbodiesel V6 engine which puts out 258lb ft (350Nm) torque. Features "chassis revisions to enhance driver control" and is a hugely improved car. 2.3HOT now has 250bhp and same 350Nm torque as diesel. Gets to 60 in 6.5, goes on to 155mph, does 32mpg in the combined cycle and emits just 209g/km CO_2. A tax-efficient quick car for company drivers. To further appeal to CO_2 BIK conscious company drivers, SAAB has added the 120bhp 2.2GM 16 valve chain cam four cylinder Ecotec diesel. 120bhp is developed at 4,000rpm and 280Nm (207 lb ft) from 1,500rpm. Top speed of the saloon is 124mph, 0–60 is 10.4 seconds, 40–60 in 4th is 6.7 seconds, 50–70 in 5th is 10.0 seconds and the estate isn't far behind. Combined consumption of the saloon is 42.8mpg and C02 175g/km. Figures for the estate are 40.1mpg and 178g/km. Prices start at £19,995 for the saloon and £12,195 for the estate. BIK base rates work out at 20% and 21% respectively.

More online at www.saab.co.uk

What's bad: Vectra-based, so not a true SAAB, but has subframe mounted steering rack. No hatchback apart from estate. Early production did not share the latest thinking on front suspension with the 9–3. Had peculiar lurch understeer. Later cars still understeer, but much more progressively. In June 2001 SAAB was rated by Motor Warranty Direct as Britain's joint 4th worst out of 22 marques for warranty claims (check online at www.warrantydirect.co.uk) This conflicts with the J.D. Power survey findings above.

What to watch out for: No known major problem areas yet apart from recall below. Check the mileage carefully. Listen for timing chain rattle on four cylinder SAAB engines. Trend SAAB (0115 937 7200) has an economical technique for replacing timing chains of 4 cylinder SAAB engines in situ by re-threading the chains. Better to go for a later model with the 2001/2002MY improvements.

Recalls: 300 x 2002MY 9–5s recalled because batch of steering knuckle joints could develop hairline cracks and possibly fracture. Joints replaced on 400 2002MY 9–5s awaiting sale at dealers.

900 (1993 to 1998)

What's good: Excellent safety features. Hatchback, with big boot and proper passenger protection against load. Five 3–point safety belts. Good side protection. Interesting clutch-free 'Sensonic' five-speed box (but dropped for 9–3). Trend SAAB (0115 937 7200) has an economical technique for replacing timing chains of 4 cylinder SAAB engines in situ by re-threading the chains.

What's bad: Cavalier based with bulkhead mounted steering rack, so not a true 'Saab'. Disappointingly soggy steering, handling, roadholding and ride quality. Comes a bit more alive with turbo, but spins its front wheels readily and still not a car you'd ever choose for handling finesse. Bulkheads apt to crack around steering rack mounting points. In June 2001 SAAB was rated by Motor Warranty Direct as Britain's joint 4th most expensive out of 22 marques for used car warranty claims (check online at www.warrantydirect.co.uk)

What to watch out for: Timing chains of 4-cylinder Saab engines need clean oil or can give problems at around 60,000 miles. (GM V-6s have belts, best replaced at 60,000 miles.) Clean oil also essential for turbo life. Turbos best run on fully synthetic. Put the car through a £70 check at a SAAB dealers, then buy a used Saab warranty. Average performance in NCAP crash tests. Make sure aircon blows cold if fitted. Listen for steering creaks and look for cracks around steering rack bulkhead mounting points, a £700 job to repair. Abbot Racing of Spinnels Farm, Manningtree (tel: 01255 870636) have a means of mounting the rack more rigidly, and also replacing the soft rubber suspension bushes which not only solves the problem but makes both Cavaliers and SAAB 900s steer and handle much better. Make sure reverse gear selects easily as some 900s have developed internal gearbox and gearbox linkage faults, possibly associated with the SAAB reverse gear ignition lock.

Recalls: 1994 (VIN R2000001–R2028886): delayed braking action. 1994 (5–door-VIN R2000001–R2022754): cracking of driver's seat rails. 1995 (VIN R2027373 to S2009903 and S7000001 to S7013081): welds missing from seat frames. 1997 (1996–97 build: 21,661 cars): corrosion on the throttle housing can cause a sticking throttle. Relevant parts to be replaced with brass items which cannot corrode. 4/10/2001: 4,109 900 hatchbacks and convertibles recalled because build up of static may set off passenger airbag. Grounding wire to be fitted between airbag module and car body.

900 (to 1993)

What's good: Eccentric, 'classic' SAAB looks. Much loved by the entertainment industry and often the car of the star. Convertibles best, despite scuttle shake. 185 bhp Ruby Turbo (last of the line) is now an appreciating classic. Understeer can be overcome by judicious left-foot braking. Heavy, solid and capable of mega mileages if looked after properly. Hatchback has long, flat luggage area. Rear bumper makes a good seat for events. Nice old cars with bags of desirable character. A late convertible or a Ruby Turbo could hold its value quite well and may even eventually appreciate.

What's bad: Lots of understeer. Timing chains and tensioners tend to need replacing every 60,000 miles. Trend SAAB (0115 937 7200) has an economical technique for replacing timing chains of 4 cylinder SAAB engines in situ by re-threading the chains. Even non-turbos are fairly thirsty. Parking brake of pre-1988 cars worked on front discs and was never satisfactory – often an MOT failure point and expensive to fix. Autobox was only a three-speeder.

What to watch out for: Rattling timing chains, dirty oil, cracked cylinder heads (check for mayonnaise under the oil cap), cracked turbo manifolding (remember, it glows red hot), can be gear-selector problems, check suspension bushes, front hubs and driveshafts carefully. Make sure turbo not 'coked' as Saab-sourced replacements are expensive. Make sure big bumpers have not been used as buffers. Check that aircon blows cold.

Recalls: 1996 (900 convertible 1993–1995: old shape): check for loss of steering control.

9000CD (1988 to 1997)

What's good: Booted, better looking 9000CS, so same general comments apply. Truly enormous boot. Trend SAAB (0115 937 7200) has an economical technique for replacing timing chains of 4 cylinder SAAB engines in situ by re-threading the chains.

What's bad: As 9000CS. In June 2001 SAAB was rated by Motor Warranty Direct as Britain's joint 4th most expensive out of 22 marques for used car warranty claims (check online at www.warrantydirect.co.uk)

What to watch out for: As 9000CS.

Recalls: (See list under 9000CS)

9000CS (1986 to 1998)

What's good: Great cars, none better than the 170 bhp 2.3 eco turbo which covers the ground quickly and still returns 32 mpg. Capable of huge mileages if looked after properly. Decent 'big car' handling. Innocuous looks. Wonderful seats. Good, old-fashioned 4-speed automatic does what you want and doesn't 'hunt'. Full-on 2.3 turbo Carlsson puts out 220 bhp, which is very nearly too much. Trend SAAB (0115 937 7200) has an economical technique for replacing timing chains of 4 cylinder SAAB engines in situ by re-threading the chains.

What's bad: Ride quality a bit firm, but made up for by the excellent seats. Direct ignition module can give trouble. ABS pump needs fresh brake fluid every year. Timing chains oil-sensitive (best run on fully synthetic, particularly turbos). 2.0 eco turbo not as well suited to autobox as 2.3i or 2.3 eco. V6 best avoided. Subject to quite a lot of recalls. Automatic doesn't seem to last. Tends to fail due to a bush wearing in the pump and rebuilds cost £1,800 (new box

£3,500). In June 2001 SAAB was rated by Motor Warranty Direct as Britain's joint 4th most expensive out of 22 marques for used car warranty claims (check online at www.warrantydirect.co.uk)

What to watch out for: Timing chain rattles. Smoky engines (especially turbos). Check for white smoke from blown head gasket or cracked head. Look under oil cap for mayonnaise. Huge discs are expensive to replace (feel them through the wheels). Look for wear in front suspension bushes, hubs and driveshafts. Best put though a £70 pre-check at a Saab dealers, then purchase a comprehensive used Saab warranty. Make sure aircon blows cold.

Recalls: 1994 (VIN N1041085–N1049024 and P1000001–P1015289): fuel leak. 1994 (9000/Turbo-VIN N1000001–N1049024, P1000001–P1042386, R1000001–R1027659): oil leak and faulty brake light switch on some models. 1995: (*manual with TCS): VIN N1000001 to N1049024, *P1000001to P1042386, *R1000001 to R1026535: loss of brake pressure and/or ABS. 1999: 1993/94 build (5,300 cars): possibility of moisture corrupting computer chips which control passenger airbag trigger mechanism.

9X Coupe (from 2003?)

What's good: Began as a concept car, but now thought likely to reach production by 2003 on one of GM's new platforms. Concept car has 300bhp 3.0 litre V6 putting out 302lb ft torque at 2,200rpm and six-speed sequential manual gearbox. 0–60 in 5.9 seconds. Top speed limited to 155mph.

What's bad: Too soon to say.

What to watch out for: Too soon to say.

SANTANA

Anibal (from 2002)

What's good: Basic, inexpensive and practical Land Rover 110 SIII based 4x4 built by Santana which used to assemble Land Rovers in Spain and also assembled Suzukis. Simple leaf springs with parabolic option for greater comfort. Four cylinder 125bhp 2.8 litre Iveco diesel engine giving 88mph and 28mpg. Front and rear disc brakes. Seats closer to centre than Landy Defender. 5 or 9 seats in total. Roll up and down side windows. Selectable two wheel drive, four wheel drive, low range and diff locks. From £13,000.

More online at www.fourtecuk.com or www.santanauk.com; tel: 01362 860303.

What's bad: Obviously a work vehicle rather than a motorway cruiser.

What to watch out for: If buying used, off road damage, though farmers are far less likely to damage their 4x4s than off road enthusiasts.

SEAT

Alhambra (1996 to 2003)

What's good: Seat's version of Galaxy/Sharan, all built on the same line in Portugal. All have air conditioning, but otherwise fairly basic trim. VW 2.0 litre petrol and 1.9 litre TDI 90 110 or even chipped 130 engines. Also 125 bhp 1.8 20v and 150 bhp 1.8 20v Turbo. Three-year unlimited mileage warranty. More cheerful trim than Galaxy and Sharan. Basically the same Sharan was a Three-Star performer in NCAP crash tests (6 points front impact; 15 points side impact). Attractive Y2K facelift includes new 115 bhp TDI PD and 204 bhp VR6 – both with four-wheel-drive option. Six-speed VAG gearboxes now standard throughout the range. List prices cut September 2000 to start at £17k for 2.0 litre 7 seater S with 7 three-point seatbelts, a/c, ABS, driver, passenger and side airbags, roof rails, luggage cover, electric mirrors and 3-year 60,000–mile warranty.

SEAT online self-help group: www.seatcupra.net

What's bad: Trim quality and damage from family use may let the vehicle down. Below-average 'customer satisfaction'. On early models water can enter car via ventilation, soak the underfloor and get into the ECU which controls the electric windows and alarm system. On later models, this ECU has been moved. May also soak the pollen filter preventing ventilation air entering the vehicle and leading it to steam up. The cure is to unblock the vent plenum chamber drain pipes. Aircon vulnerable to front end shunts. Also shifted in later models. TDIs can blow turbos and catalytic converters. Have also been manual gearbox problems with TDIs and one report of gearchange cables separating on a 1996 2.0 litre petrol model. Automatics can lock in 'park' when the brake switch fails. Insulation of cables to lights and wiper in rear door can crack. Galaxy from same family came last in J.D. Power 'P' reg. survey and Sharan second bottom, but by 'R' reg. had improved. Air mass meters on TDI 110s can suffer failure through corrosion.

What to watch out for: Lowest list prices mean most likely of Galaxy

TDI 90 family to have been used as a taxi, so look for signs of clocking. Make sure servicing up to date and warranty still in place. Make sure 7–seaters have rear compartment heater. Spec was progressively improved. Later Alhambra TDI 110 has aircon and pop up picnic trays on backs of front seats. Make sure manual Ford gearbox isn't 'clonky'. Pre 1999MY key-lock immobiliser models suffer same security design fault as Passats, A4s and early Golf Mk IVs. Thieves can pop out the lock barrel then use the same screwdriver to turn lock so all the windows open and alarm sensors are disabled.

Recalls: 1997: brake pads may overheat. 13/1/2000: 80,000 Galaxys, Alhambras and Sharans VIN TV000001 to YV509825 recalled to check for contamination of brake fluid through master cylinder vent. Brake master cylinders of older cars to be replaced.

Arosa (from 1997)

What's good: Cheap, well-equipped, very cheerful small cars, all with power assisted steering. Decent ride quality. Originally, numerous 'option packs' included comfort pack, safety pack and even aircon. Later restricted to base and SE spec. 1.4 litre four-speed auto one of the cheapest autos with PAS (1.4 manual introduced later at same price). Tall body good for entry and exit by the elderly. 1.7 litre SDI with unpainted bumpers the most practical city car, capable of 65 mpg. Initially built at Wolfsburg; now Barcelona. 'SE' version replaced 'Comfort Pack'. Three-year unlimited mileage warranty. Did well in German TUV front offset crash test. New 118 mph 100 bhp 1.4 16v petrol engine and 106 mph 75 bhp, 66 mpg 75 bhp 1.4 litre TDI now in UK. 1.4TDI sensibly priced at £9,995 and £8,995. Cute new SEAT corporate front for 2001. Price of 1.0 base model cut to £5,995 in April 2002. Good, friendly dealers. Both 1.7SDI and 1.4TDI emit 119g/km CO_2, so qualify for £80pa VED from April 2002.

SEAT online self-help group: www.seatcupra.net

What's bad: Handling not to standard set by Ford Ka, but it's okay. Clutch cables stick and may break. Door mirrors feel a bit cheap. Clutch replacement unusually expensive on 1.0 version (more than

£500). Quite a few problems both from Wolfsburg and Barcelona production. UK unlikely to get 1.2 litre '3L' super economy diesel because UK diesel tax is too high to justify the cost.

One reader's comments on his Arosa 1.7SD:

"Diesel MPG average: 72 mpg (I commute on the A1 when there's no traffic at 60–65 MPH). Best was 80.2 MPG. Fuel log kept. Warranty claims: 11 non-scheduled visits in one year. Front tyre wear due to incorrect toe-in setting at factory. Seems to be a SEAT problem as a friend with a new Arosa TDI had a similar problem. Door mirrors are useless: cannot be adjusted from inside the car. Replaced by just as bad. Minor oil leaks due to improperly fitted gasket. Chronic Stereo static (still not fixed after 6 visits). Squeaky rear suspension (may be bushes-not yet investigated). Dealer support: Friendly, yes. Expensive: Very. Standard 10,000 mile "there-was-nothing-to-adjust" service was over £225, reduced to £165 after serious complaining. My wife's Mk IV Golf had a full VW 2 year service, laser 4-wheel alignment and fluid changes and I still got change from £222. Oil change is a shocking £80, but takes 15 minutes and parts costs £30. Cambelt change due next year and will cost a whopping £312 which is odd since the belt is under a plastic cover and is easily accessible, and that includes access to the idler pulley. I will take the car to France for this work which is 30% cheaper (while on a booze-cruise). Overall: An excellent small car. Very comfy, fair handling, good build quality (except mirrors). Overpriced main dealers."

What to watch out for: The 'Comfort Pack' of height-adjustable seats, parcel shelf, better trim etc. costs £245 new and is so good it's worth paying an extra £300 for second-hand. Make sure servicing up to date and warranty still in place. Have been known to misfire so make sure the cat isn't torched by having it MOT emissions checked.

Recalls: SEAT has admitted a cold weather fault with the 1.4 automatic, manifesting itself in a loud noise when changing up from 1st to 2nd gear. Replacement parts are fitted free. June 2002: 120,000 Polos, Lupos and Arosas built during 1998 and 1999 recalled because cracks in the brake vacuum pipe could lead to loss of servo assistance to the brakes. Recall hotline: 0800 711811.

Cordoba (from 1994)

What's good: Saloon, two door 'coupe' and estate version of Ibiza. Saloon also became the Polo saloon. Excellent 1.6 litre 100 bhp petrol engine. Cordoba Vario estate is the best-looking of the range and is available with TDI 90 or TDI 110 engines. Same revisions as Ibiza from September 1999. Good, friendly dealers. SEAT online self-help group: www.seatcupra.net

What's bad: Cordoba coupe is ugly. Cordoba saloon has a bouncy ride. Vario estate is not a true estate because it has a high load lip to give the body rigidity.

What to watch out for: VW's 'self adjusting' clutch cable that can lead to a slipping clutch. Make sure servicing up to date and warranty still in place.

Ibiza (1985 to 1993)

What's good: These did used to shift a bit on Spanish roads. Had 'Porsche-design' engines, VW gearbox, good handling. Not bad looking in a chunky sort of way. 1,193cc had 63bhp and 5 speed gearbox; 1,461cc had 85 or 90bhp and 100bhp with fuel injection. Only the very last had cats which cut the power of the injected 1.5 to 98bhp. Haynes manual 1609, ISBN 1 85010 609 6. SEAT online self-help group: www.seatcupra.net

What's bad: Not very well made. Rust-prone Fiat Ritmo underpinnings. The last of the pre-VW SEATs. Neglect has nearly always taken its toll on the car's looks.

What to watch out for: Rust, fall-apart trim, rattly dashboards, groaning wheel bearings, total lack of maintenance by people who buy them for next to nothing and chop them in as a '£500 minimum part-exchange'. Avoid the old pushrod engined 42bhp 900 unless it's for nothing and has a long MOT.

Recalls: 1994 (1985–1991 VIN 09045074–D119002): fuel leak.

Ibiza (1993 to 1999)

What's good: The development car for the current Polo, essentially the same underneath but slightly longer wheelbase. Neat shape.

Sporty image from rally success. Fun 'Mediterranean' image. Ibiza TDI 90 noisy, but goes well, handles well, ideally geared for city driving, does 55 mpg even at 80 mph. Think of Seats as 'fun' Volkswagens. Later cars came with three-year unlimited mileage warranties. TDI recommended. Good, friendly dealers. SEAT Online self-help group: www.seatcupra.net

What's bad: No protection strip means doors vulnerable to damage in supermarket car parks. Build not quite up to Wolfsburg standards. Costs a fortune to replace the exhaust system of the 1.4. The public knows the TDI is good, so none are ever cheap.

What to watch out for: Lots of model variations: 1.3s, then much better 1.4s, etc. You need a 'Parker's Guide' or 'The Book' to find out just how much of a saving you're making. Make sure servicing up to date and warranty still in place. If exhaust blows don't buy because replacement exhaust costs a fortune as subframe needs to be detached to fit it.

Ibiza (1999 to 2002)

What's good: Reworking of the 1993 model, itself the first manifestation of the Polo platform, from the 'A' pillar forwards. Better handling and improved ride comfort from new 'silentblock' mounted front suspension. Interior design and quality much improved. Range includes 156 bhp 1.8 petrol turbo which is a fantastic town car. While TDI 110 with switchable traction control gives true Gate performance plus 55 mpg economy. Remember, SEATs are 'fun' Volkswagens, and Ibizas are more fun to drive than Polos. 68 bhp SDI diesel from October 1999 launch at a reasonable £8,995 with PAS. New 'tax-break' 1.0 litre 16v 70 bhp engine from early Y2K. Three-year unlimited mileage warranty. TDI 110 recommended. 'Cool' models with a/c at no extra charge from spring 2000. 156 bhp Cupra model from October 2000 actually has more power, excellent brakes with Brembo callipers and costs just £12,995. TDI 110 listed in January 2002 price-list at £11,995 with Sport trim. Emits 138g/km CO_2 and has standard a/c. Good, friendly dealers. Three Stars in Euro NCAP crash tests.

180bhp Cupra R new for 2001 giving 0–60 in 7.2 seconds and top speed over 140mph. SEAT online self-help group: www.seatcupra.net

What's bad: Re-engineering the brake servo for RHD meant no UK 1.8 Cupra Turbo until spring 2000 and no TDI 110 until late 2001. Steering wheel still only adjustable up and down and seats still only have old rocking adjustment of Golf Mk II Gate. Replaced by new Ibiza on Skoda Fabia floorpan in 2002. Official 180bhp Cupra R very expensive at £18,900. Cupras eat front tyres. Exhaust system of 1.4 costs a fortune to replace.

What to watch out for: Build quality complaints include: battery earth lead bolt becoming unscrewed, windscreen wiper spindle unwinding itself and damaging bonnet, ECU unit becoming detached from its under dash mounting. If exhaust blows don't buy because replacement exhaust costs a fortune as subframe needs to be detached to fit it.

Ibiza (from 2002)

What's good: The most exciting looking car on VAG's Fabia/Polo/Ibiza OA4 platform on sale in UK from 1st May 2002. The new Ibiza has the most powerful diesel in the A04 line-up: none other than the PD 130bhp combined with the same six-speed gearbox as the Golf. Performance is 0 – 60 in about 9 seconds, 130mph top speed and 56mpg economy which is likely to be a realistic figure because this engine gives its best on-road performance between 2,000 and 3,000rpm. 6th gear gives 37.5 mph per 1,000 rpm. Price: £13,495. Other engine options include the new 64bhp 1.2 litre VAG 3 cylinder chain-cam lightweight, from £7,995 but without ABS, a/c and only a centre rear seat lap belt; a pair of 1.4 16 valvers with 75 or 100bhp, and a PD 100bhp TDI. Rumoured to be getting a full line-up of engines, including a 1.8 turbo and the 170bhp 2.3 V5. Cupra R version to follow in 2004. Though it shares traditional, high-waisted chunky looks with the current Ibiza, the new car is 77mm longer, 58mm wider and 19mm taller with 56mm extra rear legroom and a 267 litre boot. Prices from £7,995 for the 1.2

(£8,495 with a/c) to £13,495 for the TDI 130 six speed. See road-test online at www.honestjohn.co.uk

More online at www.seat.co.uk

SEAT online self-help group: www.seatcupra.net

What's bad: The 1.2 I tried did not feel as good as the VW Polo, possibly because it was one of the first RHDs built and may have been set with too much toe-in. Also noisier than Polo.

What to watch out for: Too soon to say.

Ibiza MPV?

What's good: New Ibiza-based mini MPV apparently planned for late 2002. May be built by Emelba, who built a SEAT Panda based mini MPV in the early 1980s. Can't confirm or unconfirm.

What's bad: Too soon to say.

What to watch out for: Too soon to say.

Leon (1999 to late 2003)

What's good: Great looking Golf IV-based 5–door hatch, essentially a shortened Toledo, pronounced 'Lay-on'. Not unlike a latter-day Alfasud. Shares Toledo's superior road feel and handling. Galvanised body with 12-year warranty. 3-year mechanical warranty. UK engine range from 75 bhp 1.4 16v to 147 mph 180 bhp 1.8 20v turbo six-speed (or the 143 mph Haldex-clutched four-wheel-drive version), and including the usual 90 bhp and 110 bhp TDIs. 4WD Haldex clutch allows use of different circumference wheels and for the car to be towed with two wheels off the ground. At £14,995 the 180 bhp 20VT Sport is a fantastic performance buy and more fun to drive than the four-wheel-drive. Switchable traction control not too intrusive. Even has Brembo front brake callipers. 204 BHP V6 four-wheel-drive Cupra 4 and 150 bhp TDI PD 4 announced at September 2000 Paris Show but LHD only and not coming to UK. Cabrio version seen testing. Built in Brussels and Martorell. Old VAG 8v 1,595cc 100bhp engine emitting 187g/km C02 (£155pa VED) substituted by new more fuel efficient 16v 105 bhp with 109lb ft torque emitting 170g/km CO_2 (£140pa VED) for

2001 model year. This is the bargain of the Leon range as it comes with air-conditioning, ABS, alloy wheels, front and side airbags, remote central locking and electric front windows all as standard for £10,980. Generally good, friendly dealers. 22nd from top of 100 models for reliability in *Auto Express* 2002 survey. Hand-built 210bhp front-drive Cupra R arrived in July 2002 offering 147mph performance with 0–60 in 6.9 seconds for £16,995. Mods over and above standard 180bhp Cupra R include twin force fed intercoolers, 18 alloy wheels, four-pot Brembo front brake callipers, faster steering at 2.5 turns lock to lock and SEAT's Agile Chassis Concept (ACC) of special spring and damper rates and revised suspension geometry. ABS with EBA and TCS remain standard. ESP remains switchable. Comes with standard climate control, six-speed box, leather steering wheel, sports seats and a six stack CD player. Colours are Ovni Yellow, Flash Red, or Ebony Black. Warranty is 3 years or 60,000 miles on the mechanicals; 12 years on the body. Highly recommended.

SEAT online self-help group: www.seatcupra.net

What's bad: Drain holes in door bottoms can get blocked with wax and water can leak into the car between the inside door structure and the black ancillaries panel. These panels need to be removed and properly resealed or damp will make a real mess of the driver's footwell. Vent into car via plenum chamber may also not be properly sealed. Seals around the rear lamp clusters can also let in water. And tube can come of rear screen washer, depositing washer fluid in boot. Two complaints of ECU failures on 20VTs, both replaced under warranty. One complaint of faulty temperature sender in 110TDI sending wrong message to ECU leading to increased fuelling and poor mpg. One complaint of badly misaligned suspension on delivery. Complaints of intermittent loss of power on 105bhp 1.6 16v, apparently due to a software glitch. Complaint of wrong, much higher final drive ratio in one 2002MY Leon 20VT, which blunted its performance especially in 6th.

What to watch out for: Obviously the 180 bhp 1.8 litre engine is not going to last for ever. 100bhp per litre is a lot of power.

Recalls: 28/2/2001: Build 1/10/2000–30/11/2000 Passenger airbag may not inflate correctly due to leak in pressure reservoir of gas generator. Passenger airbags to be replaced. 2001: On LHD 20VT4s (four wheel drive) built up to March 2000, the bottom rear hub carrier ball joint can corrode and seize, leading to the lower suspension arms snapping at the hub ends. (No 20VT4s officially imported.)

Leon II (from late 2003)

What's good: New Leon from mid to late 2003 based on PQ35 Golf V platform with its own distinctive look based on Walter de'Silva Salsa. 3 and 5 door options. The plan is to give it sportier handling than the Golf V, though, as with current Leon, SEAT chassis improvements may feed their way through to the Golf itself. Multi-link rear suspension. Engines may include 86bhp FSI 1.4, 116bhp FSI 1.6, 150bhp FSI 2.0; 185bhp 2.0T, 150bhp TDI and 240bhp 3.2 V6. More certain to include 75bhp 1.4 16v and 102bhp 1.6 16v. To be launched at Frankfurt Show in autumn 2003.

What's bad: May be too much sulphur in UK petrol for FSIs (see Golf V).

What to watch out for: Too soon to say.

Marbella (1988 to 1995)

What's good: Cheap skate for cheapskates, especially in Spain where they sold for not much more than £3,000 new. Terra Vista combi van the best version. SEAT online self-help group: www.seatcupra.net

What's bad: Hideous Panda re-style. Based on old Seat Panda, not post-1988 Fiat Panda, so has old 903cc pushrod engine and old unimproved suspension. Rust-prone. Poor quality trim. Like Panda, clutch cables snap.

What to watch out for: Rust, front struts, wheel bearings, smoky and rattling engines. (The rattle is usually the timing chain tensioner.) Front suspension problems (check for uneven tyre wear). Don't touch one with a catalytic converter. Could you really live with a car this ugly that makes you look so much of a miser?

Tango

What's good: SEAT's Street Ka rival is an Arosa sized roadster concept car enticingly dubbed the SEAT Tango. It's only 3,685mm long (12 ft 1 inch), has no hood, and adopts an Elise style minimalist approach inside with exposed frame tubes based on the structure of the SEAT World Rally Car. Power is from the familiar 180bhp 1.8 litre 20v turbo engine fed through a six-speed gearbox. Top speed is claimed to be 146mph with a 0–60 of less than 7 seconds which will be quicker than the Ford Street Ka.

More online at www.seat.co.uk

What's bad: Will it make production? If it does, then some versions will probably be toned down. But will be good to see a genuinely competitive rival to the Street Ka on the market at the same time.

What to watch out for: Too soon to say.

Toledo (1991 to 999)

What's good: Jetta-based family hatchback with enormous boot. Had mid-life facelift in 1995. Most models very well equipped for their price bracket. TDI 90 is a good package with decent performance and economy at (for the UK anyway) a sensible price. SEAT online self-help group: www.seatcupra.net

What's bad: Not a great looking car. Seat built a special Taxi-spec diesel Toledo. That big hatchback did nothing for the car's structural rigidity.

What to watch out for: Toledos that began their lives as taxis. VW's 'self adjusting' clutch cable that can lead to a slipping clutch. Leaks from ill-fitting tailgate (it's big, so twists out of shape easily). Check all electrics, including lights. Make sure servicing up to date and warranty still in place.

Recalls: 1996: cooling fan motor may seize, leading to overheating in traffic or on hills.

Toledo (from 1999)

What's good: Golf IV-based family saloon. Really good looking in the manner of the Alfa 156. Much sportier than Skoda Octavia, using lessons learned on the Skoda. Better steering and handling than Golf IV and Bora due to 15in alloys with 195/65 tyres, stiffer four-door body and softer suspension settings. Good ride quality, comfortable, rattle-free, galvanised body with 12-year warranty; otherwise 3-year unlimited mileage warranty. 170bhp V5 has a perfect set of gear ratios and is lot of car for £16,995. But 52 mpg TDI S 110 with standard aircon and alloys was the best buy. Good, friendly dealers. Recommended.

SEAT online self-help group: www.seatcupra.net

What's bad: Deep boot, but you have to post your luggage through a narrow slit. V5 gives nice, progressive power but lacks the grunt of the old VW VR6. Drain holes in door bottoms can get blocked with wax and waterproof door membranes can lift, leading to ingress of water into car.

What to watch out for: Too soon to say.

Recalls: 28/2/2001: Build 1/10/2000–30/11/2000 Passenger airbag may not inflate correctly due to leak in pressure reservoir of gas generator. Passenger airbags to be replaced (only 11 cars affected).

SKODA

Estelle (1977 to 1990)

What's good: Some people liken the oversteering handling to that of a Porsche. Engine in the back means you leave engine noise behind you. Decent-sized front boot. Pocket money cheap.

What's bad: Skoda 'skip' image dating from the days when these cars were assembled by convicts. Fall-apart trim. Becoming difficult to obtain spares (VW doesn't want to know about this model). Only buy with a long MOT and be prepared to throw the car away at the first sign of any expense.

What to watch out for: Paying more than £100 for one. Screeching gearboxes, iffy electrics (check all lights and indicators – I've seen new Estelles where the indicator cables were cross-connected). Cheapskate home maintainers will have used the cheapest oil, changed it grudgingly and never bothered to change the coolant. But buy a car from an obsessive DIYer with a Haynes manual and the chances are he'll have sorted out all the faults.

Fabia (2000 on)

What's good: First incarnation of the new VAG AO4 floorpan to be shared with the new Polo and SEAT Ibiza. Chunky good looks. High quality electro-galvanised construction. Height- and reach-adjustable steering wheel and height-adjustable driver's seat giving huge range of adjustment. Switchable passenger airbag. Safety 'door open' red lights in both front doors. Engines include an aluminium pushrod 68 bhp 1.4 litre petrol based on the old Favorit/Felicia 1.3; a 101 bhp 16v 1.4 from the Polo/Lupo and the 64 bhp 1.9 litre SDI diesel. New 100bhp TDI PD engine with 177lb ft torque arrived in November 2000 priced from £11,300 to £12,000 according to trim. Will eventually get VAG's new 1.2 litre 3 cylinder chain cam 65 bhp petrol engine and VAG's 75 bhp 1.4 litre 16v. Good ride and handling (much better than pre-A04 Polo). Decent-sized boot. Full-sized 'spare'. Very easy to park and manoeuvre. Nice radio with pop-out volume knob. Optional a/c even on 68 bhp 1.4.'Classic', 'Comfort' and 'Elegance' trim levels. Ten-year body warranty. *What Car* Car of the Year. Friendly, sensibly priced dealers. Very good Four-Star rating in Euro NCAP crash tests. Prices from £7,500 for 1.4 Comfort. Kombi estate car with 100bhp TDI PD engine arrived March 2001. Booted four door saloon arrived Summer 2001. 2.0 litre 8v 115bhp arrived late in February 2002 at £11,900 with Elegance trim, giving Golf IV Gate performance for £3,000 less. Skodas come with a three year UNLIMITED MILEAGE warranty. 6th Top in 144 car 2002 JD Power/*What Car?* Customer Satisfaction Survey of V and W reg. cars. 'Silverline' and 'Blackline' Specials for July 2002 with alloy wheels, electric sunroofs and metallic paint, but with 68bhp pushrod 1.4 engine for £8,295,

What's bad: More expensive than outgoing Felicia. Slow, overlight, lifeless but very accurate steering. Lack of character. 1.4 8-valve slow and thirsty at just 30.28 mpg. 1.0 very slow. High quality but extremely dull 'parts-bin' dashboard with nowhere to put things. High rear door sills contribute to strength, but make rear seat entry/exit difficult for the elderly. High boot sill. No external hatchback latch. Centre rear belt only two-point. ECU is mounted on the engine compartment scuttle and could be subject to moisture ingress. Reports of ECU failures. Very soft engine mountings result in occasional 'clunks' and affect the steering. Euro 4 throttle damping takes some crispness out of throttle response, especially on 1.4 16v, but there are no problems exiting junctions, etc. No auto option at UK launch. Complaints of water leaks from ventilation plenum chamber into driver's footwell, head gasket failure on 1.4 8v and misaligned auxiliary drive belt on 1.4 8v. Further complaints about 1.4 8v include poor throttle response, mechanical unreliability, fuses blowing in immobiliser circuit due to a fuel pump fault, engine coolant loss due to bottom hose seal failing and, in around 5% of cars, coolant loss through head gasket due to insufficiently torqued stretch bolts. (Coolant loss meant one owner needed a new waterpump, cylinder head gasket and coolant reservoir as a result of overheating.) Several incidences reported of glass in rear hatchback shattering.

What to watch out for: Make sure the 1.4 8v is not losing coolant and has not overheated through loss of coolant in the past, possibly due to friction on the bottom hose as a result of soft engine mountings.

Recalls: Faulty relay can result in electric windows opening about one minute after doors are locked with the key. These relays are in the process of being replaced under a low priority recall. 11/5/2001: Build November 2000: Passenger airbag may not inflate correctly due to leak in pressure reservoir of gas generator. Passenger airbags to be replaced. (Only 10 cars affected: same fault as on SEAT Leon and Toledo.)

Favorit (1989 to 1995)

What's good: Gave a massive boost to Skoda's image. Handles quite well. Decently engineered. A good, sound, practical low-budget car. Much better than a Lada. Very cheap.

What's bad: Memories of Skoda image die hard. Build quality still 'pre-VW'. Fall-apart trim, grotty plastic, iffy electrics (particularly lights). Soft brake pedal (like old Polos). Engines start to smoke if oil not changed regularly and decent oil not used. Starter motors fail and can chew up the starter ring. The down pipe of the heating duct inside the car gets detached and it is very difficult to get back on.

What to watch out for: Penny-pinched home servicing using the cheapest oil. Duff cats on catalysed models. Does the owner impress you as someone who really knows how to look after a car?

Recalls: 1994 (VIN P0670305–R0916381 and P5019665–R5043486): wheel bearing failure.

Felicia (1995 to 2000)

What's good: Looks like a Favorit, but really a VW Polo in Skoda clothes. PAS now available with 1.6 petrol and 1.9 diesel engines. Sound, practical cars. Well built. Excellent paint quality, good shut lines. Strangely, high quality trim and plastics seem as if they're deliberately made to look cheaper than those of Polo. 1.3 versions cheap, but the engines feel it. Haynes manual available from March

1999. 3-year warranty means dealer servicing for first three years but dealers are friendly and sensibly priced. An amazing 3rd from top in 'R' reg. J.D. Power Customer Satisfaction Survey. Still 16th from Top in 144 car 2002 JD Power/*What Car?* Customer Satisfaction Survey of V and W reg. cars.

What's bad: Skoda image not good for the status conscious. Old-fashioned single-plane door and ignition key up to April 1998 grille facelift, when it was replaced by twin-plane key. Diesel version a bit front heavy for standard width tyres – can lose adhesion. Very limited model range from early 2000 with most models discontinued. Pop-up sunroofs tend to leak.

What to watch out for: Owners home-servicing using the Haynes manual from March 1999 may take short cuts and will miss any rectification work carried out by Skoda dealers on TSBs. Check soundproofing under carpets for damp from leaking sunroofs.

Recalls: 1998: (models with airbags): wiring for airbag may chafe. 2001: Recall by Continental Tyres for free replacement of CT22 tyres on Felicias because they may split.

Octavia (from 1998)

What's good: Galvanised body has 10-year warranty. VW Golf Mk IV underpinnings. Excellent 1.6 litre 100 bhp, 1.8 litre 125 bhp petrol engines and 1.9TDI with 90 or 110 bhp. Very well built. Estate car much better than saloon. 2.0 litre VAG 115 bhp engine replaces non-turbo 1.8 20v from autumn 1999. 150bhp 1.8 20v Haldex clutched 4x4 estate from February 2001 priced at a reasonable £16,200. 180bhp RS front drive from April 2001 at low £15,100 OTR got a great reception from journalists. 4x4 150bhp hatchback introduced in October 2001 at £15,500. Good, friendly dealers. 12th from top in 2001 *Top Gear*/JD Power Customer Satisfaction Survey of S and T reg. cars. 24th from top of 100 models for reliability in *Auto Express* 2002 survey. 3rd equal from Top in 144 car 2002 JD Power/*What Car?* Customer Satisfaction Survey of V and W reg. cars. Four star score in 2001 NCAP crash tests.

What's bad: Still a Skoda in the eyes of the golf club secretary. Looks like a Passat with the back wheels in the wrong place. Early

LHD examples understeered heavily and late models can still be frightening in icy conditions, especially TDI with its heavy, torquey engine. 180bhp RS has only a 5-speed, not 6-speed gearbox and not as good to drive as SEAT Leon 20VT. Power loss on TDI 110s down to same problem as on Golf Mk IV. VAG acknowledges a fault with the ECU (038 906 018 BM) and specifies an upgraded unit (038 906 018 GQ) at £695.00 + VAT. According to VAG technical, this problem will eventually occur with all ECUs of the 'BM' part number.

What to watch out for: Plastic water pump impellers on early 1.8 20v engines fail. Newer water pumps have metal impellers.

Recalls: 2000: LXi models built May '98 to Jan '99: incorrect ABS servo fitted could lead to brakes locking up. 25/6/2001: Fuel tank may leak. Check for leaks and replace tank where necessary. 2001: On Octavia 4x4s built up to March 2000, the bottom rear hub carrier ball joint can corrode and seize, leading to the lower suspension arms snapping at the hub ends.

Superb (from May 2002)

What's good: New big Skoda based on stretched Chinese market Passat floorpan and 4,803mm (15 ft 9 in)long. 2.0 litre UK priced from £14,200 including air-conditioning, CD player, metallic paint and five three-point seatbelts. VAG engine options start with VW's old 2.0 litre 115bhp petrol, the Passat's 150bhp 1.8T, a TDI PD 130 diesel and a 193bhp 2.8 V6. Line up might also include the Passat's 155bhp V6 TDI and 170bhp V5. Expect automatic option with some but not all engines. 150bhp 1.8T drives well.

What's bad: Too soon to say whether Skoda badge will work positively or negatively.

What to watch out for: Too soon to say.

SPYKER

C8 Spyder

What's good: Stunning new aluminium space framed sports car from Holland that revives the old Dutch car maker's name. (Spyker was corrupted to Spijker, but Spyker is the correct original name.) The new car has a 400bhp 4,172cc Audi V8 also developing a healthy 354 lb ft torque. Top speed is estimated at 187mph and 0–60 in just over 4 seconds. Variable F1 suspension. New glass-topped Laviolette coupe version announced February 2001. Maker's website: www.spykercars.com

What's bad: Looking for initial deposits of £2,500 to allocate a chassis number. Car will then be tailor made to customer's requirements and final price will depend on what these are. Standard C8 has no weather protection.

What to watch out for: Too soon to say.

STRATHCARRON

SC-5A

What's good: Terrific new minimalist sportscar from the family of motoring Lord, David Strathcarron. 125bhp 1200cc motorcycle derived engine and very low weight of 550kgs should give amazing performance and handling. Price £22,450 on the road. 160bhp racing version to come in January. Entry level SC-6 at £19,995 to arrive in March. Maker's website: www.strathcarron.com

What's bad: Sadly, the venture didn't succeed and only very few were made.

What to watch out for: Too soon to say.

SSANGYONG

Korando (from August 1997)

What's good: Short wheelbase two door 4x4 estate, combining the looks of the Jeep CJ5 and the old Toyota Land Cruiser. 14ft 3in long by 6ft 1in wide, weighs 1,810kg and pulls 2,800kg. MB design 5 cylinder 2,874cc diesel developing 96bhp or 2,293cc 138bhp four cylinder petrol. 5-speed manual or option of 4 speed autobox on 2.3 petrol, high and low ranges on both. Production ended March 1999. Then Daewoo took over, building the 138bhp 2.3 petrol and dropping the non turbo in favour of the 118bhp 2.9 turbodiesel from the Musso. Still listed in June 2002.

What's bad: The model hardly got of the ground in the UK before rumours spread about the collapse of Ssangyong. So, as with the Musso, this meant bargain prices to get the stocks shifted. Nothing special at all to drive, but a usefully high towing weight for hard work.

What to watch out for: If it's been towing, check what it's been towing. Before buying, make sure you can find someone local to service it.

Musso (from May 1995)

What's good: Big UK (Worthing) designed 5–seater 4x4 with elevated back seats. 15ft 3in long by 6ft 3in wide, weighs 1,875kg and pulls 2,300kg. Complicated model history began with MB design 5 cylinder 2,874cc diesel developing 94bhp. Power of this went up to 98bhp in May 1996 and this engine continued alongside a 118bhp turbo launched December 1997. Also offered from Jan 1997 with 3199cc 217bhp twin cam six cylinder petrol engine and from June 1997 with 2,293cc 138bhp four cylinder petrol. 5-speed manual or 4 speed autoboxes, auto only on 3.2 petrol. Production ended March 1999. Then Daewoo took over, building just the 138bhp 2.3 petrol and 118bhp 2.9 turbodiesel models, still listed in June 2002.

What's bad: Bankruptcy blight took its toll on UK stocks and Mussos were sold at huge discounts in 1998 and 1999. This had a devastating effect on residual values to anyone who originally paid the full price, particularly if they bought a 94 or 98bhp 2.9 diesel.
What to watch out for: Usual 4x4 checks, and make sure you can find someone local to service it.

SUBARU

Forester (1997 to 2002)

What's good: Impreza-based four-wheel-drive estate with boxier body and more ground clearance than Impreza. Self levelling rear suspension. 175 bhp Turbo very good. 8th from top in 'R' reg. J.D. Power Customer Satisfaction Survey. Forester S-Turbo down to £20,494 from October 2000. S and T reg. cars came 14th in 2001 *Top Gear*/JD Power Customer Satisfaction Survey. From December 2001, 2.0 litre 125PS model is available with Sport bodywork at £16,995 otr. 15th from Top in 144 car 2002 JD Power/*What Car?* Customer Satisfaction Survey of V and W reg. cars.

What's bad: Exhaust system hangs quite low and could be vulnerable on bumpy tracks. Second-hand examples quite hard to find. One report of rear suspension of 1997 Forester collapsing, and later discovered not to have been self-levelling.

What to watch out for: Check for underside damage from 'off-road' use. Check for uneven tyre wear due to damaged suspension. Feel through the wheels for scored rear discs. Check the mileage carefully. Make sure has self levelling rear suspension or likely to be an independent import not to UK spec.

Forester II from October 2002

What's good: All-new Forester on sale in UK from October 2002. Much better looking, classier, more integrated design. Possibly the first genuinely good looking car from Subaru. The company has also gone for a quality feel. Will be same size as the outgoing model. US models went on sale first with the 2.5 litre flat-four. UK versions will have a choice of 125PD 2.0 litre flat four or 177PS 2.0 litre flat four turbo. Improvements are listed as better fuel economy, better aerodynamics, greater engine and transmission refinement, enhanced safety, greater interior width, more legroom and better handling.

More online at www.subaru.co.uk

What's bad: Too soon to say.
What to watch out for: Too soon to say.

HM-01 Hybrid Concept

What's good: Based on the Japanese market Pleo microcar, the HM-01has a 658cc four cylinder petrol engine driving the front wheels via a CVT transmission. But its rear wheels are driven by a 42 volt electric motor. The speed at which the front and rear wheels are driven is synchronized electronically. When the car is cruising on the over-run, the momentum of the rear wheels is converted into electric power by a high power 3kW alternator in the rear drive unit and re-charges the batteries. Length is 3,425mm; width: 1,425mm; height: 1,475mm. Engine power is 45bhp at 6,000rpm and 43 lb ft (58Nm) torque at 5,200rpm. The operating voltage of the rear drive is 42 volts; maximum torque 106 lb ft (144Nm); maximum power output 5kW (6.7bhp).

More online at www.subaru.co.uk

What's bad: Not yet scheduled for production, but likely to be.
What to watch out for: Too soon to say

Impreza (1993 to 2000)

What's good: Saloon or hatchback semi-estate bodies. Came top of *Top Gear*/J.D. Power 'N' and 'P' reg. Customer Satisfaction surveys, and 2nd to Legacy in 'R' reg. survey. Excellent reports from owners. 23rd from top of 100 models for reliability in *Auto Express* 2002 survey. Engines are 88 bhp 16v 1.6 flat four, 101 bhp 1.8 litre 16v flat four and 113 bhp 2.0 litre. Auto optional on 1.8 and 2.0. 2.0 obviously the best engine, but 1.6 much cheaper. Recommended.

Users and import buyers website: www.scoobynet.co.uk

What's bad: There was a 1.6 litre two-wheel-drive version from 1994–96. Change of piston skirt design in 1997 led to knocking noise on start up – usually cured under warranty by replacing just one piston. Clutch wear is common because drivers do not adjust their driving technique to the requirements of a four wheel drive car.

What to watch out for: Don't bother with two-wheel-drive versions. All Subarus are prone to scoring of the rear discs. Try and feel them through the wheel when cold. Check underside with torch for rocky lane accidents. Check for uneven tyre wear. Make sure clutch not slipping.

Impreza (from 2000)

What's good: New car from late 2000 after a very long model life by Japanese standards. Same choice of 5–door semi-estate or 4–door saloon. List prices start at £13,950 for 1.6TS Sports Wagon. New six-speed gearbox for WRX turbo at £21,495 for saloon and £21,995 for Sports Wagon. 23rd from top of 100 models for reliability in *Auto Express* 2002 survey.

   Users and import buyers website: www.scoobynet.co.uk
What's bad: Plain ugly.
What to watch out for: Too soon to say.

Impreza Turbo (1994 to 2000)

What's good: Saloon or hatchback 'semi-estate' bodies. Quick with standard 208 bhp engine, improved to 215 bhp in March 1999. But special import WRX STis offer 240–280 bhp and two-door WRX has up to 300 bhp. These cars are very fast indeed. 1999 UK 'special' 236 bhp RB5 offers a terrific drive. Officially imported two-door WRX P1 with 277 bhp, 4.7 second 0–60 and 155 mph at 7,500 rpm priced at £31,495. Impreza Turbos outsell the non-turbo Impreza in the UK, with 13,000 sold. If you can find an RB5, that's the one to go for. 23rd from top of 100 models for reliability in *Auto Express* 2002 survey.

   Users and import buyers website: www.scoobynet.co.uk
What's bad: In short supply so WRXs command substantial 'overs'. Impreza P1 just beaten by Mitsubishi EVO V1 in *Autocar* head-to-head test. Reports of clutch and gearbox failures and spate of big end failures which has led Motor Warranty Direct to refuse extended warranty cover.
What to watch out for: Large proportion of available cars are

independent imports, borough in either new or used. Watch out for Japanese modifications for which you can't easily get replacements in the UK. Change of piston skirt design in 1997 led to knocking noise on start up – usually cured under warranty by replacing just one piston. Check for underside damage from 'off-road' rally stage excursions. Check for uneven tyre wear. Feel through the wheels for scored rear discs. Smoke from exhaust could mean burned out turbo oil seals. These cars really need 3,000–mile fully synthetic oil changes. All WRXs are non-approved grey imports, so make sure they're legal with proper SVA certificates. To avoid the old SVA 50–car quota, some may have been 'cloned' (more than one car on the same registration). Be very careful not to pay official UK import price for a grey import standard model Impreza Turbo.

Talk to Protech: www.protech-uk.co.uk

Impreza WRX STi (from 2002)

What's good: Fully European Type Approved 261bhp Subaru Impreza WRX STi. UK sale date January 2002. Active Valve Control engine puts out 261.5bhp at 6,000rpm and 343Nm (253 lb ft) torque at 4,000rpm fed through a six speed gearbox to the car's four wheel drive system. 0 to 60 takes 5.2 seconds and top speed is 148mph. Further mods over standard Impreza Turbo include larger 17 inch Brembo brake discs, 17 inch wheels with fatter 225/45 tyres, uprated suspension with inverted struts, front and rear Suretrac limited slip diffs, and a faster 2.6 turn steering rack. There will be two versions: one with a Prodrive upgrade.

Subaru's UK 3 year or 60,000 mile warranty will apply. Prices, fuel consumption and CO_2 output will be announced closer to the on sale date. Achieved very good ratings in 2002 American Insurance Institute for Highway Safety crash tests: top of small car category for side impact and 'best pick' in 40mph front offset test. £2,000 of mods from Prodrive now add 39bhp giving the STi a full 300bhp.

More online at www.subaru.co.uk

Users and import buyers website: www.scoobynet.co.uk

What's bad: No beauty contest winner, otherwise too soon to say.

What to watch out for: Too soon to say.

Justy (1989 to 1996)

What's good: Cheap, small, reliable four-wheel-drive hatchback. Multipoint injected, catalysed 73 bhp 1,189cc 3-cylinder engine from September 1992 (3–door chassis 007401; 4–door chassis 009601) the best, but previous 67 bhp engine avoids the cat. Not great to drive, but light weight of 770kg makes it excellent in the snow.

What's bad: CVT automatic transmissions fail and a replacement costs the wrong side of £2,000.

What to watch out for: Avoid automatics unless running properly and going for buttons. Look for suspension, drivetrain, engine damage underneath from rocks. Be very suspicious of uneven tyre wear. Make sure drivetrain doesn't shriek or scream (expensive to fix). Have it emissions tested to make sure cat converter not smashed. Interior damage from children, dogs or farm animals should be obvious.

Justy (1996 to 2001)

What's good: Now Suzuki Swift-based and built in Hungary, with four rather than three cylinders and no unreliable auto option. 1,298cc. 67bhp.

What's bad: Hungarian build quality not the world's best. Interior trim not particularly tough. Sold in small numbers, so may have been built a long time before first registration date.

What to watch out for: 1,298cc Suzuki Swift engine has been known to suffer from cracked cylinder head. Be suspicious of uneven tyre wear. Try to get it on a ramp for a good look underneath, or take a torch. Check for oil leaks, bent suspension, dents in underside. Check the build date.

L-Series (to 1992)

What's good: A Texas bank got 600,000 miles out of one. Can represent a cheap, reliable car for those who need four-wheel-drive in the winter. 1,595cc, 67bhp to 73bhp; 1,781cc, 80bhp to 90bhp; 1,781cc Gate 105bhp; 1,781cc RX Turbo 136bhp.

What's bad: Starting to get really old now and onto their third or fourth owners. May be impossible to check history. Suspension bushes go. Remember, Japanese cars are designed to be very reliable for up to 7 years. They aren't built to last longer than this.

What to watch out for: Avoid turbos (too old now to expect them to be reliable). Rust. Broken front subframes. Any signs of having been used by a farmer (bits of straw under the carpet, strange dents, farmyard smells). If it has seat covers, look underneath – especially the top of the back seat. If tyre wear is uneven, best to walk away unless car is sub-£300.

Legacy (from 1990)

What's good: The most sensible large country estate car you can buy. Spacious, strong and reasonably economical (25–28 mpg). Facelifted in April 1994 and in October 1996. Clever 'hillholder' brake system. Low transmission range very useful for crawling along in a traffic jam. Avoid the 2.0DL or 2.0DLSE (Feb 92_-April 94) which has only part-time four-wheel drive and lower rear roof line. New American-built Legacy from December 1998 has revised floorpan with less suspension intrusion into load area. Did very well in USA Insurance Industry offset crash tests. Came top in J.D. Power 'R' reg. Customer Satisfaction Survey. Fresh price cuts October 2000 bring latest 2.0GL estate down to £15,995. 3.0 litre 207bhp Outback H6-3.0 automatic expensive at £26,995, but a brilliant tow car. 148bhp 2.5 Outback a sensible compromise. Was voted 2001 Towcar of the Year over £25,000 and best 4x4 towcar by the Caravan Club. Mileages of 300,000 + have been recorded even in the UK. Handling improvements for 2002, a/c standard across the range and prices starting at £15,750 for the 2.0GL saloon. 13th equal from Top in 144 car 2002 JD Power/*What Car?* Customer Satisfaction Survey of V and W reg. cars. Recommended.

What's bad: Spartan interior. Frameless side windows. Propensity to score rear discs. Cheap, old shape 'Classic' models dropped from line-up in autumn 1999 and new models were £2,000 dearer. Used prices rose strongly after J.D. Power result.

What to watch out for: Have been known to sit around on dockside compounds for years before finding buyers, so registration date may be 18 months later than build date. Always check the rear discs for scoring. If it has a tow-hook, check whether it's been pulling a single or a double horsebox. Use a torch to peer underneath just in case it's been up a rough track and suffered serious damage from a rock. Mk Is from 1989–94 are getting old now. Second or third owner may have skimped maintenance and used it for hauling animals. Have a good look under load area carpeting for dents. If the car has seat covers, take them off – a dog may have eaten the seats underneath.

Legacy Turbo (1991 to 1994)

What's good: Nicknamed in the trade the Subaru 'Lunacy', with 197bhp four cam flat four turbo engine these are very quick yet full five-seaters and the estate is a full-size estate car.

What's bad: They do get crashed. Getting old now for a turbo.

What to watch out for: Accident damage. Twisted shell. Suspension and or steering damage from 'falling off the road'. Smoke from exhaust could mean turbo oil seals have gone.

SVX (1991 to 1996)

What's good: Strange looking 226bhp 3,319cc flat-six 2+2 alternative to an XJS, a BMW 840/850 or a Mercedes SL. Four wheel drive. Four speed autobox. 15ft 2in long by 5ft 10in wide. Weighs in at 1,610kg.

What's bad: Very limited market and only a few Subaru dealers ever specialised in them.

What to watch out for: Difficult to get parts and make sure you can fins someone who knows the model to service it before committing any cash.

SUZUKI

Alto (from late 2002)

What's good: Awaiting information. May be MR-Wagon (see below).

What's bad: Too soon to say.

What to watch out for: Too soon to say.

Alto 1.0GL (1997 to late 2002)

What's good: Not bad looking for a tiny car. 53 bhp 993cc four-cylinder engine. Five-speed manual or three-speed auto option. 735kg.

What's bad: May be bought as a marginal retirement car. Built in India. Perodua Nippa is better value. Auto dropped in June 1999.

What to watch out for: Dings in the very thin sheetmetal. Premature rusting.

Alto FX, GL, GLA (1981 to 1997)

What's good: Cheap, tiny, basic car with 40 bhp 796cc 3-cylinder engine and 4-speed manual gearbox or optional 2-speed autobox. Weighs in at just 630kg. It was UK's cheapest auto at £4,000. Park anywhere and can still provide marginal motoring.

What's bad: Very small indeed. Noisy. Too slow for the motorway. Very light build, so rusts easily. Model dropped from UK line-up between 1992 and 1997. Car shown is a Dutch market example of around 1995. Not quite under the microcar B1 licence weight limit of 550kg.

What to watch out for: Rust will seriously weaken the structure. Suspension gets tired quickly. Uneven tyre wear a more-than-usually bad sign.

Baleno (from 1995)

What's good: Range of 3–door hatch, 4–door saloon, 5–door estate, all with same 1.6 litre engine. Power steering. Decent equipment levels. Owners like them. Got the 'ladies prize' at the 1996 Birmingham Motor Show.

What's bad: Comparatively poor NCAP crash test results, but not tested with standard UK spec. Driver's airbag. Bland to drive with overlight steering. No image. New model arrived August 1998.

What to watch out for: No known problem areas. But not many of these cars about.

Cappuccino (1993 to 1995)

What's good: Tiny 679–725kg sports car just 10ft 10in long and 4ft 7in wide. Powered by turbocharged 657cc engine developing 64bhp and getting it to 60 in 11.3 seconds. Top speed limited to 83mph. Red lined at 9,300rpm, but peak power at 6,500rpm. Top composed of folding canvas back with two hard top panels overhead. Owners club online: www.score.org.uk

What's bad: That revvy engine can do itself in and some parts are hard to find.

What to watch out for: Paying too much for an old grey import. Best to contact the owners club for advice first.

Grand Vitara (from 1998)

What's good: By UK standards, quite well priced at just over £16,195 for the 2.5 litre V6 5–door. 2.0 litre 86bhp Turbodiesel option with 5–door body. Seats of 5–door fold flat to make double bed. £800 clip-on tent available. 2.0 Litre 126 bhp GV2000 3–door manual or 4-speed automatic launched spring 2000 to compete with Honda's much sharper HRV.

What's bad: Still not a great drive. 4th from Bottom in 144 car 2002 JD Power/*What Car?* Customer Satisfaction Survey of V and W reg. cars.

What to watch out for: Too soon to say.

Grand Vitara XL-7 from Sept 2001

What's good: New Grand Vitara 4x4 now capable of carrying seven passengers. Lists at £19,995 and boasts a standard 170bhp 2.7 litre V6 engine and the choice of 5-speed manual or 4-speed automatic transmissions. Length: 4,700mm (15 ft 5 in); width: 1,780mm (5 ft 10 in); height: 1,740mm (5 ft 9 in). Gross vehicle weight: 2,260kg and maximum braked towing weight: 1,850kg. Luggage capacity with 2nd and 3rd rows of seats folded: 1,492 litres. Turning circle is a tight 11,800mm (39 feet) for this class of vehicle. The 2.7 litre V6 develops 170bhp at 6,000rpm and 231Nm (170 lb ft) torque at 3,300rpm. Combined fuel consumption for the manual is 26.2mpg and emissions 260g/km. Figures for the automatic are 23.5mpg and 285g/km. Importantly, the engine has a timing chain rather than timing belt for long term reliability.

Front suspension is independent by MacPherson strut; rear is a solid axle on five-link trailing arms.

More online at www.suzuki.co.uk

What's bad: Too soon to say.

What to watch out for: Too soon to say.

Ignis (from 2001)

What's good: New small car aimed at same market as Toyota Yaris and priced from £6,995. 3– or 5–door hatchbacks with 88 bhp 1.3 litre 16-valve VVTi engine. All have power steering, twin airbags, split folding rear seats and oddments tray under boot floor. High and flat load deck will suit older drivers. Optional a/c, ABS, automatic transmission.

What's bad: You sit up high and this adversely affects the car's centre of gravity. Otherwise too soon to say.

What to watch out for: No serious problems reported.

Jimny (from 1998)

What's good: Cute-looking with decent off-road ability. Reasonable performance (0–60 in 13.6 secs; top speed 100 mph) from 1,298cc 80 bhp engine). Separate chassis for strength. Part-time four-wheel-drive on the road driving rear wheels only for economy. 4-speed auto option. Soft-top version launched at Barcelona Show in May 1999 weighs 1,048kg and can tow 1,300kg.

What's bad: Noisy and unrefined. Poor 'on-road' manners, especially with large wheels and tyres. 15th from Bottom in 144 car 2002 JD Power/*What Car?* Customer Satisfaction Survey of V and W reg. cars.

What to watch out for: Too soon to say

Recalls: 2/11/2001: 4,068 Jimny hard and soft tops built 1/4/1998 to 31/10/1999 recalled because bolt holding gear selector yoke to gear selector shaft may loosen and fall out. High tensile replacement bolt to be fitted and torqued to tighter setting.

Liana (from July 2001)

What's good: New monobox hatchback from Suzuki, from Summer 2001. 4,230mm (13ft 9ins)long; 1,690mm wide (5ft 6ins), 1,550mm (5ft 1.5ins) high and high hip points of 23ins at the front and 24.5ins at the back make it particularly easy to get in and out of. Engine is a 1,586cc 'all alloy' twin-cam putting out a healthy 102bhp at 5,500rpm and 106 lb ft (144NM) torque at 4,000rpm. Combined fuel consumption is 39.8 mpg for the 5-speed manual and 35.8 for the 4-speed automatic. CO_2 outputs are 171g/km (£140pa VED) and 192g/km (£155pa VED. Prices are £9,995 for the GL and £11,495 for the GLX, which has ABS with EBD, air-conditioning, alloy wheels and a CD player as standard. Bodies are 80% galvanized (unusual for a Japanese car) and covered by a 12 year no perforation warranty. The mechanical warranty lasts 3 years or 60,000 miles, backed up by 24 hour roadside assistance. Undercuts new, non-galvanised Honda Civic by a wide margin.

More online at www.Suzuki.co.uk

What's bad: Strange looking from the back.

What to watch out for: No problems reported.

MR-Wagon concept car

What's good: Cute little town car from the same mould as the Daewoo Matiz. Good looking enough to be a hit.

What's bad: No specific plans for its future, but could be coming 2002. Might even be the new Alto.

What to watch out for:

SJ 410/413 (1982 to 1995)

What's good: The smallest, cheapest off-roader you can buy in the UK. Relatively light weight of 850kg helps in snow and 'soft' conditions. 970cc engine puts out 45bhp; 1,324cc has a stronger 64bhp and also available with longer wheelbase. Continued to be built by Ssangyong in South Korea at least up to 2000, but with two wheel drive and high-top hard-top.

What's bad: Santanas are Spanish built; SJs are Japanese; Katanas are built by Ssangyong in South Korea for Indonesia and called Jimnys. 410/413 Superseded by Japanese 'Jimny' late in 1998. Can suffer cracked cylinder heads after 50,000 miles (look for emulsified oil under oil filler). Not at all nice to drive on the road, but okay as a holiday villa runabout or as an off-road working car where small size is important. Surprisingly thirsty for a small engine.

What to watch out for: Uneven front tyre wear means the tracking's out, so has the front suspension been damaged? Has it been off-roaded (much more likely than Vitara because these are classed as a working vehicle). Check drivetrain for oil leaks. Make sure it slips easily into four-wheel-drive (transfer boxes have been known to take in water and corrode inside). Listen for gearbox rattles, especially with the clutch disengaged. Check everywhere for rust, especially the hood mechanism the joints of which can rust up and snap. Check under matting on cargo floor for rust in the seams. Take care on corners.

Swift (1985 to 1993)

What's good: 101 bhp Gate 16v only weighed 750kg so was fast and furious. Most had 67bhp 1.3. Odd 1,590cc 91 bhp GLX four-

wheel-drive saloon lasted from March 1990 to January 1993
What's bad: Cylinder heads of 8-valve 1.3s and 1.6s can crack.
What to watch out for: Cracked cylinder head on 8-valve 1.3. Gate 16v likely to have been thrashed – expect heavy tyre wear but look out especially for uneven wear. Country-bought GLX four-wheel-drive saloons may be damaged underneath.

Swift (from 1993)

What's good: Cheap, especially 1.0 litre 52bhp GC 5–door version. Low weight of 740kg (3–dr), 770 kg (5–dr). Also 67bhp 1.3, but 100bhp 1.3 Gate 16v still only weighs 835kg and by far the best. 12ft 3in long, 5ft 2in wide.
What's bad: Built in Hungary. Cylinder heads of 1.3 8vs can crack. Gate 16v dropped from line-up in October 1996. Ex-rental 1.0GCs took forever to sell into the trade.
What to watch out for: Cracked cylinder head.
Recalls: 15/12/2000: 300 Swift 1.0 and 1.3 litre models recalled because fasteners of steering rack and inboard engine mounting may not have been tightened correctly. If these come undone, the driver could lose control of the car. All models to be checked and fasteners correctly tightened and torqued. 2/3/2001: Build 11/8/2000–30/11/2000 Crankshaft position sensor cable may be worn away by offside driveshaft. Clip to be fitted to stop this happening.

Vitara GV 1600 (from 2001)

What's good: Cheaper lead-in Vitara to slot between Grand Vitara and Jimny, and also offer a mid-size soft top. Has 1,590cc 92bhp engine, high and low range, selectable four wheel drive. Comes with SWB 12ft 9in soft top body or as 13ft 9in 5–door estate. All have PAS.
What's bad: See other Vitaras.
What to watch out for: See other Vitaras.

Vitara LWB (1993 to 1998)

What's good: JX and JLX 5–door long wheelbase Vitaras. Tall body easy to get in and out of. Quite good looking. Will carry 4/5 and their luggage. Was originally the only 4x4 of its size. Range includes a 95 bhp 16-valve 1.6 petrol, a 70 bhp turbodiesel, manual and automatic and a 134 bhp 2.0 litre 24-valve V6. Manuals have high and low range gears and selectable four wheel drive. Autos have selectable four wheel drive. All have power steering.

What's bad: Not a brilliant drive.

What to watch out for: Usual 4x4 checks: is it a town car or a country car? Has it been towing? (If so, what?) Check steering gear for play and damage from kerbing (even on town cars). Has it been rolled or turned on its side? Brake callipers can stick (need servicing, not replacing). Avoid if drivetrain unduly noisy. Back seat and backs of front seats may have been crocodiled by dogs. Drive carefully, especially round corners. Prone to cracked cylinder heads due to silting and clogging of oil and waterways(see Vitara SWB).

Recalls: 1994 (Sep 1993–Jul 1994 build): wheel bearing failure. 1997 (July-Dec '97 build): steering shaft could detach. 8/5/2000: Vitara V6 and diesel built June '95 to Sept '96: chance that flexing of suspension strut mounting turret may cause strut studs to shear. Reinforcement plates to be fitted to strut turrets and top mountings.

Vitara SWB (1988 to 1997)

What's good: Hard or soft tops. 1.6 litre 8-valve engine range has four outputs: 74 bhp, 79 bhp and 80 bhp. High/low range gears and selectable four wheel drive. A bit of a hairdresser's favourite (especially convertible) and not many of these cars don't go off road. Some but not all had PAS.

What's bad: UK cars Spanish built. Cylinder heads can crack. Poor oil feed to rocker shaft may lead to premature wear. Not terrible, but nothing special to drive. Early JX SWB models did not have PAS.

What to watch out for: Prone to cracked cylinder heads due to silting and clogging of oil and waterways, so look for low header tank coolant level and emulsified oil under the oil filler cap.

Avoid ludicrous fat-wheeled, running-boarded 'customisation' because it's like wearing a chest wig and pedestrians will laugh at you helplessly. Make sure the four-wheel-drive works. Clean oil, changed every 3,000 miles, is essential to avoid blocking oil feed. Brake callipers can stick (need servicing, not replacing). Avoid if drivetrain unduly noisy. Back seat and backs of front seats may have been crocodiled by dogs. Drive carefully, especially round corners.

Recalls: 1994 (Sep 1993–Jul 1994 build): wheel bearing failure. 1997 (July–Dec '97 build): steering shaft could detach. 1998: (Oct '91–Oct '93 build): front seatbelt stalk may fracture.

Wagon R+ (1997 to 2000)

What's good: Chain-cam little screamer of a 64 bhp 996cc engine revs to nearly 8,000 rpm. Light controls. Easy to drive. Holds its own on the motorway – just. Much more elbow room than Daihatsu Move. Not as small as you think it's going to be. Shopping basket, bucket hidden under passenger seat. Reasonable legroom in the back. 3-year warranty. More powerful 68 bhp 1.2 litre engine, front-end restyle and automatic option from June 1998, still qualifies for reduced-rate VED. Joint 17th from Top in 144 car 2002 JD Power/*What Car?* Customer Satisfaction Survey of V and W reg. cars.

What's bad: Daft looking, but not as daft as the Daihatsu Move. Severe understeer. Little feel from power steering. Wouldn't like to be hit by a Toyota LandCruiser while driving one. Can have short front disc life due to corrosion of discs on lightly braked town-used cars.

What to watch out for: Make sure it's not coming apart at the joints. Reports of handbrake binding on after being left overnight and requiring replacement springs.

Recalls: 8/11/2000: 3,490 Wagon Rs built 1/2000 to 8/2000 recalled because handbrake lever pawl may not rotate freely leading to handbrake slipping off after having been applied. Replacement handbrake assembly to be fitted where necessary.

Wagon R+ (2000 on)

What's good: All-new structure and built in Hungary. Similar in concept to original, but much better looking. 76 bhp chain-cam 1,298cc engine with 85 lb ft torque. 14in wheels. Basically the same as the Vauxhall Agila. To get Fiat's 60 bhp, 1.2 litre 100 mpg CDI diesel engine in 2002. Joint 17th from Top in 144 car 2002 JD Power/*What Car?* Customer Satisfaction Survey of V and W reg. cars.

What's bad: Cars registered before 1/3/2001 don't qualify for reduced rate VED, otherwise too soon to say.

What to watch out for: Too soon to say.

Recalls: 8/11/2000: 3,490 Wagon Rs built 1/2000 to 8/2000 recalled because handbrake lever pawl may not rotate freely leading to handbrake slipping off after having been applied. Replacement handbrake assembly to be fitted where necessary. Further 1,542 Wagon Rs built 14/6/2000 to 15/9/2000 recalled because fasteners on the steering rack, rear suspension and near-side engine mounting may not have been tightened to the correct torque and could become detached. Fasteners to be tightened to correct torque.

TOYOTA

Allion (from late 2002)

What's good: Replacement for the Avensis, launched in Japan in January 2002, and a much sleeker, more exciting looking car. To have 1.5 litre and 1.8 litre VVTi petrol engines and the 2.0 litre D-4D. Manual, torque converter auto or CVT transmissions to be offered. Bound to handle much better than the outgoing Avensis because it will be the last car in Toyota's line-up to benefit from the company's change in suspension strategy. May not have Allion name when it comes to the UK in late 2002.

What's bad: Too soon to say.

What to watch out for: To soon to say.

Avensis (1997 to 2002)

What's good: A much improved Toyota Carina E. Same range of lean-burn engines. 1.8 litre the most frugal (40–45 mpg) and fitted with Michelin Energy tyres as standard. Much better looking than Carina E with all-new panels which hide its slab sides and high waist. Three proper lap and diagonal rear seatbelts. New 16v common rail direct injected 2.0 litre diesel, called 'D-4D' for 2000 MY, more economical than lean-burn petrol engine. Launch advertising campaign left impression of a high-quality car. Range includes a useful estate. Has a 3-year manufacturer warranty, and 5-year extended warranty on expensive Lambda probe. Nice unaggressive 'smiley face' cheers up other drivers. In June 2001 Toyota was rated by Motor Warranty Direct as Britain's 3rd most claim-free used marque. Second most reliable car in 2001 Fleet News Survey of 620,000 fleet cars mostly under 3 years old. (check online at www.warrantydirect.co.uk) BMW, Toyota and Ford jointly suffered the fewest breakdowns attended by German ADAC during 2001. 14th from top of 100 models for reliability in *Auto Express* 2002 survey. Toyota had fourth lowest average cost in warranty claims for cars up to 10 years old in 2002 Warranty Direct index, check online at www.performanceindex.co.uk

What's bad: Still Carina E-based, so it's not going to set your pants on fire with excitement. Lean-burn engines require same economy driving style of high revs with small throttle openings – not holding high gears and labouring the engine. Pre-2000 MY diesels pointless. Lost its 'smiley face' for 2000 model year. Some reports of premature clutch and gearbox failures. Isolated report of problems with immobiliser. Steering racks of early build 1997 cars can be prone to leaks (Toyota has replaced these FOC at 4 years old). On later cars a clunk from the rack is easily cured by re-greasing. Rear drum brake cylinders can also start to seep fluid. To be replaced by new Allion, already in Japan and in UK by end of 2002.

What to watch out for: Nearly-news likely to have been ex-rental. Look for minor damage from rental car carelessness. May have been kerbed, so check for uneven tyre wear and damaged hubcaps. Some problems experienced with steering column; subject to TSB and replaced FOC if owners complain. Make sure clutch still has plenty of bite and feel carefully for any gear-change problems. Look for leaks at ends of PAS rack on early cars. Steering clunks cured by regreasing on later cars.

Avensis Verso from August 2001

What's good: Avensis Verso on sale from 1st August 2001 offers seven seats in two-three-two layout and ample luggage space for seven, all within a length of 4,560mm (15ft 3ins). Engine choice is a 2.0–litre timing-chain VVT-i petrol engine offering 147bhp at 6,000rpm and maximum torque of 142 lb ft (192Nm) at 4,000rpm. Top speed of the manual is 119mph with a 0–60 of 11.2 seconds. (Auto 112mph and 0–60 12.0 seconds). Fuel economy is 32.8 mpg on the EU combined cycle with a CO_2 output 202g/km for the manual and 213g/km for the automatic (both £155pa VED). Alternative engine is a 114bhp 2.0 litre D-4D common rail diesel engine stumping up 184 lb ft (250Nm) torque from 1,800 to 3,000rpm giving the Verso a top speed of 112mph and a 0–60 of 12.2 seconds. Fuel economy is 43.5mpg on the combined cycle and CO_2 output 173g/km (£150pa VED). For BIK purposes, the tax bases are 22% of list price for the petrol manual; 24% of list for the petrol automatic and 19% of list for the diesel. Clever packaging of the spare wheel under the front passenger floor helps result in a low centre of gravity and a low overall height of 1,675mm (5ft 6ins). This leaves space for an underfloor rear luggage compartment helping to give 282litres of luggage space with all seats in place or a massive 2,422 litres with all five rear seats removed. All five rear seats can be bi-folded or removed entirely. The rear compartment length is a useful 2,104mm (6ft 11ins). Standard kit on all models includes ABS with EBD and Brake Assist, lap and diagonal seatbelts for every seat, air-conditioning and a Thatcham Category 1 alarm/immobiliser and a single CD player. In addition, GLS models have rear air-conditioning, 16 inch alloy wheels, roof rails, turn-by-turn satellite navigation, front fog lamps and leather steering wheel and gear knob. In a test by German magazine Auto Motor und Sport, the Avensis Verso was found to have the shortest, safest braking distances of any MPV. Passengers are not squeezed for shoulder width and three adults can sit across the second row in comfort. Interior width is 1,505mm, with shoulder width of 1,446mm, 1,456mm and 1,340mm in front, second and third row seats respectively. Headroom is equally useful at 1,048mm, 1,012mm and 911mm respectively. While drivers of all shapes and sizes can be accommodated. The drivers seat slides through 240mm and has 44mm of height adjustment. The steering column is adjustable for tilt. List prices are £17,795 for the GS VVT-I manual; £18,795 for the GS VVT-I automatic; £18,795 for the GS D-4D manual; £19,795 for the GLS VVT-I manual; £20,795 for the GLS VVT-I automatic; and £20,795 for the GLS D-4D manual. All include a full three year or 60,000 mile warranty and a 12 year no rust through perforation warranty. Colour choice is solid Pure White or metallic Silver Steel, Merlot Red, Island Green, Carlo Blue, Basalt Grey, Orb Gold or Teal Aqua. All are trimmed in Kirkfell Grey cloth. Highly rated by George Fowler, 'Motormouth' of the *Star*.

More online at www.Toyota.co.uk

What's bad: No serious criticisms.

What to watch out for: No reports of any problems.

Camry (1987 to 1991)

What's good: Ultra reliable sub Granada sized front drive saloon 14ft 10in long (estate 15ft 1in) with 126bhp 1,998cc twin-cam 16 valve four or 158bhp 2,507cc 24 valve V6. 5-speed manual of 4-speed auto on four; auto only on V6. Seem to go on and on and on.
What's bad: Body parts are getting to be a problem.
What to watch out for: Rust. Difficult to obtain bits that could mean an MOT failure.

Camry (1991 to 1995)

What's good: Large saloons and estates with extra rear-facing bench on 15ft 8in long US-built estate, making it a 7–seater. Good 134 bhp 2.2 litre four (manual or 4-speed auto) and smooth 185 bhp 3.0 litre V6 (auto only). Spacious inside and comfortable. Very reliable for first 5–7 years. Depreciates rapidly so makes an excellent value-for-money used buy. Rear seat of 7–seater estate is vinyl so sticky sweets and other child mess wipes off. In June 2001 Toyota was rated by Motor Warranty Direct as Britain's 3rd most claim-free used marque (check online at www.warrantydirect.co.uk) BMW, Toyota and Ford jointly suffered the fewest breakdowns attended by German ADAC during 2001. Toyota had fourth lowest average cost in warranty claims for cars up to 10 years old in 2002 Warranty Direct index, check online at www.performanceindex.co.uk
What's bad: Estates discontinued and saloons only available to order from Sept 1995.
What to watch out for: Not much goes wrong, so look for signs of abuse, such as towing something heavy or carrying heavy loads. Make usual checks of front suspension geometry – look for signs of uneven tyre wear and reverse turn in both directions to check for driveshaft clonks.

Camry (1996 to 2002)

What's good: Very good-looking large four-door saloon, high spec, badged as a Lexus in some markets. Three proper three-point rear seatbelts. 2.2 litre down on power slightly to 128 bhp; V6 slightly up to 188 bhp. Available in standard or 'Sport' trim (lowered, with bodykit and 17in alloys). Far better than Scorpios or Omegas, but top models getting expensive. Four-Star NCAP crash test rating among the best. S and T reg. cars came 10th in 2001 *Top Gear*/JD Power Customer Satisfaction Survey. In June 2001 Toyota was rated by Motor Warranty Direct as Britain's 3rd most claim-free used marque (check online at www.warrantydirect.co.uk) BMW, Toyota and Ford jointly suffered the fewest breakdowns attended by German ADAC during 2001. Toyota had fourth lowest average cost in warranty claims for cars up to 10 years old in 2002 Warranty Direct index, check online at www.performanceindex.co.uk

What's bad: Over-light steering not quite in the BMW league. No 'image'. No estate. Depreciates steeply over first three years.

What to watch out for: No problem areas known, but wise to buy with full Toyota service history. (If not available, why not? No history disqualifies the car from its 3-year warranty.)

Camry (from 2002)

What's good: All Camry made its Euro-debut at Frankfurt Motor Show on 11th September 2001 and reached the UK in November. America's favourite car now has more interior room, similar refinement and comfort and the option of two engines: a 2.4 litre VVT-i which offers best in class fuel consumption of 32.8mpg on the combined cycle, or a 3.0 litre V6 auto with a top speed of 140mph and a 0–60 of 8.9 seconds.

The design is completely new and builds on the model's attributes of class-leading comfort and refinement. Offers a "carefully engineered balance of ride, comfort and performance". Inside, has 7 per cent more interior space, higher levels of interior quality and "executive class features". Low noise levels and a "world-class safety system".

Smaller 2.4 litre VVT-i engine develops 150bhp at 5,600rpm and 161 lb ft (218Nm) torque at 3,800 to 4,200rpm. Manual gets to sixty in 9.1 seconds, goes on to 130mph, delivers an excellent 32.8mpg in the combined cycle and emits 206g/km CO_2. 2.4 four-speed auto does the sixty dash in 10.2 seconds, reaches 124mph, sips petrol at the rate of 29.2mpg on the combined cycle and emits 233g/km CO_2. 3.0 litre V6 pumps out 184bhp at 5,300rpm and 201 lb ft (273Nm) torque at 4,300rmp. Auto only, it gets to sixty in 8.9 seconds, runs to 140mph, gives you 25.7 miles per gallon on the combined cycle and emits 263g/km CO_2. Maximum braked towing weight of all models is 1,600kg.

External dimensions are: length: 4,815mm, width: 1,795mm, height 1,500mm. Boot capacity is a big 587 litres. Dual stage SRS airbags are standard equipment for driver and passenger, as are side-airbags. SRS curtain shield airbags help protect the heads of both front and rear seat passengers. Brake system offers ABS, electronic brake force distribution and brake assist as standard features. Five 3–point seatbelts. Front seatbelts come with pre-tensioners and force-limiters, the rear seats offer ISOFIX mountings for child seats. Equipment includes full multi-information display, rain-sensitive automatic windscreen wipers and automatic climate control, amongst many other features. UK Prices: £19,494 to £27,495. On sale date: November 2001.

More online at www.toyota.co.uk

What's bad: Front three-quarter look not as good as side on.

What to watch out for: No complaints yet.

Carina E (1992 to 1997)

What's good: Derbyshire-built upper-medium-size cars with quite powerful and particularly frugal 1.6 litre and 1.8 litre engines (40 mpg plus). Easy for anyone to drive. Useful estate cars. Decent build quality but not quite up to UK Honda and Nissan standards. Built to do a high mileage in a short time with no trouble. BMW, Toyota and Ford jointly suffered the fewest breakdowns attended by German ADAC during 2001. Toyota had fourth lowest average cost in warranty claims for cars up to 10 years old in 2002 Warranty Direct index, check online at www.performanceindex.co.uk

What's bad: Fairly ugly slab-sided body with high waistline. Reliability and 'customer satisfaction' factor not quite up to levels set by Japanese Corolla and previous Carina II. Unresolved damping causes handling problems. Lean-burn engines require unusual economy driving style of high revs with small throttle openings – not holding high gears. Front tyre wear can be heavy: 14,000 miles or so. Diesel nothing special. Reports of early transmission failure, wiper motor failure and suspension bush failure.

What to watch out for: Check for missed services, clocked ex-fleet cars (could have had the haircut years ago). Once they're a few years old, must have six-monthly oil changes. Had its fair share of immobiliser problems, cured by new keyfob transmitter. Rear shocks can spring a leak. Expect a few behind-dash rattles. One report of timing belt failure at 39,000 miles, so change at 35,000 miles rather than the recommended 63,000 miles. 'Lean burn' lambda sensor failure quite common (£416 a pop). Toyota guaranteed them for 5 years, but after that you're on your own. Power steering rack prone to premature failure leading Toyota to extend the warranty on it to 5 years as well. Since production ended in November 1997, these 5 year warranties will run out in November 2002 on the youngest Carina Es. On 1.8 models, fuel injection throttle butterfly is prone to sticking after a cold start due to combination of worn butterfly spindle bearings, varnishes and dirt in throttle body and different co-efficients of expansion of throttle body casting and butterfly. Was a four year warranty on this assembly which ended November 2001 for the youngest Carina Es. Repair cost is £631 at a Toyota dealer, so don't buy a Carina E with a sticking throttle.

Recalls: 1996: anti roll bar linkages may fail (first sign us a rattling noise). (Was covered under 3-year warranty. Only affected 2% of cars.) 1997 (Sept '93–Jan '96 build): stop lights may fail. 2000: rear axle hub may detach.

Carina II 16v (1988 to 1992)

What's good: Fantastic reputation for 'high mileage, trouble-free' motoring. Easy to drive, good engines, good automatic. Available as saloon, hatch or estate. 94bhp 1.6 or 126bhp 2.0 litre. 5-speed manual or 3-speed auto. Still proving reliable for some owners even though the cars are years past their sell-by date.

What's bad: Bland to drive. 'Feel-free' steering. I.6 engine sounds strained at speed. Ride quality not wonderful. Getting old now.

What to watch out for: Be very suspicious of any of these with a tow hook. Will probably have been pulling a large caravan. Starting to get a bit old for a Japanese car now, so look for rust, saggy suspension, shocked shock absorbers. Expect failures such as water pumps, oil pumps, brake cylinders, etc. Check timing belt for recent replacement. Highly likely to have been mini cabbed. Parts are expensive because in Japan cars of this age were scrapped years ago.

Celica (1985 to 1991)

What's good: Smart, front-drive coupes with 1,998cc twin cam 16 valve 147bhp engines. 14ft 3in long by 5ft 7in wide and from a substantial 1,280kg. California built cabrio from 1987 to 1988. Turbo GT Four with 182bhp from 1988 to 1991. Can last well.

What's bad: Getting old now. Steering light and not as involving as the European sports car norm. Turbos of GT4s can crack, gearboxes can give trouble, head gasket and big end problems not unknown.

What to watch out for: Rust: first places to go are the front wheel arches. Spares can be a problem. Best to join the club. Be very careful if buying a GT4 because it's highly stressed and an old car now.

Celica (1991 to 1994)

What's good: Weird-looking coupe. 201 bhp to 205 bhp GT-Four has warts and growths over its bonnet area. 'Carlos Sainz' GT-Four was collectable. Very quick, with excellent rally pedigree – notorious for being banned for a year for ingenious flouting of air restrictor rule. Basic front-wheel-drive models have 158 bhp, which is enough. Handle well. Good to drive. Toyota had fourth lowest average cost in warranty claims for cars up to 10 years old in 2002 Warranty Direct index, check online at www.performanceindex.co.uk

What's bad: It really is ugly in an organic way – like something designed for 'Alien' by H. Gigor. All models have a firm ride. The interior is black as a coal mine. Reliability of front-drive models is typically Toyota, but GT-Four power train comes under strain.

What to watch out for: GT-Four is a gearbox breaker. Must have specialist service history, but even then gearbox may fail. All need six-monthly oil changes, preferably using fully synthetic oil. Watch out for used RHD imports from Japan. May not be fully up to UK spec.

Celica (1994 to 2000)

What's good: Very good-looking car, especially the convertible. GT-Four has 240 bhp. Front-drive GT has 173 bhp. Cut-price 1.8ST much slower with just 114 bhp, but this is enough for cruiser types. Good seating position and good steering. Typical Toyota reliability. 12th from top in 'R' reg. J.D. Power Customer Satisfaction Survey. In June 2001 Toyota was rated by Motor Warranty Direct as Britain's 3rd most claim-free used marque (check online at www.warrantydirect.co.uk) BMW, Toyota and Ford jointly suffered the fewest breakdowns attended by German ADAC during 2001. 9th from top for reliability in *Auto Express* 2002 survey. 13th equal from Top in 144 car 2002 JD Power/*What Car?* Customer Satisfaction Survey of V and W reg. cars. Toyota had fourth lowest average cost in warranty claims for cars up to 10 years old in 2002 Warranty Direct index, check online at www.performanceindex.co.uk

What's bad: Strange set of gear ratios and generally a softer car than the previous Celica. Doesn't handle or hold the road as well.

What to watch out for: GT-Four may follow in footsteps of old model and break its gearbox. Must have specialist service history (from Toyota or Japanese performance car specialists such as Intech or Protech) All need six-monthly oil changes, preferably using fully synthetic oil. Watch out for used RHD imports from Japan brought in at half the UK price. May not be fully up to UK spec. Watch out for 1.8s disguised as 2.0s. Could have been a drug dealer's car.

Celica (from 2000)

What's good: Entire car has been re-thought. Now 101 mm shorter with much better steering and handling than previous car. Six-speed manual or sequential four-speed auto. Standard 1.8 VVT-i has 140 bhp, but 1.8 litre Celica 190 has 192 bhp, and 133 lb ft, giving

0–60 in 7 seconds and a top speed of 140 mph. Best colour is dark metallic blue. List prices cut to from £16,995 for 140bhp but increased from £19,995 to £20,495 for Celica 190. Probably the best handling front wheel drive car you can buy, and the extra 52 bhp of the 190 makes it better still. By far the best 2.0 litre coupe. Highly recommended. BMW, Toyota and Ford jointly suffered the fewest breakdowns attended by German ADAC during 2001. 9th from top for reliability in *Auto Express* 2002 survey. 13th equal from Top in 144 car 2002 JD Power/*What Car?* Customer Satisfaction Survey of V and W reg. cars. Recommended.

What's bad: Not much leg or head room in the back.

What to watch out for: Grey imports not to UK spec.

Corolla (1983 to 1987)

What's good: World's best selling car by a long way. Simple 1,295cc 65bhp engine with front drive and rear wheel drive on estates. 13ft 7in long, 5ft 5in wide, light weight of 890–925kg. 5-speed manual with 3 speed auto option. 74bhp from March 1985. GT rear wheel drive 2–door coupe with 1,588cc 122bhp twin cam engine from Feb 1984 to August 1987 and 3–door front drive GT hatch with same engine from March 1985 to August 1987. Haynes manual: 0683.

What's bad: Getting really old now. Likely to have had a long hard life and to have served time as a mini cab.

What to watch out for: Almost bound to have been owner-maintained. But so cheap, if it runs and has a long MOT you can buy it to run until its ticket runs out.

Corolla (1987 to 1991)

What's good: Next generation of front drive Corolla. Tried and proven 1,390cc 74bhp, 1,587cc 94bhp and 1,587cc GTi-16 123bhp engines: saloon, hatchback and estate car bodies. four wheel drive estate 1988 to 1991. Pre-cat. Haynes manual: 1683. 1.6 Executive quite smart. Capable of high mileage and staggering long-term reliability.

What's bad: Light steering. Uninvolving to drive. Thin sheetmetal.

Yet weight up quite a lot on previous Corolla: now 1,050 to 1,185kg.

What to watch out for: Should be cheap, but not quite throwaway, so don't pay too much for an ex-minicab. Rust quite badly (surprisingly, worse than previous model).

Corolla (1992 to 1997)

What's good: The world's most popular car (even though Corolla can mean different cars in different markets). Blandly efficient and extremely reliable over first 5 years or so. Easy but dull to drive. 87 bhp 1.3 quite powerful, but economical. 1.6 has 113 bhp. Autos on 1.3s are 3-speed; on 1.6s are 4-speed. Full range of hatchbacks, saloons and estates. Well regarded and hold their value well. Has been top or near top in J.D. Power Customer Satisfaction Surveys. In June 2001 Toyota was rated by Motor Warranty Direct as Britain's 3rd most claim-free used marque (check online at www.warrantydirect.co.uk) BMW, Toyota and Ford jointly suffered the fewest breakdowns attended by German ADAC during 2001. Toyota had fourth lowest average cost in warranty claims for cars up to 10 years old in 2002 Warranty Direct index, check online at www.performanceindex.co.uk

What's bad: Too bland, too dull for enthusiasts (this is not a criticism – they are deliberately made this way).

What to watch out for: Early cars had 6,000–mile service intervals and all need an oil change every 6,000 miles or every 6 months (whichever comes first) if you want to them to last. Quite likely to have been mini-cabbed and clocked, so look for excessive back seat wear and tear, worn door mechanisms, etc. Look for signs of a tow hook as may have been towing something too heavy. Estates may have had a hard life visiting cash & carrys for small businesses. Look for signs of sagging rear springs, damage to trim inside load area.

Corolla (1997 to 2002)

What's good: The market took to the somewhat jokey re-style. Looks by far the best as a 3–door in silver. Huge range of cars offered as 3–door or 5–door hatches, 4–door saloon, 5–door estate. Five- or six-speed manual gearboxes, or three- or four-speed automatic. GS models all have aircon. Limited range of engines – just an 85 bhp 1.3 16v, a 109 bhp 1.6, or a 71 bhp 2.0 litre diesel. Manufacturer 3-year warranty. Five lap and diagonal seatbelts. Three-Star above-average performance in NCAP crash tests. Restyled at the front for 2000 with new 95 bhp 1.4 litre and 109 bhp 1.6 litre VVT-i engines, 90 bhp 1.9 HDI diesel and six-speed gearbox for 1.6SR. List prices cut to from £8,995 still with three year warranty as from October 2000. Seventh from top in 'R' reg. J.D. Power Customer Satisfaction Survey, but see 'What's Bad' for latest model. S and T reg. cars came not quite so good 18th in 2001 *Top Gear*/JD Power Customer Satisfaction Survey. Came top in this year's German ADAC reliability survey. In June 2001 Toyota was rated by Motor Warranty Direct as Britain's 3rd most claim-free used marque. Sixth most reliable car in 2001 Fleet News Survey of 620,000 fleet cars mostly under 3 years old. (check online at www.warrantydirect.co.uk) BMW, Toyota and Ford jointly suffered the fewest breakdowns attended by German ADAC during 2001. 13th from top of 100 models for reliability in *Auto Express* 2002 survey. 10th from Top in 144 car 2002 JD Power/*What Car?* Customer Satisfaction Survey of V and W reg. cars. Toyota had fourth lowest average cost in warranty claims for cars up to 10 years old in 2002 Warranty Direct index, check online at www.performanceindex.co.uk

What's bad: 1997–1999 1.3G6 6-speed manual with ABS is a bit of an oddity. 1.3 with 3-speed auto is fairly slow and can lead to worrying moments when overtaking (no 1.4 auto in the Y2K range). Very 'Corolla'-like to drive, so expect bland efficiency rather than fun. British-built Y2K models proving to be less reliable than predecessors with reports of front wheel bearing and ECU failures. Complaints that instruments of Y2K restyle are difficult to read in daylight.

What to watch out for: Repaired accident damage (a surprisingly high proportion seem to be involved in minor 'dings'). Still a new car so to remain under warranty will have needed to be serviced on time by a Toyota dealer.

Corolla (from 2002)

What's good: All new Corolla range unveiled at the 2001 Frankfurt Motor Show and launched in the UK on 2/1/2002. As well as a three-door hatchback, a five-door hatchback, a saloon, and an estate, in line with the Yaris and Avensis, there is an MPV called the Corolla Verso and, like the Yaris, there is a high performance 189bhp T Sport. Three and five-door hatchback models built in the UK at Burnaston. Engine choice includes two 2.0–litre common-rail diesel engines (89bhp and 109bhp), and a selection of three VVT-i (Variable Valve Timing–intelligent) petrol engines, ranging from a 95bhp 1.4 through a 108bhp 1.6 and a 139bhp 1.8–litre version. At the top of the range, the 189bhp 1.8 T Sport features VSC (Vehicle Stability Control), Brake Assist and the same 1.8–litre VVTL-i (Variable Valve Timing and Lift–intelligent) high performance engine used in the Celica T Sport, linked to a 6-speed gearbox. Prices from £10,795 for the T2 3–door 1.4 hatch to £16,995 for the T Spirit 1.8 Verso auto. 2.0 109bhp D-4D Spirit 5–dr emits 154g/km, VED band B (£130), combined consumption 48.7mpg, price £15,995. 2.0 89bhp D-4D T3Verso emits 164g/km, VED band B (£130), combined consumption 47.8mpg, price £15,495. 189bhp T Sport 6-speed does 140mph, gets to 60 in 8.2 seconds, emits 198g/km CO_2, VED band D (£155), combined consumption 34.mpg, price £15,495. All models have electric power steering. A useful cross the range extra is 'City Collection' which consists of parking sensors and bumper corner protectors at £285.95. Another useful extra is Toyota's Traffic Avoidance System which combines satellite navigation with electronic traffic avoidance, alerting the driver to congestion on his or her route and feeding them around it. Previous model was 13th from top of 100 models for reliability in *Auto Express* 2002 survey. Seems too light at first, but actually drives and handles very well indeed. Recommended. See road test of 1.6 T Spirit online at www.honestjohn.co.uk

More online at www.Toyota.co.uk

What's bad: Too soon to say, but probably very little. In its first pix, the standard 5–door model looks remarkably like a Skoda Fabia.

What to watch out for: No complaints yet.

Recalls: May 2002: 6,600 UK market 3 and 5–door Corollas built at Burnaston recalled for bolts on rear stub axles to be re-torqued.

Eco Spirit Cubic (ES3) concept only

What's good: Toyota's ES3 (Eco Spirit Cubic) prototype is probably the most efficient, environmentally friendly four-seater car yet built. With its aluminium and resin body the car weighs just 700kg and has a Cd value of 0.23. The engine is a turbocharged 1.4–litre direct-injection diesel engine combined with a continuously variable transmission (CVT). The exhaust system includes a Diesel Particulate-NOx Reduction System and emissions conform to Euro IV for petrol engines. An idling stop mode automatically shuts off the engine when the vehicle is stopped, and regenerative braking technology is included to achieve higher efficiency. While the use of improved Toyota Super Olefin Polymer and biodegradable plastic greatly improve recyclability. The key to the ES3ft s outstanding fuel economy of 104.6mpg (2.7 litres/100km) and CO_2 emissions of 71g/km is a highly efficient powertrain, combined with a light and aerodynamic body. The main powertrain is a 1.4–litre, direct-injection, common-rail diesel with variable geometry turbocharger and charge-air intercooler, mated to a continuously variable transmission. The common-rail direct injection system is electronically controlled to deliver reduced emissions and lower noise and vibration levels. A newly developed CVT, with a torque converter, contributes to ES3 fuel efficiency. It also helps keep emissions low and adds to the enjoyable driving performance. A braking energy regenerating system is used to convert vehicle deceleration energy to electric energy for storage in a capacitor. The stored electric energy is used for auxiliary electric loads and for restarting the engine. This allows for reduced engine workload in generating the required volume of electricity, thus, providing further reduction in fuel consumption. The ES3 is very aerodynamic with a target drag coefficient of Cd0.23, despite its length of only 3.52 metres. The front features an optimised cooling intake and a special bumper configuration that flows smoothly to the body side and bottom. The roofline flows gently downward to the rear, while the rear sides narrow, forming a sheer back. The floor height is raised to increase the amount of airflow under the car and the underfloor surfaces have been smoothed to increase airflow speed. An raised rear floor provides great improvement of airflow convergence at the rear end of body. In addition, an optimally shaped rear under spoiler, bracket type door mirrors, flat wheel covers and the shape of the rocker covers all contribute to outstanding aerodynamics and exceptional stability at high speeds. Dimensions are: length 3,520mm; width 1,630mm; height 1,460mm. In simplified form, may become the Peugeot/Toyota joint venture basic car (see Peugeot 007).

More online at www.Toyota.co.uk

What's bad: So far, no more than a concept, but could be put into production (the Toyota Prius was).

What to watch out for: Too soon to say.

FXS Concept Car

What's good: First Shown at the Tokyo Motor Show from 26–10–2001, FXS is short for Future Experimental Sports, a two-seater roadster with a curvy body. In Toyotaspeak. "The FXS has been designed under the theme of a simple and sexy form with a sense of presence and has a wide and low slung body that expresses beauty on wheels, contrasting areas of brilliant lustre against those of elusive shade. Its full leather interior is highlighted by touches of chrome and bluish-white illuminated dials set within a deep blue background." Engine is the 4.3 litre V8 from the Lexus LS430, mated to a six-speed sequential manual transmission. Suspension is double-wishbone all-round. Toyota is showing 16 other concept vehicles at the show, so production of this one is probably unlikely.

What's bad: Concept Car only.

What to watch out for: Too soon to say.

Landcruiser Amazon (from 1996)

What's good: Huge, big, restyled VX 'Landbruiser'. Power of 4.2 litre diesel rose from 165 bhp to 201 bhp with 317 lb ft torque. Still with gear-driven overhead camshaft, so no belts or chains to worry about. Official combined fuel consumption 25.4 mpg. Also even more powerful 4.5 litre V8 version. Seven forward-facing seats. List prices cut by £3,000 in October 2000. S and T reg. cars came 20th in 2001 *Top Gear*/JD Power Customer Satisfaction Survey. In June 2001 Toyota was rated by Motor Warranty Direct as Britain's 3rd most claim-free used marque (check online at www.warrantydirect.co.uk) BMW, Toyota and Ford jointly suffered the fewest breakdowns attended by German ADAC during 2001. Toyota had fourth lowest average cost in warranty claims for cars up to 10 years old in 2002 Warranty Direct index, check online at www.performanceindex.co.uk4.2 diesel recommended.

What's bad: Too big to be safe for the school run. 202 bhp 4.5 litre V8 does just 17 mpg combined.

What to watch out for: If history is not impeccable, highly likely to have been clocked. Avoid oilwell-emptying petrol version. Lots of strange spec imports around, some five rather than seven seaters.

Landcruiser Colorado (1996 to 2002)

What's good: 3 litre 123 bhp 4-cylinder diesel manual or automatic, or 176 bhp 3.4 litre V6 petrol automatic with cruise control. Most have five doors. Re-styled for 2000 model year. List prices cut by £2,500 in October 2000. New 3.0 litre common rail direct injected diesel engine from 1/2/2001. The new engine puts out 161bhp but, more importantly for a 4x4, a stonking 253 lb ft torque (343Nm) at just 1,600 rpm. Prices start at £23,795, rising to £31,695. Fuel consumption is quoted at 30.1mpg on the combined cycle and CO_2 emissions 287g/km. In June 2001 Toyota was rated by Motor Warranty Direct as Britain's 3rd most claim-free used marque (check online at www.warrantydirect.co.uk) BMW, Toyota and Ford jointly suffered the fewest breakdowns attended by German ADAC during 2001. Toyota had fourth lowest average cost in warranty claims for cars up to 10 years old in 2002 Warranty Direct index, check online at www.performanceindex.co.uk

What's bad: 3–door version dropped September 1998. Cylinder heads of early 3.0 diesels are prone to failure and cost £2,000 to replace. Toyota replaced many FOC and solved the problem by 1999.

What to watch out for: Check history very carefully and don't buy from itinerants. Make sure cylinder head hasn't failed by looking for muck in expansion tank, emulsion under oil filler cap and white smoke from exhaust. Make sure the Colorado you're buying isn't really a Prado, unless, of course, it's at the much lower Prado price.

Landcruiser Colorado (from late 2002)

What's good: New Colorado due end of 2002, will have benefited from the continuous development of the old one. Awaiting information, but almost inevitably will be tough and reliable.

What's bad: Too soon to say.

What to watch out for: Too soon to say.

Landcruiser VX (1990 to 1996)

What's good: Huge, big, brutal 165 bhp 4.2 litre diesel capable of towing a Jag on a trailer at 100 mph. Has gear-driven camshaft rather than belt or chain. Seven forward-facing seats. Auto available, but manual best. In June 2001 Toyota was rated by Motor Warranty Direct as Britain's 3rd most claim-free used marque (check online at www.warrantydirect.co.uk) BMW, Toyota and Ford jointly suffered the fewest breakdowns attended by German ADAC during 2001.

What's bad: Almost certain to have been used as a towcar, probably pulling something heavy. A lot used by people of no fixed abode to tow chrome plated caravans. Clocking is rife. Too big to be safe for the school run.

What to watch out for: If history is not impeccable, highly likely to have been clocked. Avoid oilwell-emptying petrol version.

MR2 (1985 to 1990)

What's good: Better-executed Fiat X19 successor, with revvy 1.6 litre twin-cam set sideways in the middle. Super handling, great fun to drive and just enough performance not to be dangerous. Good value new. Held its price extremely well. Has developed a cult following.

What's bad: So many were thrashed and crashed or rusted out that good ones are now regarded as classics and fetch top money ('Parker's Guide' prices are usually about right.) No bootspace of any significance.

What to watch out for: They rust badly. Smart, fresh paint is likely to hide basinfuls of 'pudding'. Feel all round the edges for crumbly bits. Look inside the front boot for rust, fresh paint and signs it has been front ended. Brake balance is all-important on these cars – not enough bias to rear and the front wheels will lock up in the wet. DIY kerbside servicing can't do a proper job as they need to be up on a ramp. Driveshafts start to clonk, diffs whine, gearbox bearings get noisy, valve stem seals go, electric window and headlight motors fail. Check tyres for uneven wear – may signify crash, kerbing or simply misalignment. Check floorpan for leak damage from T-bar roof.

MR2 (1990 to 2000)

What's good: Bigger, much more powerful car than the original. Moved into a different league. Base model had just 119 bhp, but 'GT' had 158 bhp. Improved from March 1992 with bigger 15in alloys, better suspension, Yokohama tyres. The real improvements came in March 1994 with better suspension, ABS and power boosted to 174 bhp. Ex Japanese market MR2 Turbo imports with 225bhp plus seen at UK auction for as little as £3,000. March 94–August 96 is the model to have. In June 2001 Toyota was rated by Motor Warranty Direct as Britain's 3rd most claim-free used marque (check online at www.warrantydirect.co.uk) BMW, Toyota and Ford jointly suffered the fewest breakdowns attended by German ADAC during 2001. Toyota had fourth lowest average cost in warranty claims for cars up to 10 years old in 2002 Warranty Direct index, check online at www.performanceindex.co.uk

What's bad: A much more 'lardy' car than the original: 300kg heavier at 1,275kg. 1990–92 models had a reputation for swapping ends, especially in the wet. 92–94 variable rate power steering can be a liability on a mid-engined car and power catalysed down to 154 bhp. After 1994 boost, power cut back to 168 bhp from August 1996. Front suspension geometry easy to knock out of alignment by potholes or road humps, leading to heavy front tyre wear. Rear suspension adjustment rusts up and seizes. New, cheaper lightweight replacement arrived in 1999 in spirit of MX5 and original MR2.

What to watch out for: Grey Japanese second-hand imports may not pass UK emissions tests. (Turbos are all grey imports). Check all wheels for uneven tyre wear which could be due to accident damage, falling off the road, potholing, kerbing or may simply be misadjusted alignment. Full service history essential – either Toyota or Japanese performance car specialist. Needs 6–month services with fully synthetic oil. Make sure front brakes aren't snatching (needs new front-to-rear compensator, but may need new discs as well). Feel the state of the discs through the wheels and budget accordingly. Timing belt needs to be replaced every 30,000–40,000 miles and belt-driven water pump and tensioners at least every 70,000–80,000 miles, but belt replacement is a comparatively cheap £190 (engine does not have to come out).

MR2 (from April 2000)

What's good: MR2 went back to its routes and became a sporty spyder once again. All new 1.8 litre 140 bhp VVT-i engine. 0–60 in 7.9 seconds; tops out at 130 mph. Soft top has glass rather than plastic rear window and is very easy to raise and lower. Low weight: just 975kg, like original MR2. Combined mpg figure 38.2 mpg. UK cars have Thatcham 1 security system. Extra-cost sequential manual 5-speed sports shift works the right way round: lever back to change up; forwards to change down, but better still using press buttons on the steering wheel. This is the best version to drive because it enables you to more fully exploit the fantastic handling. A good driver in one of these can keep up with an average driver in a Mitsubishi EVO VI. Huge fun. Options include hard top, air conditioning, leather seat facings. Prices cut to from £17,995 still with three year warranty from October 2000, but available from trade Sales of Slough and Motorpoint of Derby at £14,999 without the extra two years warranty. Much better drive than MGF. Hold their value well. BMW, Toyota and Ford jointly suffered the fewest breakdowns attended by German ADAC during 2001. Toyota's UK base price cut by £850 to £17,130 from January 2002.

What's bad: Hardly any luggage space at all: just two small compartments behind the seats and barely enough for a briefcase under the bonnet. Power steering unnecessary. Small and low, so drivers need to be aware that other drivers may not see them. Demand ensures high used prices.

What to watch out for: Imports lack the Thatcham 1 security system.

Paseo (1996 to 1998)

What's good: Small non-sports coupe 13ft 82 long by 5ft 5in wide and reasonably light at 92okg. Had an 89bhp 1,497cc engine and five speed manual box. Pop-up and removable glass sunroof. Power steering on ST model. ABS on Si. Seems to be a car for the elderly who want Toyota reliability and coupe looks without performance. Same engine with reduced output is used to power the Prius. Toyota had fourth lowest average cost in warranty claims for cars up to 10 years old in 2002 Warranty Direct index, check online at www.performanceindex.co.uk

What's bad: Didn't get much of a reception from the car magazines and not many sold. Might start to be a parts problem quite soon.

What to watch out for: No feedback.

Picnic (1997 to 2001)

What's good: Scenic-sized six- or seven-seater. Seems to handle quite well. 2.0 litre 126 bhp engine same as RAV-4. Same five-speed manual or excellent four-speed auto as well. 2.2 litre IDI turbodiesel gives more mpg at expense of performance. GS is basic model with 7 seats. GLs and GXs have aircon and ABS. Four-star performer in NCAP crash tests (10 points front impact; 15 point side impact). Second-best MPV and 9th from top overall in 'R' reg. J.D. Power

Customer Satisfaction Survey. In June 2001 Toyota was rated by Motor Warranty Direct as Britain's 3rd most claim-free used marque (check online at www.warrantydirect.co.uk) BMW, Toyota and Ford jointly suffered the fewest breakdowns attended by German ADAC during 2001. Toyota had fourth lowest average cost in warranty claims for cars up to 10 years old in 2002 Warranty Direct index, check online at www.performanceindex.co.uk

What's bad: No luggage space when all six or seven seats in use. Seats don't fold very cleverly, but rear pair can be removed. Clutch on diesel Picnics reported to be short-lived and troublesome.

What to watch out for: Unlikely to have been a taxi. Most likely to have been privately owned. Trim may have received 'deposits' from very young children, sticky sweets may be stuck in seams. Dogs may have crocodiled the upholstery. Check clutch of manual diesels carefully.

Previa (1990 to 2000)

What's good: One of the bigger MPVs with room for up to 8 and their luggage inside. 15ft 7in long by 5ft 11in wide and weighing from 1,730kg. 135bhp 2,438cc four cylinder engine under the floor and rear wheel drive. 5-speed floor-change or 3-speed plus overdrive column shift auto. Good build quality. Oldest are now affordable and can be 'de-catted' if necessary to save expense. Was also a slightly narrower Japanese market Lucida Emina which looked the same and could be had as a diesel automatic 4x4. In June 2001 Toyota was rated by Motor Warranty Direct as Britain's 3rd most claim-free used marque (check online at www.warrantydirect.co.uk) BMW, Toyota and Ford jointly suffered the fewest breakdowns attended by German ADAC during 2001. Toyota had fourth lowest average cost in warranty claims for cars up to 10 years old in 2002 Warranty Direct index, check online at www.performanceindex.co.uk

What's bad: Only one sliding side door on the nearside. No diesel, supercharged petrol or 4x4 in UK. Only one petrol engine (but ripe for an LPG conversion). Auto holds its gears for a long time, can be frenetically noisy and a bit juicy.

What to watch out for: One sliding rear door may preclude use as a taxi under some local authority rules. Airport taxis do huge mileages they may not show. 8–seater versions best. 6 'captain's' chairs pointless. Cylinder head gaskets can go if coolant not changed every two years. Look for mayonnaise under oil filler cap and in coolant expansion tank (though, since these are remote from the engine, it may not have reached that far). White exhaust smoke also indicates head gasket problems. Rear diffs eventually whine. Interior may have been trashed by kids or 'crocodiled' by dogs. Catalytic converters go eventually. On the GS, the single pop-up sunroof was fitted at port of entry. Sometimes they ran out, so no sunroof on a GS does not necessarily mean a non UK car. Diesel 4x4s are all Lucida Emina grey imports. Slightly narrower than Previa.

Previa (from 2000)

What's good: Huge, all-new Previa now with sliding rear doors on both sides. Still offered as a six-, seven- or eight-seater. Plenty of room for luggage, even with eight passengers aboard. Has 2.4 litre VVT-i petrol engine developing 154 bhp and 166 lb ft torque. Now front rather than rear-wheel-drive with 5-speed manual or 3-speed column shift autobox with press-button overdrive. 0–60 in around 11 seconds for either with 115 mph top speed. Official 'combined' fuel consumption 30.0 mpg manual; 26.9 mpg auto. 114bhp 2.0 litre D-4D diesel engine option offering 184lb ft torque (250Nm) at 1,800 rpm with 5-speed manual box from May 2001, list prices of diesels from £21,450. 191g/km CO_2. Combined mpg 39.2.
What's bad: Rear bench seat of eight-seater not completely removable. Severe roll understeer. Doesn't like two sudden changes of direction in a row.
What to watch out for: No serious problems reported. Lots of independent imports about, new and used, so make sure you know what you're paying for.

Prius (from 2000)

What's good: The first hybrid car on general sale and a proper 4/5 seater hatchback. 1,496cc 58 bhp VVT-i engine feels bigger.

Combined dash-mounted automatic transmission selector and parking brake. Excess power output charges a bank of nickel-metal hydride batteries, which are also charged by regenerative braking when descending hills. These feed a 40 bhp electric motor. The engine switches itself off at rest and the car moves off on its electric motor, starting its ic engine when needed. It works remarkably well and the car even has a lively feel to it. Very low carbon dioxide emissions of 114g/km – already meets Euro 2005 emissions limits. Annual VED from March 2001 just £90 (dropped to £60 from April 2002 due to low 114g/km CO_2). London Congestion Charge exempt. Official urban fuel consumption figure an incredible 61.4 mpg. Air conditioning and CD radio included in UK price of £16,495. First 200 sold in UK qualify for £1,000 Powershift grant bringing the price down to £15,495. BMW, Toyota and Ford jointly suffered the fewest breakdowns attended by German ADAC during 2001. Highly recommended. Dedicated website: www.prius.co.uk

What's bad: Beaten to the UK market by the two-seater, much sportier Honda Insight. Real life economy doesn't seem to match the government figures.

What to watch out for: Just don't expect to equal the government figures, especially if the car is used mostly about town where the hybrid system doesn't get a chance to work properly.

RAV 4 (1994 to 2000)

What's good: The first fashion 4x4 that really was car-like to drive. Strong performance from 126 bhp twin cam 2.0 litre Celica engine. Manuals have a centre diff lock; autos don't. Autobox is typically excellent Toyota with good ratios and is fully controllable (does 60 in second). 5–door versions are more practical and handle better, 3–doors are faster and more fun. Nice low rear load height for dogs, etc. Reasonably economical (30 mpg). Typical Toyota reliability. In June 2001 Toyota was rated by Motor Warranty Direct as Britain's 3rd most claim-free used marque (check online at www.warrantydirect.co.uk)BMW, Toyota and Ford jointly suffered the fewest breakdowns attended by German ADAC during 2001. Top for reliability in *Auto Express* 2002 survey. Toyota had fourth lowest

average cost in warranty claims for cars up to 10 years old in 2002 Warranty Direct index, check online at www.performanceindex.co.uk
What's bad: Not great in an 'elk avoidance test'. Rear seat of 5–door slopes forwards and is situated over rear wheels, so not comfortable. Suspension wishbones hang too low for serious off-roading.
What to watch out for: Bent suspension wishbones. Uneven tyre wear. Don't buy one with silly, over-large wheels and ridiculous running boards or you'll lose a lot of money on resale. Make sure you know what you're buying and don't pay full UK retail price for an independent import.

RAV 4 (from 2000)

What's good: Freshly restyled swb 3–door and lwb 5–door. Choice of front-wheel-drive with 1.8 litre VVT-i engine and 123 bhp or four-wheel-drive with 2.0 litre VVT-i and 148 bhp. Rear seats now slide, fold, double fold or can be removed altogether. Official 'combined' fuel consumption: 1.8 is 38 mpg; 2.0 is 32 mpg; 2.0 auto is 30.36 mpg. Typical Toyota reliability. List prices reduced to from £13,495 (1.8 2WD short wheelbase) from October 2000 still with three year warranty. D-4D common rail direct injected diesel engine option from September 2001 in both three and five door bodies. Main benefits are an EU combined fuel consumption figure of 39.8mpg and a CO_2 output of 190g/km (£160pa VED; 23% list price BIK tax base) for the three door. D-4D develops 114bhp (85kW) at 4,000rpm and offers constant torque of 184 lb ft (250Nm) across the power band from 1,800rpm to 3,000rpm giving a top speed of 106mph and a useful 0–60 of 11.9 seconds. This broad torque band is also very useful for off-roading, of course. D-4D RAV4s from £15,995 (NV Three-door) or £17,495 (NV Five-door), including a full three year or 60,000 mile mechanical warranty. No automatic option for the D-4D. BMW, Toyota and Ford jointly suffered the fewest breakdowns attended by German ADAC during 2001. Top for reliability in *Auto Express* 2002 survey.
     More online at www.Toyota.co.uk
What's bad: Soundly beaten off road by the Nissan X-Trail, but that's not the point.

What to watch out for: No serious complaints. But again, make sure you don't pay UK money for an import lacking things like Thatcham I security system.

Space Cruiser/Town Ace (1983 to 1995)

What's good: Compact at 14ft 1in by 5ft 6in and offering up to 8 seats inside. 1,812cc 78bhp engine from 1983 to 1985; 1,998cc 88bhp from then on. Five on the tree manual or three speed + overdrive auto. Twin sunroofs, alloy wheels and moquette cloth trim add to the ambiance. Space Cruiser replace by Previa in UK in 1990, but Lite Ace van based Town Ace continued in Japan and other Far East markets. Many have found their way to the UK, usually with diesel engines, four wheel drive and automatic transmission. Can be reliable. Used to be favoured by mini-cabbers before they graduated to Lucida Estimas.

What's bad: Basically, a forward-control van with driver and front passenger sitting either side of the engine. Strange seating configuration, but can include swivelling centre seats so the passengers in the back can face each other. Often had privacy glass and/or curtains. They drive like a van with a continually pitching motion, not like a car. Can cost fortunes in repairs. Not recommended.

What to watch out for: Spacecruisers are all old and are usually rusty. Town Aces were usually bought as scrap for next to nothing in Japanese auctions, shipped over to the UK and resold for £4,999 at the roadside. Often clocked. No chance of checking the history. Variable parts availability, so look out for bodging under the bonnet.

Starlet (1990 to 1996)

What's good: Toyota's smallest car (in the UK anyway). Very light weight, starting at 710kg. Good little 12-valve 1.0 litre 54 bhp and 1.3 litre 74 bhp engines. 1.0 litre dropped in January 1993. Totally reliable for the first five years. 3-year warranty. In June 2001 Toyota was rated by Motor Warranty Direct as Britain's 3rd most claim-free used marque (check online at www.warrantydirect.co.uk) BMW, Toyota and Ford jointly suffered the fewest breakdowns attended by German ADAC during 2001. Toyota had fourth lowest average cost in warranty claims for cars up to 10 years old in 2002 Warranty Direct index, check online at www.performanceindex.co.uk

What's bad: No power steering. Not very well packaged. Limited rear seat and load area. Expensive new.

What to watch out for: Lots of 'specials' such as 'Kudos'. Tend to be owned by uninterested people who want no more than a very small, reliable car. Make sure it has been serviced regularly and that the owner hasn't 'forgotten'. Look for evidence of parking dings, behind-bumper damage. May need a cambelt change.

Starlet (1996 to 1999)

What's good: Better styled, better value and better packaged. New 1,332cc 74 bhp engine and 3-speed automatic option. PAS standard on 5–dr manual and 3–dr and 5–dr auto. Heavier, but still a reasonable 830kg. Totally reliable for the first five years. 3-year warranty. Wider range appeals to wider range of buyers than before. S and T reg. cars came 15th in 2001 *Top Gear*/JD Power Customer Satisfaction Survey. In June 2001 Toyota was rated by Motor Warranty Direct as Britain's 3rd most claim-free used marque (check online at www.warrantydirect.co.uk) BMW, Toyota and Ford jointly suffered the fewest breakdowns attended by German ADAC during 2001. Toyota had fourth lowest average cost in warranty claims for cars up to 10 years old in 2002 Warranty Direct index, check online at www.performanceindex.co.uk

What's bad: Sporty SR version not exactly sporty.

What to watch out for: If a 3–door manual, check that optional PAS has been fitted. Must have Toyota service history for remaining warranty to apply. Not much point in buying a used independent import of one of these unless you want air-conditioning and the price is right.

Yaris (from 1999)

What's good: New small Toyota 3 & 5–door hatch replaces Starlet, initially all with same 68 bhp 1.0 litre 16v VVTi iron block engine, but 85 bhp VVTi alloy 1.3 and 4-speed auto option from October 1999. Low parts prices, good reparability, low insurance groups, combined finance and servicing package, three-year 60,000–mile warranty, slide-forward back seat, option of 'Free-Tronic' automatic clutch with 5-speed gearbox. High seats make it easy for the elderly to get in and out of. Praised by road testers for its excellent steering, good handling and the roominess of its interior (far better than a Polo in all these respects). Unusual central digital speedometer set in a tunnel is clear and easy to read. Light years ahead of the Starlet it replaced. Price competitive with alternatives on UK market. Did reasonably well in German TUV front offset crash tests. Excellent Four-Star-plus rating in Euro NCAP crash tests. European 1999 Car of the Year. Prices cut to from £6,995 from October 2000, still with three year warranty. 1.5 T Sport launched March 2001 with sub 9 second 0–60 and 119mph top speed at a price of £11,995. S and T reg. cars came second in 2001 *Top Gear*/JD Power Customer Satisfaction Survey. High used values. New 74bhp, 125lb ft torque chain-cam 1,364cc D4–D diesel from March 2002 offers 12.6 seconds 0–60, 106mph top speed, 67.3mpg combined economy and 113g/km CO_2 output for prices from £8,395 in S trim with PAS. Engine is quiet, smooth with linear power delivery. Handling good. A great little car to drive. BMW, Toyota and Ford jointly suffered the fewest breakdowns attended by German ADAC during 2001. 3rd top for reliability in *Auto Express* 2002 survey. Top in 144 car 2002 JD Power/*What Car?* Customer Satisfaction Survey of V and W reg. cars. Toyota had fourth lowest average cost in warranty claims for cars up to 10 years old in 2002 Warranty Direct index, check online at www.performanceindex.co.uk highly recommended. See also Yaris Verso mini-MPV

What's bad: Annoyingly, 5–door versions only available in GS trim. This pushes starter price of D-4D 5–door to £9,895. Now also built in France and quality may suffer. Bonnet is prone to paint chips. 'Space saver' emergency wheel not liked by Brits. Can't yet be bought used at bargain prices.

What to watch out for: Build quality problems starting to emerge.

Recalls: 18/4/2000: 19,639 Yarises built Jan 1999 to Jan 2000. Brake proportioning valve may cause car to become unstable under braking. Modified valve to be fitted. 29/8/2001: 700 Yaris models built between February and June 2001 recalled because bolts on rear axle can become loose. (Source '*Auto Express*' 29/8/2001.)November 2001: Production period – June 18 to July 12 2001. Modification to Airbag (Install plate to airbag connector). 8/8/2001: 697 Yaris models recalled because bolts securing left and right hubs to axle beam may not have been tightened to the correct torque. Check and tighten as necessary.

Yaris Verso (from 2000)

What's good: Weird looking but very useful mini-MPV, ideally suited to the needs of the elderly. 85 bhp VVTi alloy 1.3 litre engine and 4-speed auto option. Supremely easy to step in and out of, with huge front-to-back grab handles to help. Rear door is side hinged on the right-hand side and sufficiently low for loading wheelchairs, etc. Removable false floor to rear enables the long-legged to be comfortably accommodated. Rear side seats fold away under this false floor, but narrower centre seat needs to be removed and stored. Easy to drive. Height-adjustable steering wheel. Handles surprisingly well with good steering and good front end grip (better than a Zafira). Automatic cruises at a relaxed 3,000 rpm at 70 mph. Very clear digital instrumentation. 3-year warranty. Discounted prices from £8,499 at Trade Sales of Slough (but don't include 3 year warranty). My recommended choice for elderly drivers and the disabled. Also see 'Toyota Yaris' above. S and T reg. cars came second in 2001 *Top Gear*/JD Power Customer Satisfaction Survey. Best colour: solid bright red. New 74bhp, 125lb ft torque chain-cam 1,364cc D4–D diesel from February 2002 offers 13.5 second 0–60, 99 mph top speed, 56.5mpg combined economy and 133g/km CO_2 output, from £11,395. BMW, Toyota and Ford jointly suffered the fewest breakdowns attended by German ADAC during 2001. 3rd top for reliability in *Auto Express* 2002 survey. Recommended.

What's bad: Looks not to everyone's taste. Quality from French factory may not match Far East built cars. Bonnet prone to paint chips. Quite a lot of rattles from dual height rear parcel shelf. First timers need to be careful folding the seats as fingers can be trapped.

Doors feel tinny and the car doesn't have any side protector strips – which it needs. Big gap between 4th and 3rd on automatic. Accessory Protection Pack includes door mats, mud flaps and door rubbing strips, but the strips fit too low to offer proper protection to the doors. 'Space saver' emergency wheel not liked by Brits. An ignition quirk on the petrol engined model can feel like the clutch is slipping on first pull away of the day.

What to watch out for: Build quality problems starting to emerge.

Recalls: 29/8/2001: 700 Yaris models built between February and June 2001 recalled because bolts on rear axle can become loose. (Source *'Auto Express'* 29/8/2001.)November 2001: Production period – June 18 to July 12 2001. Modification to Airbag (Install plate to airbag connector).

TVR

TVR

What's good: Hairy-chested all-British sports cars we can now feel proud of. Compact new AJP8 engine is utterly brilliant. New AJP6 'Speed Six' and Tuscan are promising, with 350 bhp 4,185cc six putting out 320 lb ft torque allied to six-speed gearbox. Older models still used modified Rover/Buick pushrod V8s. S1s, S2s and S3s had Ford pushrod V6s with 187 bhp (S3C). Late cars reliable and well put together. Some owners do 25,000 miles a year in them. Buy one and you buy into a club. Tuscan racing series well worth a watch. Company run by the hands-on owner, Peter Wheeler.

What's bad: Lack of problems by no means guaranteed. Many cars have an extremely hard ride and are very noisy. Cerbera coupe with AJP8 has very little flywheel effect and revs like a racing car which can catch out the unskilled with snap oversteer. S and T plate Chimaeras 13th from bottom in 2001 *Top Gear*/J.D. Power Customer Satisfaction Survey.

What to watch out for: Only buy from true enthusiasts or from TVR specialists. Be prepared to spend a few grand to get a used car the way you want it. Use your judgement or get the car checked by a TVR expert. HPI or AA/Experian history check also well advised as the car could have been bought on the drip, after which the 'owner' hit hard times. Block porosity of older 4.6 litre Rover V8s is a sign that these engines may have been over-bored. Check oil and coolant very carefully.

Recalls: 31/8/2001: 846 Cerberas and Tuscans built 16/12/1996 to 8/5/2001 recalled because build up of corrosion adjacent to front wheel bearing bore can cause the aluminium suspension upright to crack. Suspension uprights to be replaced with a new design where necessary and extra cover plate to be fitted to uprights showing no visible corrosion.

VAUXHALL

Agila (from 2000)

What's good: Five-door minibox based on Suzuki Wagon R. 12-year anti-perforation warranty. Same 1.0 litre 58 bhp and 1.2 litre 75 bhp engines. Upright and easy for the elderly to get in and out of. To receive Fiat's 60 bhp, 1.2 litre 100 mpg CDI diesel engine in 2002 or 2003. Three year warranty from October 2000.

What's bad: See Suzuki Wagon R. Four, not five, seats.

What to watch out for: As Suzuki Wagon R. Consumers Association members have reported transmission problems, fiddly head restraints and noisy suspension.

Astra (1984 to 1991)

What's good: Well-liked and still good enough to form the basis of the 1994–1997 Daewoo Nexia. 3–door and 5–door hatches and estates. Also spawned the rather ugly Belmont saloon. Engines from 54bhp 1.2, through 75bhp 1.3 (grew to 1.4 in 1990), 82bhp and 90bhp 1.6s, 112bhp 1.8s, 115bhp 2.0 GTE 8v and 150bhp 2.0 GTE 16v. GTE 16v was quick in a straight line. Nicely judged end-of-the-line SX and SXE hatches and estates. Hatchbacks were 13ft 1in long, 5ft 5in wide, weighed 840kg to 1,032kg. Also a convertible from May 1987 to June 1993.

What's bad: Solid blue and solid red paint both oxidise. Lacquers on metallics peel off. Hard, jiggly ride not matched by good handling and road feel. Dodgy digital instruments on GTEs. ABS pumps very expensive to replace. Belmont saloon is hideous. Pretty convertibles suffer severe scuttle shake. Getting old now and rusting.

What to watch out for: Could have done 400,000 miles, particularly diesel estates, so look for all the signs. Clutches stick (may need a cheap new cable or may have damaged bulkhead). Suspension bushes wear. Main problem is camshaft wear, which can be terminal for the engine. Listen for thrashing noises and look for signs of oil weeping from top of engine. Fuel evaporation problem with all late injected models. Check for driveshaft wear by doing reverse-turns in both directions. Split driveshaft boots are common and an MOT failure point. Regular 3,000–mile oil changes essential. If not, engines will sludge up and rattle. Cambelts must be changed every 35,000 miles; tensioners every 70,000 miles. Always lift the boot carpet and look for signs of accident damage repairs because bodyshells are very difficult to pull back into proper alignment. Check the floorpan of convertibles for rust caused by leaks.

Astra (1991 to 1998)

What's good: Model designation is 'F Type'. Not bad looking and with metallic paint gives impression of reasonable quality. Heavier than previous Astra at 930kg to 1,150kg. Estate car the most practical in the class. Convertible from June 1993. Useful improvements for 1995 ('V' grille) model year include power steering across the range and 'low pressure turbo' GM diesel. 67bhp LPT diesel estate the best buy and deservedly the most popular. 69bhp 1.6 E-Drive petrol engine slow, but very economical (45 mpg): a good choice if worried about diesel price increases. 'High torque' 60 bhp 1.4 8v the most popular engine, but even more short of puff than E-Drive. 89bhp 16 valve 1.4 and 99bhp 1.6 16v engines much more perky. GSi down on power on to 134bhp. 13ft 4in long but fatter 5ft 11in wide.

What's bad: Better than the Escort when it came out in 1991, but not much better. 4–door versions look hideous. Over-light power steering and severely lacklustre handling, even on 'Sport' and 'GSi' versions. 16 valve versions criticised for sticking valves – usually the owner's fault for driving short distances from cold starts on the cheapest petrol (switching to a high detergent petrol might cure the problem in a few hundred miles). On 1.4 16v, timing belt also drives the water pump, so if this fails it will lead to timing belt failure. Most likely reason for the water pump to fail is lack of water (coolant) so check this regularly. See Recalls re GF50 plastic timing belt pulleys. Misting up may be caused by cable from flap control to flap coming off or failure to fit replacement pollen filter into its seal correctly, allowing water to enter cabin and soak carpets. Door mirrors are 'snap-off', not sprung.

What to watch out for: Sagging rear suspension on hard-used ex-fleet estates. Kerbing damage to front suspension (look for uneven tyre wear). Worn front suspension bushes and steering joints. Damaged suspension arms from jacking by them. Unpleasant clutch action (might be cured cheaply with a new cable). Electric front windows can stick. Valve gear gets noisy with mileage and ambitious 9,000–10,000 mile oil changes. Valves of 16vs may stick if run on cheap detergent-free petrol. Unfortunately Vauxhall's cure for this seems to have been to ream out the valve guides a bit too much with the result that many 16v 1.6s have become oil burners. Petrol engine cambelts need changing every 35,000–40,000 miles. Floor around handbrake mounting and driver's seat mounting can crack (symptom: having to pull handbrake right up). This could be the reason why more than a few *Telegraph* readers complain of being unable to release the handbrake of Astras with drum rear brakes. Ex-Vauxhall Masterhire cars on full service contracts come with very comprehensive computerised service histories, itemised down to light bulb replacements. Watch out for dodgy histories in kerbside or auction sale cars. More likely than most to be clocked.

Recalls: 1995: fuel pipe, airbag. 1995 (TD: VIN S5000001 to S5241939; S2500001 to S2707652 and S8000001 to S8216827): chafing of wiring harness and possible fire risk. 1995: airbag may fail to inflate in an accident. 1995: static sparking during refuelling. 1997 (1993–1996 1.4 & 1.6 16vs only): 1999: possibility of failure of one or all of three GF50 plastic cambelt idler pulleys on 16v engines 1993–96, which can snap cambelt. Changed as an 'in service mod' when cambelts are changed at 35,000–40,000 mile intervals. (Vauxhall Recall Helpline: 01189 458500 or 01582 427200). 17/4/2000: 620,000 F-Type Astras built 1991–1999 recalled to check for water contamination of brake fluid and to fit rubber grommet to underside of bonnet. Customers to be advised that brake fluid is hygroscopic and a service item to be regularly replaced.

Astra (from 1998)

What's good: New G Type Astra vastly better than previous F Type. Steering, handling, roadholding now class-competitive. Longer at

13ft 6in, wider at 6ft 6in (including mirrors). Heavier at from 1,079kg upwards. Better steering feel than four-cylinder Golf Mk IVs. Three proper three-point rear seatbelts standard across the range. Ski-hatch to boot. Useful 'head up' information display. Four stars for secondary safety in 1999 NCAP tests. Long-lived direct-injected chain-cam 81bhp 16-valve small turbo 'DI' diesel works well in this car allied to excellent 4-speed autobox: gives 45 mpg. DI boosted to 99bhp DTi in September 2000. Decent build quality. Most UK cars built in UK at Ellesmere Port. Aircon often fitted. 160 bhp 2.0 litre GSi from autumn 1999. 187bhp turbo from May 2002. 147 bhp 2.2 litre chain cam four available from September 2000, plus uprated 125 bhp 1.8 petrol and uprated 85 bhp 1.6. Three year warranty from October 2000. Price cuts brought Astra 1.6i Club 5–door with a/c down to £11,225. 1.7 16v DI Eco emits just 119g/km CO_2, so is the largest diesel car to qualify for reduced rate £80pa VED from April 2002. 89bhp 1.4 16v, 74bhp 1.6 8v and 99bhp 1.6 16v also available as specific LPG fuelled models.

What's bad: Nondescript , 'hamster'-like road-hugging styling. Ride quality may be too firm for some. Is regarded as 'also ran' to Golf Mk IV and Ford Focus and does not hold its value as well. (This is something for the second-hand buyer to take advantage of.) DI 16v diesel has reputation as an oil burner. The real reason may be that oil collects in the 16v head and takes a long time to drain back to the sump. Dip within an hour of stopping and you will get a falsely low reading leading you to overfill with fresh oil which then gets burned. Diesel automatic dropped from line-up. DIs seem to need new mass/airflow sensors every 36,000 miles. Water leaks (see below). A problem seems to have developed with the ECUs of early 1.4 and 1.6s which are being replaced FOC on cars up to 4 years old. Springs fail in rear brake compensators and are not available as a separate part. A new compensator is £150 fitted. Timing belt and tensioner changes re-scheduled from 80,000 miles to 40,000 miles on engines which have them.

What to watch out for: Nearly-new examples likely to be ex-rental, so look for signs of careless driving such as kerbing. Check front tyres for uneven tread signifying suspension misalignment. A batch of faulty sealant left some mid-1999 Astras prone to condensation inside the headlights and foglights. Make sure it does have aircon and that the aircon blows cold. Lift front carpets and check for water underneath. The cure is either re-sealing the front bulkhead or re-sealing the pollen filter carrier. Blower fans fail. May also mist up because vent flap mechanism has broken. See recalls about noisy power steering pumps. The old Vauxhall Cavalier & Vectra steering column failure seems to have re-emerged with the G Type Astra, though Vauxhall will usually pay the replacement costs. One report of premature cat failure at 3 years and 35,000 miles. In this case, Vauxhall paid 50%.

Recalls: Depending on source of supply, some models developed noisy power steering pumps. Free-of-charge replacement programme spring 1999. 14/7/2000: 3,008 3–door models built between January 1998 and October 1998 recalled for replacement of front seat adjuster spring which can lose its tension. (Press release received 15/7/2000.) 2001: TSB about voltage spikes from the alternator damaging the camshaft sensor. This is prevented by unpicking the wiring loom and re-routing the cam and crankshaft sensor cables together around the front of the airbox, keeping them away from the alternator.

Astra Coupe/Convertible (from 2000)

What's good: Debut car for Vauxhall's new family of chain cam ECOTEC petrol engines (has 2.2 litre 147 bhp version). Decent performance. Three year warranty from October 2000. 190bhp Turbo version launched November 2000 at £18,995 will clock up 151mph. Convertible from Spring 2001 is much prettier than the coupe. Turbo Convertible from March 2002 offers same performance as turbo coupe but with soft top at £19,995. It's the quickest four seater convertible for the money.

What's bad: Ordinary coupe dull to look at and very disappointing to drive. Rattly, crashy, felt unfinished. Turbo is much better to drive, but all are utterly shamed by the Toyota Celica. Turbo has belt cam 2.0 litre engine. Timing belt and tensioner changes re-scheduled from 80,000 miles to 40,000 miles on engines which have them.

What to watch out for: Too soon to say.
Recalls: 2001: TSB about voltage spikes from the alternator damaging the camshaft sensor. This is prevented by unpicking the wiring loom and re-routing the cam and crankshaft sensor cables together around the front of the airbox, keeping them away from the alternator.

Astra Signum from 2004

What's good: Started as a concept car with engines up to a 4.3 litre 330bhp V8. But now thought to be the basis of the next Astra. Engine range from FIAT sourced 1.3 diesel to GM's 211bhp 3.2 V6.
What's bad: Too soon to say.
What to watch out for: Too soon to say.

Calibra (1989 to 1998)

What's good: Good-looking, practical Cavalier-based four-seater coupe with a big, golf-bag-sized boot. Some good engines in the line-up. Some very fast, very powerful cars such as 201bhp six-speed 4x4 turbo. Some nice trim combinations. 168bhp 2.5 V6s with leather and white instruments on 'R' plates can represent a lot of coupe for the money. Usefully had a lever behind the headlights to switch from left dip to right dip for continental driving (explained in the driver's manual).
What's bad: Hard to see out of and very difficult to reverse. Though it handles better than the Cavalier it still suffers from the understeering limitations. Front-drive Calibras will always come off the road front-first. Six-speed gearbox on 4x4 turbo fails and costs a fortune to replace. Bulkhead may crack around steering rack mountings. On 2.0 litre 16v models a problem can develop with the idle adjustor control valve necessitating replacement and modifying by the fitting of an oil separator. Plug leads deteriorate and are ridiculously expensive to replace.
What to watch out for: Ex-Vauxhall Masterhire cars previously on service contracts come with trustworthy print-out of full service history, including cambelt changes every 36,000–40,000 miles.

Listen for steering creaks and look for cracks around steering rack bulkhead mounting points, a £700 job to repair. Abbot Racing of Spinnels Farm, Manningtree (tel: 01255 870636) have a means of mounting the rack more rigidly, and also replacing the soft rubber suspension bushes which not only solves the problem but makes the car steer and handle much better.

Recalls: 1999: possibility of failure of plastic cambelt idler pulley GF50 on 16v engines 1993–96, which can snap cambelt. Changed as an 'in service mod' when cambelts are changed at 35,000–40,000 mile intervals. (Vauxhall Recall Helpline: 01189 458500 or 01582 427200) June 2000 recall of V6 models due to crankshaft fault.

Carlton (1986 to 1994)

What's good: Solid, German-built saloons and estates capable of mileages of 300,000 or more with little trouble. Big, comfortable, well-liked by many owners, particularly 'Strasbourg' box automatics. 15ft 4in long, 5ft 10in wide, weighed between 1,166kg (1.8GL saloon) and 1,471kg (3.0iCDX estate). Strong loyalty factor. Good handling and ride. Pre-August 1992 may be pre-cat (check for fuel filler restrictor). Estate car has a huge capacity. Line-up included 2.3 litre diesels with 74bhp and 100bhp. 201bhp 3.0GSi 24v is quick. 360bhp twin-turbo Lotus Carlton is seriously quick. Dubbed by Jasper Carrott "the family car for the Fittipaldis."

What's bad: Power steering a bit vague. Can suffer from electrical glitches. Diesels are lacklustre. Obstructive manual gearboxes. Starting to look old. ECU connector block prone to hairline cracks which allow moisture in and lead to intermittent faults which could hot spot a 'cat'.

What to watch out for: Clocking, obviously, because these cars take the miles so well. Some engines require timing belt replacement every 35,000–40,000 miles. Others have chains. Vital to check special rear shock absorbers in estates as these are expensive. Want to see evidence of regular maintenance, including biannual autobox ATF and filter change. Beware of clonky or noisy manual boxes – they're expensive to rebuild. Oil breathers of four-cylinder engines sometimes get blocked. Noisy valve gear often denotes missed oil changes. If it has a tow hook or signs of one having been fitted, be extra careful. Watch out for clocked ex-taxis.

Cavalier (1981 to 1988)

What's good: First front-wheel drive Cavaliers. Saloon, hatchback or estate built with Australian Holden body panels. 75bhp 1,297cc, 90bhp 1,598cc, 115bhp 1,796cc and 130bhp 1,796cc SRi 130. 14ft 4in long, 5ft 6in wide, 920kg to 1,091kg. four or five speed manuals or three speed autobox. Can last well. Can be kept going long after the end of its design life. Haynes manual 0812.

What's bad: No PAS. Getting old now.

What to watch out for: Selling for next to nothing on the strength of how much ticket and rent left. Make the usual old car checks.

Cavalier (1988 to 1995)

What's good: Popular, reliable, good build quality, comfortable, cheap spares, cheap servicing, cheap and easily replaced clutch. Good, smooth, economical 81bhp Japanese (Isuzu) turbodiesel engine. Huge range of engines from 75bhp 1.4 to 204bhp turbo 4x4. 150bhp 2.0 16vs were a popular choice. Four speed 2.0 autos had long gearing and were surprisingly economical. hatchback 14ft 3in long and 6ft 2in wide (inc mirrors). Typical weight 1,200kg. Cheap-to-replace ABS from 1994.

What's bad: Stodgy handling. Rust in seam on rear wheelarch. Brakes can develop judder. Door mirrors are 'snap-off', not sprung. Combined alternator/brake vacuum pump of turbodiesels is very expensive. ABS pump of early SRis is eye-wateringly expensive (more than the cars are worth). Lost steering-wheel height adjustment when gained drivers airbag in early 1993. Six-speed gearbox on 4x4 turbo fails and costs a fortune to replace. GF50 plastic timing belt tensioners can fail on 16-valve engines built August 1993–January 1996. Lower front suspension arms may have been damaged by use as jacking points. Bulkhead may crack around steering rack mountings. Plastic fuel filler pipe between cap and tank can develop hairline cracks leading to petrol fumes entering the cabin when the tank pressurises. On 2.0 16v models a problem frequently develops with the idle stabilisation control valve, necessitating the fitting of an oil separator. Alternator belt passes around engine mounting which requires dismantling before it can be changed. Job is fiddly and takes a couple of hours. Crankshaft position and camshaft sensors and associated wiring and connectors also prone to faults. Multipin connector to ECU prone to condensation water ingress.

What to watch out for: ABS light on early SRis (make sure it hasn't been disconnected). Signs of clocking as lots of 200,000–milers have received haircuts. Damage from being jacked up by front suspension arms. Timing belts not changed at 36,000–40,000–mile intervals. Camshaft wear on 1.6 litre 8-valve engines. Serious engine oil leaks. Track rod end wear. Shot shock absorbers. Juddery braking due to warped front discs. Non-fused wiring can rub against base of battery holder and cause a short. Alternator may short out due to ingress of water through worn rubber steering rod sleeves. Choke mechanism of 1.6 carburettor models fails: may be no more than blocked water heating passage, or may require £100 repair kit. Creaking from steering may indicate cracks in bulkhead at base of steering column – especially on V6s. It's a £700 job to repair. Abbot Racing of Spinnels Farm, Manningtree (tel: 01255 870636) have a means of mounting the rack more rigidly, and also replacing the soft rubber suspension bushes which not only solves the problem but makes both Cavaliers and SAAB 900s steer and handle much better.

Recalls: 1994: (1.7 TD Mar 1992–Mar 1994 VIN NV201488–R7560941): loss of braking efficiency. 1995: static sparking during refuelling. 1999: possibility of failure of plastic cambelt idler pulley GF50 on 16v and V6 engines 1993–96, which can snap cambelt. Changed as an 'in service mod' when cambelts are changed at 35,000–40,000 mile intervals. (Vauxhall Recall Helpline: 01189 458500 or 01582 427200)

Combo kombi (from 2002)

What's good: Opel Corsa derived utilitarian MPV along same lines as Berlingo Multispace, Peugeot Partner Combi, FIAT Doblo Combi,

Renault Kangoo Combi, etc. Sliding rear side doors. Side hinged rear doors. Huge amount of space. And very attractive looking. Will be more than £10,000 in Germany and this price premium might keep it out of the UK on a Vauxhall badge. Also up against in house competition from the Meriva.

What's bad: More expensive than competition.

What to watch out for: Too soon to say

Corsa B (1993 to 2000)

What's good: Ageing design but still a different and practical shape for a supermini. 12ft 3in long by 5ft 3in wide. Weighs from 835kg to 960kg. Plenty of room in the back of the 5–door version. Doesn't make demands on the driver. Good engines, especially the ultra-economical chain-cam 57bhp Suzuki 1.0 litre 3-cylinder 12-valve, often badged 'Breeze'. 49bhp and 66bhp 1.5 litre Isuzu diesels and 59bhp 1.6 litre GM diesel. Most powerful was 107bhp 1.6 16v GSI. Generally reliable, last well and cheap to run.

What's bad: Still based on the Nova floorpan, so stodgy and characterless to drive. 1.4s have suffered cat problems. Awarded Two-Star NCAP crash safety rating in 1997. Short runs may lead to sticking valves on 16-valve models (usually cured by switching to a high detergent petrol). See 'Recalls' about timing belt pulleys which need renewing at least every 40,000 miles. On 1.4 16v timing belt also drives the water pump, so if this fails it will lead to timing belt failure. Most likely reason for the water pump to fail is lack of water (coolant) so check this regularly. Reports of repeated failures of heater matrixes. Central locking can fail due to failure of a small, brittle, badly designed casting (part 90540614). Costs less than £6, but £50 + VAT to get it fitted.

What to watch out for: Could have been a courier's car or a driving school car ('Engineering Education Trust' on the V5 = BSM). Clutch cables can be troublesome (cheap to replace). Heavier diesel engines promote high front tyre and suspension wear. All Corsas prone to front suspension wear. Check driveshafts for clonks by reverse turns in both directions. Cracking around door hinges on 'A' pillars of 2–door models (also look for cracks in the paint on 'B' pillars – an

MOT failure point). Feel front discs for grooves, 'shouldering' and wear. GTEs may have been thrashed by kids. Beware of any noises from the water pump (see 'What's Bad'). Check front carpets for damp signifying failed heater matrix.

Recalls: 1995: static sparking during refuelling. 1997 (1993–1996 1.4 & 1.6 16vs only – 27,000 cars): Possibility of plastic cambelt idler pulley breaking which can snap cambelt. 1998 (diesel K to N reg: 26,000 cars): live cable may rub against bonnet hinge, lose insulation and cause a fire; (1.0 12v, P to R reg: 8,000 cars): cable may touch engine inlet manifold. (Vauxhall Recall Helpline: 01582 427200) 1998: Vauxhall Corsa diesel (K to N reg: 26,000 cars): live cable may rub against bonnet hinge, lose insulation and cause a fire. (3/6/98.) Vauxhall Corsa 1.0 12v (P to R reg: 8,000 cars): cable may touch engine inlet manifold. (3/6/98: Specific Helpline: 01189 458500.)February 2000: Safety recall to reinforce front seat rails and replace fatigued or worn front seatbelt buckles. 9/3/2001 500,000 cars recalled to fit reinforcing plates to front seat runners to prevent rails from fracturing. 9/3/2001 also recalled again to replace seat belt buckles with quality assured buckles.

Corsa C (from 2000)

What's good: New model arrived Autumn 2000, similar but prettier than before. Now 12ft 3in long and 6ft 3in wide (including mirrors) Weight up to from 980kg to 1,190kg. Electro galvanized bodies with 12-year no perforation warranty, active front head restraints, 'Dynamic Safety' chassis, combined information and entertainment system. Three three-point rear seatbelts. Engines include 125 ps 1.8i 16v and 74bhp 1.7 DTi. 57bhp 1.0 litre 3 cylinder 12v and 74bhp 1.2 litre Ecotec 4 cylinder 16v are both chain-cam Suzuki engines, so no belts and GF50 tensioners to worry about. 5-speed 'Easytronic' semi-automatic on 1.2 16v similar to the system in the MCC Smart and avoids a power-sapping torque converter. Three Stars in Euro NCAP crash tests. Three year warranty. List price examples: £7,995 for 1.0 12v Club; £9,995 for 1.2 litre 16v SX1; £11,495 for 1.4 litre 16v SRi, all inclusive of three year warranty and first year's insurance. Corsa Improvements for 2002 include: A £300 'Protection Pack' optional on Comfort, Elegance, SXi and SRi models. This comprises side airbags, full size side curtain airbags and a 'smart' passenger seat which detects if someone is sitting in it and if not disarms the passenger airbag. A further £300 upgrades standard air conditioning on Elegance and SRi models to full climate control and the package also includes a heat reflecting windscreen. £100 buys a set of 10 spoke ally wheels for Elegance models. The 74bhp 1.7DTi 16v diesel engine is now available in SXi models, offering excellent 60.1mpg economy on the combined cycle and emitting just 127g/km CO_2 which qualifies it for the £110pa diesel VED bracket. List prices are £10,750 for the 3–door and £11,250 for the 5–door, but with Vauxhalls you should always look for a serious discount. A 65bhp version of the same 16 valve diesel engine is available in Club models where it also offers 60.1mpg in the combined cycle. List prices are £8,950 for the 3–door Club 1.7Di 16v and £9,450 for the 5–door Club Di 16v. The £8,495 Club 1.0 12v 5–door offers 50.4mpg in the combines cycle and its 134g/km CO_2 output should keep it in the lowest £100 VED bracket for several years to come. Achieved an excellent four star rating for crash safety in 2002 NCAP tests.

More online at www.vauxhall.co.uk

What's bad: Timing belt and tensioner changes re-scheduled from 80,000 miles to 40,000 miles.

What to watch out for: Too little feedback to say, which is a good sign given the popularity of the model. Some doubt about clutch life of Easytronic.

Recalls: 30/4/01: Replace front passenger airbag control unit so it interacts properly with child safety cradle 'smart' deactivation function. 19/12/2001: Recall of 8,662 Corsa three and five door 2002 models sold in UK since September 2001 to check front seat adjustment locking mechanism for fatigue and possible wear. Replace if necessary. w/e 6/1/2002: Recall announced in Germany for 1.7di and 1.7dti due to a battery cable fault.

Frontera (from 1991)

What's good: Not bad looking, in a chunky sort of way. Right car at the right time when launched in 1991 to feed 4x4 fashion fad.

Initially well-priced as alternative to a Cavalier. Held value well until the public started to wonder why they were driving crude old-fashioned 4x4 trucks instead of proper cars. Reasonably competent off-road. 1998 'round the World' endurance run helped improve public perception of reliability. Range revamped for 1999 with 113 bhp 2.2 direct injected diesel or 204bhp 3.2 litre V6. Sport V6 listed at £19,995 does 114mph, 0–60 in 9.5 seconds but just 15.9mpg in the EC urban cycle. Three year warranty from October 2000. 2.2DTi and 3.2 V6 have maximum towing weight of 2,400kg

What's bad: Five door version achieved no more than an average three star 62% rating for crash safety in 2002 NCAP tests with very poor pedestrian protection. Really no more than a dressed-up Isuzu pick up. Legion of quality problems. Short-lived direct injected 2.8 Isuzu diesel withdrawn due to emissions problem. 2.3 and 2.2 petrol engines guzzle petrol. If you want a chunky 4x4 to use as a day to day car the Honda CRV, Toyota RAV4, Hyundai Santa Fe and Land Rover Freelander are vastly superior. Has been rock bottom in J.D. Power Customer Satisfaction Surveys and still second bottom in the 'R' reg. survey. S and T platers 4th from bottom in 2001 *Top Gear*/J.D. Power Customer Satisfaction Survey. 2.2 litre direct injected diesels can Some 2.2 litre DI 16v models thought to use a lot of engine oil, but oil from the 16v heads takes a long time to drain down and dipstick can give a falsely low reading. Repeated alarm system problems reported by readers. In April 2001 a shortage of rear windscreens for the 5–door model with over 400 on back order. Vauxhall dealer advice has been to try and get one from a breakers. Timing belt and tensioner changes re-scheduled from 80,000 miles to 40,000 miles on engines which have them. Third worst after FIAT/Alfa and MGF for breakdowns attended by German ADAC during 2001. Not recommended.

What to watch out for: Is it a townie's car (never gone off road) or is it a farmer's car? Big difference in likelihood of damage to underside and drive train. Has a towing hook been fitted at some time? If so, what has it been towing? (Anything from a one horse horsebox to a mobile catering stand, so look for saggy rear suspension, groaning rear diff., noisy wheel bearings). Look for oil leaks from engine and drive train. Check that it tracks straight. Look for wear in front suspension and steering joints. Listen for big-end rattles, noisy tappets (signs of insufficiently frequent oil changes). Check dipstick for clean oil.

Recalls: 1995: VIN NV500400 to RV628644: faulty bonnet safety catch. 1996 (Sport): fit heat shield between exhaust system and petrol tank (fire risk). Replace catches for removable roof section. Spring 1999: warning issued to all known owners to take vehicles to Vauxhall dealers at 4 years or 40,000 miles for a replacement timing belt and timing belt idler wheel. 1999: all 'new' Fronteras built from June 1998 to September 1999 (6,557 vehicles) officially recalled for a check on steering components. This recall was repeated in 2001 to correct 'steering to the left'. 2001: TSB about voltage spikes from the alternator damaging the camshaft sensor. This is prevented by unpicking the wiring loom and re-routing the cam and crankshaft sensor cables together around the front of the airbox, keeping them away from the alternator.

Meriva MPV (from 2003)

What's good: Five seater Corsa C based mini MPV. One of GM's stars in concept form at the September 2001 Frankfurt Motor Show. Now set to launch at the autumn 2002 Paris motor show and to go on sale early 2003 to rival Honda's Jazz and Ford's Fiesta Fusion. The three rear seats slide forwards individually or can be completely folded away similar to those of the Zafira, providing a flat floor. The Meriva is a compact 4,042mm (13ft 3in) long and will come with a range of diesel and petrol engine options from 1.6 to 1.8 litres with outputs of 75PS to 125PS. (The diesel is the 75PS 1.7 16v DI.) The car will be built at the existing Corsa factory at Zaragosa, Spain, up the road from Seat and down the road from VW's Polo plant near Pamplona.

More online at www.vauxhall.co.uk

What's bad: Too soon to say.

What to watch out for: Too soon to say.

Monterey (1994 to 1999)

What's good: Badge-engineered Isuzu Trooper.

What's bad: Slow seller and lots hung around unsold in compounds for more than a year. See Isuzu Trooper.

What to watch out for: See Isuzu Trooper.

Recalls: See Isuzu Trooper.

Nova (1983 to 1993)

What's good: One of the better 'older' superminis. 3–door is nicest and most valuable, but also available as 5–door and 2– and 4–door saloon. Most had decent ohc engines. Easy DIY. Haynes manual 0909. Lots of cheerful trim combinations on updated range from 1990. 11ft 11in long by 5ft wide. Quite light from 740kg to 850kg. 49bhp and 67bhp Isuzu 1.5 litre diesels from 1989. 101bhp GTEs 'caught on' among young 'Max Power' and 'Revs' readers, who spend thousands of pounds doing them up. Insurance hikes mean they do the same with 1.2s, the stereos of which may be more powerful than the engines.

What's bad: Stodgy handling and indifferent ride. 3–door not very space-efficient. Combined alternator and brake vacuum pump of Isuzu diesel is expensive to replace. Getting old now.

What to watch out for: Rust. May have been couriers' cars (especially diesels) and could have been clocked back at anything up to 12 years ago. DIY servicing may have been incompetent or skimped. Really needs an oil change every 3,000 miles or every 6 months, whichever comes first. Main problem is camshaft wear, which can be terminal for the engine. Listen for thrashing noises and look for signs of oil weeping from top of the engine. Early 80s fuel pump problems should have been rectified in service by now. Check for driveshaft clonks by reverse turning in both directions. Look for split driveshaft gaiters. Expect to have to replace some front suspension bushes. If it has an aftermarket 'pop-up' sunroof, expect water leaks and check carpets. Rust starts in area of hatchback and rear wheel arches. Always lift boot carpets (especially in saloons) to check for repaired accident damage, rust, or both. 'SR' gearboxes don't last long. Interiors weak on all but post-1990 facelift models.

Dashboards fall off. If the brakes of the 1.5 litre Isuzu turbodiesel lack servo assistance, you're in for a £600 combined brake vacuum pump and alternator.

Omega (from 1994)

What's good: Well equipped, comfortable, handles well with more road feel than Senator. both 2.5 litre and 3.0 litre V6s nice to drive. 150 mph 207 bhp 3.0 MV6 was almost good value by UK standards at list price of £24,445. Big at 15ft 10in long and 5ft 10in wide. Also heavy, from 1,410kg to 1,808kg. Manual boxes better suited to engines than Senator manuals. Get a white, grey or otherwise dark coloured one and the cars in front will still think you are a police car. Three-Star NCAP crash test rating. Comprehensively facelifted and re-engineered in autumn 1999 with option of new 2.2 litre chain cam 146 bhp four-cylinder engine offering 151 lb ft torque. Three year warranty from October 2000. 2.5 litre 6 cylinder BMW diesel supplemented then replaced by GM's own 2.0 and 2.2DTi four cylinder diesels from January 1998. Comprehensively facelifted in October 1999 for 2000 model year. 144bhp 2.2 Sport added to range at £19,995 in September 2001. Combines 2.2 chain cam VX220 engine with MV6 chassis.

What's bad: Poor paint quality on some early cars. Large number of quality problems and complaints, often over BMW powered 2.5 litre straight six diesel. The police had great difficulty getting their kit into the limited dashboard and front-of-engine space. Started looking at Volvo T5s instead. New front-wheel-drive Omega from 2002. Timing belt drives water pump, so seizure of water pump wrecks engine. Some 2.2 litre DI 16v models thought to use a lot of engine oil, but oil from the 16v heads takes a long time to drain down and dipstick can give a falsely low reading. Timing belt and tensioner changes re-scheduled from 80,000 miles to 40,000 miles on engines which have them (all apart from 2.2 litre petrol and diesel and BMW 2.5 diesel). Side bumpstrip trim on rear doors of pre-facelift cars can come into contact with partially opened front doors and become irreparably bent. 8th from Bottom of 100 models for reliability in *Auto Express* 2002 survey.

What to watch out for: Electrical and electronic problems (check everything works, including computer and especially ABS warning light). Check the a/c, heating and ventilation system on all settings because broken flap controls are common and very expensive to repair due to complex dismantling involved. Ignition igniter coils vulnerable to water ingress and condensation. BMW diesel must have had 4,500–5,000 mile oil changes (easy for busy company drivers to forget). Serious reliability problems of Opel badged version (exactly the same as the Vauxhall) reported by ADAC (the German breakdown organisation) in its 2001 report. Idle air control valve problem that affects 2.0 16v Cavaliers and Vectras also affects Omegas with the same engine. Excess wear on inside edge of front tyres usually due to worn front suspension wishbone bushes. Pre 2000 model MV6ft s have attractive twin spoke Irmscher 17 inch alloy wheels which don't survive potholes. If possible make sure they run true by seeing them spun on a balance machine. Replacements cost £230 each. Post 2000 MV6 wheels cost half this, take the same size tyres (235 45ft s) and are much stronger.

Recalls: 1995: static sparking during refuelling. 1995 (16v: VIN R 1000001 to S1155206): fuel feed pipe may chafe. Reposition and clamp into place. 1999: possibility of failure of plastic cambelt idler pulley GF50 on 4 -cylinder 16v engines 1994–98, which can snap cambelt. Changed as an 'in service mod' when cambelts are changed at 35,000–40,000 mile intervals. (Vauxhall Recall Helpline: 01189 458500 or 01582 427200) General problem of ignition steering wheel lock failure, usually replaced FOC. June 2000 recall of V6 models due to crankshaft fault. 2001: TSB about voltage spikes from the alternator damaging the camshaft sensor. This is prevented by unpicking the wiring loom and re-routing the cam and crankshaft sensor cables together around the front of the airbox, keeping them away from the alternator.

Senator (1987 to 1995)

What's good: The policeman's favourite police car. 16ft long, 5ft 9in wide, weighed from 1,370kg. Highly successful 1987 re-style looked longer and lower than Carlton and garish 'chip-cutter' grille is just right, especially pitched against bland looking Granada. High-spec 204bhp 3.0 24v CD obviously the best (not all had leather). Glovebox of air-conditioned CD can be used as a fridge or drinks cooler. Later 148bhp 2.6 12v CD is okay, 177bhp 3.0 12v also okay. The police liked these cars so much, they stored them and some did not come into service until 'M' reg. Enthusiastic Owners Club (see clubs directory at www.honestjohn.co.uk). The model lived on in Australia until 1990 as the Holden Calais 2.6 with curiously bland, maybe police spec trim.

What's bad: Top spec 3.0 24v CDs with less than 75,000 miles now very rare. Lots of electrical glitches on CDs, particularly autobox electrics. Early 140bhp 2.5 12v lacked essentials such as proper engine cooling. Police spec had no sunroof or aircon, wind-up windows and manual five-speed boxes. They're not that easy to drive because the engine lacks the expected low down torque. All the cheap ex-police versions have now been auctioned off. Getting old now.

What to watch out for: Re-trimmed ex-police cars. Repaired accident damage on ex-police Senators. Police cars are very well maintained, usually with new clutches and 'cats' at around the 80,000–90,000 mile mark. Check all electric windows and sunroof (if fitted). Make sure aircon blows cold (if fitted). Privately owned cars may have suffered skimped maintenance, leading to camshaft wear. Beware of Senators used for 'private hire' (i.e. taxis). Servotronic steering should have 'over centre' feel (more steering effect at extremes of lock). Check for evidence of having had a tow bar. Bounce each corner, especially the back two as springs may have sagged and left shocks in a state of shock. Try to feel the discs through the wheels and budget for replacement accordingly. Timing chain tensioners on privately-owned cars not serviced and driven to police standards tend to fail at around 90,000 miles and the timing chains themselves at 100,000–110,000 miles.

Sintra (1997 to 1999)

What's good: Vauxhall's large MPV. Previa-sized, with advantage of two sliding rear side doors. Powerful 201 bhp 3.0 litre petrol V6, 141 bhp 2.2 litre petrol four. 1998 introduced 2.2 litre direct Injected diesel the most sensible choice, but a bit short of low-down grunt.

What's bad: American built, so trim not up to European standards. Not especially different or particularly attractive. Blitzed in the market place by the Chrysler Voyager. Poor two-and-a-half star performer in NCAP crash tests (3 points front impact; 15 points side impact). Came rock bottom in 'R' reg. J.D. Power Customer Satisfaction Survey and rock bottom again in 'S' and 'T' reg. J.D. Power Customer Satisfaction Survey. Not recommended.

What to watch out for: Has it been an airport taxi? (Late introduction of diesel means this is unlikely.) Watch your fingers when fiddling with the seats (see recalls).

Recalls: 1998: Catches for removing rear seats may sever fingers. Covers to be fitted to seat release lever mechanism. 2001: TSB about voltage spikes from the alternator damaging the camshaft sensor. This is prevented by unpicking the wiring loom and re-routing the cam and crankshaft sensor cables together around the front of the airbox, keeping them away from the alternator.

Tigra (1994 to 2000)

What's good: Cute, cleverly repackaged Corsa. 'Girly' car image. Decent pair of 89bhp 1.4 litre and 104bhp 1.6 litre 16v engines. Reasonably economical. Enough of a sports car for less demanding drivers. Three year warranty from October 2000.

What's bad: All it really is underneath is a Corsa. 'Girly' car image (if you're not a girl). Glass hatchbacks leak. Can suffer from sticking valves if used for short runs on petrol lacking adequate detergent. Rear seats too small for adults. Came close to bottom in 'R' reg. J.D. Power Customer Satisfaction Survey. Timing belt and tensioner changes re-scheduled from 80,000 miles to 40,000 miles. Production ended October 1999.

What to watch out for: Must be serviced regularly (preferably every 6 months). Look for uneven tyre wear. Broken wheel trims or damaged alloys denote a kerb-prone driver, so expect suspension and steering damage. Feel front discs for grooves, 'shouldering' and wear.

Recalls: 1997 (1993–1997): possibility of GF50 plastic cambelt idler pulleys breaking which can snap cambelt. (Vauxhall Recall Helpline: 01189 458500 or 01582 427200). February 2000: Safety recall to reinforce front seat rails and replace fatigued or worn front seatbelt buckles. 9/3/2001 recalled again to fit reinforcing plates to front seat runners to prevent rails from fracturing. 9/3/2001 also recalled again to replace seat belt buckles with quality assured buckles.

Vectra (1995 to 2002)

What's good: Half a step forward from the Cavalier. Reasonable build quality, comfortable ride, cheap spares, smooth ride. Especially good on motorways. 14ft 8in long; 5ft 7in wide. From 1,185kg to 1,427kg. Smooth, economical 81bhp Japanese (Isuzu) turbodiesel engine in early diesels. Important improvements for 1997 model year include height-adjustable steering wheel, better seats and Trafficmaster. Standard aircon from Sept '97 in lieu of sunroof. Long-lasting chain-cam direct-injected 81bhp 2.0 litre DI 16v engines in later diesels. Vastly improved SRi and GSi models from spring 1998 with steering and front suspension modifications developed jointly with Saab. Major facelift in spring 1999 made it a better, but not better-looking, car. Most UK cars built at Luton. Bargain model 1.6 16v Expression with a/c launched 24/8/2000 at £10,995 OTR. 147 bhp 2.2 litre chain cam four replaces 2.0 in Vectra from 2001, plus uprated 125 bhp 2.2 DTi 16v diesel and uprated 125 bhp 1.8 petrol. 2.5 V6 grew to 2.6 litres with same power but more torque. Three year warranty from October 2000. New prices announced on 7–11–2000 from £13,250 for 1.6i 16v Club to £20,945 for 2.6i V6 CDX estate, with 147bhp 2.2LS competing directly against 125bhp Mondeo 1.8LX at £14,595. Suspect 20,000 mile oil change regime introduced at the same time. 145mph 2.6 GSi with bigger brakes, priced at £18,595 from Spring 2001.

What's bad: Until the 1998 improvements, a whole step backwards from the Cavalier. Still only a three star performer in 2001 NCAP crash safety tests. Clutch replacement remains a five- to-six-hour job involving engine removal instead of the simple half-hour job it was on the Cavalier. Earlier cars suffer stodgy handling with severe understeer, which is not entirely cured even in the latest 1999 model Vectras. Terrible driver's seat on early models with no steering wheel height adjustment (corrected from 1997 model year). Styled door mirrors give limited view. DI 16v has undeserved reputation as an oil burner. What actually happens is that oil collects in the 16v head and takes a long time to drain back to the sump. Dip within an hour of stopping and you will get a falsely low reading leading you to overfill with fresh oil. 2001 model year ex-fleet cars which have been subject to 20,000 mile oil changes will not be as good a second-hand buy as cars which have had their oil changed every 6 months or 7,000 miles at most. Plug leads deteriorate and are ridiculously expensive to replace. Whole dash needs to come out to replace odometer bulb. DIs seem to need new mass/airflow sensors every 36,000 miles. Timing belt and tensioner changes re-scheduled from 80,000 miles to 40,000 miles on engines which have them. Internal roof stiffener bars on estate models can become unglued due to heat and cold on the roof and cause a rattle. 15th from Bottom of 100 models for reliability in *Auto Express* 2002 survey. See 'What to Watch Out For' for a lot more faults. Clarkson was right first time. Hand on heart, I cannot recommend these cars. **What to watch out for:** Ex-Vauxhall Masterhire cars come with trustworthy print-out of full service history, including cambelt changes every 35,000–40,000 miles. Vectras from other fleets might have been clocked, so be sure to check mileages properly. Older SRis on Firestones may suffer premature tyre wear. Best tyres for older non-sporty Vectras are Pirelli P6000s. Best for new SRis and GSis are Yokohamas. Front suspension can wear prematurely. Make sure ABS light comes on, then goes out when it should. If engine misses, may have faulty ECU and cat may be hot spotted. Alternatively, may be camshaft or crankshaft position sensor: a £150–£170 job, but a lot more if the misfire has spiked the cat. Or may simply be moisture in the connectors (a very common Vauxhall/Opel problem). May suffer steering column rattle. May have been run on cheap petrol and suffering sticking valves as a result. Readers also report problems with air-conditioning systems and window regulators. If idle speed of 1.6. 1.8 or 2.0 petrol engine is 1200–2000 rpm the problem is the idle adjustor control valve (Air Intake Control Valve). Needs cleaning with fuel system cleaner but if that doesn't work it needs replacing at £113 + VAT and modifying by fitting an oil separator. Tends to happen at 60–70k miles.

Recalls: 1996 (8/95 to 2/96 build: 40,000 cars): check front seatbelt mounting bolts and tighten if necessary. 1997 (1995–1996 1.6 16vs only-27,000 cars): Possibility of failure of plastic cambelt idler pulley GF50, which can snap cambelt. Changed as an 'in service mod' when cambelts are changed at 35,000–40,000 mile intervals. 1997 (Jan-May '96 build): Fuel pipe may come off at tank. 1998 (all 200,000 built before July 1998): handbrake cable subject to premature wear. Modified cable free replacement service. 1998 (automatics only): in service modification to autobox ECU mapping. 1999: possibility of failure of cambelt idler pulley on petrol engined 'P' to 'R' reg. Vectras (Vauxhall Recall Helpline: 01189 458500 or 01582 427200) June 2000 recall of V6 models due to crankshaft fault. 2001: TSB about voltage spikes from the alternator damaging the camshaft sensor. This is prevented by unpicking the wiring loom and re-routing the cam and crankshaft sensor cables together around the front of the airbox, keeping them away from the alternator.

Vectra II (from June 2002)

What's good: All new Vectra, code name J3200, on SAAB/GM Epsilon platform with more chunky styling and 12 year body warranty arrived in 2002. Particularly different styling for estate models. Bigger than first Vectra, with 60mm longer wheelbase and 50mm wider track. Engines are chain-cam ECOTEC units developing 122bhp to 145bhp on petrol and 99bhp to 123bhp on diesel. Also a 3.2litre 208bhp V6. Most petrol engines already comply with the Euro 4 emission limits. All new Vectras fitted with improved active head restraints on the front seats; full-size curtain airbags; three-point belts for all seats; Vauxhall's patented pedal release system; electronically-controlled ABS with cornering brake control and brake assist. Optional enhanced electronic stability programme called ESP Plus. Five-speed manual gearboxes and all-new five-speed automatic gearbox offering sequential gear changes. 1.8 litre new Vectra engine will also be available with an optional CVT (continuously variable automatic transmission). Torsional stiffness is up 74 per cent on previous Vectra. All new Vectras have a new 'IDS' chassis system featuring a new multi-link rear axle, aluminium components for lower unsprung weight and electro-hydraulic power steering bringing significant improvements in ride and handling which are major bugbears of the current Vectra. Electronic Stability Programme (ESP) is standard throughout. Passive safety measures include front, side and curtain airbags, breakaway pedal box and active head restraints developed by GM's SAAB division. £200 million has been invested in GM's Ellesmere Port production plant where most UK RHD Vectras will be built under GM's 'flex' facility system. The other Vectra plant is Russelsheim in Germany. The general consensus of opinion between '*Autocar*' and '*Auto Express*' is that the car has an excellent ride quality but, while handling is a huge improvement on the old Vectra, it is still not quite up to Mondeo standards.

Achieved an excellent four star rating for crash safety in 2002 NCAP tests.

More online at www.vauxhall.co.uk

What's bad: At time of writing, still awaiting a drive.

What to watch out for: Too soon to say.

VX220 (from 2000)

What's good: Elise-based Lotus-built mid-engined sports car powered by 147bhp chain-cam ECOTEC 2.2 litre engine. Three year warranty. Comparatively low Group 16 insurance. No power steering. Massive kickback through the steering wheel You feel and are aware of everything the car is doing. More forgiving than the Lotus Elise and with a more powerful engine. Wonderful, crude race-car feel to the gearchange. An absolute hoot to drive, and a better choice than the facelifted Elise. Recommended.

What's bad: Very limited production run, so beware of paying over the odds, otherwise too soon to say.

What to watch out for: Have been plenty of Lotus build quality faults and some rejected cars are being re-offered via the auctions.

Zafira (from 1999)

What's good: Seven seats in a body the same length as an Astra hatchback. Rearmost fold into floor. Centre seats fold and push forward, giving a completely flat load bay. 1.6 litre and 1.8 litre 16v engines on launch; long-lived chain-cam 50 mpg DI came later. Very impressive build quality with an immensely solid feel and no rattles at all even on a 10,000–miler. Galvanised body guaranteed not to rust for 12 years. Drives nicely as long as you don't push too hard. Did quite well for driver and front passenger protection in TUV/*Auto Bild* offset crash tests. Uprated 125 bhp 1.8 petrol from September 2000. Three year warranty from October 2000. Option from February 2001 of 147bhp 2.2 litre engine from VX220 which puts out 150lb ft torque and gives the Zafira a 9.0 second 0–60. £16,245 for 2.2 Comfort; £17,495 for 2.2 Elegance. Automatic option. 190bhp 138mph Zafira Turbo announced at Geneva Motor Show. Scored an impressive 12 out of 16 points for frontal impact and full marks for side impact in German ADAC crash tests. Prices cut from Spring 2001, from £12,995, but check out www.broadspeed.com online for some amazing deals on imported Opel Zafiras. 189bhp 2.0 litre turbocharged ECOTEC Zafira seven seater finally hits the streets in November 2001 at £19,995. Zero to 60mph is 7.6 seconds. Maximum torque of 184 lb ft (250Nm) is maintained from 1,950rpm all the way to 5,400rpm where maximum power of 189bhp (192PS) is developed. Fuel consumption is a reasonable 27.9mpg on the combined cycle and the engine conforms with Euro 4 emissions limits. But CO_2 output is a far from brilliant 243g/km, giving it a BIK rating of 31% x £19,995, or £6,198 and a £2,479 pa tax bill for a 40% tax payer. 125bhp 2.2DTI started arriving as imported Opels in July 2002. Recommended.

More online at www.vauxhall.co.uk

What's bad: Gearlever just a touch too far back, and flop-down driver's armrest gets in the way. Suffers usual roll understeer on tight bends and on long sweepers taken too fast. No DI automatic due to weight problems. DIs seem to need new mass/airflow sensors every 36,000 miles. 138mph 7–seater Turbo may be difficult to insure. Did badly in 2001 NCAP MPV Crash Tests achieving only a 65% mark due to "unstable" body and pedal box intrusion. Also low two points for pedestrian safety. (But see contradictory ADAC crash test results above.) DI 16v has reputation as an oil burner. What often happens is that oil collects in the 16v head and takes a long time to drain back to the sump. Dip within an hour of stopping and you will get a falsely low reading leading you to overfill with fresh oil which then gets burned. Timing belt and tensioner changes re-scheduled from 80,000 miles to 40,000 miles on engines which have them. 10th from Bottom of 100 models for reliability in *Auto Express* 2002 survey.

What to watch out for: Lift front carpets and check for water underneath. The cure is re-sealing the front bulkhead.

Recalls: 25/4/2000: 268 RHD 2000 model year DI models recalled for check on fuel line in engine compartment which could rupture in a front end crash. Fuel lines to be replaced with ones of improved specification.

VOLVO

240/260 (1978 to 1993)

What's good: Built like a tank. Pioneered a lot of secondary safety features. 15ft 7in estate cars have long load decks and will take fairly large items of furniture if you don't mind blotting out your rear view. Capable of Starship Enterprise mileages. 2,127cc carb engine had 107bhp; 2,127cc injected engine put out 123bhp, both with 4-speed manual or 3-speed auto; 2,316cc carb engine had 110bhp; with 4 or 5-speed manual or 3-speed auto; 2,316 with injection put out 116bhp. 2,316 GLT injected engine had 136bhp. Later 1,986cc injected engine had 118bhp or 111bhp with cat. 2,809cc injected V6 had 155bhp. Didn't weigh as much as a tank, though: from 1,270kg to 1,470kg.

What's bad: A dinosaur to drive. Some drivers think that the safety features make them 'safe', but heaven help the rest of us. Hidéous looks. Appalling steering. Horrible handling. Wallows like a hippo in a mudbath. Load platform is high and rear overhang too long which make an overloaded 240 estate doubly dangerous.

What to watch out for: Kerbed front suspension (all too easy with no steering 'feel' at all). Saggy springs. Soggy shock absorbers. Rust does eventually attack these cars.

340/360 (1982 to 1991)

What's good: Strangely popular among Brits. Early cars were all 1.4 litre Renault pushrod powered CVT autos. Later cars mostly manual with option of 1.7 litre Renault overhead cam engine from the 11 and 19 or Volvos's own 2.0 litre in two stages of tune. Many mechanical parts cheaper from Renault dealers than from Volvo dealers. Easy to change clutches of manuals because box is a transaxle and the engine and clutch are at the front. 1.4 has a decent twin-choke Weber carb and, because it's an ancient pushrod unit, a timing chain rather than a belt.

What's bad: Getting very old hat now and being replaced by most owners with Rover 400s or Swindon built Honda Civics. Can rust badly. I.7s susceptible to distributor problems due to ingress of damp. Cured by special Renault/Volvo plastic bag.

What to watch out for: These days 80ft s cars to be bought only as £50 to £100 bargain bangers to use up the 'ticket and rent' (MOT and VED), but you might find a cherished 1990 or 1991 model which could be worth preserving.

440/460 (1989 to 1997)

What's good: Came after 480 on same floorpan. Plenty of attention to secondary safety. Crude but effective Renault diesel. 1.8 CVT automatic probably the best combination. Many former 340/360 owners liked their 440s and 460s just as much and mourn the passing of this car.

What's bad: Booted 460 an aesthetic compromise. Poor Dutch build quality of early production from factory in Born. Ride quality not brilliant, especially of 460 with a laden boot. May rust prematurely. 440 1.7 and 1.8 conventional automatics suffer same problem of primary drum splitting as Renaults.

What to watch out for: Rust, especially in body seams. Oil-consuming 2.0 litre versions may have required 'mod 2371ft , carried out 'in-service' by Volvo dealers. Look for at least four years' official Volvo dealer servicing to make sure 'in-service' improvements were carried out. PAS not always fitted, but can be retro-fitted for about £600. Late, facelifted 440s and 460s the best.

Recalls: 1994: 440/460 2.0 litre (440 VIN 419000–602090; 460 VIN 419001–602089; 480 VIN 586300–590058): airbag may deploy accidentally. 1996: 440/460 (1991–1995): fire risk from faulty electrical connections.

480 (1987 to 1995)

What's good: Coupe version of 440/460 on same floorpan from same factory in Born reached the market first. Owners seem to like them with a passion. The last of the line were the best with very comprehensive spec, including air conditioning. Galvanised, so rust not a big problem. 1.7 had 109bhp of 122bhp with turbo. 2.0 had 110bhp.

What's bad: Poor Dutch build quality led one magazine to dub it 'the coupe from hell'. But the car was progressively improved and almost all problems will have been solved 'in service'. Seals above rear side windows start to leak.

What to watch out for: Oil-consuming 2.0 litre versions may have required 'mod 2371ft , carried out in-service by Volvo dealers. Look for at least four years' official Volvo dealer servicing to make sure 'in-service' improvements were carried out. Check aircon blows cold (if fitted). Make sure no water under the carpets.

Recalls: 1994: 480 2.0 litre (VIN 586300–590058): airbag may deploy accidentally. 1996: 480 (1991–1995): fire risk from faulty electrical connections.

740/760 (1984 to 1990)

What's good: Built like a tank. Better looking than antiquated 240 in a curious 1970s American way. 'Genteel', very middle-class, 'respectable' image (but see 'What's bad'). 7 seat option. 15ft 8in long, 5ft 9in wide, weighed from 1,270kg to 1,525kg. Engine line-up included 1,986cc 121bhp injected four from 1988 to 1990; 2,316cc 114bhp/117bhp carb four from 1984 to 1991; 2,316cc 121bhp injected four from 1987 to 1991; 2,316 131bhp injected four from 1986 to 1990; 2,316cc 155bhp twin cam 16v four from 1989 to 1990; 2,316cc 182bhp turbo four from 1986 to 1989 (down to 170bhp to 1990); 2,383cc 109bhp turbodiesel six from 1986 to 1990; 2,849cc 156bhp V6 from 1982 to 1987 (170bhp from 1987 to 1990); 2,383cc 122bhp turbodiesel six from 1983 to 1990.

What's bad: Ugly looks. Horrible handling. Very mixed image: genteel and middle-class, but, on the other hand, sometimes driven by very aggressive drivers. High-intensity high-level rear brake light on automatics must be fitted with low-intensity bulb or will dazzle the driver behind in a traffic jam (technically an offence under the RVLR 1989). Duff old PSA V6 (don't buy a 760 with a 'V' engine). The market is for Volvo estates, and saloon versions are very hard to sell. Old estates that began with antiques dealers end up with painters and decorators. Saloon has very small boot due to fuel tank intrusion. All now at least 11 years old.

What to watch out for: Steering and front suspension damage from 'kerbing'. Baggy suspension on estates from carrying ludicrously heavy loads. Fluid drips near back wheels could be leaking rear shocks. Engine and exhaust system damage from 'short run syndrome'. With 3,000–mile oil changes engines will do 300,000 miles plus, but most of the other bits won't. Previous owners may have replaced alternators, water pumps and starter motors but may have offloaded the car because the gearbox or diff is about to give up. On autos check ATF: should be red, not grey-black. High risk of clocking or having run 100,000 miles 'unhooked'. Cats are £600, but can be ditched because all 740s are pre-August '92. Front crossmember can crack, leading to chafing of battery cable and possible underbonnet fire.

Recalls: 1995: VIN 37400 to 39877 and 16300 to 38007: battery short circuit leading to possible fire risk.

850/S70/V70 (1992 to 2000)

What's good: The first sporty, modern Volvo. Changed Volvo's image completely, especially when estates were entered for 1994 Touring Car Championship. T5s are seriously quick. T5 saloons or estates replaced Senators on many police fleets. Ex-police two-year-olds available for around £4,500 (West Oxfordshire Motor Auctions, tel: 01993 774413). TDIs not far off T5 performance and give 35 mpg economy. Rock-solid build quality. Good, predictable, safe handling. More fun to drive than any previous Volvo. Changed the image of the company. Original S70 earned Three-Star NCAP crash test rating. Late 1999 mods earned Four-Star NCAP rating. Engine range began with 2.0 litre 10 valve at 126bhp, 2.0 litre 20 valve at 143bhp; 2.4 10 valve at 140bhp; 2.4 20 valve at 170bhp; 2.5 TDI at 140bhp; 2.3 AWD turbo at 195bhp; 2.3 T5 at 225bhp; 2.3 T5R at 250bhp. Bi-fuel (lpg) 144bhp 2.4 10valve engines also available. S70 was 10th from top in 'R' reg. J.D. Power Customer Satisfaction Survey but, strangely, V70 was only 34th. Yet V70 was joint 20th from Top in 144 car 2002 JD Power/*What Car?* Customer Satisfaction Survey of V and W reg. cars.

What's bad: Daytime running lights can dazzle other drivers. Estates are only commodious if you load them to the roof. Hard ride and sharper steering came as a shock to old-school, traditional Volvo owners. Front tyre wear of TDI, T5 and T5R can be severe: manuals 6,000–8,000 miles; autos 12,000–14,000 miles. TDI timing belt drives water pump and, if water pump fails, so does belt. Complaints of failed heater matrixes and early front wheel bearing failure. Serious reliability problems reported by ADAC (the German breakdown organisation) in its 2001 report. Spate of aircon evaporator failures at 2 to 4 years old. £1,000 job to put right. More on the online bulletin board at www.volvoclub.org.uk

What to watch out for: Kerb-damaged front suspension and front driveshafts. Front tyre wear. Retrimmed, clocked ex-police cars. Make sure aircon blows freezing cold (see above).

Recalls: 1995: VIN 078000 to 120420 and 175000 to 220678: fault with jack which could allow the car to fall. 1997 (1996 and 1997 model years): check for sticking throttle. 1997 (19,400 TDI models built 1995 and 1996): TSB to Volvo dealers worldwide warning of leak in rubber hose from brake vacuum pump to servo could cause loss of brake servo assistance. Many cars were never checked for this. 2000: S70 & V70 1997 and 1998 model years: side airbags may inflate for no reason. Headlamps may fail. 2001: TDI brake vacuum pipe problem made subject of a safety recall in the UK affecting 1,300 UK imports.

940 (1992 to 1997)

What's good: Lots of 'passive' safety features. One of the first cars with a built-in rear child seat and three three-point rear seatbelts. Really an updated 740. 16ft long by 5ft 9in wide. Weighed 1,366kg to 1,451kg. & seat option. Engine range: 2.0 litre 111bhp; 2.0 litre turbo 155bhp; 2.3 litre 130bhp; 2.3litre LPT 135bhp; 2.3 litre turbo 165bhp; 2.3 litre HPt 170bhp; 2.4 litre turbodiesel six 109bhp and 122bhp. Genteel, very middle-class, respectable image (but see 'What's Bad').

What's bad: Boring to drive. Flabby handling. Very mixed image: middle-class, but, like 740, sometimes driven by very aggressive drivers. High-intensity high-level rear brake light on automatics must be fitted with low-intensity bulb or will dazzle the driver behind in a traffic jam (technically an offence under the RVLR 1989). The market is for Volvo estates and saloon versions are very hard to sell. Rumoured problem with 1995–1997 cars that the throttle can stick and the brake servo can fail. Not something you want with an automatic.

What to watch out for: Steering and front suspension damage from 'kerbing'. Engine and exhaust system damage from 'short run syndrome'. Front crossmember can crack, leading to chafing of battery cable and possible underbonnet fire.

Recalls: TSB to check throttle operation and brake servo of 1995–1997 build cars.

960 and S90 (1994 to 2000)

What's good: The ultimate 'Q' car. Stonking 204 bhp twin-cam 3.0 litre straight six makes this old dowager really fly. Sports car drivers simply can't believe their eyes. Not over-dear once they've done a few miles. Became S90/V90 for 1997 model year.

What's bad: Volvo image may or may not be what you want. Ridiculous damage-prone protruding alloy wheels fitted 1996 (though low-profile tyres hugely improved handling).

What to watch out for: Some 960 24vs have suffered from cracked cylinder heads. Check very carefully for water and oil leaks and for signs of water and oil mixing. Check for steering and front suspension damage from 'kerbing'. Look for engine and exhaust system damage from 'short run syndrome'.

C70 (from June 2000)

What's good: Good-looking coupe launched June 1997 with 240 bhp 2.3 litre T5 engine. Convertible and lower powered variants followed. Smallest engine 163 bhp 2.0 litre light pressure turbo.

What's bad: Daytime running lights can dazzle other drivers. Expensive. 2.0 litre LPT not really powerful enough. Serious reliability problems reported by ADAC (the German breakdown organisation) in its 2001 report. Failure of electric hood motors of convertible not unknown and if this happens in some positions the boot cannot be opened to hand crank the hood up or down.

What to watch out for: Kerb-damaged front suspension and front driveshafts. Front tyre wear. If checking out a convertible, run the hood up and down several times to satisfy yourself that the mechanism is fault-free. And, obviously, check the hood carefully for tears.

Recalls: 2000: C70 1997 and 1998 model years: side airbags may inflate for no reason. Headlamps may fail.

S40/V40 (1996 to 2003)

What's good: Top in class for secondary safety in NCAP crash tests. Turbo versions are very fast. 1.8 litre 125 bhp GDI versions economical. Always had three three-point rear belts. Plenty of places to store oddments inside. Significant, much needed suspension improvements from spring 2000. 5-speed 2.0 turbo automatic is a real flyer. LPG options from June 2001, but the car is noticeably less lively on LPG and the tank takes a lot of boot-space. S40LPG: £17,020; S40SE LPG: £18,842; V40LPG £17,870; V40SE LPG £19,692.

What's bad: Bright, quartz iodine daytime running lights can dazzle and infuriate other drivers, especially at 'traffic calming' points. If you switch to sidelights to avoid this you get no lights-on warning when you leave the car. Ride, steering, handling and roadholding not up to expectations created by good-looking body and clever marketing. Lots of early production quality problems at Dutch factory, later rectified. Not the car the image leads you to expect. Pre-spring 2000 cars had indifferent handling and overlight steering. Bottom front suspension ball joints tend to wear prematurely. Problems of valves carbing up on T4s and also on lesser injection models driven on petrol with inadequate detergent content. Main wiring loom passes in front of radiator and is protected by a split plastic tube which can let in water leading to severe corrosion by road salt blowing a 40 amp fuse and putting out heater, aircon and indicator circuits (see recalls). Sender for digital petrol gauge prone to failure.

What to watch out for: Minor accident damage buckles the inner-wing structure. Car may have been badly repaired to save cost. Check front suspension bottom ball joints. Problems emerging with valve gear of Mitsubishi 1.8GDI engines, possibly due to insufficiently frequent oil changes.

Recalls: Volvo has an 'in service' cure for intermittent poor running, applied if owners complain. 2000: 2000 model-year cars: front brake callipers may crack and leak fluid. 14/6/2001: on 2001MY cars a diode in the climate control system may not be sufficiently durable leading to fan stopping working. Additional heater fan cable harness with climate control diode to be fitted. November 2001: TSB issued with fix for cold start ignition problems on 1.8 engines.

S50/V50/C50 (from 2003)

What's good: New 50 Series Volvo to replace 40 Series and be based on C1 floorpan of next Ford Focus. Will have range of Ford and Volvo engines from Ford's 1.6 Zetec S to Volvo's 2.4 litre 250bhp T5. Saloon, estate and coupe bodies. To be built at a Ford plant rather than at the Volvo/Mitsubishi Nedcar plant, Volvo's share of which is being sold to Mitsubishi. Focus floorpan suggests will be a much better handler than Carisma based S40/V40.

What's bad: Too soon to say.

What to watch out for: Far too soon to say.

S60 (from 2000)

What's good: Good looking new front-drive mid-range model from autumn 2000 sharing styling of S80 but narrower and with coupe-like rear roofline. Impressively solid, with decent handling and roadholding. All engines turbocharged from 180bhp 2.0 litre through 200 bhp 2.4 litre to 250 bhp T5. Prices from £19,995 for 2.0T. But 200bhp 2.4T is the best all round model and even works well with the standard automatic transmission. An S60 T5 set a new record by averaging 135.1 mph for 24 hours around the Millbrook bowl on 14th October 2001, driven by the Channel 4 'Driven' team. LPG and CNG options from June 2001. S60 S LPG £20,670; S60 SE LPG £22,620; S60 S CNG £21,495; S60 SE CNG £23,445. Volvo's own lightweight 163bhp common rail diesel from Summer 2001 offers 251 lb ft (340Nm torque)from 1,750rpm, combined consumption of 43.5mpg, CO_2 of 171g/km and prices of £20,745 for the S or £22,945 for the SE. Insurance Group 14. Awesome S60 T6 manual reported to be on the way with 320bhp and all-wheel drive (but will the engine fit?). S60R from September 2002 has 300bhp.

What's bad: Not much legroom in the back, particularly for the centre passenger.

What to watch out for: Too soon to say.

Recalls: TSB issued early 2002 to fix intermittent fault with remote central locking.

S80 (from 1998)

What's good: Front-wheel-drive 960 replacement. Good-looking, dignified, rounded body. Same 204 bhp 2.9 litre straight six; 140 bhp 2.5 litre TDI, 144 bhp 10v and 170 bhp 20v 5-cylinder engines from S70. Flagship S80 T6 has 273 bhp 2.8 litre twin turbo and 4-speed Tiptronic auto. T6, 2.9 and TDI are all good to drive with lots of grip and nice steering. 2.4 litre is 'softer' and more vague, but still okay. All have excellent radios with knobs for volume, channel changing and function/waveband selecting. Integrated hands-free car phone system (you simply insert your SIM card into a slot in the dash). Lots of bottle, cup and can holders. Very good 29 point Four-Star 85% NCAP crash safety score. After top results in US-NCAP and Insurance Institute of Highway Safety has been nominated 'The World's Safest Car'. S and T reg. cars came 16th in 2001 *Top Gear*/JD Power Customer Satisfaction Survey. LPG and CNG and options from June 2001: S80 S LPG £22,835; S80 SE LPG £24,510; S80 S CNG £23,635; S80 SE CNG £25,310. Volvo's own lightweight 163bhp common rail diesel from Summer 2001 offers 251 lb ft (340Nm torque)from 1,750rpm, combined consumption of 43.5mpg, CO_2 of 172g/km and prices of £22,335 for the S or £24,235 for the SE. Insurance Group 13. The S80 D5 is really good to drive, handles well, goes well and at 31mph per 1,000 rpm is a very relaxed cruiser. Four star score in 2001 NCAP crash tests. 200bhp S80 2.4T introduced for 2002, priced from £23,855 for the manual and from £24,955 for the auto. Low CO_2 of 222g/km for the manual and 242g/km for the auto make this 143mph car with a 0–60 of 7.7 seconds very attractive to company car drivers who will pay £2,580 in BIK over 2002/2003 for the manual. Joint 17th from Top in 144 car 2002 JD Power/*What Car?* Customer Satisfaction Survey of V and W reg. cars. Much more likeable than the spec suggests.

What's bad: In the diesel, the 2.9 and the T6 you feel every ridge and draincover – not something traditional Volvo owners are used to. High first-year depreciation for a new car of 46%. Top auction bid on a 17,000–mile year-old £26,000 SE 140 was £14,150. Expensive to repair after a low-speed crash – could lead to rising insurance costs.

What to watch out for: Lots of build quality niggles. One report of an S80 having to go back to the supplying dealer 17 times.

Recalls: August 2000: 116,000 S80 models (5,500 in UK) recalled because front suspension ball joint can work loose or fail. 2/4/2001: left and right rear outer seatbelt bottom fixing bolts and rhs child restraint anchor bracket may be loose or may have been incorrectly torqued. Re-torque as necessary. November 2001: German recall of 200 CNG dual fuel S80s due to problem with switching between fuels. None of these cars reached Britain through official channels. TSB issued early 2002 to fix intermittent fault with remote central locking.

V70 Estate (from 2000)

What's good: The best looking estate car you can buy. Confusingly, based on the new S80, but replaces the 'old' V70. Satisfying to drive. Wide range of engines including petrol turbos up to 250 bhp, Audi's 140 bhp straight five TDI and a new TDI. Widely praised for convenience features. XC is a four-wheel-drive cross-country version on raised suspension with 200 bhp petrol turbo engine. 200 bhp V70T is a nice drive. Excellent medium wave radio reception and a really good integrated hands-free mobile phone system (£900 option). All you have to do is slip in the SIM card from your pocket cellphone, key in your pin and you're in business. 250 bhp T5 model very popular with police forces, so look out for bargain high-milers in white from 2002. LPG and CNG options from June 2001: V70 S LPG £24,455; V70 SE LPG £26,255; V70 S CNG £25,255; V70 SE CNG £27,055. Volvo's own D5 lightweight 163bhp common rail diesel from Summer 2001 offers 251 lb ft (340Nm torque)from 1,750rpm, combined consumption of 42.2mpg, C02 of 177g/km and prices of £23,955 for the S or £25,955 for the SE. Insurance Group 13. V70 AWD four-wheel-drive gets diesel engine early in 2002 and diesel automatic option from summer 2002. Should be an excellent towcar. 300bhp V70R from September 2002. Joint 20th from Top in 144 car 2002 JD Power/*What Car?* Customer Satisfaction Survey of V and W reg. cars. Recommended.

What's bad: See S80. Poor steering lock can make it difficult to swing into a parallel parking space. Bright, quartz iodine daytime running lights can dazzle and infuriate other drivers, especially at 'traffic calming' points. If you switch to sidelights to avoid this you get no 'lights on' warning when you leave the car. If you leave the daytime running lights on they eat bulbs. Serious reliability problems reported by ADAC (the German breakdown organisation) in its 2001 report. Getting a reputation for flattening batteries due to some kind of immobiliser fault which Volvo dealers seem unable to trace (see April 2001 recall which could be the culprit). Also a locking problem, which particularly affects the rear hatchback lock.

What to watch out for: See S80, but depreciation will always be lower for an estate car. Make sure all the door locks work properly, especially the rear hatchback lock (see recalls).

Recalls: August 2000: V70 models recalled because front suspension ball joint can work loose or fail. 2/4/2001: Possible faults in rear door wiring harnesses may prevent child safety locks working. Check for effective operation and replace wiring harness if necessary. 2/4/2001: left and right rear outer seatbelt bottom fixing bolts and rhs child restraint anchor bracket may be loose or may have been incorrectly torqued. Re-torque as necessary. TSB issued early 2002 to fix intermittent fault with remote central locking.

V90 (from 2005)

What's good: Low, wide estate car, a bit like Audi's concept car for the new A8. Apparently to b powered by new transverse 3.0 V6 with 225bhp, or a 3.2 V6 common rail diesel. To have 1,900 litres of floor to ceiling loadspace.

What's bad: Too soon to say.

What to watch out for: Too soon to say.

XC90 (from Autumn 2002)

What's good: New four wheel drive Volvo based on wide-body S80 that's a cross between an estate car and a big 4x4 SUV. High ground clearance. Seven forward facing seats. 163bhp, 340Nm torque D5 diesel or 272bhp, 380Nm torque twin-turbo straight six petrol engines. Unveiled January 2002 at Detroit Show; UK launch: Autumn 2002. UK Prices: D5S £28,400; D5S Geartronic: £29,650; T6S Geartronic: £31,640; D5SE: £30,400; D5SE Geartronic: £31,650; T6SE Geartronic: £33,640. Prices undercut Audi Allroad, which only has five seats.

What's bad: Too soon to say.

What to watch out for: Too soon to say.

VW

A000 from 2004

What's good: New back to basics small car to replace Lupo and cost around £4,000. Also to be a Skoda version.

What's bad: Project canned due to lack of enthusiasm by the Chinese (the car's principal market) who found the car too small and basic for Chinese consumers. Going to build Lupo in China instead.

What to watch out for: Too soon to say.

Beetle (from 1998)

What's good: Golf Mk IV-based and an instant cult car in the USA and Europe. Standard engine is updated 8-valve 2.0 litre from Golf III, which is pleasantly torquey and suits town work. TDI 90 engine available and 100 bhp 1.6 petrol. Four-Star performance in NCAP crash safety tests. As with Golf Mk IV, gains serious roadholding and handling improvements for 2002 model year. Also a 150bhp 1.8T and a 170bhp V5, which is a hoot to drive. 100bhp TDI PD diesel from early 2001 with a/c for £14,175. Low 143g/km CO_2 output. Prices cut March 2002 to Beetle 1.6 102bhp: £11,750 OTR; Beetle 2.0 115bhp: £13,495 OTR. Convertible from Summer 2002 to give model a new lease of life.

What's bad: No more than a Golf Mk IV in a beetle shell, which is nothing like as practical as that of the Golf. Very little room in the back seats. Small luggage capacity. UK prices started at £15,775 for LHD with a/c, alloys and a full spec including a bud vase. Strictly a fashion accessory 'fun' car. Difficult to park. Batch of 500 non air-conditioned 2.0 litre models dumped on UK market Summer 2001. Dull to drive before 2002 model year handling improvements. Enthusiasm seems to have switched to the MINI.

What to watch out for: Grey imports started arriving in the UK in 1998. Trade imports restricted to 50 by SVA, so don't buy a non-registered Beetle or you won't be able to register it. Look out for parking damage at the ends. Don't buy without a/c.

Recalls: May 1998, first 12,000 recalled in USA because wiring could become trapped by battery, overheat and catch fire. April 2002: German recall of all Beetles with standard ABS (no problem with those with ABS + EDS, ASR, ESP.)

Beetle rear engined (from 1946)

What's good: Still being imported from Brazil by www.beetles-uk.com 1600cc fuel injected and catalysed flat four. Prices from £7,995 for basic LHD. Convertibles £16,995. Three year importers warranty. Used examples also available. Parts costs: Complete unleaded engine £1,695; set of seats: £595; complete bodyshell, painted, wax-injected and with headlining: £2,995.

What's bad: Handling, lack of speed.

What to watch out for: Tied to Beetles UK for parts, etc.

Bora (1999 on)

What's good: Good-looking saloon version of Mk IV Golf with stiffer suspension and V5 engine available from launch. Superb set of gear ratios in V5 giving nice, linear acceleration. Big boot. Higher specs than Toledos with similar power outputs. Galvanised body has 12-year warranty. 2.8 V6 4–Motion introduced early 2001. 150bhp V5 increased to 170bhp with new cylinder head. Cut-price 2.0 litre S version, non PD TD 110 and 150bhp 1.8 petrol turbo versions launched to expand the range in May 2001. TDI PD 130 replaced TDI PD 115 in early Summer 2001 at price premium of £275. Very low CO_2 emissions of 146g/km. 5-speed Tiptronic available with PD 130. TDI 100PD also available in Bora from October 2001 with CO_2 output is slightly lower at 143g/km. Prices are £14,270 for the S, £15,870 for the SE and £17,060 for the 5-speed SE Tiptronic which emits 176g/km CO_2. New for 2002 a 150bhp TDI PD six-speed offering 236lb ft (320Nm) torque, 0–60 in 8.4 seconds and a top speed of 134mph. 34mpg on the combined cycle and 149g/km C02. Priced at £17,995 in Sport trim with lowered suspension, ASR traction control, walnut wood trim, sports seats with lumbar support, 3x3 point rear seat belts, dash controlled CD autochanger and air-conditioning. 21st from top of 100 models for reliability in *Auto Express* 2002 survey. All Boras fitted with ESP in addition to ABB with EBD from June 2002 (see recall announcement).

What's bad: More expensive than Seat Toledo and Skoda Octavia siblings. Stiffer suspension might be an advantage on open roads in the dry, but lacks 'bite' and can make the overlight steering feel a bit frightening when turning in on a wet bend. Bora estate not available in the UK. See Golf Mk IV for longer list of problem areas. Some earlier Mk IVs with lowered suspension could ground their sumps on road humps.

What to watch out for: See Golf Mk IV.

Recalls: 26/2/2001: Build October and November 2000: Passenger airbag may not inflate correctly due to leak in pressure reservoir of gas generator. Passenger airbags to be replaced. (149 cars affected: same fault as on SEAT Leon and Toledo and Skoda Fabia.) 1/12/2001: Limited recall of seven Golf and Bora 4–Motion models built 1/2/1997 to 28/2/2000 because moisture can enter rear axle ball joints causing corrosion of the joints leading them to seize and the suspension transverse arm to snap. Ball joints and transverse arm to be replaced. April 2002: German recall of all Boras with standard ABS (no problem with those with ABS + EDS, ASR, ESP.) By June 2002 this became a Worldwide recall.

Brazil Type 2 Bay Window

What's good: Surfers favourite vehicle. Still being imported new from Brazil by www.beetles-uk.com Available as a panel van with side doors from £9,000 + VAT; as a bus from £12,999 including VAT; or as a 2 or 4 berth elevating roof Rio camper from £15,999 including VAT. Powered by 1.6 litre injected and catalysed flat four engine. Three year importers warranty. LHD or RHD.

What's bad: On original examples, rust (see two owners reports below).

What to watch out for: Comments on these old Bay Windows from The Back Room, the online forum at www.honestjohn.co.uk:

'Your main enemy is rust. Look under the front seats, in the wheel arches front and rear, the sills and the door hinges. And make sure (that's *really* sure) that the chassis hasn't been patched up with filler. If there is *any* sign of a repair, such as a patch of new-ish underseal or suchlike, ask to see receipts or photographs of the repair and if you have any doubt at all walk away. There are a lot of rusty old heaps out there with gleaming new paint ready for the summer. If you can get one with an oil temp. gauge (the oil is also the coolant) so much the better. If not, it might be worth having one fitted. Later models (post-1972 I think) are better in a crash and have disc brakes, although many earlier ones will have had them fitted anyway.' (Thanks to Chris.)

'You do need to worry about the body work. Signs of rust, accident repair, previous damage etc. If it's going on a ramp, my experience would suggest that any problem will probably be visible: inside the wings, under the carpets, around the fuel tank, front bulkhead, etc. Check which camper conversion it is and who it was done by.' (Thanks to Mark from Brazil.)

Caravelle (from 2003)

What's good: New Caravelle based on practical new T5 van. Floorpan also to be used for new Microbus.
What's bad: Too soon to say.
What to watch out for: Too soon to say.

Caravelle T4 (to 2003)

What's good: VW's front engined Transporter in short and long wheelbase estate car format. Various trim options, such as Multivan with curtains and seats that convert to a bed. Bags of room inside. Useful 5 cylinder TDI diesel offering up to 35mpg and reasonable 80–90mph cruising. Quite nice to drive with TDI engine. Good view. You see hazards ahead over the roofs of normal passenger cars. 2.5TDI can be chipped to give higher performance. Also a VR6 version as well as 1.9 TDIs.

Much improved after 1996 facelift. Metallic paint is best.

What's bad: Big. Built at van plant at Hanover to van standards, which is basically to run reliably to a high mileage in a short time. Paint and rustproofing not to car standards, though improved hugely after 1996 facelift. Sold only by VW commercial vehicle dealers, so service reception isn't like a VW franchise. VR6 is a heavy drinker. Earlier non-TDI models were awful to drive. Only available from VW commercial vehicle dealers. VR6 is a heavy drinker. TDI's timing belt drives water pump and, if water pump fails, so does belt. Injection distribution pump timing difficult and expensive to re-set when renewing timing belt.

What to watch out for: When buying used, look for rust and paint defects. Best engine is the 5 cylinder 2.5 TDI, but remember it needs frequent expensive timing belt and tensioner replacements, and a new timing belt driven waterpump every 80,000 miles.

Corrado (1989 to 1995)

What's good: 136bhp 1.8 16v, 160bhp 1.8 G60 supercharged, 115bhp 2.0 8v, 136bhp 2.0 16v. But the engine to have is VW's VR6, here in superb 2.9 litre 190 bhp form. Excellent front-drive handling. Best bought for sensible money LHD in Germany. VR6 recommended.

What's bad: They were part of the drug dealers 'uniform', so don't be surprised if low lifes edge up to the car and flash money at you. Can suffer more than their fair share of niggly faults. Demand exceeds supply, so these cars are expensive. Cheaper used German imports will, of course, have been driven at 150 mph on the Autobahn and will suffer stone damage to the body and paint. Parts prices are high with very few cut-price alternatives.

What to watch out for: Pre-digital odometers easy to clock. VR6s fashionable among drug dealers 1996–97, often evidenced by 'flash' modifications. If aircon fitted, make sure it blows cold. Superchargers of G60s wear out (can be reconditioned by Jabbasport from £320, tel: 01733 571769). Check water level in expansion chamber and look for emulsified oil under oil cap as engines tend to blow head gasket at about 60,000 miles. Very hard to re-surface narrow angle V6 block and head and coolant in combustion chambers leads to burned out piston crowns. Problem also emerging of stretched timing chains on VR6s and chains actually breaking at around 90,000 miles.

Recalls: 1996 (4-cylinder cars 1988F-1989G): bypass valve to be inserted into heater pipe; heater matrix to be replaced if degraded. 1996 (VR6 1993–95): cooling fan motor may seize.

Golf Mk 1 GTI (1975 to 1983 to 1993)

What's good: Giugiaro designed, the original and lightest GTI, just 805kg, first with Bosch injected 1.6 but the one to go for is the 112bhp 1.8 fitted for the last three months of production. A real flying machine and still exhilarating, only bettered by the Peugeot 205GTi which handled, braked and looked even better. Now a collectors piece with the best examples worth £12,000 +. Converting to 1.8 or 2.0 litre 140bhp 16v engine adds rather than reduces value. Some also running latest 1.8 20v four. The Mk 1 cabrio continued right through to December 1993 after which it was replaced by the Mk III cabrio. A small batch of the very last Mk 1 cabrios has official retro-fitted PAS. 12ft 3in long by 5ft 3in wide.

What's bad: Rust. All Mk 1 Golfs rust and though rustproofing was improved by the introduction of RHD GTIs they can still be bad. Complicated right to left brake linkage robs brakes of feel and makes action unpleasant. Notchy 'across the gate' gearshift. (The first LHD Golf GTis were 4-speeders). No power steering even on cabrio unless retro fitted using LHD Scirocco Gate 16v parts or a kit from TSR of Bridgwater. Old, but a classic.

What to watch out for: Accident damage, rust, and the general quality of the inevitable modifications.

Golf MK II (1983 to 1992)

What's good: Image. 16v the one to have. Unlikely to rust in the glued rather than welded seams. Long-life engines, exhausts, batteries, shock absorbers. Euro Car Parts (0541 506506) supplies cheap parts. The older they are, the less replacement parts they seem to need – almost as if the originals were designed to wear out.

Bigger than Mk 1 at 13ft 1in long by 5ft 6in wide, and heavier too at 835kg to 1,000kg.

What's bad: Rattles. Needs a cambelt change every four years or 40,000 miles and a tensioner change every 80,000 miles. Plastic door membranes go, leading to soggy carpets. Water pumps, clutches, front strut top bearings, etc. have only average life. Clutch cable self-adjusters go, leading to premature clutch wear. Hubs go in 8–12 years (80,000–120,000 miles). Underfloor fuel pump on fuel-injected cars springs a leak after 9–10 years. Water pumps last 5–10 years. Radiators last 5–10 years. Rear disc callipers on Gate can go and cost £300 each. Pneumatic central locking starts to fail on rear doors after 11 years. Steel wheels can fleck with rust after 6 years. Getting old.

What to watch out for: Make sure heater matrix bypass has been installed (major recall 1995–97). Check oil filler cap for black sludge (oil not changed regularly enough) or mayonnaise (cylinder head gasket problems). Check driveshafts by reversing car on full lock in both directions. Easily clocked so look for signs of more miles than the odo shows. Rear discs rust first, become pitted and fail MOT. Clutches last 70,000–80,000 miles on average, less with town driving. Driver's seat upholstery should last 12 years and 100,000 miles before starting to wear through. Bonnet slam panel should be matt black, not body colour. After 12 years, cam cover of all but 16v should have lost almost all its paint unless owned by someone particularly fastidious. Engines should look scruffy, not 'steam cleaned', because steam cleaning washes off rustproofing. Look for a square white sticker showing the vehicle identification number on the inside of the boot sill. No sticker is a sure sign that the car has been rear-ended. Went hydraulic tappets in 1986: cheaper to service. Rusts first on top of scuttle between screen and bonnet.

Recalls: 1995 (Golf 1.6 & 1.8 1983A to 1989G): bypass valve to be inserted into heater pipe; heater matrix to be replaced if degraded. 1996 (Golf 1.3 1983A to 1989G): bypass valve to be inserted into heater pipe; heater matrix to be replaced if degraded.

Golf MK III (1992 to 1997)

What's good: Strong image. High residuals. Best engines are 90bhp TDI, 150bhp 2.0 16v and 174bhp 2.8 VR6 engines. Also 100 bhp 1.6 fitted to last Golf GLs. Now 13ft 2in long and 5ft 7in wide. Weighs from 1,000kg to 1,155kg. Euro Car Parts (0541 506506) supplies cheap parts.

What's bad: Strong image not completely justified. Three-door models flex quite badly (five-door models are better). Handling and roadholding not brilliant by 90s standards. 4-speed autobox can have problems, Since VW dealers charge £4,000 for a new one, this is best sorted by an independent specialist. Often no more than an oil control valve. Though car may remain solid and rust-free, many replacement parts will be needed over 10-year life. More than its fair share of recalls.

What to watch out for: Premature clutch wear due to faulty self-adjusting cable. Oil-burning TDI engines. Clocking. See Mk II. Also reports of wiring faults developing in electric window circuits, lights, rear window demister, so check all electrics carefully before buying (see recalls). Problems emerging of stretched timing chains on VR6s and chains actually breaking at around 90,000 miles. On 5-door models, look for rust on the hinge face of the rear door frames.

Recalls: 1995 (Golf Gate, 16v, VR6, Convertible: VIN 1HPW 439315 to 1HSW 418237 and 1ERK 000001 to 1ESK 025159): headlamp failures. Headlight switch on RHD models can overheat, leading to headlight failure. 28,000 cars affected. 1996: (1993–95 build): cooling fan motor may seize. 1997 (single headlight models). January 1997 recall for headlight failure. Headlight switch on RHD models can overheat, leading to headlight failure. 9,700 cars affected. 1997 (1994–97 build): September 1997 recall for headlamp modification for all cars. Total 150,000 cars affected. 1997 (1991–94 models with electric front windows: 16,000 cars): insulation on power cable may chafe and short-circuit. Needs protective shield in cable opening of door. 1997 (Aug '93–Jan '97 build): engine wiring loom may overheat.

Golf MK IV (1998 to 2003)

What's good: Status and strong used values. Much better looking than Mk III. UK market cars have high equipment levels, including ABS. 3-year manufacturer and dealer warranty. More room, safer and better handling than Mk III. Now 13ft 8in long by 5ft 8in wide and weighing from 1,163kg to 1,306kg. (V6 4–Motion even heavier.) Super-efficient and quick 110 bhp TDI available for first time in UK. Later 115 bhp TDI with six-speed gearbox even quicker and 35 mph/1,000 rpm makes it even more economical at speed. 100 bhp 1.6 petrol good 'cooking' engine. 150 bhp VR5, later uprated to 170bhp, makes a wonderful noise, has a good set of gear ratios. 204 BHP V6 six-speed 4 motion is the spiritual successor to the Mk III VR6, and a much better car with grippy four-wheel-drive chassis. Joint top of the class for secondary safety in NCAP crash testing after side airbags fitted from August 1998. Excellent car-like estate not the biggest in its class but feels very classy. The qualities of these cars grow on you. Galvanised body has 12-year warranty. Mk V Golf cabrio due in 2002 with folding steel top. V5 uprated in late 2000 with new 20 valve cylinder head, raising power to 170bhp and torque to 166lb ft. (NB Like the VR6, the V5 is a narrow-angle V5 with a single cylinder head for both banks.) More price competitive in UK after December 2000 price cuts and newfound willingness of dealers to discount. PD 130 TDI replaced PD 115 TDI in early Summer 2001. Very low CO_2 emissions of 146g/km. 5-speed Tiptronic available with PD 130. Serious roadholding and handling improvements to Mk IV range for 2002MY. Now as good as the SEAT Leon. GT TDI PD 130 is a great drive with 52mpg economy. See VW Triple test at www.honestjohn.co.uk. 'Pumpe Duse' 100bhp TDI replaces the old conventionally injected TDI 90bhp. Facts and figures are: 100bhp at 4,000rpm; 177lb ft (240Nm) torque at 1,800rpm; top speed 117mph; zero to 60mph 11.0 seconds; combined economy 52.3mpg; and CO_2 output 146g/km. Prices are £14,200 for the S, £15,320 for the SE and £16,510 for the 5-speed SE Tiptronic automatic (which emits 178g/km CO_2). The same engine is available in the Golf estate with marginally lower performance and an increased CO_2 output of 149g/km. Prices are £14,840 for the S, £15,960 for the SE and

£17,130 for the 5-speed SE Tiptronic (which emits 178g/km CO_2). Ninth most reliable car in 2001 Fleet News Survey of 620,000 fleet cars mostly under 3 years old. New for 2002 a 150bhp TDI PD six-speed offering 236lb ft (320Nm) torque, 0–60 in 7.6 seconds and a top speed of 134mph. 34mpg on the combined cycle and 149g/km C02. Prices: £17,425 for the 3–door and £18,045 for the 5–door. Prices include GTI Turbo trim, sixteen inch Montreal II alloys, lowered suspension, ASR traction control, black wood trim, sports seats with lumbar support, 3x3 point rear seat belts, CD player and air-conditioning. VW issued a new price list for Golfs on 1–3–2002 and, for the first time in the UK, a base 1.4E 3–door comes in at under £10,000. This is a cut of £720 on the previous price but, more significantly a full £2,000 less than when the Golf IV was launched back in November 1997.

More online at www.volkswagen.co.uk

What's bad: Steering originally very light but much improved for 2002 model year. Modification to 'B' pillar delayed production. Cable gearchange on all but 1.6 and 1.4, and have been problems with early 1.6 and 1.6 gearboxes. Original 1.8 20v and 1.8 20v Turbo work well but don't involve the driver. 1.8 20v replaced by old 115 bhp 2.0 litre 8 valver in 1999. Not everyone likes the relatively hard seats. Plastic coating rubs off the armrests of the doors and looks terrible. The back of the car gets very dirty. Alarm sensitivity on early production corrected by unnecessary pillar-mounted sensors (all drivers had to do was shut off the air supply to inside the car). Front door lock barrels of 1998 Golf Mk IVs can be prised out with a screwdriver and the windows opened without activating the microwave alarm. (Higher spec Golfs from 1999 on have ultra sonic alarms which can only be deactivated by the remote fob.) Heavy, so slower than Mk III when fitted with the same engines. Some TD 110s had a problem of stalling while coasting to a standstill from about 15 mph in neutral. The cure was to replace the ECU, but if the car was a personal import out of its 12–month pan-Euro warranty, the owner had to pay. This problem now seems to be coming back on high mileage TDI 110s. VAG acknowledges a fault with the ECU (038 906 018 BM) and specifies an upgraded unit (038 906 018 GQ) at £695.00 + VAT. According to

VAG technical, this problem will eventually occur with all ECUs of this part number, so a second hand part may only be only a short term cure. Glass headlamp lenses of GTI and Highline models break easily and cost £260 to replace. Best protected by £25 headlamp protectors from VW dealers. Quite a few build quality niggles emerging, especially on South African (SA VIN cars), such as squeaking seats, rattling window mechanisms inside doors which can fail entirely, clutch bearing failure, flywheel failure, trim panel for sunroof falling off rails, side window glass coming out of carriers, pipe to rear washer coming off and staining ceiling trim. Also reports of complete failure of ancillary electrics and problems with six speed gearbox on TDI 115. Supply problem in Autumn 2001 particularly of TDI PD 130s due to a strike at the South African factory from which a proportion of RHD UK market Golf Mk IVs are sourced. Getting reports of problems with V6 4–Motions: excess tyre wear, pulling to the left, same problem with printed circuit boards of self levelling Xenon headlights as occurred with Honda Accord Type R (same supplier). In damp weather, which then turns to freezing weather, the soft door seals are apt to freeze up and either make the doors impossible to open or tear when the doors are opened. Silicone grease is the answer. Audi A3 problem of leaking rear brake fluid union finding its way into early Mk IV Golfs. Some earlier Mk IVs with lowered suspension could ground their sumps on road humps. Mass Airflow Sensor problems common on 1.8T. For 1.8T problems and their solutions, check online at http://forums.vwvortex.com/zeroforum?id=27 Starting to get reports of gearbox problems on mechanical shift 1.4s and 1.6s. New Golf Mk V including 7 seater mini MPV due in 2002. Faulty power steering switch on 1.6 can cause hunting of engine and erratic idle. Poor performance and fuel economy of Y and 51 reg. 1.6 16vs may be due to fault with ECU, cured under warranty by dealer replacing the ECU.

What to watch out for: RHD personal imports not to full UK spec – especially estate cars. Some TDI 110s suffered a low-speed running problem which could only be cured by a modified flywheel and inlet manifold and in some cases a re-chipped ECU. See faults list above. On early Mk IVs look for rear brake fluid leaks as hydraulic connection to rear brake callipers can corrode due to types of metals used. Look under engine for damage to sump from road humps.

Recalls: Announced *Daily Telegraph* 1/10/98: 9,500 Mk 1V Golfs from SE spec upwards fitted with volumetric alarms recalled to fit less sensitive volumetric sensors. (Not actually necessary because problem can be solved by using ventilation control to shut off outside air.) 1999: 70 early production 115 PDs recalled to replace pistons because they were not properly coated with a Teflon-like material in production. 22/1/2001 (Estate only): Welding faults on the seams of the ISOFIX mounting bars may occur. ISOFIX mounting bars to be re-welded. 26/2/2001: Build October and November 2000: Passenger airbag may not inflate correctly due to leak in pressure reservoir of gas generator. Passenger airbags to be replaced. (149 cars affected: same fault as on SEAT Leon and Toledo and Skoda Fabia.) 1/12/2001: Limited recall of seven Golf and Bora 4–Motion models built 1/2/1997 to 28/2/2000 because moisture can enter rear axle ball joints causing corrosion of the joints leading them to seize and the suspension transverse arm to snap. Ball joints and transverse arm to be replaced. April 2002: German recall of all Golfs with standard ABS (no problem with those with ABS + EDS, ASR, ESP.) Led to Worldwide recall in June 2002.

Golf Mk V (from 2003)

What's good: Code name A-5 on PQ35 floorpan, this is the new Golf Mk V to be revealed at the Paris Motor Show in autumn 2002 for sale from August 2003. Engines may include 86bhp FSI 1.4, 116bhp FSI 1.6, 150bhp FSI 2.0; 185bhp 2.0T, 150bhp TDI, 240bhp 3.2 V6 and possibly a 175bhp V5 TDI. Will include entry level 75bhp 1.4 16v and 102bhp 1.6 16v. Multi-link rear suspension. To be launched at Frankfurt Show in autumn 2003.

What's bad: Launch of FSIs may be delayed in the UK because they depend on petrol which is almost 100% sulphur free (less than 10 parts per million).

What to watch out for: Too soon to say.

Golf Mk V 7-seat MPV (from late 2002)

What's good: VAG's 5 or 7 seat Zafira and Peugeot 307SW competitor due now at Paris Show autumn 2002 with sales starting in Germany by the end of 2002, to be priced from around £13,000 in UK. Engines may include 116bhp FSI 1.6, 150bhp FSI 2.0; 185bhp 2.0T, 150bhp TDI. Will be 4,380mm long, 1,8770mm wide. Scoop pictures in '*Autocar*' issue 11/4/2001. '*Auto Express*' carried a different image with disguised headlights in issue 671, 19–25 September 2001.

What's bad: Too soon to say.

What to watch out for: Too soon to say.

Jetta (1983 to 1992)

What's good: Underrated 'Golf with a rucksack'. Stiffer body so handles better than a Golf with fewer rattles. 139bhp 16v seriously quick, does 60 in 2nd gear, and gets there in 7 seconds. 'Long life' bodies, exhausts, batteries, shock absorbers. 14ft 2in long by 5ft 5in wide. Weighed from an amazingly light 725kg (for the 2.3) to 1,010kg (for the 16v). PAS standard on 'big bumper' versions from August 1989. Euro Car Parts (0541 506506) supplies cheap parts.

What's bad: Dowdy image. See under Golf Mk II.

What to watch out for: See Golf Mk II.

Recalls: 1995 (1.6 & 1.8 1983A to 1989G): bypass valve to be inserted into heater pipe; heater matrix to be replaced if degraded. 1996 (1.3 1983A to 1989G): bypass valve to be inserted into heater pipe; heater matrix to be replaced if degraded.

Lupo (from 1999)

What's good: High build quality. 11ft 7in long by 5ft 5in wide. Same car as Seat Arosa, built at Wolfsburg, with cute front-end styling, much nicer interior, twin airbags, height-adjustable driver's seat and steering wheel as standard. Formed basis of '3–litre car' – capable of 100kms on three litres of petrol, equal to 94 mpg. 1.4s have new twin-cam 16v engine. 1.7SDI charming, economical and not too slow – a far better bet than the 1.0 litre petrol version. 100

bhp 1.4 16v Sport from September '99. 75 bhp 1.4 direct injected diesel option. Lupo FSi with direct injected petrol engine giving 105 bhp and 56 mpg shown at 1999 Frankfurt Show. Lupo did well in German TUV/*Auto Bild* front offset crash test. Four-Star NCAP crash safety rating. Six speed gearbox and alloy body panels for 125bhp Lupo Gate at no extra cost from mid 2001. Now does 127mph, 0–60 in 8 seconds. Price of base model 1.0 cut to £6,995 in April 2002. Both 1.7SDI and 1.4TDI emit 119g/km CO_2, so qualify for reduced £80pa VED from April 2002.

What's bad: Prices higher than Seat Arosa. Power steering a £450 option on 1.0 litre base model. 1.0 litre horribly, painfully slow.

What to watch out for: Problem of breather pipes failing on 1.4S models built in 2001. VW modifying the part.

Recalls: June 2002: 120,000 Polos, Lupos and Arosas built during 1998 and 1999 recalled because cracks in the brake vacuum pipe could lead to loss of servo assistance to the brakes. Recall hotline: 0800 711811.

Microbus (from 2005)

What's good: VW concept vehicle is 4,722mm long, 1,904mm high and 1,909mm wide. (Note that its height disqualifies it for the best discounted fares on the Eurotunnel Shuttle.) Power comes from VAG's 236bhp 3.2 litre V6, as found under the bonnet of top versions of the latest Audi A4. Torque is 236lb ft and the gearbox is a five-speed Tiptronic. Interior design features include a dash mounted gearshift lever, seven TV/video plasma screens and three rows of seats the centre pair of which swivel. June 2002 announcement that will definitely go into production at VW's Hanover commercial vehicle plant to replace the Portugal built Sharan. Will share floorpan of next Transporter. Production versions may differ from concept in engines and trim level. Options likely to include 175bhp TD, four wheel drive. Code named 'Kombi Bully' before the marketing boys took over.

More online at www.volkswagen.co.uk

What's bad: Too soon to say

What to watch out for: Too soon to say

Passat (1982 to 1988)

What's good: Audi 80 derived hatchback, estate and 4–door saloon (badged Santana). Santana still built in China. Hatchback 14ft 7in long; estate 14ft 11in long; both 5ft 6in wide and weighing from 950kg. Strong, nicely built and have clocked up mega mileages of 500,000 plus. 85bhp 1.6; 90bhp 1.8; 54bhp 1.6 diesel; 70bhp 1.6 turbodiesel; 115bhp 5 cylinder 2.0. 5-speed manual with option of 3-speed auto on 1.8 and 2.0GL5. 1.8 estate quite well balanced and handles surprisingly well.

What's bad: No power steering on 1.6, 1.8 and diesels and steering is very heavy indeed. All engines overhang the front wheels and the 2.0 is a severe plough-on understeerer.

What to watch out for: Resist rust very well. The seats seem to wear out long before the running gear. Listen for clicking driveshafts because just one replacement will cost you more than the car is worth. Lots of these cars saw out their days as 'work cars' full of plumbers or builders kit and often overloaded.

Passat (1988 to 1997)

What's good: Estates have excellent rear legroom, are comfortable and handle well. 15ft long by 5ft 7in wide and weighing in from 1,125kg to 1,250kg. Engines now transverse, not overhanging. Was a 174 bhp VR6, briefly, 1993–95. TDI 90 best compromise engine. Estates hold value well. Saloons worth £2,000 less. Aircon available in lieu of sunroof.

What's bad: Good, well-specified estates hard to find and still sell for strong money. All diesel models may have been cabbed. Saloons have dowdy image.

What to watch out for: As Golf/Jetta/Vento. Make sure aircon blows cold. Make sure not cabbed. A lot of this model Passat began their lives on rental fleets. Problems emerging of stretched timing chains on VR6s and chains actually breaking at around 90,000 miles.

Recalls: 1995 (VIN3ARE 0000001 to 3ASE 142536): headlamp failures. 1996 (4-cylinder Passats 1988F-1989G): bypass valve to be inserted into heater pipe; heater matrix to be replaced if degraded. 1996 (1993–95 build): Cooling fan motor may seize. VW Passat (Dec '95–Mar '98): may be airbag activator fault.

Passat (1997 to 2000)

What's good: The best perceived quality in its class; really a class above. High quality plastics and velours, nicely put together. Much more status than a Mondeo or Vectra. 15ft 4in long by 5ft 9in wide. TDI 90 and 110 engines better than 1.8 20v, but 20v turbo will do 140 mph – and brake from 140 mph safely. Very low levels of wind and road noise. Excellent economy from TDI 90 and 110 – many owners will better 50 mpg. Comparatively good performance in NCAP crash tests. Improved 115 bhp, 210 lb ft TDi for 2000 model year. High spec, reasonably priced SEL trim versions launched summer 2000 from £15,570 OTR for 1.8 20v to £17,110 OTR for TDI 115 PD. Galvanised body has 11-year warranty. Trim lasts well. Properly looked after, these cars can stay looking new for years. Fourth most reliable car in 2001 Fleet News Survey of 620,000 fleet cars mostly under 3 years old.

What's bad: Went back to overhanging engine design. Steering a bit too light, especially on motorways. Vague feeling can be partially cured by fitting aftermarket Bilstein dampers. Imprecise gearshift. Hasn't lived up to its quality promise. Since 1997, Ford Mondeos have been far more reliable. Yet perceived quality still leads to high residuals making Passats expensive used buys until they hit high mileages. Alarming number of build-quality faults and problems, such as leaks from screen area, under-dash rattles, seatbelts failing to free-reel, rear shock absorbers failing, whining 4-speed automatics when mated to 1.8 litre 20v engine (1.6 auto, diesel auto and 5-speed Tiptronic OK). Front door lock barrels of 1997–1998 Passats can be prised out with a screwdriver and the doors opened without activating the microwave alarm. (Passats from 1999 on have ultra sonic alarms which can only be deactivated by the remote fob.) Cats fail on TDIs built before August 1998. Came lower than Mondeo and Freelander in 'R' reg. J.D. Power Customer Satisfaction Survey. Heavy salted road spray may make front brakes feel spongey. In Germany, deflectors are available FOC to cure this (*Auto Bild* magazine 24/11/2000). Poor AM radio reception. Reports of corroded rear brake seals and failing front suspension wishbones at around four years old. Wishbone replacement is a £500 to £700 job. Plenum chamber seal fails allowing water in which can lead to electrical failures and eventually collects in rear footwell. Complaints of rear doors not latching properly and doors flying open.

What to watch out for: Needs to be the right colour (not white, solid green or solid blue). Check very carefully for signs of water leaks (feel footwell carpets for damp). May be a structural leak, or may be because the a/c condenser drain pipe is blocked leading to water being dumped into the footwell. Listen for rattles. Check front tyre wear. Blue exhaust smoke from diesel indicates faulty turbo oil seals. Plastic water pump impellers on early 1.8 20v engines fail (newer water pumps have metal impellers). If dash warning light stays on permanently, it's usually because a wrong button has been pressed on the VAG 1552 electronic interrogator when the car was in for a service.

Recalls: 1998: 11,450 cars built May-November 1997 recalled due to potential fault affecting front seatbelts. Involves replacing complete belt units. 1998: Passat Synchro (Dec '97–Apr '98 build): throttle and brake hose problems; 11,450 Passats built between May and November 1997 recalled due to potential fault affecting front seatbelts. Involves replacing complete belt units. 2000: March '98–August '98–built Passats recalled because steering track rod ends could work loose. £500 factory accessory removable towbar has been recalled twice. March 2001: Worldwide recall of 560,000 1999 model year A4s, A6s, A8s and VW Passats to replace steering ball joints (track rod ends). Announced *Auto Bild* 11/3/2001. German 'Worldwide recall' of all VW Passats from 1996 to July 2001, Audi A4s from 1994, Audi A6s from 1997 to replace faulty front lower wishbones. Recall announced in *Auto Bild* 25th/26th August 2001. The ball joint can fail and the two other flex connections can fail. (These are the long arms that go from the bottom of the front hubs to the body.)

Passat (2001 to 2004)

What's good: Much more than merely facelifted Passat looks classy and hides very comprehensive improvements under the skin. Now with a 12 year body warranty. Steering gives slightly better road feel. Sloppy gearchange improved. New engine range begins with 2.0 litre 8 valve 115bhp shared with Golf Mk IV Gate, but at a low price of £14,495 which includes ABS, climate control, Thatcham 1 alarm immobiliser and much more. TDI 130 S is an excellent car for company drivers because it combines a low CO_2 output of 154 g/km with a low on the road price of £16,310. Has no less than 228 lb ft torque and goes like a steam train. Range also includes a 100bhp TDI PD, a 150bhp 1.8 petrol turbo, a 150bhp V6 TDI, a 170bhp V5 and a 193bhp V6 4Motion four wheel drive. 6 speed manual gearbox on TDI PD 130 Sport and TDI V6 Sport. Others have 5 speed manual, 5 speed Tiptronic auto or 4 speed auto. Will be a 280bhp W8 4Motion capable of 0–60 in 6 seconds and 150mph top speed for less than £30,000 by the end of 2001. TDI PD 130 voted Diesel Car magazine Car of the Year. Full road test and comprehensive range and spec description in the road tests at www.honestjohn. co.uk. 150bhp petrol turbo S versions of saloon and estate introduced May 2001 with 5-speed Tiptronic auto option. Achieved 4–star Euro NCAP crash safety score. Fourth most reliable car in 2001 Fleet News Survey of 620,000 fleet cars mostly under 3 years old. 115bhp 8 valve 2.0 litre engine replaced by the 130bhp 20v 2.0 litre as used in the new Audi A4 in May 2002. 0–60 comes down from 10.9 seconds to 9.6 seconds, top speed goes up from 124mph to 130mph, fuel economy improves from 32.8 mpg to 34.9 mpg on the combined cycle, and CO_2 emissions are down from 206g/km to 194g/km. Price for the S spec with standard a/c goes up by £155 to £14,850, but because CO_2 emissions are down company car drivers will actually pay less BIK tax than for the old car. The Passat S Estate with the 2.0 130bhp engine is priced at £15,800. Three 3–point rear seatbelts standard spec from mid 2002.

What's bad: Gearchange still not as good as cars like the Mondeo and a lot worse than the very precise cable shifter in the Chrysler PT Cruiser.

What to watch out for: Too soon to say.

Recalls: Worldwide recall of all VW Passats from 1996 to July 2001 to replace faulty front lower wishbones. Recall announced in *Auto*

Bild 25th/26th August 2001. The ball joint can fail and the two other flex connections can fail. (These are the long arms that go from the bottom of the front hubs to the body.)

Passat (from 2004)

What's good: New transverse-engined Passat based on stretched PQ35 floorpan with wide range of engines from 115bhp 1.6FSI petrol through to a 240bhp 3.2 petrol V6. 100bhp, 130bhp, 150bhp TDI PD 1.9s.

What's bad: Too soon to say.

What to watch out for: Too soon to say.

Passat W8 (from December 2001)

What's good: 4.0 litre all-wheel-drive 275bhp Passat W8 at the promised starter price of £29,900 for the six-speed manual saloon, which doesn't get here until March 2002. Tiptronics available from December 2001 at £31,325 for the saloon and £32,275 for the estate. (Six-speed manual estate: £30,850.) High standard spec includes ESP (electronic stabilization programme), 17 inch Madras alloy wheels, six airbags, bi-Xenon self levelling headlights, Nappa leather upholstery, walnut inserts, Climatronic air conditioning, six disc CD autochanger, rain-sensing wipers, automatic dimming rear view mirror and metallic or pearl-effect paint. Top speed of all versions is limited to 155mph, and 0–60 acceleration varies from 6.3 seconds for the manual saloon to 7.8 seconds for the Tiptronic estate. Towers should note that maximum torque is 273 lb ft (370 Nm) at 2,750rpm. Drives, grips and handles very well with a lovely 'whoopy' engine note.

More online at www.volkswagen.co.uk

What's bad: Combined consumption varies from 21.7mpg for the Tiptronic saloon to 21.2 for the manual estate. Unusually, Tiptronics slightly more economical than manuals. CO_2 emissions vary from 312g/km to 317g/km (again, the manuals come out worst) so you'll be paying 40% tax on 35% of between £29,900 and £32,275. Manuals also reported to be awful to drive with a slow, imprecise gearchange and an ECU/engine/gearbox mismatch that makes them difficult to drive smoothly.

What to watch out for: Too soon to say.

Phaeton (from late 2002)

What's good: Project Code D1 now has the model name Phaeton. This is VW's flagship model to be built at its Lower Saxony plant near Dresden and scheduled to arrive in the UK by the end of 2002. At 5,055mm (16ft 7ins) it's longer than a standard MB S Class. Engine choice starts with a 3.2 litre V6 offering 241bhp and 232ln ft (315Nm) torque, includes the 4.0 litre 270bhp W8 scheduled for the top Passat and is topped off by a 6.0 litre V12 with 420bhp and 406lb ft (552Nm) torque. But the engine creating the most interest is a 5.0 litre V10 TDI which develops 313bhp and a mammoth 553lb ft (750Nm) torque. A beefy new six-speed autobox has been developed specifically for the car, while the V10 and V12 will be four-wheel rather than merely front-wheel drive. Official Euro launch will be at the Geneva Motor Show in March 2002. UK prices are likely to range from around £37,500 to around £65,000. Will probably become the State car for China. Think of it as the development car for the new 200mph Bentley GT coupe.

More online at www.Volkswagen.co.uk

What's bad: Squint at it a bit and it looks horribly like a Peugeot 607.

What to watch out for: Too soon to say.

Polo (1981 to 1991)

What's good: Reasonable build quality whether put together in Germany or Spain. 12ft long by 5ft 2in wide. Extremely light weight, from just 700kg. Steel 'factory' sunroof a desirable extra, adds £200 to price. Euro Car Parts (0541 506506) supplies cheap parts.

What's bad: Weak front suspension. Not very roomy. Tiny boot. Surprisingly heavy steering. No brake servo prior to 1991 facelift. If water pump seizes, will usually snap cambelt. Catalysed and just 45 bhp from 1.0 litre version from 1991 model year.

What to watch out for: Piston-slapping tiny mileage shopping cars, serviced 'every two years whether they needed it or not'. (They need an oil change every six months.) Pre-hydraulic cam cars (pre-'86) more expensive to service. Need cambelt changes every 36,000–40,000 miles or every 4 years, preferably tensioner too. Sump pan can rust, especially if engine has been 'steam cleaned'. A dirty engine with peeling paint on the cam cover is a good sign. Check spec carefully. Some 1.3 CLs were 4-speed, not 5-speed and starting to get reports of gearbox failures. Will eventually rust, so check round the edges especially the door bottoms and the front bib. Normal for cam covers to lose their paint. Engines should look scruffy, not 'steam cleaned', because steam cleaning washes off rustproofing.

Tips from Keith Stockdale (in The Back Room, the online forum at www.honestjohn.co.uk):
- Check the petrol tank, especially at the join between the filler neck and main tank.
- Check how it starts and runs from cold it should be a really smooth steady idle with little noise from the hydraulic tappets.
- When it is warm it should idle nicely also. These cars can have more than their fair share of idle running problems.
- Check that the heater fan does not squeal.
- Polos eat front disks for breakfast, so have a good look at them.
- Check around the door handles for break in damage. Thieves ram a screwdriver between handle and body to get in.
- Run the car until the cooling fan kicks in and check for water leaks.
- Check the gearbox for oil leaking from the gearchange input shaft, I have not seen any that don't leak yet!! If it is and you buy it, fill it up with gearbox oil ASAP. There will be hardly any oil in the box.
- Check the clutch for smooth light action. Any roughness in the pedal action or noise from the release bearing could mean trouble. At this age the diaphragm will go before the friction material. The clutches are cheap and easy to change though. But the clutch mechanism (to press the release bearing to the diaphragm) is expensive and a stiff pedal may mean the parts are shot.

- Check the rear silencer. Although it may be modified on the newer models and not as prone to rusting.
- Take the top of the air filter housing (is it a carb model?) and check for excessive oil in the filter housing. Walk away if there is. By excessive I mean a small puddle of liquid oil, not the usual congealed light coating of oil.
- Check for accident damage. Realistically at that age the car is likely to have incurred some accident damage. Will be more rust in areas which have been badly repaired.

Polo (1991 to 1994)

What's good: 3–door Polo restyled and fitted with 45bhp single-point injected and catalysed 1,043 engine plus 4-speed manual box and option of 5-speeds.Also a 55bhp 1.3 on which 5-speeds became standard in November 1991. 75bhp multi-pint injected 1.3 GT always had 5-speeds as did supercharged 113bhp G40 for which there was even a race series. Available with vertical tailgate or sloping 'coupe' tailgate throughout. Useful option of steel wind open sunroof. These cars last well and there are still plenty about.

What's bad: Last knockings of old 3–door Polo with all its deficiencies, but GT and G40 were fun

What to watch out for: Mainly rust in front valence and doors, and need regular timing belt, belt tensioner and waterpump replacements as water pump is driven by timing belt.

Polo (1994 to 2000)

What's good: Strong UK image. A bottle green two-door Polo with a sunroof has been described as 'the most middle-class car you can buy'. (Bottle green is the 'right' colour and two rather than four side doors says 'it's a second car'.) 12ft 2in long by 5ft 5in wide and weighing from 955kg to 1,080kg. All have good, fairly upright driving position, second only to the Fiat Punto. Big car ride (much better than Punto). 3-year dealer warranty, necessitating VW franchise servicing. Comparatively good performance in NCAP crash tests. Cordoba Vario-based estate launched spring '98.

Facelifted inside and out for 2000. Very well thought of by independent VW dealers and service agents who regard them as 100% reliable.

What's bad: Gearchange quality varies. Despite VW's best efforts, Spanish build quality in general can vary. PAS not available even as an option on early 1.0 versions. 1.4 automatic not really powerful enough and can develop upshift problems from 1st to 2nd which can sometimes be successfully cured by changing a solenoid (see SEAT Arosa which has the same engine and gearbox). Surprisingly old-fashioned dashboard. Sky high used prices. 1.9 diesel not very economical when pushed. Ugly Cordoba-based saloon versions not as comfortable as hatchbacks, but have big, deep boots. 1.9SDi diesel frugal but noisy. Dashboard shows its age compared to much more cheerful Lupo. Did quite badly in 'R' reg. J.D. Power Customer Satisfaction Survey. Was 115th in 'S' and 'T' reg. survey, behind the Rover 600 and way behind the Ford Fiesta. Has appetite for front tyres, front brake discs and front pads. Reports of rusting of the doors of 1994–1999 Polos and also rust spots developing on the door frames. Reports of side windows falling off carriers into doors.

What to watch out for: Paying too much for a two- or three-year-old. Particularly paying too much for a used Polo saloon, which is really nothing more than a Seat Cordoba. Very variable gearshift quality. Faulty self-adjusting clutch cables may cause premature clutch failure. Electric windows can play up. Check front discs and pads as tend to need replacing every 30,000 miles. If buying a 1994–1999 Polo, check the doors and door frames carefully for rust, especially under the window rubber and at the bottoms of the doors. Also look for rust spots on the front valence where they could have been caused by stone chips.

Recalls: 1996 (to June 1996 build): faults in steel wheels may lead to loss of tyre pressure. June 2002: 120,000 Polos and Lupos built during 1998 and 1999 recalled because cracks in the brake vacuum pipe could lead to loss of servo assistance to the brakes. Recall hotline: 0800 711811.

Polo (2000 to 2002)

What's good: See above. Still the most status you can buy in a small ordinary hatchback, but silver now the best colour. Apart from attractive new front and interior, the car looks the same as the previous Polo but is actually 75% new with stiffer shell, tighter shut lines, higher specs (PAS and ABS on all models) and a huge range of engines from 1.0 litre 50 bhp to 1.6 litre 16v with 125 bhp. The new three-cylinder pump injector 1.4 TDI is amazing, offering 75 bhp and 144lb ft torque which makes it quick off the mark as well as very economical, from £11,670 in UK. Four-Star rating in Euro NCAP crash tests. Have seen a year old Polo sell at public auction for 86% of its new list price. Both 1.7SDI and 1.4TDI emit 119g/km C02, so qualify for £80pa VED from April 2002.

What's bad: Expensive, ranging in price at launch from £8,290 to £14,460. Gearchange quality still varies. Gate feels top heavy on corners and does not inspire confidence. Spanish rather than German build quality. Complaint that lacquer on Gate alloys is prone to peel off. To be replaced by new model on Fabia floorpan in 2002. Poor performance and fuel economy of Y and 51 reg. 1.6 16vs may be due to fault with ECU, cured under warranty by dealer replacing the ECU.

What to watch out for: Too soon to say.

Polo (from 2002)

What's good: Fine new Polo on A04 platform goes straight to the top of its class. Not innovative, versatile or spacious like the Honda Jazz. But feels beautifully put together and is a cheerful little car that's also bags of fun to drive. New 65bhp 1.2 litre chain-cam engine is the one to go for. Squeezes 47.1 miles out of a gallon but is also eager and perky. Huge line up of engines and options take base prices from £9k to £14k but can whip past £15k with a few extras. 75bhp 1.4TDI from £11,055. £7,995 55bhp base E versions arrived earlier than anticipated in late March 2002. Has ABS, PAS, height and reach adjustable steering wheel and Group 1 insurance. Also 100bhp 1.4 16v, from £12,400 in three door Sport trim. All have power steering and ABS and passenger airbag switches off. Auto available on 75bhp 1.4 only.

Achieved an excellent four star rating for crash safety in 2002 NCAP tests. Spyder also reported to be on the way to compete against Street Ka and VAG's own SEAT Tango.

What's bad: Though prices start sensibly it's very easy to spend over £10,000 and the car and lacks the innovative interior of the Honda Jazz.

What to watch out for: Too soon to say.

Polo Caddy Kombi (from 1998)

What's good: Kombi version of Polo/Ibiza/Cordoba-based Caddy van. 75 bhp 1.6i petrol and 60 bhp 1.9 SDI. Very spacious in the back and surprisingly good fun to drive. Now with option of 90 bhp TDI.

What's bad: Doesn't ride as well, isn't as practical and isn't as cheap as a Citroën Berlingo Multispace Forte HDI 90 at £8,995.

What to watch out for: Second-hand examples which have led an extremely hard double life as weekday van and weekend transport for the family and its dogs.

Scirocco Mk II (1983 to 1991)

What's good: Like the Mk 1 Scirocco, still based on the original Mk 1 Golf floorpan. Decent handling. Quite spacious inside. Variety of engines from standard 75bhp 1.6 to hot 136bhp 1.8 litre 16v, the first VAG car to get the new 16v engine. This is the one to have, but it's a rare car and only ever had power steering in LHD format. Other engines included a 90bhp carburettor 1.8 and the fuel-injected 112bhp 1.8 from the Golf Gate.

What's bad: Usual Mk1 Golf problems such as a curious across the gate gearchange and spongey brakes due to a complicated linkage from the brake pedal on the right hand side of the car to the master cylinder on the left hand side (obviously not a problem with LHDs). They also rust, but nothing like as badly as Mk 1 Golfs.

What to watch out for: Wear their miles well so are often clocked. But the newest is going to be at least ten years old and less than £750 so the main thing to look for is rust and anything likely to lead to an expensive repair, such as a clutch replacement.

Recalls: Same general cooling system recalls as other VWs: first to fit pressure release valve to the tubing, then to replace the heater matrix if it sprung a leak.

Sharan (1995 to 2003)

What's good: VW-badged Galaxy carries the most prestige and holds its value best. Got the 110 bhp TDI engine before Galaxy or Alhambra. Also first to offer 110 bhp TDI with 4-speed autobox. 1.8 20v from spring '98. Falling used values led to price cuts and VW dealers offering 'S' reg. TDI 110 'S' specs with aircon for £16,450 at 4–6 months old. Three-Star performer in NCAP crash tests (6 points front impact; 15 points side impact). Y2k revamp includes six-speed TDI 115PD and six-speed 204 bhp MPV-6 (also with 5-speed Tiptronic and/or four wheel drive). Another range restructuring in March 2002. All Sharans now come with ABS, a/c, four airbags, six speed gearbox, remote locking, alarm, trip computer and roof rails. Prices start at £18,395 for 2.0SL to £26,205 for 204bhp Carat V6 6-speed with 4Motion. Top spec autos are Carat V6 Tiptronic front wheel drive at £25,840 and Carat TDI PD 115 Tiptronic at £24,365. Cheapest TDI PD 115 six speed is the SL at £19,785 and 178g/km CO_2.

What's bad: VW 2.0 litre 8v petrol engines not as good as Ford's 2.0 and 2.3 litre twin-cams. Began to suffer from over-supply in 1998. Below average 'customer satisfaction'. On early models water can enter car via ventilation, soak the underfloor and get into the ECU which controls the electric windows and alarm system. On later models, this ECU has been moved. Aircon vulnerable to front-end shunts. Also shifted in later models. TDIs can blow turbos and catalytic converters. Have also been manual gearbox problems with TDIs. Came second bottom in 'P' reg. J.D. Power Customer Satisfaction Survey, but by 'R' reg. had improved. S and T platers 18th from bottom in 2001 *Top Gear*/J.D. Power Customer Satisfaction Survey. Pre 1999MY key-lock immobiliser models suffer same security design fault as Passats, A4s and early Golf Mk IVs. Thieves can pop out the lock barrel then use the same screwdriver to turn lock so all the windows open and alarm sensors are disabled. Problems emerging of stretched timing chains on VR6s and chains actually breaking at around 90,000 miles. Joint 16th from Bottom in 144 car 2002 JD Power/*What Car?* Customer Satisfaction Survey of V and W reg. cars. Air mass meters on TDI 110s can suffer failure through corrosion.

What to watch out for: RHD imports not to UK spec, missing important items such as air conditioning, rear seat heating, etc.

Recalls: 1997: (built Jan '96–Apr '97): problems with optional child seats. 1997 (built Dec '95–July '96): brake pads may overheat. 1998: (Aug '96–Feb '98 build): loss of power due to wiring loom failure. 13/1/2000: 80,000 Galaxys, Alhambras and Sharans VIN TV000001 to YV509825 recalled to check for contamination of brake fluid through master cylinder vent. Brake master cylinders of older cars to be replaced.

Touareg (from 2003)

What's good: New high riding 4x4 estate car from VW due in the UK summer 2003. Will be 4,750mm long, 1,930mm wide and 1,720mm high. To have choice of 4.2 V8 petrol, V6 petrol, V10 TDI and 2.5 litre V6 TDI engines. Transfer box has low ratio range and three locking diffs and with short overhangs the offroad capability should be high. Top speed of most powerful versions limited to 155mph. Designed to compete with BMW X5, MB ML, Porsche Cayenne and Range Rover.

What's bad: Unfortunate name in the UK. Sounds a bit like 'toe-rag'.
What to watch out for: Too soon to say.

Vento (1992 to 1996)

What's good: Like the Jetta, underrated and consequently cheap. Euro Car Parts (0541 506506) supplies cheap parts. TDI is roomy, sensible, economical and quite quick. VR6 (if you can find one) is a performance bargain. More rigid body shell and better protection from rear end impacts than Golf Mk III. Still called Jetta in the USA and got a bit of a boost by co-starring in 'The Fast and The Furious'.

What's bad: UK market treated them just like the Jetta. Otherwise see Golf Mk III. VR6 needs suspension mods to drive well.
What to watch out for: See Golf Mk III.
Recalls: (See Recalls for Golf Mk III)

Index

The Good Garage Guide, the Car Clubs Directory and the Car by Car Breakdown are compiled alphabetically for easy reference. For these sections, only manufacturers (Car Clubs) and specialists (Good Garage Guide) are indexed here.

Index

Index

Index

Talbot (*Car Clubs* entry) 163
Tata 30
Tatra (*Car Clubs* entry) 164
telediagnosis 89
telematics 89
three litre cars 53–4, 63–4
timing belt tensioner 34, 70, 195
Torcars (*Car Clubs* entry) 164
Tornado (*Car Clubs* entry) 164
Torotrak 60, 71
Toyota 30
  (*Car Clubs* entry) 164
  (*Good Garage Guide* specialists) 105, 111
  Avensis 26, 55, 83
  Camry 26, 83
  Carina 55
  Corolla 26, 71, 83, 111
  Prius 73, 92
  Yaris 1, 71, 93
trade licence/trade plates 81–2
Transport 2000 66
Trident (*Car Clubs* entry) 164
Triumph (*Car Clubs* entry) 165–6
Turner (*Car Clubs* entry) 166
TVR 30, 42, 43
  (*Car Clubs* entry) 166
  (*Good Garage Guide* specialist) 98
  Tuscan Speed Six 42
tyre pressure gauge 48
tyres
  information 14
  symbols 56–7
  tyre pressures 14
  wear rating 57

understeer 54–5
USA 14
  car terminology 74
  see also American cars
used cars 183–99
  advertisements and websites 12, 184–5
  agreeing a price 199
  buying from a company 185–6
  buying from a dealer 186–7, 190
  buying privately 183–4
  car history checks 6, 9, 191–2
  home traders 190–1
  imports 205–9
  inspections 193–6, 197–8
  'nearly new' cars 20–3, 176
  older cars 86, 198–9
  road test 196–7

service history 195–6
supersites 189–90
warranties 199

Vanden Plas (*Car Clubs* entry) 166
Vauxhall 14, 30
  (*Car Clubs* entry) 166–7
  (*Good Garage Guide* specialists) 102, 118, 121
  Astra 26, 71, 83
  Corsa 26, 71, 83, 92
  Meriva 26
  Network Q 186
  Omega 14, 26, 83
  Vectra 1, 26, 31, 71, 83
VCAR *see* write-offs
Vehicle Excise Duty (VED) 22–3
  120g/km cutoff 92–3
  disc display 90
Vincent-HRD (*Car Clubs* entry) 168
Volvo 26–7, 30, 31, 71
  (*Car Clubs* entry) 169
  (*Good Garage Guide* specialists) 101, 104, 107, 112
  S40 83
  S60 83
  S70 83
  S80 71, 83
  S90 83
  V40 83
  V70 83
  V90 83
VW 14, 17, 30
  (*Car Clubs* entry) 168
  (*Good Garage Guide* specialists) 100, 101, 102, 104, 111, 112, 120, 121, 123, 124
  Beetle 42
  Bora 26, 83
  Golf 24, 26, 71, 83
  Lupo 63, 71, 93
  Passat 26, 71, 83
  Polo 26, 71, 93
  Retailer Approved Used Cars 187
  Sharan 26, 83

websites, motor related 4–14, 188–9
Westfield 30
windscreens
  MOT screen test 80
  treatments 11, 14
Wolseley (*Car Clubs* entry) 169
write-offs 48–9, 58–9

762